Praise for *Jugaad Innovation*

"We are entering an age when humanity's grand challenges are being solved by a new generation of 'do-it-yourself' innovators employing jugaad-style thinking. Today the entrepreneurial spirit of your very own employees, customers, and partners—empowered by new technologies—can literally change the world. X PRIZE has proven the value of jugaad by leveraging this bottom-up approach of 'better, faster, cheaper' to the point of sending a man into space for a fraction of what NASA spends. This compelling new book, *Jugaad Innovation*, articulates how you can start to accomplish amazing things on a shoestring. It is a vital read."

> **—Peter H. Diamandis**, founder and chairman, X PRIZE Foundation

"*Jugaad Innovation* throws cold water in the faces of CEOs, reminding them of the immense power of grassroots, do-it-yourself, cheap, quick, simple innovation. This is one of the most important lessons that emerging markets are teaching the West."

> **—George F. Colony**, CEO, Forrester Research

"*Jugaad Innovation* goes farther than conventional business books that chart consumer growth in Brazil, Russia, India, and China. It explains how emerging economies are pioneering the art of 'frugal engineering,' then provides practical tips on how Western companies—from tech startups to multinational industrial corporations—can likewise do more with less. A provocative and entertaining read for 21st century business leaders."

> **—Carlos Ghosn**, CEO, Renault-Nissan

"The authors have it right: highly structured innovation processes can't deliver all the breakthroughs required by today's 'speed of business.' What's called for are new practices that work *with*—not against—the forces that drive our hypercompetitive world. *Jugaad Innovation* lays out the new principles that you—and every forward-thinking leader in your company—need right now."

> **—Charlene Li**, founder, Altimeter Group; bestselling author, *Open Leadership*

i

"Businesses must move away from the top-down organizational hierarchies that have defined the past and transform themselves into social enterprises built on bottom-up, agile models based on collaboration. *Jugaad Innovation* shows how you can enable your entire ecosystem—employees, customers, and partners—to make significant contributions and drive hypergrowth. An important book for anyone who wants to compete in the future."

—Marc Benioff, chairman and CEO, salesforce.com; bestselling author, *Behind the Cloud*

"CEOs tend to manage innovation like an orchestra conductor—with a traditional, hierarchical, and prescriptive approach. *Jugaad Innovation* shows how to innovate like a jazz band—with improvisation, creativity, and agility. Both styles are necessary on today's global stage."

—Doreen Lorenzo, president, frog

"I've long argued that the role of business is to make the world a better place. In the new economy, this requires true innovation—bold ideas, gutsy people, and extraordinary actions. Need a new roadmap? Fresh inspiration? Accessible tools? It's all in this remarkable book, *Jugaad Innovation*. Get a copy for yourself and every member of your team today."

—Kevin Roberts, CEO worldwide, Saatchi & Saatchi; bestselling author, *LoveMarks*

JUGAAD INNOVATION

THINK FRUGAL,
BE FLEXIBLE,
GENERATE BREAKTHROUGH GROWTH

Navi Radjou   Jaideep Prabhu   Simone Ahuja

Foreword by
Kevin Roberts
CEO Worldwide, Saatchi & Saatchi

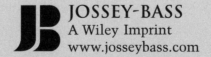
JOSSEY-BASS
A Wiley Imprint
www.josseybass.com

Published by Jossey-Bass
A Wiley Imprint
One Montgomery Street, Suite 1200, San Francisco, CA 94104-4594
www.josseybass.com

Jossey-Bass books and products are available through most bookstores. To contact Jossey-Bass directly call our Customer Care Department within the U.S. at 800-956-7739, outside the U.S. at 317-572-3986, or fax 317-572-4002.

Wiley also publishes its books in a variety of electronic formats and by print-on-demand. Some material included with standard print versions of this book may not be included in e-books or in print-on-demand. If the version of this book that you purchased references media such as CD or DVD that was not included in your purchase, you may download this material at http://booksupport.wiley.com. For more information about Wiley products, visit www.wiley.com.

Library of Congress Cataloging-in-Publication Data
Radjou, Navi.
  Jugaad innovation : think frugal, be flexible, generate breakthrough growth / by Navi Radjou, Jaideep Prabhu, and Simone Ahuja.—1st ed.
      p. cm.
   Includes bibliographical references and index.
    ISBN 978-1-118-24974-1 (hardback); ISBN 978-1-118-28323-3 (ebk);
  ISBN 978-1-118-28347-9 (ebk); ISBN 978-1-118-28600-5 (ebk)
  1.   Technological innovations—Case studies. 2.   Adaptability (Psychology)—Case studies. I. Prabhu, Jaideep C. II. Ahuja, Simone. III. Title.
HD45.R245 2012
658.4′063—dc23
                                                                        2011050766

Printed in the United States of America
FIRST EDITION
HB Printing 10 9 8 7 6 5 4 3 2 1

*To our parents, who taught us to be frugal and flexible,
and encouraged us to follow our hearts*

CONTENTS

FOREWORD

Ideas and creativity are the heart of my business, so when a book like *Jugaad Innovation* comes along, reframing as it does the language and methodology of innovation, it's time to get excited. As the authors note, this is a time of increasing complexity and greater scarcity of resources, of fractured financial models in the West, and confidently emergent economic powerhouses in the East and the South. What is revelatory is that the authors surface a new set of principles—from emerging markets such as India, Brazil, China, and Kenya—for breakthrough innovation that we must take notice of and start adopting if we are to regenerate growth.

I first met one of the authors —Jaideep Prabhu—at Judge Business School, University of Cambridge, when I was CEO-in-Residence. One of the joys of my role was meeting people like Jaideep and listening to their nascent ideas for making the world a better place. With his collaborators, Navi Radjou and Simone Ahuja, Jaideep has brought the concept of jugaad to life with the full color and exuberance that is India.

This is a radically optimistic book and one that aligns with several strands of my own academic inquiry and gut instincts following forty years in business. My mantras unfold like this: be purpose inspired; change comes from the edge; devote yourself to world-changing ideas; emotion leads to action; creativity overcomes scarcity; in tough times, you need to win ugly. Their principles are parallel: be heart powered; seek opportunity in adversity; do more with less; include the margin; remain asset light; the world is too complex for the mind alone. My touchstone for innovation is "fail fast, fix fast, learn fast." Theirs: "fail cheap, fail fast, fail often."

Jugaad Innovation journeys through several of emerging markets' most innovative initiatives, from low-tech street corner entrepreneurs in the Philippines meeting the needs of a local community to large industrial conglomerates in India and China seeking to improve the lives of hundreds of millions of people. The authors track a number of Western companies that have mirrored jugaad methods—Procter & Gamble and PepsiCo are two companies I have worked for—but on the whole conclude that "the Western innovation engine has become too rigid, insular, and bloated ... consumes a lot of resources and makes a lot of noise but produces little of significance." Ouch.

Jugaad is therefore both a wake-up call for mature companies with over-developed processes of institutional innovation, and a primer for how to be resourceful with scarce resources. In my home country of New Zealand, the jugaad equivalent is called "#8 wire." In the early agricultural and industrial development of New Zealand, farmers and business people couldn't wait for the months it took for replacement parts or new machinery to arrive on the boat from Mother England—so they improvised solutions, made it up. It was amazing what could be achieved with a simple piece of fencing wire.

"Scarcity is the mother of invention" say the authors. Austerity is the new operating system both for many companies and indeed countries. Frugality is the framework of managers; re-using and recombining is a way of life for the characters who populate the pages of *Jugaad Innovation*, and it is a practice that we in the wasteful West need to learn and then get used to. In my business—communications, marketing, and advertising, aka selling—the advent of social media has slashed the type of budgets we were once used so. Creativity is our greatest savior. Great ideas are budget blind, it's just that we have little practice of working in this environment. Jugaad lights a path.

Where *Jugaad Innovation* really pumps my blood is in its discussion of "intuiting the latent needs of consumers." Steve Jobs had this intuition and designed new products that people never imagined but are so obvious when they're in your hands. A classic frugalist, he defined presence as absence; he took away—the keyboard, the mouse, the computer box; he reduced and eliminated. My book *Lovemarks: The Future Beyond Brands* took the position that companies, if they were up to it, would be able to place themselves into the hearts of customers, be invited in, and be able to clearly answer the killer question that every customer has: "how will you improve my life?" The chest-thumping of companies who claim to put customers at the heart of what *they* do have the equation back to front. As the authors state, "your heart knows what your mind doesn't." They advocate "following your heart" with intuition, empathy, and passion; my trifecta is "mystery, sensuality, and intimacy."

The final element of jugaad to highlight is what I call "mental toughness." The authors refer to "building up your firm's psychological capital to boost its confident resilience." At Saatchi & Saatchi we have a founding statement of purpose: "Nothing Is Impossible." To this I added "One Team One Dream." Having crazies with purpose on your side is great; having unguided crazies is not. Just as I have invented, adapted, and stolen methods and techniques for organizing and keeping 6,000 people on the straight and narrow, these authors offer us a host of how-to's. You can't have a book about resourcefulness without resources, and *Jugaad Innovation* is generous in its roadmaps.

Until this book, the commonest currency I had with India was cricket. I captained cricket teams through my school years, beguiled by the mysteries of the googly (look it up on, um Google; it's a type of delivery bowled by a right-arm leg spin bowler) and the blatant power of hitting a six over square leg. Now I have jugaad, and my relationship with India and with innovation is reborn.

Grasmere, England   Kevin Roberts
February 2012   CEO Worldwide
                                                          Saatchi & Saatchi

CHAPTER ONE

JUGAAD
A Breakthrough Growth Strategy

We reached Ramakrishna Nagar, a village in the desert of Gujarat, a state in Western India, after travelling 250 miles from Ahmedabad, the state's capital. Our team—a Silicon Valley management consultant, a business school professor from the University of Cambridge, and the founder of a Minneapolis advisory boutique and media firm—had set out a few months earlier on an extensive research and travel project. Our mission: to discover new approaches to innovation in emerging markets such as India that could help Western firms take on the complexity of our tough and turbulent times.

We came to Gujarat to meet with Professor Anil Gupta at the Indian Institute of Management (IIM) in Ahmedabad.[1] Professor Gupta runs Honeybee Network, a non-profit organization that identifies and cross-pollinates grassroots innovation all across India. Over more than two decades, Honeybee had populated a database with over ten thousand inventions of grassroots entrepreneurs who have created ingenious solutions for pressing socioeconomic problems in their local communities. Professor Gupta suggested we meet with one of these rural entrepreneurs.

As we left an arrow-straight concrete highway to follow narrower and increasingly cratered gravel roads, the temperature rose to a debilitating 120 degrees. Stepping out of our air-conditioned jeep, we could feel the weight of the desert's oppressive heat.

Mansukh Prajapati greeted us warmly outside his workshop.[2] A potter by trade, Prajapati had for years been experimenting with clay to produce a variety of durable goods, many of which were on display in the office outside his "lab." We were parched—and grateful when he asked

1

us if we wanted water. We had run out, and there wasn't any sign of a store or kiosk nearby to restock. He reached around to a faucet, handed us cups, and, beaming with pride, said, "Please, have this cold water—from my fridge."

Baffled, we looked more closely at the terra-cotta box in front of us. It was made entirely of clay, except for a glass door and a plastic faucet at the bottom. While sipping the refreshingly cool water, we looked around and found no electrical cord, no battery—just clay. Amused by our expressions, Prajapati explained how this clay fridge—the Mitticool (*mitti* means "earth" in Hindi)—works: water from an upper chamber seeps through the side walls, cooling the lower food chamber through evaporation. The fridge consumes no electricity, is 100-percent biodegradable, and produces zero waste during its lifetime. An ingenious invention!

But this inventor and his personal story are even more impressive. Prajapati doesn't work for NASA or Whirlpool, and he doesn't have a Ph.D. in quantum physics or an MBA from Stanford. In fact, he didn't even finish high school. His R&D lab—a simple open-air room with clay in various shapes and forms arrayed on the floor and an oven tucked away in the corner—is a far cry from the sprawling campuses of GE and Whirlpool, which swarm with hundreds of engineers and scientists.

In 2001, an earthquake had devastated Prajapati's village and the surrounding area. Reading a report of the devastation in the local newspaper, he noticed a photo caption: "Poor man's fridge broken!" The photo featured a smashed earthen pot commonly used by villagers to fetch water and keep it cool. And though the newspaper had called it a fridge in jest, it triggered Prajapati's first eureka moment. *Why not use clay*, he thought, *to make a real fridge for villagers—one that looks like a typical fridge, but is more affordable and doesn't need electricity?* Over five hundred million Indians live without reliable electricity, including most of the people in Prajapati's village.[3] The positive health and lifestyle benefits of owning a fridge in a desert village where fruit, vegetables, and dairy are available only intermittently would be tremendous.

Prajapati's training as a potter, coupled with his intuition, told him that he was on to something. He experimented for several months and eventually had a viable version of the Mitticool that he began selling to people in his own village. The fridge—which costs around US$50—was a hit. Prajapati worked tirelessly on design improvements, and began selling Mitticools across India, and then internationally. He couldn't keep up with the rising demand and had to find ways to scale up—fast.

Then he had a second eureka moment. Why not transform pottery from an artisanal craft into an industrial process? He could leverage his traditional knowledge of pottery to mass-produce goods that met modern consumer needs. So Prajapati first developed an entirely new and more efficient method of working with clay. Then he began training women in his village in these industrial pottery techniques and finally hired them to work in his new factory. Soon a "mini" Industrial Revolution in pottery was launched in this remote Indian village.

Mitticool was the first product that Prajapati mass-produced in his factory. He soon built other products from clay, such as a nonstick frying pan that retains heat longer than other frying pans and costs a mere US$2. From one man and one idea has grown a frugal yet fruitful industry, one that employs large numbers of people in his own community and serves consumers in India and abroad. Prajapati's groundbreaking inventions, which deliver more value at less cost, have earned him accolades from all over the world—including from the president of India. And *Forbes* magazine recently named him among the most influential rural Indian entrepreneurs, one of few to have made an impact on the lives of so many.[4]

JUGAAD: THE GUTSY ART OF IMPROVISING AN INGENIOUS SOLUTION

The Mitticool, an idea born out of adverse circumstances, shows how a resilient mindset can transform scarcity into opportunity. Combining limited resources and a never-say-die attitude, Prajapati tapped into his empathy and passion for his fellow community members to conjure up an ingenious solution that improved lives in Gujarat and beyond. Not only did he produce a cheap and effective cooling device, but he also created jobs for dozens of undereducated women. In doing so, Prajapati is both driving environmental and socioeconomic sustainability in his community and ensuring the financial sustainability of his own business. Prajapati embodies the true spirit of *jugaad*.

Jugaad is a colloquial Hindi word that roughly translates as "an innovative fix; an improvised solution born from ingenuity and cleverness." Jugaad is, quite simply, a unique way of thinking and acting in response to challenges; it is the gutsy art of spotting opportunities in the most adverse circumstances and resourcefully improvising solutions using simple means. Jugaad is about *doing more with less*. (We feature articles and videos on jugaad on our companion website, JugaadInnovation.com.)

Jugaad is practiced by almost all Indians in their daily lives to make the most of what they have. Jugaad applications include finding new uses for everyday objects—Indian kitchens are replete with empty Coke or Pepsi bottles reused as ad-hoc containers for dried legumes or condiments—or inventing new utilitarian tools using everyday objects, like a makeshift truck cobbled together with a diesel engine slapped onto a cart (interestingly, the origin of the word jugaad, in Punjabi, literally describes such makeshift vehicles).

The word jugaad is also applied to any use of an ingenious way to "game the system." For instance, millions of cellphone users in India rely on "missed calls" to communicate messages to each other using a pre-arranged protocol between the caller and receiver: think of this as *free textless* text messaging. For example, your carpooling partner may give you a "missed call" in the morning indicating he has just left his house and is on his way to pick you up.[5] Hence, the word jugaad carries a slightly negative connotation for some. But by and large, the entrepreneurial spirit of jugaad is practiced by millions in India simply to improvise clever—and completely legitimate—solutions to everyday problems.

In this book, we delve into the frugal and flexible mindset of thousands of ingenious entrepreneurs and enterprises practicing jugaad to creatively address critical socioeconomic issues in their communities. Jugaad innovators like Mansukh Prajapati view severe constraints, such as a lack of electricity, not as a debilitating challenge but as an opportunity to innovate and overcome these very constraints.

The entrepreneurial spirit of jugaad is not limited to India. It is widely practiced in other emerging economies such as China and Brazil, where entrepreneurs are also pursuing growth in difficult circumstances. Brazilians have their own word for this approach: *gambiarra*.[6] The Chinese call it *zizhu chuangxin*.[7] The Kenyans refer to it as *jua kali*.[8] The French have a term too—Système D.[9] Throughout this book we profile jugaad entrepreneurs from Argentina, Brazil, China, Costa Rica, India, Kenya, Mexico, the Philippines, and elsewhere who have created simple yet effective solutions to address vexing problems that their fellow citizens face. We hope to shed light on how these jugaad innovators think and act—and identify the valuable lessons we in the West can learn from them.

JUGAAD IN THE WEST

While jugaad is currently the dominant form of innovation in emerging markets, in the West it is practiced only in isolated instances. And although the 1980s TV series *MacGyver* popularized the American jugaad spirit—also known as *Yankee ingenuity*—very few Western *corporations* actually practice jugaad today.[10] Yet jugaad was once a big part of Western innovation too. It was the flexible mindset of jugaad-style innovators that catalyzed growth in Western economies like that of the United States during the Industrial Revolution.

For instance, in 1831 a self-educated Virginian farmer named Cyrus McCormick introduced his newly invented mechanical grain reaper. The reaper promised to free farm workers from back-breaking labor and address the problem of scarce food supplies that plagued his community. When McCormick was born in 1809, over 80 percent of Americans were dependent on agriculture for their livelihood (by 1970 that figure had dwindled to just 4 percent).[11] In early nineteenth-century America, farmers harvested grain crops by hand, requiring many laborers to complete the task. Cyrus McCormick's father had wanted to make life easier for his fellow farmers. He spent twenty-eight years trying to develop a machine that could automate grain harvesting, but he gave up after multiple unsuccessful attempts. When his son Cyrus was barely twenty-two, he took over his father's invention and tinkered with the machine to make it work. In his family barn, which served as a makeshift workshop, he spent many months tweaking the design for an automated grain-harvesting machine, using limited resources and hand-made components. Finally, in 1831, he came up with a workable and elegant version of the mechanized reaper, capable of harvesting more grain than five men could gather using the earlier cradles.[12]

The reaper wasn't even Cyrus McCormick's first invention. Despite little education, at age fifteen he had invented a lightweight grain cradle that could cut and stack grain more efficiently. A few years later he developed two new types of plow. Nineteenth-century America—struggling with a scarcity of resources, yet fertile with opportunities—teemed with jugaad entrepreneurs like Cyrus McCormick whose clever inventions brought great benefits to the society at large.[13]

Yet Cyrus McCormick's most famous jugaad invention—the mechanized reaper—wasn't an instant commercial success. His fellow farmers, accustomed to manual methods of harvesting, were initially skeptical about the usefulness of this unfamiliar machine. McCormick struggled for years to sell his machines. He found success through further flexible jugaad thinking: pioneering the practice of word-of-mouth marketing, he got his first few customers to recommend his reaper to other potential customers. Eventually, sales of his reapers picked up, and McCormick shifted production to a factory in Chicago. His machines started selling well and dramatically improved agricultural practices across the country. In the process, McCormick also laid the groundwork for many innovative sales and marketing practices—like assessing customers' credit-worthiness and offering a "money-back guarantee"—that are now standard practices of Western businesses across industries. McCormick proved to be not only an ingenious technical inventor but also a great *business model* innovator. And although McCormick's life was filled with adversity—from factory fires to patent disputes—he always bounced back with resilience. McCormick's jugaad inventions enabled scores of American workers to shift from farming to factory work—thus accelerating the Industrial Revolution.[14]

Among the many early American jugaad innovators, the best-known may well be Benjamin Franklin. Franklin experienced scarcity and learned about the virtue of frugality firsthand, growing up in a large Puritan family of nine brothers and seven sisters.[15] When he was just ten years old, Franklin left school and started working in his father's candle and soap shop to help support his family. Early on, Franklin developed a knack for using limited resources to devise ingenious and frugal solutions to tackle the everyday problems of his contemporaries. Franklin's legendary ingenuity was fueled by his genuine empathy for his fellow citizens. One of his most practical inventions was the Franklin stove.[16] During the eighteenth century, homes in the United States were primarily heated by inefficient fireplaces that spewed smoke while much of the heat they generated escaped up the chimney. They were also hazardous, as their sparks could trigger fires that quickly devoured wood-built homes.

Franklin's jugaad innovation to tackle this problem was a new type of stove with a simple hooded enclosure in the front and an air box in the rear. The new stove and its reconfiguration of the flues enabled a more efficient fire, one that consumed 75 percent less wood and generated twice as much heat.[17] The Franklin stove delivered "more with less." An early advocate of open source technology, Franklin turned down the patent offered for his original design, stating that altruism rather than profit was his driving motive for developing the efficient stove. He wanted all Americans to benefit from his invention. In fact, Franklin patented *none* of his inventions. In his autobiography, he wrote that "as we enjoy great advantages from the inventions of others, we should be glad of an opportunity to serve others by any invention of ours; and this we should do freely and generously."[18] As a serial jugaad entrepreneur, his approach to innovation was always inclusive: his ingenious but simple inventions—including the lightning rod, bifocals, and a carriage odometer—enhanced lives throughout the colonies.

America's founding fathers, as well as its creative farmers, industrial pioneers, and scientific explorers in the nineteenth and early twentieth centuries—from Ben Franklin to Cyrus McCormick to the Wright brothers—were historic practitioners of jugaad in the West.

These ingenious entrepreneurs spurred the Industrial Revolution in Western nations, building a strong foundation of economic leadership that lasted for decades. In the twentieth century, however, especially after World War II, Western nations gradually lost touch with this jugaad spirit as they matured into postindustrial economies and became attached to a systematized, predictable way of life and work. Improvised ingenuity—the essence of jugaad—took a back seat to a more formally structured approach to innovation.

HOW THE WEST LOST ITS JUGAAD

In the twentieth century, as North American and European economies expanded, Western corporations began to institutionalize their innovation capabilities, creating dedicated R&D departments and standardizing the business processes needed to take their ideas to market. They focused on *managing* innovation, just as they managed any other business activity. This industrialization of the creative process led to a *structured* approach to innovation with the following key characteristics: big budgets, standardized business processes, and controlled access to knowledge.

But this structured innovation approach, which helped Western firms become highly successful in the second half of the twentieth century, has three clear limitations in the fast pace and volatility of the twenty-first century: it is too expensive and resource consuming, it lacks flexibility, and it is elitist and insular.

The Structured Approach Is Too Expensive and Resource Consuming Western firms have come to believe that their innovation system—like any industrial system—will generate more output (inventions) if fed more input (resources). As a result, the structured innovation engine is capital intensive. It requires an abundant supply of financial and natural resources at a time when both are increasingly scarce. The approach is designed to deliver "more with more"—that is, firms charge customers a hefty premium for overengineered products that are expensive to develop and produce. For instance, the thousand companies in the world that invest the most in innovation—many of which are Western firms—spent a whopping $550,000,000,000 (yes, that's US$550 billion!) on R&D in 2010 alone.[19] But what did they get in return for all this expense? Not much, according to research conducted by the management consultancy Booz & Company. They found that the three Western industries that spend the most on R&D—computing and electronics, healthcare, and automotive—struggle to generate a steady stream of groundbreaking inventions, despite their hefty R&D investments. Hence there is *a weak correlation* between how much money your firm spends in R&D and how well it performs in terms of developing and marketing products that generate a significant financial return. To put it bluntly, *money can't buy innovation*. Fittingly, a Booz & Company report carries a photograph of a dejected-looking CEO wearing a T-shirt that reads: "We spent $2 billion on R&D and all we got was this lousy T-shirt." The caption illustrates well the frustrations of Western corporate leaders facing, on the one hand, huge financial constraints, and on the other, immense pressures from shareholders to deliver growth.[20]

The pharmaceutical industry is one sector where the "bigger is better" R&D strategy is clearly running out of steam. Big Pharma's spending on R&D ballooned from $15 billion in 1995 to $45 billion in 2009.[21] Yet the number of new drugs launched annually has dropped by 44 percent since 1997.[22] This is especially bad news for Big Pharma, given that between 2011 and 2016 drugs worth a whopping $139 billion are set to go off patent.[23] To further complicate things, Big Pharma in the United States is facing a growing backlash from politicians and the public as health care costs spiral out of control, even as fifty million Americans continue to lack basic health insurance.

The drug industry is not an exception. The U.S. auto sector spent $16 billion on R&D in 2007 alone.[24] But American automakers nevertheless trail their Japanese, Korean, German, and even Chinese and Indian rivals, as frugal consumers worldwide clamor for more compact, fuel-efficient, and environmentally friendly cars. The U.S. market share of the Big Three—Chrysler, General Motors, and

Ford—has steadily declined, from 70 percent in 1998 to 44.2 percent in 2009.[25] In December 2008, the cash-strapped automakers asked the U.S. government for a $34 billion bailout to cover employee health care expenses and prevent bankruptcy and massive layoffs.[26] Since December 2009, the U.S. government has given $82 billion in aid to the Big Three—including $62 billion to General Motors and Chrysler alone (both carmakers filed for bankruptcy protection).[27]

The Structured Approach Lacks Flexibility   With so much money invested in R&D, Western firms have become risk averse in their approach to innovation. They have implemented standardized business processes such as "Six Sigma" (an integrated set of management techniques designed to decrease production defects and increase operational efficiency by standardizing processes) and "stage gate analysis" to manage and control their innovation projects. These structured processes were expected to drastically reduce uncertainty—and risk of failure—from the entire innovation process and make R&D projects more predictable in both execution and outcomes. But these structured business processes and methods are unfit to deliver the agility and differentiation that enterprises need in a fast-paced and volatile world.

Take Six Sigma—the well-known management strategy pioneered by Motorola in 1986 and the corporate dogma of leading Fortune 500 firms such as GE and Boeing. Six Sigma is a set of practices designed to improve quality by eliminating defects. With a Six Sigma process implemented, there is a statistical expectation that 99.99966 percent of the products manufactured will be free of defects. Six Sigma works marvelously when you are seeking to institutionalize "sameness," and this comes in handy when you are mass-producing widgets in a predictable environment. But Six Sigma is like a straitjacket: once you get in, you are stuck, and when things start to change, you can't move (let alone dance).[28]

Built around stable and predictable processes, programs like Six Sigma cannot enable the rapid change that companies need as they seek to mass customize products and services, satisfy increasingly diverse and finicky customers, and keep up with technology shifts. Worse, the orthodox Six Sigma culture weeds out "positive deviance"—the uncommon strategies used by those pioneering employees in a company who use unconventional and counterintuitive methods to solve vexing business problems that can't be addressed using traditional approaches.[29] But, as Malcolm Gladwell points out in *Outliers*, positively deviant behavior and ideas are what actually drive game-changing innovation.[30] That explains why George Buckley, CEO of 3M—where an outlier named Art Fry invented the now-indispensable Post-it® Notes by sheer serendipity—rolled back several Six Sigma initiatives at 3M in a bid to revive innovation in the firm. Buckley points out: "Invention is by its very nature a disorderly process. You can't put a Six Sigma process into that area and say, Well, I'm getting behind on invention, so I'm going to schedule myself for three good ideas on Wednesday and two on Friday. That's not how creativity works."[31]

The Structured Approach Is Elitist and Insular   Throughout the twentieth century, Western firms built large R&D labs that employed hundreds of top scientists and engineers, based on a belief that "knowledge is power" and that controlling access to it was key to success. Thus innovation became an elite activity controlled by a few high priests: engineers and scientists working under conditions of secrecy in in-house labs close to headquarters. Only these chosen few were invited into the R&D department and given the resources and permission to innovate. Any new knowledge they generated was closely guarded. Collaboration with other employees—let alone outsiders—was shunned. The assumption was that to dominate markets through innovation one needed two things: top-of-the-line technology and ownership of the best intellectual property, both of which could be bought with enough money. However true that assumption might have been in an earlier industrial era, it is far less valid now. Part of the old belief was that only a bunch of smart Ph.D.s could *invent* new things. But in today's consumer-driven economy we know that it's more important to *commercialize* technology, which requires knowledge of fields such as design and marketing—skills that engineers and scientists may not necessarily have.[32] As Bob McDonald, CEO of Procter & Gamble, explains: "For us, innovation is not invention. It's the conversion of a new idea into consumer delight and, ultimately, into revenues and profits. If an idea or technology cannot be successfully commercialized, it's not an innovation."[33]

Further, in an interconnected world powered by social media, the intellectual property that one can buy isn't the only source of new ideas. Finding, sharing, and integrating globally dispersed knowledge among all levels of employees is just as important, if not more so. Consider this statistic: as of this writing, every Facebook user creates, on average, ninety pieces of content per month, contributing to more than thirty billion pieces of shared content—ranging from family photos to web links to posts—across the Facebook social network.[34] The power of innovation has shifted from the professional class to the masses. Creativity has been democratized—thanks to social media tools like Facebook. As strategy consultant and author Gary Hamel says, "The underlying principles on the Web of natural hierarchy, transparency, collaboration and all the rest—those characteristics are going to have to invade management. The idea of a hierarchy that fundamentally empowers the few and disempowers the many is more or less dead."[35]

Yet top-down R&D systems are often unable to open up and integrate such bottom-up input from employees and customers. Younger, creative employees use new technologies like social media in order to brainstorm ideas, creating a virtual watercooler. Structured organizations often find it hard to integrate these methods of innovation into their business model. The chief information officer of a large engineering services firm told us, "Many of our younger employees brainstorm new ideas on Facebook. As a result, Facebook has become the virtual brainstorming place where people gather and hatch ideas. I really don't know how to funnel those ideas back into our corporate R&D systems."

Bottom line: the processes, systems, and mindsets that underpin the structured approach to innovation are now failing. Although in years past corporations were able to survive and even thrive with this approach, it was designed to help them compete and win in a relatively stable, slower, and predictable world of abundance—one that no longer exists. Today's highly complex and turbulent business environment demands a new approach to innovation and growth—one that is frugal, flexible, and participative.

COMPLEXITY STRETCHES WESTERN FIRMS' ABILITY TO INNOVATE

In a global survey conducted by IBM in 2010, 79 percent of the 1,500 CEOs surveyed said that they anticipated greater complexity in the future environment.[36] Worryingly, fewer than half of these CEOs believed that their firms were prepared to respond creatively to this increasing complexity. The main reason is that Western firms' structured approach to innovation is ill-equipped to help them innovate *faster, better, and cheaper* as they seek to cope with five major components of complexity—scarcity, diversity, interconnectivity, velocity, and breakneck globalization.

Scarcity Even as Western economies struggle to emerge from the global recession, access to financial capital remains restricted for small and midsize companies—which account for two-thirds of job creation in the United States—while consumers struggle to obtain loans from risk-averse banks.[37] For instance, America's consuming middle class, which accounts for two-thirds of national spending and forms the bedrock of the U.S. economy, is feeling the pinch. Between 2000 and 2010, the inflation-adjusted income of middle class American households dropped by 7 percent. In late 2011, an astounding 46.2 million Americans (or 15 percent of the U.S. population) were living in poverty and nearly 50 million lacked health insurance.[38] Not surprisingly, in 2011 only 65 percent of Americans believed their children would be able to achieve the American Dream—down from 69 percent in 2008.[39]

In times like these, it's unrealistic to expect Western governments to come to the rescue of their citizens, as they are feeling the squeeze as well: U.S. public debt, for instance, has increased by over $500 billion, on average, every year since 2003. As of early August 2011, the total public debt of the United States was a whopping $14.34 trillion dollars.[40] In the UK, public sector borrowing skyrocketed to £175 billion (US$253 billion) or 12.4 percent of GDP in 2009—the highest level of borrowing among all developed nations.[41] Heavily indebted Western governments have no choice but to cut down on public services, and this will only further hurt already stretched Western consumers.

Meanwhile, natural resources like oil and minerals are becoming more scarce and consequently more expensive. While everyone frets about the escalating price of oil, another precious resource—water—is also becoming increasingly scarce. One out of three U.S. counties faces a risk of water shortages in coming decades, and fourteen states, including California and Texas, face an extreme threat to their water sustainability.[42]

Further, the outlook of Generations Y and Z marks a significant change in both the workforce and the consumer base. These frugal and environmentally conscious young consumers are more comfortable working with scarcity and seem to instinctively follow jugaad in their daily lives. They innately appreciate the need to do more with less, having experienced firsthand the worst economic times since the Great Depression. The MacArthur Research Network on Transitions to Adulthood and Public Policy conducted five hundred interviews with twenty-somethings on their cost-conscious lifestyle and concluded that their "frugality could last a lifetime."[43]

All three trends—financially constrained consumers and governments, dwindling natural resources, and greater numbers of frugal Gen Y and Z consumers wanting low-impact environmental products— have put scarcity on the agenda for Western companies, forcing them to find frugal ways to grow with less. The raw materials necessary to make new products will cost more in the future, and consumers' financial constraints will drive them to look for low-cost products that still deliver results in an eco-friendly way.

Diversity The workforce of most Western companies is now more diverse than ever before. The Gen Y (also known as the Millennials) and

Gen Z—with their distinctive values and expectations—are now joining Generation X and the baby boomers at work. The COO of a large Silicon Valley–based tech firm told us, "For the first time in my life, I now manage workers across four generations—which is more difficult because we have to accommodate the diverse values and expectations of our multigenerational workforce."

Meanwhile, traditionally homogeneous markets are now more fragmented, as consumers from minority groups seek solutions tailored to their unique needs. For instance, Hispanics already account for more than one-third of California's population and are expected to become a majority in that state by 2042.[44] As a result, corporate leaders have to learn to reconcile the varying values and expectations of their diverse workforce and consumer communities they serve. Unfortunately, the structured approach to innovation—rigid, insular, elitist, and promoting *uniformity*—is limited in its ability to deal with a world of diversity.

Interconnectivity Cloud computing, mobile technologies, and social media have created new ways for companies to connect and engage deeply with their current and prospective customers and partners alike. Indeed, the United States is turning into what Daniel Pink calls a "free agent nation," one in which a growing number of professionals are escaping "corporate fortresses" by leveraging professional social networks like LinkedIn to freelance their skills.[45] Technology has fostered a growing need for creative freedom among employees and citizens by forcing CEOs to open up their business models and organizational structures to make the most of a connected society and workforce. Specifically, the rigidity of the structured approach limits the use of more flexible ways of innovating that involve groups *outside* the firm, such as consumers and partners. And the insularity of the structured approach limits the involvement in innovation—even *within* the firm—of employees who are not strictly tasked with doing R&D.

Velocity The speed of change is increasing on multiple fronts—technological, market, and competitive. In particular, product life cycles are getting shorter, putting pressure on corporations to launch new products faster than ever and to keep ever-more-demanding consumers satisfied. For instance, the Apple iPad 2 was released even before there was viable competition for the iPad 1. And in the era of Twitter and Facebook, the reputations of companies (and governments) can be destroyed at lightning speed—as evidenced by Wikileaks. This accelerating pace—and the associated ambiguity about what the future holds—forces CEOs to delegate decision making to frontline employees, to respond swiftly to unexpected opportunities and challenges in their environment. But the insularity and rigidity of the structured approach to innovation limits the extent to which CEOs can use more decentralized approaches that rely on empowered employees to cope with changes effectively and quickly.

Breakneck Globalization   The rapid rise of emerging markets like India and China magnifies the impact of scarcity, diversity, interconnectivity, and accelerating change. For instance, the Chinese middle class, already three hundred million strong, is expected to double over the next decade. More consumers worldwide entails a greater strain on existing resources and hence a dwindling of resources available to Western firms. For example, India and China together are expected to contribute to over 50 percent of the increase in global energy demand between 2010 and 2035.[46] In 2035, China will be consuming nearly 70 percent more energy than the United States. Meanwhile, by 2020 one global worker in four will be Indian. Accenture, a U.S. management consulting firm, already employs more than sixty thousand workers in India, making this its largest workforce in the world. A more global workforce means both more competition for firms that operate primarily in Western markets and a more diverse workforce at Western multinationals expanding into emerging markets. More competition from emerging market firms will place greater pressure on Western firms to innovate, especially for emerging market consumers (who are likely to be more frugal). And more diversity in the workforce will drive Western firms to be more flexible in their organizational structures and processes to accommodate diverse values, cultures, and expectations. The structured approach to innovation isn't well suited to dealing with these pressures of globalization. Its expensive, even profligate, nature limits its ability to deal with increasing scarcity. And its rigidity and insularity limit its ability to deal with diversity and velocity, on the one hand, and to fully exploit the potential of interconnectivity, on the other.

Deep scarcity, major demographic shifts, rapid technological change, and accelerating globalization are creating the most complex business environment since the Industrial Revolution. In this context, the old models of innovating are breaking down. As we mention earlier, fewer than half of the 1,500 global CEOs surveyed in the IBM poll believe that their firms are prepared to respond creatively—and effectively—to this escalating complexity.

The Western innovation engine has become too rigid, insular, and bloated to remain effective. It consumes a lot of resources and makes a lot of noise, but—for many companies—it produces little of much significance. If this condition of dysfunction continues much longer, there is a risk that it will cripple the West even as it emerges from tough economic times and seeks to grow.

It is clear that the West must build a new innovation engine that allows it to innovate faster, better, and cheaper. To do so, Western firms must find new sources of inspiration. Emerging markets are a great place to start.

SEARCHING FOR THE HOLY GRAIL OF INNOVATION

When we began our research in 2008, we predicted that the so-called BRICs—Brazil, Russia, India, and China—might be a good place to look for a new approach to innovation.[47] We had each come to this realization in our respective professions—academia, consulting, and media—and this interest brought us together in the shared quest that has culminated in this book.

In early 2008, Simone began extensive background research and ethnographic work for a documentary film series exploring innovation in India. During her work she came across Navi, then an analyst at Forrester Research, and asked him to act as an innovation consultant to the film series. Navi had written extensively about—and consulted on—innovation in both Western and emerging markets. In late 2008, Navi decided to focus all his attention on emerging markets and joined Jaideep at the University of Cambridge's Judge Business School to set up the Centre for India & Global Business. Jaideep, after spending most of his academic career studying innovation in the West, had also begun to turn his attention to the increasingly important role of emerging markets in the global innovation ecosystem.

When we began our quest, the emerging economies had grown in the previous decade from one-sixth to a quarter of the world economy. Even in 2008, at the height of the global recession, India and China were growing at 7 percent and 9 percent, respectively. Goldman Sachs, among others, had predicted that these nations would continue to grow between 3 percent and 5 percent per year until 2050, dominating the world economy for the next forty years.[48]

The BRIC economies' vastness (both geographically and demographically), their diversity, and their pervasive scarcity of resources all add up to a challenging state of affairs that would trouble even the most seasoned business leaders. However, the very fact that the BRIC nations have been grappling with complexity and instability for so long seems to give them an edge and a kind of immunity in volatile and adverse circumstances. What is in the immune system of these emerging economies that makes them so resilient? And what might business leaders in these countries be able to teach their counterparts in the West?

To find the answers we studied the *mindset* and *principles* of innovators who were driving growth in the BRICs. If Western leaders could acquire a similar mindset and principles, then they could potentially develop the same immunity to complexity—and quickly identify emerging business opportunities in their own mature economies.

Among the BRICs, we chose to study India first because, after China, it is the fastest-growing economy in world. Further, many—including Goldman Sachs and Ernst & Young—predict that India not only will economically outpace China soon but will continue to grow faster than the other BRICs for several decades to come.[49] Most important, India is as complex as they come. The country faces scarcity on a grand scale across the board: from water, food, and energy (over five hundred million Indians lack regular electricity) to access to education and health care. Its chaotic democracy is characterized by a Kafkaesque bureaucracy and mind-boggling diversity; its population of 1.2 billion is expanding at 1.3 percent a year.[50] Despite all the chaos and complexity, the Indian economy is growing strongly in challenging economic times. If Indians have managed to grow "in spite of complexity," then there must be something there worth learning from.

On our many trips to India we met dozens of grassroots entrepreneurs and visited over a hundred enterprises, large and small. What we saw amazed us. The country is bursting with ingeniously simple yet effective innovations. After more than three years of extensive field research, searching for the holy grail of innovation all over the country, we came to a realization: all the thrifty innovators we encountered shared a unique mindset—the jugaad mindset.

Expanding our research to other countries, we found that the entrepreneurial spirit of jugaad, far from being a purely Indian thing, is really universal. Other emerging markets, from Latin America to Africa to Eastern Europe to Asia, have their own versions of jugaad. (In our companion website, JugaadInnovation.com, we showcase several of these jugaad innovators.) Because these emerging economies share the same adverse conditions that drive jugaad in India, they also excel at this improvisational and frugal art of responding to complexity. What then are the shared, underlying principles of this jugaad mindset?

THE SIX PRINCIPLES OF JUGAAD—AND THEIR BENEFITS TO THE WEST

We found that jugaad can be distilled into six guiding principles, which anchor the six practices of highly effective innovators in complex settings like emerging economies. The six principles are:

- Seek opportunity in adversity.
- Do more with less.

- Think and act flexibly.
- Keep it simple.
- Include the margin.
- Follow your heart.

   Collectively, these six principles of jugaad help drive resilience, frugality, adaptability, simplicity, inclusivity, empathy, and passion, all of which are essential to compete and win in a complex world. Adopting these principles could also help Western firms innovate and grow in a highly volatile, hypercompetitive environment.

Seek Opportunity in Adversity Jugaad entrepreneurs perceive harsh constraints as an invitation to innovate. Modern-day alchemists, they transform adversity into an opportunity to bring value to themselves and their communities. For instance, Kanak Das, who lives in a remote village in northeast India, grew tired of riding his bicycle on roads full of potholes and bumps. Rather than complain, he turned this constraint to his advantage by retrofitting his bicycle with a makeshift device that converts the shocks it receives into acceleration energy—allowing his bicycle to run faster on bumpy roads. Similarly, Enrique Gómez Junco, a Mexican engineer turned jugaad entrepreneur who founded Optima Energía, was unfazed by the skepticism he faced when he first attempted to convince risk-averse companies to buy his sustainable energy solutions. Instead, this adversity motivated him to adapt his business model and come up with a compelling new value proposition—that is, customers can buy his energy savings solutions with no up-front payments—which enabled him to convert those initially skeptical companies into loyal customers. (You will learn how Junco reframed adversity to achieve a breakthrough in Chapter Two.)

   This ability to reframe adversity as a source of innovation and growth is vital for any organization to survive and thrive. And as we discovered, some of these alchemists also work for large Western corporations such as 3M. For example, in Chapter Two we show how 3M is capturing big growth opportunities in an extremely adversarial business environment by rekindling and unleashing the jugaad spirit of all its employees.

Do More with Less Jugaad innovators are highly resourceful in the face of scarcity. Unlike many Silicon Valley entrepreneurs, raising capital is the least of their worries. The practitioners of jugaad work with what they've got. Doing more with less is in striking contrast to the "bigger is better" R&D approach used in the West—an approach that has been unsuccessful in making basic services like education and health care affordable to more people. Indeed, this frugal principle can help firms in both emerging and developed economies optimize the use of scarce financial and natural resources while delivering high value to a greater number of customers.

In Chapter Three you will meet two jugaad entrepreneurs—Gustavo Grobocopatel of Los Grobo (Argentina) and Sunil Mittal of Bharti Airtel (India)—who have developed frugal business models to cost-effectively deliver agricultural and telecom services, respectively, to the masses. Similarly, you will learn how PepsiCo is reinventing its business model as an affordable and sustainable provider of nutritious foods and beverages—in a proactive response to both the growing consumer demand for healthy food and the scarcity of natural resources like water.

Think and Act Flexibly Jugaad is the antithesis of structured approaches such as Six Sigma. Jugaad entrepreneurs' flexible mindset constantly questions the status quo, keeps all options open, and transforms existing products, services, and business models. Unconstrained by structured processes, jugaad innovators can quickly respond to unexpected changes in their environment. Jugaad innovators don't just think outside the box: they create whole new boxes. Their nonlinear thinking often yields breakthrough ideas that turn conventional wisdom on its head and help to shape entire new markets and industries. As we explain in Chapter Four, that's the case with Ratan Tata, chairman of the Tata Group, who foresaw a big market for extremely affordable cars and went on to successfully launch the $2,000 Nano in 2009—proving wrong those skeptics who had belittled his vision as a pipe dream. When the original plans failed to deliver sales, leaders at Tata Motors (the automotive unit of Tata Group) had to think on their feet and improvise new manufacturing, distribution, and marketing strategies for the Nano.

Jugaad innovators also *act* flexibly. In Chapter Four we describe how Zhang Ruimin, the entrepreneurial CEO of Haier, a fast-growing Chinese appliance manufacturer, has made Haier's organizational structures flat, thus empowering frontline employees to swiftly sense and respond to changes in customer demand and innovate faster, better, and cheaper than rivals. Closer to home, we explain how the New York Times Company is exhibiting flexible thinking by proactively embracing social media and mobile technologies, rather than being disrupted by them.

Keep It Simple Jugaad isn't about seeking sophistication or perfection by overengineering products, but rather about developing a "good enough" solution that gets the job done. Creative simplicity is jugaad's key principle. Western firms that are engaged in an "arms race" to out-innovate each other by cramming more technology and features into their products and services should make simplicity a key tenet of *their* innovation projects—just as entrepreneurs in emerging markets do. For instance, the open-source software company Ushahidi has developed an elegantly simple solution—the Ushahidi Platform—that relies on mobile SMS (text messaging) to coordinate bottom-up responses to cataclysmic events such as hurricanes, earthquakes, or epidemic outbreaks. The Ushahidi Platform was pioneered in Africa and is now being widely deployed worldwide—including in the United States—as a simple yet highly effective crisis management tool. In Chapter Five you will discover how large Western companies such as GM, Philips, and Siemens, as well as next-generation companies such as Google and Facebook, are using simplicity to ensure that their solutions are accessible and easy-to-use by a large number of users.

Include the Margin Western firms typically vie to serve mainstream customers; in contrast, jugaad entrepreneurs intentionally seek out marginal, underserved customers and pull them into the mainstream. Such entrepreneurs conjure up radically affordable solutions to meet the needs of these underserved markets. Their inclusive business models engage low-income and nontraditional communities, not as passive consumers but as active value cocreators. For instance, Dr. Liu Jiren, chairman and CEO of Neusoft, China's largest IT solution and service provider, is concerned about the health of eight hundred million Chinese living in rural areas who, says Dr. Liu, are going to "get older and sicker before they get wealthier."[51] Dr. Liu's genuine concern for China's marginal segments led him to develop inclusive technology solutions—such as telemedicine applications—that deliver affordable health care to millions of rural Chinese.

Similarly, Abhi Naha has founded Zone V, a company that seeks to empower the 284 million blind and partially sighted people worldwide by providing them with cellphones specially designed to meet their particular needs. Naha's aspiration is to build a world in which "lack of sight doesn't mean lack of vision."[52] In Chapter Six we explain why and how Procter & Gamble is fundamentally shifting its business model to serve the "un-served and under-served consumers"—marginal segments that increasingly include middle-class consumers in the United States whose purchasing power is being squeezed by the lack of growth in their income over the last decade.

Follow Your Heart Jugaad innovators do not rely on focus groups or formal market research to decide what products to make—nor do they worry about how investors will react to their new product strategies. They know their customers and their products intimately—and ultimately, they trust and follow their hearts. Specifically, jugaad entrepreneurs employ intuition, empathy, and passion—qualities that are increasingly just as important as analytical thinking in navigating a global environment that is ever more diverse, interconnected, and unpredictable. For instance, Kishore Biyani—founder of Big Bazaar, one of India's largest and most successful retail chains—did not use management consultants to validate his idea of launching retail stores that look, feel, and even smell like chaotic street bazaars. When he launched his new store format, he trusted his intuition—fired by his empathy for Indian consumers—more than any analysis. By intuitively sensing the latent needs of consumers in a high-aspiration society like India, Biyani conjured up an innovative retail model that is hard for rivals to replicate.

Similarly, Steve Jobs was the prototypical jugaad innovator in the West. He always heeded his intuition rather than relying on analytical thinking to innovate and grow. The result, as we explain in Chapter Seven, was a series of disruptive inventions such as the iPad, a product that consumers, analysts, and media initially were convinced had no market.

The heart is also the seat of passion. Jugaad entrepreneurs such as Diane Geng and Sara Lam, cofounders of the Rural China Education Foundation (RCEF), are motivated not by money or an "I want to go IPO and become a millionaire" mentality. Rather, as we detail in Chapter Seven, Geng and Lam were driven by a deep passion to make a difference in their communities. It was this passion that led them to develop a radically new approach to providing rural youth in China with a quality education. Also, a growing number of Western firms now recognize that the best way to motivate—and retain—knowledge workers is not by giving them bonuses, but by giving them the freedom to pursue projects that they are passionate about. In Chapter Seven we describe how frog, a global design and innovation consultancy, launched an initiative called Centers of Passion that lets its creative workers worldwide initiate or join projects in which they find a deep sense of meaning and purpose—well beyond sheer intellectual or even emotional satisfaction.

JUGAAD: A COMPLEMENT TO STRUCTURED INNOVATION

As Western firms strive for continued growth, they have much to gain from adopting and practicing these six principles of jugaad—seeking opportunity in adversity, doing more with less, thinking and acting flexibly, keeping it simple, including the margin, and following the heart. For too long, the Western model of innovation has been like an orchestra: top-down, rigid, and driven by upper-level employees. This model works well in a stable world of plentiful resources. But given the complex and unpredictable business environment that Western companies are about to face in the coming years, they need an alternative approach, one more akin to a jazz band: bottom-up, improvisational, fluid, and collaborative while working within a framework of deep knowledge. Jugaad represents that alternative.

It's important to note, however, that jugaad isn't relevant for all situations and contexts. In particular, jugaad shouldn't *replace* Western companies' existing structured approach to innovation; rather, jugaad should *complement* it. In this book, we argue that jugaad is an important tool that Western companies can add to their existing innovation toolkit. We explore each of the underlying principles of jugaad and show how they can fortify a structured approach to innovation and achieve growth by adding frugality and agility.

In particular, in Chapter Eight we discuss the advantages and limits of jugaad innovation, and the specific contexts in which jugaad is particularly effective (that is, complex and volatile environments). We describe how Western companies can mesh the agile and resilient spirit of jugaad with the more structured approach to innovation. For leaders of Western companies entrenched in a structured approach to innovation, the idea of adopting jugaad can seem daunting. We make that adoption process easier by helping corporate leaders prioritize the specific jugaad principles they need to adopt most urgently. We do this by matching the benefits of each of the six principles with the needs and context of organizations.

To illustrate how Western firms can accelerate their adoption of jugaad, we describe how a large western multinational—GE—is attempting to integrate a jugaad approach into its structured innovation approach steeped in Six Sigma practice. In sum, we show that jugaad can enrich the innovation toolkit of Western firms so they can effectively grow and succeed in a world of complexity and scarcity.

In our companion website (JugaadInnovation.com) you will find additional tools and roadmaps for prioritizing—and accelerating—the adoption of jugaad principles in your own organization.

A GROUNDSWELL JUGAAD MOVEMENT IS GROWING IN THE WEST

Over the last three years we have drawn on our business experience, academic training, and multimedia expertise to document and understand how emerging market innovators—from grassroots entrepreneurs such as Mansukh Prajapati to pioneering CEOs like Ratan Tata—think and act. We have written extensively about these innovators—and their jugaad principles—in our blog on the *Harvard Business Review* website. We have featured them in the PBS documentary film series *Indique: Big Ideas from Emerging India*.[53] Finally, we have drawn on the principles of jugaad to help organizations around the world implement them in order to innovate better, faster, and cheaper. The response to these efforts from readers, corporations, viewers, and clients around the world has been overwhelming.

Western leaders—inured to a world of relative abundance and used to operating for so long in a relatively predictable environment—have the most to learn from jugaad. We have consulted with Western companies that have begun to implement the principles of jugaad—companies that enjoy a culture that promotes openness and adaptability and that have harnessed the creativity of employees, customers, and partners alike. These companies have found that jugaad has given them the agility needed to sense and respond to rapid shifts in the highly volatile environments in which they operate—and deliver more value to customers at less cost.

Although it's been a long time since the previous, nineteenth-century era of jugaad in the West, we may now be coming full circle, as some firms begin to appreciate and adopt its principles again. In the coming chapters, we will illustrate how forward-thinking Western companies across diverse sectors—such as 3M, Apple, Best Buy, Facebook, GE,

Google, IBM, PepsiCo, Procter & Gamble, Renault-Nissan, and Wal-Mart—have already adopted the principles of jugaad, to their great advantage. These vanguard companies are combining the frugal and resilient spirit of jugaad with more structured traditional approaches to innovation to generate breakthrough growth.

But corporate leaders are not the only ones rediscovering the spirit of jugaad in the West. In Chapter Nine, we describe how a groundswell movement—led by creative citizens, forward-thinking entrepreneurs, venture capitalists, and non-profit organizations—is gaining momentum across Western societies. And increasingly, governments and universities are supporting such a jugaad ecosystem as well. For instance, the White House Office of Social Innovation and Civic Participation, set up by President Obama in early 2009, is enabling grassroots entrepreneurs across America to devise bottom-up solutions to address pressing socio-economic issues in their local communities. Similarly, Stanford University's Entrepreneurial Design for Extreme Affordability program is training future engineers and business leaders in how to develop high-quality products at low cost—such as an infant warmer that costs less than 2 percent of the cost of a traditional incubator—for use in both emerging markets and the United States. This emerging ecosystem not only creates an environment for jugaad innovators to thrive in but also helps Western firms in their own efforts to adopt jugaad. By joining this *external* groundswell movement, Western firms can accelerate their *internal* adoption of jugaad—and profit handsomely from it.

In the rest of this book, we present a vision of how whole swaths of Western economies—from education and healthcare to energy and manufacturing to retail and financial services—can be rejuvenated by embracing jugaad. At the heart of that vision, however, lie those six fundamental principles of jugaad *innovation*. We turn to an exploration of each of these principles in the following chapters.

CHAPTER TWO

PRINCIPLE ONE
Seek Opportunity in Adversity

It has done me good to be somewhat parched by the heat and drenched
by the rain of life.

— HENRY WADSWORTH LONGFELLOW

In the late 1980s, Tulsi Tanti moved to Surat, in the Indian state
of Gujarat, to set up a textile unit. Like other entrepreneurs in India,
Tanti found himself faced with infrastructural bottlenecks. The biggest
of these was the power supply. Expensive and unpredictable, power
proved a major barrier to growth. His profit margins were only around
5 percent, while energy accounted for a staggering 40 to 50 percent of
total operating costs.

Instead of giving in to this problem, Tanti focused on finding a
solution to it. He began to experiment with various types of boilers.
He looked at different kinds of power generators. He tried out different
combinations of boilers and generators. And then he realized that all
these were, in one way or another, dependent on fuel, gas, or oil. So
he thought, "Why not find a solution that doesn't require fuel?" This
launched him on a search for an alternative source of power that was
both reliable and sustainable.

In 1990, he invested in two wind turbines to supply electricity to his
textile unit. It soon became clear that this was the solution he had been
looking for. Now he had a power supply that was literally harnessed
from thin air. After the initial investment in the turbines was recovered,
his operating costs would be low and predictable. The "fuel" came at
no cost. And there was plenty of it.

With time, Tanti began to see the wider implications of his solution. Wind had the potential to power more than just Indian textile factories. It could meet the global demand for a steady supply of affordable energy: 44 percent of 1.2 billion Indians live outside the electricity grid, and worldwide more than 1,400 million people lack access to electricity.[1] Tanti saw this huge challenge as a vast untapped opportunity. So he set out to capture this opportunity by creating Suzlon Energy in 1995.

"As an entrepreneur," says Tanti, "I firmly believe that at the heart of every challenge lies an opportunity. Entrepreneurs are a league of people who are able to turn obstacles into profitable solutions."[2] This statement pretty much captures the essence of the resilient mindset that drives jugaad innovation.

Today Suzlon is the world's fifth largest wind energy solution provider. The company employs more than thirteen thousand people and provides a full spectrum of wind power solutions in over thirty countries on six continents. In the space of two decades, Tanti has gone from being dependent on an erratic and expensive supply of energy to creating—through innovation—a plentiful supply of it for millions worldwide.

Reflecting on this astounding growth, Tanti says: "The journey called Suzlon, embarked upon sixteen years ago, was my solution to an obstacle. The beginnings were humble, and the odds were against me, but my dreams were big. And when dreams are pursued with conviction and fortitude, they not only become a reality, they are a force that guides you and shapes your life and those of the people around you."

Jugaad innovators like Tulsi Tanti are adept at taking on the arduous challenges that emerging markets pose and reframing them as opportunities to learn, innovate, and grow. These innovators respond to even the most adverse circumstances by demonstrating resilience, ingenuity, and an aptitude for risk. Seeking opportunity in adversity is often the first and most critical of the six principles that jugaad innovators have to apply. After all, jugaad innovators face adversity from the very beginning of their innovation journeys; if they are unable to apply the principle of seeking opportunity in adversity at the outset, they will be unlikely to move on to discover and apply the other five principles of jugaad.

A resilient jugaad mindset can also enable Western executives to systematically turn adversity into an opportunity for innovation and growth. In this chapter, we show how Western organizations can unlearn practices that worked in a bygone era of relative predictability and find new ways to succeed in a future of adversity and constant change. But first we explore why and how jugaad entrepreneurs seek opportunity in adversity.

A HARSH ENVIRONMENT NURTURES RESILIENCE

Entrepreneurs and managers in emerging economies face adversity at every turn. Take India as a case in point. Even starting a business there is a daunting task. Doing so takes an average of 165 days (compared to 9 in the United States). Securing the necessary licenses to construct a simple warehouse is complex, time consuming, and costly, involving 34 procedures over 227 days and costing 1,631 percent of the country's per-capita income.[3] Running a business is even harder. Property rights are often unclear or hard to ascertain, so acquiring land is fraught with difficulties. Labor laws are restrictive or complex or both, and can be a minefield to navigate. Due to India's federal structure, there are currently 47 national laws and 157 state regulations that directly affect India's labor market.[4] Hiring and firing of workers presents its own challenges. New taxes may be instituted and applied at any time.

On top of all this bureaucracy, political upheavals are a fact of life. A local government with a policy favoring business may fall overnight and be replaced by another that favors agriculture over industry. Land that was granted to a company to set up a factory may be confiscated and returned to the original owners or fall under litigation. Court cases are expensive and drag on for years, often with no clear resolution in sight.

But perhaps there is no greater challenge to starting a business in India than its poor infrastructure. Jugaad entrepreneurs in India—as in other emerging markets like China, Africa, and Brazil—do not have access to many of the basic things that are taken for granted in the West. Roads can be poor, heavily congested, or nonexistent (40 percent of India's villages do not have access to all-weather roads).[5] Education and training systems are patchy, so skilled personnel are hard to come by. Health care services are scant, and workers who get sick may stay out of work for long periods.[6]

Emerging markets like India also face acute shortages of resources: natural, human, and financial. It can be hard to raise capital. Banks are typically conservative, and venture capital and angel investor networks are underdeveloped. As a result, jugaad innovators cannot afford to invest in capital-intensive equipment. Jugaad innovators also typically serve a market that is economically deprived: 80 percent of Indians live on less than $2 a day; 26 percent of Brazilians live below the poverty line; 230 million African households are *unbanked*—that is, they do not have a bank account; and nearly 40 percent of rural Chinese can't afford basic medical treatment.[7, 8, 9] (The extent of scarcity in emerging markets is so dire that how innovators respond to it constitutes the second principle of jugaad—do more with less—which we discuss in Chapter Three.)

Trying to operate in such a harsh environment could drain the energies of even the toughest business person. Yet jugaad innovators are unfazed by the reality that surrounds them. Indeed, it is this very harshness that gives them their particularly resilient mindset. Extreme *external* circumstances seem to heighten their *internal* resolve to succeed. As with Tulsi Tanti, rather than becoming passive victims of current circumstances, jugaad innovators are driven to take charge of events and steer them in a direction of their own choosing. For them, adversity exists largely in the mind.

Dr. Thomas Müller, a psychologist who specializes in crisis management, observes that in a crisis some people simply attempt to go back to how things were before. In the process, they make compromises for the sake of security. Others, however, withstand the pressure and ask themselves, "If I go one step further, what's the opportunity to be exploited?"[10] Jugaad entrepreneurs belong to this second category. When confronted with adversity, they don't retrench but embrace the difficulties and learn from the experience.

Armed with resilience, perseverance, and a willingness to learn, jugaad innovators strive to respond to the harsh world they face and find opportunities for growth and expansion in it. In doing so, they are able to create a better world, not just for themselves but also for their communities.

REFRAMING THE HALF-EMPTY GLASS AS HALF FULL

Jugaad innovators find opportunity in adversity in three ways: reframing challenges as opportunities for growth, making constraints work for them, and constantly adapting to a changing environment by improvising solutions to challenges they face along the way. In this section, we examine each of these strategies and look at specific examples of each.

The first and perhaps most important strategy of jugaad innovators is *reframing—that is, changing the lens through which they perceive the situation they face.* Jugaad innovators perceive and interpret the world differently from the rest of us.[11] Their ability to reframe means they are likely to see the glass half full even when everyone else sees it as half empty. Indeed, one may think of jugaad innovators as modern-day alchemists who *mentally* transform adversity into opportunity.

An example of such an alchemist is O.P. Bhatt, former chairman of the State Bank of India (SBI), India's largest and oldest bank, with more than two hundred thousand employees and twenty thousand branches across India. O.P. Bhatt was appointed its chairman in 2006. A lifelong banker, he was deeply aware of the immense creative potential of SBI's large employee base and was eager to find ways to unleash it. But he also knew that his hands were tied in many ways. The SBI is partially owned by the Government of India, which in turn is run by risk-averse bureaucrats who vet every hiring and firing decision. (In fact, it's virtually impossible to fire anyone once he or she gets a job in a government-owned Indian enterprise.) As Dr. Prasad Kaipa, a CEO coach who has advised Bhatt, points out: "It was clear to Bhatt from the start that he could neither 'get the right people on the bus nor get the wrong people off the bus.' It was also obvious to him that he lacked the resources to financially motivate his managers to take risks and drive innovative projects (Bhatt himself was paid less than US$1,000 a month)."[12]

These challenges, though significant, did not faze Bhatt. Instead, he used a jugaad approach to ignite the genius within SBI. First, he drew on his superior communication skills to rekindle his employees' feelings of pride about SBI, a bank with a distinguished two-hundred-year-old history. Then, through an in-house training program called Parivarthan (Sanskrit for "transformation"), he instilled a new sense of commitment into SBI staff across all levels and departments. In time, the program began to bear fruit: SBI employees felt more empowered, demonstrated greater creativity, and took customer service to new heights. Across the country, employees began to devise bold and ingenious solutions to problems they had always faced but had never felt the desire or had the support to address. For example, in the city of Hyderabad, within five months Mr. Sivakumar, the local head of SBI operations, launched an SMS-based customer complaint unit of four people to deal with seven thousand complaints—thus building a loyal customer base receptive to the bank's future marketing and promotional initiatives.[13]

By reframing a seemingly adverse situation as an opportunity, Bhatt unleashed the creative genius in his employees. And the payoff was huge. In four years, SBI increased its market share from 16.5 percent to 19 percent, doubling its stock price and boosting customer satisfaction—and all this in a mature and highly competitive market. In this period SBI also won many international awards for its stellar performance.

As Bhatt's story shows, jugaad innovators don't find opportunity *in spite of* adversity; for them, adversity often *is* the opportunity. They perceive constraints not as a debilitating deterrent but as a creative stimulus. Indeed, their creative juices begin to flow when they are confronted with a seemingly insurmountable challenge.

The second way jugaad innovators find opportunity in adversity is by *making constraints work for them rather than against them*. In Chapter One we introduced Kanak Das, a jugaad innovator who hails from Morigaon, a village in the northeast Indian state of Assam. Like many Indians, Das rides a bicycle to work. And, as in many parts of India, the roads he travels on are full of potholes and bumps. These not only gave him back problems but also slowed him down considerably. Das knew there was little or nothing he could do to improve the quality of these roads. So instead he posed a quintessentially jugaad question: "What if I can actually find a way to make my bike run *faster* on these cratered roads?" That question inspired him to retrofit his bicycle so that every time the front wheel hits a bump, a shock absorber compresses and releases energy to the rear wheel. By converting the energy in the shock absorber into a propulsive force, his bicycle can run faster on bumpy roads.

"Making the bumps work for you" is how Professor Anil Gupta of the Indian Institute of Management in Ahmedabad refers to Das's ingenious solution. Gupta is a passionate advocate of grassroots innovations in India. He notes, "You have hybrid cars today that generate energy from brakes, but not from shock absorbers: it is a whole new concept that Kanak Das has pioneered."[14] The National Innovation Foundation, where Gupta serves as executive vice-chairperson, has helped patent Das's invention. Who knows where this might lead? In the not-too-distant future, cyclists all over the world may benefit from Kanak Das's jugaad innovation. Already, engineering students at MIT are using Das's invention as inspiration for how to convert the energy generated by shock absorbers in automobiles into acceleration.[15]

The third way that jugaad innovators seek opportunity in adversity is by *being quick to act in response to the opportunities they see*. Not only did Kanak Das and O.P. Bhatt *think differently* in response to adversity, but they also *acted quickly* to adapt their models and strategies to the challenges in their environments. Jugaad innovators aren't attached to old business models and will let go of past successes if conditions require this. This ability to constantly adapt and reinvent themselves—with a crystal clear focus on the future—is key to jugaad innovators' long-term survival.

An example of such adaptability is Enrique Gómez Junco, a Mexican engineer turned jugaad entrepreneur.[16] In the late 1980s, Junco was driven by a vision to create a sustainable energy business. In 1988 he set up a company called Celsol to sell thermosolar panels to Mexican businesses, especially hotels. But he found it hard to crack this market: it was highly regulated, subsidized, and dominated by monopolies, and he had trouble finding capital to finance Celsol. Rather than give up on his vision, Junco shut down Celsol and launched a new venture—Optima Energía—in 2000. Optima's initial plan was to sell energy technologies to building owners and facility managers to help them use electricity more efficiently and save on energy costs. These energy-saving technologies would also provide an environmental benefit, as commercial buildings account for 7 percent of man-made carbon dioxide emissions worldwide. But again he failed. Optima's value proposition didn't impress facility managers much, because it required them to make a large up-front investment that would not yield significant returns in the short term.

This new setback shifted Junco's perspective once again. He realized that as an engineer he had fallen in love with technology for its own sake, and in the process had forgotten about his customers. His customers, he realized, didn't care how good his technology was: what they wanted was to save money. Immediately he knew that he had to shift his positioning again: from being a high-risk, niche *technology* vendor to being a low-risk, end-to-end *business solution* provider.

Armed with this insight, in 2004 Junco went back to the drawing board and reinvented his company's value proposition. Rather than merely selling a technology, Optima began offering an integrated solution to risk-averse commercial building operators. Specifically, Optima would sign a performance-based contract with a client to implement an energy efficiency project that could potentially save the client up to 50 percent in energy costs. The client would not have to invest a dime, however. Instead, Optima would directly finance the installation of the relevant technology in partnership with leading financial institutions, including the World Bank's International Finance Corporation.[17] The client would then use the initial savings in energy costs generated by the project to pay back Optima's capital investment over a ten-year period. All additional savings would then be split between Optima and the client. Optima has been especially successful in selling this value proposition to major hotels—in particular, the energy-hungry resorts located along the coastline of the Gulf of Mexico.

After reinventing his business model twice, Junco finally realized his vision of saving clients' energy costs while protecting the environment.[18] Since its founding, Optima has consulted with more than 120 different clients and implemented its turnkey solutions in more than fifty facilities. The firm has saved its customers $100 million, 16 million cubic meters of water, 230 million kilowatts of electricity, 41 million liters of natural gas, and 14 million liters of diesel. Junco is now planning to take his integrated solution into other sectors—especially manufacturing and public services (such as municipalities), where the market for energy saving is an estimated $7 billion in Mexico alone.[19] Optima began its life as a clean technology provider but has evolved into a successful financial services provider that happens to be in the energy sector. Junco's adaptability allowed him to overcome adversity. For his unrelenting efforts to drive greener construction and provide clean energy in Mexico, Junco was selected by the World Economic Forum as one of the 100 Global Leaders for Tomorrow; he also received the Wharton Infosys Business Transformation Award in 2006.[20]

Jugaad entrepreneurs like Junco approach innovation—indeed, approach life in general—as a potentially never-ending experiment. Trial and error is an important part of the process; individual failures and successes are merely way stations on a longer journey. As such, jugaad allows innovators like Junco to adapt, evolve, and continuously reinvent their ideas over time.

To sum up: jugaad innovators are experts at reframing challenges as opportunities, making constraints work for them, and adapting to changing circumstances by improvising solutions along the way. Jugaad innovators develop these strategies in response to the sometimes extreme forms of adversity they face in the business environment in emerging markets. But what relevance do these strategies have for Western firms, given the very different nature of the business environment in developed economies? We now explore how adversity is increasingly an important factor in the Western business environment and the implications of this for Western business leaders.

BUCKLE UP, WESTERN FIRMS:
MAJOR ADVERSITY AHEAD

It would be easy to assume that jugaad innovators' reframing of adversity and adaptation to a constantly changing environment is not relevant to innovators, entrepreneurs, and business people in the West. After all, the West is prosperous. Western firms and their leaders don't have to struggle in a constantly turbulent political and economic environment or worry about poor infrastructure and scarce resources. Compared to emerging economies, the West is relatively stable. Or has been, until now. Ominous signs indicate that the West is poised to experience a sustained period of turbulence and painful change in the years to come. Let's look at the major sources of adversity that Western companies now face:

• *A worsening macro-economic situation.* The already anemic U.S. and European economies may soon become comatose as demand fails to pick up in spite of umpteen stimulus packages. The International Monetary Fund (IMF) predicted that the U.S. economy will grow by just 1.8 percent in 2012 and expects the Euro-zone economy to limp along at 1.1 percent.[21] This poor growth will place severe constraints on the capital that companies will have access to in the years to come. In general, the poor macro-economic climate will force Western firms, large and small, to find new ways to put scarce capital to better use in the coming decade.

• *An avalanche of new regulations to come.* In addition to health care and financial services, other industries—from automotive to food to energy—are likely to face a host of new regulations from legislators in the years to come. For instance, the U.S. carmakers reluctantly agreed to an Obama administration plan to push for stringent federal fuel economy standards that would double efficiency targets to fifty-four miles per gallon by 2025.[22] These stringent regulations will place further constraints on businesses—forcing them, in the coming decade, to radically change their current practices and even their business models to meet new regulatory requirements.

- *Tectonic shifts in demographics.* European firms have to contend with a rapidly aging workforce. For instance, Germany will lose five million workers—or 12 percent of its total workforce—over the next fifteen years due to retirement.[23] And U.S. firms have to contend with the growing diversity of their multigenerational, multi-ethnic workers and consumers. This will put pressure on employee recruitment and retention and make it hard for Western firms to meet the diverse needs of a heterogeneous customer base.

- *The social computing revolution.* The explosive growth of social media networks such as Facebook and Twitter—which enable improvised and informal grassroots interactions among hundreds of millions of users worldwide—is challenging the corporate orthodoxy embodied in hierarchal communication, linear planning methods, and insular approaches to innovation.

- *The accelerating scarcity of natural resources.* Natural resources such as oil and water that have hitherto been cheap and plentiful in the West will become scarcer in the years to come. According to a report by Ceres, sectors such as agriculture, food and beverage, hi-tech, and pharmaceuticals could be severely affected by water shortfalls. For instance, a water-related shutdown at a semiconductor factory operated by Intel or Texas Instruments could cost them $100–$200 million in missed revenues during a quarter. This grim outlook led Nestlé chairman Peter Brabeck-Letmathe to comment: "I am convinced that ... we will run out of water long before we run out of fuel." This increasing scarcity will force companies to find sustainable methods to generate more energy or food using less of these increasingly expensive resources.[24]

- *Unforgiving competition from emerging markets.* Western firms are facing stiff competition in North American and European markets from low-cost rivals in emerging economies. For example, Chinese consumer product companies HTC and Haier are giving Nokia and Whirlpool a run for their money by introducing feature-rich cellphones and kitchen appliances at low prices that greatly appeal to cost-conscious Western consumers.

All these challenges are generating constraints within the environment in which Western firms operate. These constraints could paralyze Western leaders and cripple their decision-making processes, but they could also galvanize Western leaders into innovating for growth. For the latter to be the case, Western leaders must learn to reframe the adversity they face not as a debilitating challenge (or "risk," as management consultants call it) but rather a unique opportunity to innovate and grow—just as Tulsi Tanti, O.P. Bhatt, and other jugaad innovators have done.

But doing so is more challenging than it looks. Faced with harsh challenges like those just mentioned, Western firms tend to gravitate toward adopting one of four responses to adverse situations. They fail to notice adversity or simply ignore it, they try to tackle it head-on, they address it with old frames of reference, or they think too small or incrementally in response to adversity. But all of these responses are counterproductive in today's business environment. Here's why:

• *Failing to notice—or ignoring—adversity until it's too late.* Western CEOs often fail to read the writing on the wall, because of complacence, inertia, or overconfidence. Gary Hamel, author of *The Future of Management*, notes that many Western executives don't pay sufficient attention to the early warning signs of big shifts in demographics, technology, and regulation—thus missing out on a great opportunity to proactively innovate their business models to take advantage of these shifts.[25] Instead, corporate leaders generally react to problems only after things have gotten out of control and their companies are up against the wall. For instance, right after the September 11, 2001, terrorist attacks, when the U.S. economy plunged into the red, U.S. carmakers failed to recognize a structural shift in American consumers' behaviors. Consumers were looking not just for cheaper cars—which GM and Ford offered with tons of rebates and 0-percent financing—but for *better* cars that were fuel-efficient and eco-friendly. Consequently, U.S. automakers failed to invest early in innovation to make energy-efficient cars—losing out to forward-thinking German and Japanese rivals.

- *Tackling adversity head-on, rather than seeking to leverage it.* When faced with the possibility of harsh constraints, Western CEOs often attempt to neutralize them rather than find a way to use them to their advantage. For instance, when facing regulatory constraints, many CEOs choose to oppose such constraints and lobby to have them repealed or delayed. We see this with large pharmaceutical companies that face shrinking drug development pipelines and a patent cliff, competition from emerging markets' generics manufacturers, and a U.S. government keen to reduce health care costs. Many of these firms have chosen to lobby to keep their business model intact, extend patents, and keep foreign competition out rather than respond innovatively to these challenges—for instance, by fundamentally rethinking and changing their business models.

- *Addressing new problems with old frames of reference.* Successful executives often resemble generals fighting an earlier war. They fight new battles using strategies that may have achieved victory in the past but are toothless in the present changed conditions. For instance, consumer goods companies continue to rely on traditional mass-marketing strategies like TV advertising, even though it is clear that consumers want to engage brands in a two-way dialogue using social media tools such as Facebook and Twitter.[26]

- *Thinking small when facing big challenges.* According to Adam Richardson, author of *Innovation X* and creative director at frog, a global design and innovation consultancy, most executives play it safe when confronted with extreme conditions.[27] Thus, in response to hypercompetition or rapid technological or market change, they are more likely to come up with incremental innovations and "me too" products, rather than reach for the big untapped "white spaces" in the market that are up for grabs. For example, Borders recognized the Internet's potential early on but failed to take adequate advantage of it; its e-commerce initiatives were tepid at best. In fact, when the Borders.com site was launched in 1998, it allowed readers to only check the availability of books but not to actually purchase them. Eventually Amazon established its dominance, and Borders folded in 2011.

Tempting as it may be to dismiss adversity as an emerging markets problem alone, there is increasing evidence that adversity is moving westward. But even if Western firms and leaders recognize this fact, they may fail to deal with it effectively, for the reasons just discussed. If Western firms and leaders want to avoid the pitfalls of these four counterproductive responses to adversity—and wish to truly turn challenges into opportunities—they would be wise to learn a thing or two from the resilient mindset of jugaad innovators such as Tulsi Tanti, O.P. Bhatt, Kanak Das, and Enrique Gómez Junco. We now turn to a discussion of how they might do so.

LEARNING TO CAPITALIZE ON ADVERSITY

Western leaders can systematically turn adversity into an opportunity to innovate and grow by adopting the resilient mindset of jugaad innovators and their coping strategies.

Recognize That the Glass Is Always Half-Full   Western leaders can learn from jugaad innovators how to turn adversity on its head and get it to work in their favor. The key to doing so is being able to reframe challenges as opportunities and use constraints as a spur to innovate. But one cannot reframe (that is, see that the glass is actually half-full) while one operates in a state of fear. Fear only clouds one's perspective and inhibits one's reactions. Rather, when facing crises and challenges, leaders must cultivate a sense of equanimity and demonstrate what Justin Menkes, author of *Better Under Pressure*, calls "realistic optimism."[28]

Menkes, who works for the executive search firm Spencer Stuart, studied more than two hundred candidates for the CEO position and interviewed over sixty current and retired CEOs in his research. He found that a key attribute that enables leaders to achieve their potential (and that of their organizations) is "realistic optimism"; that is, the ability to clearly recognize the risks that threaten survival and yet remain confident that the company will prevail. In other words, at the first sight of a dark cloud, successful CEOs don't pull out the umbrella but strive instead to identify the silver lining around the cloud—just as jugaad innovators do.

For instance, many Fortune 500 CEOs feel threatened by the explosive growth of social media (as of this writing, over 250 million Tweets are sent each day and Facebook has more than 800 million members), especially after witnessing the damage done by Wikileaks. They fret about how social media tools, when placed in the wrong hands, can be used to spread false rumors, damage brands, and ruin corporate and personal reputations within hours. In contrast, as early as the year 2000, well before Twitter and Facebook saw the light of day, Procter & Gamble's top management identified the tremendous potential of social networking tools. They wholeheartedly embraced these tools as a new *social engagement* platform on which to build and sustain a meaningful dialogue with consumers in the digital economy of the twenty-first century. In the past, when developing new products, Procter & Gamble's R&D teams used to rely on expensive, time-consuming focus groups and physical prototyping to test their new ideas. Now they use social media tools like Affinnova to test dozens of new product ideas with hundreds of customers voting online on their favorite features. Thanks to this real-time collaboration with customers, Procter & Gamble can swiftly weed out unprofitable product ideas early on and dedicate R&D resources to developing product concepts that customers like the most.[29] Likewise, Procter & Gamble has turned the viral marketing power of social networks to its advantage—by converting satisfied customers into "word of mouth marketers" of the firm's brands in cyberspace. For example, the company has built Vocalpoint—an online community of more than six hundred thousand socially engaged mothers it can tap for early feedback on new promotional campaigns before launching them nationally—helping to get each marketing message right the very first time. Vocalpoint members also generate positive buzz on social networks for Procter & Gamble's upcoming products.[30] Thanks to this reframing of social media and their business value, Procter & Gamble has not only boosted customer loyalty but has also established new industry-leading practices in social engagement—well ahead of its rivals. The firm has even packaged its social marketing skills to create Tremor, a software service sold to other companies such as Kellogg, Sears, and MasterCard seeking to harness the power of word-of-mouth marketing to boost their own brands.[31]

Realize Extreme Conditions Are Fertile Soil for Extreme Innovation Taking a cue from jugaad innovators, Western corporate leaders should view extreme conditions—such as massive technology shifts, draconian regulations, or competitive threats that come out of the blue—as an opportunity to develop radical innovations that disrupt industries and shape whole new markets. Marc Benioff, chairman and CEO of salesforce.com, is one such Western innovator. In 1999, Benioff founded salesforce.com in his San Francisco apartment with a bold vision: he wanted to make the business software—which enterprises use to manage their customer interactions—affordable and accessible to more companies. He envisioned using the Internet as a platform to deliver business software to corporations as a *service*, rather than as a product—as it had been so far. The idea was that firms would subscribe to software applications hosted by salesforce.com on a "pay-as-you-go" basis and access them using just a web browser rather than having them installed on employees' PCs—thus avoiding the expensive license fees and maintenance costs charged by large software vendors like Oracle, Siebel, and SAP.

Yet in 2001, just as salesforce.com was about to take off, the dot-com bubble burst and the stock market plummeted. Large corporations perceived Benioff as yet another dot-com entrepreneur peddling snake oil and refused to buy into his vision of Software as a Service (SaaS). Benioff and his startup were ridiculed by large competitors who questioned the security and scalability of the SaaS model. In April 2001, Tom Siebel, CEO and founder of Siebel, a large business software vendor, predicted that salesforce.com would be out of business by 2002.[32]

But Benioff persisted in the face of all this adversity. He saw a silver lining in the dark economic cloud that engulfed corporate America in the early 2000s. He realized that his cost-conscious potential customers—small to large firms—were confronted with their *own* challenges. In particular: (1) they were struggling to extract more value from their software investments without breaking the bank, and (2) they wanted their existing software solutions to quickly adapt to rapidly evolving business needs. Unfortunately, firms were stuck with software applications that were too expensive to maintain and not flexible enough—and they had trouble conceptualizing what an alternative solution might be.

Sensing an opportunity, Benioff started evangelizing to potential customers the merits of the SaaS model—rather than touting salesforce.com's capabilities. He passionately articulated the value of SaaS, not only to frugal technology buyers but also to flexibility-seeking C-level executives. For instance, he explained to corporate leaders how—with the explosion of mobile devices—the SaaS model could enable their employees to access their business applications anywhere, anytime—something that could not be done with the traditional, centralized software delivery model. Benioff also tirelessly promoted the SaaS model to the press, analyst firms, and other influential tech industry figures. Eventually, large businesses warmed to SaaS and began to buy into Benioff's vision—and into salesforce.com. Thanks to Benioff's persistent evangelizing of SaaS, a groundswell movement was ignited in the tech sector. As more software developers recognized the benefits of the SaaS model, they started building more solutions using the model—spawning a whole new software ecosystem that made the model self-sustainable.[33]

Salesforce.com was comfortably positioned to lead this SaaS movement—and it did. Salesforce.com's subscriber base grew by 1,500 percent in the following seven years, and it currently serves more than 100,000 customers.[34] Averaging an annual revenue growth of 36 percent in recent years, salesforce.com expects to reach a $3 billion annual revenue run rate during its fiscal year 2013.[35] Benioff has set for salesforce.com a "$10 billion vision," which he believes "consists of customer success."[36]

The SaaS movement that Benioff initiated has since evolved and is now known as "cloud computing" (an appropriate name, considering it was born out of Benioff's ability to see a silver lining in every dark cloud). The cloud computing market, which was worth $40 billion in 2010, is predicted to balloon to $241 billion by 2020.[37] All the major software vendors who initially ridiculed salesforce.com's business model have since jumped onto the cloud computing bandwagon—and those who didn't have disappeared (salesforce.com's archrival Siebel was bought by Oracle in 2005).

Benioff believes that extreme conditions can generate ground-breaking innovation: "salesforce.com is a living example of how resilient entrepreneurs—and corporations—can transcend the extreme difficulties they face and turn them into opportunities for success."[38]

Build Psychological Capital to Boost Confident Resilience

Leaders cannot build a resilient organization without a resilient work-force. Fred Luthans, professor of organizational behavior at the University of Nebraska-Lincoln, puts it this way: "The true value of a company is no longer its tangible assets or even its technological processes: it lies in its human capital and underlying psychological capital—neither of which is open to imitation. Anyone can buy technology or obtain money from financial markets; but we cannot buy motivation, engagement, confidence, resiliency, hope, optimism."[39]

It's not enough for business leaders to be optimistic, resilient, and adaptable. They also need to *empower employees at every level* to think and act like jugaad innovators—by embracing ambiguity, tolerating risks, and being willing to learn from challenges rather than trying to wish them away. Franck Riboud is one such leader, keen to boost his firm's psychological capital. Riboud is the CEO of Danone—a French multinational that is one of the world's largest suppliers of dairy products and bottled waters (its dairy products are branded as Dannon in the United States). Riboud believes that his ninety-two-year-old company is confronted with two major challenges: (1) consumers worldwide are clamoring for healthy, nutritious food items that are affordable and sustainably produced; and (2) the biggest business opportunities in coming decades will come from emerging markets—such as Mexico, Indonesia, China, Russia, and Brazil—where Danone needs to innovate, and adopt, new business models to effectively capture the exploding growth opportunities. These two challenges are making the business environment in which Danone operates highly complex, simultaneously creating more constraints while opening new opportunities. As Riboud explains: "Our future hinges on our ability to explore and invent new business models and new types of business corporations."[40]

To navigate this complex environment, Riboud recognizes that Danone needs a more adaptable workforce with a resilient mindset. To succeed in a "multipolar" world characterized by multiple centers of growth, Riboud is gradually transforming Danone—a very traditional French firm with most decision-making power and R&D activity concentrated in Europe—into a *polycentric organization* with a decentralized decision-making structure and a globally distributed R&D network.[41] Such a polycentric structure will empower frontline managers worldwide—especially in fast-growing emerging markets like China and Brazil—to address local challenges and opportunities by improvising robust solutions just as jugaad innovators do—all the while sharing innovative ideas and best practices through peer-to-peer knowledge networks.[42, 43] Unlike other multinationals that compel employees worldwide to do things *the right way* (using rigid and highly standardized processes), Riboud is motivating its global workforce to do *the right thing* (by embodying the companywide values of openness, enthusiasm, and humanism).[44] By decentralizing decision making and R&D operations—all the while enabling collaboration and knowledge sharing among regional units and maintaining high standards of social and environmental sustainability—Danone has been able to increase its organizational flexibility and successfully expand in emerging economies, which account for 60 percent of Danone's future growth.[45]

This, however, is only half the story. Riboud's real objective in creating a polycentric, multipolar organizational structure is to initiate a veritable *revolution of the mind* within Danone's leadership team. As Western economies enter an age of scarcity and complexity, Riboud wants to cultivate in his Western managers a whole new way of thinking and acting under constraints—a resilient mindset that is prevalent in

emerging markets like Brazil and China. In particular, Riboud wants
Danone's senior managers in the West to innovate frugally and flexibly
under severe resource constraints—by learning from jugaad innovators
in emerging markets who know how to turn adversity into an opportunity
to innovate. Riboud explains: "Until recently we assumed that the richest countries would be the main source of innovation. As I see it, it's the
countries with strong growth that should inspire us."[46] For instance,
building a micro dairy product factory in Bangladesh requires the same
amount of capital that one needs to buy a house in France—a fact that
inspired Danone's Western leaders to adopt radically new solutions to
reduce operating costs in big traditional plants without compromising
quality. Riboud believes that by adopting a flexible mindset, Danone's
Western leaders can not only reduce manufacturing costs but also
dramatically improve product design, marketing, and distribution across
the company.

In recent years, despite challenging market conditions, Danone has
posted financial results that have exceeded targets: with sales up nearly 7
percent in 2010, the firm is among the best performers in the food industry worldwide. Riboud is convinced that Danone has found the right
business model to succeed in today's complex global economy. More
important, Riboud believes that Danone's unique culture, which emphasizes pragmatism, adaptability, and local decisions—what he calls being
"quick on your feet"—is a huge advantage in adverse circumstances.
Interestingly, one of the six big "emerging markets" that Danone is
targeting is ... the United States. Unlike other Western CEOs who
complain about the moribund U.S. economy, Riboud sees huge opportunities for his yogurt products in the United States, where per-capita
yogurt consumption is still low compared to European markets.[47]

Approach Big Challenges with a Growth Mindset   According
to Carol Dweck, professor of psychology at Stanford University, most
leaders operate with one of two mindsets: a fixed mindset or a growth
mindset. Leaders with a fixed mindset believe their qualities—and
others'—are carved in stone, compelling them to stick to tried and tested

solutions to challenges. In contrast, leaders with a growth mindset believe that their basic qualities can be nurtured and improved through efforts. Jugaad innovators are endowed with a growth mindset: they confidently focus on building the future, rather than clinging to the safety of the past.

We believe that as the business environment becomes increasingly complex and adversarial, it is vital that corporate leaders cultivate a *growth mindset*. This is critical because when leaders face adversity with a fixed mindset, their minds are clouded by fear or pride, they tend to innovate incrementally, and their efforts yield limited results. A growth mindset instead helps leaders approach even big challenges with optimism and curiosity—enabling them to generate breakthrough innovation that delivers more sustainable results in the long term. Specifically, those with a growth mindset are willing to let go of old business models and embrace new ones to maintain long-term success.

IBM is one company that has been successful in cultivating a growth mindset among its leaders. IBM celebrated its one hundredth anniversary in June 2011. The company has survived two world wars, the Great Depression, the 1970s oil crisis, the dot-com boom and bust, and even the current global economic recession. Over the past century, the firm's leaders have used a growth mindset to proactively disrupt the company many times over, completely reinventing its business model again and again. Thus IBM has gone from selling tabulators to typewriters to mainframes to networked PCs to software and services—effectively riding one technology wave after another.[48] Compare this with HP, IBM's rival in Silicon Valley, whose leaders seem to have waited too long to reinvent the firm's seventy-year-old business model. With stock prices plummeting and a leadership crisis under way, HP's top management seriously considered selling its PC business in late 2011 but finally decided to retain it.[49] The leadership of IBM has been more proactive; in the early 2000s, they recognized that although the company had invented the PC, its PC business was rapidly being commoditized by the emerging Internet-based computing model. In 2004, IBM's former CEO Sam Palmisano make the radical decision to sell its PC business—freeing resources so the company could move up the tech industry value chain.[50] Here is how Palmisano explains his decision: "In 1981 the PC was an innovation. Twenty years later it had lost much of its differentiation. It was time to move on—to the future. This enterprise (IBM) has always moved to the future. Continual forward movement is, in fact, inherent in IBM's value proposition, our business model. The frontier of what is truly innovative keeps moving ... and that compels us not to sit still."[51]

Tap the Power of Networks to Tackle Big Market Threats

Rather than deal with adversity by relying exclusively on internal resources, corporate leaders can benefit from working with customers, partners, and even competitors to cocreate innovative solutions. Take Pfizer: CEO Ian Read is breaking out of the Big Pharma R&D mold and trying to think and act like a nimble jugaad innovator. Rather than depending exclusively on internal R&D for innovation, under Reed's leadership, Pfizer is multiplying R&D alliances with external partners. In some ways, Pfizer has no choice, as it faces a double whammy: its drug development pipeline is drying up even as it faces growing pressure in the United States and Europe to rein in skyrocketing health care spending. Seeing the writing on the wall, Read cut 24 percent of Pfizer's own R&D spending—an act deemed sacrilegious by Wall Street analysts—and is shifting the resulting savings into new partnerships with academic labs and nimble biotech firms worldwide.[52] For instance, the firm recently struck a licensing deal with Biocon, the Indian bio-pharma company, to market the latter's diabetes treatment products in both emerging and developed markets.[53]

To sum up: Western companies and their leaders can find opportunity in adversity in a number of ways, including

- Recognizing that the glass is always half-full
- Realizing extreme conditions are fertile soil for extreme innovation
- Building psychological capital to boost resilience
- Approaching big challenges with a growth mindset
- Tapping the power of networks to tackle big market threats

Although many individual leaders and their companies have employed one or more of these coping strategies, few firms and their leaders have employed many—if not all—of these strategies consistently over time. An exception is 3M; under several legendary leaders over 110 years the company has applied many of these robust strategies to turn adversity to its advantage and continually stimulate growth. We turn to a detailed case study of 3M with a view to understanding how the company and its leaders were able to seek and find opportunity in adversity in a sustained way over a long period of time.

HOW 3M'S JUGAAD SPIRIT BUCKED THE RECESSION

Founded in 1902, 3M has come to epitomize American ingenuity. Over the course of a century, its prolific inventors have churned out breakthrough products that have become part of Americana: Scotch® Tape, Scotchgard™ Protector for Fabric & Upholstery, Thinsulate™ Insulation, and Post-it Notes. 3M's jugaad innovators like Art Fry—who invented the Post-it Note—have produced scores of useful products that have made life easier for millions of consumers across the globe.[54]

What makes 3M so innovative can be summed up in two numbers: 30 percent and 15 percent. Both figures are deemed sacrosanct by 3M's management and employees. Decades ago, recognizing that its consumer products face rapid obsolescence, 3M set itself the goal of generating 30 percent of its total revenues from new products it had introduced in the preceding five years. This bold goal—known within 3M as the New Product Vitality Index (NPVI)—helped create an innovate-or-die culture that sustains a constant sense of urgency among 3M designers and engineers who continually develop hundreds of new products each year (3M currently boasts a portfolio of seventy-five thousand products). Interestingly, some of 3M's most successful products to date were invented by its engineers in their "spare time." Indeed, way back in 1948, long before the idea was popularized by Silicon Valley firms like Google, 3M launched the 15-percent program—a radical initiative that allows 3M employees to use 15 percent of their paid work time to pursue their dream projects—especially left-field jugaad innovations.[55] The 15-percent program's objective was to loosen up the corporate culture and make it nimble and risk-tolerant—allowing 3M employees to swiftly sense and respond to new market opportunities in a dynamic bottom-up fashion. 3M's management has been totally supportive of many maverick innovations that have come out of this 15-percent program—whether they succeed commercially (like Post-it Products) or not.

After proving its mettle as an exceptional corporate innovator for nearly a century, 3M experienced declining performance in the late 1990s. The nimble Midwestern manufacturer had become too big, complacent, and risk-averse—resting on its laurels rather than creatively shaping the future. Its stock price took a hit, and its sales and profits began to decline. When faced with such adversity, corporate leaders can demonstrate either a fixed mindset, by playing it safe and seeking incremental change, or a growth mindset, by seeking opportunity in adversity and turning it to the company's advantage. In 3M's case, a leader with a growth mindset would have deepened 3M's existing commitment to jugaad thinking and innovation and used it to fashion a more radical response to adversity.

In 2001, 3M hired Jim McNerney as CEO to revive 3M's fortunes. McNerney, who had previously worked at GE (he had been a front-runner to replace Jack Welch), brought in management discipline and streamlined the bloated firm's cost structure by implementing Six Sigma management techniques. This significantly boosted 3M's profitability: its operating margins shot up from 17 percent in 2001 to 23 percent in 2005. The highly structured Six Sigma processes—which emphasize predictability and sameness—worked wonders in 3M's factories by making production systems more cost-efficient. Initially, it seemed as if this structured approach to reviving 3M's fortune was working. But the same structured approach had the opposite effect when McNerney applied it in 3M's R&D labs to standardize and systematize the *innovation* process and make it faster and cost-effective. Six Sigma arguably choked 3M's free-flowing jugaad creativity. In the process, Six Sigma failed to tap into the psychological capital of 3M's innovators, whose ingenuity and resilience to adversity had been built up over several decades. Rather than dreaming big and producing breakthrough products, 3M's engineers became risk-averse and played it safe—by generating incremental innovations that met Six Sigma performance goals. 3M's management began to frown on disruptive ideas proposed by its jugaad innovators. As a result, 3M's sales revenues and reputation as a cutting-edge innovator began to flag. By 2005, 3M's share of revenues derived from new products had gone from its traditional 30 percent to only 21 percent. Its ranking in Boston Consulting Group's Most Innovative companies list gradually slipped as well, from number one in 2004 to number seven in 2007.[56] It felt as if 3M's jugaad spirit had waned.

Faced with the adversity of declining revenue and brand reputation, George Buckley, who had replaced McNerney as CEO in 2005, focused on reviving 3M's risk-tolerant jugaad culture. In particular, Buckley began rolling back Six Sigma initiatives—and reinstituted the 15-percent program, giving 3M engineers more flexibility and freedom to pursue radical ideas without fear of retribution. Buckley acknowledges: "Perhaps one of the mistakes that we made as a company—it's one of the dangers of Six Sigma—is that when you value sameness more than you value creativity, I think you potentially undermine the heart and soul of a company like 3M."[57]

Buckley had to move fast, as several of 3M's products were becoming outmoded or increasingly commoditized. It was facing growing competition from agile competitors in all its major product segments. But 3M was facing an even bigger challenge: rapidly shifting customer preferences. In today's digital environment, consumers value aesthetics as much as function in the products they buy—as demonstrated by the huge success of the well-designed iPhone. This new reality made 3M's leadership realize that while the company was great at *engineering* products, it had to get better at *designing* them in an appealing fashion.

Sensing an opportunity in this situation of adversity, 3M decided to broaden its traditional jugaad mindset to include not only great technical performance but also great design. To drive that transformation, 3M hired Mauro Porcini as head of global strategic design. The flamboyant and passionate thirty-seven-year-old Italian, who reports directly to the head of R&D for 3M's Consumer & Office Business, runs a large team that is attempting to make both 3M's existing and new products more visually appealing without sacrificing their technical performance.[58]

We met Mauro at his sleek new office at 3M's headquarters in Saint Paul, Minnesota. The crisp white walls and décor and the curved fuchsia-colored path paving the way to Mauro's office offered a creative oasis that stood in stark contrast to the claustrophobic brown cubicles in the rest of the building. Porcini, whose stylish sartorial esthetic also stood out, explained to us the challenge 3M is now facing and how his team is helping address it:[59]

> Customers are no longer just "buying" products—rather, they are seeking new *experiences* that delight them. They want to establish an emotional bond with the products they buy—even if it's an ordinary household item or office product. This challenge presents an opportunity for 3M to rethink the way we develop products. We are learning to pay more attention to aesthetics—rather than obsessing about functional excellence. We are also changing the way we engage with customers. When you listen to customers, you merely react to needs; when you empathize with customers, you anticipate their needs; but when you truly love your customers, you *surprise* them by introducing them to products they couldn't even fathom.

Porcini points to Apple as a company in love with its customers: by marrying superior design with excellent engineering, Apple keeps surprising—and thrilling—customers with each new product it launches. "Companies like Apple and Target have proven that good design can help capture not only bigger market share but also customer mindshare and 'heart share.' 3M's new challenge is to find ways to increase our customer 'heart-share' by using superior design to differentiate our products in a crowded market."[60]

Porcini's team of jugaad designers are given carte blanche to rejuvenate 3M's signature office and consumer products by giving them a bold, sexy look. For instance, they gave a facelift to 3M's fifty-year-old transparent Scotch Tape Dispenser by creating a high-heel tape dispenser. Porcini himself redesigned an existing multimedia projector by making it sleeker, and "something consumers want to touch": it was an instant hit. Some award-winning products that Porcini helped develop at 3M include the MPro150 Pocket Projector, the Scotch Pop-Up Tape Dispenser with precut strips, and the Scotch Pet Hair Remover. Porcini's designers are now actively involved in new R&D projects from the very beginning—thus influencing both business and technical decisions associated with new product development. Porcini quips: "3M used to be known as a company of 'maverick engineers.' Now we also want to be famous for housing 'maverick designers.'"[61]

Crushed by the Six Sigma juggernaut in the early 2000s, 3M reignited its jugaad spirit by giving its employees more creative freedom and by integrating left-brain functional excellence with a right-brain design sensibility. These efforts have paid off handsomely. They have helped rebuild the psychological capital of 3M's innovators, which, in turn has given 3M resilience in the face of subsequent adversity. Although 3M's sales revenues fell during the recessionary year of 2009, they have bounced back since, increasing 15 percent to $26.7 billion in 2010 (one of the highest growth rates ever achieved in 3M's hundred-plus-year history). In 2010, 3M posted a record operating profit of $5.9 billion, with margins of 22.2 percent. By 2010, 3M was once again generating 30 percent of its revenues from new products—and that percentage may even reach the mid-30s in 2012. 3M now launches about 1,200 new products a year. George Buckley notes with satisfaction: "Even in the worst economic times in memory, we released over one thousand new products."[62] 3M seems to have found a sticky growth formula fit for the postindustrial economy—as evidenced by a 2011 survey conducted by Booz & Company with global executives, who ranked 3M as the third most innovative firm in the world—right after Apple and Google.[63]

CONCLUSION

In an increasingly complex business environment that throws all kinds of challenges at companies, demonstrating resilience in the face of adversity and turning it to one's advantage is a new competence that business leaders must urgently develop.

Although it is difficult to adopt as many different strategies designed to turn adversity into opportunity as 3M did, it is certainly not impossible. As 3M and the various other Western companies featured here prove, strong leadership is key to getting these resilient strategies to work.

But seeking opportunity in adversity is only the first of the many jugaad principles that Western leaders—and their organizations—can apply to succeed in a unpredictable and fast-moving global economy. Of all the forms of adversity that emerging economies and Western firms face, none is as severe or threatening to survival and growth as scarcity. How jugaad innovators respond to scarcity by "doing more with less"—and what Western leaders can learn from this frugal principle—is the subject of our next chapter.

CHAPTER THREE

PRINCIPLE TWO
Do More with Less

If I had one dollar to spend, I would invest in solving the biggest problem today— the economics of scarcity.

— JEFFREY IMMELT, CHAIRMAN AND CEO, GENERAL ELECTRIC[1]

Gustavo Grobocopatel is a fourth-generation Argentinian farmer of Russian-Jewish extraction. For three generations his family pursued a small-scale, subsistence model of farming in Argentina. Grobocopatel's dream was to break out of this mold and do something more ambitious. But his vision was hindered by scarcity from the very start.[2]

First, Grobocapatel had difficulty accessing large tracts of land. Although Argentina is a vast country, endowed with rich soil and a favorable climate, farmland is actually hard to come by. Only 10 percent of the land is arable—and much of the arable land is controlled by a few owners who are reluctant to part with it.[3]

Next, Grobocopatel faced a shortage of the skilled labor needed to scale up his business. Farming is labor intensive, as people are needed to fertilize, sow, tend, and harvest crops. In Argentina such labor is in limited supply, is not formally organized, is spread out across the country and can be costly to hire, especially during peak harvest seasons.[4]

Third, Grobocopatel didn't have the capital to buy the farm equipment he needed to achieve scale without using labor. Funding opportunities to bootstrap new businesses are very limited for entre-preneurs in Argentina.[5]

Instead of giving in to these challenges, Grobocopatel conceived and then implemented an ingenious business model. He overcame the scarcity of land by *leasing* it rather than acquiring it. He dealt with the scarcity of labor by *subcontracting* every aspect of farm work to a network of specialized service providers, giving him access to "freelance" laborers he hires only when they are needed. And he overcame the cost of owning equipment and the lack of access to capital by *renting* the equipment needed from networks of small local companies.

By cleverly leveraging a grassroots network of 3,800 small and medium-size agricultural suppliers, Grobocopatel's company, Los Grobo, operates as an *asset-light* company, and in this way is able to *do more with less*. Overcoming the skepticism of his peers, this jugaad entrepreneur has proven the value of his "more with less" model. In 2010, Los Grobo became the second largest grain producer in Latin America, farming over three hundred thousand hectares, trading three million tons of grain per year, and generating US$750 million in revenue—all without owning land or a single tractor or harvester. Having succeeded in Argentina, Los Grobo is now exporting its "frugal farming" model to Brazil, Uruguay, and Paraguay, and helping farmers there produce more with less in their local contexts.

Emerging markets are teeming with innovators like Grobocopatel. Faced with scarcity across the board, these jugaad innovators have mastered the art of doing more with less. In this chapter, we get inside the minds of jugaad innovators and the enterprises they run to better understand how they create more value with fewer resources. Although many factors hinder Western companies from adopting a "more with less" approach, doing so is increasingly imperative—as the American and European economies stagnate and face growing resource constraints. Indeed, Western firms that succeed in adopting frugal innovation methods to create affordable offerings are very likely to gain a significant competitive advantage over their peers in the tough economic times ahead.

SCARCITY IS THE MOTHER OF INVENTION

To even a casual observer, the most striking thing about jugaad innovators in emerging markets is their frugal mindset. These entrepreneurs and managers—whether they come from Argentina, Brazil, China, India, Kenya, Mexico, or the Philippines—are constantly looking for new ways to do more with less and deliver greater value to customers at a lower cost. What makes this mindset so fundamental to jugaad innovators, and why are they so good at getting "more for less"? We believe that such a mindset is a rational response to the pervasive scarcity in their environment. For jugaad entrepreneurs, being frugal is not a luxury—it's the key to survival.

While Silicon Valley entrepreneurs typically operate in a resource-rich environment, jugaad entrepreneurs face scarcity of every possible kind. First, they must contend with the scarcity of capital. Quite simply, the availability of financial resources in emerging markets is limited. Banks are conservative, and venture capital and angel investor networks underdeveloped. For instance, 80 percent of South African entrepreneurs report difficulties in accessing funding.[6] Thus, jugaad innovators cannot afford to invest in capital-intensive R&D equipment. This partly explains why a country like India spends only 0.8 percent of its GDP on R&D (compared with 3 percent in developed countries), and why the private sector's share of this spending is only 20 percent.[7]

Second, jugaad innovators must deal with the scarcity of natural resources. Raw materials in emerging markets—from water to electricity—are expensive and hard to obtain reliably. This makes setting up and running new businesses—especially in the manufacturing sector—costly and difficult.

Third, jugaad entrepreneurs face a scarcity of qualified talent. Emerging markets like India, Brazil, and China have huge populations. But only a small percentage of these populations are qualified professionals who can use or deploy the offerings of emerging market entrepreneurs. According to a survey conducted by ManpowerGroup, 67 percent of enterprises in India and 57 percent of those in Brazil have difficulty finding qualified technicians, sales representatives, engineers, and IT staff. As a result, it is hard to sell complex medical devices in rural areas with few qualified doctors. Or to sell PCs to village schools where teachers lack computer literacy.[8]

Finally, jugaad innovators face a scarcity of quality infrastructure. The poor roads and limited transportation options in emerging markets make it difficult to get goods and services to far-flung places in a timely fashion. Moreover, the cost of doing so becomes a huge challenge, limiting the reach of markets in emerging economies.

In addition to pervasive scarcity, jugaad innovators also have to contend with a frugal and demanding consumer base. This consumer base has low disposable income. For instance, three hundred million Indians earn less than $1 a day. Many of these people either go without or are very careful about what they buy. This forces jugaad innovators to radically rethink price points. Their offerings have to be extremely affordable, not just barely so.

These consumers are also very value conscious. They may be low earners, but they also are high "yearners." Given their high aspirations, these consumers reject new offerings that do not deliver significantly higher value than existing offerings do. This puts a lot of pressure on jugaad innovators to develop higher value offerings at a lower price.

Finally, the consumer base in emerging markets is huge and diverse. Markets like China, Brazil, and India have millions of consumers. But these consumers are not homogeneous. To deliver higher value to a large and diverse base, jugaad innovators have to find clever ways of deriving both economies of scale *and* scope in whatever they do.

The pervasive scarcity and the demanding nature of the consumer base make jugaad innovators masters of frugality. Let's consider some of the ways in which they manage to do more with less.

BEING RESOURCEFUL IN A RESOURCE-SCARCE ENVIRONMENT

Jugaad innovators are able to get more from less by applying frugality to every activity they perform at every step along the value chain.

They are frugal in how they design products, how they build them, how they deliver them, and how they perform after-sales maintenance. Their frugality shows up not only in their parsimonious use of capital and natural resources but also in how they maximize their limited time and energy: rather that doing everything themselves, they rely extensively on partners to perform various operations, thus saving time and energy. The following are some frugal approaches employed by jugaad innovators to gain more from less.

They Reuse and Recombine Rather than creating something entirely new, from scratch, jugaad innovators are more likely to reuse or seek new combinations of existing technologies or resources both to come up with new solutions and to commercialize them in markets. For instance, Zhongxing Medical, a Chinese medical device maker, borrowed Digital Direct X-ray (DDX) equipment technology from its parent company (Beijing Aerospace)—which wasn't using it effectively—and reengineered DDX for use in everyday applications like chest X-rays. As a result, its X-ray machines cost just $20,000 to build, compared to $150,000 for the equivalent GE and Philips models (which use DDX only for high-end applications). By creating low-cost, mass-market applications out of an underused technology, Zhongxing cornered 50 percent of the Chinese X-ray machine market—forcing rival GE to cut its prices by 50 percent while Philips, unable to compete, withdrew from this segment altogether.[9]

Similarly, jugaad innovators in African countries are leveraging existing cellphone networks to devise frugal business models that make services like health care and banking affordable to more people. In Kenya, for instance, only 10 percent of the population has access to banking services. Yet mobile penetration is over 50 percent. Sensing an opportunity, Safaricom, a local telecoms service provider, 40 percent owned by UK-based Vodafone, launched a service called M-PESA in 2007. M-PESA is an SMS-based (text message) system that enables people to spend, save, and transfer money using their cellphones at a fraction of the cost of money transfer services like Western Union—and *without* having a bank account. Users of M-PESA can convert cash into electronic money that is stored on their cellphones at any one of hundreds of M-PESA outlets, including village mom-and-pop shops that act as M-PESA agents. On receiving an M-PESA user's cash, the agent texts the equivalent amount in electronic money (e-money) to the user's phone. The user can then text a part or all of this e-money to either an M-PESA agent or to another M-PESA user. All the e-money in circulation is backed up by real money in a bank account owned and managed by Safaricom. This safeguards the system against fraud while obviating the need for users to have their own bank accounts. As of this writing, over fourteen million Kenyans—or 68 percent of the country's adult population—have subscribed to M-PESA. This is much more than the number of people who have bank accounts![10] Migrant workers in Kenyan cities now routinely use M-PESA to safely and cost-effectively transfer earnings to their families who live in remote villages.[11]

They Remain Asset-Light   A second strategy that jugaad innovators use to get more from less is to leverage the capital assets of others to scale up their business model. This is precisely what Gustavo Grobocopatel did in Argentina. But Grobocopatel is hardly an exception. Many jugaad entrepreneurs in emerging markets choose to operate an "asset-light" business model with as few fixed assets as possible on their balance sheet. Thus, instead of owning physical assets, they rent or share them. This approach not only makes their cost structures lean but also allows them to quickly scale operations up or down to meet shifts in demand without investing in additional assets.

For instance, Indian cellphone companies like Bharti Airtel used this frugal strategy not only to get started but also to turn their industry into one of the largest and most competitive in the world. In the early 2000s, as the mobile revolution was taking off in India, Airtel was short of both the capital and the technology it needed to scale up its business. Undeterred, Airtel's chairman Sunil Mittal used a jugaad approach to getting more with less: he boldly decided to outsource all but key marketing and branding activities to partner companies that had capital, technology, or both.[12] Today, IBM manages Airtel's IT infrastructure while Ericsson and Nokia Siemens Network (NSN) manage its network infrastructure. (This might just be one of the first examples of Indian companies outsourcing to Western ones, with both benefiting hugely from the process.) Today Airtel—which boasts over 170 million subscribers—is the world's largest "asset-free" telecom service provider. It is also the first mobile carrier that dared to outsource all its core network infrastructure; most telecom operators prefer to own and manage this in-house given its strategic nature. Its frugal operating model enables it to deliver better value to its customers at less cost. By transforming fixed technology costs into variable costs, Airtel not only succeeded in getting more for less, it also did so at breakneck speed—at times signing up as many as ten million subscribers per month.

They Leverage Existing Networks for Distribution A third "more with less" strategy that jugaad innovators use is focused on solving the "last mile" problem—that is, the difficulty of reaching far-flung customers in an economical way. Rather than investing in expensive logistics networks, jugaad entrepreneurs leverage existing networks to cost-effectively deliver their products and services to people in hard-to-reach markets. In particular, they rely on grassroots partners in local communities to reach more customers and personalize their offerings for them. These grassroots distribution partners are often micro-entrepreneurs themselves. By building on already developed and trusted social networks in emerging markets, jugaad innovators can compensate for the poor state of the physical infrastructure there. More important, by enrolling grassroots entrepreneurs as their channel partners, jugaad innovators drive their own financial sustainability while also creating new economic opportunities in local communities.

For instance, toothpaste maker Colgate Palmolive scaled up its logistics network to serve remote villages in India by creating a mobile network of young people. Mounted on bicycles carrying a few oral care products, these salespeople go from village to village with their "micro-stores on wheels"—thus solving the last mile problem. This solution costs less to Colgate than setting up physical distribution in these villages would. Plus it delivers more value to local communities—improving their health and providing jobs for local youth.[13]

Similarly, MicroVentures in the Philippines—cofounded in 2006 by Bam Aquino, nephew of former President Corazon Aquino—is making a wide range of consumer products and services accessible to consumers at the *base of the* (socioeconomic) *pyramid* (BOP).[14] Rather than setting up its own distribution network—a costly and nearly impossible task, given the fragmentation of the BOP market spread across hundreds of villages—MicroVentures leveraged an existing ad-hoc logistics network made up of eight hundred thousand *sari-sari* (mom-and-pop) stores. These tiny stores—found across the entire seven-thousand-island Philippine archipelago—are operated by entrepreneurial women who set them up as an extension of their homes.[15] MicroVentures applied what is known as the *conversion franchising* model which consists in converting already existing, independently owned stores into members of a standardized and branded network known as the Hapinoy Program.[16] By converting and upgrading some of the existing sari-sari stores into branded Hapinoy Community Stores, MicroVentures rapidly scaled up its distribution network: ten thousand sari-sari stores have joined the Hapinoy Program since 2007—a figure that Aquino predicts could go up to a hundred thousand in the coming years. It's worth noting that a number of sari-sari stores that have joined the Hapinoy Program are also members of CARD MRI, the largest microfinance institution in the Philippines, with whom MicroVentures had established a synergistic partnership.

The women who own sari-sari stores enjoy many benefits by joining the Hapinoy Program:

1. They pay less for their supply of goods, because MicroVentures can—by aggregating demand from multiple Hapinoy stores—negotiate bulk prices from consumer goods manufacturers.
2. They can generate more income by selling a broader variety of goods and value-added services—such as mobile payments—sourced from MicroVentures' partners.
3. They learn how to professionally run their businesses—and scale them up—by receiving personalized training from MicroVentures

in areas such as inventory management, marketing, leadership, and personal development.

Aquino explains:

> Rather than building a new logistics network from scratch, our business model leverages the *human network* of micro entrepreneurs—the women who own sari-sari stores. By building on an existing grassroots distribution infrastructure, we have created a sustainable solution that benefits all members of BOP communities. First, BOP consumers gain access to a greater variety of affordable goods and services. Second, sari-sari store owners in villages increase their income levels by joining the Hapinoy Program—and learn how to improve their own lives and meaningfully contribute to their communities. And third, more micro-producers in villages can now extend their market reach by joining our distribution network. Our vision is to turn the Hapinoy Program into the social equivalent of an iPad: a platform that gives our network members [the women micro-entrepreneurs] access to hundreds of "social apps"—i.e., products and services offered by our partners. Our network members can pick and choose specific apps [products/services] that deliver the most value to their local communities. [17]

HELPING CUSTOMERS GET MORE VALUE

By relying on a frugal operating model, jugaad innovators strive not just to reduce their own costs, but also to pass value on to consumers. Thus, unlike their counterparts in the West, they do not typically focus on wowing customers with products that have cool features or the latest technologies. Instead, they pursue functionally minimalist solutions that offer superior value to customers—often transforming their lives in the process. Simply put, they help their customers get more value for less cost by offering them quality products and services at highly affordable prices.

For instance, in 2010, KPIT Cummins Infosystems, an Indian engineering and IT services provider, unveiled Revolo, a low-cost plug-in parallel hybrid solution for cars. (Revolo is the brainchild of Tejas Kshatriya, an engineer who works for KPIT Cummins. Kshatriya came up with the idea while stuck in a traffic jam in Mumbai in 2008.) By installing the Revolo kit in their cars, owners of cars that run on gas can cost-effectively convert their existing vehicles into fuel-efficient, high-performance hybrids. The conversion kit—which includes a rechargeable battery pack, an electric motor, and a pulley—can be retrofitted into most cars in just six hours by a KPIT Cummins–certified mechanic.

Revolo works best in stop-and-go city traffic, as it captures the kinetic energy generated every time the brakes are applied and stores it in its batteries for later use. Tests show that the Revolo technology boosts fuel efficiency by over 35 percent and reduces greenhouse gas emissions by at least 30 percent. Most important, at a price between $1,300 and $3,250 for the Indian market—and around $5,000 when sold in Western markets—the Revolo system costs 80 percent less than other hybrid car options.[18] Revolo can be plugged into any car, whatever its brand or age, without interfering with the carmaker's transmission configuration. KPIT estimates that, when used at an average daily run of thirty-one miles, the Revolo conversion kit pays for itself in less than two years. Hence Revolo is a win-win for both car owners and auto manufacturers. Ravi Pandit, CEO of KPIT Cummins, notes: "With Revolo, we found an affordable and retrofittable solution to transform a gas-guzzling car into an environmentally mindful, fuel-efficient, high-performance hybrid. With Revolo, car owners get more value at less cost."[19]

KPIT Cummins is negotiating licensing deals with several U.S. and European carmakers that are eager to initially offer Revolo as a branded aftermarket service to their existing car users—while exploring the long-term possibility of incorporating Revolo as a standard feature in their future models. Large-scale commercial production of Revolo is expected to begin in 2013.[20] It is worth noting that it cost KPIT less than $2 million to develop the Revolo technology—much less than the $1 billion it costs, on average, to develop a new car.[21]

How do jugaad innovators know what is of value to their customers and how much customers will be willing to pay to get that additional value? Rather than considering these questions in the abstract in an R&D

lab, jugaad innovators spend time in the field, observing and interacting with potential customers to identify their latent needs and requirements. Only then do they zero in on the essential features of a solution that are most relevant to their unique customers. In other words, they first seek to identify the *appropriateness* of a solution. Armed with these insights into what customers need rather than want, jugaad innovators design, from the ground up, an appropriate product or service—as well as a business model—that can best fulfill these needs. Very often they don't get it right the first time. But by trial and error and rapid experimentation, they eventually settle on the set of features—and the business model—that is likely to deliver the highest value at the lowest price for their market.

To understand this better, let's consider another jugaad example, one that can make a life-or-death difference to many people around the world. Twenty million babies are born prematurely or with a low birth weight each year worldwide, and four million of them die, most in developing nations. Those who survive often suffer from low IQ, diabetes, and heart disease when they reach adulthood. Many of these deaths and ailments could be averted by simply keeping these premature babies warm. Unfortunately, current options for warming babies in developing nations are either expensive or unsafe. The incubators sold in Western countries cost up to $20,000 and require electricity—which is unreliable in developing nations. And ad-hoc solutions like positioning babies under bare light bulbs are simply risky.

Jane Chen, Linus Liang, Naganand Murty, and Rahul Panicker cofounded Embrace to come up with an affordable infant warmer for use in developing countries, one that costs far less than incubators available in the West. The founders came up with the idea for Embrace's frugal business model while they were all attending Stanford University's Entrepreneurial Design for Extreme Affordability program. After producing an initial prototype—a stripped-down version of traditional incubators powered by electricity—they traveled to Nepal to test it in an urban hospital. But they soon found that 80 percent of babies that die prematurely in developing nations like Nepal are born at home in villages, far from well-equipped hospitals and without access to regular electricity.[22]

That insight led them to fundamentally rethink who their *users* really were. Realizing that their customers were doctors and parents in villages, they set out to identify what product features would bring the most value to these rural users. That inquiry led them to design a *portable* infant warmer that looks like a tiny sleeping bag and gives mothers greater mobility and more intimate contact with their babies. The bag in turn contains a pouch of a wax-like phase-change material (PCM) that keeps babies warm for up to six hours at regular body temperatures. Not only is this infant warmer intuitive to use, but it requires only thirty minutes of electricity to heat up the PCM pouch—using a portable electric heater that comes with the product. Further, this design dovetails well with the recommended practice of "kangaroo care," whereby a mother holds her baby against her skin (hence the company name "Embrace").[23] Most important, the Embrace portable infant warmer costs less than 2 percent of the cost of incubators available in Western markets.

In 2011, Embrace piloted this product in India, where 1.2 million premature babies die each year. Early results have been very encouraging. A preliminary study validated Embrace's safety and efficacy with twenty infants. Embrace then undertook a more extensive clinical study of 160 premature babies. In one instance, a two-pound baby born to parents from a village near Bangalore, in Southern Indian, was kept in the Embrace infant warmer for twenty days and began to gain weight—bringing great joy to its parents who had lost two babies previously.

Embrace uses rapid prototyping techniques to get customer feedback on new product features fast and zero in on the product attributes that are of highest relevance and value to rural customers. For instance, after noticing that mothers in Indian villages didn't trust numerical displays that indicate whether the temperature is right, Embrace replaced the numerical scale with symbols indicating "OK" or "Not OK." Similarly, Embrace is planning to release a future version of its product targeted at mothers who live in far-flung villages with no electricity at all: in this version, the PCM pouch will be heated—and thus "recharged"—using a heating device that runs on *hot water* (instead of electricity).

Embrace is also experimenting with different pricing models—such as a rental option—to make its product affordable in countries like India where hundreds of millions in villages live on less than $2 a day. "Entrepreneurs often fall in love with their original product idea or business model and fail to listen to customers," Chen explains. "We, on the other hand, have no qualms about modifying our product features and pricing again and again till we find a solution that delivers the highest value to our customers at the lowest cost for them. For us, innovation is a dynamic process that never ends."[24]

Embrace is currently negotiating partnerships with multinational pharmaceutical and medical device companies such as GE. The company is also working with local NGOs to piggyback on their extensive distribution networks to make the Embrace infant warmer accessible to as many hospitals and clinics as possible in countries like India. Finally, Embrace is testing its infant warmer at the Lucile Packard Children's Hospital at Stanford University: the entrepreneurs believe there is a big market for Embrace's product in the United States where infant mortality rates are among the highest in the developed world. Embrace has set itself a bold target of saving the lives of over one hundred thousand babies over the next three years, as well as preventing illness in over seven hundred thousand babies.

In sum, jugaad innovators are able to find abundance in scarcity—and to share that abundance with customers and other stakeholders who also face scarcity. Jugaad innovators may lack financial, natural, and technological resources, but they compensate by finding ingenious ways to leverage social networks and their intimate knowledge of customers to create and deliver more value at less cost. In many ways jugaad innovators embody Theodore Roosevelt's belief that "all the resources we need are in the mind."

WELCOME TO THE AGE OF AUSTERITY

Prestigious Western organizations such as GE and Lucile Packard Children's Hospital at Stanford are adopting Embrace's low-cost incubators, even though they clearly have access to many high-performing incubators in the West. These forward-thinking Western organizations recognize that a frugal approach is increasingly critical for survival in the age of austerity that is upon us. The warning signs are all around. Indeed, these signs are not very different from the more general indicators, discussed in Chapter Two, of increased adversity in Western economies. Nevertheless, it's worth examining the specific factors that are shaping a new culture of austerity in the West. These include

• *Increasingly frugal customers.* The recession has made Western middle-class consumers far more cost-conscious than they were in the boom years of the housing bubble. Similarly, in business-to-business markets, power is shifting from buyers who value features and functionality to those who prefer value pricing. For instance, in hospitals the technology buyers are no longer doctors (who typically favor technically superior but overpriced medical devices), but instead cost-conscious purchasing managers.[25]

• *Dwindling natural resources.* Because the oil and water needed to produce energy and food are in short supply, Western companies are motivated to identify more efficient ways of using these scarce resources. Also, Western consumers are becoming environmentally conscious and voting with their wallets for eco-friendly brands that use less of those natural resources.

• *Government regulations.* More policies are being put into place to deal with financial and environmental pressures. For instance, to deal with its huge budget deficit, the U.S. government is asking Big Pharma to make more drugs available to more Americans at a lower cost. Similarly, increasingly stringent environmental regulations are forcing U.S. carmakers to develop cars that deliver more miles with less fuel and lower greenhouse emission.

• *Competition from low-cost rivals from emerging markets.* Across industries, Western companies are facing competition from low-cost emerging market companies. For example, Western pharmaceutical companies are threatened by generic drug makers from Brazil and South Africa who produce and sell cheaper medicine; Western automakers are being challenged by low-cost car manufacturers from India and China who are producing affordable electric vehicles and ultra-compact cars; and Western cellphone companies such as Nokia and Apple are being taken on by low-cost Chinese cellphone makers such as HTC and Huawei.

• *Rivalry from agile Western startups.* Western start-ups with high-value offerings for cost-conscious consumers are popping up across industries, from hospitality to consumer goods to fashion. In the process, these start-ups are stealing customers from larger players. For example, Warby Parker, founded by four Wharton MBAs while still at B-School, is trying to break the oligopoly—steeped in the old "more for more" business model—that controls the global eyewear industry. The startup offers fashionable high-quality prescription eyewear for just $95, a fraction of what high-end eyewear manufacturers charge.[26] It provides more value to consumers by allowing for home try-ons of different frames and contributes to a larger cause by donating one pair of glasses for each pair it sells.

In the West, frugal consumers and competitors are rewriting the rules of engagement for manufacturers and retailers alike—pressuring them to develop goods and services that are affordable and eco-friendly. As a result, Western businesses are being forced to rethink how they address the aspirations and needs of their value-conscious customers. But doing so will not be easy.

FOR MOST WESTERN COMPANIES, BIGGER IS STILL BETTER

In the new era of scarcity, Western companies must learn how to produce greater value with fewer resources. Despite the benefits of doing more with less, Western companies face significant obstacles in adopting this approach.

For a start, the top management in many companies is wedded to a previously successful "more for more" strategy. To differentiate their products from competition, large Western companies are used to spending huge sums on R&D to develop expensive, often overengineered products for which they charge customers a hefty premium. In the past, this strategy worked because customers were able to afford such premiums, and these premiums in turn enabled companies to recoup their large R&D investments. However, this "bigger is better" approach is no longer sustainable, as Western companies face greater resource constraints and cost-conscious consumers in the West shift from premium products to value-for-money offerings.

Not only is top management wedded to a "more for more" strategy, but senior managers in Western companies also lack the incentive to pursue opportunities in low-income segments. They perceive these segments as too small, unprofitable, or both. Moreover, the margins that companies can charge in value segments are typically low. So, even though the numbers of potential consumers in low-income segments may be large, these markets need up-front investment and require time to develop and grow. Therefore, senior managers who are under pressure from shareholders to deliver quarterly results are not motivated to make these long-term investments in growing value markets.

On the R&D side, Western engineers have come to equate complexity with progress. These engineers come to work every morning with a desire to push the boundaries of technology. For many of them, "doing less" would seem a step back rather than forward. As a result, they tend to design products that cost more and that are overloaded with features that customers don't necessarily want. For example, the most effective way of making cars fuel efficient and inexpensive is to make them lighter. But the pursuit of technology for its own sake—and the need to differentiate cars from each other—has resulted in their getting heavier with time. Specifically, designers add more electronics to cars to deliver ever more bells and whistles. This increases their weight, drag, and hence fuel inefficiency, which in turn makes them more, not less, expensive.

Arguing against this trend, John Maeda, president of the Rhode Island School of Design, says: "It's not necessarily beneficial to add more technology features just because we can. R&D engineers must make frugal simplicity the core tenet of their design philosophy. They must design for the 'real world' by practicing what I call 'radical incrementalism'—which is doing more with less. Wouldn't it be nice if rather than complimenting their R&D teams with 'Wow! You worked so hard to come with this new product with all the bells and whistles: it is amazing!' CEOs told R&D engineers 'Wow! You did almost nothing—and yet produced a 'good enough' product that gets the job done: Congratulations!' "[27] (In Chapter Five we discuss the importance of simplicity when designing new products and services.)

Engineers may be the ones who *create* more expensive products by piling on complex functionality and features that customers don't want. But sales managers have a role to play too: more often than not they love to sell these expensive products. In fact, they typically lack the motivation to *sell* affordable products, fearing that these products might draw consumers away from their more expensive offerings. After all, selling cheaper products doesn't help them earn larger commissions. Further, a common misconception among sales managers is that the market for low-cost products is "too niche" and therefore doesn't deserve time and effort to build. But they fail to recognize that even mainstream customers are now turning away from premium products and seeking affordable solutions that deliver better value at lower cost. Seventy-eight percent of U.S. online consumers say that they are willing to switch from their current brand to a private label for personal goods primarily because the price is lower.[28] And 22 percent of the customers shopping at dollar stores earn $70,000 or more annually. When even Middle America begins patronizing thrift stores, the trend is undeniable. (In Chapter Six we explore the impact of the shrinking American middle class on businesses.)

Despite these changes in consumer behavior, however, marketing executives in large companies still equate "low-cost" with "poor quality" and are concerned that promoting low-cost offerings will damage their company's brand. But marketing executives must recognize that, in this new age of austerity, with a rapidly dwindling middle class, the notion of "premium" is being redefined as "more value for the money" even in middle to high-end markets.

Thus, Western companies face a conundrum: they are confronted with a growing number of frugal consumers clamoring for affordable solutions, yet their existing corporate culture and incentive systems are not designed to deliver more with less. As scarcity deepens in the West, Western corporate leaders will have no choice: they will have to bite the bullet and infuse their organizations with a frugal mindset. A jugaad approach could be just the way to undertake such a transformation.

HOW WESTERN COMPANIES CAN FIND ABUNDANCE IN SCARCITY

To compete and win in the dawning Age of Scarcity, Western CEOs must boldly revamp their companies' R&D approaches, business models, and incentive systems for sales and marketing—all of which were designed for success in the Age of Abundance. Rather than caving in to Wall Street's demand for short-term gains, CEOs of Western companies must restructure their organizations to boost their long-term ability to continually design and deliver affordable and sustainable solutions to frugal consumers. Here are some suggestions for undertaking such systemic changes.

Tie Senior Management's Compensation to Frugal Performance   It's not enough for CEOs to adopt a frugal mindset and strive to do more with less. They must also encourage their senior managers to follow suit. One way to do that is by linking senior executives' compensation to performance metrics aimed at driving frugality. Take the case of Ramón Mendiola Sánchez, CEO of Florida Ice & Farm Co., a large food and beverage producer and distributor in Costa Rica that is deeply committed to sustainability. In 2008, Mendiola set up a balanced scorecard with a set of key performance indicators (KPIs) to track how well his company was reducing its consumption of natural resources such as water while simultaneously delivering more value to customers and other stakeholders. He linked these KPIs to his senior executives' compensation so they have some skin in the game: 50 percent or more of their compensation is tied to their meeting—or exceeding—these KPIs. Mendiola is leading by example—he has linked 65 percent of his own pay to the balanced scorecard that combines financial, social, and environmental KPIs to compute a "triple bottom line" of people, planet, and profit.

This strategy has been successful: since its implementation, Florida Ice & Farm's senior executives have found creative ways to do more with less by motivating their employees to improve manufacturing and distribution processes and help local communities better conserve natural resources. Under Mendiola's leadership, Florida Ice & Farm has reduced the amount of water it requires to produce a liter of beverage from 12 liters to 4.9—and aims to soon further reduce it to 3.5 liters. It has also eliminated solid waste from all its operations and is well on its way to meeting its target of becoming "water neutral" in 2012 and "carbon neutral" by 2017.[29] Meanwhile, the company achieved a compound annual growth rate of 25 percent between 2006 and 2010—twice the industry average. Mendiola notes: "By using incentives, we motivate our employees at every level to get creative and invent frugal and sustainable ways to deliver significantly more value to all our stakeholders by using far fewer natural resources—while saving substantial amounts of money for our company."[30]

Senior Management Must Challenge R&D to Do More with Less   The recession is forcing many Western CEOs to cut their R&D spending with the hope of increasing their innovation performance at lower cost. But this will happen only when engineers and scientists are offered challenging projects that give them the incentive to do more with less. For instance, in the late 1990s, Louis Schweitzer—former CEO of the French carmaker Renault—visited Russia, where he found that low-cost domestic cars like the Lada—that cost merely €6,000 (US$7,800)—were outselling his company's €12,000 (US$15,600) cars. Following this visit, Schweitzer challenged his R&D team to come up with a modern, reliable, and affordable car for less than €6,000. As Schweitzer recalls: "Seeing those antiquated cars, I found it unacceptable that technical progress should stop you from making a good car for €6,000. I drew up a list of specifications in three words—modern, reliable and affordable—and added that everything else was negotiable."[31]

The result was the Logan, a no-frills car priced at €5,000, which, since its 2004 launch, has become Renault's cash cow across recession-wary European markets as well as in many developing economies. Interestingly, Schweitzer's successor Carlos Ghosn—who coined the term "frugal engineering" in 2006—is now pushing Renault's R&D team in France to do *even more with less* to compete effectively with low-cost carmakers from emerging market such as Tata Motors (which developed the $2,000 Nano).[32]

Marketing Executives Should Create Separate Brands for Their Affordable Offerings   To avoid brand dilution, Western companies need to create distinct brands for distinct segments. Given that they might already have well-established brands for higher-priced segments, they should develop distinctive *new* brands for their affordable segments. Doing so will reduce the problems of brand dilution while ensuring greater market coverage. For instance, the Starwood Group opened two affordable but chic hotel chains—Aloft and Element—to cater to value-conscious consumers.[33] Similarly, in an attempt to reach mainstream consumers, high-end designer Vera Wang has recently adopted a three-tiered branding approach: the top tier includes her pricey luxury bridal wear, the middle tier is made up of her eponymous line sold at accessible prices, and the bottom tier includes casual budget-priced brands—such as Simply Vera—that are selling like hotcakes through mass-market retailers like Kohl's.[34] Finally, high-end restaurateurs and star chefs have now adopted a low-cost venue—the food truck, traditionally used by hot dog vendors—to dish out gourmet items at affordable prices. In New York City you now find food trucks that sell lobster rolls, Van Leeuwen's artisanal ice cream, and even sophisticated dishes put together by celebrity chefs.

Create Incentive Systems for Salespeople to Sell Affordable Products   Western companies must recognize that jugaad innovation isn't just about *designing* affordable products. It is also about successfully *selling* these products in the marketplace. But successful selling won't happen as long as salespeople have the incentive to sell only big-ticket items. Instead, companies will have to align their sales force's incentive systems with the corporate strategy of doing more with less. Companies can address this issue by reorganizing their sales force along brand lines, with different salespeople responsible for the low-end and high-end segments. This will also help reduce any internal resistance based on the fear of cannibalization. Even better, healthy internal competition between divisions could drive sales and marketing personnel responsible for different brands to be more innovative in how their reach and keep their respective customers. Consider that for decades Procter & Gamble maintained a homogeneous sales structure, selling premium products to mainstream middle-class consumers. But as the purchasing power of middle-class Americans declines, P&G has restructured its sales force into two distinct groups that separately target high-income and low-income segments.[35]

Design Affordable Solutions from the Ground Up R&D teams should move away from pursuing overengineered "perfect products" and focus instead on developing "good enough" solutions. By "good enough" solutions we don't mean stripped-down versions of existing high-end products. Such solutions could leave customers feeling shortchanged and less than satisfied. And although a stripped-down approach could help reduce costs in the short term, companies will pay the price later, as designers will have to return to the drawing board and undo the problems caused by such quick-fix solutions. Rather, Western engineers need to create affordable solutions from the *ground up*. And emerging markets can help with this: they offer Western engineers a great training ground on which to practice such frugal innovation. Indeed, a few forward-thinking Western companies across sectors are increasingly using their R&D teams in emerging markets like India and China to develop minimalist solutions from the ground up that deliver higher value to customers. For example, when GE Healthcare's R&D engineers in India had to come up with low-cost alternatives to the company's high-end ECG machines to serve local needs with limited means, they didn't attempt to strip down GE's existing product to meet local price points. Instead, they went back to the drawing board and, based on deep observation of customers, they developed the MAC i, a radically affordable, portable ECG machine with basic features and a long battery life that is priced at around \$500—one-twentieth of the cost of ECG devices available in the West.[36] Similarly, Nokia's 1100 model, an ultra-low-cost cellphone with a simple interface and a flashlight to help users see their way in the dark, was designed from the ground up for emerging markets. This product has been a huge seller in India and Africa, where millions of people who live beyond the reach of the electricity grid find a simple feature like a flashlight invaluable.

Engage Eco-Aware Consumers in the Sustainability Dialogue

An explosion of social media tools, such as Facebook and Twitter, has given rise to well-informed and powerful consumer communities around the world. Often, the consumers who participate in these communities congregate on product fan pages or websites created by other consumers, far beyond the reach of the company that offers these products. Frequently, participants in these user communities are young, frugal, and environmentally conscious. They aren't just looking for a deal; they're searching for—and willing to champion—products that fit into their personal value system. These consumer communities can help build brands they favor, or cause the demise of brands they disapprove of. Companies should proactively engage with such communities on issues like sustainability and resource scarcity—and use such engagement to identify ways to do more using fewer natural resources. Doing so will not only help companies shape their own strategies but also bolster their brand and help them differentiate themselves from competitors. Because most companies have been slow to understand how to work with user communities online, those companies that succeed in doing so can stand out from the competition and garner long-term brand loyalty.

Partner Extensively   Partnering with key external players offers a powerful way for companies to get more out of their limited R&D dollars. Partners can cost-effectively bring companies better ideas than they already have, help companies develop existing ideas more efficiently, or enable them to commercialize these ideas more extensively and at lower cost. An outstanding example of a company that has used partners to improve its R&D efficiency is Procter & Gamble (P&G). In 2000, A. G. Lafley, then P&G's CEO, noted that "for every P&G researcher there are 200 scientists or engineers elsewhere in the world who are just as good—a total of 1.5 million people whose talents we could use."[37] Lafley wanted to tap into this global brainpower so P&G could innovate more widely, radically, and rapidly than before—without investing more in internal R&D. To do so, he set a challenge for his until-then internally focused R&D organization. Within ten years P&G was to move from being a research and develop (R&D) company to being a connect and develop (C&D) organization, one that sourced as much as 50 percent of its new product ideas from *outside* the company. To achieve this ambitious goal, Lafley opened up P&G's old R&D model to the creative input of a wide array of external stakeholders—customers, suppliers, universities, venture capitalists, and think tanks. In one instance, P&G found a cost-effective and speedy external solution to the problem of printing trivia questions in edible ink on Pringles chips. Rather than solving the problem internally (as they would have done in the past, thereby costing the firm a fortune), P&G used its links with universities around the world to identify a professor in Bologna, Italy, who had already developed a means of printing on pizza and bread. P&G then worked with this professor to adapt his solution to printing on Pringles chips. This collaboration yielded a commercially successful P&G product without incurring huge in-house R&D expenditure.

Our research shows that the strategies just outlined are among the more common ones adopted by Western companies who are embracing the jugaad approach to innovation. These frugal strategies are also the ones that we are increasingly called on to share with Western leaders who seek our advice on incorporating a "more with less" approach in their organizations. Of all the invitations we've received to consult on this jugaad principle, one stands out as particularly memorable.

PEPSICO: A REFRESHING APPROACH TO DOING MORE WITH LESS

In January 2010, we had lunch with Indra Nooyi, chairman and CEO of PepsiCo, Inc. and, according to *Fortune* magazine, one of the world's most powerful women.[38] Nooyi had read an article in *Bloomberg*

Businessweek that profiled our research on jugaad, and she was eager to discuss how PepsiCo had infused the efficient and innovative mindset that is jugaad's trademark into its operations.[39]

Jugaad innovation is definitely on top of Nooyi's mind—and for a strategic reason. PepsiCo's products are made, manufactured, or sold in more than two hundred countries. They cover consumer preferences and needs that evolve on an ongoing basis. Given that the macro-economic environment is in a constant state of change, PepsiCo must be ready to refresh and diversify its products to meet the needs of a dynamic marketplace—especially in light of the growing consumer demand for healthy and nutritious food.

Understanding the demonstrated potential of the global packaged-nutrition market—valued at $500 billion and growing—PepsiCo, the second largest food and beverage business in the world, has expanded its vast product portfolio to include foods and beverages that deliver positive nutrition.[40] Today, PepsiCo provides foods and beverages that are "good-for-you" (featuring brands such as Quaker and Tropicana), complementing its "fun-for-you" (with brands such as Pepsi and Lay's) and "better-for-you" (including brands such as zero-calorie Pepsi Max and Propel Zero) portfolios. This expansion into products that deliver positive nutrition is in line with Performance with Purpose, PepsiCo's guiding principle.

For PepsiCo, Performance with Purpose means delivering sustain-able growth by investing in a healthier future for people and the planet. Specifically, four planks make up Performance with Purpose: financial performance, human sustainability, environmental sustainability, and talent sustainability.[41] It is this push for sustainability, both financial and societal, that stimulates jugaad innovation at PepsiCo.

Nooyi has brought in the right talent to enable PepsiCo's expansion into the nutrition area. To hone PepsiCo's focus on nutrition, Nooyi appointed Dr. Mehmood Khan—an M.D. whose experience includes serving at the Mayo Clinic as the director of the Diabetes, Endocrinol-ogy and Nutrition Clinical Trial Unit and as consultant physician in Endocrinology—as PepsiCo's chief scientific officer as well as CEO of its Global Nutrition Group (GNG).[42] Khan's crossover role, which is unique in the global food and beverage industry, enables him to translate the science of nutrition—in which he is an expert—into commercially viable products. Khan's goal as head of GNG is to grow PepsiCo's portfolio of good-for-you products to $30 billion in net revenue by 2020 by increasing the amount of whole grains, fruits, vegetables, nuts, seeds, and low-fat dairy in its global product portfolio. For instance, Khan's GNG team is researching ready-to-eat—and even drinkable—breakfast products that combine fruit, dairy, and grains like oats.

With the goal of identifying *frugal business practices*, PepsiCo also set up the Global Value Innovation Center in India in late 2010. Here is how Tanmaya Vats, who heads the Center, explains his mandate: "We want to discover disruptive business practices that can significantly lower the cost of operations in our supply chain—in manufacturing and distribution. We look for radical ways to reduce the *capital intensity* in our business model—by, for instance, developing cost-effective and eco-friendly capital equipment that delivers significantly more value and yet costs drastically less than currently available solutions."[43] Rather than reinventing the wheel, Vats's unit is partnering extensively with jugaad innovators worldwide—such as academic institutions, researchers, entrepreneurs, and domain experts—who have already invented—or helped in inventing—jugaad solutions for making manufacturing and distribution processes more efficient. Once a promising jugaad innovation is identified for reducing capital intensity, Vats's unit will then work with various business units at PepsiCo to help adopt and roll it out globally.

Nooyi is also using a "bottom-up" approach to dealing with scarcity. She is empowering her employees in different regions to experiment with out-of-the-box solutions that address scarcity in their local supply chains.

One of the critical resources fundamental to PepsiCo's business is water. There is a clear need for PepsiCo to achieve water use efficiency to both improve product outputs and provide access to safe water for those in water-distressed areas. In India, an environment of severe water scarcity prompted members of the PepsiCo India team to investigate ways to reduce water use throughout the supply chain. For example, they developed an eco-friendly agronomic technique called *"direct seeding"* of rice paddies. Here is how direct seeding works. In India, rice is traditionally cultivated by sowing seeds in a small nursery where they germinate into seedlings. The seedlings are then manually transferred into the main field and grown with four to five inches of water at the base of the crop for the first six to eight weeks, mainly to prevent weed growth. Direct seeding, in contrast, avoids three basic water-intensive operations—puddling (compacting the soil to reduce water leakage), transplanting, and growing in standing water—thereby saving on average about 30 percent of the usual water requirement in paddy cultivation, or approximately 900 kiloliters (238,000 gallons) of water per acre. In addition, direct seeding cuts greenhouse gas emissions by 70 percent.[44] In essence, direct seeding helps farmers increase their yields while reducing their water input and saving time. While experimenting with direct seeding, the PepsiCo India team members relied heavily on jugaad. For instance, rather than designing their direct sowing machine from scratch, they repurposed an imported peanut planter powered by a normal tractor—and had their repurposed machine prototyped and built by a small local manufacturer.

Impressed by the success of the direct seeding experiment, PepsiCo's management picked up this grassroots innovation and piloted it on a larger scale across a few Indian states over a three-year period. The pilot was a huge success—farmers were raving about the results, which generated cost savings of more than 1,500 rupees (US$33) per acre, thus raising net revenue/return per acre. In 2010 alone, through direct seeding, PepsiCo India saved more than 7 billion liters (1.85 billion gallons) of water, which helped make it *water positive* in India—meaning that the company was saving more water through frugal initiatives such as direct seeding than it was consuming in the rest of its business.[45]

Nooyi is also fostering some healthy competition among its regional business units to encourage them to embrace the "do more with less" principle.[46] For instance, PepsiCo's beverage plants in India draw about two-fifths of their energy consumption from renewable sources such as biomass and wind turbines. The jugaad example set by the PepsiCo India team is serving as inspiration for—and is being replicated in—other regions, including in the United States, where PepsiCo Frito-Lay's Casa Grande, Arizona, facility has achieved "near net zero" status, running primarily on renewable energy sources and recycled water while producing nearly zero landfill waste.[47]

In the end, PepsiCo's pursuit of efficient and responsible use of resources is what allows the company to deliver on its Performance with Purpose promise, using jugaad principles. As Nooyi told us: "We need to bring a frugal mindset to the United States, which is going to face scarcity of all sorts in coming decades. PepsiCo and other U.S. companies need some jugaad thinking to come up with economical and healthy solutions that deliver better value to our customers—and do so in a responsible way."

By reframing scarcity as an opportunity to drive disruptive innovation—a key attribute of jugaad thinking—Nooyi is positioning PepsiCo for sustainable success in a global economy characterized by eco-aware, frugal, and health-conscious consumers. Indeed, if Nooyi's experiment with "doing more with less" succeeds, PepsiCo's efficient business model will revolutionize the global food and beverage sector for many years to come.

CONCLUSION

As we've seen, because emerging markets face scarcity on a grand scale and across the board, jugaad innovators who operate within them are masters of frugality and the art of doing more with less. Western companies, however, are facing scarcity too—as they confront dwindling natural resources and value-conscious and demanding consumers. To survive in this dawning age of austerity and scarcity, Western leaders need to learn from jugaad innovators like Gustavo Grobocopatel of Los Grobo (Argentina) and Sunil Mittal of Bharti Airtel (India) how to get more from less by applying frugality to every link of the value chain. Western leaders can also learn from Jane Chen (Embrace) and Ravi Pandit (KPIT Cummins) how to help their customers get more value for less cost by offering them quality products and services at very affordable prices.

Practicing frugality, however, requires a fundamental shift in how Western companies think and operate. Western leaders need to eschew their traditional "bigger is better" R&D approach. They need to radically overhaul their R&D structure and incentives systems to create and sustain a frugal *culture* in their organization that espouses "doing more with less" as its core value—just as Indra Nooyi is doing at PepsiCo.

However, jugaad innovators aren't focused only on frugality and responding to adversity. To do more with less and turn adversity into opportunity, they also draw on another key principle of the jugaad approach: thinking and acting flexibly.

CHAPTER FOUR

PRINCIPLE THREE
Think and Act Flexibly

*One cannot alter a condition with the same mindset that created it in the
first place.*

—— ALBERT EINSTEIN

With an estimated sixty-two million diabetics—a statistic expected
to increase to a hundred million by 2030—India now has the second largest number of people with diabetes in the world, after China.[1]
The disease is being diagnosed particularly frequently in Indian villages,
where 70 percent of Indians live. One person who has successfully
responded to this alarming trend is Dr. V. Mohan, a globally renowned
diabetes expert and chairman of Dr. Mohan's Diabetes Specialities Centre based in Chennai, capital of the South Indian state of
Tamil Nadu.

Dr. Mohan operates a mobile telemedicine clinic in some of the
remotest villages of Tamil Nadu. Care for rural patients is provided by a
network of primarily urban doctors who are supported by rural technicians and grassroots community health care workers. These technicians
travel in a van equipped with telemedicine technologies that permit transmission of diagnostic tests via satellite uplink even in areas too remote
for Internet connectivity. From their offices in Chennai, Dr. Mohan
and other doctors can see and communicate remotely in real time with
patients through video monitors, while tests conducted in the van, such as
retinal scans, are transmitted within seconds for immediate evaluation.

"Why should patients come to the doctor when it could be the other way around?" Dr. Mohan explains. "I asked myself: What if I can come up with a service that allows physicians to *remotely* consult patients without either group having to travel?"[2]

Turning this vision into reality required Dr. Mohan to improvise new solutions for the various obstacles he faced along the way. For instance, he decided *not* to use regular doctors and nurses to run most of the operations in his mobile clinic. Doctors and city technicians are expensive; employing them in his van would have strained his frugal business model. Even if he could bring in health care providers from the city, retaining them would be hard. So Dr. Mohan recruited young people from small towns with only a high school education (or less) and gave them highly focused training so they could carry out specific functions, such as using the equipment in his van. Meanwhile, Dr. Mohan also trained local people in villages to provide simple follow-up care for his diabetes patients. They could, for example, go from home to home enquiring whether a patient is reducing daily sugar intake or has visited the van for follow-up care. Because Dr. Mohan could not afford to pay these young people for their work, he convinced them instead to volunteer by appealing to their sense of goodwill for the community and their pride in being able to help. To that end he gave them crisp white uniforms as well as formal recognition, including the title "Dr. Mohan's Diabetes Ambassador." All these actions enhanced their status in their communities and boosted their employability. Finally, unlike other health organizations that have access to expensive communications technology from vendors like Nokia and Cisco, Dr. Mohan had to improvise a way to equip his van with cost-effective communication capability. To do so, he partnered with the Indian Space Research Organization (ISRO, India's equivalent of NASA)—which has produced and launched dozens of satellites for socially relevant applications—to get free satellite communications for his ingenious telemedicine service in remote areas where neither mobile nor wireless services are available.

Jugaad innovators like Dr. Mohan constantly employ flexible thinking and action in response to the seemingly insurmountable problems they face in their economies: they are constantly experimenting and improvising solutions for the obstacles they face, and adapting their strategies to new contingencies as they arise. In this chapter, we delve into the minds of jugaad innovators to understand why and how they think and act flexibly. We then examine what constrains Western companies from thinking and acting flexibly—despite the growing pressure to do so—and what they stand to gain by overcoming such constraints. We end the chapter with a discussion of how Western companies can adopt such flexibility in their own innovation initiatives.

JUGAAD INNOVATORS ADAPT TO SURVIVE

Anyone who has attempted to negotiate street traffic in India (or in any other emerging market, for that matter) knows instinctively the importance of thinking and acting flexibly. The sheer unpredictability and diversity of life on the road demands such flexibility. Vehicles come in all shapes and sizes and travel at a range of speeds. Animals and pedestrians compete with buses, trucks, cars, scooters, and cycles. The terrain can be of varying quality and topography: roads, such as they are, may be dug up or undergoing repairs. Vehicles are likely to veer in and out of lanes (if there are any), and all this with the liberal aid of horns (though not necessarily with any other type of signaling). Paradoxically, a linear and orderly approach to driving in such an environment would lead to an accident. The only way to survive is, ironically, to accept the unpredictability of everyone else on the road and to respond by being similarly adaptable—in both thoughts and actions.

As with the roads, so too with the economic environment in emerging markets. The sheer diversity, volatility, and unpredictability of economic life in emerging markets demands flexibility on the part of jugaad innovators. It demands that they think outside of the box, experiment, and improvise: they must either adapt or die. In many ways, this diversity, volatility, and unpredictability also *enables* flexible thinking and action on the part of jugaad innovators.

Through our interactions with jugaad innovators, we have identified four crucial ways in which they think and act flexibly in response to the environment they face. We explore each of these in detail.

Jugaad Innovators Think the Unthinkable   There is mind-boggling diversity in emerging economies. The heterogeneity of populations in these markets demands unconventional, nonlinear thinking. Traditional approaches and cookie-cutter solutions to complex challenges are unlikely to work. Jugaad innovators therefore dare to challenge many ingrained beliefs and turn conventional wisdom on its head. Dr. Mohan, for instance, questioned a convention of the medical industry. Why should patients come to visit the doctor, when it can be the other way around? That radical question then led him to consider an original solution that allows physicians to remotely consult patients without *either* party having to travel.

Harish Hande is another jugaad entrepreneur who dared to think the unthinkable, and succeeded. Hande, who founded India's Solar Electric Light Company (SELCO) in 1995, set out to provide solar energy to the rural poor of India with the intention of debunking three popular myths: (1) poor people cannot afford sustainable technologies, (2) poor people cannot maintain sustainable technologies, and (3) social ventures cannot be run as commercial entities.[3] Having installed his solar energy solution in more than 125,000 rural households in India, Hande has successfully busted these three myths by demonstrating his flexible thinking in three particular areas: (1) financing his business, (2) pricing his services, and (3) distributing and maintaining his solution.

Take financing: Hande started his business in 1995 with very little seed money, as conservative banks and cautious venture capitalists deemed his unproven business model in an unproven industry (solar energy) too risky. Undeterred, Hande bootstrapped SELCO with his own money—$30, to be precise. With it he purchased his first solar home lighting system, which he then sold. With the revenues, he then bought additional systems, which he also sold, and so on.

Hande, however, soon hit a wall. As he penetrated deeper into rural India, he learned that his potential consumers—many of whom earn $1 to $2 a day—could not afford the up-front costs of buying and installing his solar lighting systems. Even if these systems somehow got installed, there was no economical way for him to maintain them for rural consumers scattered across multiple villages. To overcome these twin problems, Hande applied flexible thinking to improvise a truly creative solution that involved a network of small-scale entrepreneurs in rural communities. These grassroots entrepreneurs would own and maintain the solar panels as well as the batteries they could charge in their stores. The entrepreneurs would then rent out the batteries to end consumers daily on a pay-per-use basis—and collect payment every day. This ingenious business model made SELCO's solution affordable and accessible to scores of rural customers who couldn't make an up-front investment in SELCO's solution. These customers included mom and pop storeowners, small-scale farmers, and women who work from home. SELCO's approach also created an incentive for local entrepreneurs to distribute and maintain the equipment over time. Using this approach, SELCO was able to scale up the distribution of its solar lighting system to over one 125,000 households within a few years. It now aims to serve 200,000 households by 2013.[4] For thinking the unthinkable—that is, that poor people can indeed afford and maintain renewable energy solutions—Hande was awarded the World Economic Forum's Social Entrepreneur Award in 2007 and, in 2011, the Ramon Magsaysay Award, considered by many to be Asia's Nobel Prize.

Jugaad Innovators Don't Plan—They Improvise Emerging markets are characterized by high volatility. Economic circumstances are constantly changing. Growth rates are often in double digits, and the competitive landscape is often shifting. New laws and regulations are constantly being put into place, and policy is constantly evolving. So jugaad innovators need to experiment as they go along and be willing to try multiple options, rather than adopting one approach at the start and sticking to it thereafter. Unlike their counterparts in Silicon Valley, jugaad innovators do not attempt to work everything out in advance or rely on a business plan to determine the mid- to long-term roadmap for their new ventures. Instead, they improvise their next course of action as circumstances change, and they do so from within a framework of deep knowledge and passion. Their approach is in fact more akin to a jazz band than to an orchestra: everything is improvised, fluid, and dynamic. As such, their strategies are organic and emergent rather than predetermined. Jugaad innovators' flexible thinking—their ability to improvise—serves them especially well when confronted with adversity.

Given their propensity for improvisation, jugaad innovators don't rely on forecasting tools like scenario planning, as many Western companies do, to assess future risks. They believe in Murphy's Law—anything that can go wrong will go wrong—so what's the point of anticipating every single obstacle that might appear down the road? Jugaad innovators don't have a Plan B, let alone a Plan C. Rather, when confronted with an unexpected hindrance, they rely on their innate ability to improvise an effective solution to overcome it, given the circumstances at that time.

A good example is that of Tata Motors, the maker of the $2,000 Nano car. The Nano was the brainchild of Ratan Tata, chairman of the Tata Group (Tata Motors' parent company), who conceived it as an affordable, comfortable, and safe alternative to the perilous two-wheelers that often carry entire families on Indian roads. In 2006, Tata Motors announced that the Nano would be manufactured in Singur, West Bengal, an East Indian state. The factory was to be built on land acquired from farmers by the state government in a bid to boost local industry. Tata Motors intended to roll out its first Nanos from the Singur plant in late October 2008.

In 2007, however, local farmers began protesting against the acquisition of land for the factory. The dispute rapidly escalated into a political issue—and caught Tata Motors off guard. As the protests intensified through 2008, Ravi Kant, then managing director of Tata Motors (and later its nonexecutive vice chairman) made a bold decision. He set aside his firm's prior manufacturing plans and swiftly shifted the production of the Nano to Sanand, in the investor-friendly state of Gujarat, on the other side of the country. He didn't hire a management consultant to advise him on the move; he just trusted his instinct that this was the right thing to do, given the circumstances.[5] In just fourteen months (compared to the expected twenty-eight months for the Singur plant), Tata Motors built a new factory in Sanand, Gujarat. The new factory began production of Nanos in June 2010.[6]

One year later, Ravi Kant and his team had to demonstrate the ability to adapt to rapidly changing circumstances yet again: the Nanos weren't selling as well as expected. Monthly sales had fallen well below the optimistic forecast of twenty thousand units. Rather than being disappointed by the Nano's lackluster performance, Tata Motors' leadership used this early market feedback to improvise a plan to shore up sales. Ratan Tata originally envisioned a distributed supply chain model whereby Tata Motors would dispatch flat packs to local entrepreneurs across the country, who would do the final assembly of Nanos close to customers—thus creating gainful employment in local communities. With flagging sales, however, this original vision had to be revised: Tata Motors' executives went back to the drawing board and quickly revamped Nano's logistics network to a more straightforward one, which involved manufacture and assembly at one site in Gujarat, and distribution through a traditional dealer network throughout the country. But again Tata Motors hit a snag: rural customers—such as farmers—were not venturing into Tata Motors' showrooms in small towns. Among other things, they felt intimidated by dealers dressed in suits and ties.

This setback led Tata Motors' management to redesign their rural showrooms to make them more informal—for example, by staffing them with casually attired salesmen who could pitch the Nano to farmers over a cup of *chai*. Tata Motors also launched a nationwide TV campaign and began offering consumer financing at highly attractive rates to lure frugal Indian consumers. By constantly adapting and refining its business model—and implementing changes within weeks, not months—Tata Motors invigorated sales of the Nano, which, although still lower than expected, are gradually beginning to pick up.[7] Indeed, it is very likely that the future success of the car will depend on more such quick adaptation and flexible thinking by the managers of Tata Motors.

Jugaad Innovators Experiment with Multiple Ways to Reach a Goal Unpredictability is the norm in emerging markets. Because of diversity and rapid change, it is hard to predict how consumers will respond to new products and services—and how new business strategies will perform in, say, rural markets. Jugaad innovators may have a single-minded vision of where they want to get to, but they must be willing to try different paths to get there. Specifically, they must be willing to keep experimenting in order to attain their goals—and they must be flexible enough to quickly switch from one path to another along the way.

Dr. Mohan, for instance, experimented with a number of different ways to frugally yet effectively engage rural communities both as consumers (patients) and employees. When he first sent his expensive technicians from his city hospital to work in remote villages, he found that these technicians—although highly competent—would soon leave, wanting to return to city life. Learning this, he developed a training curriculum in his city hospital to impart to young men and women from villages the basic skills they need as health care workers. After about three months, these newly trained health care professionals would return to their rural homes, where they were more likely to want to remain. This in turn helped reduce costs and turnover in Dr. Mohan's model. Dr. Mohan had a similar experience with his attempts to work with nontraditional partners to develop a cost-effective telemedicine platform. Although he initially contemplated partnering with more typical—and expensive—technology providers, Dr. Mohan eventually linked up with ISRO, which provides his roaming telemedicine van with a free satellite uplink to his clinic in the city of Chennai.

Jugaad Innovators Act with Speed and Agility In emerging markets, new threats and opportunities can emerge from out of the blue. This forces jugaad innovators to not only think but also *act* flexibly. By demonstrating agility, jugaad innovators can deal with unanticipated challenges faster and seize unexpected opportunities—such as changing customer needs—more swiftly than their competitors. Zhang Ruimin is one such jugaad innovator who thinks *and* acts quickly.

Zhang, introduced in Chapter One, is the CEO of Haier, a Chinese consumer goods company that is making appliance manufacturers like GE and Whirlpool nervous. Under Zhang's leadership, Haier has, in the space of a decade, made huge inroads into North American and

European markets by selling quality appliances at lower prices than those of Western suppliers like Whirlpool and GE. Armed with its "value for money" strategy, Haier is disrupting the consumer goods market not only in mainstream segments like air-conditioners and washing machines but also in niche segments like wine coolers. For instance, Haier launched a $704 wine cooler that is less than half the cost of industry leader La Sommelière's product. Within two years of this launch, Haier has grown the market by a whopping 10,000 percent and now controls 60 percent of the U.S. market by value.[8]

What makes Haier so innovative is not just its cool products, but also its flexible organizational structure. Zhang believes that in the Internet era, appliance makers like Haier need to shift from mass production to mass customization—and start thinking and acting nimbly, as Facebook and Google do. As Zhang explains: "The focus on promoting your cost or price advantage has shifted to a focus on service differentiation, mostly centering on customer experience."[9]

To sense and respond to his retail customers' needs faster than rivals can, Zhang came up with a jugaad innovation: he radically redesigned Haier's organization, which currently employs over fifty thousand people worldwide. Specifically, he replaced Haier's organizational pyramid with a loosely coupled network of more than four thousand self-managed, cross-functional units (including R&D, supply chain, sales, and marketing) that interact directly with customers and autonomously make decisions. Each unit operates as an independent profit center and is evaluated as such. Zhang refers to this organizational innovation—which empowers autonomous units of frontline workers to sense and respond to consumer demand—as "making a big company small"—that is, allowing a big company like Haier to maintain the unique flexibility of a small startup.[10] To make this bottom-up, customer-centric organizational structure work, Zhang shifted the role of managers from being commanders and supervisors into being supporters and providers who ensure that the independent units have the resources they need to meet customer demand as promptly as possible. He doesn't want managers to be in charge, as they aren't directly in touch with customers.[11]

Haier's organizational agility enables it to react swiftly to rapidly changing—or unexpected—customer needs, and to innovate faster, better, and cheaper than its rivals. For instance, in China, any call placed to Haier's national customer service center is answered within three rings and a technician is dispatched to your house within three hours—even on Sundays. A few years back, one such call came from a farmer in a remote village in Sichuan province who complained about the constantly clogged drainpipe in his washing machine. The Haier technician who went to investigate found that the farmer was using the machine to wash the mud off his freshly harvested potatoes; it was this mud that was causing the clogging. "Most companies would react by saying 'This machine is not designed for this purpose,'" explains Philip Carmichael, Haier's president, Asia-Pacific, "but Haier's approach was to say, 'This guy (farmer) isn't the only one who's tried to wash potatoes. Is there a way to adapt this product to this requirement? Maybe we can make a machine that actually washes potatoes and clothes.'"[12]

Haier's flexible thinking was spot on: it turns out that millions of farmers across China routinely use their washing machines to clean their vegetables. Sensing a big market opportunity, Haier's cross-functional teams quickly acted on their intuition by developing a washing machine with larger pipes that could also handle vegetables. The product was a big hit among farmers. But Haier's creative teams didn't stop there. They also invented a washing machine that can *peel* potatoes and even designed a model for herders in Inner Mongolia and the Tibetan Plateau to help churn yak milk into butter! These inventions eventually inspired Haier to introduce, in 2009, a washing machine able to wash clothes *without* detergent. That groundbreaking innovation helped propel Haier to the number one position in the laundry equipment market not only in China but also around the world.[13]

Jugaad innovators—such as Haier's employees—are highly adaptable. They are capable of thinking on their feet and acting with great agility. Being nimble-minded and nimble-footed serves them well in the context of emerging markets, which are characterized by extreme unpredictability. Western leaders confronted with increasing volatility and uncertainty in their own business environment must also learn to think and act flexibly—but, as we discuss next, that's easier said than done.

WHAT MAKES WESTERN FIRMS SO INFLEXIBLE?

Being flexible and coming up with new business models—as Dr. Mohan, Harish Hande, Ratan Tata, and Zhang Ruimin have done—is increasingly critical for Western firms, not only to enter and grow their businesses in emerging markets but also in Western markets. However, many Western companies continue to operate their businesses as usual, paying little attention to the impending upheaval in their home environments. We believe that Western firms' inability to think and act flexibly in response to change has five chief causes: complacency; binary logic; an aversion to risk; disengaged employees; and rigid, time-consuming product development processes. Let's look at each in detail.

Complacency   As we discussed in Chapter Two, according to Carol Dweck, a professor of psychology at Stanford University, individuals typically have one of two mindsets:[14]

- A fixed mindset—that is, they believe their qualities and others' are carved in stone
- A growth mindset— that is, they believe that their basic qualities can be nurtured and improved through effort[15]

Every corporation also has one of these mindsets, and many Western companies tend to suffer from the fixed type. Such a rigid mindset often comes from structured innovation processes and, ironically, past successes, which can breed complacency and sow the seeds of failure. Specifically, the complacency that comes from past successes blinds companies to the fact that every challenge is unique and requires a different approach for success. Consequently, when faced with new challenges, companies tend to reapply "tried and true" solutions rather than develop radically new ones. As Prasad Kaipa, a CEO coach and leadership expert explains, "The same core competence that made Western companies so successful in the early stages of their lifecycle eventually also becomes their Achilles' heel—or their 'core incompetence' that eventually brings them down."[16]

Shashank Samant, president of GlobalLogic, a company that provides R&D services to large technology vendors, observes that

> Many large tech firms have become victims of their own success: they first rose to success by riding the wave of one major technology cycle—which typically lasts seven to eight years—but they don't know how to ride the next wave. They fail to understand that the innovation born out of the previous cycle isn't relevant in the new emerging cycle: they are as reluctant to go back to the drawing board and invent next-generation solutions as they are unwilling to unlearn their past generation best practices. The bad news is that technology cycles are now getting shorter and shorter—forcing incumbents to unlearn and relearn even faster.[17]

GlobalLogic recently partnered with a U.S. tech company to overhaul its fifteen-year-old product, which was invented before the web era. This technically superior product was very successful in its early years but eventually lost its edge when younger users, who prefer the cleaner interface of Facebook and Google, deemed its user interface clunky. The company hired GlobalLogic to give its product a facelift so that it would appeal to a new generation of users. GlobalLogic's developer team—made up of twenty- and thirty-something software programmers from India and Ukraine—designed a user interface that was as easy to use as Facebook's. Their demo wowed top managers of the U.S. tech firm. However, one middle manager anxiously raised his hand and said: "This new user-interface looks great. But it doesn't comply with our fifteen-year-old software development standard back in the United States." He didn't realize that the very purpose of partnering with the IT outsourcer *was to get rid of that clunky old standard* and introduce a new one fit for the twenty-first century. In the end, the tech company stuck to its old user interface—forgoing an opportunity to reinvent its product for adoption by Generation Y and Z users. Complacency often leads to an inability to get rid of old thinking patterns and entrenched behaviors. This often sounds the death knell for individuals and organizations, especially when they are confronted with complexity.

Binary Logic   Western companies and their leaders often operate in a black-and-white world that confers a sense of predictability on things. Competitors are "bad" and partners are "good." Regulations are typically "bad for business," whereas protectionist policies are "good." And although some companies may like "doing good" as part of their corporate social responsibility (CSR) initiatives, they worry primarily about "doing well" in their core for-profit businesses. Such binary thinking—anchored in deep-seated assumptions—prevents companies from reconciling polarities, a process that could, ironically, yield disruptive innovation. Doreen Lorenzo, president of the global design and innovation consultancy frog, points out: "We are entering a 'gray world' where things are no longer black or white—as yesterday's competitors can become tomorrow's partners—but exist in multiple shades of gray. So many shades can be disconcerting at first, but then you realize they represent as many opportunities for disruptive innovation."[18]

An instance in which shades of gray were at first disconcerting but later recognized as an opportunity is the case of Big Pharma. Many Western pharmaceutical companies have traditionally ignored the low-income segments in emerging markets because these consumers were too poor to afford their drugs. But these companies failed to adapt to changing circumstances and recognize a truth we pointed out in Chapter Three: although the poor are low earners, they are also high *yearners*—a counterintuitive fact of life in emerging economies.[19] Unlike Harish Hande of SELCO, in the past Big Pharma didn't take the time to experiment with for-profit business models that would allow them to cost-effectively manufacture and deliver drugs to the four billion low-income consumers worldwide.[20] Only now, as Western markets have become saturated and increasingly regulated, is Big Pharma scrambling to find innovative ways to reap the "fortune at the bottom of the economic pyramid"—a fortune that continues to elude them.[21]

Risk Aversion   Many Western companies do not attempt to develop radically new products, as they are afraid that these products will cannibalize the market for their existing offerings. Even if they do develop such products, many companies fail to commercialize them, even as nimble competitors encroach on their core markets. This is such a common phenomenon that Clayton Christensen of Harvard Business School has dubbed it the "innovator's dilemma."[22] This problem is compounded by the fact that the tenure of CEOs is shrinking, forcing them to deliver short-term results rather than drive long-term transformational changes. For instance, the average tenure of the CEO of a hospital is less than six years—not enough time to invest in bold innovations like Dr. Mohan's initiative, which may take several years to show results.[23]

Perhaps the most obvious example of the "innovator's dilemma" is Kodak. Over a ninety-year period, the company succeeded by selling cheap analog cameras and making most of its revenues from selling and processing photographic film. Even though Kodak actually invented the digital camera, it failed to adapt its old business model, suited for the analog world, to the world of digital cameras, a world in which users could easily print their photographs at home or store and distribute them digitally, online. Similar rigidities in thinking and action—shaped by risk aversion—are responsible for the failure, if not the actual demise, of brick-and-mortar book retailers like Borders in the face of the breakthrough business models of online retailers like Amazon.com.

Disengaged Employees   Some Western companies dabble in "intrapreneurship" (also known as "skunkworks") and "jamming"—initiatives that encourage employees to think flexibly and come up with unconventional ideas for new products or processes. Unfortunately, the bright ideas that come from these initiatives are rarely implemented, because of either management's lack of commitment to them or their fear of cannibalization. Worse, employees may even be punished when their ideas fail commercially. As a result, employees grow cynical or fearful: they begin to feel that their flexible thinking is underappreciated, and they start playing it safe. All this further encourages groupthink, and nobody dares to question or change the status quo. Over time, everyone is content with incrementally innovating existing offerings, rather than investing time and effort in truly disruptive innovation. Employee disengagement grows and cripples the firm's innovation engine.

In support of this view, a Gallup survey in late 2011 found that only 29 percent of American workers feel engaged in their jobs, meaning only 29 percent work with passion, feel their input is appreciated, and have a deep connection to their company. A full 52 percent say they don't feel engaged in their jobs. Most worrisome of all, the remaining 19 percent say they are actively disengaged.[24] This widespread employee disaffection is both the symptom and the cause of the rigid, inflexible approach to innovation in many Western firms.

Rigid, Time-Consuming Product Development Processes

Of course, several Western companies do think flexibly—and come up with truly innovative ideas. But even these companies struggle to commercialize their trailblazing ideas fast enough, for two reasons. First, they take a long time to conduct market research to validate their idea and an equally long time planning and developing a product to get it "right." Second, they are paralyzed by rigid go-to-market processes like Six Sigma and the fact that departments such as R&D and marketing, whose cooperation is needed for innovation, tend to work independently of each other in corporate silos. Eric Schmidt, Google's executive chairman, points out that employees who work too long at any company get inculcated in a repeatable development process that eventually becomes too rigid and stifles their creativity and innovation. Schmidt says: "Real innovation is hard to do when you have a process culture with Six Sigma [that is, extremely low-defect manufacturing]. Risk management is around the process, keeping it the same."[25]

In a fast-moving business environment that is ripe with ambiguity, where customer needs shift overnight and product lifecycles get truncated by aggressive competitors, it's not enough to think flexibly—companies must also *act* flexibly. Tim Harford notes in his book *Adapt*: "The world has become far too unpredictable and profoundly complex ... We must adapt—improvise rather than plan, work from the bottom up rather than the top down, and take baby steps rather than great leaps forward."[26] For instance, it takes Western cellphone makers like Nokia and Motorola many months to plan, develop, and launch what often is an "overengineered" cellphone. In contrast, agile Chinese and Indian rivals like HTC, Huawei, and Spice rely on rapid experimentation: they crank out "good-enough" models within *weeks* and keep improving their design with each subsequent model using real-time market feedback.[27] The secret weapon of these Asian innovators is their organizational flexibility. HTC, Huawei, and Spice routinely employ cross-functional development teams that eliminate communication gaps among the key players responsible for product development and launch—much like Haier, as discussed earlier. Similarly, Google has organized itself as a flexible and dynamic network of small teams that can quickly react to market needs—by building and launching new products in rapid-fire fashion. "[At Google] we don't have a two-year plan. We have a next week and a next quarter plan," explains Eric Schmidt, Google's executive chairman.[28]

LEARN TO IMPROVISE

To break free from the constraints that keep Western companies inflexible—complacency, binary thinking, risk aversion, disengaged employees, and rigid processes—Western companies must learn to improvise, experiment, and adapt their business models to changing circumstances. But breaking free is not easy: pressures to deliver strong short-term quarterly results often deter management from thinking radically. Still, there are many strategies that Western companies—knee-deep in traditional, structured processes and approaches to innovation—can employ to cultivate and sustain flexible thinking and action.

Break Rules and Shift Values When Necessary   Even conventional beliefs and values have a shelf life: there is nothing eternally wise about them. Breakthrough innovation occurs when commonly held beliefs and values are challenged, not reinforced. For instance, in many companies, flexible thinking is sacrificed at the altar of "corporate values." These companies often fail to realize that their corporate values *have lost their value* as the times have changed—and need to be overhauled to reflect new market realities and major societal shifts. In July 2003, to prevent such ossification from setting in, IBM's then-CEO Sam Palmisano organized "ValuesJam"—a three-day-long online brainstorming session in which all employees were invited to renew and update IBM's century-old value system.[29] This collaborative exercise recontextualized the very notion of innovation—IBM's core value—as something measured not by the number of patents filed or products shipped but by the impact that IBM makes on society. This ability to reassess where the company stands and this willingness to change its direction led IBM to embark on its Smart Planet initiative, which uses technology to build sustainable communities worldwide.[30]

Don't Let Inflexible Investors and Customers Dictate Your Innovation Agenda   Because external stakeholders often tend to be conservative or lack the perspective to appreciate vision or foresight, it is probably best not to seek their validation for bold new products and services. Recall what Henry Ford famously said: "If I had asked customers what they wanted, they would have said 'faster horses.'" More recently, Apple didn't do extensive market surveys to come up with the iPad. This may have been just as well, given that many consumers, analysts, and media experts were convinced that there was no market for the product. Yet the iPad turned out to be a breakthrough innovation now eagerly copied by Apple's rivals.[31]

Create Time and Space for Employees to Improvise and Experiment   Companies can hardly expect employees to think flexibly while they maintain their regular routine and operate in their usual work environment. To be able to think and act flexibly, employees need dedicated time and an inspiring space to experiment with new ideas. Google is a good example of a company that allows employees ample time for improvisation. It employs a 70/20/10 model for organizing work: its employees spend 70 percent of their time on core business tasks, 20 percent on related projects, and 10 percent on projects totally unrelated to their core work. Many of Google's commercially successful innovations such as Google Maps and Google Mail were developed by employees during the 20 percent of the time spent outside their day-to-day activities—when they were able to unleash their outside-the-box thinking.[32]

Recognizing the company could do still more to encourage such creative thinking, Google launched a new experimental incubator in January 2011 dedicated to building mobile, social, and location-based applications. The incubator is located in San Francisco—an hour away from Google Headquarters in Mountain View—and operates with a small team of twenty people empowered to think flexibly and to "hatch new startups" in Google. Heading the team is John Hanke, who ran Google Maps for six years. "Our goal will be to pump out prototypes quickly and see what sticks," says Hanke. Of course, many of the ventures conceived at this incubator will fail, but some will succeed and evolve into billion-dollar businesses for Google. By giving its employees a safe place to experiment—and fail—Google can sustain the flexible thinking that leads to truly breakthrough innovation.[33]

Get Outside Your Comfort Zone to Gain New Perspectives

To truly think flexibly, managers need to be taken out of their comfort zones and exposed to new situations that challenge them to think differently. DuPont sent its senior executives to rural India, where they received a somewhat humbling revelation. None of their expensive technological solutions, designed for Western urban markets, seemed relevant to low-income Indian villagers. This experience forced these DuPont executives to go back to the drawing board and cocreate with local communities a whole new set of affordable and sustainable solutions designed for fast-growing emerging markets like India.[34]

Partner with Flexible Thinkers   Sometimes the best way to develop a new mindset is to seek inspiration from outside your company.

Thus one way to nurture flexibility is to partner with other companies that are already flexible and agile. For instance, electronics retail giant Best Buy has deep ties with Silicon Valley start-ups that tend to innovate faster and better than the large electronics vendors that supply Best Buy. As a result, Best Buy is able to bring groundbreaking technologies to market much faster than even its large electronics suppliers can. For instance, after getting an early look at Sling Media's Slingbox (a technology that lets consumers pipe TV programming from their homes to their mobile devices wherever they are), Best Buy brought this innovation to market months ahead of its competition.[35]

IBM is another company that partners with nimble thinkers. Although it employs three thousand in-house research scientists and engineers and files more patents annually than any other company, IBM has nevertheless opened "collaboratories" in leading universities worldwide. In these collaboratories, IBM technologists work closely with agile-minded university researchers to cocreate cutting-edge technologies. These technologies include smart electricity grids, resilient transportation networks, and cost-effective health care delivery solutions with the potential to have a big social and economic impact globally.[36]

Experiment with Multiple Business Models   Often companies become too attached to a successful business model and find it nearly impossible to let go of it, let alone to explore alternative options. But competition can spring from unexpected corners and disrupt your business model overnight. Flexible thinkers keep all options open—and experiment with multiple business models simultaneously. The Indian biotech company Biocon, for instance, has developed an insulin treatment for diabetes that it commercializes through direct channels in emerging markets but licenses to Pfizer for deployment in Western markets.[37] Similarly, Amazon.com, aware of the potential for its own online model to be disrupted by digital e-readers, has been flexible in developing and promoting a new business model around its own e-reader, the Kindle, while maintaining its dominance in online retailing.[38]

Fail Cheap, Fail Fast, Fail Often   A corollary of the willingness of jugaad innovators to continually experiment is their willingness to fail cheap, fail fast, and fail often. Fernando Fabre, president of Endeavor, a global nonprofit that supports high-impact entrepreneurs from emerging markets, highlights the fact that jugaad entrepreneurs typically do not take *large* risks. Based on a detailed study it conducted on fifty-five high-impact entrepreneurs across eleven countries, Endeavor found that, unlike Silicon Valley entrepreneurs—who, backed with venture capital, go for broke (it's either the next Facebook or it's not worth doing)—emerging market entrepreneurs start with what they have (not much) and who they know (friends and family). They rarely do something so rash as mortgaging their houses. Consequently, they have small initial budgets to work with—which, rather than cramping their style, forces them to experiment in a frugal manner that does not result in large losses (that is, they fail cheap). Their initial budgets also force them to change tack as soon as one means to achieving their goal shows any signs of not working (that is, they fail fast). Finally, given their willingness to try out different means to reach their goals, they are willing to do so several times over in an iterative fashion (that is, they fail often).[39]

Western innovators have much to gain from adopting these practices of jugaad entrepreneurs. They can look to Google and Best Buy for inspiration. At Google, failure is widely celebrated—especially if you fail fast and cheap. For instance, in June 2011 Google pulled the plug on two high-profile projects—Google Health and Google PowerMeter—which were launched, respectively, in May 2008 and February 2009. The company mentioned its "inability to scale" as the main reason to shut down these two projects.[40] Similarly, in early 2011 Best Buy shut down its big-box stores in China a mere five years after entering the country—citing stronger-than-expected local competition and the fact that its Westernized store format failed to appeal to Chinese consumers. "We experimented with a new approach in China," explains Kal Patel, former president of Best Buy's business in Asia. "It was worth trying—given the sheer size of the Chinese consumer market. But it didn't work—so we pulled the plug before we incurred too much loss. We tried to be flexible in both entering and exiting China. It's vital that you fail early and cheap in unpredictable markets like China."[41] In contrast to Best Buy, other Western manufacturers and retailers continue to pump billions of dollars into expanding their presence in China even though they are steadily losing their market share to local rivals.

BREAK DOWN ORGANIZATIONAL SILOS TO GAIN SPEED

Flexible thinking must go hand in hand with flexible action. In today's fast-paced environment, with product lifecycles growing ever shorter, companies need to break down organizational silos so they can convert breakthrough ideas into breakthrough products faster. Facebook understands this: although its subscriber base has grown to more than eight hundred million users, the company still employs only about thirty-five designers, using a flat organizational structure.[42] These designers work closely with marketing executives, engineers, writers, and researchers in multidisciplinary teams that can convert bright design ideas into new user experiences within hours. Soleio Cuervo, the second designer that Facebook CEO Mark Zuckerberg hired in 2005, says, "When I started, it was only a handful of product designers. Now, engineers work with us directly. We don't throw documents at them with specs. We all focus on the site's user experience versus the code."[43]

Breaking down internal silos is even more critical when you are trying to quickly bring to market brilliant ideas from external sources. For example, Procter & Gamble has established a mechanism called Connect & Develop to fast-track the sourcing and commercialization of bright ideas from creative external partners. Now P&G can launch promising products within months rather than years. One such product is the Pulsonic toothbrush, which P&G codeveloped with a leading Japanese firm. P&G brought this product to market twice as fast as it would have if it had tried to build the product on its own. In October 2010, Bob McDonald, CEO of P&G, set a bolder target for his company: to triple the impact of Connect & Develop so it can potentially contribute $3 billion to the company's annual sales growth. "We want the best minds in the world to work with us to create big ideas that can touch and improve the lives of more consumers, in more parts of the world, more completely," explains McDonald.[44]

ALL THE NEWS THAT'S FIT TO DIGITIZE

The New York Times Company (NYTC) has successfully demonstrated its ability to think and act flexibly by providing dedicated space and time for its creative employees to experiment with radical new ideas. From 2007 to 2009, U.S. newspapers saw an estimated 30-percent drop in revenues from online and offline circulation and advertising. With the Internet slowly killing print media and sucking away advertising revenues, NYTC decided to reinvent itself.[45] In January 2006, it set up an R&D department—the first ever in the media industry—staffed with thirteen members whose primary focus is to anticipate the future—and imagine the unthinkable.

The department identifies emerging consumer and technology trends, such as social media, e-readers, and mobile devices, and formulates strategies for NYTC to proactively embrace them, rather than being disrupted by them. "It is not a product development group," clarifies Michael Zimbalist, vice president of research and development operations at NYTC, describing his team's mission. "It is much more focused on monitoring trends and identifying opportunities."[46]

Foreseeing the potential of Facebook, in 2007 the R&D team launched an application to push content (including a daily quiz as bonus material) onto the social networking site. Today, the *Times* boasts far more followers than any other newspaper on Facebook and Twitter. NYTC's jugaad innovators also linked *Times* content to Google Earth maps to show locations mentioned in stories. Recently, they created Cascade—a data visualization tool that provides a time-based view of how *Times* stories and op-eds virally spread in Twitter's social universe as soon as they go live. Cascade helps NYTC identify critical information such as influential Tweeters and determine the best times of the day to publish a story online.[47]

Zimbalist strongly believes that newspapers need to go beyond the print and even basic web and use platforms such as social networks, smartphones, TV, and even smart cars of the future to reach all users. His team seeks to gain insight into how people consume media content on different platforms and helps NYTC make forays into new platforms.

Predicting an imminent future when all devices will be connected via the Internet, Zimbalist's team of jugaad innovators is working to enable readers to access the newspaper's content across multiple interconnected platforms. Here is one possible scenario that NYTC's jugaad innovators are trying to enable: In the future, a reader may start an article on the *Times* website on her desktop at the office in the late afternoon, continue reading it on her iPhone as she leaves works, listen to an embedded podcast in her car on her way back home, watch an accompanying video on the HDTV in her living room, and finally forward the article to friends via her personal laptop. "[We are] investigating the ideas at the edges of today and thinking about how they're going to impact business decisions tomorrow," notes Zimbalist.

In addition to its adaptable and creative R&D team, NYTC has found other ways to encourage flexible thinking among all its four thousand employees. It now hosts internal technology and innovation challenges to encourage employees to think flexibly and come up with a jugaad way to use technology to address a vexing business issue. Recently, NYTC launched beta620.newyorktimes.com, a public website described as "a springboard for the creativity of our software developers, journalists and product managers, who will use it as a platform to showcase new and exciting ideas for the *Times*."[48] Its readers are strongly encouraged to provide feedback on the jugaad inventions showcased on this site.

By harnessing the ingenuity of all its employees, NYTC is building an army of jugaad innovators who can conquer the increasingly complex and unpredictable publishing world—by improvising cutting-edge solutions that can sustain the firm's growth in the highly connected web economy. In the process NYTC is reinventing itself as a nimble, social-media-savvy, multiplatform digital content provider.

CONCLUSION

A baffling number of uncontrollable and unknowable forces determine the future of our increasingly complex business world. In the midst of this uncertainty, long-term plans become toothless—even dangerous—and rigidly structured processes prevent us from coming up with the next big thing and responding quickly to competitive threats. To thrive in this volatile world, the ability to think and act flexibly is crucial.

In emerging markets, jugaad innovators facing daily uncertainties have become masters of flexibility: frequently challenging conventional thinking, coming up with entirely new value propositions, experimenting with various ways to achieve their goals, quickly responding to changing circumstances, improvising new solutions, and modifying their plans as they go. Western companies and entrepreneurs have much to gain by adopting such flexibility and using it as a foil to their own more structured approach to innovation.

Jugaad innovators like Dr. Mohan and Harish Hande aren't just flexible thinkers and doers, however. They are also masters of simplicity. Facing mind-boggling complexity in their daily lives, they are driven to *simplify* their products and services to make them more affordable and accessible to their customers, and to simplify their customer interactions to deliver a superior user experience. Yet, jugaad innovators' simple solutions are not simplistic. Quite the contrary: adhering to Leonard da Vinci's credo that "simplicity is the ultimate sophistication," jugaad innovators pursue what mathematicians call "elegance" in their solutions. Keeping it simple is the subject of the next chapter.

CHAPTER FIVE

PRINCIPLE FOUR
Keep It Simple

I would not give a fig for the simplicity on this side of complexity, but I would give my life for the simplicity on the other side of complexity.

— OLIVER WENDELL HOLMES

Dr. Sathya Jeganathan is a pediatrician in Chengalpattu Government Medical College, a rural hospital in South India. Infant mortality used to run high at her hospital: on average, 39 out of every 1,000 infants died at birth. This statistic, unfortunately, did not differ greatly from overall neonatal mortality rates in India where, of the roughly 26 million children born each year, 1.2 million die during their first four weeks of life.[1]

Wishing to decrease infant mortality in her hospital, Dr. Jeganathan first tried to import incubators made in the West. But she soon found the setup cost of these incubators prohibitively high, and the staff and maintenance needed to operate the equipment unsuited to rural India. Undeterred, she applied some jugaad thinking. She decided to design her own incubator, one that was simple, inexpensive, and easy to use. Teaming up with neonatal nurses and local electricians, Dr. Jeganathan developed a minimalist incubator from a wooden table made of locally harvested wood, a Plexiglas top, and standard 100-watt light bulbs (rather than radiant coils) to maintain the baby's temperature. Thanks to its simple design, the incubator cost only $100 to build and was easy to maintain.

Once Dr. Jeganathan had the first working prototype of the incubator constructed and implemented in her hospital, infant mortality was cut by half. Now she is working closely with the Lemelson Foundation, a U.S.–based organization that supports entrepreneurs in emerging markets, to fine-tune and rescale her invention so it can be distributed across other rural hospitals in India.[2]

U.S. lawmakers seeking to address America's health care crisis might find Dr. Jeganathan's incubator story interesting. U.S. medical device makers spend billions of R&D dollars trying to push the frontiers of science and technology—only to come up with highly expensive and complex equipment that requires highly trained technicians to operate. In the process, these device makers often forget the basic needs of end users. After all, why make things simple when they can use their R&D dollars to make them more complicated? High-end incubators sold in the West, like those Jeganathan originally sought to buy, have many high-tech features and can cost up to $20,000. Yet they meet the same fundamental need as Dr. Jeganathan's ingeniously simple $100 machine: they keep babies warm.

In this chapter, we look at how jugaad innovators like Dr. Jeganathan are at the forefront of a *low-tech* revolution devoted to finding "good enough" solutions. Rather than offering overengineered products, jugaad innovators in emerging markets offer products that are easy to use and maintain and address customers' fundamental needs. By designing for the most basic universal needs, jugaad innovators appeal to a wider spectrum of consumers and thus dominate the sectors they operate in.

In contrast, Western companies have long embraced a "bigger is better" approach to innovation. However, consumers are increasingly put off by the complexity of technology, especially in products like consumer electronics and automobiles that they encounter daily. More important, Western consumers across income levels are "downshifting"—opting for a simpler, more meaningful life. Western companies who respond now to these consumer and societal changes are likely to benefit in the long run. In this chapter, we discuss how some forward-thinking companies like Google, Facebook, GE, General Motors, Siemens, and Philips are leading this response by building simplicity into their products and services—as well as into their organizational design—and, in the process, creating deep and lasting relationships with consumers.

THE PRACTICAL BENEFITS OF SIMPLICITY

Jugaad innovators find success in emerging markets by pursuing simplicity in the products and services they offer. They are motivated to do so because this allows them to develop quick yet effective solutions for consumers grappling with complexity in their daily lives.

Simple products offer three advantages to jugaad innovators:

- *They are cheaper to make—and therefore more affordable.* Resources in emerging markets are scarce and expensive. Simple products—with fewer features—require fewer resources and are therefore easier and cheaper to produce and deliver. Jugaad innovators can pass on these savings to customers in the form of lower prices, making simpler products more affordable and thus more successful in the marketplace.
- *They are easier to install and maintain.* Emerging markets face a lack of skilled workers to install and maintain complex products. For example, in India, 26 percent of adults are illiterate and therefore cannot read basic instruction manuals, let alone complicated ones. The limited availability of skilled workers means that companies cannot create highly engineered products that require skilled staff to set up and maintain.
- *They can satisfy a wider audience.* Emerging market customers are diverse in their needs and in their ability to use and maintain products. To reach as wide an audience as possible, jugaad innovators are compelled to design products that take into account the buying power, literacy, and technical aptitude of the least able members of the population. Designing simple products is the key to achieving universal appeal across diverse groups.

THE ART OF SIMPLICITY

Jugaad innovators in emerging markets rely on several strategies to design products that are simple to use and maintain. To begin with, they focus more on customers' *needs* than on their *desires*. They employ a functional approach to product and service design and try to develop practical solutions that address well-defined customer needs. They are not in the business of coming up with cool features that appeal to customers' wants. Instead, jugaad innovators aim to make and deliver a good enough solution with limited functionality rather than one with a dazzling array of features.

For instance, to address the high cost of electricity in Filipino slums, Illac Diaz invented an ingeniously simple solution: Isang Litrong Liwanag (A Liter of Light), is a scheme that brings an eco-friendly solar bottle bulb to underprivileged communities across the Philippines. The solar bottle bulb (SLB) is simply a recycled plastic bottle filled with bleach-treated water (to prevent formation of mold) that is fitted snugly into a hole in the corrugated roof of makeshift homes in shantytowns. The water in the bottle refracts the sun's rays producing the equivalent of a 55-watt light bulb. An SLB produces more light than a conventional window might let in. And, unlike windows, the bulb doesn't break or leak during the typhoon season. The SLB is made from recyclable materials; is very easy to assemble, install, and maintain; and helps create new jobs in underdeveloped communities, as slum dwellers can now work in their normally dark homes during the day. More important, an SLB can be installed for just $1.[3] Diaz's vision is to deploy SLBs in one million homes across the Philippines by the end of 2012.[4]

Jugaad innovators like Diaz don't try to guess what would make their products simple by sitting in an R&D lab. Rather, they spend a great deal of time with customers in their natural setting to observe and identify what would make a product or service easier for them to use. Nokia, for example, employs ethnographers who spend long periods of time living with customers in emerging markets to understand their latent needs. In one case, Nokia's ethnographers studied migrant workers in Indian slums, the shantytowns of Ghana, and the *favelas* of Brazil to figure out how technology could make their lives easier. They were humbled to discover that regular cellphones were too expensive, flashy, and complex for slum-dwellers to buy and use and that the devices couldn't withstand the dusty, no-electricity environment where these people worked and lived. Armed with this insight, Nokia's researchers set out to develop a simple solution that would blend into the lives of these target users. The result was the Nokia 1100, a rugged cellphone with a minimalist design that allows calling and texting, withstands dust, and can be recharged within a few minutes. When Nokia's researchers noticed that many of these customers use their cellphone's bright screen as a light source, they included a flashlight in the 1100 design—making it very popular among, for example, truck drivers in Asia and Africa who use it to repair their vehicles at night. The Nokia 1100 was launched in 2003 and became an immediate hit: it appealed to not only low-income consumers but even middle-class users looking for an uncomplicated cellphone. The Nokia 1100 has sold 250 million units around the world, making it the best-selling cellphone ever.[5] *Foreign Policy* magazine calls the Nokia 1100 "the most important cellphone on the planet."[6]

When creating simple products that meet the immediate needs of their customers, jugaad innovators typically design them *from the ground up*. They avoid "defeaturing"—a practice often pursued by Western multinationals, which involves taking products designed for affluent Western consumers, stripping them of nonessential features, and then selling them at somewhat lower prices to consumers in emerging markets. These defeatured products typically fail in emerging markets because they are not fundamentally designed to take into account the inherent constraints of the local markets' socioeconomic context.

For instance, many Western tech giants like Intel, Microsoft, and HP, as well as academic institutions like MIT, have tried to build a low-cost PC for emerging nations.[7] But none of these projects has succeeded because these PCs were either too complex to use or too expensive to buy, or they failed to meet specific local requirements. On October 5, 2011, however, Kapil Sibal, the Indian minister of communications and information technology, launched a $60 tablet (promoted as "the world's cheapest tablet") that was ideally designed to meet local requirements.[8]

Called the Aakash ("sky" in Sanskrit), it was developed by DataWind, a UK-based tech startup, in partnership with several leading Indian technical universities, with local needs and constraints in mind.[9] The initial market for the Aakash will be students—from primary schools all the way to universities—who will receive the first ten thousand units at the subsidized price of $35 per unit. The Aakash boasts a simplified user interface and is preloaded with educational software developed in local languages.

The Aakash clearly cannot match the computing power or the features of Apple's iPad (which costs $500) or Amazon's Kindle Fire (priced at $200). However, it was designed with a different set of users in mind—Indian students, who needed a simple and practical computing device. The Aakash meets those needs very well. First, it provides basic capabilities students need, like web browsing, video, Wi-Fi, and word processing software. Second, the Aakash runs on Google Android and other open-source technologies, which are cheaper and easier to maintain than proprietary technologies. Third, the Aakash comes with a solar charging option, a huge advantage in many parts of India where the electricity supply is either nonexistent or unreliable. Fourth, the Aakash touchscreen makes it easier for students to navigate educational content and makes learning more intuitive and fun. In sum, the Aakash is *simple*. It is part of the Indian government's broader initiative to extend broadband access to twenty-five thousand colleges and four hundred universities across India. Given its simplicity and affordability, the Aakash has the potential to become a runaway success, not only in Indian schools but also in academic institutions abroad. Even U.S.–based experts who tested the Aakash in their labs gave it rave reviews.[10]

It is worth pointing out that jugaad innovators infuse simplicity into not only how they design products but also how they interact with customers, from the sale of their products and services to their delivery and after-sales support. Such *service innovation*—that is, innovation in the way jugaad innovators interact with customers, deliver services to them, or use technology to support them—is crucial to simplifying and enriching the user experience throughout the solution's lifecycle. In particular, many jugaad entrepreneurs who sell products to the base of the economic pyramid in emerging markets rely on a grassroots network of distributors and technicians who make it easier for customers in villages to learn more about a product, get it installed quickly, and have it maintained without hassle. For example, SELCO, introduced earlier as a company that provides solar lighting to over 125,000 Indian village homes, relies on a vast network of grassroots entrepreneurs who install and repair SELCO's solar lanterns on very short notice—even in the most far-flung villages.

Finally, jugaad innovators ensure that their solutions are simple but not *simplistic*. There is an important distinction between the two. Jugaad innovators follow Albert Einstein's exhortation to "make everything as simple as possible, but not simpler." In other words, jugaad innovators don't necessarily try to simplify the nature of the problem the customer is facing. Doing so runs the risk of producing simplistic solutions, ones that may appear simple in the short term but prove ineffective in the long run. Instead, jugaad innovators often embrace complexity but mask it from customers by giving them a simple user interface. In other words, rather than simplifying the problem the customer is facing, jugaad innovators often simplify the *use* of the solution. As a result, they produce robust and resilient solutions that address users' complex needs, comprehensively and sustainably.

For instance, Ushahidi, which originated in Kenya, is a simple solution that relies on mobile SMS (text messaging) to coordinate grassroots responses to cataclysmic events like hurricanes, earthquakes, or epidemic outbreaks. According to the company website, the Ushahidi platform enables "the gathering [of] crisis information from the general public [and] provides new insights into events happening in near real-time"—in the aftermath of, say, an earthquake.[11] Via text messages, the general public can learn—and inform others—where food and medical supplies are located, and receive SMS alerts when missing persons have been found. Within hours of a cataclysmic event, Ushahidi can help coordinate relief efforts in a highly targeted fashion: medical supplies and food can be dispatched precisely to those locations that need them the most, based on real-time information gathered by thousands of people at the scene. Contrast this with the traditional hit-or-miss relief management approach that is onerous and time-consuming: as relief workers lack precise information on which specific locations need help the most, they plan their relief efforts in a top-down fashion and take a scattershot approach to distributing food and supplies. Ushahidi has been used successfully to rapidly and optimally coordinate relief efforts in the aftermath of the 2010 earthquakes in Haiti and Chile. It was also used by the *Washington Post* to map out blocked roads and other information in the wake of the winter storms that hit Washington, DC in 2010.[12]

The problems Ushahidi is trying to solve are overwhelmingly complex, such as helping people affected by an earthquake or tsunami rapidly locate the food and medical supplies they need. Traditional crisis management tools tend to tackle such huge problems only superficially or partially because the tools are *too* simplistic, as explained earlier. But Ushahidi is able to address complex issues like disaster management *in their full depth and breadth* with relative ease—thanks to an elegantly simple, user-friendly, yet comprehensive bottom-up solution that leverages the power of crowdsourcing.

THE BACKLASH AGAINST COMPLEXITY

The trend toward simplicity is also growing quickly in the West. Although Western technology is more developed and Western consumers are more sophisticated and affluent than their counterparts in emerging markets, there are several reasons why Western companies may benefit from keeping things simple:

• *Customers are clamoring for simplicity*. At the dawn of the twenty-first century, Western customers are increasingly overwhelmed by technology-driven complexity. For instance, 65 percent of Americans complain that they "have lost interest in purchasing a technology product because it seemed too complex to set up or operate."[13] Similarly, having overindulged in technology in the past two decades, Fortune 500 companies now want simpler IT systems that are affordable and easy to deploy and maintain. These technology-jaded users now increasingly equate simplicity with sanity.

- *Generations Y and Z and baby boomers are rebuffing advanced technologies.* The members of generations Y and Z, who are willing to trade high pay for flexibility and work/life balance, also eschew complex offerings in favor of simplicity. For instance, a study at Stanford University found that a majority of graduate students actually prefer the average-quality MP3 version of a song played on their iPods to the high-quality CD version, even though the latter is technically superior.[14] Similarly, large numbers of retiring baby boomers—confronted with health issues such as deteriorating eyesight and arthritis—are put off by complex consumer electronic devices that have too many features and are too complicated to use.

- *More citizens in the West are downshifting their lifestyles.* A grassroots cultural movement known as *voluntary simplicity* is growing across the US.[15] The movement calls for voluntary practices such as reducing one's material possessions or increasing self-sufficiency in order to achieve a simpler, richer, and more meaningful quality of life. Studies show that 15 to 28 percent of Americans have already voluntarily adopted simplified lifestyles.[16]

- *Overengineered products cost a lot of R&D money and time.* In a time of scarcity, Western companies can no longer afford to invest lavishly in R&D to come up with complex products bloated with features that require lengthy development cycles. As a result, several Fortune 500 companies are slashing their R&D budgets (which amounted to a whopping $550 billion in 2010), reducing their products to a more rational number, and simplifying their product development processes to gain in efficiency and speed.[17]

- *Nimble rivals are stealing market share using simplicity.* Visionary companies such as Google and Facebook are democratizing technology by making it simple and accessible—and thereby stealing market share from technology rivals who produce overengineered, counterintuitive products. Similarly, business software companies like SAP and Oracle face competition from cloud computing vendors like salesforce.com, which simplify the lives of tech buyers by reducing all the headaches associated with expensive software upgrades.

"WHY MAKE IT SIMPLE WHEN WE CAN MAKE IT COMPLEX?"

Despite growing evidence that consumers want simplicity in the products and services they buy—and despite the fact that overengineering products is no longer sustainable, as R&D budgets are increasingly being slashed in the West—many Western companies nevertheless find it hard to make simplicity a key tenet of their product development and commercialization processes. There are several reasons for this.

First, Western companies often believe that customers aren't willing to pay a premium for products unless these products are loaded with features and functions. Specifically, the fear of losing the power to charge high prices and earn high margins makes companies shy away from simplicity.

A second, related reason is that complexity has been lucrative in the past. "New, improved" versions of products and services have allowed Western companies to differentiate their new offerings from their own (and other companies') existing ones. That has helped companies convince customers to keep upgrading—or replacing—existing products with ever more complex ones. This in turn has helped companies secure growth and a steady stream of revenues as well.

Third, Western companies are often stuck in an endless innovation war with each other: a perpetual battle of one-upmanship, with each company forced to out-innovate others in order to convince shareholders and customers that they are still "in the game."

Fourth, companies don't always design products with end users in mind. In his book *The Laws of Simplicity*, John Maeda, president of the Rhode Island School of Design, declares that it's high time we "humanize technology."[18] Currently technology development is anything but human-centric. Many of the features in new products are determined not by deep customer observation but by the guesswork of R&D and marketing teams, driven by their desire to create a better version than the last one, often regardless of whether it adds value for the consumer or not.[19]

Finally, innovation metrics in Western companies—such as the number of patents filed each year and the percentage of revenues dedicated to R&D—currently measure and reward cleverness, not customer value. The value of a product should not be measured by the number of patents associated with it.[20] Rather, it should be measured by the experiential value it delivers to end users. For many users, the best experience is a simple, seamless one. Yet most Western companies continue to use the number of patents they file as a key yardstick to measure how innovative they are.

Shifting the emphasis from R&D-driven complexity to customer-valued simplicity, however, will require companies to make some fundamental changes in the way they develop products.

HOW TO SIMPLIFY YOUR PRODUCTS— AND YOUR ORGANIZATION

Pursuing complexity for its own sake is increasingly self-defeating. Not only are customers moving away from complexity and toward simplicity in products and lifestyle, but R&D costs are high and rising, so pursuing complexity is an increasingly expensive proposition for companies. In such a context, it would be wise for Western business leaders to go back to the drawing board and find ways to enshrine simplicity into their value propositions and business models. The following strategies may help Western companies respond to the new economic reality by placing simplicity at the heart of what they do.

Redesign the Entire Organization Around Simplicity

Western companies cannot design simple products while keeping their business operations complex. For instance, a customer may love the ease of use of a firm's products but hate the convoluted sales process she has to go through to buy the product. Companies must therefore simplify *every* interaction with their customers throughout the product lifecycle—from the initial purchase to the actual use and even to the product's disposal—by streamlining not only their R&D and manufacturing but also their sales and customer service processes.

One company that has done just that is the electronics giant Philips, headquartered in Amsterdam. In fact, the company redesigned its entire organization—from R&D to manufacturing to customer support—to serve customers better, using the simplicity principle. This process began in the early 2000s when Philips received a big shock following the results of a piece of market research it had commissioned. For more than a hundred years, the company had built a reputation for exceptional technical performance, one that has yielded market-shaping inventions such as the compact tape cassette and compact disc. Yet the two thousand consumers it surveyed globally were now telling Philips that technical superiority wasn't what drove them to buy an electronics product. If anything, consumers felt intimidated by the growing complexity of technology: 30 percent of home-networking products were returned, as users didn't know how to set them up; and nearly 50 percent of people postponed their decision to buy a digital camera, deterred by its complexity.[21] As Stefano Marzano, CEO and chief creative director of Philips Design, observes: "People are ready for unobtrusive technology."[22]

Sensing an opportunity, Philips' management team decided to reinvent its entire organization around simplicity—from the inside out. The conglomerate pruned its portfolio of businesses from five hundred to seventy and reduced the number of divisions from seventy to five. It simplified customer service so end users got the same experience, irrespective of the Philips business they were dealing with. Philips even extended simplicity to its corporate communications: no PowerPoint presentation was allowed to exceed ten slides, and all its annual reports since 2009 have been made available only online. In a way, Philips embraced voluntary simplicity as a new organizational principle.[23]

By first internalizing simplicity and then actively living it, Philips was able to authentically engage customers in a discussion about simplicity. The company launched a rebranding campaign themed "Sense and Simplicity"—which has since become its corporate motto.[24] It even set up a Simplicity Advisory Board made up of five leading global experts in healthcare, lifestyle, and technology to help the company deliver on its "Sense and Simplicity" promise.[25] It began to proactively infuse the end user's perspective into every aspect of new product development, from ideation to prototyping and even packaging. For instance, Philips' R&D team quickly redesigned the packaging for a new flat-screen TV so the TV could be removed from a carton lying horizontally—a decision made after pilot users struggled to pull the heavy set out of an upright box.[26] In recent years, Philips has launched a steady stream of user-friendly products that have won rave reviews from customers and industry experts for their ability to marry simplicity and performance. In 2011, Philips bagged a record twenty-eight iF product design awards for its new products that seamlessly marry advanced technologies, sustainability, and a consumer-friendly design. These products included the Daily Duo vacuum cleaner and the Econova LED TV.[27]

Distill Customer Needs to Their Bare Essence—and Design Simple Products Around Them Simplicity advocates insist that "user-centric design" boosts the ease of use of products and services. Although this is true, it is important to remember that the urgency of customer needs varies widely. Western companies should zero in on consumers' most acute need (or pain point) and build a solution around *that* need above all others. A master of this approach was Apple cofounder Steve Jobs. Jobs elevated simplicity to an iconic status in computing. In many ways, Jobs was the Michelangelo of the digital age: he could take a piece of hardware, chip away the nonessential pieces, and design wonderfully simple-looking products like the iPod, the iPhone, and the iPad. In a rare interview, Jobs once told *BusinessWeek*: "Innovation emerges when saying no to thousands of things to ensure that we do not take the wrong path or try to do too much."[28]

Design Simple Offerings from the Ground Up Rather than stripping down existing high-end products—that is, defeaturing them—companies need to design and build products from the ground up so they truly embody the spirit of simplicity. This not only appeals to customers but also helps reduce costs and helps companies come up with more long-lasting breakthroughs in their innovation process.

One company that has learned the ineffectiveness of defeaturing the hard way is Siemens AG. Headquartered in Germany, Siemens is a global powerhouse in electronics and electrical engineering, operating in the industry, energy, and health care sectors. Founded by an engineer in 1847, Siemens employs around 30,100 researchers who come up with about forty inventions each working day. It holds a total of 57,900 patents and filed 4,300 patents in 2010 alone.[29] Siemens sells highly engineered products—ranging from power generators to high-speed trains to MRI machines to wind turbines—to business users ranging from small to large enterprises as well as local and national governments. Siemens competes head-to-head with GE worldwide across all its businesses.

Seeking to escape the recessionary economic climate in the West, Siemens has been aggressively expanding in the booming emerging markets, and especially in Brazil, Russia, India, and China. Over the last five years Siemens has more than doubled its sales in emerging markets; these markets now account for 30 percent of the company's global sales revenues.[30] Siemens's initial go-to-market strategy in emerging countries consisted of stripping down its existing Western products—such as its expensive and overengineered MRI machines and power turbines—and adapting them to local requirements. But this "product localization" strategy didn't sit too well with clients in emerging markets who complained that these localized products were still too costly and complicated to use and maintain. As Armin Bruck, managing director of Siemens's Indian subsidiary acknowledges: "Entry-level users want simple user interfaces. They do not need or appreciate bells and whistles."[31] This market reality led Peter Löscher, Siemens's global CEO, to recognize that his company's products required a different kind of innovation in emerging markets. "What counts here [in emerging markets] is simplicity, not sophistication," he notes.[32]

In 2005, the financial and labor constraints of emerging markets led Siemens to come up with a bold new product strategy called SMART, which stands for Simple, Maintenance-friendly, Affordable, Reliable, and Timely-to-Market. Siemens defines SMART as finding new ways to use old technologies and developing solutions that are "good enough" for an initial market segment, while allowing them to be improved. Besides cost-effectiveness, the SMART philosophy emphasizes ease of setup, operation, and maintenance.[33] As Armin Bruck points out: "Our new [SMART] product initiative has been set up to design simple products to meet the entry-level requirements [of emerging markets]."[34]

SMART products are being designed cost-effectively from the ground up in emerging economies such as India and China, using entirely local R&D talent that owns end-to-end responsibility for developing these products. The Chinese R&D team, for instance, has produced low-cost medical equipment like X-ray machines that can easily be deployed and operated by hospitals in small Chinese towns where skilled technicians are hard to find. Similarly, Siemens's R&D engineers in India are developing small local power grids that can use multiple sources of energy—from solar to coconut shells—to supply electricity to a typical Indian village of fifty to one hundred households. These micro power plants can be set up easily and require limited maintenance.[35] Siemens estimates the market potential for SMART products in India alone to be about €12 billion (US$15.6 billion).[36]

Siemens currently employs 15,500 R&D engineers across emerging markets, many of whom are involved in SMART product development projects. Over 150 products have already been generated in the SMART category since its launch in 2005. In India alone, Siemens has over sixty SMART products in the pipeline and plans to launch half of them in 2012.[37] The company finds that by designing SMART products from the ground up in emerging markets it can save 20 to 40 percent in development costs, compared to adapting or locally producing products designed in the West. Although SMART products are positioned as entry-level products in Siemens' global product portfolio, they are highly profitable. Thanks in part to SMART products, Siemens generated €22 billion (US$28.7 billion) in revenues from entry-level markets in fiscal 2010, *double* the amount it earned in fiscal 2005. Entry-level markets now account for 30 percent of Siemens's total global revenues—up from 20 percent in 2005.[38] Even better, Siemens intends to sell these entry-level SMART products to recession-weary customers in the United

States and Europe who are looking for simple and affordable solutions. For instance, Siemens's Indian engineers—in partnership with German engineers—have developed Fetal Heart Monitor, a device that monitors the heartbeat of fetuses in the womb. This device uses simple but ingenious microphone technology instead of expensive ultrasound. As such, the device holds great market potential in both emerging and developed economies.[39]

Embrace the Universal Design Philosophy to Boost the Usability of Offerings   Universal design is a philosophy that celebrates humanity's diversity and exhorts companies to design products that are usable by as many people as possible.[40] Examples of universal design include buildings with access for all instead of a separate entrance for those with disabilities, unisex facilities where both men and women have a place to attend to a child's needs, and graphics on signs that can be recognized and understood by anyone regardless of language.

OXO, the consumer product company, is one of America's most ardent corporate advocates of universal design. Over time, OXO has built a well-deserved reputation for simplicity, and the company offers products that are both technically superior and easy to use. How does OXO pull it off? It zeroes in on the essence of the problem shared by a large number of customers across demographic segments and then designs user-friendly products that precisely meet customers' latent needs. This approach has helped OXO produce many best-selling products whose simplicity appeals to a wider audience—including kitchenware such as a salad spinner that can be used with one hand, liquid measuring cups that can be read from above without bending over, and kettles with whistle lids that open automatically when tipped to pour.[41] OXO even applied its universal design thinking to develop an easy-to-use syringe for patients of all ages with rheumatoid arthritis who struggle to administer self-injections.[42]

Get Engineers and Industrial Designers to Work Together
Bringing down the Berlin Wall may have been easier than dismantling

the mental wall that keeps technology-enamored engineers and user-centered designers separate. Yet that mental wall must be torn down in order to achieve a proper balance between complex function and simple design. Companies must recognize that incorporating simplicity up front during the product conceptualization phase is *several* times more cost-effective than doing it as an afterthought in the later stages of the development process. Recognizing this fact, forward-thinking companies such as Google and Facebook encourage engineers and designers to work in cross-functional teams from the very start to ensure that performance is not sacrificed for the sake of simplicity—and vice-versa. At Facebook, for instance, communication and product designers, engineers, writers, and researchers all work together in multidisciplinary teams that create new product features with a shared goal: keep improving the user experience without sacrificing simplicity (see the detailed case study on Facebook later in this chapter).

Simplify Product Architectures and Reuse Platforms Across Products   R&D engineers are like craftsmen: they often like to create their own technologies or components from scratch, even if comparable technologies or components are readily available in the market. But this "reinvent the wheel" approach often leads to long product development cycles and results in expensive, overengineered products. In a resource-constrained economy, however, it is vital to reuse readily available components to make "good enough" products that get the job done. One way to do that is to simplify product architectures and reuse similar parts across multiple products in a portfolio.

Mary Barra is attempting to do exactly that at General Motors (GM). Barra, the highest-ranking female executive in GM's history, is in charge of design and engineering for all GM cars worldwide. Her boss, Dan Akerson, GM's CEO, has given her a tough assignment: shave several months off GM's three- to four-year-long product development cycle, reduce development and production costs by 25 percent, and make every GM car look cool and appealing. Barra is tackling this herculean task with gusto, weeding out complexity from GM's notoriously complex

R&D processes by enshrining simplicity as a core tenet of GM's new product development approach.[43]

Two factors have historically plagued GM's R&D processes. First, given its decentralized culture, different brands across multiple geographies were all running independent, often redundant R&D projects. This led to a proliferation of product platforms and higher costs. Second, GM's engineers had a predilection for creating every new car from scratch. This made the whole product development process lengthier and costlier. The result was a disorganized, underoptimized global R&D organization as complex as a jigsaw puzzle.

Barra is striving to streamline and simplify this chaotic structure by creating *global platforms*. These will allow every GM brand to be built off the same core architecture, whether it is produced in the United States, Europe, China, India, or Brazil. Such global platforms will allow engines and subsystems to also be shared across brands—gaining huge cost savings and faster time-to-market for all new GM models worldwide. Currently, only 30 percent of GM's products share global core architectures. By 2018, however, Barra wants 90 percent of GM's models to be built on global platforms.[44]

Platform sharing is only one facet of Barra's great simplification strategy. The other facet is called *lightweighting* (aka *mass reduction*). The goal is to simplify the core architecture itself in order to make cars that are significantly lighter. Lightweighting happens when you make hundreds of small reductions of mass in the entire product architecture; for instance, by replacing heavy steel and aluminum with lighter carbon fiber. The net result will be far better fuel efficiency, an obsession with carmakers like GM since U.S. legislators passed a new law in July 2011 imposing stringent mileage requirements. U.S. automakers, including GM, are engaged in a race to improve their cars' current average 27.5 miles per gallon performance to 54.5 mpg by 2025—as required by the new law.

At the outset, Barra's efforts to simplify GM's development processes may appear to stifle the creative freedom of its R&D engineers. However, these constraints could provide the spur for developing a jugaad mind-set at GM by fostering healthy "coopetition." Indeed, one can imagine GM's R&D teams across the United States, Europe, and Asia collaborating to simplify the core product architecture—while simultaneously competing with each other as jugaad innovators to show which region can develop the hippest and most affordable, user-friendly, and sustainable cars, all using the same simplified core product architecture.[45]

Make It Simple, Not Simplistic   Simplicity is often the most powerful antidote to complexity. But simple does not necessarily mean simplistic—realistically, complexity can be neither ignored nor avoided. Rather, innovators must embrace the complexity of a problem and then find a simple way through or around it. Consider the Google search engine. The technology behind it is the stuff of rocket science: the search software can solve, in less than a second, an equation of more than five hundred million variables to rank eight billion web pages by relevance. But the three hundred million users who do two billion searches every day on Google are totally oblivious to the complex algorithms executed behind the scenes every time they choose Search. Google's minimalist and intuitive home page cleverly hides the highly complex functionality of its search engine.[46]

According to Marissa Mayer—currently Google's vice president of location and local services and previously in charge of the search site's look and feel, a role in which she acted as Google's "simplicity cop": "Google has the functionality of a really complicated Swiss Army knife, but the home page is our way of approaching it closed. It's simple, it's elegant, you can slip it in your pocket, but it's got the great doodad when you need it." Building on this metaphor, Mayer compares Google's competitors' products to "an open Swiss Army knife"—which can intimidate users and even potentially harm them. It's this obsessive attention to simplicity that helps explain why Google controls a nearly 60 percent (and growing) share of the search market.[47]

In sum, Western companies can gain in simplicity by focusing on customer needs, rationalizing their product architectures, streamlining their R&D processes, and boosting collaboration between designers and engineers—just as Siemens, GM, and Google have done. Ultimately, to make simplicity part of their DNA, Western leaders must redesign their entire organizations around simplicity—a bold move undertaken by large corporations such as Philips and digital-age start-ups like Facebook.

HOW FACEBOOK IS LEADING THE LOW-TECH REVOLUTION

Facebook, the social networking site, understands the importance of creating an interface of simplicity for the rich social media content it provides to its hugely diverse user base. By making simplicity the lynchpin of its product design strategy, Facebook has developed an easy-to-use social networking site that has rapidly conquered the hearts of more than eight hundred million users worldwide.

Nearly half the U.S. population has a Facebook account. *Entertainment Weekly*, in placing Facebook on its end-of-the-decade "best-of" list, wondered: "How on earth did we stalk our exes, remember our co-workers' birthdays, bug our friends, and play a rousing game of Scrabulous before Facebook?"[48]

Facebook's huge popularity and global appeal stem largely from its hyper-simplified user interface. Compared to some other flashy sites, Facebook may even feel anachronistic. The website has a clean look: easy-to-navigate content, few menu options, and no glitzy graphics. Creating new content on Facebook is a breeze; you don't need to be an expert web developer to do so. This may explain why, as of this writing, the average Facebook user creates over ninety pieces of content per month, adding up to more than thirty billion pieces of shared content across the network. In sum, Facebook's interface is so simple that even kids can use it, and so they do! According to ConsumerReports.org, there are 7.5 million children under thirteen with Facebook accounts.

Facebook's minimalist interface is not an act of randomness: it was intentionally designed using a frugal and inclusive principle called "social design." Unlike traditional software design that produces abstract technology algorithms, social design develops new features based on how real people interact in the real world. The proponents of social design seek to improve the way people build human-to-human—rather than human-to-interface—connections on the Web. As Kate Aronowitz, Facebook's director of design, explains:

> Simplicity is key in creating "social design," which is really just about designing products around people. So when we talk about design, we're not just talking about color schemes and shapes—we're also talking about product design that puts people at its center. For instance, a lot of people look at Facebook's muted blue and white color scheme and wonder where design plays a role. The real art here is that the product falls into the background so that people remember their interactions with their friends, not the site itself. Ultimately, the challenge of social design is in creating a product that seamlessly enhances both online and offline interactions.[49]

To deliver such authentic experiences to users, Facebook designers use everyday English words, rather than jargon or buzzwords, for features on the site. As Christopher Cox, vice president of product, explains: "In 2005, we decided to create a photo product that we called Photos. Other people at the time were using names like Flickr, Picasa, Photobucket, right? Very niche-y. Instead, we use common words. We recede into the background. We design a place where there aren't new objects to trip over. Photos are photos. Chat is chat. Groups are groups. Everything just is."[50]

"Receding into the background" doesn't come easy to Silicon Valley start-ups, which generally like to impress users with their technological prowess. But on Facebook, the user is king. And this user can be logging in from New York, Cape Town, Mumbai, or Ulan Bator. In an effort to accommodate the mind-boggling diversity of its soon-to-be one-billion-user base, Facebook prefers to opt for the most universal basics when introducing new features—so that any user in any continent can intuitively understand and use them regardless of age, cultural background, and technical ability. Take, for example, the

Like, Comment, and Share features that let you share your opinion of a photo, link, or status update. These inconspicuous and easy-to-use features have been a huge hit with users worldwide, irrespective of the language they speak. In many ways, the Facebook vocabulary is providing the building blocks for a long-elusive universal language that strives to unite humanity while simultaneously celebrating its diversity.

Reena Jana, a former editor at *BusinessWeek* who has extensively studied Facebook's design culture, notes that the "plainness" of Facebook's site may appear unsophisticated to the cognoscenti of the design world—museum curators and creative directors—who view the interface as "cold" and "unengaging." But Jana believes these design experts are evaluating Facebook using traditional frames of reference, whereas Facebook is creating a whole new design paradigm—one that seeks to replicate offline human connections online by keeping them straightforward and genuine.[51]

By favoring simplicity over sophistication, Facebook is initiating a veritable revolution in the global technology sector—one that could be called the "low-tech revolution."

CONCLUSION

Jugaad innovators accommodate the tremendous diversity of customer needs in emerging markets by integrating simplicity into their culture and their solution design—much as Philips, Siemens, Google, GM, and Facebook are doing in the West. This simplicity makes their solutions affordable and accessible not only to mainstream customers but also to those who live on the margins of society. Indeed, driven by empathy and a sense of social equity, jugaad innovators often use their creativity to devise inclusive business models that profitably meet the needs of the underserved consumer segments that are ignored by traditional enterprises. In the next chapter, we explore how by "including the margin" jugaad innovators can extend the reach of their offerings to a much larger audience in a socially equitable *and* economically viable fashion.

CHAPTER SIX

PRINCIPLE FIVE
Include the Margin

We need a system of inclusive capitalism that would have a twin mission: making profits and also improving lives for those who don't fully benefit from market forces.

—— BILL GATES, CHAIRMAN, MICROSOFT CORPORATION

In 2004, Dr. Rana Kapoor quit his job with a multinational company to start an inclusive bank: one that would sustainably serve the financial needs of the broadest possible swath of consumers. Dr. Kapoor felt strongly that banks should be servants of a country's economy rather than its arrogant masters. His vision of serving the needs of the Indian economy extended to the six hundred million Indians who had no access to a bank. To turn his vision into reality, he staffed his new venture—a "responsible bank" he named YES BANK—with some of the industry's most brilliant minds. He invited these recruits to apply their creativity to meeting the financial needs of average Indian families and businesses.[1]

Over the years, YES BANK has pioneered many initiatives to make financial services accessible to the masses—either directly or through intermediaries. It uses sophisticated financial tools—so far available only to big businesses—to develop offerings for small and medium enterprises and nonprofit organizations. Specifically, it borrows cutting-edge products used in high-end investment banking and adapts them for development banking—by, for example, securitizing the microloans of microfinance institutions (MFIs) and selling them to institutional

131

investors as convertible debentures. In doing so, these MFIs gain access to additional capital, which allows them to lend money to even more people.[2]

YES BANK—founded by a jugaad entrepreneur—is particularly keen to support the development of micro entrepreneurs who have so far been excluded from the traditional banking system. To that end, the bank has developed several simple but effective financial inclusion tools to streamline access to capital for micro entrepreneurs. For instance, YES BANK noticed that there was no viable solution in the market for credit appraisal of micro entrepreneurs who neither maintain formal business records nor file business details with authorities. To address this shortcoming, the bank developed the Credit Appraisal Toolkit (CAT): an Excel-based data analysis tool that compares details orally provided by a micro entrepreneur applying for a loan against those collected earlier from his or her peers for a better and quicker credit approval decision.[3]

More important, YES BANK's inclusive model—fueled by jugaad innovation—is profitable. Even though 46 percent of the bank's loans are extended to underserved segments of the Indian economy, it still earns 2 percent over its cost of lending, whereas most banks earn 1 to 1.5 percent less than what lending costs them. Riding on the back of his successful banking model, Dr. Rana Kapoor intends to grow YES BANK's revenues from $4.6 billion today to $30 billion by 2015. Dr. Kapoor points out: "At YES BANK, our primary focus is enabling social sustainability, which in turn helps drive our business sustainability. We serve the marginal segments of our society not as part of a CSR initiative, but as a core component of our inclusive business model. I don't see any contradiction between doing good for my society and doing well for my shareholders."

Emerging markets are full of jugaad innovators who, like Dr. Rana Kapoor, are successfully including marginal segments of their society, both as consumers and as employees. These innovators are showing how including the margin not only enables greater social good but also makes great business sense: it is profitable and drives innovation.

In this chapter we look in detail at how and why jugaad innovators include the margin.

Many Western companies, in contrast, often ignore marginal consumers and employees. They view these groups as unprofitable, too complex to serve, or not sufficiently valuable to include in their innovation processes. And this is despite growing diversity in the West—due to an aging workforce and expanding ethnic minorities—and the increasing number of economically marginalized even in the middle class. In this chapter, we also explore how Western companies can learn from jugaad innovators like Dr. Rana Kapoor to profitably include marginal groups.

INCLUSION: A MORAL IMPERATIVE THAT MAKES BUSINESS SENSE

To understand what drives jugaad innovators like Dr. Rana Kapoor to include marginal consumer segments in their for-profit business models, we need to first understand the environment in which jugaad innovators operate. As we've discussed in previous chapters, emerging markets possess three features—scarcity, diversity, and interconnectivity—that together constitute an imperative to include the margin.

First, as we pointed out in Chapter Three, emerging markets are characterized by pervasive *scarcity* on many fronts. Because of underdeveloped infrastructure, ineffective governments, and accelerated population growth, millions of people in Africa, India, and Latin America lack access to basic services like health care, education, and energy. In India alone, over six hundred million mostly rural citizens are excluded from the banking sector, and a nearly equal number live outside the reach of the electricity grid. There is an upside, however, to this widespread scarcity: millions of excluded citizens equals millions of potential customers. For entrepreneurs willing to rise to the challenge, the choice to include the margin promises many potentially lucrative opportunities to build entirely new businesses.

Second, many emerging economies are also characterized by mind-boggling *diversity*. The sheer social, economic, and cultural heterogeneity of these populations (India alone has 22 recognized languages and over 2,500 dialects) exacerbates the challenges posed by scarcity. Thus exclusion cannot be addressed with a one-size-fits-all approach—wherein, for example, a single product or service serves the majority of the population—an approach that is often favored by large corporations. Instead, inclusivity requires an approach to innovation that is sensitive to individual differences and local circumstances. The intellectual and creative challenge of serving the diverse needs of a large number of people in an economical way is a great spur to jugaad innovators.

Third, deepening *interconnectivity* in emerging markets both amplifies the sense of exclusion and offers interesting ways to reduce it. Even poor people in remote villages in Africa or India now have access to cable TV and can see what they are missing out on. This ability to see what the world has to offer drives them to aspire for better and more things. Pervasive cellphone ownership—India alone adds ten million cellphone subscribers a month, a majority of whom are in rural areas—creates many new opportunities for inclusion. For instance, even small entrepreneurs can now leverage mobile computing as a cost-effective platform to deliver education, health care, and financial services to the masses.

In sum, scarcity, diversity, and interconnectivity are together driving jugaad innovators like Dr. Rana Kapoor to build their businesses around the needs and aspirations of marginal consumers and employees. But *how* do these innovators successfully and profitably include such marginal groups and what underpins their ability to do so?

COCREATING VALUE WITH THE MARGIN

Jugaad innovators like Dr. Rana Kapoor are uniquely attuned to respond to the external pressures and opportunities they face. They often live close to marginal segments, they perceive these segments' unmet needs first-hand, and they have an intuitive grasp of how to meet them. They also have a sense of fairness that drives them to make basic services like education, health care, and energy accessible to all. Finally, jugaad innovators believe in what Bill Gates calls "creative capitalism"—that is, they know how to employ for-profit business models to bring about social change.[4] Jugaad innovators work with these traits to successfully reach the excluded in the following ways.

Approaching Marginal Groups as Whole New Markets

Jugaad innovators don't merely treat marginal groups as one more segment on which to dump their existing products. Instead, they approach marginal groups as whole new markets that need to be served with entirely *new* business models. For instance, large technology vendors boast about the accessibility features built into their existing products to enable the physically challenged to use them. But few of these companies come up with new products—let alone whole new business models—dedicated to serve, say, blind people.

A notable exception is Abhi Naha of the cellphone company Zone V. After two decades of executive-level experience in the tech sector, Naha founded Zone V with the express intention of developing cellphones for exclusive use by blind and partially sighted people worldwide.[5] Globally, there are 284 million blind and partially sighted people, two-thirds of whom are women.[6] Naha is particularly determined to empower blind women through mobile technology—especially in developing nations where such women are outcasts and are excluded from educational and economic opportunities.

In 2013 Zone V will introduce three models of cellphones. The first model will be a high-end smartphone with a simplified user interface targeted at elderly people in Europe (and later in the United States) with regular eye sight—but which can also be used by blind and partially sighted people. The second will be a mid-range smartphone primarily for blind and partially sighted people in urban areas of emerging markets. And the third will be a basic low-cost phone with valuable features for blind people who live at the bottom of the socioeconomic pyramid. All three models will be codeveloped and comarketed with a global network of design, manufacturing, and distribution partners.

Naha estimates the global cellphone market for blind and partially sighted people as well as regular-sighted senior citizens to be more than €1 billion (US$1.36 billion). Zone V will operate as a for-profit company and will initially target blind and partially sighted people in Western economies with easy to use yet beautifully designed cellphones. Some of the profits from the sales in Europe and the United States will help Zone V create ultra-low-cost phones that will be supplied to blind women in India and Africa on a not-for-profit basis. Abhi Naha is truly a visionary. What else can one say of someone who aspires to create a world in which the lack of sight does not mean a lack of vision?

Helping Everyone Climb Up Maslow's Hierarchy of Needs

Jugaad entrepreneurs recognize that even low-income consumers have high aspirations and are eager to climb up Maslow's hierarchy of needs. (According to the American psychologist Abraham Maslow, people face a hierarchy of needs: basic requirements such as food and safety come first, followed by higher level needs such as belonging, status, and esteem, with self actualization at the top.)

Jugaad innovators do not, therefore, short-change low-income consumers on quality: they know that although these consumer are low earners, they are high *yearners*. As such, jugaad innovators strive to offer marginal segments products of value that are nonetheless affordable. For example, as mentioned before, YES BANK has adapted high-end investment banking products for development banking—which in turn help microfinance institutions (MFIs) gain access to additional capital so they can offer micro loans to even more people.

Likewise, Zone V is infusing even its low-cost phones with high-end design to make them more desirable to blind women in developing nations. To that end, Naha has hired Frank Nuovo as Zone V's chief designer. Nuovo is the former chief of design of Nokia and the co-founder of Vertu—Nokia's offering for the luxury phone segment (which represents a $1 billion market)—where he remains principal designer. While continuing to design diamond-encrusted phones for the super-rich, Nuovo has joined Zone V determined to make luxury affordable and accessible to the masses. In particular, he is designing phones for Zone

V that are cool yet inexpensive and that deliver a high-end experience to blind consumers at the bottom of the pyramid—giving them a phone they can be proud to own and that can help elevate their status within their community (see Chapter Three for more examples of how jugaad entrepreneurs deliver more value at a lower cost for more people).

Although people at the bottom of the pyramid do worry about meeting their basic needs, like food and shelter, they also have *higher order* needs such as being entertained or looking beautiful. Many companies, especially multinationals, fail to see this. Rama Bijapurkar, the Indian marketing guru and author of *Winning in the Indian Market*,[7] says: "Every kid—poor or rich—has a right to be entertained. It is a basic right. Yet Western theme parks, with their steep entry fees, tend to exclude low-income people. Such an exclusive business model won't work in an emerging market like India where three hundred million people still earn $1 a day—and yet want to be entertained."[8]

As if speaking directly to this point, Xavier López Ancona, a Mexican entrepreneur, founded KidZania in Mexico City in 1999 to make entertainment more inclusive—as well as increase its educational value. KidZania is a reasonably priced indoor theme park where four- to twelve-year-old kids play at being adults in a realistic, safe, and fun environment. At KidZania, kids perform "real world" jobs—as doctors, TV anchors, firefighters, police officers, pilots, or shopkeepers—and are paid in "kidZo" currency that they use to buy goods and services. In their role-play, kids get guidance and support from adult "Zupervisors." Built to scale for kids, KidZania is complete with paved roads, cars, buildings, an active economy, and real-world establishments like hospitals, banks, fire stations, and supermarkets. The success of the Mexico City park—ten million children have visited it to date—encouraged Ancona to open more parks not only in emerging-market cities like Jakarta and Dubai but also in Tokyo, Seoul, and Lisbon. To date, twenty million people have visited KidZania parks worldwide. Walt Disney Parks and Resorts and Six Flags had better watch out: KidZania is planning its U.S. entry in the near future.[9]

Similarly, in the early 1990s, Heloísa Helena Assis—known as Zica—recognized the basic need of underprivileged women to look beautiful. A former hairdresser who grew up in a family of thirteen children in the *favelas* (urban slums) of Rio de Janeiro, Brazil, Zica was aware that these women couldn't afford to go to expensive beauty salons or spas in cities that charge a premium for services like hair care. She also noticed Brazilian women tended to go to hair salons to straighten their curly hair. Zica thought: "What if I could come up with a product—and a unique process for applying it—that can enhance Brazilian women's curly hair, rather than straighten it? That would help these women find beauty in their natural looks." After several experiments on her own curly hair, she came up with the right formula—a cream that could hydrate and relax it and preserve its natural structure without straightening it.[10] She patented her proprietary formula under the name Super-Relaxing. As a logical next step, in 1993 Zica opened a hair salon in Rio de Janeiro named Beleza Natural, where she could test her Super-Relaxing formula on real customers. The formula and the salon were a hit. Zica immediately expanded her business and opened more salons with three other partners.

Beleza Natural currently operates twelve salons, located in Rio de Janeiro, Espírito Santo, and Bahia, primarily targeting low-income women. These salons are all operated by local community women. Each salon serves up to a thousand customers a day, treating up to forty clients at a time through a fast seven-step process. The salons now also sell a complete line of hair care products—developed by Beleza Natural's manufacturing unit, Cor Brasil, in partnership with leading researchers in top Brazilian universities.[11] Beleza Natural currently serves over seventy thousand customers, and the company's sales revenues are growing at 30 percent a year. Since 2005, Beleza Natural has increased its revenues by 918 percent and has expanded its workforce by 214 percent—today employing more than 1,400 people. "Above all, we sell self-esteem," explains Assis. "I saw an opportunity to make all Brazilian women feel beautiful, [regardless of] their financial means."[12]

Cocreating Value with Customers and Partners Throughout the Value Chain

Jugaad innovators don't view customers as merely passive users of their products and services. Recognizing the diversity of customer needs, they invent new solutions from the ground up by working closely with marginal groups to identify their unique needs. They then engage local communities and partners to set up a grassroots value chain to locally build, deliver, and support their solutions—making these solutions in turn affordable, accessible, and sustainable.

For instance, to effectively serve the six hundred million unbanked Indians, YES BANK is constantly experimenting with new technology-powered inclusive business models that tap a vast network of partners. The YES MONEY service is one such initiative. As part of this initiative, the bank has teamed up with various payment platform companies like Suvidhaa Infoserve and Oxigen Services which offer payment services through about two hundred thousand mom-and-pop retail stores in urban and rural areas. YES BANK has helped these companies to deploy a specialized "domestic remittance" module, allowing, for example, migrant workers in cities to send money to their families in far-flung villages through the National Electronic Fund Transfer (NEFT) system. Compared to money order remittance services (offered by India Post, a government undertaking), YES MONEY is about five times cheaper and five times faster. YES MONEY also offers a cost-effective alternative to Western Union. Moreover, the majority of the fees collected are passed back to the payment platform companies and the retailers—creating value for all partners in the YES MONEY ecosystem.[13]

Like YES BANK, Zone V is positioning its products as tools for economic empowerment rather than for passive consumption. Zone V's phones can therefore enable blind women in rural India to manage not only the finances of their households but also those of their neighbors and the village council. In this way, the individual phone becomes a vehicle for driving socioeconomic growth in an entire community. To make all this happen, Zone V will rely on a host of partners. It has outsourced its design and manufacturing to contract engineers and manufacturers and relies on nongovernment organizations (NGOs) like Sightsavers to distribute its phones in emerging markets like India—especially in rural areas. More important, Zone V will create a platform for third-party software developers to develop "inclusive apps" for its phones. These apps will be available at different price points depending on the customer segment and the phone being used. Naha believes that many mobile app developers will be motivated to create solutions that meet the basic needs of blind people worldwide.

In emerging markets, jugaad innovators often partner with state-level and local governments to make health care, education, and financial services more inclusive. For instance, GE Healthcare has signed a performance-based service contract with the government of the Northwestern Indian state of Gujarat. Under the terms of this public-private partnership agreement, GE-trained partners will operate and maintain all the medical equipment installed in government-run hospitals in the smaller cities of Gujarat. Rural hospitals, for their part, won't need to invest in expensive equipment or scramble to recruit qualified technicians. Nevertheless, they will be guaranteed higher equipment uptime and lower utilization costs—all of which will translate into cost-effective and high-quality care for rural patients.[14]

Scaling Up Personalized Solutions with Technology

Jugaad innovators cleverly employ technology—especially mobile computing—to reduce the cost of delivering services to marginal segments. They also leverage technology to customize their offerings on a large scale. A case in point is Reuters Market Light (RML), a mobile phone service developed by Thomson Reuters in India. RML delivers to farmers customized and localized weather forecasts, local crop prices, agricultural news, and other relevant information (namely relevant government aid schemes), in the form of three SMS messages sent daily to their mobile phones in the local language. Such customized and timely information enables farmers to better plan their activities such as irrigation, fertilizer use, and harvesting. As a result, farmers can better manage risks and improve their decisions regarding when and where to sell their produce to maximize profit. The service costs a mere 250 rupees (US$5) for a three-month subscription. As of 2011, some 250,000 Indian farmers from over fifteen thousand villages had subscribed to RML. Thomson Reuters estimates that over a million farmers across at least thirteen Indian states have benefitted from the RML service. Moreover, farmers have reaped substantial returns from their investment in RML. Some have realized up to 200,000 rupees (US$4,000) in additional profits, and savings of nearly 400,000 rupees (US$8,000) with an investment of only US$5 in subscription costs.[15]

Another jugaad innovator using technology to bring low-cost services to the masses is Dr. Liu Jiren, chairman and CEO of Neusoft, China's largest IT solution and service provider. Dr. Liu, a former professor of computer science, is worried that the Chinese, thanks to sustained double-digit economic growth, "have accumulated lots of wealth in the past two decades, but have also accumulated lots of diseases as they got richer."[16] It is estimated that ninety million Chinese suffer from diabetes and two hundred million may be suffering from cardiovascular diseases. The explosion of chronic diseases—which are particularly devastating for low-income Chinese in rural areas—is forcing the government to invest in a health care system that has so far been deficient or nonexistent in the rural areas, which lag behind urban areas in medical resources and health care infrastructure. But Dr. Liu warns: "If the Chinese government were to build a health care system to serve 1.3 billion Chinese modeled on the United States [where health care spending is projected to account for 20 percent of GDP by 2020] we will need a huge budget which will soon bankrupt our country. We need an alternative health care model that is smart, affordable, and inclusive. We need a model that focuses on—and enables—disease *prevention* rather than treatment."[17]

For its part, Neusoft has developed several low-cost but high-tech solutions, such as affordable health monitoring devices and telemedicine solutions for rural hospitals to serve low-income Chinese patients. More impressively, Neusoft has developed a cutting-edge wristwatch for chronic disease patients to use as a mobile health monitor. On a regular basis, the watch collects bio indicators from sensors attached to the patient's body. This dynamic data is sent to Health Cloud, a cloud computing–based expert system. Health Cloud analyzes the data using a health care knowledge database and offers customized advice to the patient in terms of exercise plans and diet regimen, thus helping the patient make healthy lifestyle changes.[18] For instance, if you are overweight, the system will suggest a three-month jogging plan, monitor and report back your progress daily, and even suggest improvements when needed.

Dr. Liu notes that in a rapidly aging China—where family ties are important and the over-sixty-five population is projected to increase from 130 million in 2010 to some 222 million by 2030—these wristwatches and home health monitors have become popular gifts from young Chinese to their parents.[19] Through these gifts, young Chinese can remotely track their parents' health—through daily reports on their mobile phones—and proactively tend to their well-being. Dr. Liu believes that Neusoft's ability to serve marginal groups (such as the elderly and the rural poor) faster and cheaper by harnessing affordable technologies like cloud computing gives the company an advantage over Western multinationals. He says: "We don't have the resources of a large multinational corporation, but we identify opportunities in underserved markets early on and execute fast on them by harnessing the power of technology—especially cloud computing, which significantly lowers the cost of service delivery in sectors like health care."

Jugaad innovators like Dr. Liu successfully include the margin by approaching marginal groups as whole new markets, helping everyone climb up Maslow's hierarchy of needs, cocreating value with customers and partners throughout the value chain, and making clever use of affordable technology to scale up their personalized solutions. As Western nations become increasingly diverse, however, there is a growing urgency for Western companies to pay close attention to the margin.

THE MARGIN IS BECOMING THE MAJORITY

In coming years, "marginal" segments in the West will no longer be marginal; they will become bigger, possibly *much* bigger. And the number of marginal consumers will increase across a number of dimensions: age, ethnicity, and income.

Take age. In the next fifteen to twenty years, the number of Americans over sixty-five will double. In the same period, the number of Americans over eighty-five will triple. This shift will be even more dramatic in Europe. The continent already has nineteen of the world's twenty demographically oldest nations. By 2030, nearly 25 percent of Europeans will be older than sixty-five, up from about 17 percent in 2005. As a result, the U.S. Census Bureau estimates that by 2030 the European Union will experience a 14-percent decrease in its workforce and a 7-percent decrease in its consumer populations.[20] All this means that American and European companies will need to tend to a rapidly aging workforce and learn to serve aging consumers—many of whom belong to the assertive baby boomer generation which is used to getting what it wants given the sheer strength of its numbers.

The good news is that this senior market is a highly lucrative one. In the UK, the over-fifties spent £276 billion (US$437 billion) in 2008, making up around 44 percent of total family spending in Britain.[21] In the United States, the over-fifties' annual after-tax income is estimated to be $2.4 trillion, accounting for some 42 percent of all after-tax income.[22] The bad news is that existing products and services are often not tailored to aging consumers' needs. Ian Hosking, senior research associate at the Engineering Design Centre at the University of Cambridge's Department of Engineering, points out: "Aging populations exhibit an increasing variation in functional capabilities such as vision, hearing, and dexterity. In general these abilities reduce with age. Even though it may seem obvious to design inclusive products, many products are targeted at young, able-bodied users. As a result, they are neither accessible nor desirable to older users. At the same time, the products that we use every day seem to grow ever more complex to operate."[23] Western companies will miss out on a big market opportunity if they fail to adapt their offerings to the requirements of the rapidly aging consumer base in the United States and Europe.

Western populations are not only aging, they are also becoming more diverse and multicultural. For instance, the percentage of children in the United States with at least one foreign-born parent rose from 15 percent in 1994 to 23 percent in 2010. Similarly, more than half of the growth in the U.S. population between 2000 and 2010 came from the increase in the Hispanic population, which rose 43 percent to 50.5

million during that period; these Hispanic consumers are likely to form the majority in states like California within a generation. It is estimated that the Hispanic consumer group has a collective buying power of about $1 trillion.[24] The Census Bureau projects that the share of ethnic and racial minorities will reach 54 percent of the total U.S. population and surpass that of non-Hispanic whites by 2042—eight years sooner than expected.[25]

The demographic makeup of Europe is also bound to change rapidly. Muslims, who currently account for 5 percent of the overall population of the European community (reaching 10 percent in France), are expected to account for 20 percent by 2050.[26] But long before that, countries such as Britain, France, Spain and the Netherlands will have surpassed that figure. As the working-age population rapidly decreases, European governments will have no choice but to liberalize their immigration policies if they wish to sustain their economic competitiveness. This growing ethnic and cultural diversity of Western populations will force corporations to innovate their products and services to meet the differing needs of minority consumers.

Another key factor contributing to the diversity of Western populations is the rise of Generation Y and Z workers, with their idiosyncratic values and expectations. Many studies show that Gen Y and Z employees consider themselves widely misunderstood in the workplace and feel alienated—primarily because the hierarchical structures and top-down communication styles of Western corporations are at odds with the collaborative spirit of Gen Y and Z workers. Unless Western companies find an innovation mechanism to keep their Gen Y and Z employees fully engaged, these young workers are likely to feel marginalized and leave for organizations that truly capitalize on their creative talents.

Finally, there has been a dramatic shift in income in the United States, where the lingering recession has pushed more people into poverty. In 2010, 15.1 percent of Americans (or 46.2 million people) were living below the official poverty line, the highest level since 1993 (in 2009, the percentage was 14.3 percent).[27] More worryingly, America's consuming middle class, which accounts for 70 percent of national spending and forms the bedrock of the U.S. economy, is shrinking. According to Pew Charitable Trusts, nearly a third of Americans who belonged to the middle class as teenagers in the 1970s have slipped below it as adults.[28] The study highlights the relative ease with which even Americans who started life with advantages can end up in low-income, low-opportunity circumstances.

And although it has become easier to be downshifted economically, it has become harder to climb back up the socioeconomic ladder. Median incomes in the United States have remained stagnant for the last thirty years. (In 2010, the median U.S. household income was $49,445, down slightly from $49,777 in 2009.) Adjusted for inflation, the middle-income family earned only 11 percent more in 2010 than it did in 1980, whereas the richest 5 percent in America have gained a 42-percent income boost. In sum, the bottom 60 percent of U.S. households experienced an income reduction in 2010, whereas households making $100,000 and above enjoyed an increase in income. As a result, the 5 percent of Americans with the highest incomes now account for 37 percent of all consumer purchases.[29]

An economy rife with such inequality and downward mobility—the so-called "plutonomy"—is simply not sustainable.[30] In an op-ed entitled "The Limping Middle Class," Robert Reich, former U.S. secretary of labor, warns: "When so much income goes to the top, the middle class doesn't have enough purchasing power to keep the economy going without sinking ever more deeply into debt—which, as we've seen, ends badly."[31] Fifty million Americans currently don't have medical insurance, and a whopping sixty million Americans are unbanked or underbanked—which means they are unable or unwilling to avail themselves of the full gamut of financial services offered by traditional banks. One can expect these numbers to go up significantly in coming years as economic conditions worsen. For a growing number of disenfranchised middle-class Americans, the American dream will remain just that: a dream.

What does all this mean for Western corporations? The marginal groups that have traditionally been perceived—and therefore ignored—as the "long tail" of the consumer economy (that is, as niche segments) are rapidly becoming the "fat tail" (that is, dominant consumer groups).[32] These groups can no longer be ignored. Companies that actively embrace them, and form their businesses around their needs, are likely to find, just as jugaad innovators in emerging markets are finding, that doing so increasingly makes business sense. Indeed, it will increasingly be possible to include the margin (do good) and make a profit (do well) at the same time. But there are several factors holding back Western companies from including the margin in their business strategies. We explore these factors in the next section.

WHY WESTERN COMPANIES VIEW MARGINAL GROUPS AS UNPROFITABLE

Even though marginal segments are increasingly economically important, many Western businesses still shy away from serving them for three key reasons, each of which is related to either the unwillingness or the inability of Western companies to view marginal groups as profitable.

First, many Western companies view creating products and services for segments that are typically marginalized as a social mission rather than a core business opportunity. They tend to use their philanthropic arms to reach out to, say, low-income groups or ethnic minorities. But such exercises invariably become part of companies' corporate social responsibility (CSR) activities, while the for-profit business focuses on "mainstream" customers. For instance, many leading Western banks have set up foundations and CSR programs through which they partner with non-profit organizations like Operation Hope to serve the banking needs of the disenfranchised, yet in their core business these banks continue to serve middle-class and wealthy clients. Similarly, many companies have diversity programs that celebrate diversity in the workforce and customer base, but they rarely succeed in implementing employee engagement strategies specifically tailored to diverse groups.

Second, Western companies' current, often entrenched business models are not designed to meet marginal customers' diverse needs. To truly serve marginal customers and make a profit, companies would need to build entirely new business models specifically tailored to such groups. Unfortunately, most companies are reluctant to do this; they prefer to tweak their existing offerings and business models to serve the diverse needs of marginal customers. Such attempts, being halfhearted, are often doomed to fail. Thus companies fail to come up with a compelling and unique value proposition for marginal customers.

Third, a short-term outlook prevents Western companies' long-term investments in products and services that serve marginal groups. Companies that worry about quarterly performance aren't motivated to invest the time and resources needed to design business models that target marginal segments; the returns on such investments, they feel, are unlikely to materialize for a number of years. The financial services sector is a prime example. According to the FDIC, sixty million Americans are either unbanked or underbanked.[33] The big banks have yet to address the need of this large marginal group. Rob Levy, manager of innovation and research at the Center for Financial Services Innovation (CFSI), explains why: "Some large banks are aware of the market potential that over sixty million unbanked and underbanked American consumers represent. But to effectively serve those consumers, banks will need to design entirely new products, marketing strategies, and distribution channels to meet the needs of this consumer segment. While this kind of comprehensive approach to the underbanked market may realize positive returns and strong customer relationships in the long run, it may not yield gigantic profits in the first few years of operation. It can, therefore, be hard for banks to justify such long-term investments to shareholders."[34]

This reluctance of Western companies to include the margin is unfortunate. It means these companies are literally and figuratively leaving money on the table, and exposing themselves to competition from unexpected quarters on many fronts.

WESTERN COMPANIES WILL FACE INCREASED COMPETITION IN CORE MARKETS

As we've noted, with the ranks of those in the marginal segments growing, the "long tail" is increasingly becoming the "fat tail." And as long as large corporations continue to view marginal segments as unprofitable, opportunities will open up for new players to step in and fill the vacuum created in this sizable and growing market. As a result, established Western companies will soon face competition, even in their core markets of middle-class and affluent consumers, from a range of players.

Frugal Innovators from Emerging Markets   Companies from emerging markets such as HTC and Haier are already giving Western consumer goods companies a run for their money by offering low-cost, high-value cellphones, fridges, and wine coolers to financially stretched Western consumers. Similarly, Western carmakers need to worry about the upcoming launch in the U.S. and European markets of Tata Motors' US$2,000 Nano, as the car is poised to capture the hearts (and wallets) of cost-conscious Western consumers clamoring for affordable, fuel-efficient transportation.

Goliaths from Unrelated Industries   Leading players across industries are facing competition from big players from other industries who are encroaching on their home turf by serving marginal segments. For instance, Wal-Mart, Inc. is challenging banks on their home turf by opening 1,500 Money Centers that serve many of the basic financial needs of low-income consumers—allowing them to transfer money, buy prepaid debit cards, pay bills, and cash checks (not to mention allowing them to use this cash, along with complimentary coupons, to shop within the same store). Walmart Money Centers are highly successful because they are accessible (they are located very close to where consumers live), intimate (consumers regularly visit the Walmart store for their grocery purchases and trust the brand), and affordable (Walmart charges only $3 for cashing checks up to $1,000 and only $3 for buying or reloading its prepaid card).[35]

Encouraged by the success of its Money Centers, Wal-Mart is launching even smaller kiosks called Express Centers in more far-flung locations. As Rob Levy of CFSI notes: "While many are talking about financial inclusion, Wal-Mart is actually championing it using an innovative business model that eschews product complexity in favor of simplicity and convenience that enhance the user experience."[36]

Nimble Start-Ups   By exclusively focusing on mainstream markets, large companies ignore lucrative opportunities in marginal segments and expose themselves to competition by nimbler start-ups. Again, take the financial services sector: not only do incumbents have to contend with a giant retailer like Wal-Mart encroaching on their turf, but they also need to ward off rivalry from nimble start-ups like PayNearMe. PayNearMe helps the 24 percent of American households who have neither a debit nor a credit card to buy stuff on Amazon, purchase bus tickets on Greyhound's website, or pay by cash offline at a 7-Eleven outlet. Danny Shader, a serial entrepreneur who founded PayNearMe, observes that "the 'underbanked' is a giant underserved market. We're making it better, faster, and cheaper for them to transact."[37] Visa and MasterCard are paying close attention to PayNearMe, given that $1.2 trillion worth of consumer purchases were conducted using cash in 2010.

   Marc Andreessen, cofounder of Netscape and general partner of the venture capital firm Andreessen-Horowitz, believes that "asset-light" tech start-ups—such as PayNearMe, which conducts millions of dollars in financial transactions without owning a single bank branch—are in the process of invading and overturning established industry structures. Andreessen believes that we are in the midst of a radical and wide-ranging technological and economic shift in which software companies are about to take over large swathes of the economy. He notes: "Over the next ten years, I expect many more industries to be disrupted by software, with new world-beating Silicon Valley companies doing the disruption in more cases than not."[38] Increasingly, these Silicon Valley entrepreneurs are targeting marginal segments that have long been ignored by brick-and-mortar companies in capital-intensive sectors such as health care, telecom, finance, education, and energy. It is this sharp focus on marginal segments that will lead to big revenue gains and growth for the companies who target them.

HOW TO MAKE BIG MARGINS BY
INCLUDING THE MARGIN

Jugaad entrepreneurs offer many powerful strategies that Western companies can learn from in their attempts to include the margin profitably. Specifically, Western companies can adopt the following strategies.

Carry Out Social Inclusion with a Business Mindset   Nonprofit CSR programs that serve marginal groups are redundant if your company is also striving to meet the needs of the same groups using a for-profit business model—just as jugaad innovators in emerging markets are doing. To avoid such corporate cultural schizophrenia, Western corporate leaders need to pull the plug on their CSR efforts and get serious about social inclusion by making it a strategic *business imperative* for all their departments and senior managers. These leaders could emulate Ramón Mendiola Sánchez, CEO of Florida Ice & Farm Co., a large food and beverage producer and distributor in Costa Rica. As explained in Chapter Three, Mendiola merged his business, social responsibility, and environmental strategies into a single integrated corporate strategy, which is carried out by employees at all levels in ways that bring benefits to all stakeholders.[39]

Cater to the Expanding Low-Income Western Consumer Base   The economic downturn is set to keep the financial squeeze on middle-class Americans and Europeans for some years to come. This hollowing-out of the middle class means that Western companies that traditionally served this mainstream market will need to radically shift their innovation strategies—or lose out to low-cost rivals. Rather than spending R&D on premium products with high-end features, these companies will need to create value-for-money products that are accessible to the growing low-income consumer base in the United States and Europe. This is a wise strategy that companies such as the French carmaker Renault are currently following. These companies are stepping up their R&D and marketing efforts to launch a slew of products tailored for budget-conscious Western consumers. For instance, Renault is rapidly extending its low-cost Dacia brand—that includes the Logan, the highly successful sedan that sells for about $10,000—by adding the Logan van, the Logan pickup, and even the Dacia Duster SUV to the portfolio. Aimed at cost-conscious European car buyers, these no-frills Dacia vehicles—manufactured in Renault's factory in Romania—use fewer parts and boast a simplified design, yet are affordable and robust. Low-cost vehicles in the Dacia portfolio have rapidly become Renault's cash cow, contributing to over 25 percent of its sales revenues in 2010, up from 20 percent in 2008. That percentage could be higher in coming years, given that 59 percent of Europeans under thirty—and 54 percent of Europeans over fifty—claim to be ready to buy a low-cost car.[40] Renault envisions expanding its low-cost product portfolio even further in the future by adding more models that will be developed by the company's rapidly expanding R&D team in India—a country that, according to CEO Carlos Ghosn, boasts deep expertise in what he calls "frugal engineering."[41]

Create an Inclusive Work Culture   As their workforce becomes increasingly diverse and global, Western companies must ensure that no worker feels marginalized due to age, social background, or job title. Companies must strive to foster an open and inclusive culture anchored by a participative management style. This helps to foster a creative and motivated workforce, one that can tap into different domains of expertise in devising new products and services and that feels empowered and encouraged to do so. ThoughtWorks is one such company that has successfully cultivated a transparent and inclusive work culture. This software consultancy, headquartered in Chicago, has experienced revenue growth of 20 to 30 percent a year, by charging premium fees to its loyal blue-chip clients such as JetBlue, L.L.Bean, and DaimlerChrysler. The company's secret: a flat organizational structure that allows its one thousand global employees to have an equal say in all major corporate decisions. Roy Singham, founder and chairman, notes: "We want to be the flattest company in the world. The janitors in China should be the strategic equals of the CEO in Chicago. And how do intellectuals collaborate in the twenty-first century? Self-organizing in small teams, poly-skilled, decentralized, non-authoritative."[42] ThoughtWorks' "hypertolerance" of diversity begins with a stringent recruitment process that ensures, says Singham, that "no bigot, sexist, or homophobe gets in." Singham observes, "In the twenty-first century, inclusivity won't happen through authority or some artificial 'diversity' program. Rather, the CEO must embody the spirit of inclusivity by nurturing an 'obnoxiously' transparent culture where every decision and strategy can be debated openly, without fear."[43]

Recognize That Marginal Segments Are Not Marginal Minds
By labeling marginal customers and employees "too poor" or "too old," companies lose an opportunity to tap into the rich knowledge and wisdom these marginal groups might contribute to the organization. Take the baby boomers, for instance. On January 1, 2011, the very first baby boomers started to turn sixty-five, an age beyond which employees are deemed "unproductive" by most employers. Yet companies such as Boeing and Eli Lilly have recognized that although at sixty-five their employees' hair may be gray, their "gray matter" remains of considerable value. Recognizing this fact, in 2003 Procter & Gamble and Eli Lilly (along with Boeing) launched YourEncore.com, an innovation community that connects retired scientists and engineers with organizations seeking to leverage their expertise to solve challenging technical problems. Fifty companies—including many Fortune 500 companies—are now members of the YourEncore network, which provides a great platform for retired scientists to continue doing the work they love by matching them to short-term projects at member companies.[44]

Use Technology to Lower the Cost of Inclusion   Just like jugaad innovators in emerging markets do, rather than invest in expensive brick-and-mortar delivery infrastructure, Western companies need to harness the power of social media, cloud computing, and mobile telephony to cost-effectively deliver their products and services to marginal consumers. For instance, health care insurers UnitedHealth Group and Blue Cross and Blue Shield—in partnership with technology vendors such as Cisco—are piloting cost-effective telemedicine programs that allow patients in Minnesota and Colorado to talk to health care professionals remotely as a low-cost alternative to expensive in-person visits from doctors to patients who live in rural and underserved areas. If successful, these virtual solutions could be deployed in several other states across the United States. According to a study by the Center for Information Technology Leadership, a non-profit research center in Boston, the widespread implementation of telemedicine solutions could save the U.S. health care system more than $4 billion annually just by reducing transfers of patients from one location, such as a nursing home, to provider offices or hospitals.[45] Affordable, accessible telemedicine solutions also significantly reduce hardship for financially stretched American patients and their families.

Partner with Non-Profit Organizations Corporations rarely partner with non-profit entities outside their CSR initiatives (initiatives that, as we argued earlier, need to be integrated with the company's core business strategy). But a new generation of non-profit ventures is willing to work with businesses to cocreate for-profit business models that improve the lives of marginal citizens while also generating a profit. For instance, the Center for Financial Services Innovation, a policy research and advisory organization based in Chicago, advises large banks on how to design inclusive business models that can profitably serve the roughly sixty million Americans who are either unbanked or underbanked.

Secure C-Level Buy-In to Drive Systemic Business Model Changes Given that inclusivity requires fundamental and systemic changes in how companies operate, top management's commitment is vital to enabling and sustaining such business model transformation within companies. For instance, GE's Healthymagination program—aimed at making health care services affordable and accessible for the masses—is overseen by CEO Jeff Immelt himself. Through his leadership, Immelt is personally driving a shift in GE's culture from that of an R&D-driven high-end product company to a community-focused inclusive solution provider (see Chapter Eight for more details on GE's Healthymagination initiative).

Adopt—and Adapt—Proven Best Practices from Emerging Markets As we described earlier in this chapter, emerging markets—because of scarcity, diversity, and interconnectivity—are increasingly a breeding ground for solutions that include the margin. If you have learned how to financially include the six hundred million Indians who are unbanked or offer affordable medical treatment to the hundreds of millions of Indians who lack access to basic health care, you are likely to have gained valuable insights into how to serve the sixty million unbanked and underbanked Americans and the fifty million Americans who lack health insurance.

By using emerging markets as a breeding ground for inclusive innovation, Western companies can not only grow their businesses in those markets but also learn lessons and develop products and services that they can adapt to serve marginal groups in the United States and Europe. Johnson & Johnson, for example, is currently sponsoring Text4baby, a text messaging service that provides pregnant women and new mothers in low-income families with valuable information about how to care for their health and give their babies the best possible start in life. Text4baby was inspired by successful mobile health initiatives undertaken in emerging markets such as Mexico and Kenya.[46] (In Mexico, VidaNET is a free service that sends text messages to HIV patients to remind them to take their medication on a regular basis.) Text4Baby is literally a lifesaver in the United States, where each year five hundred thousand babies are born prematurely and nearly twenty-eight thousand children die before their first birthday. (According to the World Health Organization, babies born in the United States have a greater probability of dying in their first month than babies in much of the developed world.[47]) By late 2011, over two hundred sixty thousand women had signed up for Text4baby—a number expected to reach one million by the end of 2012.[48]

Embrace Inclusive Design Principles It is easier to factor in inclusivity up front, during the design phase of innovation, rather than to try and retrofit or reengineer existing products and services to appeal to marginalized segments of the market after the fact. To learn these new inclusive R&D skills, companies should consider joining academic initiatives like the Inclusive Design program at the University of Cambridge's Department of Engineering or recruiting graduates from Stanford University's Entrepreneurial Design for Extreme Affordability program and Santa Clara University's Frugal Innovation Labs. (We describe these programs in more detail in Chapter Nine.) In addition to helping Western companies gain access to the next generation of inclusive innovators, these programs can give Western companies early access to new technical solutions, results of pilot tests in the field, and knowledge of how to go about doing inclusive innovation more generally. For instance, the Engineering Design Centre at University of Cambridge's Department of Engineering is helping organizations such as the BBC, Bayer Healthcare, Roche, Nestlé, Royal Bank of Scotland, Bosch, Siemens, and Marks & Spencer design mainstream products and services that are accessible to, and usable by, as many people as reasonably possible (but especially the elderly) without the need for special adaptation or specialized design. There are already 130 million people over fifty in the European Union; by 2020, one in two European adults will be over fifty. Designing products and services that these consumers love to use is not only socially responsible but also makes great economic sense.

Western companies can no longer afford to ignore marginal segments, which are poised to grow in size and significance in the coming decades, as the workforce and the customer base in the West become increasingly diverse and the purchasing power of the U.S. middle class continues to shrink. Recognizing the commercial potential of these marginal groups, Western companies must start designing entirely new products and services that meet their particular requirements—just as Renault is doing. To effectively market and distribute these offerings to these segments, companies need to take advantage of technologies such as social media and mobile computing and to forge partnerships with non-profit organizations. More critically, to optimally serve marginal segments in the long run, Western companies need to enshrine inclusivity into their corporate culture and their business models, just as Wal-Mart is doing. As Johnson & Johnson did, Western companies can jump-start these inclusion initiatives by adopting proven solutions and business practices from emerging markets.

Western companies, however, need to move fast—or else they risk leaving opportunities open for nimble rivals from around the world to jump in. This threat is precisely why consumer goods giant Procter & Gamble is proactively reinventing its business model to serve marginal groups—especially low-income consumers.

HOW PROCTER & GAMBLE INCLUDES THE MARGIN PROFITABLY

For decades, Procter & Gamble (P&G) has concentrated on developing household goods for the vast American middle class. But today the company is changing the way it does research, distribution, and marketing so that it can better serve the needs of cash-strapped Americans. Specifically, P&G wants to build a whole new business by tapping into what it calls "un-served and under-served consumers." Thus, for the first time in thirty-eight years, in 2010 P&G launched a new dishwashing soap in the United States. The soap had the Gain name and scent, formerly reserved for laundry detergent, and was offered at a bargain price (compared to the company's slightly more expensive Dawn Hand Renewal dish soap). Since 2008, when the recession deepened, P&G's cheaper brands—such as bargain-priced Luvs diapers and Gain laundry detergent—have sold better and posted faster market-share gains than its premium-priced Pampers and Tide brands.[49]

Seeing a clear trend, P&G is stepping up its research into the swelling ranks of low-income American households. In doing so, the company seeks to ward off growing competition from low-cost suppliers across its product lines. Between 2008, when the recession began, and 2011, P&G's fabric-softener sheets business (which includes the Bounce brand) lost 5 percent of its market share to Sun Products and private-label brands. Rivals such as Church & Dwight and Energizer Holdings, which supply the low-cost Arm & Hammer detergent and Schick shaving blades, respectively, are stealing market share from P&G's pricier brands such as Tide and Gillette.

With a sense of urgency, P&G's CEO Robert McDonald is accelerating the company's R&D efforts to come up with a rich pipeline of "value for money" products that cater to budget-conscious Americans—making this a strategic priority for P&G. "We're going to do this both by tiering our portfolio up in terms of value as well as tiering our portfolio down," McDonald explains.[50]

Although P&G has successfully served the bottom of the socio-economic pyramid in emerging markets, its executives in the United States never imagined they would one day be selling to this segment in America. "This has been the most humbling aspect of our jobs," says Phyllis Jackson, P&G's vice president of consumer market knowledge for North America. "The numbers of Middle America have been shrinking because people have been getting hurt so badly economically that they've been falling into lower income groups."[51]

CONCLUSION

The growing diversity of the workforce and the customer base in Western societies, combined with the shrinking purchasing power of the middle class, are forcing Western companies to find innovative ways to serve marginal segments—segments that now carry more economic weight than ever before. But jugaad innovators don't include the margin on a mere whim or for philanthropic purposes. Rather, innovators like Dr. Rana Kapoor of YES BANK include the margin because it makes business sense for them to do so.

Perhaps of greater interest, jugaad innovators are driven to include the margin by passion, intuition, and empathy. Indeed, they pour their hearts into their inclusive innovation initiatives, as they are able to intuitively connect with marginal groups and empathize with their needs. This genuine empathy confers authenticity on their inclusion initiatives and makes these projects more sustainable. Like Bill Gates, jugaad innovators are passionate about creating a system of inclusive capitalism—one that can harmoniously reconcile the twin goals of making profits and improving people's lives. Empathy, intuition, and passion are at the core of the final principle that drives jugaad innovation: "Follow your heart."

CHAPTER SEVEN

PRINCIPLE SIX
Follow Your Heart

Your time is limited, so don't waste it living someone else's life. Have the courage to follow your heart and intuition. They somehow already know what you truly want to become. Everything else is secondary.

— STEVE JOBS

Unlike Western CEOs, Kishore Biyani doesn't rely on expensive management consultants to advise him on his next strategic move. Biyani owns Big Bazaar, one of India's largest grocery and home goods retail chains or "hypermarkets." When Big Bazaar opened its first store in India, Biyani was advised to follow the traditional, Western approach to retailing, using neatly organized aisles and soothing music. But that format didn't go down well with Indian shoppers who found it all a bit too sleek and unnatural. After all, Indians are used to shopping in noisy, disorganized street markets. Biyani then realized that the Big Bazaar stores should live up to their name: they must look—and even smell—like bazaars. When we visited him in his office in Mumbai, he told us, "Initially we took the advice of management consultants who made us follow the Walmart model. But we soon discovered that this didn't work in the Indian context. We realized what we had to do was to be ourselves, and follow our *intuition*."[1]

Guided by his intuition, Biyani swiftly reconfigured his stores to have the chaotic look and feel of Indian street markets: cluttered aisles, store clerks in casual clothing, and bins of vegetables with some bad items thrown in to make customers feel they had scored when, for instance, they found the perfect onion. And rather than standardize their offerings across all stores, he made sure that each Big Bazaar outlet stocked a product mix that fit local needs. Further, these needs weren't identified by expensive market researchers, but by regional store managers with an intuitive and empathetic understanding of local preferences.

"Common sense retailing" is what Biyani calls this customer-centric approach. And it's worked. We visited several Big Bazaar stores across India. Typically crowded, they have the feel of a buzzing Moroccan souk. Biyani continues to experiment and tweak his business model. Not surprisingly, Big Bazaar is now India's largest hypermarket.

Jugaad innovators in emerging markets rely more on their intuition than on analysis to successfully navigate a highly complex, uncertain, and unpredictable environment. They use their gut intelligence and innate empathy for customer needs to innovate breakthroughs that defy conventional wisdom. Their undying passion acts as the fuel that sustains their efforts to make a difference in the lives of the communities they serve.

In this chapter, we discuss why and how Western executives, inured to data-driven decision making, can benefit from relying more on their intuition to succeed in an increasingly complex world. Rather than second-guessing what customers want by sitting in a remote R&D lab, Western innovators need to immerse themselves in customers' native environment so as to better empathize with customer needs. Most important, we show how, rather than merely seeking to harness their employees' brainpower, Western companies can learn to tap into their employees' "heartpower," thus unleashing the passion of individual employees and channeling it into innovative pursuits that serve a larger purpose.

YOUR HEART KNOWS WHAT YOUR MIND DOESN'T

The heart is the seat of passion, intuition, and empathy. Jugaad innovators in emerging markets possess these qualities in abundance. The challenge is twofold: how to develop these qualities in the first place and then how to nurture them. We have found that several key aspects of the complex environment in which jugaad innovators operate make them particularly passionate, intuitive, and empathetic.

Jugaad entrepreneurs are regularly exposed to the harsh conditions in which their fellow citizens live—whether these involve regular electricity failure, water rationing, or poor access to health care and education. Whatever they may be, these extreme conditions arouse the empathy of jugaad entrepreneurs, who feel they must do something to improve the often harsh conditions around them. Thus jugaad innovators don't just sit around after witnessing others' pain; rather, they convert their compassion into passion by seeking solutions to alleviate this pain. Yet these solutions are not charity work—they are built around sound for-profit business models. As such, empathy forms the cornerstone of jugaad innovators' practice of an altruistic form of capitalism that is shaped by enlightened self-interest. Adam Smith captured well the importance of empathy as a vital ingredient of entrepreneurial innovation. In his pioneering work *The Theory of Moral Sentiments,* Smith argued that although man generally tends to be selfish, "there are evidently some principles in his nature which interest him in the fortune of others, and render their happiness necessary to him, though he derives nothing from it, except the pleasure of seeing it."[2]

In some cases, jugaad entrepreneurs innovate to meet their *own* needs—and to alleviate their personal pain. For instance, after Venkat Rangan heard his father constantly complain that his brokerage company couldn't execute stock transactions as fast as he liked, Rangan decided to do something about it. He founded INXS Technologies, a software product company based in Chennai, South India, which has developed one of the world's largest mobile trading platforms. The platform, called MarketSimplified, currently helps speed transactions through mobile phones not only for Rangan's father but also for millions of customers of the world's leading brokerage houses that use MarketSimplified.[3]

Another reason why jugaad innovators follow their hearts—more than their brains—is that they are forced to think on their feet all the time. It's hard—even counterproductive—to logically analyze a highly complex situation and make rational decisions when things are changing constantly. Emerging markets are fast-paced and volatile. Confronted daily with do-or-die situations, jugaad innovators have learned to make decisions on the fly, using their well-honed intuition rather than relying solely on analysis and logic. For instance, as soon as he saw signs that a Westernized retail format for Big Bazaar was faltering, Kishore Biyani quickly dropped it and embraced a new one—without waiting for an opportunity to do market research. If he had failed to respond as quickly as he did by heeding his intuition, it is quite possible that his business would have gone under.

The harsh conditions in emerging markets kindle jugaad innovators' creative empathy and passion, and the unpredictability of the local environment forces them to make rapid-fire decisions based on intuition rather than rational analysis.

THE GUTSY ART OF ACTING ON WHAT FEELS RIGHT

Jugaad innovators like Kishore Biyani and Venkat Rangan are a self-confident and brave breed: they dare to *act on* what they feel is right. They don't seek validation or approval from customers or investors for their visionary ideas, and they tend to ignore naysayers. They know intuitively what the right solution for an unmet market need is. Only after they have introduced their pioneering solution do others recognize its true value. In other words, jugaad innovators valiantly forge their way into uncharted territory using the heart as a compass.

For instance, Diane Geng and Sara Lam, two Harvard-educated Chinese-Americans eager to reconnect with their ancestral roots, decided to spend time in Chinese villages where eight hundred million people or 60 percent of China's population live. In these villages, Geng and Lam noticed that up to 90 percent of the youth dropped out of middle school without any occupational skills—and with a clear disdain for their communities. Geng and Lam also learned that the reason why rural youth either never attended or did not complete high school was not financial difficulty but (1) the irrelevance of the school curriculum to their life needs and (2) ineffective teaching that encouraged rote learning rather than creative thinking. As a result, Chinese villages were deprived of skilled young workers who would otherwise find creative ways to sustain the socioeconomic growth of their communities.[4]

Geng and Lam recognized this was going to be a major issue for China, given its rapidly aging population (by 2030, 16 percent of the Chinese population will be over sixty-five—up from 10 percent in 2011). Driven by empathy, they decided to do something about the situation. Their intuition told them that the solution lay in improving the "software" of the rural education system—such as curriculum and teacher quality—rather than fixing the "hardware," such as building more schools and offering scholarships (as most NGOs and government agencies in China do). So Geng and Lam launched the Rural China Education Foundation (RCEF), a community-led grassroots initiative that recruits and works with local teachers in villages. RCEF creates new student-centered curricula that impart life-relevant skills to students, using practice-based learning methods that foster creativity and keep students engaged. By providing rural youth with a quality education that is practical and relevant to their life needs and skills, RCEF hopes to ensure China's future economic stability.

When asked what drives jugaad entrepreneurs like her to do something bold like RCEF, Lam had this to say: "A sense of urgent need and mission. A feeling that something must be done. Compassion and an intolerance for injustice. The willingness to take the first step and to do what you can with what you've got. It's easy to think 'All I need is this much more funding, or that many more people, then I can start.' "[5]

Jugaad innovators also succeed in following their hearts because they rely heavily on their social intelligence to guide their decisions. Jugaad innovators are street smart and possess very high "cognitive fluency"—which means that, rather than relying on spreadsheets to make decisions, they rapidly process large amounts of sensory information from the real world and improvise decisions in an intuitive and dynamic fashion based on emergent patterns.[6] Jan Chipchase and Ravi Chhatpar, who work for frog, the design and innovation consultancy, and have interacted extensively with innovators in emerging markets agree. Chipchase is frog's executive creative director of global insights, and Chhatpar is strategy director at frog and founder of its Shanghai studio. Both point out that, for instance, many Chinese innovators in the consumer electronics sector who practice *zizhu chuangxin*, the Chinese version of jugaad, don't use focus groups to determine ahead of time what features to include in their new products.[7] Rather, they spend a great deal of time on the street, observing what products customers actually use, and learning about which competitors' products are selling well and why. These innovators then use their deep customer insight to prioritize and quickly decide which features to include in their own products. In the process, they gain an intuitive sense of what customers want and thus can anticipate their needs.

Their deep customer insight also enables jugaad entrepreneurs to connect with customers at an emotional level—and establish higher customer intimacy in the process. Kevin Roberts, CEO of the global advertising agency Saatchi & Saatchi, discusses this very connection in his book *Lovemarks*.[8] Noting that intimacy is a key ingredient of winning over consumers, and highlighting the importance of empathy, commitment and passion in achieving intimacy, Roberts says: "It's the thoughtful touch, the surprises, that connect with a consumer's heart."[9] Jugaad innovators tap into this empathy-based customer intimacy to gain deeper insights into the core issues that customers are grappling with and the broader socioeconomic context in which they live. These rich insights allow jugaad innovators to then devise solutions that have a meaningful impact on customers' daily lives.

For instance, Anil Jain, managing director at Jain Irrigation Systems Ltd., has come up with a series of innovative solutions that have dramatically improved the productivity of the small-scale Indian farmers who make up a large segment of the Indian population. He attributes this success to the high emotional quotient of his employees: "We intentionally hire salespeople whom we call 'sons of the soil' "—that is, people with an agricultural background who can relate to and empathize with the company's customers—the farmers.[10] These employees help elevate transactional customer relationships to transformative relationships. For instance, in their initial interactions with their customers—the farmers—Jain Irrigation's salesmen don't try to "pitch" solutions to them; rather, they try to instill pride in the farmers by cocreating innovative solutions with them. Such shared innovation is sustainable because it is shaped by empathy and a passion shared by all stakeholders. Thanks to this customer-centric engagement approach, Jain explains, his company has been able to successfully shift its business model from "contract farming" to "*contact* farming," a model that delivers disproportionately higher value to farmers.

While jugaad innovators trust their intuitions, they also conduct rapid experimentation to validate them. Rather than making forecasts or predictions, jugaad innovators test their intuitions in the real world to get rapid feedback. As such, they use experiential learning (that is, learning by doing) to hone their intuition and innovate continuously over time. Take Bam Aquino's Hapinoy Program in the Philippines, introduced in Chapter Three. The program empowers women owners of sari-sari stores (mom-and-pop shops) in the rural islands of the Philippines by identifying new business opportunities for them and giving them the tools and skills needed to capitalize on these opportunities. Aquino told us that although he relies on his intuition to identify what additional services he can bring to the women in the Hapinoy Program's network, he also relies on rapid prototyping to validate his intuition: "We do lots of small pilots. We drop bad ideas early on and identify good ideas that have legs and focus our efforts on scaling them up."[11] For instance, the Hapinoy Program recently piloted a project with a large pharmaceutical company to sell its over-the-counter medicine on a per-tablet basis through some of the sari-sari stores in far-flung villages that belong to the Hapinoy network. The pilot was successful, and is now being scaled up across the network." On the other hand, Aquino had a strong intuition that mobile remittances—sending money to family members via cellphones—would be a great service that the Hapinoy Program could offer throughout its sari-sari store network, but the pilot project revealed some limitations. The organization found that adoption of the mobile remittance service depended on the level of access to banking services—which varied widely from area to area. So the mobile remittance service was deployed selectively in some areas only. Aquino explains: "We use rapid prototyping to validate our intuitive ideas and reach one of three decisions: kill the idea, selectively scale it up in some parts of our network, or totally scale it up all across our network." Acting in congruence with their intuitive feelings—and staying true to their passion—gives jugaad innovators such as Kishore Biyani, Diane Geng, Sara Lam, Anil Jain, and Bam Aquino an edge over competitors. And this can lead to eventual success in the marketplace.

KEEPING THE FIRE ALIVE

How do jugaad innovators manage to sustain their passion? By practicing what one might call "detached engagement." Although deeply engaged in their innovative projects, jugaad innovators remain detached from the outcomes. They don't let either failure or success affect their passion. For instance, Kishore Biyani didn't allow the failure of his first retail business model to dampen his passion for delivering a better retailing experience to Indian customers; he just moved on and tried other business models.

Jugaad innovators are indefatigable in pursuing their interests because their passion transcends the intellectual and emotional realms: they frequently believe they are carrying out a critical mission that serves a larger purpose. In Indian philosophical terms, jugaad innovators believe they are following their *dharma*—the personal obligations or duties that one is called upon to perform in his or her lifetime with diligence and detachment. Dr. Prasad Kaipa, a CEO coach and senior fellow at the Indian School of Business, explains: "Mahatma Gandhi famously said that 'Happiness is when what you think, what you say, and what you do are in harmony.' By aligning these three elements—thoughts, words, and actions—with heart and spirit, jugaad entrepreneurs derive a sense of fulfillment by serving a larger cause. This is truly the secret of their undying passion."[12]

Take the case of Dr. Devi Shetty, a reputed Indian heart surgeon who treated Mother Teresa. Dr. Shetty is the founder of Narayana

Hrudayalaya, a heart hospital in Bangalore, India, where hundreds of low-income people receive heart surgery every week. Dr. Shetty started the hospital because he believes that, as a physician, he has a moral duty to make health care affordable and accessible to everyone, regardless of their caste, creed, religion, or income.[13] It is a compassionate sense of duty that sustains the passion of Dr. Shetty and his fellow physicians at Narayana Hrudayalaya. In doing his duty and being true to his profession, Dr. Shetty is clearly following his heart (visit JugaadInnovation.com to learn more about Dr. Devi Shetty and his compassionate health delivery model).

Not only are jugaad innovators able to sustain their own empathy and passion, but they also actively seek to ignite the passion and empathy of others. These qualities can be contagious: jugaad entrepreneurs are very good at inspiring employees, customers, and partners to rally around the cause—thus forming "passion networks." For instance, to secure his managers' buy-in for his visionary ideas, Big Bazaar's Kishore Biyani doesn't rely on traditional corporate communication tools such as PowerPoint presentations. Instead, he has a "chief belief officer"—Devdutt Pattanaik—who concocts stories inspired by the rich storehouse of Indian myths to fire up managers' passion and enlist their support for transformational changes in the company.[14] Similarly, driven by his own passion, Bam Aquino is igniting the passion of women entrepreneurs in the Philippines through the Hapinoy Program, which encourages them to dream big and scale up their mom-and-pop stores. The women who succeed in doing so in turn become passionate advocates of Aquino's idea—and the Hapinoy Program—and evangelize it to other women business owners in nearby villages—thus forming a "passion network" whose ripple effects are felt all across the Philippines.

THE WORLD IS TOO COMPLEX FOR THE MIND ALONE TO GRASP

In the coming years, Western corporate leaders—inured to data-driven analysis and rational decision making—will find it helpful, if not crucial, to follow their hearts as much as their brains. In this section, we discuss the reasons why we believe this is likely to be the case.

Pure Logic Will Not Suffice In an unpredictable environment, Western companies can't solve problems using data when the problems themselves are ill defined and good data is likely to be unavailable. As Dan Pink argues in *A Whole New Mind*, the left-brain's linear, analytical, computer-like thinking—controlled by what we call our "mind"—is insufficient to help us decipher, let alone navigate, our increasingly complex and ambiguous world.[15] Rather than relying purely on logic, therefore, Western executives must learn to innovate by also tapping into what Jack Welch calls their "gut intelligence"—a creative intuition honed by years of experience.[16]

Research in neuroscience, cognitive psychology, and behavioral economics increasingly shows that the emotions play a major role in helping humans solve complex problems in situations of ambiguity and uncertainty. Rather than being untrustworthy, emotion and intuition may actually help people make wiser decisions than if they were guided by rational considerations alone. As Malcolm Gladwell shows in *Blink*, in many cases spontaneous decisions can often be as good as, if not better than, carefully planned and considered ones.[17]

Gen Y Employees Are Looking for Meaning Western employees—especially Gen Y or Millennial workers—are no longer motivated by money alone: they want to work for an organization that puts their creative skills to use for a larger cause. Firms that leverage Gen Y's brainpower only to please shareholders are likely to lose out to rivals who channel Gen Y's *heartpower* into innovative projects that actively engage them and benefit the company as well as society at large. In a recent survey conducted by EuroRSG, 92 percent of Millennials agree the world must change, and 84 percent consider it their duty to drive this change. Nearly 82 percent believe they have the power to make it happen.[18] With 50 percent of the world's population under the age of twenty-seven, it is imperative that Western companies find creative ways to harness the passion and entrepreneurial dynamism of young people driven to make a difference in the world.

Customers Yearn for Authentic Relationships   According to
Forrester Research, only 5 percent of consumers agree with advertising claims; the other 95 percent consider them to be dishonest
and inauthentic. Forrester also found that a growing number of
consumers—empowered by peer-to-peer social computing tools like
blogs and Facebook—trust other consumers *more* than they trust
brands.[19] In the hyperconnected age of Twitter and Facebook, customers can swiftly punish brands that disingenuously attempt to "sell"
to them rather than engage them in a respectful and empathetic relationship. The good news, according to Josh Bernoff and Charlene Li,
coauthors of *Groundswell*, is that Western consumers do trust brands that
they feel truly empathize with their needs. The authors argue that the
onus lies with companies to demonstrate genuine empathy in their
interactions with customers—by respectfully engaging them as value
cocreators rather than passive users of their offerings.[20] Indeed, 96
percent of North American consumers are more likely to purchase
products from a company that listens to—and acts on—their advice.[21]

Unfortunately, many Western companies don't realize that by
encouraging or even allowing employees to follow their hearts and
by creating emotionally engaging experiences for customers, they can
help drive innovation and growth. And the companies that do recognize
this may find it difficult to institutionalize such a culture and make it
fundamental to the organization and its practices.

INDUSTRIAL-ERA BUSINESS PRACTICES KEEP HEARTS LOCKED OUT

In the postindustrial experience economy in which complexity is
the norm, customers seek intimate and authentic relationships with
brands, and Gen Y employees look for meaning in their work, it
pays to be empathetic, intuitive, and passionate—and to take advantage of your organization's heartpower. Yet Western companies have
trouble cultivating—and demonstrating—their heartpower because
they remain attached to industrial-era business practices and structured innovation approaches. These practices and approaches—which

overemphasize left-brain thinking and rational behavior—hinder Western leaders' ability to make intuitive decisions, and prevent their companies from building empathetic connections with customers and igniting and harnessing the passion of creative employees.

R&D: Isolated and Disconnected from Real-World Customers

R&D engineers who operate in isolated labs do not spend time immersed in the world of customers and thus cannot empathize with them. Further, at many Western companies, R&D performance is still measured by the number of patents produced (an indicator of left-brain prowess) rather than the quality of the customer experience delivered (an indicator of right-brain empathetic creativity). But as Matt Bross, an American who runs Huawei's R&D, notes: "There are no breakthrough technologies, only breakthrough *market applications*."[22] R&D's inventions, groundbreaking or otherwise, will fail at launch if they don't address a well-defined source of customer pain. Understanding customer pain requires empathy for, and collaboration with, customers. Unfortunately, R&D tools and techniques, used for scientific discovery in the lab, were not conceived to capture consumer insights such as latent buyer needs, let alone to dynamically engage end users in designing and testing new products. This explains why 80 percent of new consumer products fail after launch—they often lack market relevance, leading Tim Brown, CEO of IDEO, a top design and innovation consultancy, to conclude: "[R&D] design may have its greatest impact when it's taken out of the hands of designers and put into the hands of everyone."[23]

Firms Often Seek Refuge in Numbers—and Shun Intuition

The business world abhors surprises and craves predictability: forecasts, plans, and budgets are all meant to "control" the future and confer a sense of stability—leaving no room for intuitive improvisation. It is easier for a CEO to justify to investors a decision to invest in a new product or service if the CEO has lots of data to back it up. But investors are less likely to buy into an innovation project if you tell them that it's your gut telling you that the project merits investment.

Companies' overreliance on data—rather than intuition—leads them to make two strategic mistakes. First, they tend to axe many projects too early because they can't find enough data to support their commercial viability. (Conversely, they don't realize that by the time they have collected all the data needed to justify an innovation project, the window of opportunity for commercializing it may already have closed.) Second, companies prefer to invest in incremental innovation rather than breakthrough innovation because the former is easier to justify to investors. This attitude explains why nearly 90 percent of R&D projects in consumer product companies are aimed at sustaining existing products—by developing, for instance, line extensions—rather than investing in new-to-the-market products.[24] This leaves the door open for a competitor to disrupt the market with a groundbreaking offering.

Marketing Executives Don't Emotionally Connect with Customers   Marketers often want customers to understand their value proposition, when it should be the other way around. For instance, consumers are sending this message to suppliers of premium consumer goods: "My values have shifted. I now value simplicity and affordability: can you deliver on that?" But consumer good companies lack the empathy to positively respond to this plea; instead they continue to make and sell high-priced goods to middle-class Americans. As a result, frugal consumers find their suppliers insensitive to their economic woes and take their business elsewhere. Kevin Roberts warns marketers: "In the [old] Era of New marketing, it was all about your product. In the Age of Now it is all about the mastery of emotional communication; not manipulation, but of having relationships. In the Age of Now it's all about the single question consumers have of you: 'How will you improve my life?' Answering this is to deliver priceless value."[25]

Outdated Human Resource Management Doesn't Engage Next-Generation Employees   Companies continue to rely primarily on financial incentives (such as bonuses) to motivate their employees rather than giving them the space and time to pursue their passion in a constructive manner. Not surprisingly, according to a Gallup survey, only 29 percent of Americans work with passion, and a full 52 percent say they do not feel engaged by their jobs. John Hagel, cochairman of the Deloitte Center for the Edge and coauthor of *The Power of Pull: How Small Moves, Smartly Made, Can Set Big Things in Motion*, offers the following piece of advice to heads of human resource management: "One thing I would do is to start systematically measuring the passion levels of my employees. I've developed a strong view that one of the keys to motivating individuals is to help them connect to their passion for their profession. Monitoring passion level gives you the ability to provide rapid performance improvement. Passionate people are deeply motivated to improve themselves and drive themselves to the next level of performance."[26]

HOW WESTERN FIRMS CAN FOLLOW THEIR HEARTS

In an environment that favors more structured and data-driven approaches to innovation, following one's heart in business today poses several challenges for Western managers and companies. By drawing on the experience of jugaad entrepreneurs, however, there are several ways in which Western leaders can develop a culture of empathy and passion within their companies.

Send Senior Management to "Empathy Development Bootcamps" Empathy is like a muscle; it can be developed in senior executives by exposing them to diverse perspectives. For instance, Allianz Global Investors runs a dedicated training center in its headquarters in Munich, Germany, where senior executives from Allianz as well as client companies attend training programs in communication, team building, and leadership—all of which are conducted by visually impaired trainers in the dark or by hearing impaired trainers in a soundproof space.[27] The goal of these programs is to increase self-awareness among senior executives, the idea being that one cannot empathize with others unless one has direct knowledge of them and one has realized and acknowledged one's own limits.

Ignore Market Researchers and Investors to Innovate Radically C-level executives need moral courage to follow their hearts—and this often entails ignoring market researchers and investors when it comes to disruptive innovation. Specifically, to avoid getting caught in an inflexible web of structure and demands for data, senior executives shouldn't rely solely on the approval of external stakeholders when launching truly disruptive products and services. Relying on external approval in this way could either delay or altogether prevent corporate leaders from pursuing truly breakthrough ideas. For instance, when developing new products or formulating new strategies, Apple's Steve Jobs rarely bothered to get validation from financial analysts, media pundits, or even consumers. He was more interested in following his heart than in merely seeking to please analysts and market watchers.

Embrace Customer-Centric Design Principles R&D engineers and scientists need to get out of their labs and immerse themselves in the environment that surrounds their customers, to truly understand their needs: this is the basis of customer-centric design. As we've noted, companies like Nokia and Intel employ ethnographers who spend months living with underserved customers in emerging markets to identify their latent needs and design meaningful solutions that can make a significant impact on customers' daily lives. These solutions (such as Nokia's 1100, which has sold over 250 million units worldwide) carry the potential of turning into breakthrough products with huge commercial potential. Firms eager to build their internal skills in human-centered design can do so by hiring specialized consultancies such as IDEO, frog, LUNAR, or Continuum. Companies that can't afford these design consultants can use social media tools like Facebook and crowdsourcing techniques to engage "lead users"—that is, the early adopters among consumers. These lead users can help companies identify mainstream customers' unarticulated needs and help cocreate new products, services, and experiences that fulfill those needs.[28]

Engage Your Customers in a Heart-to-Heart Conversation

Researchers in fields from neuroscience to psychology, behavioral economics to marketing, all agree that emotions are as powerful a driver of consumer behavior as rationality and calculation. In many cases, emotions may even be the only driver of consumer behavior. In others, they may be more dominant. In still others, the emotions may play a complementary and reinforcing role to that of reason.[29] All this has profound implications for CMOs and marketers more generally. In a world where brands have achieved parity on features, price, distribution, and even design, engaging customers' emotions becomes a crucial way for marketers to differentiate their offerings from those of others.

Kevin Roberts of Saatchi & Saatchi has long been passionate about engaging customers' emotions. Roberts says that a major breakthrough in his thinking came from the insight that reason leads to conclusions, whereas emotion leads to action. Following this insight, Roberts felt certain that emotional, not rational factors were the key to the next round of competition and that the future would be won on relationships, not just transactions. This conviction led Roberts to create the notion of "lovemarks" to replace "brands." He felt certain that "if people loved something rather than merely liked it, they would be loyal beyond reason, beyond price, beyond recession." Hence the notion of lovemarks: a "future beyond brands, infused with mystery, sensuality and intimacy. Delivering premium margins because people don't merely like them, they love them."[30]

Starbucks provides another example of this kind of emotional connection with consumers. The company revolutionized how coffee was bought and sold by engaging customers emotionally rather than through price or convenience. Prior to Starbucks, the mass market was mostly about "instant coffee," bought off the shelf, and with price discounts. But following a trip to Milan, Starbucks' Howard Schultz, who joined as director of retail operations and marketing in 1982, realized that coffee was much more about passion, emotion, and lifestyle than about price, convenience, and a warm drink. By creating a "third space" between home and work, and using coffee as the means to fill that space, Starbucks was able to engage consumers emotionally and create a global business in the process.

Lululemon Athletica also engages customers at an emotional level. The company has used this ethos to develop a cult-like following for its high-end yoga gear and generate remarkable sales—over 52 percent compound annual growth in the roller-coaster economy between 2005 and 2009. It has achieved this largely through the creation of a unique customer-centric culture—built both within stores and through a community-based marketing approach—that is quickly being copied by Nike, Gap, and Nordstorm, among others. The company identifies local yoga ambassadors who embody the "lulu lifestyle" and outfits them with their gear. Every week, the store pushes aside racks and shelves, and mats are unrolled so these ambassadors can provide free yoga classes in stores. Their easily identifiable red shopping bags are decorated with phrases and aphorisms such as "breathe deeply" or "friends are more important than money." Although yoga has been around for millennia, Lululemon has driven a trend that makes yoga practitioners feel they are a part of a community and a larger vision—and keeps consumers coming back for more.

Create "Centers of Passion" Across Your Organization

Firms must empower employees to publicly share and discuss ideas they are passionate about—however controversial and disruptive these ideas may be. And to bring these ideas to life, they must help build communities of customers and partners around them. For instance, frog has launched "centers of passion" across its global network of design studios where employees can freely discuss their left-field ideas and engage with colleagues, customers, or external partners who share similar passions. Robert Fabricant, vice president of creative at frog and the driving force behind this enterprise-wide initiative, explains: "We want to turn an individual employee's passion into a 'community of passion' where people with different perspectives can identify ways to convert their personal passion into a practical reality. These passions are the seeds of transformational solutions that can be used to enhance existing initiatives or launch entire new practice areas. The aim is to create a groundswell movement within frog by cross-pollinating and cross-fertilizing personal passions across our organization."[31]

Frog has set up a website where its employees can share their passions with the world. In one of these videos, Denise Burton, a frog fellow, describes her passion:

> Connecting people has always been my passion. Even as a kid, whenever there was a fight in the playground I was the one who always brokered peace among fighting kids and reconnected them. As I grew up, I recognized how technologies like the World Wide Web and RFID can not only help connect [millions of] people but also [billions of] devices together. I always dreamed of "connected experience"—a seamless world where people and devices are interlinked. Even after I joined frog, it long remained a dream. But now I think frog's clients are finally ready for my dream: it's no longer a blue-sky idea. The timing is right to turn "connected experience" into a viable commercial reality.[32]

Encourage Employees to Trust Their Gut—and Validate with Rapid Experimentation   CEOs need to follow the lead of Kip Tindell, CEO of The Container Store, a leading U.S. housewares chain, who not only relies on his *own* intuition to guide his business decisions but has also enshrined intuition as one of his company's "Foundation Principles."As Tindell explains: "We just beg and plead and try to get employees to believe that intuition does have a place in the work force. After all, intuition is only the sum total of your life experience. So why would you want to leave it at home when you come to work in the morning?"[33]

Both Google and Facebook encourage employees to trust their gut by beta-testing their intuitive ideas—and then adopting those that achieve significant customer uptake into their mainstream product line. Despite the power of intuition, it is important to note that however much you trust your intuition, it is unlikely to *always* be right. Therefore the best way to minimize the risks of investing in the wrong products and services is to test your intuitive ideas early on in the marketplace—and use customer feedback to continually iterate design or drop the offering altogether if customer interest is tepid.

APPLE: A HEARTPOWERED CORPORATION

Steve Jobs, cofounder and former CEO of Apple, was perhaps the world's most effective practitioner of the "follow your heart" principle. Jobs helped Apple disrupt the consumer technology industry several times over, first with the iPod and iTunes, then with the iPhone and most recently with the iPad. But Apple didn't do extensive market surveys to come up with the iPad. This may have been just as well, given that many consumers, analysts, and media experts were convinced that there was no market for it. But Jobs had a knack for reading the market and was well known for anticipating customer needs without relying on analysts' predictions or focus groups.

More important, Jobs depended on his company's heartpower, as measured by the quality of customer experience delivered, rather than its brainpower, as measured by the number of patents filed. Indeed, it is telling that Apple ranked eighty-first in the 2010 Booz & Company's ranking of companies by their R&D expenditures. As a percentage of its revenue, Apple spends a *fifth* of what Microsoft spends. Yet it is the world's most valued brand today; and, in the same Booz & Company study mentioned earlier, Apple was ranked as the most innovative company in the world.[34] Credit for this goes to three qualities that Jobs consistently demonstrated throughout this his career at Apple.

Jobs Was Intuitive   Steve Jobs was always a dreamer who envisioned the future of technology well before competitors—or even customers—did. He let his intuition identify big opportunities and reveal the pathways to seize them (interestingly, according to Jobs's biographer Walter Isaacson, Jobs learned to trust his intuition during an introspective trip to India in 1974).[35] As such, he was able to shape—and lead—entire new markets again and again. For instance, when he returned to Apple in 1997 after a twelve-year absence, he happened to meet a designer named Jonathan Ive. Ive was dejected because his latest invention—a monolithic monitor that had all the computer functions integrated into it—had been rejected by Apple's managers who viewed it as too avant-garde. But Jobs was immediately smitten by Ive's invention—in it, he saw the future. He promised Ive that they were about to start a long-term partnership that would change the world of computing forever. Ive later became Apple's head of design; the invention that Jobs helped bring to market was the iMac.[36]

Because he always followed his intuition, Jobs never sought out or relied on external validation for his decisions—from either investors or customers. In fact, in an interview with *Inc.* magazine in 1989, Jobs said: "You can't just ask customers what they want and then try to give that to them. By the time you get it built, they'll want something new."[37] Jobs practiced customer-*minded* innovation, honed by intuition, rather than customer-*driven* innovation, shaped by rationality.

Jobs Was Empathetic   Steve Jobs never had to purposefully listen to end users to understand their needs. His identification with users was so great that he used himself as Apple's first and foremost customer. And he was often the customer of the future rather than of the present. This helped him design superlative customer experiences not so much to please external users as to please himself. Indeed, it seems as if he spent his entire career trying to address his *own* needs as a technology user, rather than thinking and acting like a technology provider as most of Apple's rivals do. You could call this self-empathy or self-directed compassion.

Jobs Was Obsessively Passionate   Steve Jobs wasn't just a passionate leader—he was an *obsessively* passionate one. He was obsessed with delighting customers with amazing products that marry ease of use and superior technical performance—and with over-the-top customer service to boot. His unabashed passion for excellence in everything pushed Apple's employees to outdo themselves and meet his stringent quality expectations. Jobs's perfectionism is enshrined in Apple's product development principles, such as "Pixel Perfect Mockup" (any prototype needs to be designed hyperrealistically to look and feel as close as possible to the end product) and "10 to 3 to 1" (for every new feature, Apple engineers design without restriction ten entirely different mockups, then narrow them down to three, and eventually settle on a final one).[38] Of course, Jobs's detractors thought that his passion for excellence bordered on insanity (the marble for the floor at the New York Apple store was allegedly shipped to his California office first so he could examine the veins). But as the saying goes, the difference between genius and madness is success.

In his 2005 commencement address at Stanford, Jobs had this to say to the graduating students: "You can't connect the dots looking forward. You can only connect them looking backwards, so you have to trust that the dots will somehow connect in your future. You have to trust in something—your gut, destiny, life, karma, whatever—because believing that the dots will connect down the road will give you the confidence to follow your heart, even when it leads you off the well-worn path, and that will make all the difference."[39]

Tim Cook, Steve Jobs's successor, is more operations focused, given his supply chain background—and he seems more driven to managing the present rather than predicting the future. However, Cook may be just what Apple needs now that the role of chief empathy officer and chief intuition officer has shifted from a single individual—Steve Jobs—to thousands of passionate jugaad innovators at Apple. To help these employees channel their ingenuity into shaping the future of computing while maintaining Apple's successful legacy, you need a leader who is solidly anchored in the *present*. Tim Cook might well be just that person.

CONCLUSION

Jugaad innovators like Kishore Biyani and Steve Jobs are truly gutsy in many respects: they have courage and the willingness to take risks, they trust their intuition, and they are passionate about what they do, believing that they are pursuing a higher cause in the process.

Following one's heart—the seat of empathy, intuition, and passion—is the last of the six principles that jugaad innovators follow. But following these principles alone is insufficient for an enterprise to be able to implement the jugaad approach to innovation. As we explore in the next chapter, to sustain the adoption of jugaad and its six principles, corporate leaders must understand what changes are needed at the *organizational* as well as the individual level.

CHAPTER EIGHT

INTEGRATING JUGAAD INTO YOUR ORGANIZATION

Company cultures are like country cultures. Never try to change one.
Try, instead, to work with what you've got.

— PETER DRUCKER

So far, we've shown the many ways in which practicing the six principles of jugaad innovation—seeking opportunity in adversity, doing more with less, thinking and acting flexibly, keeping it simple, including the margin, and following your heart—can help Western companies generate and sustain breakthrough growth in today's complex environment. But jugaad innovation is not a panacea to be applied to all innovation problems in all situations; despite its clear benefits, it also has some clear limitations. Indeed, jugaad isn't a *substitute* for the traditional, structured approaches to innovation most commonly used in Western companies; rather, jugaad is a useful *complement* to this approach.

In this chapter, we discuss the advantages and limitations of jugaad innovation and the contexts in which it is best applied. We describe how Western companies can combine the agile and resilient spirit of jugaad with more structured approaches to innovation, and how they can prioritize the jugaad principles they need to adopt most urgently.

WHEN DOES JUGAAD WORK BEST?

The relevance—and ultimate success—of any new business tool, practice, or approach depends on the context in which it is applied. When adopting any new tool or approach, companies should apply it not indiscriminately in all circumstances but selectively, in situations where the tool or approach is most appropriate. Companies must demonstrate similar discernment when implementing jugaad innovation—applying it in specific contexts that best lend themselves to this approach. We have found that jugaad innovation delivers the most impressive results when it is practiced in complex and volatile environments with the following characteristics:

• *Rapid changes.* Jugaad has particular potency in highly volatile settings where product lifecycles are shorter, demographic patterns are shifting, competition can come from anywhere, or governments are constantly changing policy and unleashing new regulations. For instance, the fast-paced consumer electronics industry, with its short product life spans, requires flexible thinking and rapid-fire action, which jugaad innovation can handily deliver.

• *Widespread resource scarcity.* Jugaad is most relevant to companies, sectors, or countries where capital is limited and access to natural resources is constrained. For example, the resource-hungry food and beverage industry as well as the automotive sector—confronted with scarcity of water and oil—need jugaad innovation to revamp their supply chains so they can do more with less.

• *Frugal and diverse customers.* Jugaad can be most powerful in markets where cost-conscious customers are seeking affordable products and want them to be tailored to their particular needs. For instance, the consumer products and health care sectors need jugaad innovation to discover ways to include marginal segments and build empathetic and personalized relationships with their diverse customers.

• *Industry immaturity.* Jugaad is important in sectors that are still nascent and where market mechanisms and industry standards aren't established. For example, in sunrise sectors like clean tech and biotech—which are highly unpredictable—jugaad innovation can help companies seek opportunity in adversity, turning it to their advantage.

• *Exploding interconnectivity.* Jugaad has relevance in industries that are undergoing a technology revolution and where free social media tools and ubiquitous cellphones are making communication cheaper and collaboration easier. Banks, for instance, can apply jugaad innovation to devise inclusive business models that leverage mobile technologies to cost-effectively serve marginal segments such as the sixty million unbanked or underbanked Americans.

These extreme conditions typically have been more prevalent in emerging markets like India, China, and Brazil than in the United States or Europe. As we discussed in previous chapters, however, Western economies have also begun to exhibit many of these aspects of scarcity, diversity, unpredictability, and interconnectivity. Given these developments, jugaad may be just what the doctor ordered for Western companies too: a pill that can boost their immune system, ward off complexity, and help them innovate and grow. But how should companies with an established, structured approach to innovation go about dealing with jugaad? Should they abandon the structured approach altogether? Or should they integrate it with the jugaad approach? If they choose to do the latter, how should they integrate the two approaches?

THE HAMMER VERSUS THE SCREWDRIVER

Despite the limits of the structured approach to innovation—particularly in complex, unpredictable contexts—companies shouldn't abandon these traditional structures and processes as they still hold value in certain conditions. Rather, companies with structured approaches to innovation—built around big budgets, large R&D teams, and standardized and linear product development processes—should expand their innovation toolkit with jugaad. As the global environment gets ever more complex, companies will need more than a single tool to deal with complexity. Instead of always using a hammer to deal with problems, they might find it useful to use a screwdriver too from time to time. If the structured approach to innovation is the hammer, then jugaad could well be the screwdriver.

The key issue for companies, therefore, is to know *when* to use the hammer and when the screwdriver. For that, they need to understand the capabilities and benefits of both tools and how they complement each other.

The traditional structured innovation approach brings three major benefits:

1. *Volume-oriented economies of scale:* Large R&D teams and vast supply chain resources enable companies to scale up new products and distribute them to millions of undifferentiated customers. As such, structured innovation—when successfully executed—delivers *volume-oriented* economies of scale for standardized products and services in homogenous markets.

2. *Infusion of "hard" capital:* Structured innovation favors "big risks, big rewards" R&D projects undertaken by companies with huge resources. As we explained earlier, many of these mega-budget projects fail. Yet the few projects that do succeed can occasionally lead to disruptive technologies or groundbreaking products (such as blockbuster drugs) that can help companies increase revenues and profits and expand market share—generating "hard" capital and tangible assets that can be reflected in the balance sheet.

3. *Efficiency:* Standardized processes like Six Sigma can help companies execute innovation projects more effectively and efficiently, *provided the environment is stable.*

The jugaad approach extends these benefits by bringing additional value in the following ways:

1. *Value-oriented economies of scope:* As populations grow more diverse and markets become more fragmented, jugaad enables companies to

tailor solutions to the specific needs of multiple customer segments. Jugaad innovation helps deliver more *value* to individual customers in heterogeneous markets.

2. *Infusion of "soft" capital:* We are entering a postmaterial era in which employees and customers are seeking meaning more than material benefits per se. By adopting jugaad, companies can unleash the passion of employees and engage customers in meaningful relationships. In this way, companies can accumulate "soft" capital—namely, higher employee productivity and customer loyalty. These intangible assets will sustain the company's competitive edge, as they are harder for competitors to replicate than more tangible assets, like technology.

3. *Flexibility:* In an increasingly volatile business environment, managers need to think on their feet to overcome unexpected challenges. The resilient jugaad mindset can help managers overcome harsh constraints by improvising robust solutions using limited resources.

To summarize: jugaad is like a booster, extending a company's ability to cope with volatility and do more with less in highly constrained settings. Ultimately, in order to simultaneously deal with low-volatility, resource-rich settings as well as high-volatility, resource-constrained settings, companies need to have *both* sets of capabilities: the volume-oriented economies of scale, hard capital, and efficiency of the structured approach to innovation, as well as the value-oriented economies of scope, soft capital, and flexibility of jugaad.

The challenge for companies is to know when to apply which approach—that is, when to use the hammer and when the screwdriver. This in turn requires leaders to create an organizational context in which both approaches can exist in harmony without one being favored over the other at all times. Tim Leberecht, chief marketing officer of frog, observes, "Companies need to give themselves the freedom to swing to both extremes—that is, from highly structured innovation to free-flowing jugaad—rather than settling in the middle trying to achieve an elusive 'balance.'"[1]

Such organizational flexibility can be visualized metaphorically as a pendulum whose dynamic movement enables companies to explore a wide range of options to meet the innovation requirements of the rapidly evolving marketplace. For leaders, this means they need to cultivate the wisdom to know when to be like Miles Davis and improvise innovation and when to be like Leonard Bernstein and orchestrate it.

Managing the creative tension between jugaad innovation and a structured approach can prove disruptive. Bringing in the new approach can conflict with companies' existing organizational structures and practices such as resource-intensive R&D models, time-consuming product development processes, mass-marketing techniques, and hierarchical management structures. Yet this creative tension between the "yin" (structured) and "yang" (unstructured) aspects of innovation is healthy and worth nurturing: it can even yield tremendous benefits for organizations. In an increasingly complex world, managing polarities—that is, extremes—is rapidly becoming a core competence for Western leaders. And there is no better way to develop it than by integrating jugaad into their organizations and learning how to balance and integrate multiple—and conflicting—approaches to innovation.

HOW GE SUCCESSFULLY INTEGRATES JUGAAD AND SIX SIGMA

GE, a large conglomerate that heavily relies on structured approaches like Six Sigma, has managed to integrate the jugaad approach into its existing organization and, in the process, learned to swing with this "innovation pendulum." There is a strategic reason behind this. The $150 billion industrial goliath that employs three hundred thousand people worldwide is striving hard to become agile and resilient in the face of growing complexity. The company is doing so by shifting its business model from that of an R&D driven company to that of a customer-focused organization.

GE's radical transformation is driven by CEO Jeffrey Immelt. Unlike his predecessors—such as the legendary Jack Welch—who had an operations or engineering background, Immelt's background is in sales and marketing, the first CEO with such a background in GE's 120-year history. Because he has spent most of his career interacting with customers, Immelt understands intuitively the importance of being customer-focused, agile, and responsive. In particular, through extensive interaction with customers, Immelt gained the following important insight: GE's customers no longer value just how well GE engineers its products, but also how well GE *serves* them throughout the product lifecycle. Plus they expect GE to deliver these quality products and services faster and cheaper.

For GE, this means that the ability to sense and respond swiftly to customers' requirements is as critical to success as engineering prowess is—if not more so. Recognizing that this new market reality calls for higher speed, agility, and cost-efficiency, Immelt is encouraging every GE employee to innovate and think differently by adopting the frugal and democratic principles of jugaad. And, as we'll now describe, this push is working.

GE Healthcare, one of GE's units, is a clear example of the massive cultural transformation GE is undergoing—and the resulting benefits. GE Healthcare operates in the West and in emerging markets, in an industry that is extremely complex, supercompetitive, highly regulated, and undergoing a great deal of change. Despite these challenges, GE Healthcare is managing to innovate by successfully practicing the six principles of jugaad to compete and win in a complex world of adversity, scarcity and unpredictability.

GE Seeks Opportunities in Adversity The PET/CT scanners produced by GE Healthcare (hereafter simply "GE") are high-end devices used for cancer diagnosis and treatment. The devices themselves are expensive. They also require a cyclotron—which is as costly as a PET/CT scanner—to generate a radioisotope called fludeoxyglucose (FDG) that is injected into patients to help produce the diagnostic images that can precisely locate the disease. In India, large hospitals have traditionally imported FDG for use with their PET/CT equipment.

But this process is expensive and time-consuming—and quite beyond the reach of small-town and rural hospitals. Seeing an opportunity in these adverse circumstances, GE worked with private diagnostic centers and local airlines to domestically produce FDG and deliver it within hours to small-town hospitals around the country.[2] This just-in-time supply chain for FDG delivery is now fully operational and is being scaled up. In addition, GE has connected with Nueclear Healthcare, an Indian company, to set up a network of 120 advanced molecular imaging centers all across India by 2015. These types of affordable and accessible solutions for early cancer detection are of huge value to India, where cancer is one of the leading causes of death and the incidence of the disease is growing alarmingly fast. The number of cancer patients in India, currently about 2.5 million, is expected to increase five-fold by 2025.[3]

Despite the challenges of working in a country like India, where logistics can be highly unreliable, GE has succeeded in making high-quality cancer diagnosis and treatment available to even low-income communities across the country. Terri Bresenham, president and CEO of GE Healthcare India, says: "Our studies and pilot programs helped us imagine and innovate solutions that are appropriate and affordable. However our 'jugaad' innovations are not limited to technologies. We also focus on parallel needs in healthcare delivery; the scarcity of affordable capital, digitization for networking urban centers of excellence with tier-II and tier-III towns, and key partnerships with local suppliers, medical colleges, and state governments."[4]

GE does more with less   GE recognized that its bulky and expensive electrocardiogram (ECG) devices were unaffordable for physicians in emerging markets like India, China, and Africa. The company also realized that these devices were impractical in these markets, as doctors could not carry them on their motorbikes or bicycles when visiting patients in far-flung villages. Plus, villages often didn't have electricity to power these ECG devices. Recognizing the problem and aware of the need for this device in rural areas, GE's researchers in India invented in

2008 the MAC 400—a portable electrocardiogram that costs one-tenth and weighs one-fifth of its current equivalent in Western markets. The compact MAC 400—priced at \$1,000—boasts a super-long battery life and uses several off-the-shelf components. Its rugged printer, for instance, is an adapted version of the portable ticket machine used in Indian bus kiosks. As a result, MAC 400 is easy to use and maintain in dusty rural environments and delivers more value at a lower cost.[5]

After successfully deploying MAC 400 in emerging markets such as India and China, GE rolled out this FDA-approved device in the United States for applications such as emergency roadside assistance.[6] After introducing MAC 400 in 2008, GE outdid itself in 2010 by launching the MAC i, an ECG device that is lighter than MAC 400 and is priced at around \$500—potentially bringing the cost of ECG tests down to just \$0.20 each.[7]

GE Thinks and Acts Flexibly   GE's recession-weary clients are reluctant to pay millions of dollars up front for big-ticket items like power turbines, aircraft engines, and medical equipment. This reality has forced GE to think flexibly. Accordingly, the company has transformed its business model from that of a product supplier to that of a total solutions provider, offering clients more financing options in the process. In particular, rather than selling its products outright, GE also now rents them out, using a "pay as you go" pricing model. Alternatively, the company works with partners to operate and maintain products for a fee under a performance-based service contract. For instance, in India, GE has implemented a flexible pricing model known as "pay-per-scan" that enables frugal medical diagnostic centers to rent GE's diagnosis equipment like CT scanners—instead of buying them at a high price—and to pay a variable fee depending on the total number of scans conducted each year.[8]

GE is also demonstrating its flexible thinking by revamping its relationship with government bodies. While many Western companies complain about escalating government regulations—and thus view the government as a barrier to increasing business performance—GE is forging win-win public-private partnerships (PPPs) with governments worldwide. For instance, in India, GE has partnered with state and local governments and specialized service providers that operate diagnostic imaging facilities equipped with GE's equipment at public hospitals—especially in rural areas. Such a win-win PPP model has helped increase the efficiency of state-run hospitals, which are spared the need to invest in expensive equipment or scramble to recruit qualified technicians—yet can provide affordable, high-quality care for rural patients.[9]

GE is not only empowering its executives to think flexibly but also enabling them to *act* flexibly. Indeed, GE has started redesigning its rigid, top-heavy organizational structure to allow for jugaad innovators in its regional units to sense and respond to local opportunities faster. In particular, the heads of GE operations in emerging markets are being given latitude to make strategic decisions without seeking approval or resources from headquarters.[10] Now these regional leaders can quickly fund and execute promising jugaad ideas, such as the just-in-time delivery of FDG to hospitals and clinics equipped with PET/CT scanners.

GE Keeps It Simple   Having traditionally overengineered products, GE's R&D teams are now learning the virtues of simplicity. GE's top engineers found that physicians in rural areas of emerging markets like India, who use only a thermometer and stethoscope, had no use for their bulky, hard-to-use ultrasound machines. Yet these physicians were not technology averse—they all carried cellphones. With this information, GE's engineers had a jugaad idea: what if they could design an ultrasound machine as compact and simple to use as a cellphone? The result was Vscan, a portable ultrasound device that weighs merely one pound, is as small as a smartphone, and has a user interface as simple as an iPod's. Vscan has been a huge success in both developed countries and emerging markets. Immelt believes this simple but powerful device will one day become as indispensable to physicians as the thermometer and stethoscope. Indeed, a study conducted by

Scripps Health validated Vscan's ability to accurate diagnose structural heart conditions. The study called Vscan the greatest invention since the two-hundred-year-old stethoscope (which was invented in 1816), because Vscan allows the physician to "see" a patient's heart, leading to more accurate diagnoses. Dr. Eric J. Topol, chief academic officer at Scripps Health and principal investigator on the study, explains: "Approximately twenty million echocardiograms are conducted in the United States every year, each costing $1,500 or more and requiring a return appointment for a hospital or clinic echo laboratory for an extended session of about forty-five minutes. A pocket echocardiogram [like the Vscan] could significantly reduce costs and improve the quality of the patient experience."[11]

GE Includes the Margin In 2009, GE launched Healthymagination—a strategic initiative overseen by Immelt that aims to make high-quality health care affordable and accessible to more people, especially underserved communities around the world, including in the United States. As part of Healthymagination, GE has, for instance, partnered with P&G, Johnson & Johnson, Anthem, and UnitedHealthcare to pilot a government-funded community program in Cincinnati that aims to improve health delivery while reducing costs. Cincinnati's health statistics are alarming: over 12 percent of the population lacks health insurance, and the mortality rate is higher than the national average—causing health care spending to increase at 8 percent annually. The Beacon Community program will set up an electronically connected, citywide health care system called HealthBridge that aims to reduce the cost of care and improve quality and efficiency metrics targeted at diabetes, primary care, childhood asthma, and congestive heart failure. If this grassroots model in Cincinnati is successful, GE intends to apply it to other communities across the United States—thus making health care accessible to marginal segments. As part of the Healthymagination initiative, GE is making its low-cost, easy-to-use devices like the MAC 400 and Vscan more widely available to less-specialized community health workers—such as those in rural areas of the United States.[12]

GE Follows Its Heart   GE has traditionally served business customers such as airlines, hospitals, factories, and governments. But given his commercial background, Jeff Immelt recognized the importance of developing empathy for *end users*—those whom its business clients serve. To that end, Immelt has tasked Beth Comstock, GE's chief marketing officer, with increasing GE's emotional quotient by engaging these end users in a meaningful dialogue. Comstock is now connecting GE's left-brain R&D engineers more closely with end users through an empathy-building initiative called "market back"—that is, first identify end users' needs, and then co-create new solutions, in partnership with business customers and partners. These market back solutions are designed from the ground up in local markets rather than being pushed down by senior executives in headquarters, so they fit specific local contexts better. They are quickly rolled out and tested using immediate customer feedback. For instance, GE's R&D engineers are immersing themselves in village clinics in India and Bangladesh to develop empathy for rural patients and understand how to come up with health care solutions that are affordable and accessible for low-income communities worldwide. Comstock notes: "Global perception and expectation of innovation is changing and businesses would be short-sighted not to change with it. And that means looking at innovation in both the science lab and the 'real world' lab. From the top down to the masses up. And from pure profit to profit with a purpose. Companies that embrace this new model for innovation today will be better positioned for growth tomorrow."[13]

By internalizing the six principles of jugaad, GE is developing the flexible and inclusive mindset needed to improvise empathetic solutions that are affordable and sustainable for a larger number of people. But where does Six Sigma fit into all this? Six Sigma enhances—and helps magnify—the value of GE's jugaad inventions. In particular, GE leverages structured Six Sigma processes, first to improve the *quality* of its jugaad inventions so they meet international standards (in the same way it obtained FDA approval for its MAC 400 and Vscan devices), and then to rapidly *scale up* these jugaad inventions—taking advantage of GE's impressive global manufacturing and distribution capabilities—so they can be made available to a larger number of customers worldwide, thus accelerating the market adoption of jugaad inventions.

In sum, GE is a successful example of how a Western company, by embracing jugaad, can think flexibly, act nimbly, and harness the ingenuity of its vast base of employees, customers, and partners to drive breakthrough innovation and growth. More important, GE has shown how to mesh the bottom-up, unstructured approach of jugaad innovation with a more traditional, structured approach to innovation in the context of an advanced global organization.

But GE is not alone in achieving this synergistic blend. Hundreds of organizations are effectively integrating jugaad into their organizations—enabling them to innovate faster, better, and cheaper. And so too can you and your company. But to make the most of jugaad, you need to prioritize your efforts to adopt this new frugal and flexible approach to innovation.

GETTING STARTED WITH JUGAAD

Jugaad can disrupt business as usual—for the better. As with any disruptive change, however, companies can adopt jugaad in one of two ways: in one fell swoop or in small chunks. Large corporations led by visionary leaders, such as 3M, GE, PepsiCo, and Procter & Gamble have the resources and the willpower to reinvent the *entire* organization around the six jugaad principles. But the majority of Western companies—and their leaders—may be intimidated by the thought of such a wholesale adoption. For those companies and their executives we offer two suggestions:

1. *Prioritize the jugaad principles you need to adopt.* Not all jugaad principles are of equal importance to all organizations. At the corporate level, you need to let industry dynamics and your company's strategic requirements determine which of the six jugaad principles is most critical for

your business success. For instance, if you are a premium retailer that sells luxury items, doing more with less and including the margin may not be of critical relevance; however, keeping it simple may be crucial to streamlining the service experience for high-end customers. If you are a consumer product supplier like Procter & Gamble or Whirlpool, you may choose to primarily do more with less by creating new frugal products for buyers whose purchasing power is waning. Similarly, Western companies in industries undergoing major turmoil, such as pharmaceuticals and automotive, would be wise to seek opportunity in adversity and think and act flexibly in order to radically reinvent their obsolete business models.

At an individual level, your functional role may determine the critical mix of jugaad principles that will add most to your career. For instance, we would suggest to marketing executives and R&D directors—who tend to think with the logical left brain—that they follow their hearts in engaging customers and cocreating solutions that delight them. Human resource managers may also find the "follow your heart" principle relevant to their jobs. At a time when 71 percent of employees in corporate America feel disengaged at work, HR managers need to create a work environment that encourages employees, especially free-spirited Millennials, to pursue their passion in the workplace—just as companies like Apple, Google, and frog are doing.

2. *For each principle you choose to adopt, aim first for the low-hanging fruit.* Once you have decided which principles are of strategic importance to you, you can adopt each of them in small, manageable stages. If "keep it simple" appeals to you, you can begin by simplifying the design of your products and making them easier to use and maintain—as Siemens did by launching their SMART initiative. If, on the other hand, you are willing to be bold, you can do what Philips did: simplify *all* your business processes and your *entire* organization—but especially your customer interactions. Likewise, if you are attempting to "do more with less" you can demonstrate frugality by first *reusing* components across existing product lines—just as GM is doing with its "global (vehicle) platforms"

initiative. Later, you can develop your frugal mindset by emulating GE—that is, by designing entirely new, very affordable, high-quality products. Finally, if you are an enlightened bank willing to "include the margin"—that is, the 60 million Americans who are unbanked or underbanked—you can first partner with an organization like the Center for Financial Services Innovation (CFSI) and pilot financial inclusion solutions in a few U.S. cities before scaling them up nationally. Of course, you would have to hurry as you do this, because nimble start-ups and Wal-Mart are already encroaching on your turf by offering basic banking services to underserved communities.

In our companion website (JugaadInnovation.com) we showcase additional tools that can help you prioritize how you implement jugaad and guide you in how to do so effectively.

Prioritizing and adapting the six principles most relevant to your business will help you build buy-in for jugaad across the organization and successfully integrate its most relevant principles into your enterprise—enabling you to use jugaad as a powerful tool to accelerate innovation and growth. The most critical factor, however—one that can make or break the successful adoption of jugaad in an organization—is leadership. Without strong commitment and backing from senior leaders, starting with the CEO, a potent yet disruptive approach like jugaad will fail to take hold in organizations accustomed to the structured approach to innovation.

DRIVING JUGAAD ADOPTION: THE CEO'S AGENDA

Ultimately, jugaad won't take hold in a corporation without active support from the very top. Growth-seeking CEOs have a key role to play in driving the adoption of jugaad across their enterprise. Based on our knowledge of many companies' experiences, we've created a list of dos and don'ts for CEOs seeking to integrate jugaad into their organizations.

Don't Try to Implement Jugaad in a Systematic, Top-Down Fashion   In these recessionary times, CEOs may view jugaad as a silver bullet for driving innovation-led growth. They may be very tempted to adopt—and even impose—jugaad as a new "best practice" that can quickly be implemented in a top-down fashion. Yet such an attempt is more likely than not to fail. You don't roll out jugaad across your organization the same way you roll out a Six Sigma process or an enterprise software tool. Jugaad is neither a process nor a tool nor a scientific method that can be deployed in a top-down way. In spirit and practice, jugaad is closer to a fluid art and culture than a rigorous science. More important, an *organization* doesn't practice jugaad; rather, the *individuals* in that organization do so. CEOs need to exercise restraint, enabling the ingenuity that lies dormant in each one of his or her employees to emerge on its own and flourish from the bottom up.

Do Celebrate Your Existing Jugaad Innovators   Rather than trying to institutionalize jugaad, CEOs should seek instead to identify—and celebrate—those maverick employees who already think and act like jugaad innovators. These mavericks are the "outliers" who defy corporate policies and guidelines to come up with groundbreaking inventions. By publicly celebrating their achievements, CEOs can send a signal to other employees that it's OK to think and act flexibly or do more with less or include the margin. But CEOs should also acknowledge—and even celebrate—the failures of jugaad innovators—to also send the signal that failure in the pursuit of innovation is fine. For instance, Google's ethos celebrates both success and failure. Google's executive chairman Eric Schmidt explains that his company is a risk-tolerant organization where "it's absolutely OK to try something that's very hard, have it not be successful, and take the learning from that."[14]

Do Persuade Skeptical Employees by Creating a Sense of Urgency   CEOs may find it difficult to convince some employees in the United States or Europe to embrace jugaad innovation. These employees may lack the appropriate context to properly appreciate these principles and their relevance in today's complex world. For instance, R&D teams in the West, accustomed to abundant resources and devoted to pushing the technology frontier for its own sake, may find it hard to relate to the jugaad principles of do more with less and keep it simple. Here is some anecdotal evidence to that effect: after attending our workshop on jugaad, a senior executive at a Fortune 500 company pointed to the hundreds of cars in his company's vast parking lot and said, "Look: all I see is abundance, not scarcity. Why should I bother doing more with less?"

Nevertheless, engineers and scientists love challenges. And CEOs can appeal to this competitive spirit by setting R&D teams challenges that are both socioeconomic and technological. These challenges will foster a sense of urgency by creating artificial constraints that favor the emergence of jugaad ideas and "good enough" solutions. For instance, inspired by Ratan Tata (who came up with the idea for a $2,000 car), Renault-Nissan's CEO Carlos Ghosn, who famously coined the term "frugal engineering" in 2006, is challenging his French and Japanese engineers to match and even exceed the cost, performance, and speed of his Indian engineers. In one instance, Mr. Ghosn asked three different R&D teams—one each from France, Japan, and India—to come up with an engineering solution for the same technical problem. The teams came up with solutions of equal quality—yet the Indian engineers' solution cost only one-fifth of what the French and Japanese engineers' solutions cost.[15] Jean-Philippe Salar, a Frenchman who heads Renault's Design Studio in Mumbai, notes that Renault's R&D and marketing leaders in headquarters are learning to appreciate the flexible and frugal mindset of Indian engineers—who think and act like jugaad innovators do.[16] Indeed, as frugal engineering becomes key to competing and winning in the recessionary economies of the West, Renault's executives want to embrace the principles of jugaad in France.

Don't Patent Jugaad Inventions—Monetize Them As the jugaad culture blossoms in companies, it is bound to unleash a torrent of inventions—conceived by thousands of ingenious employees.

Rather than trying to patent them all—which will only cost time and money—companies should focus on *monetizing* the most promising ideas by commercializing them at speed. In this area, Asian companies are ahead of Western companies in their perception of and approach to intellectual property (IP)—as exemplified by Neusoft, China's largest IT solution and service provider. Dr. Liu Jiren, chairman and CEO of Neusoft, explains: "When we introduced our first software in China, it was immediately copied by other Chinese rivals. That's when we realized that even if I had patented an idea, someone else could have come up with a better idea. So we shifted our focus from patenting a single big idea to generating a multitude of ideas and then executing on our ideas as fast as possible. The faster we can monetize our ideas, the better positioned we will be vis-à-vis our competition."[17] Compare Dr. Liu's attitude with the practices more typical of technology companies in Silicon Valley, who tend to place greater emphasis on patenting a single big idea and desperately trying to defend it against competitors—an obsession that often leads to unending lawsuits and counter lawsuits for patent infringement. Jugaad isn't about who has the best ideas, but who is the best at *executing* ideas.

Do Use "Innovation Brokers" to Cross-Pollinate and Synergize Jugaad Ideas

Although "letting a hundred jugaad ideas bloom" is a great way to harness the ingenuity of all employees, there's a danger that companies may miss out on bigger opportunities that could emerge by recombining and integrating multiple ideas in a synergistic solution. To avoid forming "islands of creativity," CEOs need to create an "innovation brokering" function tasked with cross-pollinating and cross-fertilizing jugaad ideas across teams.

For instance, after dabbling in Six Sigma and finding that it stifled innovation, 3M swiftly returned to a more jugaad approach to innovation (see Chapter Two). Now Chief Technology Officer Fred J. Palensky oversees the cross-fertilization of jugaad ideas produced by fiercely independent inventors across the company as a whole. According to Palensky, 3M allows all technical members in its R&D group to invest 15 percent of their time and efforts in programs, interactions, teaching, and learning in areas totally outside their core activities. To enable collaboration and cross-pollination of ideas across business units, 3M has launched more than three hundred joint innovation programs that span multiple divisions. Palensky points out: "All of this creates a community of collaboration and ensures that everybody has some skin in the innovation game. And because our senior leaders have grown up in this culture, they continue to nurture and protect this highly collaborative, enterprising environment."[18]

Do Apply Jugaad to Formulate Robust Strategies   When John F. Kennedy gave voice to the bold vision of putting a man on the moon, he refrained from formulating the precise means by which to achieve that vision. Instead, he allowed the means to emerge organically through the creative input and interplay of the scientific community. Similarly, CEOs must paint a bold vision for their company's future and then trust that employees will tap into the jugaad spirit to come up with the appropriate strategy for realizing this vision. For instance, although Best Buy's vision of expanding globally was driven by top management, the precise means to execute this vision were developed by passionate employees eager to take Best Buy into foreign markets.

Do Use Web 2.0 Collaboration Tools to Harness Customer and Partner Creativity   CEOs should extend the adoption of jugaad beyond the limits of their organization and seek out bright ideas from jugaad innovators in their customer and partner communities as well. To do so, they should invest in social media technologies to engage customers and partners in a dialogue on key issues of relevance to the company. Such grassroots collaboration can help identify challenging problems and generate counterintuitive solutions.

For instance, IBM regularly conducts "jamming" sessions involving hundreds of customers and partners. These sessions help identify major socioeconomic problems, like global warming and the health care crisis, as well as promising ideas that can be developed to tackle these problems. Similarly, design houses such as frog and IDEO are now practicing crowdsourcing: using social medial tools, they are inviting jugaad innovators in cyberspace to put their brains together to solve vexing problems that afflict corporations and societies alike, worldwide.[19] These issues range from the mundane exploration of "how to make a user-friendly fridge" to more serious stuff like how to increase the number of registered bone marrow donors to help save more lives.

Bold, creative leadership is vital for the successful adoption—and integration—of jugaad in an organization. Rather than imposing jugaad as the best practice *du jour*, CEOs should strive to *facilitate* the adoption of jugaad as a grassroots movement that evolves organically and voluntarily. In doing so, CEOs will increase the stickiness of jugaad in the organization so it can deliver sustainable value to the company.[20]

CONCLUSION

Hundreds of corporations, such as GE and PepsiCo, are adopting jugaad practices and integrating them into their existing innovation approaches. But we believe that jugaad isn't applicable only to corporations; it also has relevance to non-governmental organizations (NGOs), governments, and society at large. Indeed, entire nations, especially the developed economies of the West, stand to gain from adopting a jugaad approach to innovation. The good news is that a growing number of grassroots entrepreneurs in the West—especially ordinary citizens and Generation Y—have already begun to apply jugaad to address major issues related to areas such as health care, energy, and education. As a result, a whole jugaad *ecosystem* is emerging in the United States and Europe, with the backing of forward-thinking government agencies and academic institutions.

In the next chapter we describe how corporations can actively support—and benefit from—the groundswell innovation movement unfolding across Western societies, a movement that is emblematic of a return to their jugaad roots and their rebirth as jugaad *nations*.

CHAPTER nInE

BUILDING JUGAAD NATIONS

The highest and best form of efficiency is the spontaneous cooperation of
a free people

— WOODROW WILSON

The jugaad movement is rapidly gaining traction in the West. While some Western organizations are adopting jugaad to catalyze innovation and growth, jugaad is also increasingly being practiced by a broad spectrum of individuals and groups in the West. Led by creative citizens, Millennials, forward-thinking entrepreneurs, venture capitalists, and non-profit organizations, a whole jugaad innovation ecosystem is emerging—to help Western societies improvise frugal and flexible solutions to problems of complexity and scarcity.

Larger institutions in the United States and Europe—such as governments and universities—are actively supporting the emergence of such an ecosystem—and contributing to its sustainability. This emerging ecosystem not only creates an environment for grassroots entrepreneurs to thrive in but also helps Western corporations in their own attempts to practice jugaad innovation. Indeed, corporate leaders—seeking to adopt jugaad in their organizations—can learn from other jugaad innovators in Western economies. By joining this *external* grassroots movement, Western companies can accelerate their *internal* adoption of jugaad—and profit from it handsomely.

THE INGENUITY ECONOMY

The developed world, like the emerging world, is facing its own problems in areas such as health care, education, finance, and community development. Western governments, with their bloated budgets and bureaucracies—and faced with financial meltdown—are severely constrained in their efforts to solve these problems. In such a context, entrepreneurial citizens from all walks of life in the West are increasingly taking matters into their own hands. With a flexible and frugal mindset, these citizens are seeking to address the vexing problems their societies face rather than waiting for their governments to do so.

For example, across the United States ordinary American citizens are coming up with innovative solutions to deal with challenges in health care, energy, and education. These citizen innovators are the Ben Franklins and Cyrus McCormicks of the twenty-first century: they rely on pure American ingenuity to improvise simple yet practical solutions to the problems afflicting their communities. They innovate not in a fancy R&D lab but in their homes and on the streets, doing more with less. Examples of such citizen innovators in the West include the following:

• *The Frugal Housebuilder:* In the aftermath of Hurricane Katrina, Zach Rosenburg and Liz McCartney founded the St. Bernard Project in New Orleans to make homebuilding efficient, "unfettered by prior processes and structure, by reducing construction time by 30% and costs by up to 15%."[1]

• *The Inclusive Doctor:* Dr. Vivian Fonseca, a professor of medicine at Tulane University in New Orleans, helped develop an SMS-based diabetes control solution for elderly and low-income patients that is simple to use and cost-effective.[2]

• *The Resilient Lawyer:* After graduating from law school, Brooke Richie launched the Resilience Advocacy Project to train young kids from underprivileged communities in New York to give their peers free legal advice—allowing them to discover new economic opportunities that can help them break out of multigenerational poverty.

• *The Passionate Educator:* Lily Lapenna has created MyBnk, the UK's first independent, peer-led youth banking program approved by the national banking regulator. In doing so, Lapenna is developing the next generation of financially literate and entrepreneurial citizens. Such literacy will be crucial as the UK economy struggles to avoid another recession. In just five years, thanks to its partnership with dozens of schools and youth organizations, MyBnk has evolved from a pilot project to reach thirty-five thousand eleven- to twenty-five-year-olds in under-privileged neighborhoods of London. These tech-savvy youth learn about managing money and the basics of entrepreneurship through cellphone-based games.[3]

MILLENNIALS LAUNCH THE DIY REVOLUTION IN THE WEST

The groundswell jugaad movement unfolding across the United States and Europe is receiving particular support—and active participation—from the Millennials, aka Generation Y. These North American and European youth, who have witnessed massive corporate layoffs and scandals, are cynical about large enterprises and no longer believe in job stability. They prefer to start their own companies and be their own bosses—thus becoming a do-it-yourself (DIY) generation. According to a survey conducted by The Affluence Collaborative, 40 percent of those in Generation Y plan to launch their own business, and 20 percent already have.[4] But these budding Generation Y entrepreneurs are frugal and think and act flexibly, like the fictional MacGyver. They are big believers in doing more with less. Rather than running big R&D departments, the new DIY start-up generation makes extensive use of social media tools like Facebook in an open source model to cocreate new products and services with their friends around the globe.

Nobody embodies the frugal and flexible mindset of this "do-it-yourself" generation better than Gen Y'er Limor "Ladyada" Fried.

An MIT-trained engineer, Fried is a pioneer of the open source hardware (OSHW) movement.[5] Members of this movement—mostly geeky engineers—make the source code of the electronic products they design available for free on the Web: anyone can download the code and use it to build their own products using off-the-shelf components. Any improvements or additions to the code are shared with other members of the larger community who improve the modified code and share it again with other members—and so the cycle repeats itself. This collaborative method of creation allows the entire community to do more for less—that is, create more products at a low cost, and with a reduced timeline, because members don't have to build code from the ground up every time they start a new project—they can simply reuse code that is already freely available.

Fried's nickname "Ladyada" is a tribute to Lady Ada Lovelace, a nineteenth-century English countess with a gift for mathematics. Lovelace is widely regarded as the first computer programmer in the world, having written perhaps the first algorithm intended to be processed by a machine (Charles Babbage's Analytical Engine).[6] Like Lovelace, Fried is a maverick. When Microsoft launched the Kinect, a motion-sensing input device for the Xbox 360 video game console, Fried organized a $2,000 challenge for open source Kinect drivers. When Microsoft reacted by deeming the challenge an unacceptable modification to their product, Fried responded by raising the prize to $3,000. Microsoft eventually relented and recognized that the Kinect drivers developed by the open source community were of high quality—and very likely far cheaper to develop than investing millions of dollars in R&D. Commenting on this bottom-up innovation, *Wired* magazine wrote: "When DIYers combine those cheap, powerful tools with the collaborative potential of the Internet, they can come up with the kinds of innovations that once sprang only from big-budget R&D labs."[7]

Fried is a prototypical jugaad innovator. From her modest studio in Manhattan, Fried—who labels herself a "citizen engineer"—churns out high-impact gadgets whose source code is immediately made available on her personal web site, www.ladyada.net. Her noteworthy inventions include MintyMP3, a portable music player whose body is essentially an Altoids box (you get "fresh" music with it), and the MONOCHRON clock, a device that displays a "Retro Arcade Table Tennis for Two" (à la PONG, the popular 1970s video game) while telling the time.

Fried also operates an e-commerce site—adafruit.com—that sells the kits and parts for the projects featured on ladyada.net along with other cool open source electronic products. In August 2011, Adafruit.com hit the hundred-thousandth customer mark. Reacting to this milestone, Fried and her teammates wrote on the website: "We'd like to thank all our customers that got us here and we look forward to the next 100,000 chances to make the world a better and smarter place through electronics, engineering and sharing!"

In 2011, Fried received a dual honor: she was named among the Most Influential Women in Technology by *Fast Company* and was featured on the cover of *Wired* magazine.[8] She was the first female engineer ever—and maybe the first ever jugaad innovator—to appear on the magazine's cover. Like many Gen Y'ers, Ladyada has a natural proclivity for jugaad innovation that enables her to improvise frugal and flexible solutions to even the most complex problems. Fried would have made the original Lady Ada proud.

NEXT-GEN ENTREPRENEURS RESHAPE ENTIRE INDUSTRIES

A new wave of flexible-minded jugaad innovators in the United States and Europe—many of them belonging to Generation Y—are turning the conventional practices of many industries upside down, and in the process creating affordable and sustainable products and services that are accessible to more people. Here are some of the ways that jugaad entrepreneurs in the West are reshaping entire industries.

Making Education Playful Several Western entrepreneurs are trying to put the fun back into education by making coursework more engaging if not outright entertaining. These attempts are targeted mainly at Generation Z, a cohort that is more at ease playing with Nintendo and interacting on Facebook than learning through boring old textbooks.

For instance, the Khan Academy is making the intimidating subject of mathematics cool (and fun) for thousands of students worldwide. The "academy" is, in fact, a virtual campus founded by Sal Khan, an MIT-trained former hedge-fund analyst. In 2006, to assist his cousin in New Orleans with her math homework, Khan created and uploaded onto YouTube some rudimentary video tutorials on how to do algebra. His videos quickly went viral. Within days, they were downloaded by thousands of people—students, teachers, and parents—from all over the world. Emboldened by this success, Khan began posting more math tutorials on YouTube. Tens of thousands of users devoured them in no time. Eventually, Khan quit his comfortable financial analyst's job to dedicate all his time to the Khan Academy. His mission was to provide "a free world-class education to anyone anywhere." Today, the Khan Academy offers more than 2,400 short lessons—ranging from ten to twenty minutes each—on a slew of topics ranging from algebra to venture capital. Anyone with a web browser can access them all—for free![9]

Students from West Virginia to Uganda to Vietnam are downloading Khan's videos (all of which he has produced himself) in ten different languages. The huge success of these online tutorials is due to five factors:

1. They are free and easy to access.
2. They are simple to use.
3. They are not time-consuming—by watching Khan's videos, you can learn, in less than twenty minutes, algebra basics that might take two hours to learn in a classroom setting.
4. They are highly engaging, given Khan's conversational style.
5. You can watch them and learn at your own pace without feeling left out or falling behind as in a physical classroom.

In a nutshell, the Khan academy delivers more value at a lower cost for more students worldwide—something that the traditional education system has struggled to accomplish. It's not surprising that Bill Gates has called the Khan Academy "a glimpse of the future of education."

Ntiedo Etuk is another entrepreneur who's making education fun and engaging for young people. Etuk founded DimensionU in New York to create web-based computer games that teach the fundamentals of mathematics, literature, and other essential subjects. The competitive nature of these games provides an incentive for students to play even after school hours. And so they do homework without even realizing that they are doing so![10]

Delivering Quality Health Care to Millions   As of this writing, fifty million Americans lack medical insurance. The United States spends twice as much per person on health care annually as Japan, Canada or Germany and still ranks lower in health indicators. Sensing an opportunity, a growing number of jugaad entrepreneurs in private and public organizations are trying to deliver higher-quality health care to more people at a lower cost in the United States.

For instance, the Centers for Medicare and Medicaid Services—run until recently by Donald Berwick, a Harvard-educated physician—is helping make the bloated health care system leaner. Berwick enabled this by rewarding hospitals and doctors not for the number of procedures they do or the drugs or tests they recommend but for bringing about tangible improvements in patients' health. As he explained: "How *much* doctors and hospitals do has become more important than how *well* they do." Berwick tried to change this state of affairs. Thanks to his initiatives, last year alone the Centers saved Medicare $36 million and earned physicians $29 million in bonuses and cost savings.

Berwick also helped improve the quality of health care by making it safer. For instance, one in seven Medicare patients is hurt during a hospital stay. "Too many Americans are being harmed by the care that is supposed to help them," Berwick pointed out. Rather than imposing any solutions to make health delivery safer, Berwick encouraged hospitals to come up with jugaad innovations to keep patients safe. For instance, he lauded the cardiac intensive care unit at Children's Healthcare of

Atlanta at Egleston for coming up with a deceptively low-tech jugaad innovation: a quiet zone where nurses can place medication orders without being interrupted, even during emergencies. The quiet zone was created after the hospital discovered that distracted staff members were making dangerous mistakes while ordering medicine. Berwick believes such simple and frugal innovations are what are needed to make health care safer, better, and affordable for more Americans.[11]

Enabling Financial Inclusion   As we've mentioned, sixty million Americans are unbanked or underbanked, with poor access to traditional financial services. Banks have traditionally lacked the incentive to serve these financially excluded groups as they were deemed unprofitable. And the global economic recession has only made banks even more conservative. But even as Wall Street retreats further from Main Street, hordes of entrepreneurial start-ups are rising to the challenge by conjuring up inclusive—and profitable—business models to deliver financial services to underbanked Americans.

Says Ryan Gilbert, CEO of one such start-up: "The 'too big to fail' banks are today, simply put, 'too scared to lend' to worthy consumers, due to the higher costs associated with serving non-prime consumers. There is hope, however . . ."[12] Gilbert's start-up BillFloat represents precisely that hope. By providing lower-cost, short-term consumer credit for bill payments, since 2009 BillFloat has helped thousands of consumers across the country avoid exorbitant late fees, overdraft charges, service termination, and high-interest payday loans. The continued economic downturn, combined with banks contracting the amount of available credit, makes the need for services like BillFloat greater than ever for Middle America.

Plastyc is another start-up making financial services affordable and accessible to the masses. Leveraging the power of the Internet and social networks, Plastyc offers 24x7 access to FDIC-insured virtual bank accounts and prepaid Visa cards. Cardholders cannot overdraft on these cards, as they can spend only money they have added beforehand. As a result, there are no late fees and no risk of going into debt. Plastyc's virtual accounts can be accessed from anywhere via the Internet or cellphone. Its iBankUP portal and UPside prepaid cards offer better services (at lower prices) than brick-and-mortar bank checking accounts, with more ways to receive money and no risk of spending more than you actually have.

Most impressively, jugaad innovators in financial services are catalyzing a seismic shift in Western societies: they are inculcating frugal thinking and behavior among spendthrift Western consumers by making *saving* more rewarding and fun than spending. For instance, Plastyc's prepaid cards have built-in automated savings—backed by generous rewards and no maintenance fees—to encourage even people with tight budgets to save more.

Says Patrice Peyret, CEO of Plastyc: "Underbanked and low-income people have the hardest time saving money because they don't have much of it, they have limited access to traditional savings accounts, and interest rates are too low to generate meaningful rewards. Our goal is to turn savings into a habit by making it simple, automatic and rewarding."[13]

For consumers who lack the motivation or ability to save alone and want to save with friends or partners toward a shared goal, PiggyMojo offers a web-based savings tool that uses text messages, social networks, and linked transfers from checking to savings accounts to enable a system of "impulse savings" rather than impulse spending. Here's how it works: First you set a goal for saving; for instance, a serious emergency fund or a more fun "Adopt a Pet." Then you start saving toward that goal. Whenever you overcome the impulse to buy something—like, say, a $5 mocha latte—you text or tweet "I just saved $5" to friends and family, who then cheer you on. And when your friends and family save, you get a message too—thus creating momentum and a virtuous cycle. At the end of each week, you transfer the amount you "saved" that week from your checking to savings account. By giving you an incentive to save "in the moment" and reinforcing your decision with positive feedback from various sources, PiggyMojo makes saving satisfying and fun.[14]

Elevating Entertainment to High Art—Without Breaking the Bank The so-called "creative" industries, like gaming and Hollywood, often churn out safe, relatively uninspiring sequels that consume huge budgets. In contrast, frugal artists are now making games and films that are truly creative and cost much less to develop.

Consider the case of Jason Rohrer, a game developer. Rohrer lives with his wife and three kids on a modest ranch in Las Cruces in the middle of the New Mexico desert where he creates ingenious, meaningful games with high experiential value that he gives away for free (or charges a modest fee for downloading). Rohrer and his family do not own a car; they ride bicycles. They have no insurance or mortgage; they do have a fridge, but they turn it off during the winter. This family of five has voluntarily capped its yearly expenses at $14,500—which represents the family's total annual budget. Rohrer's highly variable income—generated from modest sales of his software and donations—is a far cry from the six-digit salaries earned by top software developers in large gaming companies like Zynga.

Rohrer's frugality also extends to his professional life. His "studio" is actually a tiny office in his home where he relies on a few aging computers (including an eleven-year-old laptop that his sister gave him) to develop his mind-expanding games. "Frugality," he told us, "is indeed a business decision for me. Whenever I'm in a corporate environment, I'm bowled over by the sheer amount of waste that is part of the everyday routine!"[15]

Rohrer's fans love his games because they feel "real"—not because of hyperrealistic graphics (which would typically cost a fortune to develop) but because their stories ring true and feel genuine. Rohrer infuses his games with his own life experiences, and this in turn gives his characters and storylines authenticity. His creations deal with complex sociocultural topics such as marriage, the desire to become an artist, or balancing personal aspirations with family commitments. Whereas in commercial games superhuman heroes mindlessly shoot down monsters, aliens, and criminals, Rohrer's thoughtful characters struggle to overcome their inner demons and cope with personal dilemmas.[16]

The sophistication of the stories in Rohrer's games stands in striking contrast to the frugal simplicity of their user interface: the interface is typically minimalist, even slightly "retro," with no whiz-bang special effects like 3D. His games are rendered in low-resolution graphics—the same ones found in arcade-style games—with characters that look like pixelated gnomes. The frugal look and feel of Rohrer's games hasn't stopped them from rapidly achieving cult status among users worldwide. In 2007, within months of its free online release, Passage—Rohrer's first major game that tackled mortality as its main theme—went viral and achieved a cultlike status among top game developers. The game was even lionized by the *Wall Street Journal* and *Esquire*, which both hailed Rohrer as the pioneer of an entirely new genre of gaming that was closer to "high art" than entertainment.

Clint Hocking, creative director at Ubisoft, the world's fourth-largest game developer, is a big fan of Rohrer's. Hocking has publicly criticized his industry for failing to innovate the way indie developers like Rohrer do—developers who are making "games that matter." Says Hocking: "These games have used what is innate to games—their interactivity—to make a statement about the human condition. And we in the industry seem not to be able to do that."[17]

Thoughtful jugaad-minded individuals like Jason Rohrer live frugally while creating high-art games that are rich in meaning: they deliver better experiential value at less cost for more users. This grassroots movement toward DIY and doing more with less is catching on beyond individuals in the West and is being backed by an unlikely party: governments.

WESTERN GOVERNMENTS ARE JOINING THE JUGAAD BANDWAGON

In several Western nations, governments that used to promote big-ticket R&D projects and top-down innovation policies are recognizing the limits of these growth strategies—especially in a recessionary climate. As a result, visionary American and European policy makers are investing in—and supporting—bottom-up innovation programs. These programs are specifically designed to empower and harness the ingenuity of jugaad innovators at the community level to address pressing socioeconomic issues.

In the United States, the Obama administration has launched several initiatives to stimulate community-led innovation. Perhaps the most significant of these is the White House Office of Social Innovation and Civic Participation (SICP), which was set up by President Obama in early 2009 with an explicit mission to enable social inclusion and spur bottom-up innovations by grassroots entrepreneurs in health care, education, and energy. President Obama noted, "The best solutions don't come from the top-down, not from Washington; they come from the bottom-up in each and every one of our communities."[18] SICP acts as a catalyst to enable such community-driven solutions.

For instance, SICP collaborates with federal agencies to develop incentive-based tools—such as innovation funds, prizes, and other social capital market structures—to channel resources toward community solutions that have *already* achieved demonstrable success, with the goal of helping scale them up. In addition, SICP also acts as an innovation broker by facilitating the cross-fertilization of proven best practices across communities. Finally, SICP helps shape new public-private partnership models that will pave the way for the government to creatively engage the private sector in cocreating innovative solutions that address shared problems at the community level.

For instance, SICP coordinates the Social Innovation Fund—a public-private partnership model launched with $50 million seed capital from the U.S. Congress. The fund identifies and supports the most promising, results-oriented community programs led by grassroots jugaad innovators that can be replicated in other communities facing similar challenges.[19] It focuses on high-priority areas for the country's socioeconomic development: education, health care, youth development, and economic opportunity. The fund also partners with foundations and corporations that commit matching resources, funding, and technical assistance. One of the fund's inaugural awardees is

Venture Philanthropy Partners (VPP), founded by Mario Marino with a vision of applying a venture approach to philanthropy. VPP leads the youthCONNECT initiative—a pioneering network that brings together government, private philanthropy, and non-profit organizations to dramatically improve socioeconomic opportunities available to low-income youth (age fourteen to twenty-four) in the Washington, DC region.

Sonal Shah, the first director of the SICP, explained to us:

> The United States has traditionally approached innovation with top-down policies that focused on improving the *inputs* of the innovation system—like R&D spending—without bothering about improving the *output*—i.e., the impact of the innovation on our socioeconomic development. The SICP was set up to catalyze a new paradigm of innovation that is bottom-up and incentive-based. Rather than legislating innovation policies in a top-down fashion—the old "stick" approach—SICP is creating *incentives* for driving positive changes at the grassroots community level—the "carrot" approach. Innovations in emerging markets are happening in a bottom-up fashion led by grassroots innovators, like jugaad entrepreneurs in India. We are helping develop a similar grassroots model in the United States to effectively address our pressing socioeconomic issues. Rather than debating whether America deserves a big or small government, we should all focus our efforts on building a "democracy" with lower-case "d": grassroots democracy is what America is all about.[20]

Efforts by the U.S. federal government, such as the SICP, are being matched by projects undertaken by state and local governments. For instance, policy makers in economically depressed cities are boosting incentives to attract and retain jugaad innovators who can help reinvigorate ailing local economies. The Merrimack Valley in Massachusetts—one of the most economically depressed regions in the United States—has partnered with the Deshpande Foundation to launch the Merrimack Valley Sandbox, hosted by the University of Massachusetts in Lowell. The Sandbox brings together local colleges, non-profit organizations, and corporations to boost entrepreneurship

among students and professionals and to cultivate local leadership
through mentoring and seed funding programs. These jugaad
entrepreneurs and leaders work with local authorities to identify and
develop highly relevant solutions that bring benefit to their communities. Gururaj "Desh" Deshpande, the serial technology entrepreneur
who heads the Deshpande Foundation, says: "For innovation to have
impact, it needs relevance. Innovation plus relevance equals impact.
Innovation is getting trapped at MIT and in intellectual circles. [But]
not everybody needs to try to be MIT or Harvard. They can define a
new role of developing relevance and doing things that are good for
local business."[21]

Across the Atlantic, the British government is also keen to encourage jugaad innovators. In mid-2010, we were invited to Number 10
Downing Street to meet Rohan Silva, a senior policy advisor to Prime
Minister David Cameron. Silva had read our *Harvard Business Review*
blog on jugaad and wanted our perspective on how the British government could "do more with less"—a theme dominating UK politics as
Cameron attempts to replace "Big Government" with "Big Society"
and empower communities and citizens in the process.[22] Silva explained
that Cameron wants to see more jugaad entrepreneurs flourish in the
UK, and that he wants to encourage bottom-up solutions for making
health care, energy, and education affordable and accessible to all.

The reasons behind this are obvious. In the UK, public sector
borrowing rose to £175 billion (US$274 billion) or 12.4 percent of
GDP in 2009—a peacetime record and the highest level of borrowing
of all developed economies.[23] This dire situation has forced the UK
government to launch several initiatives—particularly in areas such
as health care and education—that seek to deliver more value for
citizens at less cost and "include the margin." For instance, the "Free
Schools" initiative empowers grassroots groups of parents and local
citizens to start their own schools, which make decisions on staffing and
curriculum design independently of local authorities. These schools will
receive public funds based on how many students enroll, with those
from poor families attracting a premium. The attempt here is to make

public money go further and to shake up the state system while also being more inclusive.

Not to be outdone by the British, the French government is also encouraging more citizens to become jugaad innovators and catalyze growth. With unemployment stuck at 10 percent, the French government is expanding efforts to liberalize France's highly regulated economy and make life easier for entrepreneurs (after all, the word *entrepreneur* is French). Thus on January 1, 2009, the French government launched the "auto-entrepreneur" initiative to allow professionals to register their small businesses online in just a few minutes and benefit from a simplified and generous tax structure, thus bypassing France's labyrinthine bureaucracy and convoluted tax system. Since its launch, more than seven hundred thousand French citizens have become jugaad innovators by signing up for the auto-entrepreneur program.[24]

France is already familiar with Système D, the French expression for jugaad-like improvised innovation. The D in Système D is short for *débrouillard,* which refers to a flexible, quick-thinking, and resourceful person who is able to extract himself from any predicament.[25] Système D is a tribute to those French entrepreneurs who rely on their ingenuity and resourcefulness to build their new businesses in spite of France's notorious bureaucracy. Now, with the auto-entrepreneur initiative sanctioned by no less than the French government itself, the country is poised to see jugaad innovation spread more broadly in the coming decade.

Such government-led initiatives to catalyze growth by enabling jugaad are receiving generous support from philanthropists and funding bodies. For instance, the New Economy Initiative for Southeast Michigan (NEI) is a unique philanthropic initiative launched in 2008 by the Ford Foundation and others. NEI partners have together committed $100 million to be spent over an eight-year period to accelerate the transformation—driven by nimble jugaad entrepreneurs—of the industrial economy of metropolitan Detroit (home to America's once-mighty carmakers) into an innovation-based economy. NEI is also supported by the Kauffman Foundation, one of America's largest foundations devoted to entrepreneurship development. In a similar vein, Venture for America (VFA)—launched in 2012—offers $100,000 each to graduates of top universities to launch their start-ups in the inner cities of Louisiana and Tennessee and contribute to local economic development. Finally, "crowd-funding" sites like Kickstarter.com enable grassroots entrepreneurs across the United States to raise funds from the general public online within days or weeks.

Jugaad has the potential to represent the truest and most creative expression of a democracy: one in which innovation is led by the people, for the people, and with the people. One could call this Democracy 2.0, a form of government in which interconnectivity and diversity are leveraged to build resilient, equitable, and sustainable societies that can meet all the challenges of complexity. A growing number of visionary policy makers in the United States and Europe are encouraging Democracy 2.0 to flourish by setting up the right incentive systems and grassroots institutions to promote jugaad innovation and growth.

TRAINING FUTURE JUGAAD INNOVATORS

Leading American and European universities are also playing their part in creating jugaad nations. They are doing so through programs that imbue the next generation of engineers and managers with a jugaad mindset and its associated principles. Specifically, these programs are creating future leaders who can think and act flexibly, do more with less, keep things simple, and include the margin. By internalizing the principles of jugaad, these future leaders will be able to design and deliver affordable and sustainable solutions that are relevant not only for developing nations but also for developed economies in the West. These academic programs are training Western youth to think and act like jugaad innovators.

Stanford University's "Entrepreneurial Design for Extreme Affordability"   At Stanford University, one of the most popular courses at the business school teaches aspiring entrepreneurs how to raise capital for their start-ups. But a growing number of MBAs are now also enrolling in "Entrepreneurial Design for Extreme Affordability," a course on frugal innovation taught by Professor James Patell and his colleagues David Beach and Stuart Coulson.

As noted by Paul Polak, author of *Out of Poverty*, 90 percent of the world's products and services are designed for 10 percent of the world's population—to meet the desires, rather than actual needs, of the richest people on earth.[26] Professor Patell's course aims to correct this imbalance. Over a six-month period, students from across disciplines—engineering, business, medicine, public policy, even law—work intensively in teams to design, prototype, and commercialize products that cost a fraction of those available in the U.S. market—and address the real needs of 90 percent of the world's population. Rather than reinventing the wheel, students are encouraged to use inexpensive, readily available, eco-friendly materials when developing their products. For instance, one team used local, recyclable parts to make infusion pumps for resource-constrained hospitals in Bangladesh at one-thirtieth of their current cost in the West. Not only is the pump inexpensive, it is also of a quality required for FDA approval. Jane Chen, Linus Liang, Naganand Murty, and Rahul Panicker—introduced in Chapter Three—are alumni of Professor Patell's program and cofounders of Embrace, which has developed low-cost infant warmers for use in both emerging markets like India and developed economies like the United States.

Professor Patell explained to us how these frugal design techniques lend themselves to application in the United States itself. For instance, one of his student teams is using sustainable architectural practices to build affordable solar greenhouses for the White Mountain Apache Tribe in Eastern Arizona. All the materials that go into these structures are 100-percent locally sourced, making them cheaper to build. Native American youth then use these greenhouses to grow fruits and vegetables using traditional agricultural practices. Thus, the greenhouses not only revitalize the local economy, they also help preserve local cultural history. Professor Patell proudly says, "Whatever my students make may seem cheap, but we ensure it is classy, useful, sustainable, and of high quality."[27] In sum, the approach delivers a lot more with a lot less (see JugaadInnovation.com for video interviews with Professor Patell, his students who participated in the White Mountain Apache Tribe project, and Jane Chen, CEO of Embrace).

Santa Clara University's Frugal Innovation Labs   At the heart of Silicon Valley, the School of Engineering and the Center for Science, Technology, and Society at Santa Clara University are jointly training—through the newly formed Frugal Innovation Labs—a new generation of engineers who won't be rushing to Facebook or Google for jobs after they graduate. Rather, these students are acquiring new competencies in engineering and management to help them design simple, affordable, and accessible solutions—based on technologies like mobile computing—that address the socioeconomic needs of underdeveloped communities in areas such as clean energy, clean water, and public health. The students are taught how to innovate under severe constraints—by doing more with less. They are also trained in how to boost the "appropriateness" of their frugal solutions by taking into account the specific needs of underserved communities as well as their unique sociocultural context.

For instance, one student team worked closely with Healthpoint Services India to improve delivery of clean water in rural communities. Healthpoint Services owns and operates a network of medical clinics—known as E Health Points (EHPs)—and clean water access points known as Waterpoints. EHPs provide families in Indian villages with basic health services—delivered via telemedicine. Although most Waterpoints are attached to EHPs, some are freestanding stations located away from EHPs in places where they are more accessible to users. The commercial sale of clean water through Waterpoints generates a steady revenue stream that helps subsidize the health services delivered in the clinics. Unfortunately, Waterpoints are currently operated manually by local operators—who may not always be attentive or honest while managing these stations. The student team from

Santa Clara University is helping address this problem by designing and implementing a telemetry solution that can totally automate water distribution at Waterpoints—enabling Healthpoint Services, in the process, to rapidly scale up the number of EHPs as well as Waterpoint units across rural India.[28]

Radha Basu, who heads the Frugal Innovation Labs at Santa Clara University, points out that these affordable solutions developed by her students can be deployed not only in emerging markets but also in developed nations like the United States that are increasingly confronted with the problems of scarcity. "For most Western firms, upwards of 50 percent of growth in the next decade will come from emerging markets. Yet none of the [more traditional] technologies developed here in Silicon Valley are appropriate to the needs of emerging market consumers," notes Basu. "Western firms need to acquire new core competencies—that we are teaching here—to not only design high-quality and low-cost products but also develop appropriate *business models* and partnership strategies to make and distribute these frugal products to the masses in emerging markets. By developing these new competencies, Western firms can not only be successful in emerging markets, but even in developed economies like the United States, which are confronted with scarcity due to the deepening economic recession."[29]

University of Cambridge's Inclusive Design Program   In the UK, the Engineering Design Centre at the University of Cambridge's Department of Engineering is going one step further than its counterparts across the Atlantic. Rather than merely training undergraduates to design products that are accessible to and usable by marginalized Western consumers (such as the elderly), the Centre, in partnership with the faculty of education at Cambridge, has piloted its programs for even eleven- to fourteen-year-old students in a number of schools.

Ian Hosking, a senior research associate at the Centre, explains:

> We have seen that students at a very young age can genuinely engage with the issue of aging and create highly innovative solutions. Studies have shown that very young children are particularly

good at divergent thinking—that is, they are able to combine unre-lated concepts from diverse domains and come up with unusual solutions in the process. Divergent thinking is key to creative prob-lem solving. Sadly, this ability seems to get lost as children get older and go through an education system that does not always foster cre-ative skills. We have formed a very successful partnership with Bill Nicholl at the faculty of education who is a leading expert in creativ-ity. Working together, we hope to reverse this process somewhat and bring the creative spark back into these children's lives.[30]

Called Designing Our Tomorrow (DOT), this innovative pro-gram has developed resources for teachers to teach an inclusive approach to design. This includes using elements from the Inclusive De-sign Toolkit (www.inclusivedesigntoolkit.com) that undergraduates in universities—as well as designers in companies—can use to develop products and services that address the needs of marginal consumers in an aging population. DOT therefore prepares school children not only for a university education but also for when they enter the workforce.

Moreover, DOT doesn't stop at education in the classroom. The output from one of the pilot schools was of such a high standard that Hosking's team arranged for the students to present their work—the design of cutlery solutions for the elderly—to a major UK retailer. Hosking says: "When I saw what the kids were doing, I was blown away. Their understanding of the issues related to aging was quite impressive. I wanted them to present their work to this retailer, not just because it would be a good experience for them but also because their ideas had genuine commercial potential for the retailer as well. This is something that we want to extend in the future to enhance the relevance of what they are being taught."[31]

The potential of DOT is spreading, with interest from other coun-tries, and the team is currently piloting the resources in one of these countries that is considering a national rollout.

Design for America Design for America (DFA) is a network of student-led studios—spanning U.S. universities like Columbia,

Stanford, Northwestern, and the University of Oregon at Eugene—that is using interdisciplinary design to revitalize U.S. cities. DFA's goal is to form a "new generation of 'creative activists' equipped with the mind-set and skills to create social impact in local communities across the United States."[32] Fifty DFA studios are expected to pop up across the United States in the next five years to address big challenges in education, health care, and the environment.

Yuri Malina, the twenty-one-year-old cofounder of DFA, told us:

> DFA was started with the observation that if you are a young American engineer or designer, you don't need to buy a $1,000 plane ticket to go to Africa or India to do development work. There are enough problems to solve right in your backyard—be they making health care safer and affordable, education better, or finding renewable energy solutions. Whether you live in San Francisco, Boston, or Chicago, you can apply your creative insights not just to design the next iPod or pair of cool sunglasses but rather to fix problems in your own neighborhood.[33]

DFA members work on "super-local" projects—meaning that all projects undertaken are located in neighborhoods accessible within the radius of a fifteen-minute bike ride from their studio. For instance, in his first project, Malina worked with a local hospital in Chicago to design a portable "roll-on" hand-sanitizer for busy physicians and nurses so they can clean their hands on the go. This is a highly practical innovation, given that, according to the Centers for Disease Control and Prevention, approximately two million people in the United States get a hospital-acquired infection (HAI) each year. Of those, roughly a hundred thousand die prematurely from this infection.[34]

Many of the engineers and designers graduating from the academic programs just described are likely to become the social entrepreneurs of tomorrow. These graduates are likely to use their frugal engineering skills to address the basic needs of underserved communities—by fixing unreliable electricity and transportation networks, making health care delivery more inclusive, and setting up sustainable water and sanitation systems. But a growing number of these graduates are also likely to join Fortune 500 companies and help ignite the jugaad spirit in these organizations as they seek to enable bottom-up innovation to address needs in global markets, the increasing scarcity of resources in the West, and growing global complexity more generally. Either way, these next-generation jugaad innovators will not operate in isolation. Given their great fondness for and deftness with social networking media, these innovators are sure to link up with like-minded innovators elsewhere, including in the emerging world—thus accelerating the rise of a global community of jugaad innovators.

THE RISE OF A GLOBAL COMMUNITY OF JUGAAD INNOVATORS

As American innovators connect with jugaad innovators in other parts of the world, especially in emerging markets, this process is helping to cross-pollinate creative ideas across regions. In time, this global community of jugaad innovators could combine, say, American and Indian ingenuity to frugally and sustainably address the major challenges facing humanity. In this section we highlight just a few of the many organizations and initiatives now at work in creating such a globally integrated network of jugaad innovators.

Ashoka and Skoll Foundation   Both of these non-profit organizations actively support thousands of jugaad entrepreneurs worldwide by giving them funding and training to address major socioeconomic challenges. Having spent millions developing the capabilities of these individual entrepreneurs, Ashoka and Skoll Foundation are now keen to promote collaboration among these entrepreneurs by integrating them into virtual communities. To that effect, these organizations have actively invested in social networking platforms—such as Ashoka's AshokaHub and Skoll Foundation's Social Edge—to cross-fertilize ideas and best practices among jugaad entrepreneurs across five continents.

Endeavor This non-profit organization has developed an unrivalled global network of seasoned business leaders who provide mentorship and strategic advice to high-impact jugaad entrepreneurs around the world—especially in emerging economies. Linda Rottenberg founded Endeavor fourteen years ago, after an Argentinian taxi cab driver with a Ph.D. in physics asked her: "How can I possibly start my own company when I don't even have a garage?"[35]

The Stanford-India Biodesign Program This initiative brings together physicians, engineers, and designers from the United States and India to cocreate affordable, user-friendly medical devices that can be deployed not only in India, where hundreds of millions of citizens lack access to basic health care, but also in the United States, where fifty million Americans lack medical insurance. Recently, a team of physicians, engineers, and designers at Stanford collaborated with their counterparts at the Indian Institute of Technology and the All India Institute of Medical Sciences in New Delhi to conceptualize and develop a low-cost bone drill—a device that, in less a minute, delivers life-saving fluids directly into the bone marrow of victims of accidents whose veins have collapsed. The device costs a mere $20 compared to $300 for the equivalent devices available in the United States.[36]

New York City's Next Idea Innovation Competition Actively promoted by New York City's Mayor Michael Bloomberg, Next Idea is an annual competition that invites teams of students from leading business and engineering schools in Europe, Asia, and Latin America to develop business plans for bold jugaad projects that will be executed in New York City and bring major socioeconomic benefits to the city. The NYC Next Idea 2009–2010 edition was won by an entrepreneurial team from the Indian Institute of Technology, Madras (IIT-M), that has devised a new system to allow utility companies and energy producers to store and distribute energy safely and efficiently through remote sites across New York's five boroughs—thus helping avoid a repeat of the 2003 blackout that crippled the city.

The New York City Next Idea competition, as well as the other initiatives just mentioned—Ashoka, Skoll, Endeavor, Stanford-India Biodesign—all aim to connect jugaad innovators in the United States with their counterparts in other countries, cross-fertilizing promising ideas across geographical boundaries to address common socioeconomic issues. One person who is highly enthusiastic about this effort is Alec Ross, senior advisor for innovation to Secretary of State Hillary Clinton. A former entrepreneur, Ross is Secretary Clinton's "tech guru." With more than 370,000 followers on Twitter, Ross is leading the U.S. State Department's efforts to find practical technical solutions for some of the globe's most vexing problems in health care, poverty, human rights, and ethnic conflict.

Speaking to us, Ross said: "Everyone is talking about the shift of power from West to East. But the real shift of power happening now is from big institutions to small institutions. Hierarchical power structures and top-down innovation models are being replaced by networked power structures and bottom-up innovation approaches. To thrive in the new multipolar world, America must relinquish its insular view of innovation and start brokering and facilitating global networks of grassroots innovators who can cocreate solutions to global problems we all share."[37]

HOW COMPANIES CAN PROFIT FROM THE GROUNDSWELL JUGAAD MOVEMENT

This emerging grassroots jugaad ecosystem—made up of activist citizens, socially minded entrepreneurs, forward-thinking governments, universities, and innovation-funding bodies—can help corporations accelerate their own adoption of jugaad. Here are some ways companies can contribute to the *groundswell* jugaad movement—and profit from it.

Support Grassroots Jugaad Innovators to Revitalize Local Economies Western CEOs who complain about the anemic economic growth in North America and Europe don't realize that they have the power to spur demand for their goods and services by supporting grassroots innovators who are striving to revitalize local economies. To do so, Western companies should partner with government bodies like the White House's SICP and non-profit organizations to harness the creative power of grassroots jugaad innovators in catalyzing community development. For instance, Charles Schwab Bank has partnered with the Center for Financial Services Innovation (CFSI) to launch the Bay Area Financial Capability Innovators Development Lab.[38] This initiative offers peer-learning and review opportunities to grassroots jugaad entrepreneurs in the Bay Area who are using innovative approaches to make financial services available to the sixty million unbanked and underbanked Americans. Similarly, Microsoft and Google are funding Code for America—a nonpolitical organization that offers fellowships to web professionals to develop applications that can help financially stretched city governments in the United States become more open and efficient in responding to citizens' needs. Code for America will replicate successful web applications across multiple U.S. cities as a way to improve governance and socioeconomic development nationwide.

Use Social Power to Innovate Faster, Better, and Cheaper

The groundswell jugaad movement is facilitated by social media tools such as Facebook and Twitter. These tools enable activist citizens—especially Millennials—to instantly organize into large online communities that bring about major change at warp speed (such as toppling governments in the Middle East or exposing corporations that indulge in inappropriate business practices). Most Western companies feel threatened by the social power of these virtual communities of jugaad innovators. But as David Kirkpatrick, author of *The Facebook Effect*, puts it: "Social power can help keep your company vital. Newly armed customer and employee activists can become the source of creativity, innovation, and new ideas to take your company forward."[39]

Ford is one company that is harnessing social power to great benefit by integrating social media into every aspect of how it designs, builds, and markets its products. "Digital suffrage is upon us," observes

Venkatash Prasad, who leads Ford's product social networking efforts. "Everyone has a right to a byte of the action, and we have embraced this might of the byte within Ford, through the use of internal and external social networks."[40] For instance, ahead of the launch of its Fiesta sub-compact car in 2010, Ford invited one hundred active bloggers—many of whom were Millennials—to test-drive the car and regularly post videos and unfiltered impressions on YouTube, Twitter, and their individual blogs. Ford's jugaad innovation in marketing—dubbed "Fiesta Movement"—paid off: it generated seven million YouTube views and forty million Tweets (mostly favorable). The grassroots media campaign generated great awareness among young car buyers for Fiesta; it also helped Ford shed its stodgy image and reposition itself as a "cool" automaker. The Fiesta has since become of one of Ford's best-selling cars ever: within ten months of its launch, the Fiesta had conquered one-fifth of the subcompact car segment in the United States. Scott Monty, Ford's head of social media, explains, "Ford doesn't have a social media strategy—it's a business strategy supported by social media."[41]

Recruit Jugaad Innovators from American and European Campuses Western companies seeking to strengthen their jugaad innovation skills—such as doing more with less and including the margin—can find those valuable skills in the next generation of American and European graduates from programs such as Stanford's Entrepreneurial Design for Extreme Affordability and the University of Cambridge's Inclusive Design program. Western companies should hire these flexible-minded students to create frugal and sustainable solutions aimed at serving the growing number of thrifty and eco-conscious Western consumers. For instance, large HMOs could engage students in the Design for America network to devise innovative solutions for making health care safer and more affordable to underserved communities in inner cities in the United States.

Harness Ingenuity Across Borders with Global Innovation Networks The global economy is growing ever more connected, thanks to social media tools like Facebook—enabling talented jugaad innovators in both Western and emerging markets to cocreate break-through solutions that no single region can develop on its own. The Stanford-India Biodesign Program described earlier exemplifies such a synergistic and *polycentric* innovation model.[42] Companies must inte-grate themselves into these global networks of jugaad innovators to take advantage of the unique skills, ideas, and opportunities available across multiple regions. For example, Xerox and Procter & Gamble each orchestrate global innovation networks that integrate the creativity of jugaad entrepreneurs in Asia with the talent of their R&D teams in Europe and the United States to cocreate high-quality and affordable products and services for global markets.[43]

By integrating themselves into the grassroots innovation ecosystem in their societies and by partnering with the various stakeholders in this ecosystem, Western companies can accelerate the adoption of jugaad in their own organizations. By joining such ecosystems, Western companies will add more momentum to—and greatly benefit from—the groundswell jugaad movement under way in the West.

A PROSPEROUS WORLD OF JUGAAD

The West is increasingly confronted with scarcity and unpredictabil-ity. As cash-strapped governments become increasingly unable to deal with these challenges on their own, ordinary citizens, forward-thinking entrepreneurs, venture capitalists, and non-profit organizations are step-ping into the breach. These grassroots jugaad innovators are using their flexible thinking to improvise frugal solutions to vexing socioeconomic problems in health care, education, financial services, and community development. However, as described in this chapter, governments are not standing idly by. From the United States to the UK and France, cen-tral and local governments are busy initiating programs to support and accelerate the grassroots jugaad movement. Universities too are joining in these efforts. Keenly aware of the problems of scarcity and volatility afflicting Western economies, several higher education institutions in the United States and Europe are training a new breed of engineers and managers to design next-generation products and services that can deal with scarcity in a frugal and sustainable manner.

All this might lead one to conclude that jugaad is finally coming to the West from elsewhere. But a longer view suggests that jugaad never actually left the West. If anything, the grassroots innovation movement we describe is emblematic of the West's *return* to its jugaad roots. America was, is, and indeed may always be the land of jugaad innovators—resilient individuals who employ flexible thinking to develop ingenious solutions with limited resources. What may have changed, if anything, is that in an increasingly interconnected world, Western jugaad innovators now no longer work on their own. Rather, through rich partnerships and by using social media platforms such as Facebook and Twitter, they are connecting with jugaad innovators elsewhere to solve our common problems.

This is all good news for Western corporations; now they can and should speed up their internal adoption of jugaad by connecting with the grassroots innovation movement unfolding across Western nations. By integrating their own organizations into local as well as global networks of jugaad innovators, Western companies can become resilient organizations that think frugally, act flexibly, and generate breakthrough growth. The sooner they do so, the better—not only for them but also for a world in a battle against scarcity of time and resources. For the challenges this brave new world poses, jugaad innovation offers a powerful solution.

NOTES

Chapter 1

1. Professor Anil Gupta, Indian Institute of Management in Ahmedabad, personal interview with Simone Ahuja, January 9, 2009.

2. Mansukh Prajapati, personal interview with Simone Ahuja, January 9, 2009.

3. "Infrastructure 2011." Urban Land Institute and Ernst & Young, 2011.

4. "Forbes Lists Top Seven 'Rural Indians.'" [http://news.in.msn.com/business/article.aspx?cp-documentid=4579411]. November 15, 2010.

5. "Stretching the Rupee to the Maximum." [http://indiandream.blogspot.com/2007/05/stretching-rupee-to-maximum.html]. May 4, 2007.

6. V. Muniz, "Campana Brothers." [http://bombsite.com/issues/102/articles/3040]. 2008.

7. Segal, A. "China's Innovation Wall: Beijing's Push for Homegrown Technology." *Foreign Affairs*, September 28, 2010.

8. Daniels, S. "Making Do. Innovation in Kenya's Informal Economy." [http://www.analoguedigital.com/docs/makingdo-download-lores.pdf]. 2010.

9. Neuwirth, R. "The Shadow Superpower." *Foreign Policy*, October 28, 2011.

10. In the *MacGyver* TV series popular in the late 1980s, the resourceful secret agent MacGyver carries no gun and relies purely on ingenuity

229

to solve complex problems using whatever limited resources he has at hand—usually duct tape and a Swiss Army knife.

11. "Cyrus McCormick." [http://web.mit.edu/invent/iow/mccormick .html]. "The 20th Century Transformation of U.S. Agriculture and Farm Policy." United States Department of Agriculture, Economic Information Bulletin, June 2005.

12. Bellis, M. "Cyrus McCormick—the Reaper." [http://inventors.about .com/library/inventors/blmccormick.htm].

13. *Inventors and Inventions*, Vol. 4. Tarrytown, NY: Marshall Cavendish, 2008.

14. "Cyrus McCormick." [http://www.pbs.org/wgbh/theymadeamerica /whomade/mccormick_hi.html].

15. "Benjamin Franklin, Entrepreneur." [http://www.benfranklin300 .org/etc_article_entrepreneur.htm].

16. "Franklin Stove." [http://web.mit.edu/invent/iow/franklin.html].

17. Bellis, M. "The Inventions and Scientific Achievements of Benjamin." [http://inventors.about.com/od/fstartinventors/ss/Franklin_invent_2 .htm].

18. Franklin, B. *The Autobiography of Benjamin Franklin: 1706–1757*. Bedford, MA: Applewood Books, 2008.

19. Jaruzelski, B., Loehr, J., and Holman, R. "The Global Innovation 1000: Why Culture Is Key." *strategy+business*, Winter 2011.

20. Jaruzelski, B., Dehoff, K., and Bordi, R. "The Booz Allen Hamilton Global Innovation 1000: Money Isn't Everything." *strategy+business*, Winter 2005.

21. Key Industry Facts About PhRMA. [http://www.phrma.org/about/key-industry-facts-about-phrma].

22. Hirschler, B. "'Last Chance' for Sickly Pharma to Deliver on R&D." [http://www.reuters.com/article/2011/02/10/pharmaceuticals-rd-idUSLDE71912R20110210]. February 10, 2011.

23. Schaper, E. V. "How Novartis Plans to Avoid the 'Patent Cliff.'" [http://www.businessweek.com/magazine/how-novartis-plans-to-avoid-the-patent-cliff-08042011.html]. August 4, 2011.

24. "Contribution of the Automotive Industry to the Economies of All Fifty States and the United States." [http://www.cargroup.org/pdfs /association_paper.pdf]. April 2010.

25. Gardner, G. "GM Cars: Good December Sales Can't Make Up for Poor 2010." *Christian Science Monitor*, January 5, 2011.

26. Isidore, C. "Big Three Want More Money in Bailout." [http://money .cnn.com/2008/12/02/news/companies/automakers_plans/index. htm]. December 4, 2008.

27. Bunkley, N. "G.M. Repays U.S. Loan, While Chrysler Posts Improved Quarterly Results." *New York Times*, April 21, 2010; "The U.S. Motor Vehicle Industry: Confronting a New Dynamic in the Global Economy." Congressional Research Service, March 26, 2010.

28. "Six Sigma: So Yesterday?" [http://www.businessweek.com/magazine /content/07_24/b4038409.htm]. June 11, 2007.

29. Pascale, R., Sternin, J., and Sternin, M. *The Power of Positive Deviance: How Unlikely Innovators Solve the World's Toughest Problem*. Boston, MA: Harvard Business School Press, 2010.

30. Gladwell, M. *Outliers*. Boston, MA: Little, Brown, and Company, 2008.

31. Hindo, B. "At 3M, a Struggle Between Efficiency and Creativity." *Bloomberg Businessweek*, June 11, 2007.

32. Tellis, G., Prabhu, J., and Chandy. R. "Radical Innovation Across Nations: The Preeminence of Corporate Culture." *Journal of Marketing*, 2003, *73*(1), 3–23.

33. McDonald, B. "Touching Lives, Improving Life: Why Innovation Matters and How to Make It Work." [http://www.pg.com/en_US /downloads/company/purpose_people/touching_lives_improving_life .pdf]. December 2008.

34. Jana, R. "Facebook's Design Strategy: A Status Update." [http://designmind.frogdesign.com/articles/facebook-s-design-strategy- a-status-update.html].

35. Kirkpatrick, D. "Social Power and the Coming Corporate Revolution." *Forbes*, September 26, 2011, p. 72.

36. "Capitalizing on Complexity. Insights from the 2010 IBM Global CEO Study." [http://www-935.ibm.com/services/us/ceo/ceostudy- 2010/].

37. Stangler, D., and Litan, R.E. "Where Will the Jobs Come From?" Ewing Marion Kauffman Foundation, November 2009.

38. Censky, A. "Poverty Rate Rises in America." [http://money.cnn.com /2011/09/13/news/economy/poverty_rate_income/index.htm]. September 13, 2011.

39. "The Great American Divide." *Time*, October 10, 2011, p. 29.

40. Wolf, Z. B., and Arnall, D. "Debt Debate for Dummies: Six Keys to Understanding the Issue." *ABC News*, July 8, 2011.

41. Kirkup, J. "Britain's National Debt to Reach £1.4 Trillion Under 2009 Budget." *Telegraph*, April 22, 2009.

42. Koch, W. "Global Warming Raises Water Shortage Risks in One-Third of U.S. Counties." *USA Today*, July 20, 2010.

43. Palmer, K. "Why Gen Y May Be Too Frugal." *US News and World Report*, March 2, 2011.

44. May, M. "Hispanics Expected to be State's Majority by 2042: Alameda County to Have Top Proportion of Asian Americans." *San Francisco Chronicle*, July 10, 2007, p. C1.

45. Pink, D. *Free Agent Nation: The Future of Working for Yourself.* New York: Business Plus, 2002.

46. "World Energy Outlook 2011." International Energy Agency, 2011.

47. The acronym BRICs (Brazil, Russia, India, and China) was coined by former Goldman Sachs chief economist Jim O'Neill in a 2001 paper entitled "The World Needs Better Economic BRICs."

48. Wilson, D., and Purushothaman, R. "Dreaming with BRICs: The Path to 2050." *Global Economics Paper No. 99*, Goldman Sachs, October 1, 2003.

49. "Ernst & Young Rapid Growth Markets Forecast (RGMF)." [http://www.ey.com/IN/en/Newsroom/News-releases/Ernst-and-Young-Rapid-Growth-Markets-Forecast]. October 24, 2011.

50. "South Asia: India." [https://www.cia.gov/library/publications/the-world-factbook/geos/in.html]. October 21, 2011.

51. Dr. Liu Jiren, chairman and CEO, Neusoft, personal interview with Navi Radjou, September 15, 2011.

52. Abi Naha, CEO, Zone V, personal interview with Navi Radjou, June 23, 2011.

53. The Best Buy–supported television series *Indique: Big Ideas from Emerging India* ran on PBS stations in 2010.

Chapter 2

1. "Access to Electricity." [http://www.iea.org/weo/electricity.asp]. 2010.

2. Tulsi Tanti, chairman and managing director, Suzlon Energy, personal interview with Navi Radjou, November 14, 2011.

3. *Doing Business in a More Transparent World. Economy Profile: India.* Washington, DC: The World Bank and the International Finance Corporation, 2012.

4. *Doing Business in South Asia 2007.* Washington, DC: The World Bank, 2007.

5. *Rural Roads. A Lifeline for Villages in India.* The World Bank, 2000.

6. Majumdar, B. "India's Poor Healthcare a Threat to Growth: Report." [http://in.reuters.com/article/2009/09/16/idINIndia-42468920090916]. September 16, 2009.

7. Granito, A. "80% of Indians Live on Less Than $2 a Day: WB." [http://www.livemint.com/articles/2007/10/16235421/80-of-Indians-live-on-less-th.html]. October 16, 2007.

8. "Population Below Poverty Line." *The World Factbook.* [https://www.cia.gov/library/publications/the-world-factbook/fields/2046.html].

9. Ratemo, J. "Airtel Kenya Unveils New Online Payment System." *Business Daily,* November 4, 2011; "High Costs Keep Patients Out of Hospitals." *Xinhua News Agency.* November 23, 2004.

10. "The Difference Defines Us: The DNA of the Entrepreneur." *Exceptional,* Ernst & Young, July-December 2011.

11. Radjou, N., Prabhu, J., Kaipa, P., and Ahuja, S. "How Reframers Unleash Innovation in Their Companies (And Beyond)." [http://blogs.hbr.org/cs/2010/07/how_reframers_are_unleashing_a.html]. July 13, 2010.

12. Dr. Prasad Kaipa, CEO coach, personal interview with Navi Radjou, November 3, 2011.

13. Radjou, N., Prabhu, J., Kaipa, P., and Ahuja, S. "How to Ignite Creative Leadership in Your Organization." [http://blogs.hbr.org/cs/2010/05/how_to_ignite_creative_leaders.html]. May 19, 2010.

14. Comments collected from Professor Anil Gupta, who spoke at "Innovation in India and China. How to Create Value from Emerging Markets"—a

conference hosted by the Centre for India & Global Business at Judge Business School, University of Cambridge, on May 19–20, 2009.

15. Thakor, P. "Villager from Guwahati Gave MIT Tech Ideas." *DNA*, December 10, 2010.

16. We collected initial details on Enrique Gómez Junco and his company Optima Energía through our interview with Fernando Fabre, president of Endeavor—a non-profit organization that provides mentorship and strategic advice to high-impact jugaad entrepreneurs such as Junco around the world. Additional details were provided later by Junco himself.

17. "IFC Investment in Optima Energía Supports Energy Efficiency in Mexico's Hotel Sector." Press release from International Finance Corporation, October 21, 2009.

18. "Our Entrepreneurs. Enrique Gómez Junco." [http://www.endeavor.org /entrepreneurs/enrique-gomez-junco/169].

19. "Mexico: Optima Energia's Novel Business Model Helps Mexican Hotels Reduce Energy Costs." [http://www.ifc.org/ifcext/gms.nsf/Attachments ByTitle/CaseStudyOptima/$FILE/Optima.pdf]. 2010.

20. "Infosys and Wharton School Announce the Wharton Infosys Business Transformation Awards 2006 for North America and Latin America." [http://wwwstage.wharton.upenn.edu/whartonfacts/news_and_events /newsreleases/2006/p_2006_11_570.html]. November 13, 2006.

21. "I.M.F. Slashes Growth Outlook for U.S. and Europe." [http:// www.nytimes.com/2011/09/21/business/global/imf-slashes-growth-outlook-for-us-and-europe.html]. September 20, 2011.

22. Edgerton, J. "Automakers Agree to 54 MPG Standard." *CBS MoneyWatch*, July 29, 2011.

23. Elliott, L., and Kollewe, J. "Germany Faces Up to Problem of Ageing Workforce." [http://www.guardian.co.uk/world/2011/mar/17/new-europe-germany-retirement-pensions-exports]. March 17, 2011.

24. *Water Scarcity and Climate Change: Growing Risks for Businesses and Investors.* A Ceres Report authored by the Pacific Institute, February 2009.

25. Hamel, G. *The Future of Management.* Boston, MA: Harvard Business School Press, 2008.

26. Stelter, B., and Vega, T. "Ad Money Reliably Goes to Television." *New York Times*, August 7, 2011.

27. Richardson, A. *Innovation X: Why a Company's Toughest Problems Are Its Great Advantage*. San Francisco: Jossey-Bass, 2010.

28. Menkes, J. *Better Under Pressure*. Boston, MA: Harvard Business School Press, 2011.

29. Overby, C. S. *The Essentials of Consumer-Driven Innovation*. Best Practices Report, Forrester Research, May 26, 2006.

30. Neff, J. "P&G's Buzz-Building Networks Thrive in Age of Social Media." *Ad Age*, October 10, 2011.

31. "New Procter & Gamble Survey of Moms Shows Teens Need More Input from Their Parents When It Comes to Spending." *New York Times*, September 8, 2011.

32. Fleschner, M. "Best Friends." [http://www.sellingpower.com/magazine/article.php?i=1168&ia=6273].

33. Hagel, J. III, Brown, J. S., and Davison, L. "Shaping Strategy in a World of Constant Disruption." *Harvard Business Review*, October 2008.

34. "Salesforce.com Announces Fiscal Second Quarter Results." [http://www.salesforce.com/company/news-press/press-releases/2011/08/110818.jsp]. August 18, 2011.

35. "Salesforce.com Announces Fiscal Third Quarter Results." [http://www.salesforce.com/company/news-press/press-releases/2011/11/111117.jsp]. November 17, 2011.

36. Hardy, Q. "A Leader in the Cloud Gains Rivals." *New York Times*, December 11, 2011.

37. Ried, S., and Kisker, H. *Sizing the Cloud*. Forrester Research report, April 21, 2011.

38. "Why Is *Behind the Cloud* a Great Book for These Times?" [http://www.salesforce.com/behindthecloud/].

39. "Psychological Capital: What Lies Beneath." *Rotman Magazine*, Fall 2008.

40. "Meeting of Minds." [http://www.danonecommunities.com/en/content/meeting-minds].

41. Radjou, N., and Kaipa, P. "Do Multinationals Really Understand Global-ization?" [http://www.businessweek.com/globalbiz/content/aug2010/gb2010086_282527.htm]. August 6, 2010.

42. "Developing Employees' Autonomy and Efficiency." [http://www.danone.com/en/axes-strategiques/developing-employees-autonomy-and-efficiency.html].

43. Global Knowledge Management at Danone. Case No. 9-608-107. Boston, MA: Harvard Business School, 2008; Shanine, K., Buchko, A., and Wheeler, A. R. "International Human Resource Management Practices from a Complex Adaptive Systems Perspective: An Exploratory Investigation." *International Journal of Business and Social Science*, April 2011, *2*(6).

44. "Our Values." [http://www.danone.com/en/company/values.html].

45. Barclay's "Back to School" Consumer Conference—Transcript. [http://finance.danone.com/phoenix.zhtml?c=95168&p=irol-presentations]. September 7, 2011; "Sustainable Development." [http://finance.danone.com/phoenix.zhtml?c=95168&p=irol-presentations]. September 7, 2011; "Sustainable Development." [http://www.danone.com/en/sustainable-development.html].

46. "2010 Growth First—Interview with Franck Riboud, CEO of Danone." [http://www.danone.com/en/company/strategy.html].

47. The Dannon Company: Marketing and Corporate Social Responsibility. Case No. 9-410-121. Boston, MA: Harvard Business School, 2010.

48. Maney, K., Hamm, S., and O'Brien, J. M. *Making the World Work Better—the Ideas That Shaped a Century and a Company*. Upper Saddle River, NJ: IBM Press, 2011.

49. Goldman, D. "HP Decides to Keep Its PC Business." *CNNMoney*, October 27, 2011.

50. Lohr, S. "Even a Giant Can Learn to Run." [http://www.nytimes.com/2012/01/01/business/how-samuel-palmisano-of-ibm-stayed-a-step-ahead-unboxed.html]. December 31, 2011.

51. "Samuel J. Palmisano. Computer History Museum." [http://www.ibm.com/ibm100/us/en/lectures/what_changes_and_what_endures.html]. August 4, 2011.

52. Pierson, R. "New Pfizer CEO Slashes R&D to Save 2012 Forecast." *Reuters*, February 2, 2011; Krauskopf, L. "Pfizer R&D Chief Upbeat Despite Smaller Budget." Reuters, March 31, 2011.

53. Krauskopf, L., and Nagaraju, B. "Pfizer to Sell Biosimilar Insulins in Biocon Deal." Reuters, October 18, 2010.

54. "A Century of Innovation." [http://solutions.3m.com/wps/portal/3M/en_WW/History/3M/Company/century-innovation/].

55. Goetz, K. "How 3M Gave Everyone Days Off and Created an Innovation Dynamo." [http://www.fastcodesign.com/1663137/how-3m-gave-everyone-days-off-and-created-an-innovation-dynamo]. Feburary 1, 2011.

56. Hindo, B. "At 3M, a Struggle Between Efficiency and Creativity." *Bloomberg Businessweek*, June 11, 2007.

57. Ibid.

58. Salter, C. "The Nine Passions of 3M's Mauro Porcini." *Fast Company*, October 2011, p. 128.

59. Mauro Porcini, head of global strategic design, 3M, personal interview with Simone Ahuja and Navi Radjou, October 7, 2011.

60. Ibid.

61. Ibid.

62. Marc Gunther, M. "3M's Innovation Revival." [http://money.cnn.com/2010/09/23/news/companies/3m_innovation_revival.fortune/index.htm]. September 24, 2010.

63. Jaruzelski B., Loehr, J., and Holman, R. "The Global Innovation 1000 Why Culture Is Key." [http://www.strategy-business.com/article/11404?pg=all]. October 25, 2011.

Chapter 3

1. Farber, D. "GE CEO Jeff Immelt: India, Globalization and the Economics of Scarcity." ZDNet, July 6, 2007.

2. Gustavo Grobocopatel, CEO, Los Grobo, email exchange with Navi Radjou, September 26, 2011.

3. "The World Factbook. Field Listing: Land Use." [https://www.cia.gov/library/publications/the-world-factbook/fields/2097.html]

4. Los Grobo: Farming's Future? Case No. 9-511-088. Boston, MA: Harvard Business School, 2010.

5. "Entrepreneurs Speak Out. A Call to Action for G20 Governments. Country Digest: Argentina." Report produced by Ernst & Young for the G20 Young Entrepreneur Summit, October 2011.

6. "Entrepreneurs Speak Out. A Call to Action for G20 Governments. Country Digest: Africa." Report produced by Ernst & Young for the G20 Young Entrepreneur Summit, October 2011.

7. "India Lags China in R&D Spending: Sibal." *Financial Express*, March 13, 2008.

8. 2001 Talent Shortage Survey Results. ManpowerGroup, 2011.

9. Zeng, M., and Williamson, P. J. *Dragons at Your Door: How Chinese Cost Innovation Is Disrupting Global Competition*. Boston, MA: Harvard Business School Press, 2007.

10. Mas, I., and Radcliffe, D. "Mobile Payments Go Viral: M-PESA in Kenya." *Capco Institute Journal of Financial Transformation*, 2011, *32*.

11. Hughes, N., and Lonie, S. "M-PESA: Mobile Money for the 'Unbankd.'" *Innovations*, Special Edition for the GSMA Mobile World Congress 2009, MIT Press, 2009.

12. Strategic Outsourcing at Bharti Airtel Limited. Case No. 9-107-003. Harvard Business School. Boston, MA: Harvard Business School, 2006.

13. Dholakia, R. R., Anwar, S. F., and Hasan, K. (Eds.). *Marketing Practices in Developing Economy: Cases from South Asia*. New Delhi, India: PHI Learning, 2010.

14. Prahalad, C. K. *The Fortune at the Bottom of the Pyramid*. Upper Saddle River, NJ: Wharton School Publishing, 2004.

15. FAQs. Hapinoy website. [http://hapinoy.com/faqs.html].

16. Weinstein, J. "Awakening a 'Sleeping Giant,' Microfranchise as a Distribution Platform." [http://www.nextbillion.net/blog/awakening-a-sleeping-giant]. February 15, 2011.

17. Bam Aquino, president, MicroVentures Inc., personal interview with Navi Radjou, September 16, 2011.

18. Doggett, S. "Low Cost 'Revolo' Hybridization Kit Could Boost India's Presence in Gas-Electric Arena." Autoobserver.com, September 13, 2010.

19. Ravi Pandit, CEO, KPIT Cummins Infosystems, personal interview with Simone Ahuja and Navi Radjou, January 5, 2010.

20. "Trailblazers, Shapers and Innovators—Model of Success from the Community of Global Growth Companies." The World Economic Forum, 2011.

21. John, S., and Sood, V. "Cleaner, Greener, Cheaper." *Mint*, July 29, 2010.

22. Steen, M. "Portable Baby Warmer Goes from Classroom Project to Nascent Organization." *Stanford Business Magazine*, Autumn 2011.

23. "Embrace—How It Works." [http://embraceglobal.org/main/product?section=howitworks].

24. Jane Chen, CEO, Embrace, personal interview with Navi Radjou, September 2, 2011.

25. Schrage, M. "Procurement's Best-Priced Deal May Stifle." [http://blogs.hbr.org/schrage/2011/12/killing-innovation-in-the-proc.html]. December 1, 2011.

26. Berfield, S. "Hip Eyewear: Warby Parker's New Spectacles." *Bloomberg Businessweek*, June 30, 2011.

27. John Maeda, president of the Rhode Island School of Design, personal interview with Navi Radjou, November 1, 2011.

28. Bradner, L. *Five Ways CPG Marketers Are Fighting the Recession.* Forrester Research report, July 16, 2009.

29. *Redefining the Future of Growth: The New Sustainability Champions.* Geneva, Switzerland: World Economic Forum, 2011.

30. Ramón Mendiola Sánchez, CEO of Florida Ice & Farm Co., personal interview with Navi Radjou, December 19, 2011.

31. "Special Report—the Race to the Modern 5,000 Euro Car." [http://www.autobrief.com/autobrief/?lng=en-us&mode=art_one&aid=635&rid=0]. June 5, 2007.

32. Ghosh, R. "Ghosn Back to Praising 'Frugal Engg.'" *DNA*, October 30, 2007; Sehgal, V., Dehoff, K., and Panneer, G. "The Importance of Frugal Engineering." *strategy+business*, Summer 2010.

33. Welch, D. "The Leaner Baby Boomer Economy." *Bloomberg Businessweek*, July 23, 2009.

34. Binkley, C. "Beyond Bridal: Vera Wang's New Look." *Wall Street Journal*, December 15, 2011.

35. Byron, E. "As Middle Class Shrinks, P&G Marketing Aims High and Low." *Wall Street Journal*, September 12, 2011.

36. McGregor, J. "GE: Reinventing Tech for the Emerging World." *Bloomberg Businessweek*, April 17, 2008.

37. Huston, L., and Sakkab, N. "Connect and Develop: Inside Procter & Gamble's New Model for Innovation." *Harvard Business Review*, March 2011.

38. Indra Nooyi, chairman and CEO, PepsiCo Inc., personal interview with Navi Radjou, January 21, 2010.

39. Jana, R. "India's Next Global Export: Innovation." *Bloomberg Businessweek*, December 2, 2009.

40. PepsiCo 2010 Annual Report. [http://pepsico.com/Download/PepsiCo_Annual_Report_2010_Full_Annual_Report.pdf].

41. Ibid.

42. York, E. B. "Dr. Mehmood Khan Taking on the PepsiCo Nutritional Challenge." *Chicago Tribune*, June 20, 2011.

43. Tanmaya Vats, head of Global Value Innovation Center, PepsiCo Inc., personal interview with Navi Radjou and Jaideep Prabhu, October 3, 2011.

44. "PepsiCo: Our Commitment to Sustainable Agriculture Practices." [http://pepsico.com/Download/PepsiCo_agri_0531_final.pdf].

45. Ibid.

46. Radjou, N., and Prabhu, J. "PepsiCo and GE Are Innovating in India." *Bloomberg Businessweek*, November 9, 2010.

47. "Frito-Lay Unveils 'Near Net Zero' Manufacturing Facility." [http://www.pepsico.com/PressRelease/Frito-Lay-Unveils-Near-Net-Zero-Manufacturing-Facility10052011.html]. October 5, 2011.

Chapter 4

1. Sinha, K. "India's Diabetes Burden to Cross 100 Million by 2030." *Times of India*, December 14, 2011.

2. Dr. V. Mohan, chairman of Dr. Mohan's Diabetes Specialities Centre, personal interview with Simone Ahuja, December 15, 2008.

3. Dr. Harish Hande, founder, SELCO, personal interview with Simone Ahuja, December 23, 2008.

4. Abrar, P. "Solar Entrepreneur Harish Hande's Solar Electric Light Company Taps Rural Schools, Homes." *Economic Times*, December 16, 2011.

5. Ravi Kant, nonexecutive vice chairman, Tata Motors, personal interview with Jaideep Prabhu and Navi Radjou, June 18, 2010.

6. A K Bhattacharya. "Singur to Sanand." *Business Standard*, August 6, 2011.

7. Baggonkar, S. "Tata Motors Goes on Nano Overdrive." *Business Standard*, November 10, 2011.

8. Zeng, M., and Williamson, P. J. *Dragons at Your Door: How Chinese Cost Innovation Is Disrupting Global Competition*. Boston, MA: Harvard Business School Press, 2007.

9. Zhang, R. "Creating New Business Models." [http://www.daonong.com /g/2011EN/Columns/20110915/32691.html]. September 15, 2011.

10. Ibid.

11. Colvin, G. "Zhang Ruimin: Management's Next Icon." *Fortune*, July 25, 2011.

12. Madden, N. "Why It's OK to Wash Potatoes in a Washing Machine." *Ad Age*, February 3, 2010.

13. Backaler, J. "Haier: A Chinese Company That Innovates." *Forbes*, June 17, 2010.

14. Professor Carol Dweck, Stanford University, personal interview with Navi Radjou, September 9, 2011.

15. Dweck, C. *Mindset: The New Psychology of Success*. New York: Random House, 2006.

16. Dr. Prasad Kaipa, CEO coach and leadership expert, personal interview with Navi Radjou, November 3, 2011; Kaipa, P. "The Flip Side of Signature Strength." *SiliconIndia*, April 2007.

17. Shashank Samant, president, GlobalLogic, personal interview with Navi Radjou, August 17, 2011.

18. Doreen Lorenzo, president, frog, personal interview with Navi Radjou, August 24, 2011.

19. Hammond, A., Kramer, W. J., Tran, J., Katz, R., and Walker, C. "The Next 4 Billion: Market Size and Business Strategy at the Base of the Pyramid."[http://www.wri.org/publication/the-next-4-billion]. March 2007.

20. Pfeiffer, P., Massen, S., and Bombka, U. "Serving the Low-Income Consumer: How to Tackle This Mostly Ignored Market." [http://www.atkearney.com/index.php/Publications/serving-the-low-income-consumer.html].

21. Prahalad, C. K. *The Fortune at the Bottom of the Pyramid.* Upper Saddle River, NJ: Wharton School Publishing, 2004.

22. Christensen, C. *The Innovator's Dilemma: When New Technologies Cause Great Firms to Fail.* Boston, MA: Harvard Business School Press, 1997.

23. Khaliq, A. A., and Thompson, D. M. "The Impact of Hospital CEO Turnover in U.S. Hospitals." Final Report prepared for the American College of Healthcare Executives (ACHE), February 2006.

24. "Majority of American Workers Not Engaged in Their Jobs." [http://www.gallup.com/poll/150383/majority-american-workers-not-engaged-jobs.aspx]. October 28, 2011.

25. Hardy, Q. "Google's Innovation—and Everyone's?" *Forbes,* July 16, 2011.

26. Harford, T. *Adapt: Why Success Always Starts with Failure.* New York: Farrar, Straus and Giroux, 2011.

27. Zhang, L. *R&D at Huawei.* Beijing, China: China Machine Press, 2009.

28. Hardy, Q. "Google's Innovation—and Everyone's?"

29. Hemp, P., and Stewart, T. A. "Leading Change When Business Is Good." *Harvard Business Review,* December 2004.

30. Palmisano, S. "Our Values at Work on Being an IBMer." IBM website. [http://www.ibm.com/ibm/values/us/].

31. Lohr, S. "Can Apple Find More Hits Without Its Tastemaker?" [http://www.nytimes.com/2011/01/19/technology/companies/19innovate.html]. January 18, 2011.

32.   Battelle, J. "The 70 Percent Solution." *Business 2.0,* December 1, 2005.

33.   Kirkpatrick, M. "Leader of Google Maps to Launch Multiple New Mobile Apps Inside Google." *New York Times,* January 14, 2011.

34.   Radjou, N., Prabhu, J., Kaipa, P., and S. Ahuja. "Indian Tales of Inclusive Business Models." *Harvard Business Review* Blog, January 5, 2011.

35.   Kal Patel, partner at VantagePoint Capital Partners and former president, Asia, Best Buy, personal interview with Navi Radjou and Simone Ahuja, August 11, 2011.

36.   Hamm, S. "Big Blue's Global Lab." *Bloomberg Businessweek*, August 27, 2009.

37.   Radjou, N., Prabhu, J., Kaipa, P., and S. Ahuja. "The New Arithmetic of Collaboration." *Harvard Business Review* Blog, November 4, 2010.

38.   Levy, S. "Jeff Bezos Owns the Web in More Ways Than You Think." *Wired*, December 2011.

39.   "How to Be a High-Impact Entrepreneur: Ten Rules for Defeating Risk and Launching a Successful Start-Up." Study conducted by Endeavor's Center for High-Impact Entrepreneurship, 2011.

40.   "Google to Pull Plug on Power Meter and Health Services." *Newsmax.com*, June 24, 2011.

41.   "Best Buy Shuts China Stores to Focus on More Profitable Brand." *Bloomberg News*, February 21, 2011.

42.   Fowler, G. "The Man Who Got Us to 'Like' Everything." *Wall Street Journal*, August 13, 2011.

43.   Jana, R. "Facebook's Design Strategy: A Status Update." *design mind*, August 2, 2011.

44.   "P&G Sets Two New Goals for Open Innovation Partnerships: Company Seeks to Triple the Impact of Connect + Develop." Press release, Procter & Gamble website, October 28, 2010.

45.   "Why U.S. Newspapers Suffer More Than Others." The State of the News Media 2011: An Annual Report on American Journalism, Pew Research Center's Project for Excellence in Journalism, 2011.

46.   Strupp, J. "New York Times' R&D Team Seeks Next Big Thing." *Editor & Publisher*, December 10, 2009.

47. Garber, M. "The New York Times' R&D Lab Has Built a Tool That Explores the Life Stories Take in the Social Space." Nieman Journalism Lab website, April 22, 2010.

48. Fiore, J. "Welcome to beta620." [http://beta620.nytimes.com/2011/08/07/intro-beta620-post/]. August 7, 2011.

Chapter 5

1. "Neonatal Mortality and Newborn Care in India." [http://mchstar.org/pdf/neonatalMortalityAndNewbornCareInIndia.pdf].

2. "Innovative Local Technology Warms the Prospects for India's Vulnerable Infants." Lemelson Foundation website. [http://www.lemelson.org/programs-grants/developing-country-program/recognition-and-mentoring-programs-ramps/india/sathya-jeg].

3. Oshima, K. "Plastic Bottles Light Up Lives." *CNN World*, August 30, 2011.

4. McGeown, K. "How Water Bottles Create Cheap Lighting in Philippines." BBC, September 18, 2011.

5. "Nokia's Cheap Phone Tops Electronics Chart." [http://uk.reuters.com/article/2007/05/03/us-nokia-history-idUKL0262945620070503].

6. Keating, J. "The AK-47 of the Cell-Phone World." *Foreign Policy*, January/February 2011.

7. Lakshman, N. "One Laptop per Child Lands in India." *Bloomberg Businessweek*, August 4, 2008.

8. Raina, P., and Timmons, H. "Meet Aakash, India's $35 'Laptop.'" India Link, *New York Times*, October 5, 2011.

9. Ahmed, M. "Mobile Web Becomes a Reality." *The Financial Express*, December 1, 2011.

10. Chima, C. "Hands On: India's $35 Aakash Android Tablet Lands in America" (exclusive). *MobileBeat*, October 26, 2011.

11. Ushahidi—Frequently Asked Questions (FAQ). [http://www.ushahidi.com/about-us/faq].

12. Giridharadas, A. "Africa's Gift to Silicon Valley: How to Track a Crisis." *New York Times*, March 13, 2010.

13. "Why Do Inclusive Design?" [http://www.inclusivedesigntoolkit.com/betterdesign2/why/why.html].

14. Capps, R. "The Good Enough Revolution: When Cheap and Simple Is Just Fine." *Wired Magazine*, August 24, 2009.

15. Glock, A. "Back to Basics: Living with 'Voluntary Simplicity.'" *O, the Oprah Magazine*, January 2009.

16. Markowitz, E. M., and Bowerman, T. "How Much Is Enough? Examining the Public's Beliefs About Consumption." *Analyses of Social Issues and Public Policy*, doi:10.1111/j.1530-2415.2011.01230.x. [http://onlinelibrary.wiley.com/doi/10.1111/j.1530-2415.2011.01230.x/abstract]. 2011.

17. "Corporate R&D Spending Rebounds in 2010, Finds Booz & Company Global Innovation 1000 Study." [http://www.booz.com/global/home/press/article/49852237]. October 24, 2011.

18. Maeda, J. *The Laws of Simplicity (Simplicity: Design, Technology, Business, Life).* Cambridge, MA: MIT Press, 2006.

19. Radjou, N. "R&D 2.0: Fewer Engineers, More Anthropologists." [http://blogs.hbr.org/radjou/2009/06/rd-20-fewer-engineers-more-ant.html]. June 10, 2009.

20. Radjou, N. *Transforming R&D Culture.* Forrester Research report. March 20, 2006.

21. "The Simplicity Imperative." [http://www.newscenter.philips.com/main/standard/about/news/speechespublications/archive/2004/article-3188.wpd]. January 9, 2004.

22. Ang, J. "Philips: Sense and Simplicity." [http://designtaxi.com/article/100322/Philips-Sense-Simplicity/].

23. Tischler, L. "The Beauty of Simplicity." *Fast Company*, December 19, 2007.

24. "Delivering 'Sense and Simplicity.'" Philips corporate website. [http://www.philips.com/about/company/brand/brandpromise/index.page].

25. "Simplicity Advisory Board." Philips corporate website. [http://www .philips.com.my/philips5philipsmy/about/brand/simplicityadvisory board/index.page].

26. Tischler, L. "The Beauty of Simplicity." *Fast Company*, December 19, 2007.

27. "The Highest Number Ever of Annual iF Product Design Awards for Philips." [http://www.newscenter.philips.com/main/design/news/press /2011/if2011.wpd]. February 8, 2011.

28. "The Seed of Apple's Innovation." *Bloomberg Businessweek*, October 12, 2004.

29. "Siemens 2011." [http://www.siemens.com/press/pool/de/homepage /the_company_2011.pdf]. October 2011.

30. "Siemens to Expand Market Share in Emerging Markets." Siemens corporate press release, June 28, 2011.

31. "Innovations for the Entry Level." [http://www.kpmg.de/WhatWeDo/ 26472.htm].

32. Lamont, J. "The Age of 'Indovation' Dawns." *Financial Times*, June 15, 2010.

33. "New Approaches for China." [http://www.siemens.com/corporate-technology/en/research-areas/smart-and-cost-innovation.htm].

34. "Innovations for the Entry Level."

35. Dr. Mukul Saxena, senior vice-president and head of Siemens Corporate Research and Technologies, Siemens India, personal interview with Jaideep Prabhu and Navi Radjou, March 26, 2010.

36. "Innovations for the Entry Level."

37. Ibid.

38. "Siemens to Expand Market Share."

39. "Less Is More." The World in 2012, *The Economist*, p. 132; Loescher, P. "Strategies to Save the Only Planet We Have." [http://blogs. reuters.com/great-debate/2011/11/03/strategies-to-save-the-only-planet-we-have/]. November 3, 2011.

40. "Principles of Universal Design." [http://www.ncsu.edu/ncsu/design/ cud/about_ud/udprinciples.htm].

41. "Universal Design." OXO corporate website. [http://www.oxo.com/UniversalDesign.aspx].

42. "OXO Gives Universal Design a Shot in the Arm." [http://www.core77.com/blog/object_culture/oxo_gives_universal_design_a_shot_in_the_arm_13772.asp]. June 16, 2009.

43. Gertner, J. "How Do You Solve a Problem Like GM, Mary?" *Fast Company*, 2011.

44. Ibid.

45. "Better by Design." *The Economist* Technology Quarterly, September 15, 2005.

46. "Simplicity and Enterprise Search." Google white paper.

47. Tischler, L. "The Beauty of Simplicity." [http://www.fastcompany.com/magazine/100/beauty-of-simplicity.html]. December 19, 2007.

48. "100 Greatest Movies, TV Shows, and More." [http://www.ew.com/ew/article/0,,20312226_20324138,00.html].

49. Kate Aronowitz, director of design at Facebook, email exchange with Navi Radjou, December 13, 2011.

50. Jana, R. "Facebook's Design Strategy: A Status Update." *design mind*, August 2, 2011.

51. Ibid.

Chapter 6

1. Dr. Rana Kapoor, CEO, YES BANK, personal interview with Simone Ahuja and Navi Radjou, January 7, 2010.

2. Anand, M., and Bhuva, R. "Banking on Innovation." *Outlook Business*, September 19, 2009.

3. Ibid.

4. Gates, B. "Making Capitalism More Creative." *Time*, July 31, 2008.

5. Abhi Naha, CEO, Zone V, personal interview with Navi Radjou, June 23, 2011.

6. "Visual impairment and blindness." [http://www.who.int/mediacentre/factsheets/fs282/en/]. October 2001.

7. Bijapurkar, R. *Winning in the Indian Market: Understanding the Transformation of Consumer India.* Singapore: John Wiley & Sons (Asia), 2008.

8. Rama Bijapurkar, marketing consultant, personal interview with Navi Radjou and Jaideep Prabhu, November 18, 2010.

9. Rubinstein, D. "Playing Grown-Up at KidZania." *Bloomberg Businessweek,* May 19, 2011.

10. We collected details on Heloísa Helena Assis (known as Zica) and her company Beleza Natural through Endeavor, a non-profit organization that provides mentorship and strategic advice to high-impact jugaad entrepreneurs such as Zica around the world.

11. Smith, G. "Brazil's Coming Rebound." *Bloomberg Businessweek*, August 6, 2009.

12. "Our Entrepreneurs. Heloísa Helena Assis." Endeavor website. [http://www.endeavor.org/entrepreneurs/helo%C3%ADsa-helena-assis/96].

13. Details on YES MONEY were provided to us by Ajay Desai, chief financial inclusion officer, YES BANK.

14. "GE Healthcare and Government of Gujarat Sign MOU for First of Its Kind Public and Private Partnership Model for Healthcare in the Country." Press release, GE Healthcare, August 2, 2008.

15. Prakash, S., and Velu, C. "Reuters Market Light: Business Model Innovation for Growth." [http://www.india.jbs.cam.ac.uk/opinion/pieces/downloads/2010/prakash_reuters.pdf]. February 2010.

16. Dr. Liu Jiren (see ch. 1, n. 51).

17. Ibid.

18. "Neusoft Unveils Health Cloud Strategy." [http://www.sinocast.com/readbeatarticle.do?id=68980]. December 22, 2011.

19. "Emerging Focus: Ageing Population in Emerging Market Economies." *Euromonitor*, May 5, 2010.

20. Hewitt, P. S. "Depopulation and Ageing in Europe and Japan: The Hazardous Transition to a Labor Shortage Economy." [http://library.fes.de/pdf-files/ipg/ipg-2002-1/arthewitt.pdf]. January 2002.

21. "The 'Grey Pound' Set to Hit £100bn Mark." Press release, Age UK, April 7, 2010.

22. "50+ Fact and Fiction." Immersion Active. [http://www.immersionactive.com/resources/50-plus-facts-and-fiction/].

23. Ian Hosking, senior research associate at the Engineering Design Centre at the University of Cambridge's Department of Engineering, personal interview with Jaideep Prabhu and Navi Radjou, September 8, 2011.

24. Abelson, J. "Suds with Splash." [http://articles.boston.com/2011-06-12/bostonworks/29650542_1_hispanic-population-p-g-hispanic-consumers]. June 12, 2011.

25. Roberts, S. "In a Generation, Minorities May Be the U.S. Majority." *New York Times*, August 13, 2008.

26. Michaels, A. "A Fifth of European Union Will Be Muslim by 2050." *The Telegraph*, August 8, 2009.

27. Censky, A. "Poverty Rate Rises in America." *CNN Money*, September 13, 2011.

28. Eichler, A. "Middle-Class Americans Often Fall Down Economic Ladder: Study." *Huffington Post*, September 7, 2011.

29. Censky, A. "Poverty Rate Rises in America." *CNN Money*, September 13, 2011.

30. Peck, D. "Can the Middle Class Be Saved?" *Atlantic*, September 2011.

31. Reich, R. "The Limping Middle Class." *New York Times*, September 3, 2011.

32. Anderson, C. *The Long Tail: Why the Future of Business Is Selling Less of More.* New York: Hyperion, 2006.

33. "National Survey of Unbanked and Underbanked Households." Federal Deposit Insurance Corporation, December 2009.

34. Rob Levy, manager, innovation and research, Center for Financial Services Innovation (CFSI), personal interview with Navi Radjou, Jaideep Prabhu, and Simone Ahuja, September 9, 2011.

35. Ibid.

36. Ibid.

37. Levy, A. "PayNearMe Targets 'Underbanked' Americans." *Bloomberg Businessweek*, May 10, 2011.

38. Andreessen, M. "Why Software Is Eating the World." *Wall Street Journal*, August 20, 2011.

39. Ramón Mendiola Sánchez, CEO of Florida Ice & Farm Co., personal interview with Navi Radjou, December 19, 2011.

40. Moffett, S. "Renault's Basic Car Detours." *Wall Street Journal*, February 2, 2011.

41. Ghosh, R. "Ghosn Back to Praising 'Frugal Engg.'" *DNA*, October 30, 2007; Sehgal, V., Dehoff, K., and Panneer, G. "The Importance of Frugal Engineering." *strategy+business*, Summer 2010.

42. Kirkpatrick, D. "The Socialist State of ThoughtWorks." *CNNMoney*, March 17, 2008.

43. Roy Neville Singham, founder and chairman, ThoughtWorks, personal interview with Navi Radjou, October 26, 2011.

44. Lallos, L. "YourEncore Keeps Retirees in the Game." *Bloomberg Businessweek*, April 15, 2010.

45. Ho, A. H. "The Telehealth Promise: Better Healthcare and Cost Savings for the 21st Century." Report prepared by the AT&T Center for Telehealth Research and Policy at the University of Texas Medical Branch, May 2008.

46. Sandhu, J. S. "Opportunities in Mobile Health." *Stanford Social Innovation Review*, Fall 2011.

47. Rettner, R. "U.S. Newborn Death Rate Tied with Qatar." Msnbc.com, August 30, 2011.

48. Miller, N. S. "National Texting Program for New Moms Continues Growth." *Pediatric News Digital Network*, December 9, 2011.

49. "As Middle Class Shrinks, P&G Marketing Aims High and Low." *Wall Street Journal*, September 12, 2011.

50. Ibid.

51. Ibid.

Chapter 7

1. Kishore Biyani, CEO, Future Group, personal interview with Simone Ahuja, October 30, 2008.

2. Smith, A. *Theory of Moral Sentiments*. Amherst, NY: Prometheus Books, 2000.

3. Venkat Rangan, cofounder and CEO, INXS Technologies, personal interview with Navi Radjou, December 28, 2010.

4. "Diane Geng and Sara Lam." [http://www.echoinggreen.org/fellows/diane-geng-and-sara-lam]. 2007.

5. Ibid.

6. Alter, A. L., Oppenheimer, D. M., Epley, N., and Eyre, R. N. "Overcoming Intuition: Metacognitive Difficulty Activates Analytic Reasoning." *Journal of Experimental Psychology: General*, November 2007, *136*(4), 569–576.

7. Jan Chipchase, executive creative director of Global Insights, frog, and Ravi Chhatpar, strategy director, frog, personal interview with Navi Radjou, August 26, 2011.

8. Roberts, K. *Lovemarks: The Future Beyond Brands*. New York: Power House Books, 2004.

9. Roberts, K. "Magic Time." [http://www.saatchikevin.com/Magic_Time/]. June 14, 2011.

10. Comments made by Anil Jain, managing director, Jain Irrigation Systems Ltd., at the World Economic Forum's Annual Meeting of the New Champions 2011 in Dalian, China, September 15, 2011.

11. Bam Aquino interview (see ch. 3, n. 17).

12. Dr. Prasad Kaipa, CEO coach and senior fellow at the Indian School of Business, personal interview with Navi Radjou, November 3, 2011.

13. Dr. Devi Shetty, founder of Narayana Hrudayalaya, personal interview with Simone Ahuja and Navi Radjou, December 14, 2009.

14. Radjou, N. "Future Group's Mythological Marketing." *Harvard Business Review* Blog Network, September 15, 2009.

15. Pink, D. *A Whole New Mind: Moving from the Information Age to the Conceptual Age*. New York: Riverhead Hardcover, 2005.

16. Welch, J., and Byrne, J. *Jack: Straight from the Gut*. New York: Business Plus, 2003.

17. Gladwell, M. *Blink: How Little Things Can Make a Big Difference*. New York: Back Bay Books, 2002.

18. "Millennials: The Challenger Generation." *Prosumer Report, EURORSG,* 2011, *11.*

19. Kim, P. *Consumers Love to Hate Advertising.* Forrester Research report, November 26, 2006.

20. Li, C., and Bernoff, J. *Groundswell: Winning in a World Transformed by Social Technologies.* Boston, MA: Harvard Business School Press, 2008.

21. *Smart CRM for CPG Manufacturers.* Forrester Research brief, May 29, 2002.

22. Radjou, N. *Transforming R&D Culture.* Forrester Research report, March 20, 2006.

23. Comment made by Tim Brown, CEO of IDEO, at the 2011 State of Design conference, April 2011.

24. Liu, Y., and Cui, T. H. "The Length of Product Line in Distribution Channels." *Marketing Science,* May-June 2010, *29*(3), 474–482.

25. Roberts, K. "Why Lovemarks Are More Valid Than Ever, or Welcome to the Age of Now." *Ad Age,* February 14, 2011.

26. Ludwig, A. "John Hagel on Empowerment, Management Fears, and Social Software in Business." *Forbes,* September 7, 2011.

27. "HR Development of the Future." [https://www.allianz.com/en/press/news/company_news/human_resources/news_2011-03-29.html]. March 29, 2011.

28. Hippel, E. v., Ogawa, S., and de Jong, J.P.J. "The Age of the Consumer-Innovator." *MIT Sloan Management Review,* Fall 2011.

29. Brooks, D. *The Social Animal: The Hidden Sources of Love, Character, and Achievement.* New York: Random House, 2011.

30. Roberts, "Magic Time."

31. Robert Fabricant, creative director, frog, personal interview with Navi Radjou, September 22, 2011.

32. "Connected Experiences—Denise Burton, frog Fellow, Austin." [http://www.frogdesign.com/about/centers-of-passion.html].

33. Tindell, K., and Bryant, A. "Three Good Hires? He'll Pay More for One Who's Great." *New York Times,* March 13, 2010.

34. "Corporate R&D Spending Rebounds in 2010, Finds Booz & Company Global Innovation 1000 Study." [http://www.booz.com/global/home/press/article/49852237]. October 24, 2011.

35. "I Learned Intuition in India: Steve Jobs." [http://www.indianexpress .com/news/i-learned-intuition-in-india-steve-jobs/864708/]. October 24, 2011.

36. Kuang, C. "What Can Steve Jobs Still Teach Us?" *Fast Company*, 2011.

37. Steve Jobs's interview with *Inc.* for its "The Entrepreneur of the Decade Award." [http://www.inc.com/magazine/19890401/5602.html]. April 1, 1989.

38. Walters, H. "Apple's Design Process." *Bloomberg Businessweek*, March 8, 2008.

39. " 'You've Got to Find What You Love,' Jobs Says." [http://news.stanford .edu/news/2005/june15/jobs-061505.html]. June 14, 2005.

Chapter 8

1. Tim Leberecht, chief marketing officer, frog, personal interview with Navi Radjou, August 5, 2011.

2. Radjou, N., and Prabhu, J. "PepsiCo and GE Are Innovating in India." *Bloomberg Businessweek*, November 9, 2010.

3. "Nueclear Healthcare Ltd (NHL) and GE Healthcare Join Hands in the Fight Against Cancer." [http://www.nueclear.com/NHL_GE.html]. December 10, 2011.

4. Bresenham, T. "Putting Innovation to Work for a Healthier India." *Economic Times*, February 3, 2012.

5. McGregor, J. "GE: Reinventing Tech for the Emerging World." *Bloomberg Businessweek*, April 17, 2008.

6. Jana, R. "Innovation Trickles in a New Direction." [http://www .businessweek.com/magazine/content/09_12/b4124038287365.htm]. March 11, 2009.

7. Chandran, R. "In India, for India: Medical Device Makers Plug In." [http://www.reuters.com/article/2010/07/05/us-india-healthcare-feature-idUSTRE6640F120100705]. July 4, 2010.

8. Joydeep Nag, CFO of GE Healthcare South Asia, personal interview with Navi Radjou and Jaideep Prabhu, December 26, 2011.

9. Ibid.

10. Radjou, N., and Kaipa, P. "Do Multinationals Really Understand Globalization?" *Bloomberg Businessweek*, August 6, 2010.

11. "Scripps Study First to Validate Usefulness of Pocket Ultrasound Device; Could Significantly Reduce Cost and Inconvenience of Traditional Echocardiograms." *PR Newswire*, July 4, 2011.

12. "Healthymagination—2010 Progress Report." GE website [http://www.healthymagination.com/progress/].

13. Comstock, B. "A New Blueprint for Innovation." [http://www.thedailybeast.com/articles/2011/01/27/ges-beth-comstock-a-new-blueprint-for-innovation.html]. January 27, 2011.

14. Siegler, M. G. "Schmidt Talks Wave's Death: 'We Celebrate Our Failures.'" *TechCrunch*, August 4, 2010.

15. Madhavan, N. "Made in India, for the World." [http://businesstoday.intoday.in/story/made-in-india,-for-the-world.html/1/5601.html]. May 30, 2010.

16. Jean-Philippe Salar, head of Renault's Design Studio in Mumbai, India, personal interview with Navi Radjou, January 24, 2011.

17. Dr. Liu Jiren (see ch. 1, n. 51).

18. "3M's Open Innovation." [www.strategy-business.com/article/00078?gko=121c3]. May 30, 2011.

19. Brown, M. "OpenIDEO Helps Solve Society's Problems Together." [http://www.wired.co.uk/news/archive/2010-08/04/openideo-brainstorming]. August 4, 2010.

20. Heath, C., and Heath, D. *Made to Stick: Why Some Ideas Survive and Others Die*. New York: Random House, 2007.

Chapter 9

1. Dickey, C. "Citizens, It's Down to You." *Newsweek*, September 11, 2011.

2. Dr. Vivian Fonseca, professor of medicine, Tulane University, personal interview with coauthors, August 25, 2011.

3. "About MyBnk." [http://www.mybnk.org/about-mybnk].

4. Anand, A. "Startup Generation Ready to Fix the Economy." MSNBC.com, August 8, 2011.

5. Anderson, C. "Q&A: Open Source Electronics Pioneer Limor Fried on the DIY Revolution." *Wired*, April 2011.

6. "Ada Byron, Countess of Lovelace." [http://www.sdsc.edu/Science-Women/lovelace.html].

7. Tanz, J. "Kinect Hackers Are Changing the Future of Robotics." *Wired*, July 2011.

8. "2011: Most Influential Women in Technology. Limor Fried." *Fast Company*, 2011.

9. Thompson, C. "How Khan Academy Is Changing the Rules of Education." *Wired*, August 2011.

10. Ryan, T. "Fostering a Love for Learning Through Game Mechanics [Future of Gaming]" [http://www.psfk.com/2011/12/fostering-a-love-for-learning-through-game-mechanics.html]. December 8, 2011.

11. Levey, N. "Pressing for Better Quality Across Healthcare." *Los Angeles Times*, October 4, 2011.

12. "BillFloat CEO Testifies 'Too Scared to Lend' a Growing Problem in Consumer Lending." *PR Newswire*, September 22, 2011.

13. "Will Plastyc Encourage the Broke to Save More?" [http://www.prweb.com/releases/prwebNew_Generation/HIgh-Reward_Savings/prweb8802732.htm]. September 16, 2011.

14. "Piggymojo, 'Impulse Saving'" [http://cfsinnovation.com/financial-capability/Piggymojo].

15. Jason Rohrer, independent game developer, personal interview with Simone Ahuja, Navi Radjou, and Jaideep Prabhu, August 16, 2011.

16. Thompson, M. "Playing God." [http://www.hemispheresmagazine.com/2011/07/01/playing-god/]. July 1, 2011.

17. Berman, J. "Can D.I.Y. Supplant the First-Person Shooter?" *New York Times*, November 13, 2009.

18. "Remarks by the President on Community Solutions Agenda." [http://www.whitehouse.gov/the-press-office/remarks-president-community-solutions-agenda-6-30-09]. June 30, 2009.

19. "Social Innovation Fund." [http://www.nationalservice.gov/about/programs/innovation.asp].

20. Sonal Shah, former director of the White House Office of Social Innovation and Civic Participation, personal interview with Navi Radjou and Simone Ahuja, September 12, 2011.

21. Huang, G. T. "Desh Deshpande on Starting Merrimack Valley Innovation Center—and Making a Global Impact from Massachusetts to India." *Xconomy*, January 6, 2011.

22. Radjou, N., Prabhu, J., Kaipa, P., and Ahuja, S. "The UK Could Rise to the Scarcity Challenge. Can Europe?" *Harvard Business Review* Blog, July 21, 2010.

23. "Tax Rise as UK Debt Hits Record." [http://news.bbc.co.uk/2/hi/8011321.stm]. April 22, 2009.

24. "La Mise en Place de L'auto-Entrepreneur: Bilan au 31 Août 2011." Press release from ACOSS, September 21, 2011.

25. Neuwirth, R. "The Shadow Superpower." *Foreign Policy*, October 28, 2011.

26. Polak, P. *Out of Poverty*. San Francisco: Berrett-Koehler, 2008.

27. Professor James Patell, Stanford University, personal interview with Navi Radjou, May 20, 2011.

28. Colvin, B., Gandhi, M., Parker, J., and Zhang, W. "Water Telemetry—Team Soochak." [http://www.scu.edu/socialbenefit/programs/frugalinnovation/upload/team_soochak.pdf].

29. Radha Basu, director of Frugal Innovation Labs at Santa Clara University, personal interview with Jaideep Prabhu, Simone Ahuja, and Navi Radjou, September 2, 2011.

30. Ian Hosking, senior research associate at the Engineering Design Centre, Department of Engineering, University of Cambridge, personal interview with Jaideep Prabhu and Navi Radjou, September 8, 2011.

31. Ibid.

32. Yuri Malina, founder of Design for America, personal interview with Navi Radjou, October 4, 2011.

33. Ibid.

34. "Monitoring Hospital-Acquired Infections to Promote Patient Safety—United States, 1990-1999." [http://www.cdc.gov/mmwr/preview/mmwrhtml/mm4908a1.htm].

35. "Our Mission." [http://www.endeavor.org/model/ourmission].

36. Dr. Rajiv Doshi, executive director, Stanford-India Biodesign Program, Stanford University, personal interview with Navi Radjou, September 6, 2011.

37. Alec Ross, senior advisor for innovation to U.S. Secretary of State Hillary Clinton, personal interview with Jaideep Prabhu and Navi Radjou, September 8, 2011.

38. "CFSI Convenes Innovators for the First Bay Area Financial Capability Development Lab." [http://cfsinnovation.com/news/article/440974]. September 26, 2011.

39. Kirkpatrick, D. "Social Power and the Coming Corporate Revolution." *Forbes*, September 26, 2011, p. 72.

40. Ibid.

41. Melin, E. "Scott Monty in Kansas City: Ford's Approach to Social Media." [http://www.spiral16.com/blog/2011/09/scott-monty-in-kansas-city-fords-appraoch-to-social-media/]. September 2, 2011.

42. Lawrence, J. "The New Shape of Innovation." [http://http://www.i-cio.com/features/july-2010/polycentric-innovation]. July 19, 2010.

43. Radjou, N., Prabhu, J., Kaipa, P., and Ahuja, S. "How Xerox Innovates with Emerging Markets' Brainpower." [http://blogs.hbr.org/cs/2010/08/how_xerox_innovates_with.html]. August 25, 2010.

ACKNOWLEDGMENTS

They say it takes a whole village to raise a child. The same applies to writing a book. We couldn't have produced this particular book without the intellectual and practical support of several people. First, we wish to thank our agent, Bridget Wagner of Zachary Shuster Harmsworth. In late April 2011, Bridget wrote to us to ask if we'd be interested in writing a book about *jugaad*—a subject we had been researching and writing about for several years. Bridget had just returned to the United States after a two-year stint working in India. Having witnessed jugaad innovation firsthand, Bridget felt strongly that this was an idea whose time had come, and she wanted to help us to introduce it to the West. Bridget worked with us tirelessly, and in just over five weeks and a dozen or so iterations, we had a winning proposal.

Next, we would like to thank Genoveva Llosa, our editor at Jossey-Bass. Genoveva has been nothing short of an intellectual partner on this journey. She immediately grasped the concept of jugaad and has been a constant source of creative ideas and crucial editorial input throughout the book development process. We would also like to thank the larger Jossey-Bass team—John Maas, Mary Garrett, and Kristi Hein—for managing the whole editing process so beautifully.

We are very fortunate to have Carolyn Monaco of Monaco Associates as our marketing manager. Her broad experience in business publishing, appreciation for the relevance of jugaad in a global context, and keen marketing insights were instrumental in successfully launching this book.

We must thank Kal Patel, partner at VantagePoint Capital Partners, and former president of the Asia Region at Best Buy, for consistently sharing potent ideas and poignant insights on creativity and innovation, and for generously supporting the *Indique—Big Ideas from Emerging India* TV series, which led us to more deeply study jugaad; Dr. R. A. Mashelkar, former director general of the Council of Scientific & Industrial Research (CSIR), for sharing his deep knowledge based on many years of dedication to the study of innovation; Dr. Prasad Kaipa, CEO coach and senior fellow at the Indian School of Business, for his cutting-edge insights into how individuals from all walks of life can ignite the creative genius that lies within them; Eddie Bowman and Sarah Bogue at Ernst & Young, for introducing us to Gustavo Grobocopatel (Los Grobo); Fernando Fabre at Endeavor, for introducing us to the innovative business models of Enrique Gómez Junco (Optima) and Heloísa Helena Assis (Beleza Natural). We are also grateful for the ideas, comments, and case studies that were generously provided by Radha Basu, Dr. Rajiv Doshi, Professor Carol Dweck, Ian Hosking, Reena Jana, Lakshmi Karan, Pradeep Kashyap, Joydeep Nag, Professor James Patell, V. Raja, Sonal Shah, and Ramesh Vangal.

We couldn't have written the book without the active input of all the jugaad innovators mentioned in our book who generously shared their professional and personal stories. Their jugaad spirit continues to inspire us.

Finally, we are profoundly grateful to family members and friends who cared about what we were doing and offered us moral support throughout—support that has helped us maintain our sanity and produce the book you now hold.

ABOUT THE AUTHORS

Navi Radjou is an independent thought leader and strategy consultant based in Silicon Valley. He is an internationally recognized voice of business innovation and leadership. Navi is also a fellow at Judge Business School, University of Cambridge, and a faculty member of the World Economic Forum.

Most recently, Navi served as executive director of the Centre for India & Global Business at Judge Business School. Previously, he was a longtime VP/analyst at Forrester Research in Boston and San Francisco, advising senior executives worldwide on breakthrough growth strategies.

Navi has been featured in the *New York Times, Wall Street Journal, Bloomberg Businessweek,* the *Economist,* and the *Financial Times.* He is a columnist on HBR.org and a sought-after speaker who has addressed the World Economic Forum, Council on Foreign Relations, the Conference Board, Harvard University, Asia Society, and more. A prolific writer, Navi has coined and popularized several business concepts, such as "global innovation networks," "polycentric innovation," and "indovation." Navi is also a coauthor of *Smart to Wise*, a book on next-generation leadership (Jossey-Bass, 2013).

An Indian-born French national, Navi earned his master's degree in information systems from Ecole Centrale Paris and also attended the Yale School of Management. He lives in Palo Alto, California. Follow Navi on Twitter @NaviRadjou.

Dr. Jaideep Prabhu is Jawaharlal Nehru Professor of Indian Business and Enterprise and director of the Centre for India & Global Business at Judge Business School, University of Cambridge. He has held positions at Imperial College London, Tilburg University (the Netherlands), and UCLA. Jaideep has a bachelor of technology degree from IIT Delhi and a Ph.D. from the University of Southern California.

Jaideep's research interests are in marketing, innovation, strategy, and international business. His current research is on the globalization of innovation and the role of emerging economies in this process. He is particularly interested in how multinationals and domestic firms are using emerging markets as a lab to do affordable and sustainable innovation for global application.

Jaideep has published in and is on the editorial board of leading academic journals such as the *Journal of Marketing* and the *International Journal of Research in Marketing*. He has taught and consulted with executives from ABN Amro, Bertelsmann, BP, BT, GE, IBM, ING Bank, KPMG, Nokia, Philips, Roche, Shell, Vodafone, and Xerox, among others. Jaideep has appeared on *BBC News24* and *Bloomberg Businessweek*, and his work has been profiled in *Bloomberg Businessweek*, the *Economist*, the *Financial Times*, *Le Monde*, *MIT Sloan Management Review*, the *New York Times*, and the *Times*. He is a columnist on HBR.org.

Dr. Simone Ahuja is the founder of Blood Orange, a marketing and strategy consultancy with special expertise in emerging markets and innovation, and content production capabilities. Headquartered in Minneapolis, with teams in Mumbai, Blood Orange uses an agile, cost-efficient content production process built on principles learned through extensive work in India, including jugaad. Simone recently developed, produced, and directed the television series *Indique—Big Ideas from Emerging India*, for which she explored how innovation in India drives socioeconomic development. Coupled with her own experience in leveraging the complementary skill sets of transnational teams, these meetings with CEOs of multinational corporations as well as grassroots entrepreneurs, heralding bottom-up, small-scale innovation, gave her a holistic, on-the-ground look at the unique methods and mindset of innovation employed in India.

Ahuja has served as an advisor to the Centre for India & Global Business at Judge Business School, University of Cambridge, and as an associate fellow for the Asia Society in New York City. She provides advisory services and keynote presentations to trade delegations, academic institutions, and Fortune 100 companies including PepsiCo, Procter & Gamble, Honeywell, General Mills, ECOLAB, Colgate-Palmolive, and Best Buy. Ahuja regularly contributes to a *Harvard Business Review* blog on HBR.org.

To learn more about the authors and their research and consulting capabilities, visit: JugaadInnovation.com.

INDEX

265

Index

Bring Jugaad to Your Organization

To generate breakthrough growth in today's hypercompetitive global economy, you need a fresh and powerful approach: jugaad innovation.

Jugaad Innovation authors can show you the way. Drawing on their deep, ongoing experience with companies in the United States and around the world, they can deliver the latest research, stories, and frameworks to help you generate quality products and services faster, better, and cheaper from within your organization. By working with them, you'll get

- Detailed case studies that underlie jugaad innovation's six powerful principles
- The best jugaad practices of today's global leaders
- An actionable roadmap for building a jugaad culture within your organization

Contact the authors directly for keynotes, workshops, or consulting advice.

Navi Radjou is an independent innovation and leadership consultant and speaker based in Palo Alto, California. He is also a fellow at Judge Business School, University of Cambridge. Navi@NaviRadjou.com

Jaideep Prabhu is the Jawaharlal Nehru professor of Indian business and enterprise and director of the Centre for India & Global Business at Judge Business School, University of Cambridge. J.prabhu@jbs.cam.ac.uk

Simone Ahuja is the founder of Blood Orange, a marketing and strategy consultancy with content production capabilities headquartered in Minneapolis and Mumbai. Simone@Blood-Orange.com

www.JugaadInnovation.com

How
to Turn
Your Ideas
into
Dollars

THE
COMPLETE
GUIDE
TO
GETTING
A GRANT

Laurie Blum

POSEIDON PRESS

NEW YORK LONDON TORONTO SYDNEY TOKYO SINGAPORE

POSEIDON PRESS

Simon & Schuster Building
Rockefeller Center
1230 Avenue of the Americas
New York, New York 10020

DESIGNED BY BARBARA MARKS
Manufactured in the United States of America

10 9 8 7 6 5 4 3 2 1

Library of Congress Cataloging-in-Publication Data

Blum, Laurie.
  The complete guide to getting a grant : how to turn your ideas into dollars
/ Laurie Blum.
      p.   cm.
  Includes bibliographical references and index.
  1. Fund raising—United States—Handbooks, manuals, etc.   2. Proposal
writing for grants—United States—Handbooks, manuals, etc.   I. Title.
HV41.9.U5B58   1993
361.7′068′1—dc20
                                                                92-45778
                                                                CIP

ISBN: 0-671-77834-X

To Gerald Howard for inspiration;
to Elaine Pfefferblit, a true editor;
to Melissa Burch, Cybèle Fisher, and Fori Kay
for invaluable research assistance;
to Ron Stone, without whom none of this
would have been possible; and, of course, to
Robert Withers

CONTENTS

INTRODUCTION

The *Guide* is intended for the average American beset by rising costs and a dwindling bank account. You hope to put your kids through college but are horrified by the expense; your elderly parent's health insurance will not cover home nursing care; you have a great idea for a business or perhaps need some expansion capital but your bank, if it still exists, has turned you down. I think it's high time that you were privy to what we fund raisers have known for years: that five billion dollars—that's right, *five billion*—exists in grant monies for individuals. With times as tough as they are, the nonprofit world is the last frontier of untapped money for the average American.

Over the years in my fund-raising practice, I have raised millions of dollars for hundreds of individuals and projects. My fees are quite steep. *The Complete Guide to Getting a Grant* will reveal my fund-raising secrets so that you too can tap into the billions of dollars available from the nonprofit sector.

An old axiom says, "Knowledge is power." My axiom is, "Knowledge is wealth." Remember, the advice that I am offering you here is exactly the same advice that I follow myself. It is the culmination of years of experience. I have organized this book in a way that's both easy to follow and fun to read. By the time you finish reading *The Complete Guide to Getting a Grant,* you will know as much about the grant process as most professional fund raisers and will be well on your way to getting yours.

You, the person for whom this book is written, have little or no experience with the grant-seeking process. I will therefore take you step by step through each stage, so that even if you are a first-time grant seeker, you can successfully win a grant. This book also contains many instructive examples of individuals for whom I have raised money.

Anyone can learn fund raising, and I'm the best example. I didn't go to school to learn to be a fund raiser, I learned fund raising by doing it. Now I am considered one of the foremost experts in my field. The point is that *anyone* can get a grant for an idea they really believe in, and *The Complete Guide to Getting a Grant* is the best place to learn how.

IT STARTS WITH
AN IDEA

You probably already have an idea—or several. If you're thinking about getting a grant, it's likely that you're interested in certain kinds of ideas—ideas that lead to action, that have the potential for causing change, for creating something that didn't exist before, for solving a problem, for making discoveries. Or you may simply have a compelling personal need, or see a need in your community, and have the idea that there must be a way to meet this need. You may want to develop your own career or interests, or pursue a project that will help your local community, your city, or a larger interest group. Your vision might reach out to the nation or even the world.

Everyone has ideas for projects, ideas for solving problems, or ideas for fulfilling needs. Some you can act on immediately—it's just a matter of making the decision, setting aside some time, and going ahead. Others require more time and resources, and that's why you're thinking about getting a grant. You may already have a very clear idea of what you want a grant for: you're a teacher and you want travel funds so that you can study Moorish architecture in Spain, or you're a mother and want to set up a day-care center in your community, or you're an inventor/entrepreneur and you want to develop a new kind of low-cost shelter that can help the homeless and put your own company on the map at the same time. Or you may have only a general idea of an area you want to work in—you want to work in documentary film, or do something in your community to help with AIDS education—but you haven't yet come up with a specific project that you want to pursue. In either case, it's worth considering what makes a good idea, for the purpose of getting a grant.

WHAT MAKES A GOOD IDEA?

What kinds of ideas attract funders? Some kinds of grants come in standard packages—they're given out for set purposes to people with very specific needs and credentials. Other grants go to people with good ideas that have never been tried before. In my work as a fundraising consultant, I've had the opportunity to help raise funds for a variety of good ideas, and I've seen certain factors that many of them have in common. Let's look at some of the qualities that can interest funders in a new idea.

- *Originality.* Funders are looking at a vast number of proposals from year to year, have already funded many, and have some firsthand knowledge of which kinds of ideas have been tried and which have succeeded. A truly original idea is certainly going to attract attention and stir interest, especially if it seems like a fresh approach to an existing problem.

I knew of a scientist who came up with what is probably one of the more original ideas I've ever come across. After much study, he had developed the theory that a specific bird living in the rain forest pecked at the bark of a certain tree, releasing a liquid secretion that the Aztecs, believe it or not, used as a form of cement in putting together structures and buildings. He'd done his research, he knew his field, and his idea was so provocative that he was able to get funding for a field trip and further research.

By originality, though, I don't mean that an idea should have no historical precedent or reference to established invention or creation. In fact, some of the most solid ideas are reactions to (or improvements upon) existing concepts. Take, for example, my own idea of "free money." Although the concept of philanthropy has existed since the time of Ben Franklin, no one before me had thought to make fundraising information available to the general public. I discovered that there was an incredible demand for this kind of information, and wrote a series of *Free Money* books that listed sources of grants for different needs—from day care to health care to business and the arts. These books were wildly successful—a total of over 300,000 copies have sold at the time of writing. This is one kind of originality: recognizing unexplored applications for an existing concept, and exploring them yourself.

In fact, it's always important for your original idea to have some point of reference, so it doesn't seem to be coming out of left field. Funders are looking for the relationship between your idea and what's been tried or explored before.

- **Problem solving.** Certain problems seem to be always with us: poverty, hunger, social and racial tensions, the need for more effective education. Other new problems arise with each decade, and different communities may have unique problems. Funders are always looking for fresh solutions to these problems, on a small or large scale. Originality plays a part here, too; good ideas often take a fresh approach to the problem at hand, and present a nontraditional solution.

One of my earliest clients, Jack Jackson, was a successful African American playwright who had won an Obie for his play *Fly Blackbird.* He was also a committed civil rights activist. After the Watts riots in the sixties, he decided that he wanted to use his expertise and experience in the arts to try to make a difference in this community, and developed the idea that the arts could be part of the solution to some of the social problems in this country.

Jack enlisted the help of Gregory Peck and others in the Hollywood community, and set up the Inner City Cultural Center in Los Angeles, where he not only trained playwrights and actors but also really started the whole idea of multiculturalism in the performing arts. He produced what was probably the first multicultural and multiracial *Hamlet,* and a number of former students of the Center are now successful members of the entertainment community.

Jack was a visionary, who saw a problem and drew on his own experience and expertise to come up with a fresh solution. Of course he didn't single-handedly solve the problems of the inner city, but he did help change the climate of the arts in this country, and provide training and opportunities to many individuals.

- **Timeliness.** This is another important factor in attracting funders to an idea. Times change, perceptions change—in the social and politial arenas as well as in the worlds of the sciences, arts, and humanities. Ideas and attitudes come into and fall out of favor. Current events can influence perceptions of social needs—just think of the effect of Sputnik on science education, or of the success of Japanese industry on workplace management theories. Funders change, too, and may shift their areas of interest to deal with perceived social problems or issues of the future. An idea that catches onto a wave of change can ride that wave to successful funding.

One organization I worked with that found its interests changing was Volunteers of America (VOA), which has had a long and distinguished record as a traditional charity with a small-town sensibility, engaged in such worthy pursuits as delivering meals to housebound senior citizens. In the early nineties, the Los Angeles chapter of VOA wanted to address what it perceived as the increasingly desperate situation of children in urban ghettos. This was at a time when the policy of the federal government was increasingly to look to business for assistance with social problems. Some officers of VOA came up with the idea of helping children in the inner cities start their own small businesses—they called it the Midas Touch Program. Kids might start a video delivery business, or decorate and sell T-shirts. The program was meant to pull kids away from the attraction of gangs, involve them in the world of work, and help them develop a sense of independence and initiative. It often made the difference between whether a child had one good meal a day or not.

We were able to enlist a good deal of support for this program. It was timely on two fronts—not only in addressing a pressing social need but doing so in a way that took into account reduced federal spending and the new emphasis on the business and private sector.

- *Compelling need.* Funders do respond to what they see as the most compelling needs, whether on a social or an individual level. On the level of broad social concerns, both public and private funders try to help with what they see as the most pressing social problems and needs—poverty, education, health care, medical research, or what have you. On the individual level, many programs support very specific kinds of individual needs, whether it's educational scholarships for Native Americans, or health care for people with heart diseases.

This is not to say that every individual need can be fulfilled, but there are many private funders who have experienced hardship or difficulties either themselves or within their own family, and who have generously donated funds to help others with similar problems. On the broad social level, funders often shift priorities and funds to address what are seen as the most pressing social needs. In the early 1980s, little funding was available to deal with AIDS research or medical assistance. As funders began to realize how compelling the problem was, they channeled more funds into these areas, and into related areas, like pediatric AIDS support, as the need became evident.

Funders' perception of need shifts to some extent with the times, following current events or well-publicized issues. At the same time, many funders remained concerned with some of the basic social needs, such as education and support of the arts. If you have a specific project, you will try in your research to locate the funders who are interested in addressing that particular need (more on this in Chapter 3). Rather than changing your project, one of the best ways to match your idea to a funder's interests is to show how your project will help serve the needs that the funder finds most compelling. When Jack set up the Inner City Cultural Center in Los Angeles, he saw that this was a community with a real need to be connected to career opportunities and the cultural mainstream of our society. He decided to address this need in a specific way by creating a program for the theater arts.

- *Outreach.* Though some funders are specifically interested in individuals and individual projects, many are looking for ideas that will affect a large number of people, whether a community or a population group. The effect could be indirect, as in certain education or arts outreach programs, or direct, as through hiring or teaching a number of individuals. The bottom line is: you are asking someone, the officers of a nonprofit entity, to give you free money to execute a project. Naturally, they want to know not only that the project will come to fruition, but also that it will reach the people it's intended to reach.

Back in the fifties, Joseph Papp had the idea that the people of New York City—the public, ordinary citizens—should be able to see more theater, that good theater shouldn't be limited to those who could pay Broadway ticket prices. So he started a program of presenting free Shakespeare in Central Park, which in turn became the New York Shakespeare Festival, which became a major cultural influence in New York, producing innovative avant-garde and multicultural work, as well as shows like *A Chorus Line* that did wind up on Broadway. Papp had both a great love for the theater and a great respect for the public. He felt the public *deserved* good theater, affordable or free, and that was the essence of his mission.

Another example: A client of mine who owned an architectural landscaping firm needed funds to hire additional workers and buy new equipment. He allied himself with a local rehabilitation center, which was trying to place recovering alcoholics in reentry jobs. Through the center, we were able to raise quite a bit of money for him to hire recovering alcoholics, and to buy some equipment as well. He found assistance for his own individual needs by reaching out to a larger group and helping meet their special needs.

One of my favorite clients was a gentleman who had become handicapped and found that while swimming and even going underwater as a scuba diver, he could function very much like everyone else. He did not feel handicapped in the water, which gave a great boost to his damaged self-esteem. So he founded the Handicapped Scuba Diving Association, which reached out to give handicapped people a renewed sense of self-esteem, as well as a great deal of pleasure.

What if you have an idea that seems to involve you alone—you want to travel, to study, to make a film or write a play? Even here, funders will be looking for outreach. If you're a high school or college teacher, wouldn't you love to spend the summer touring exotic locations, or a year teaching abroad? There are funders who will support you, not to give you a great summer vacation but to promote international educational exchange or to enrich the quality of your teaching upon return. If you want to make a film, maybe an art film or a specific documentary, you'll find that funders are concerned not only to give you a chance to create, but also to see that you will somehow share your artistic endeavor with other people—that you have a detailed plan to get your work shown on television, or tour it to community centers.

- **Multiplying factors.** As you've probably guessed by now, the factors listed above can build on one another to make a good idea even stronger.

If you come up with an idea that takes an original, fresh approach to solving a problem, is timely, and will reach out to affect many people, you may have a project that will seem almost irresistible to funders.

THE PERSONAL FACTOR

Aside from the qualities that can make an idea attractive to funders, there's one crucial factor that can make or break a funding idea. That factor is you: who you are, what experience or knowledge you possess, how you present yourself, and perhaps most significant of all, how much you care about your idea. Let's look at some of these aspects that will have a direct bearing on your success in getting a grant.

- **Your personal knowledge and expertise.** Clearly, if you are a scientist or teacher and you want a grant to do research or further study in your field, you will already have some kind of background and experience that can begin to convince a funder of your worthiness. However, this isn't the only kind of expertise that counts. Many good ideas come out of personal need and personal experience, whether from observing a need or having experienced it oneself.

You may belong to a community or a group, and be in a better position than anyone else to help solve certain problems because you know them with an insider's knowledge. My client who started the Handicapped Scuba Diving Association had a personal experience and knowledge that led him to make a unique contribution.

Or you may simply understand a need, or see an opportunity, more clearly than anyone else. Joseph Papp wasn't trained as an actor or producer. He didn't get a degree in theater, or train to be an arts administrator. But he saw a need that he believed he could address. What he had was a *vision* clear enough and strong enough to carry him through to success.

- **Can you, will you, follow through?** You must have the perceived ability to carry out your proposed project, and to follow it through to completion or fulfillment.

A funder that is giving away either public or private funds has a mandate to do so responsibly, and a commitment to do social good. When funders give grants, they expect to see the money being put to effective use. It is an honor both to apply for and to receive this money. Funders are wary in some cases of individuals who seem to have no previous experience that relates to their idea, or who may seem to lack the ability or experience to manage funds or a project. However, don't give up if you think funders might question your experience. Enthusiasm, zest, and passionate belief can count for a great deal. If you can provide a proposal that conveys a sense of true excitement about your idea and the conviction that you can carry it out, lack of experience can be overcome.

If you know you are able to carry out your project, that you are a follow-through person, who plans to be organized and responsible, there are things you can do to make your application stronger, which we'll cover in future chapters. If you've successfully managed funds or any kind of project, whether in the workplace or in your private life, you already have some evidence of your ability to follow through. If you're insecure about your abilities, you might consider collaborating on your idea, or working with an organization that can provide support in terms of financial management or other resources. But we'll return to this later.

One of the best ways to start convincing funders of your capability is to present a top-quality proposal package, containing a clear mission statement, an outline of the project that shows you've thought of every angle, and a professional and businesslike budget. We'll go over the details of this part of the process in Chapter 9.

- **Faith, conviction, and enthusiasm.** Whatever you call it—self-trust, instinct, or belief—there are certain intangibles that have more to do with your success in grant-getting than perhaps any other personal factor. You really do have to have conviction. You have to infect funders with your enthusiasm and your vision; you have to have the faith to keep going when the funding process seems endless and discouraging; you have to be able to deal with criticism and use it or reject it; and you have to believe so strongly in success that no obstacles will stand in your way.

If you do not believe in an idea 200 percent, do not pursue it. I used to work at Carnegie Hall with the Concert Artists Guild, which sponsored the debuts of young musicians. I could always tell which ones were going to make it professionally and have a career in performance, and which ones were going to end up doing something else. Those who had the drive, the need, the burning desire to realize their dream were the ones who would end up doing it—no matter if they were a little less or a little more talented than other performers. This is the kind of conviction you have to have.

This is not to say that you can't have insecurities or doubts, but that you must always believe in what you're doing, be prepared to carry it through, and be able to communicate your enthusiasm. There are exercises, books, and resources to help you focus your interests—and overcome negative thinking—and we'll mention some of them in the course of this book. If you're not an extrovert by temperament, don't despair: quiet conviction works just as well as the more flamboyant kind. But however you demonstrate it, commitment to your idea is one of the key factors that make funders take notice.

It's also one of the factors that can help you overcome lack of experience. One of my more successful clients in recent years was an African American television engineer, who wanted to start a school for minority, inner-city kids in Los Angeles to teach them radio and television production. Now, this man had not the slightest clue as to how to run a school, or how to raise money (which was why he came to me). All he had was a great dedication to his idea. Of course, as a cameraman for ABC he certainly had some qualifications, and he himself had grown up as a member of a minority group in the kind of neighborhood he wanted to target, so he also had a point of reference. His greatest asset by far, however, was his passionate belief in his idea. He was a missionary for the cause. And if you have that kind of faith, your project will succeed no matter what. The more qualifications you have the better, but a sense of passion and commitment to your idea is essential.

WHO ARE THE FUNDERS, AND HOW CAN YOU APPEAL TO THEM?

Although we'll discuss the different kinds of funders in greater detail later in this book, it's worthwhile taking a quick look right now at who the funders are and how they may react to your idea, so that you can start from the very beginning to think about how to develop your idea for funding.

WHO ARE THE FUNDERS?

Funders are actually business people looking to make an investment in a success story. They are not "ideas people" themselves, but it's their business to review, evaluate, and support ideas. They want to give money to projects that seem likely to succeed. Most funders have specific areas they are interested in; they specialize. If your idea is well thought out, designed to meet an existing need, and related to an area they are interested in, chances are funders will look favorably upon it.

Still, different types of funders will react to your project in different ways. What are these types? There are three important ones.

The Private Foundations. The most well known foundations are what I call the "Big Daddy" foundations, like the Ford Foundation, the Rockefeller Foundation, the Guggenheim Foundation, the Hearst Foundation. These have been set up by major philanthropists and wealthy business people who have created foundations to do very broad-based good. They are highly sophisticated. They give away huge amounts of money every year. The Big Daddy foundations have broad interests and many different types of funding areas. They give to education, to health, to the arts, and to many other areas. They are staffed by program officers whose job it is to deal with grant seekers in various areas. They are professionals, and usually very accessible.

The other type of private foundation is the small family foundation. The funders may be still alive, or they've died and have left their estates to be set up as foundations. These usually give much more specifically, in particular areas. For example, my ex-husband and I set up such a foundation. We gave primarily in the arts because that was my passion, and within that area we particularly gave to classical and contemporary music. We funded new pieces by composers, we funded a documentary film. We were able to support projects that we were personally interested in, which is the beauty of a private foundation.

Private foundations are usually administered by attorneys, accountants, or bank trust departments. Such individuals are not specialists, are usually not as accessible as the program officers of the Big Daddy foundations, and are often terribly overworked. The small family foundations, as a general rule, are very understaffed, and they do not have time to sit down and help you hash out or develop an idea. Often, they are set up as trusts, and are not even listed publicly, in order to avoid public solicitations. On the other hand, for these very reasons, there is usually less competition for their resources.

Corporations and Private Businesses. Corporate funders are, as a rule, much looser, and much more entrepreneurial than private foundations. They can respond to needs faster, and aren't afraid to shoot from the hip. They can often take monies out of their discretionary, marketing, or advertising budgets.

Corporations give money primarily for public relations and advertising value. This is why you see names like Mobil and Exxon on the big public television projects. They like the prestige that comes from giving to projects that will be in the public eye. Local businesses, too, will give to projects that they think will bring them some good publicity.

Businesses may also offer technical services and advice, in place of or in addition to money for your project. They can help you do a business plan, help you do budgets, or offer facilities. For example, a corporation may make space available for art exhibits at some of its buildings.

Government Agencies. Government funders may seem much more aloof. They have the responsibility of giving away taxpayers' money. As with other areas of government spending, many checks and balances have been set up to protect these public funds. So, if you apply, you'll have to adjust and conform to very specific, detailed procedures. If you follow the rules and fit into the guidelines, then you do stand a chance of government funding.

The good thing about federal dollars is that the grants are usually much larger than either private or corporate grants. The government will often give what's known as multiyear grants, which provide a predictable source of funding for several years in a row. Whereas you might need to apply to several different private funders to get all the money you want for a big, extended project, or have to reapply year after year, a decent-sized government grant might fund your whole project by itself.

Besides private foundations, corporate funders, and government agencies, there are two other kinds of funders that occasionally support individuals or organizations, though usually on a much smaller scale.

Nonprofit Organizations: Prizes and Awards. Although they do not usually give grants (they actually receive them), some nonprofit organizations give prizes and awards to individuals. There may be little or no money involved, but a prestigious award can add to your credentials, and thus contribute greatly to your fund-raising efforts. Some organizations, from local churches to rotary clubs, may offer small amounts of money or other assistance to people or projects in their local community.

Individual Donors. Individuals actually contribute the largest share of all philanthropic donations, but they often give primarily to churches and religious organizations and are not a very useful source for the individual. Some nonprofit organizations do receive support from individual donors, but they really have to dig for it, through mailings and active fund-raising campaigns. Individual donors are just not a significant source of funds for individuals, except for the extremely rare individual artist who may find a wealthy patron.

How Can You Make Your Idea Attractive to Funders?

This is the fundamental question, and in a way, my whole book is about this process. Still, you might be worrying at this point that your idea is too offbeat, too vague or personal, or even too conventional to attract funding. Or you may have started to think about how you can change your idea to match what funders want. Don't be too hasty. The key is to be flexible, but without compromising your dream. Let's consider some of the questions that might come up as you think about matching your idea to what funders want.

What Areas Are Funders Interested In?

There are over 32,000 listed private foundations in this country, and this figure does not include government agencies, which have their own distinct interests, or countless corporations and businesses that can give directly from their operating budgets to whatever projects interest them.

Because of these numbers, it's nearly impossible to summarize all the various areas of interest that funders may give to. The Big Daddy foundations, as we saw, have very broad interests. The smaller family foundations give in many areas as well. Some funders tend to support organizations and large, complex projects, while others will support individuals with unusual ideas. The conclusion? You can probably find some funder who will support your idea, but you may need to do some digging to find the precise foundation or corporation whose areas of interest coincide with yours.

It's worth mentioning that funders' priorities do sometimes change. For example, several years ago the Rockefeller Foundation was doing a fair amount of arts funding. Now it seems to be focusing more on population and hunger problems in developing countries. This reflects the changing vision of the foundation's managers and is the kind of shift that grant seekers need to be aware of. (In Chapter 3, you'll find tips for keeping up with these changes.)

Should you think about changing your idea, or even trying to come up with a new one, to fit the guidelines of a particular funder? I advise against it. I have seen too many clients, mostly nonprofit organizations, who have decided to trash a good idea and create a new program to fit a funder's existing guidelines. For an organization, it may make sense to pursue its mission in a different way. A group might give up on a job-training or education program for single mothers, and support them with a more fundable counseling program, for example, but it's always a shame to see a good idea go down the tubes. For an individual, it rarely makes sense to switch your plan.

I do think that it is very important to know the funding landscape and have some points of reference before you sit down to decide how you are going to apply for funding. Nevertheless, if you are clear in your vision and conviction about what you want to do, you should not change the focus of your project just to suit a particular foundation. There is enough variety in the nonprofit sector so that you should be able to find something that will suit your needs without altering your vision.

How to Adjust to the Funding Landscape

You will always need to take into consideration the interests of the funding organization itself. If a foundation has certain fields of interest, such as women's issues or family violence, you'll need to show how funding your idea will further this mission. Such a foundation might consider funding the operating expenses of a rescue van for a battered women's shelter, for example.

The key to the process is to stick to your vision and your convictions, while responding flexibly to the funding that exists by gearing your presentation to the interests and requirements of each funder you are approaching. I had a client a number of years back who was rather a colorful figure, an ex-CIA man who decided that he wanted to develop a low-cost geodesic dome shelter that could be used for disaster relief. He had targeted the Red Cross as the group he'd like to work with. It was a wonderful invention—it was all in one piece, it was easy to clean, it was very cost-effective to build, it could be airlifted into an area of need. The first thing we discovered, though, was that there just wasn't strong enough interest in disaster relief housing among funders.

So, what we decided to do was to go after the funding for transitional housing, and we targeted homeless organizations. We were very successful in getting seed money for a pilot project to build these geodesic domes, which we coordinated with several projects serving homeless families in Los Angeles. My client was off and running. Although he clearly went into this with a social purpose, he also started a very profitable business manufacturing low-cost housing for first-time homeowners. Though he did shift the target of his fund raising, the important thing was that he did not give up on his idea; he maintained his sense of social purpose in providing inexpensive and emergency housing, even though the recipients were different from those he had first imagined.

WHAT IF AN IDEA SEEMS JUST TOO DIFFICULT TO FUND?

It is not very often that an idea is so original that funding does not seem viable because of its novelty. If you have an invention—or an arts project—and after doing your research and putting your ideas down on paper it seems unlikely that you'll be funded, it then becomes a matter of principle whether you choose to revamp the idea to fit potential funders. But I still advise against it. The Zelig complex, as I call it, does not work in philanthropy. Your belief in your idea and its integrity are terribly important.

Still, it may seem that your idea's time has come and gone, or perhaps you are really on the cutting edge and the funding world has not yet caught up with your vision. In these cases, it's important to develop points of reference, to refresh an overfamiliar idea or educate about an unfamiliar one.

One example of the latter situation is the earliest period of funding for AIDS projects. I have done a fair amount of raising money for AIDS. Back in the early 1980s, it was next to impossible to get any money for AIDS research and even more difficult to fund support services; we simply had to keep trying to educate funders about the problem. But it took several years before the issue was enough in the public eye that more funders became open to it.

One of the more difficult projects I've raised money for was the Fund for Psycho-Neuroimmunology, which supports research into the effect of mental attitudes on physical health and the immune system. At the time, the notion that the mind and body are intimately connected was a novel one. People like Norman Cousins had helped give much wider credibility to this idea, but the scientific and medical community still looked askance at it. So I felt it was important, in writing up the proposal, to present very pertinent scientific case studies. I knew I would be submitting proposals to foundations with directors who had strong medical and scientific backgrounds, so we did careful research. We provided many points of reference, including research material from the Soviet Union, where the medical establishment had explored this idea in far greater depth. This was a case where the idea was indeed unusual, and we had to provide extra points of reference in order to raise the money.

HOW TO DEVELOP YOUR IDEA

So you have an idea, or the germ of an idea, or at least the idea of a field in which you want to work. You may have a clear sense of a personal need, or of a social problem that needs to be solved. You have some sense of how the nonprofit funding sector works, and how funders respond to ideas. How can you develop your idea, flesh it out, focus it, and polish it so that it will appeal to funders? No one gets nonprofit funding without a fully developed idea. Remember that you're not going to be calling someone on the phone and pitching your idea to them. Eventually, you'll have to fill out an application or write a letter of request. You may have to prepare a detailed three- to ten-page proposal outlining what your idea is, how it will be developed, and how it will be implemented, along with the associated financial and outreach components. So it's crucial, if you're going to do effective fund raising, to develop your idea as fully as possible, showing exactly how it will work.

Although you will need to develop a fairly specific idea to get funding, the exploration process that leads to it can begin with vague thoughts. Maybe you want to travel through Europe and you need money to do it. That's a good starting point. From there you can talk to friends or associates who have done some traveling themselves. Think about the places you'd like to visit, and what unique resources or opportunities can be found there. Talk to people in your field, and see if you can combine travel with a business, educational, or research purpose. Is there a problem in your work or profession that you could solve by making a trip?

In my work with numerous clients over the years, I've used a number of exercises that have proved very successful in helping people develop their ideas. If you've just started thinking about your idea, these exercises can help bring you to the point where you're ready to do funding research and a proposal. If you've thought through your idea pretty thoroughly, and maybe even written some form of description or proposal, these exercises can still help make your project stronger. You may have been concentrating on one aspect of your project, say, the need, and skimping on another, such as implementation.

What if your idea is already very well defined? Perhaps you even have an idea of where you're going to apply for funding. Say you want to get a Fulbright Fellowship to teach in India, and you already have an institution picked out; is there a reason to go through with these exercises? Actually, they may still help you, either in supporting your original plan or in suggesting alternative ways to realize your goals.

If the Fulbright to India—for example—is your ultimate goal, then the exercises can help you develop arguments to support your proposal. They can help you answer the questions that the Fulbright committee is sure to ask sooner or later. Why India? Why the Fulbright? How are you qualified? What are your ultimate goals? How do this specific fellowship and this specific country combine to help you accomplish those goals?

If, on the other hand, your goals are more general (you want to travel, you want to make a spiritual pilgrimage, you want to take photographs at the Ganges), then these exercises may help you come up with alternative approaches to reaching your goals. The Fulbright, after all, is a one-shot chance. Your odds are better if you apply to several different programs or funders.

What if you're involved in creative artistic or scientific work, and what you really want a grant for is the time and resources to develop an idea, write a novel, research an invention? You can't develop your idea in great detail because that's what you need the grant for. Many artistic endeavors work this way, and so do some entrepreneurial ones. I've helped raise money for numerous projects like these—visual arts projects, sculpture projects, books. In most cases, the people have credentials and have done previous work, either as artists or as business people. There are foundations that will fund work in progress and artists' colonies where you can spend time working and fleshing out an idea. Jay McInerney wrote his best-selling novel *Bright Lights, Big City* in a three-week period at the MacDowell Colony. These programs are competitive, though, and you have to have past success, or the promise of success, in order to work this out. You're not going to get $20,000 to take off time to develop an idea unless there is already interest in it, or the idea is fairly well fleshed out and what you really need is R&D money to take it further.

In any case, you'll usually need a working outline. You may not know exactly what you'll find in your research or creative process, or which direction you'll take, but you should have a logical idea of what issues you're going to deal with, what problems you'll explore, what elements you'll be working with. You'll also need to have some samples of your thinking and research to date. When you get into the project itself, obviously you'll decide exactly how you'll proceed.

YOUR CREATIVE JOURNAL

Most writers, artists, inventors, keep some kind of creative journal, where they sketch or jot down ideas on a daily basis, formed or half-formed, as they come to mind. The notebooks of Leonardo da Vinci are a famous example; he sketched and wrote notes on all his areas of interest, from fine arts and painting to engineering, military devices, and flying machines. Such a journal can be invaluable in helping you develop your ideas. Get yourself a blank notebook, and make it one that seems physically effective for you—whether spiralbound, sewn, or looseleaf, with lined or unlined pages, or maybe an artist's sketchbook. I like to use index cards in a box. Use whatever you're comfortable with. Just keep notes on ideas as they occur to you, and try to write something every day, if you can.

Start with the idea that you're already thinking about, or with the problem or issue that you want to work on. Try defining the problem—and think about how you might go about creating a solution for it. Often, the very act of writing reinforces creative thought processes, and your pen takes off with new, interrelated ideas. One of these off-the-top-of-your-head notions might be worth developing. And when you are ready to seek funding, you can use the initial notes in your Creative Journal to help shape the funding proposal. Also, you can come back to the journal later, to explore undeveloped germs of ideas and to take early thoughts in new directions.

Keep anything relevant to your idea in the journal—names of people you'd like to talk to, kinds of research you'd like to do, lists of steps that will need to be completed along the way. Just keep filling up the notebook, and be sure to look back over what you've written from time to time to recall ideas that may be worth following up on.

BRAINSTORMING—THE POWER OF FREE ASSOCIATION

Set aside some time to work with your Creative Journal, or just get a fresh legal pad, sit down, and let your mind wander freely. Take a vague idea and just free-associate—jot down everything that occurs to you in relation to that idea. No matter how silly the thought, write it down. Don't limit your thinking in any way. This is the time to be purely creative. Get rid of your internal censor; there will be more than enough time later on for you to question, evaluate, and criticize. But for now, don't be shy—no one else has to see your mental meanderings. And remember: don't be afraid to write about your personal needs and experience; this is the source of many good ideas.

If ideas are slow in coming to you, be patient. Wait for them. Meanwhile, write down everything that does come to mind, no matter how trivial it might seem. And who knows, a really crazy idea (such as using radio waves to create light) might just pay off (the E-lamp).

I've found this exercise expecially valuable for those of my clients who have come to me with a general idea of what they want to do but without the specifics. I just ask them to free-associate, write page after page of whatever comes to mind. Out of this, we can usually get the material we need to prepare a detailed outline.

UNCONSCIOUS MIND

The power of free association comes from the power of the unconscious mind. You can let this power work for you, even when you're not actively focused on your idea process. If you're feeling blocked, keep using your Creative Journal and jotting down attempts to define the problem you're wrestling with. Repeat it over and over, reword it, define it, but don't worry—you can't *force* an idea or solution into being. Let your unconscious work on the problem: when you're idle or daydreaming, or just when you're falling asleep or waking up. Your brain is still working on an unconscious level even when you are not actively concentrating. Many scientists have had this experience— you wrestle with a problem, define and redefine it, analyze it ten different ways, then the solution suddenly flashes into consciousness when you least expect it. Sometimes your mind just needs a chance to see the problem in a new way. Sir Isaac Newton needed an apple falling on his head to lead him to the concept of gravity.

POSITIVE IMAGE

This is another kind of free association that is useful if you have trouble getting past your fear of failure, or if you're all too aware of the daunting obstacles you may have to overcome. It will help you if you have trouble turning off your internal censor, the little voice that says, "This will never work." Imagine that you've already gotten that grant, that you have all the money you might need to carry out your idea. Imagine that your friends and colleagues have nothing but praise for your idea, admiration that you got the grant, and faith in your ability to carry it out. Let yourself free-associate all the steps in the process—exactly how you'll begin, what you'll do next; imagine your project well under way, what it's like on a day-to-day basis. This is a good way to get down to the details of how the project will really work.

VISUALIZE THE END POINT

The best way to start from the beginning in developing your project so that it can be funded is to visualize the end point, to see clearly where it is you want to wind up. What will be the result of actually putting your idea into practice? Say you want a travel grant to write a book about Balinese music. Think about how much time you're going to spend in Bali, what you'll do when you're there, where you'll go, who you'll talk to. Write down all these details in your Creative Journal. Or say you want to start a day-care center. How many children will you take care of? What will make your center different from others that you know of? This is a visualizing process that many creative people use.

DO A "GOOD IDEA" CHECK LIST

In this chapter we've discussed a number of qualities that good ideas and viable projects have in common: originality, problem solving, answering needs and providing goals, timeliness, outreach, points of reference. We've also talked about the personal aspects: experience, faith, and conviction, ability to follow through. Make up a check list, and write about each of these topics as it relates to your idea and your own capabilities. Write positively; find the special, unique qualities in your idea and your background. Be sure to ask yourself: Who is the audience, or who is the intended beneficiary of your project? What makes this project different from others, and at the same time, how is it related to existing ideas? What makes *you* qualified to do this project?

How to Get Your Idea into Shape for Funding

Your Creative Journal and the other exercises should have given you plenty of material to work from. Now you can begin refining and shaping your idea so that you can start the fund-raising process. There are several stages in this process. You'll need to develop a mission statement and a preliminary outline of your project, and you'll need to make the mental transition from your private dreams and brainstorming to the public sphere. You probably want to get some initial feedback and response to your idea, as part of the preparation for doing further research and writing a formal proposal.

THE MISSION STATEMENT

You are now preparing to present your idea to potential funders. You need to get that idea into clear, concise language, so that it will be easy for the funder to comprehend. Funders will have limited time to consider your proposal (they'll be looking at many), so your initial statement must be strong, to-the-point, and convincing. This is called a *mission statement*—a very simple statement of the purpose of your project, which conveys the essence of your idea in a few sentences or a short paragraph. (Some nonprofit professionals call this the *statement of need.*)

The mission statement is of crucial importance. It is the first step in selling your idea to a funder, and will create the vital first impression of your project. Writing it also helps you to focus your own thoughts about your idea, and the finished statement will serve as the jumping-off place for writing your proposal. Here are some samples of mission statements from successfully funded projects:

- To obtain funding for a special scholarship fund to enable minorities, women, and disadvantaged students nationwide to attend a special one-week media education program in Los Angeles.
- To obtain funding for the implementation of an activated oxygen technology that measurably improves the quality of water in lakes and ponds without using chemicals.
- To obtain funding for a multiyear professional electronic media training program that will use the highest quality equipment to teach young people—including ex-offenders, gang members, and at-risk youth—how to use and maintain the electronic facilities utilized in the production of radio and television programming.
- To secure funding for the reproduction and publication of lithographs, limited editions, and serigraphs of at least twelve pieces of my artwork.
- To obtain funding for the writing of a book based on a seminar that I have been conducting for four years. The seminar deals with the use of live pets and stuffed animals in the therapeutic and curative treatment of ill individuals.

Notice how brief the mission statement can be, as long as it effectively conveys what the project is and why it is unique. As we'll see later, you'll use the body of your proposal to explain your project in detail, how you will implement it, the timeline, costs, and so on. But the mission statement is the log line. It says where you're going. It should grab the readers at the foundation or corporation and set them up to be receptive to your proposal. It also forces you to be clear about your own ideas. You will find that you cannot write a proposal until you have a mission statement.

How can you boil down all those notes in your Creative Journal into a few sentences? Start by looking over your original notes on the idea, then explore possible statements on the page. Work on getting down to the heart of your idea—say what you wish to do, and include the details that make your project unique and specific. Try different wordings; figure out which words are absolutely essential in getting your idea across. Don't worry, you'll have the chance to explain in detail later on. The goal now is clarity and brevity.

MAKING A PRELIMINARY OUTLINE OF YOUR PROJECT

Once you have a clear mission statement, you are ready to write the first outline of your project. This is a working document that you may revise many times. It will help you in several ways. First, it will force you to think through the actual steps of your project clearly, from start-up to full implementation. This should enable you to begin your own evaluation of your project, so that you can see what the strong points and weak points are and which areas require further thinking. You'll begin to have your own sense of whether your project is really viable. You will also be able to show the outline to professionals or potential collaborators to get feedback and response. And it will serve as the draft document from which you begin to build your actual proposal.

What should you include? Here's a check list.

- Go back to what you know about the kinds of ideas that interest funders. Ask yourself, Do I have a unique way of solving a problem? This is one of the most important points. Not that every project is going to be unique, but you should consider what may be special about yours. At the same time, make sure you have points of reference to the familiar if your project is quite original.
- Think about outreach and ask yourself: Who is the audience, or the intended beneficiary of this project?
- Ask yourself, What is the market for or potential interest in this project?, and, What are other people doing in this area? If you don't have a real feeling for this yet, don't worry. This will come as you begin to do some preliminary research, and you can add it to your outline later.
- Explain what qualifies you to do this project, whether your experience, expertise, or special knowledge of the area. (Mention here if you're going to draw on the help of advisers or collaborators, and explain their qualifications as well.)
- Make up a step-by-step chronology of your project, beginning with the point at which you are funded, or have start-up funding. Carry it through to completion or full implementation of your project.
- Include your thoughts about any additional people who may be involved in the project, what their roles will be, at what

stage they'll be brought in, whether you have names already, whether you'll do a search.

- Include your thoughts on specific locations where your project will take place.
- Include any thoughts on additional fund raising that may be part of your project, such as ticket sales for a theater series that you want to start.

You may find that you've addressed many of these questions in your Creative Journal and brainstorming sessions. This is the opportunity to put them down in order. Don't worry too much about the format of your outline; a series of paragraphs is fine. Do be systematic; address each stage of the project in a step-by-step way. At the same time, try to be succinct. The purpose of the outline is not to include every detail or thought you have about your project, but simply to plot out the basic plan. How long should the outline be? It depends on your project. It might be three, ten, or even twenty pages for a complex, long-term project.

This is where you have to start doing your homework, and it's an essential part of the process. You cannot present funders with a one-sentence idea and expect them to hand you money on a silver platter. You'll also need to have fleshed out your idea, at least in an informal way, if you decide that you might want to work with a professional fund raiser. I have turned down innumerable potential clients because they really didn't have more than a germ of an idea. In my own practice, I love outlines—I think they work wonderfully. If someone comes in with a really good working outline, a top-notch mission statement, and a good sense of what they want, as well as having done some research in terms of "What is the market out there?," "What are other people doing?," I know the person has made a real commitment, and usually find we have a good chance to get funding.

The other great benefit of the outline is that when you work from your mission statement, and you get down three, ten, or twenty pages on paper in an organized way, you will pretty much be able to tell whether your plan is going to fly or not. You'll be able to spot weaknesses, gaps that need to be filled, questions you need to answer, areas that will need more research. You'll know what you want to find out from professionals in your field, and you'll find that people will take you more seriously, and may be more generous with their time, when they sense you've done your homework. Remember, your outline is a work in progress; you'll be adding to it and adjusting it as you continue with the next stage of the grant-getting process: going public.

MAKING THE TRANSITION FROM PRIVATE TO PUBLIC

Now that you have your mission statement and your outline, you're clear enough about your idea to begin sharing it with others and getting feedback and positive criticism that may be helpful in organizing your funding campaign. This will be part of the fund-raising preparation process that we'll explore in the next chapter.

This can be an exciting time, but it can also be difficult. So far, you have given yourself lots of creative freedom and kept your self-criticism to a minimum. Sharing your idea with other people means leaving yourself open to possible negative responses. Also, you may have some fear that someone else will steal your idea for their own profit. Some people are just more comfortable playing their cards close to the chest; others are eager to share their ideas. If you are protective about your idea, take care to choose thoughtful, considerate people with whom to discuss it. Talk to people you trust, people whose opinions you respect.

Most important, don't lose touch with the source of your passion for your idea. I've always chosen to work with ideas I'm passionate about, and I think if one is not passionate about an idea or project, one has no business taking it on. However, it's important not to let your passion cause you to get emotionally tied to a set way of doing something. Flexibility is the key here. You'll find that you need input from others who have either worked in this field before or who have some specialized knowledge. They can offer you invaluable assistance in shaping your project and getting it off the ground; but you have to remain flexible enough to be open to possible different ways of doing things.

So you're ready to start talking about your idea with others—but who should you talk to? Should you start with your family and friends? Who will really be able to help, and what exactly should you ask them for? What is the best way to present your idea to them?

Your first impulse is probably to explain your idea to your immediate family or close friends. Whether you should do this depends to some extent on how comfortable you are about sharing the idea at this point. If you are still in the early stages of development and any negative feedback might discourage you, you'll want to think carefully about who you talk to first. If, on the other hand, you are fairly confident about the idea, and other people's opinions are not likely to deter you, then go ahead. Realize that although friends and family can certainly be helpful, their comments, whether positive or negative, may not reflect the true value of your idea. They might even feel in some way threatened. In weighing their responses, take into account how well they know the field. Their suggestions may be valid, but before changing your idea to accommodate their suggestions, talk to some people with professional experience.

Talking to professionals is a very important step in going from private to public. You've spent a good deal of time thinking about your idea, and you may or may not have shared these thoughts with your friends and family. They could be invaluable collaborators, or just not that helpful. In any case, I do suggest you approach a professional in the field to get feedback that will more directly relate to the viability and originality of your project. If you want to start a day-care center in your home, talking to other day-care professionals will probably give you more valuable insights than friends or family can.

When you do consult people in relevant fields, look for those you feel you can trust, people whose opinions you usually respect, people with expertise in the field. If you're really lucky, you will find all three qualities in the same person. Avoid anyone you think may have only negative things to say; this kind of response will throw you off. Constructive criticism, on the other hand, may help you refine your idea. You will find that some individuals are better sounding boards for you than others. Keep this in mind; come back to them with other ideas. Listen carefully to their responses, weigh their suggestions against your own instincts, and make changes if you believe those changes will improve the viability or fundability of your idea.

I don't suggest you start calling up program officers of foundations at this stage. This is important, for obvious reasons. If everyone who is reading this book started doing this, the foundations would be inundated, and you can imagine the chaos that would ensue. This could mean the end of philanthropy as we know it. It's in all of our best interests that we save contacts with program officers for later on in the process, after the basic homework has been done. And there is an etiquette to contacting foundations that is important to follow.

However, I do encourage you to work with resources in your community. So, for example, if you want to start that day-care center in your home, talk to those who are operating other day-care centers in your area. You'll find that many people really like to share their expertise. That's the nice thing about the nonprofit community: it's a real community, and not as cutthroat as some commercial fields. A more gracious and more honorable style of behavior operates here, and people are fairly good about sharing information.

How can you locate people who would be helpful to talk to? This really becomes part of your fund-raising preparation, which we'll discuss in greater detail in the next chapter. For now, though, let's consider two issues that relate directly to taking your idea public: protecting your idea and dealing with criticism.

PROTECTING YOUR WORK

You may be feeling protective of your idea and reluctant to reveal it to others. Still, you will have to discuss your idea openly if you're going to pursue funding; and you'll have to get past the fear that someone might steal it. You should be careful about certain ideas, especially if a patent or copyright is involved, but you really shouldn't worry too much about theft in the nonprofit world—this is not Hollywood. I can talk about this with some assurance. My brother is a head of production in a division of a major Hollywood studio, and my sister and my brother-in-law are both successful screenwriters. So I'm fairly well versed in the workings of Hollywood from the inside. These relatives are always shocked at the way a client comes to me and discloses his or her ideas, and then we present them to a number of different foundations. They always say, "You're nuts! Why isn't someone going to steal this? It's such a wonderful idea!" The Art Buchwald/Eddie Murphy controversy over *Coming to America* has really stirred up the issue.

But the nonprofit sector has its own traditions and its own codes of behavior, going back to the time of Ben Franklin, and idea theft is simply not part of it. In my fifteen years of fund raising, I have never seen an idea stolen, and I find that rather wonderful. My colleagues attest to the same experience. To sum up: in the nonprofit world, theft is highly unlikely.

On the other hand, if you have a half-formulated idea you may want to be careful about showing it to other working professionals. If someone hears the germ of an idea, they can't help but assimilate it and utilize it, perhaps as part of a project that they're about to do. So while I don't want to alarm you to the point that you won't show your project to anyone, I do encourage you to talk your ideas through fairly specifically but not to reveal absolutely everything. Talk about your plans in a general way rather than showing a detailed outline. If you are including groundbreaking technology or some secret-ingredient recipe, just leave out the ticklish part and discuss the basic concepts. Again, I don't mean to cause serious concern that your idea might be stolen—you just need to be a little cautious.

It's important to keep this in perspective. If you are talking with professionals, remember that you're picking their brains and asking them for *their* professional insights. You have to approach this with a certain amount of mutual trust. You can't expect people to be generous with you if you play your cards too close to the chest. A filmmaker I know once joined a discussion group of other filmmakers, who had gotten together to share ideas and experiences about raising money for their projects. When it came time for the person who had actually started the group to talk about his project, he refused to say what it was. At this point, most of the others became disgusted, and the group eventually folded. Another friend meets with a group of writers who write for audiovisual programs. These people are actual competitors, they vie for the same jobs with the same companies, yet they are remarkably open with one another, sharing everything from pricing strategies to creative techniques. They realize that they each have their own unique talents and imaginations, which is what their clients pay for, and that they have more to gain from sharing experiences than they have to lose.

There are cases when you do want to be careful, and you can take advantage of certain legal protections, including patents, trademarks, and copyrights. You can't patent or copyright an idea, but you can patent a device, a chemical formula, or a specific procedure. You can't copyright a title, but you can protect the script of a screenplay, a novel, a play, a piece of music. You can protect a business name or a trademark. It's just sound business sense to take advantage of these protections if they're appropriate for your project. You can apply for most of these protections yourself and save a great deal of money that you might spend on lawyers. If you have an invention, or a for-profit business idea that is highly marketable, you should definitely apply for a patent. See the sidebar on page 40 for specific procedures.

COPYRIGHT

Copyright is a form of protection provided by federal law to the authors of original literary, dramatic, musical, and artistic works (and certain other intellectual works). Copyrightable work must satisfy the following criteria: the work must be fixed in a tangible form from which it can be reproduced; it must be the result of original authorship; and there must be at least a minimal element of creativity present.

Copyright protects only the expression of an idea, not the idea or concept itself. Names, titles, trademarks, short phrases, and slogans are not copyrightable since they lack the minimum amount of original authorship necessary for copyright. Copyrights are not available for utilitarian or functional objects.

Ownership of the copyright in a work is separate from ownership of the work. The owner of copyright has the exclusive right to do and to authorize others to do the following: to reproduce the copyrighted work in copies; to prepare derivative works based upon the copyrighted work; to distribute copies of the copyrighted work to the public by sale or other transfer of ownership, or by rental, lease, or lending; to perform the copyrighted work publicly, in the case of literary, musical, dramatic, and choreographic work, pantomimes, and motion pictures and other audiovisual works; and to display the copyrighted work publicly in the case of literary, musical, dramatic, and choreographic works, pantomimes, and pictorial, graphic, or sculptural works, including the individual images of a motion picture or other audiovisual work.

A work is protected by the copyright laws the moment it is created in a tangible form. You do not have to register the work or place a copyright notice on the work before it is published, but it is recommended that you do so.

The proper notice for copyright is: the symbol ©, or the word "Copyright," or "Copr."; the year of first publication; and the name of the copyright "owner." The duration of copyright for works being copyrighted now is generally the author's life plus fifty years.

If you register your copyright within three months after publication, you can recover statutory damages and attorney's fees if there is an infringement of the work. Registration is a straight-forward process that requires you to submit a registration form, deposit a copy of the work for which you are seeking copyright, and pay a $20 filing fee. You can write directly to the Copyright Office, Library of Congress, Washington, DC 20559, to request the necessary application forms, which are free of charge. You can also call the Hotline Number for Forms and Circulars—202-707-9100—and leave a recorded request. If you want more information about copyright, you can talk with someone at 202-479-0700. You can also request the helpful Library of Congress circular *The Nuts and Bolts of Copyright.*

PATENTS

Patents protect inventions from being manufactured, used, or sold without authorization. To qualify for patent protection an invention must be new, useful (if not a design), and nonobvious.

There are three types of patents. The first, a utility patent, is granted for any new and useful machine, process, manufacture, or composition of matter, or any new and useful improvement on these. The second, the design patent, is granted for any new, original, and ornamental design for an article of manufacture. This patent helps to protect the "look" of a particular article when copyright is not available. The third type of patent, the plant patent, is granted for the invention or discovery and asexual reproduction of a distinct and new variety of plant.

The term of a patent varies according to type: seventeen years for a utility patent, fourteen for a design patent, and an indeterminate time for plant patents. Unlike copyrights and trademark rights, you must apply for and receive a grant of patent from the U.S. Patent and Trademark Office before your work is protected by federal law. You can file a patent application with the Patent and Trademark Office, together with the filing fee (a minimum of $340 for utility patents, $140 for design patents—but both fees are reduced by half if you are a sole or independent inventor). The application is reviewed, and if all the requirements are satisfied, a patent will be issued. During the time the patent application is under consideration by the Patent and Trademark Office, the work you have applied for should be marked "patent pending." When the patent is issued, this notice must be replaced with the actual patent number, for example: "U.S. Patent No. 5,0015,089."

You can easily run up substantial costs—of several thousand dollars or more—for preparing and filing your patent application. The process can be long and it may take several years before your patent is granted. Since patent law and filing requirements are complex, it's best to seek out the advice of an expert in patent law.

TRADEMARKS

A trademark is a word, logo, or other device used to identify the source of goods and distinguish them from those manufactured or sold by others. You can create a trademark simply by adopting one and using it in connection with the sale of goods or services. A trademark can last indefinitely, provided that it continues to be used as a mark to signify the quality of products and services, and so long as the public perceives the mark as an indicator of the source and origin of the goods. As owner of a trademark, you can prevent others from using the same or a confusingly similar mark or name in connection with the sale of similar goods or services when the use would be likely to cause confusion to the public.

You do not have to register a trademark to secure protection, and can use "TM" prior to registration in order to indicate your rights in the mark. Before you can register a trademark, however, you must have a trademark clearance search made. It is advisable to hire a reputable trademark search firm, which can charge several hundred dollars for this service. Usually your lawyer, who prepares the registration application, will hire the search firm. To apply for a trademark, you must file certain forms with the Patent and Trademark Office. The filing fee is $175 for each class of goods covered by the application. You can get trademark registration forms (free of charge) by writing to the United States Department of Commerce, Patent and Trademark Office, Washington, DC 20231. You can also request their booklet *General Information Concerning Trademarks*, which provides an overview of federal trademarks and contains sample registration forms.

A federally registered trademark is valid for an initial twenty-year-term and can be renewed over and over again as long as the mark is used in accordance with the registration. In order to preserve the registration period, the owner must file an affidavit in the fifth year of use affirming that the mark is still in use. Once a registration is obtained, the owner has to continue to use the mark and must police it to prevent others from using it (or a confusingly similar name), or risk losing the rights to the mark.

You can file an "intent to use" application to reserve a mark and determine if it can be registered before investing heavily in advertising, promotion, and extensive use. However, the Trademark Office will not issue an official registration until there is a "bona fide use of the mark in the ordinary course of trade." You must actually use the mark within three years after you have filed the "intent to use" application, subject to certain six-month filing requirements.

The following notices can be used on federally registered trademarks: ®, "Registered in U.S. Patent and Trademark Office," or "Reg. U.S. Pat. & Tm. Off."

What of those people who talk for years about a project but never act on it? Do they have any right to complain if someone else acts on the same idea? Not in my opinion. I've met many, many individuals over the course of my life who had terrific ideas and never acted upon them. This brings to mind a story: A man was at a Van Cliburn concert and said, "I'd give my life to play like him." The person sitting next to him replied, "He did." And I think that really sums up the necessity of follow-through on an idea. It's not always easy. It can take a lot of time, it can take a lot of work. It can mean sacrifice. Just because someone spouts an idea does not mean they own it.

Sometimes people do pursue the same idea simultaneously, and it might seem that stealing has taken place when it hasn't. However, I think this is very rare among projects pursued by individuals. When it comes to community projects, it's a different story. I have had the opportunity to work on projects when I knew there were other people pursuing similar ideas in the same community. For example, there were a number of very similar plans for the homeless going on at about the same time in Los Angeles. There were also similar parenting projects, and similar child-abuse projects. But even these are broad categories. As a general rule, projects do parallel one another in social services and organizations. It's much more rare with individual projects.

However, this brings up a good point. What if you have worked very hard on an idea, and then discover that someone else is working on the same idea and probably will go after similar funding sources? This often happens to people who are doing their doctoral dissertations. I've known several people who have worked hard on dissertations, only to find, when they're just on the verge of submitting them, that somebody else has been there first. Do you abandon the idea completely? No, I don't think you should. I do think, if you are sufficiently committed to your idea, you ought to modify it somehow, so that you can run with it in a new direction.

DEALING WITH COMMENTS AND CRITICISM

So you bite the bullet, you contact a few people to discuss your project, and you get two totally different reactions from two different professionals. One tells you it's terrific and will be a great success; the other says it's deeply flawed and you should go back to the drawing board. Or someone tells you it's a terrific idea but needs one major change, which you feel would undermine the very reason you wanted to do the project in the first place. Now you don't know if your idea is good or bad, or if you should change it, give it up, or ignore the negative criticism and forge ahead. Don't panic—this is all part of the process.

Just as not everybody is equally skilled at giving constructive criticism, not everybody is equally adept at dealing with criticism and using it effectively. Still, you can learn to improve the way you deal with comments and criticism, so that this doesn't have to be a totally confusing, soul-wrenching process.

You can start by actively managing the process of getting feedback from the very beginning. When you talk to a professional or someone in your field, I suggest you avoid bringing up questions or reservations that you yourself may have about your idea. This may convey the sense that you're not really serious or committed to it. It's probably better to stay away from asking a point-blank question about why something doesn't seem to work, unless you feel wholly comfortable with your project, and confident in it. Until you have a clear vision and a very complete vision of where your idea is going, and how it will be realized,

I suggest you just present the project and listen; let your advisers respond of their own initiative.

When you do get a response, jot down some brief notes during the interview or immediately afterward. You might even want to consider asking to tape-record your discussion. Hearing someone react to your idea can arouse strong emotions, and you may not clearly remember every point.

After you've received some comments, especially if they're in some part critical, don't feel you have to react right away. Give yourself a cooling-off period to mull things over. You can use your Creative Journal at this point to help you absorb the feedback. Write down your adviser's comments and suggestions. Then write down your reactions to them. Do so without being overly defensive. Be honest with yourself; let the ink flow. Try this immediately after talking with the adviser, then repeat the exercise (on another page) after a cooling-off period. If you find yourself agreeing with the adviser's points, then think about making changes in your plan. If your instincts tell you to stick to your guns, by all means stick.

Don't get your feathers ruffled; criticism is usually constructive. Of course, it does occasionally come from envy, and there are people who just get an ego kick from imposing their ideas on someone else's project. But you are showing your idea to professionals who have long and vital experience in the field, and they may have been through a process that you're just starting. More often than not, they will really try to share this experience and give you constructive criticism. The best, most helpful advisers I've had have not torn things apart but have taken what worked in my idea and run with it, as well as offering constructive criticism. By that I mean, not only saying, "This doesn't work," but also, "Perhaps this is how you ought to rethink this," and, "This is what works in your idea."

I always let criticism sink in for a while. I mull it over. I think the best ideas need time to gel and time to be formed. Comments and criticism can lead to a positive reworking of an idea. But it's crucial not to be hasty in changing your plan. So if you do get criticism, don't start tearing everything apart. If an architect is designing a house for you, and you have one idea of how you think the house should be, and the architect completely revamps it, are you then going to say, "Absolutely," and totally abandon your vision? Of course not. The same holds true for your vision of your idea. Sit with the criticism for a while.

How can you tell if comments or criticism are valid? Again, you have to consider the expertise of the adviser in evaluating his or her comments. Constructive criticism from a professional in a relevant field may be quite valuable. But listen to your own instincts as well. You can also compare feedback from different advisers. This can be confusing if you get comments that contradict each other, but try to figure out what different experiences or attitudes may have caused two advisers to react differently to your idea. On the other hand, if you find that several people make the same comment or criticism, you know that this is a reaction you may get from others, including potential funders.

Still, I want to stress the importance of listening to your own instincts. I once worked with a composer named Alan J. Friedman on a show that I raised money for, and he had a wonderful expression: "Trust your goosebumps." I believe in this very strongly. Instinct and your gut reaction will give you a clue as to whether a change seems right or not. After all, it was your instinct that led you to your idea in the first place. So go with it. If it seems right, then take the criticism. If it doesn't feel right, then move on. While it's important to remain open and flexible, you must also have the strength of your convictions. Nobody does anything of any interest in the world without stirring up some negative criticism along the way. Some of it you'll just have to shrug off.

If you've come this far, you're already a long way on the road to getting a grant. You have a clear mission statement and a working outline of your project, and you've started to think about presenting your idea to others. So you are in a much stronger position than when you started. What comes next? More research, more refining, and more details. In the next chapter we'll explore the whole process of organizing your fund raising, from mental preparation to research to selling your idea.

PREPARING YOUR
FUNDING CAMPAIGN

I t all starts with an idea, but an idea by itself is not enough. You've already come a long way by developing your mission statement and an outline of your project. Now you're ready to begin your funding campaign, and to start work on actually applying for a grant. I call it a campaign, because you will have to do careful planning and research, think about potential funders, think about the money. This stage is all about laying careful groundwork so that you'll be in the strongest possible position when you do apply for a grant. How organized and effective you are at this stage will have a great deal to do with your ultimate success.

To be a successful fund raiser for your own project, you'll need to prepare yourself mentally for the process and organize your funding campaign. This is not something that you can do haphazardly. Seeking grants takes time, it takes effort, and it takes organization. You'll probably want to do some research into your own project area, and you'll certainly need to research possible funding sources. You'll need to consider the possibility of working with a professional fund raiser or joining up with a nonprofit organization. You'll need to think carefully about the budget for your project, prepare and revise a proposal, build support for your project, and communicate with funders. In this chapter, we'll outline all the steps in this process, so that you will know what to expect, and we'll get you started on some of them.

Many people use the term "grantsmanship" to refer to some of the skills and techniques that you'll learn in this chapter, but I've never liked this word. To me, "grantsmanship" conveys a mysterious "knack" that certain people have and others don't. This is just not the case. There's nothing mysterious about the techniques that lead to getting grants—anyone who's willing can learn them. To others, "grantsmanship" means a dull, scholarly, academic, scientific approach to getting a grant, and that's not what this book is about. I've always found fund raising to be an exciting and entrepreneurial activity. If you have a wonderful idea, and you really believe in it, there will be funding out there for you, no matter how quirky your project. There's nothing academic about it.

MENTAL PREPARATION

Preparing to get a grant isn't all organization; it's also important to put yourself in the right frame of mind for getting funded. This means both having a positive attitude about your ideas and abilities and having a realistic sense of the kind of commitment that's involved.

GET IN A POSITIVE FRAME OF MIND

Nothing can provide a more powerful boost to your grant getting than having a positive attitude about the value of your project and your ability to carry it out. This is the kind of intangible asset that will keep you going through the long stretch, will motivate you to pursue every lead along the way, and will ultimately infect funders with your own enthusiasm. *It's essential that you be able to think of yourself as a serious prospect for a grant.* How can you do this? How can you build your self-confidence about your project, and sustain it when the going gets tough? I'd like to suggest two approaches that are directly linked to the actual grant-getting process.

Positive Brainstorming. First, use the brainstorming techniques of Chapter 1 to focus directly on your confidence and abilities. Go back to your Creative Journal and write down every reason you can think of why you are the person to make this idea become a reality. Write down anything at all that's positive. Write about your skills and character traits. Write about past successes, of any kind. Don't censor, don't be modest, don't be shy. Don't leave things out because they're too trivial, or because you'd be embarrassed to mention them to anyone. No one is going to read this but you. If you're terrific at organizing your closets and you've categorized your CD collection by subject *and* alphabetically, then you have a skill that can certainly help you manage a research project *or* a day-care center. If you have a special rapport with kids, if you can sense their feelings and talk about their concerns, then you have another skill that will help you operate a day-care center *or* communicate with people you will need to talk to for a research project. Most people are all too good at criticizing themselves for things they don't do effectively. Instead, take some time now to look closely at the things you do well. Remember how you've succeeded in the past, and think about how these skills and experiences can support your present endeavor.

When you do this exercise, write for at least five minutes, and do it on several occasions, on different days. Go back to things you've already written—a fresh look may give you a new understanding of how this can help you. This exercise can give you a new look at yourself and help build a feeling of self-confidence that will inspire funders to place their confidence in you as well.

Just Dive In. A second approach is to throw yourself into the project. You often hear that even the most successful artistic people— actors, musicians, filmmakers—suffer from personal insecurities about their work. So what do they do? They abandon their fears by throwing themselves head first into a performance or a project that has its own momentum—playing a role, learning a piece of music, starting a new film or other project. No matter how much stage fright you have standing in the wings, once you're on stage, you've got to act. Suddenly, you realize you're doing it, and the moment of fear has passed.

I've experienced insecurities, like anyone else, but once I commit to a project that I believe in, I throw myself into the work, and my self-confidence shoots right up because I'm concentrating on the project instead of my own fears. When you have actually started doing your project, it almost takes on a life of its own. You become a servant of the project. It's like a calling: it's your duty and privilege to be the one that will make the dream come true.

Throw yourself into the work. Forget about the money for the time being, and look at what the project itself demands. Write out a timeline for the different stages. Go back and work on your outline, thinking about the steps. For example, if you want to produce a play, do you first have to get the play written or do you have to option the rights to a script that is already completed? You have to find and rent the theater, you have to hire a director, you have to help audition and hire the actors, and so on, all the way on to placing ads and getting an audience. Now, this might give you a daunting realization of the size of the task you have before you; but at the same time, it will clarify what it is you have to do. And having this down on paper will bring you one step closer to your goal. The more tangible you make your project in every way, the more it will take on a life of its own.

- **TIP:** There are countless personal-development books that promise to help you with building self-esteem and developing an optimistic attitude, self-motivation, and the like. Many can seem like gimmicks, but some have practical techniques or good psychological insights that many people have found useful. Four of these are listed below:
  - *The Seven Habits of Highly Effective People,* by Stephen R. Covey. New York: Simon & Schuster, 1989.
  - *Flow: The Psychology of Optimal Experience,* by Mihaly Csikszentmihalyi. New York: Harper & Row, 1990.
  - *Learned Optimism: How to Change Your Mind and Your Life,* by Martin Seligman. New York: Alfred A. Knopf, 1991.
  - *Wishcraft: How to Get What You Really Want,* by Barbara Sher. New York: Ballantine Books, 1983.

How Long Will It Take?

One aspect of fund raising that not everyone is familiar with—or prepared for—is the amount of time it can take to get a grant. Part of your mental preparation should be devoted to readying yourself for a long-term, sustained effort. How long will it take to get funding? It can take as little as a few weeks or as long as several years; usually it's somewhere in between. Three to six months is not unusual, from beginning your funding research to making applications to waiting for a response. If you have a large project that will involve a number of people, the fund-raising process will be more complex and take more time. If you have a simple project that involves only yourself, the process will be shorter and simpler. Funders have their own time frames. Some funders make grants on a continuous basis; others have funding cycles and make grants only once or twice a year. You'll have to research these funding cycles, and key your proposals to the funders' timelines.

Research, writing proposals, and following up all take time. If you are not willing to commit time and effort to this process, then you are not likely to follow through and execute the project even if you do get the funding. I don't mean to discourage you from applying for money, because it *is* available, and if you believe in your idea, you can get it. But your willingness to devote the necessary time to the grant-seeking process is one test of how much you really want to make your idea happen.

To go after funding effectively, you can't just target one foundation, and wait for the big yes or no. To improve your odds, you may have to submit a number of proposals or applications. You may have to build up support gradually, getting limited support from several sources to fund your idea. You will have your work cut out for you. But if you do it, someone may be willing to underwrite your vision and invest in you. It's a long haul, though, and you'll need a good amount of persistence to see you through.

There's another reason why persistence is a major virtue in fund raising. Some foundations are funny: Many will almost automatically reject a grant proposal the first time out but accept it the second or third time a revised proposal is submitted. If an idea is fundable, if it is a good idea, and if funders see you are committed to the project and likely to carry it out, sooner or later your passionate belief will make an impression.

Of course, there will be ups and downs along the way. Are you going to run into people who do not understand your idea? Yes. Are you going to meet people who think your idea cannot be realized? Yes. But you can't let this stop you. Not everyone is going to understand your vision. Funders are human beings, with personal likes and dislikes, prejudices and enthusiasms. Not everyone is going to jump up and down and think your idea is the greatest thing since sliced bread, and you have to know that going in. But if your project is well defined, and if you follow the correct procedures in applying for grants, you will surely get some positive feedback along the way that will help spur you on.

Since the grant-seeking process can stretch over a long period of time, you may find it hard to keep the ball rolling. If you're a busy person with many daily demands or distractions, you may have trouble staying focused on the process. It can be difficult to keep in touch with your long-term goals and make them a priority when short-term obligations are pressing. But there are some practical, organizational things you can do to keep up the momentum and stay focused. We'll cover them all in this chapter. One thing you can do—and I'm indebted to Barbara Sher and her excellent book *Wishcraft* for this—is keep a daily journal. She calls it an "Actions and Feelings Journal."

A DAILY JOURNAL

Get a spiralbound notebook, or whatever kind you prefer, and at the end of every day simply write down whatever you did to further your project. If you didn't do anything directly related to your project, write down what you *did* do. Maybe you did something to earn money, or you took the afternoon off to go to a movie. Don't feel guilty if you don't act on the project every day—people do have to earn money and relax. But you do want to keep your attention focused on the project for at least this one moment every day, and be able to see how work on your project continues on a week-to-week basis, even if you do take a day off here and there.

Also note down in this journal what your feelings are at the end of the day. Are you optimistic, depressed, satisfied with your progress, anxious to do more? As you look back in this journal, you'll find that some days you did a lot to further your grant seeking, other days only a little, some days you felt up, other days you felt down. But you will get a sense of steady progress. You'll see that week after week, little by little, you are moving closer to your goal. And you'll see that although your feelings can change daily, you are always pursuing your long-term desire.

How do you cope with rejection or discouragement along the way? Keep your long-term goals and inspiration always in sight. Remember that this is a labor of love. Keep visualizing what you want to achieve. If you're trying to produce a theater piece, *see* that opening night and the rave reviews. If you're trying to produce a film, picture yourself accepting that Oscar. This is not childish fantasy—it's your long-term vision, which will give shape to your project and make all that hard work worthwhile. And remember, anything you do today that furthers your project is really part of that project. A filmmaker I know says, "Raising the money for a film is just like preparing the canvas for a painting. It's really part of the process, part of the work." Just by reading this book and doing the exercises, you've already begun to make your idea a reality.

STEPS IN THE PROCESS

By now, as you fire up your grant-getting campaign, you realize that it's not just a matter of getting an idea, finding a possible funder, and writing a letter. You'll need to plan for many steps along the way. You'll need to do some research, both into the area that relates to your idea and into which funders are interested in this area. You'll need to consider whether you should be affiliated with an organization in order to get access to more funds. You'll need to work up a "marketing plan" to sell your idea to funders. You'll need to develop a realistic sense of how much money you need, and you may have to prepare several versions of a budget. You'll need to get comfortable with communicating with funders—by telephone, by letter, and in person. Let's look at these various steps.

- *Subject or "market" research—Getting feedback on your idea.* When you present your idea to funders, it's important to show that you know your subject area well. You need to be aware of what else is going on in your field and what other people are doing. You may already be well versed in your field of interest, or you may have to do some research. You may also want to talk to some professionals to get comments or feedback on your idea. We'll discuss ways you can do this kind of exploration later in this chapter.

- *Funding research.* Funding research is one of the basic steps in getting a grant. It's essential to make your applications to the correct funders, the ones that will be predisposed to take interest in your type of project. There's just too much work involved in preparing a good proposal to waste time with inappropriate funders. The next chapter—on Finding the Right Funder—will get you started. Besides researching funders, you may want to do a little bit of additional research into the fund-raising process itself.

- **Your marketing plan.** Testimonials, endorsements, and supporting documentation can all contribute to the success of your grant application. You will want to start gathering these well before you sit down to write an actual proposal. Collecting them will be part of the ongoing process, just like working on your outline and doing research.

- **Budgeting and financial planning.** Grants are based on need, and realistic budgeting is very important—not only to persuade funders to give you the grant but also so that you'll be able to put your plan successfully into effect once you get it. While some people ask for too much—and getting grants is *not* a way to get rich—it's more likely that you may ask for too little money. You should start making up a budget based on your outline, which may require some additional research. You also want to have a clear sense of your abilities for handling money, especially if your project is large and complex.

- **Affiliation.** There are thousands of foundations that make grants directly to individuals. You can apply to these directly, be approved, and receive a check. However, there are several reasons why you might want to consider affiliating yourself with a nonprofit organization. One big advantage is that you can then apply to more funders than you could as an individual. Many foundations prefer to grant funds to organizations, which pass the money along to individuals. (This is called *fiscal sponsorship*, and you can learn more about it in Chapter 4.)

  There are other advantages to affiliation. If you are working on a large and complex project, you will be able to tap into the resources and expertise of an existing organization. Even if you choose not to affiliate, there are nonprofit groups you may want to turn to for advice and assistance. Affiliation is an issue that you should consider carefully; we address it later in this chapter, and in Chapter 4.

- **Professional fund raisers.** A related question is whether you may want to turn to a professional for help with some part of your grant seeking. Can professional fund raisers guarantee that you'll get a grant? Of course not. Can they help you?

Certainly. Would it be worth it? That depends—on how organized you are, how much you can afford to spend, and how much money you are trying to raise. As someone who has worked in this field for many years, I assure you that you *can* do it successfully yourself. That is what this book is for. However, if you do want to think about working with a professional, we'll offer some tips on the subject later in this chapter.

- *Communicating with funders.* This is a big topic, which covers everything from your initial request for information (write a letter, *don't* telephone), to the way you connect your idea to the funder's mission, to possible meetings with funders. There is an etiquette to communicating with funders, and the worst thing you can do for your cause is to harass an overworked foundation officer. There are also some good reasons why you may not want to tell too much about your project right away. On the other hand, personal contact can sometimes help.

- *Your proposal or application.* In the end, it all comes down to an actual proposal or application. Different funders require different types—they can range from a simple letter to a preprinted application form to an elaborate proposal package with lots of supporting material. Nearly all of them require some of the same basic elements, such as a mission statement and a budget. When you have finished your basic outline and budget, and have done your funding research, you'll be ready to tackle your proposal. (Chapter 10 will take you through this process.)

Now that you have an overview of the whole process, let's look at some ways you can get organized to make your preparation more effective.

GETTING ORGANIZED

It's very important to be systematic about the fund-raising process. You'll need to work at it a little each week, keeping track of prospects, maintaining files, keeping a watch on deadlines, and so on. Bear in mind that when nonprofit organizations do fund raising, they have full-time staff people to do this. You will probably be applying to a number of foundations, which may have different deadlines, requirements, and application forms, and you will have to stay on top of all this. Since this is a long-term process, with many details to take care of, it's very, very important to be organized. People always ask me, What's the key to getting a grant? I think you have to learn how to be organized, and to follow through. These are two of the most important attributes of a good fund raiser.

DEVELOP A GAME PLAN

If you're going to coach a football team, you have to have a strategy. If you're starting a business, you need a business plan. If you're building a house, you need a blueprint. And so it is with the grant-getting process. You have to plan. Now that you have an outline and a timeline for your project, start to do one for your entire grant-seeking process. After fifteen years in the business, I still do this. First, draw up an outline of how you envision the process. Ask yourself how much time you'll need for research and for preparing and sending out proposals. Where are you going to do the research? How are you going to compile and keep track of what you find? Approximately how many proposals do you think you'll have to send out? Of course you won't have all the answers at first, because you're new to the game. This chapter will help you get started, and as you begin doing the research, you'll develop a better sense of how to fill in the details. You will probably revise your working plan as you go along, but you should start to develop it now.

As you begin to work up a fund-raising schedule or outline, your major steps will be: (1) to do subject and funding research; (2) to request application guidelines from funders; (3) to write the proposal and the budgets; and (4) to track the results of your applications. You're not going to have any actual deadlines until you do your research and contact foundations. So say to yourself, "I'm going to allocate the next month (or the next three weeks) to accomplish my research. Then I'll spend one week writing for guidelines, and expect to get replies during the following two weeks." Try to set aside a block of time for accomplishing each stage of the process. You can fill in the details as you learn more.

Obviously, the first step is research. If you're going to do some research into your subject area, think about where and how you will actually do it—at the library, by conducting interviews, or going to seminars—and allocate time for this. You may want to combine your subject research with your funding research. As a first-time grant seeker, you will probably need at least three to four weeks of research time, and you will have to spend some hours in the library, on the telephone, and perhaps in meetings. Get started by allocating an amount of time per week that you think you can devote to your project. Then try to block out specific time periods when you can go to the library, make calls, or work on your budget or outline. You can make a lot of progress by spending even a few minutes a day on this work, in addition to one or two larger blocks of time each week. Make appointments for yourself and enter them in your personal calendar or appointment book.

MAKE A TIMELINE CHART

At the library, you'll identify potential funders and see what their deadlines are. At this point, I suggest you draw up a timeline chart, as most professional fund raisers do.

Probably the most useful chart for you to get started with is a timeline that is divided vertically into blocks of time, usually weeks. Stationery stores sell large plastic-coated charts that you can write on with erasable colored pens. They come in different styles, some with preprinted weeks or months, but I recommend the blank charts that allow you to fill in your own time periods and categories. Block off the weeks on the chart, write in the dates, and note in each column what you plan to do that week: research, requesting guidelines, writing a proposal, and so on. You may want to divide the chart horizontally into several sections, so you can keep track of separate categories of the process—one for research, one just for proposal deadlines, one for follow-up calls, or whatever categories suit you.

At first you may just be scheduling research, but as you proceed you may find yourself filling in names of grant programs or foundations you want to apply to, along with deadlines, application requirements, and so on.

In my own work, I use a chart that is keyed to individual proposals rather than to the overall process. Once you get farther along with your grant seeking, you may want to convert your chart for this purpose or start a new one. On this kind of chart, you will list the individual foundations that you're applying to, assigning columns for the different steps in the application process and the deadlines. Column 1 might list the dates when you send off a request for guidelines, and when you receive them. Column 2 could schedule when you will write your proposals and prepare your budgets. Column 3 lists information about each proposal, such as the amount of funds requested and the expected notification date. Column 4 marks the date when you completed a proposal and sent it to the foundation. Column 5 is used to schedule a follow-up call, perhaps three to four weeks later, and to check off that follow-up call after you have made it.

I love working with charts. There's something about having your process all laid out in a big chart on the wall, with color codes and special categories, that makes it more real and more accessible (and harder to escape). It's easy to glance up and see exactly where you are in the process, what needs to be done right away, and what comes after that. You can add new information daily, and it's a good idea to set aside a time each week when you go over the whole chart, make any revisions necessary, and bring it up to date.

USE A TO-DO LIST

Buy a large week-at-a-glance appointment book, or a weekly appointment calendar, and start working with a daily and a weekly to-do list. Set aside a time each week when you will plan your weekly fundraising tasks. During this planning session, make up a to-do list for the week, and then enter the items in your appointment book or on the calendar, so that you have a specific day and time for each of them. Check the items off the weekly list as you complete them. If you find yourself spending a lot of time on fund raising, set aside a period each day to make up a daily to-do list and check off the items as you finish them.

It's natural to want to do the easy tasks first and leave the disagreeable or difficult ones for later. If you find you're falling into this habit, make a point of doing the most disagreeable task first, each day and each week. Everything will be easier from that point on. Another seductive habit is to fill up your to-do lists with easy tasks that just aren't that important, at the risk of missing the essentials. To avoid this, you've got to set priorities.

Divide your to-do list into an A and a B list, even a C list. Put the essential items on the A list, and make sure they go at the top of your daily and weekly to-dos. A deadline for a foundation is definitely an A-list item. Finishing a proposal in time to get it out for a funding deadline is an A-level priority. Perhaps getting back to someone in the community about your project is an A-level priority, while organizing your files is a B-level or a C-level priority. Of course, if you start having trouble finding things because your files are in chaos, this is going to move up to A level. You are going to have to determine which are the priorities; but if you are in business, or a homemaker, you're used to managing various demands, juggling many activities and making them all work—and this is no different.

USE A CARD FILE

I like to use an index-card file as a flexible way of keeping track of ideas and information. You can use either a large one or the smaller kind that you keep recipes in. Get a number of index tabs so that you can make separate categories for ideas, referrals, contacts, budget information, etc. Try any categories that seem useful; whenever an idea occurs to you, or you get some useful information from a telephone call, a newspaper article, or wherever, jot it down on a card and add it to your file. Keep accumulating these cards, then make time once a week to go through them and activate ideas that seem useful, or discard information that is out of date. I find this easier to use than a journal, or even a looseleaf, which fills up with obsolete material and keeps you constantly flipping back and forth. It's simple to discard and add cards, and the index tabs make it easy to find what you're looking for.

DEVELOP A RESOURCE LIST

In Hollywood, and in other lines of business too, you hear people say, "I've got a great Rolodex—I've been building it up for years." They're not talking about the little brand-name wheel that holds name and address cards, of course. They're talking about their list of contacts, names, and references—the people they know and can call on in the course of business. When you're working to get a grant, a contact list can be one of your most effective tools. This is your personal universe, the platform you'll be building from. It's important from the very beginning, when you're developing your ideas and game plan, all the way to the end, when you get your grant money and start to put your plan into effect.

It doesn't much matter how you keep your list of names and resources. You can use a Rolodex—it's convenient, with replaceable cards, and you can get one in a stationery store for about ten dollars. Or you can start with a little index-card file with alphabetical tabs.

If you're into computers, you can use an address or mailing-list program, or a database. However you store your list, it's the names you put into it that make it valuable.

SET UP A FILING SYSTEM

As you get into your research, and start writing outlines and proposals and budgets, you'll definitely need some kind of filing system. This doesn't have to be an enormous file cabinet. You can begin with one of those large plastic portable file boxes, or a cardboard file box or drawer.

You will need a box of manila file folders. You should open one file for what I call "market research," or investigative research in your field. Keep another file for funding resources. When you find relevant articles in newspapers and magazines, drop them in the appropriate file. Open a file for supporting material on your own work, including endorsements, quotes, newspaper clippings, and ideas, and a separate file for each individual funder that you're going to target, sorted alphabetically. When you write to a foundation, you'll receive a set of guidelines, perhaps an application form, an annual report, or a brochure about the funder or grant program. Drop these into the new file you've opened. You may have a dozen, or even up to twenty of these funder files, with everything you need readily accessible. You can also keep additional files for your outline, for budget information, and for your master proposal. The point is to have ready access to all the information you collect.

SET UP A HOME FUND-RAISING CENTER

If you don't have an office to work from, make sure you have all the basics at home: a desk, a telephone, your Rolodex or card file, your file box, a few basic reference books, and a typewriter or whatever you're going to use to generate your proposals.

What kind of reference books are useful to have? Well, you certainly need a good dictionary. You're going to find most of your research material in libraries, but you may want to have a few basic fund-raising references at home. You may also want to have your own copy of *Foundation Grants to Individuals*. This is put out by The Foundation Center, which is a national organization that gives information on private foundations. It may not be in your local library, as it is expensive (about $40), but there may be ways you can get access to it (see the discussion on page 96). There is also my own series of *Free Money* books, which are less expensive references and are keyed to specific subject areas. You may want to own one or two guides that are directly connected to your subject. And of course you will gradually accumulate your own collection of journals, articles, and pamphlets. (See below, Chapter 3, and the Appendix, for more details on these and other references.)

What kind of office equipment will you need? A calculator for working on budgets, and a typewriter for proposals and applications. (Of course you can always write longhand and work with a typist.) Even if you're not into computers, you may want to consider buying an inexpensive word processor. There are several models available that don't cost much more than a good electronic typewriter, and are easy to use. The advantage of a word processor is that you can save your outlines, proposals, and budgets on magnetic disks as well as on paper. In this form, you can easily revise and rework them to fit the various formats that funders may require, or to incorporate new ideas. You can write a generic request for guidelines and print out ten or twenty different copies, each personalized with its own address and greeting. You can take a proposal that you've written, add a paragraph that will address a funder's particular concern, and print it all out as a perfect original. You can use a spelling checker to make sure your proposals are letter-perfect, or even a grammar checker to clean up your writing. If you do work with a word processor, make sure that you can print out your letters and proposals on good bond paper, with type that's really "letter quality." Fuzzy, poor-quality printing will turn off funders in a hurry.

I'm not saying that you should go out and spend a lot of money on office equipment. This is not necessary if you're going to apply for a few grants and won't be preparing lengthy proposals. On the other hand, if you think you are going to be involved in a long-term process, sending out many applications, or especially if you're going to be raising quite a lot of money, good equipment can greatly increase your efficiency.

The next step beyond the simple word processor would be some kind of personal computer. These offer more sophisticated word processing, as well as special programs to help you make up budgets, organize mailings, keep track of names and addresses, and the like. Most nonprofit organizations use personal computers to assist their own fund raising. You can even use a personal computer, and a "modem" (a telephone communication device) to get access to computerized databases of funding information. Computers are a big subject, and you could use up a lot of time exploring it. But you could start with the reference listed below:

- *Introduction to Personal Computers,* by Peter Stephenson. New York: John Wiley & Sons, 1991.

TAKING YOUR IDEA PUBLIC — AND RESEARCHING YOUR FIELD

You are going to be doing three different kinds of research: (1) market research into your own field; (2) funding research to find out what kind of grants might be available to you; and, possibly, (3) some additional research into the grant-seeking process. As you start on the market research, you can also begin to get feedback from professionals about your idea. You may find it easy to pursue the different kinds of research simultaneously—doing the market research in your field leads you naturally to possible funders. In fact, you'll find that researching your own field may influence how you think about your project, and how you end up doing it.

The most important reason for doing market research is to confirm or evaluate the feasibility of your idea. You may be able to get some professionals to give you their thoughts and suggestions; it's also extremely important to know what other people have done that's different from your idea, or similar, or exactly the same. This will help you to evaluate and refine your own project, and to support it when you present it to funders—you can refer to specific success stories and failures. It will also help you to get a more realistic idea of how you will actually execute your plan when you receive funding. Remember that getting funded is only the beginning. You will want to acquire as much information as you can about how projects in your field have been accomplished, in order to have the best shot at completing yours successfully.

Researching your subject can also lead to new ways of thinking about your idea and how you will see it through. One important aspect of this is how your project relates to your immediate community: you need to know what already exists and have a realistic sense of what can still be done. For example, let's say you want to produce a play locally. The first thing you're obviously going to have to do—if you are not already familiar with this, and you have not previously applied for a grant—is to find out what other theater companies have done in the last few years in your community. You need to know what the community wants and can support. For example, if you live in Haverhill, Iowa, which has a population of 198 people, you obviously are not going to be putting on a major musical piece, because you won't have a theater to work in or the audience to support it. On the other hand, you might think of doing something in the local school, for the surrounding communities. If you live in Chicago, there will be a number of other competing theater companies, but at the same time you're going to be able to rent space more readily, perhaps from an existing theater company, and the audience is there if you can reach it.

How to Research the Market

Your first priority is to identify and contact professionals and organizations in your field who are willing to talk to you, give you their reactions to your idea, and share information about what's going on in the field or local community. How can you find these people?

Probably the best place to start is at your public library. Librarians are wonderful people: tell them what it is you are trying to research and they will certainly help. Look at the directories for nonprofit and other organizations. Use a periodical subject index, and look at back issues of the local paper. Two useful directories that you can find in many libraries are:

- *Encyclopedia of Associations*, edited by Deborah Burek. Vols. 1–3. Detroit: Gale Research Co., 1992.
- *National Directory of Nonprofit Organizations*. Rockville, MD: The Taft Group, 1990.

You can also look into regional or national publications, including professional journals, professional newsletters, and organizational newsletters. (See the Appendix, page 337, for references to some of these.) This will help you get a sense of the larger picture. Perhaps you'll learn of some very successful ideas that could work in your community but have never been tried locally. Consider joining a local or national organization that relates to your subject. Organizations not only publish newsletters that report on what their members are doing in the field, but may sponsor meetings or seminars where you can meet people and find out what they are doing on a personal basis. If you have time to participate in an organization, and perhaps even serve on committees, you'll meet others who are active in the field and knowledgeable about current trends. It depends on your available time and personal style; don't feel you have to get deeply involved with an organization unless you have the time and are genuinely interested. You may get everything you need from newsletters and a few meetings, and you can still get valuable leads from your library work.

Try to talk to the staff of nonprofits, of associations, and to those who have already worked in the field. If you do find people who will agree to talk with you, ask them to apply their own expertise. If you talk to business people, ask if they think the idea is marketable, salable, generally viable, and so on. If your adviser is a former Fulbright scholar, ask about the receptiveness of the committee to such an idea and to the format of your proposal. If your adviser is an English major, ask about your syntax and spelling, get help in tightening up your language.

It's important to have a sense of restraint and limits when talking to professionals. As a first-time grant seeker, you should take special care to avoid badgering the foundations or demanding too much from people in the community. If someone is good enough to give you an interview, don't keep calling them with follow-up questions unless they specifically invite you to. If you get a few good interviews, don't feel as though you have to talk to everyone in the business. And be sensitive to the fact that professionals have busy lives and may not always be able to speak to you. Unless you are a nonprofit professional, a well-known artist or filmmaker, or an ideas person already in the field, it can be seen as pushy or time-wasting to make too many demands. You may also find that some nonprofits are less eager than others to share information, especially when they learn you may be competing for the same funds, resources, and audience. If you have friends who work in the theater community, for example, you might be able to pick their brains, but you'll probably have to tread rather lightly. There is an etiquette to this.

What's the Best Way to Present Your Idea?

You've done a great deal of thinking about your idea by now, and you also have your written mission statement and outline. You can either show someone these, or pitch your idea orally. Your choice will depend to some extent on the people you are talking to, and whether they respond best to oral or printed material. Both approaches can be helpful to you. In talking about a project face to face, you have a lot of opportunity to explain and clarify (and if you come across a great phrase, jot it down for future use). By showing your written mission statement, you can assess its initial impact and possibly get a sense of how you might revise it for clarity and strength.

This being said, there's an important benefit you can derive from talking about your idea. I can't tell you how many times I've started to describe an idea and discovered that I really couldn't do it as well as I wanted. And if you can't explain an idea orally, all the written pages don't mean anything, because you haven't codified and clarified your project to the point that you can effectively convey it to someone else. The old Hollywood "pitch" really has something to be said for it. To get people's attention, get them interested in an idea, you do have to be able to summarize it succinctly, in a few sentences, and then elaborate on it in a systematic but still brief and concise way. There's no better way to practice getting your idea across than by simply telling it.

When you call or write to ask for an interview, be very specific as to why you want one. When someone agrees to talk with you, be sure to do your homework first, and go in with a list of questions. Know what you're going to ask. You can't pick someone's brain effectively until you have done some real thinking yourself. You need to have put your mission statement down on paper, worked up an outline, and formulated your project as well as you can by yourself. Only then will you understand exactly what areas you need to know more about. Many nonprofit people will be generous in talking about their work, but they won't like to feel they are handing it all over on a silver platter. Don't make them feel you want a free introductory lesson in the field. Show that you've done some preliminary investigation yourself. And take notes during the interview, so you can make the most of it.

When someone has been generous enough to share their experience and knowledge with you, be sure to write them a thank-you note. I am a fanatic about thank-you notes—I write them until the cows come home, and people really appreciate it. They don't get enough thank-you notes, and they'll remember yours. Then you may find that you're able to ask the person that you interviewed for a reference later on, or they may help lead you to funding. You will find some very generous and nurturing people in the nonprofit world. They are not in it for the money but to fulfill their own dreams and passions. So do show your appreciation.

What if you get negative feedback: someone says your idea can't work or can't get funded in the existing climate of your field, or needs major changes? Don't panic. Take it all in, allow yourself time to absorb the comments, then go ahead and talk to others in the field. If you start to get the same kinds of comments from several advisers, there's probably something about your idea that you need to reconsider seriously. But don't be too quick to change your idea, unless your own instincts lead you in this direction. You may want to go back and look again at the section on Dealing with Comments and Criticism in the previous chapter (page 44).

When you do get some interviews, or find printed material, follow up by organizing, sorting through, and evaluating your reserach. Obviously, you should keep a separate file or files for this. When you read through your notes, or magazine or newspaper articles, write down the most important points on a separate sheet of paper. I find this helps me to organize my thoughts. You can use these lists of key points as a jumping-off point for further research and planning.

However you pursue it, your subject research should be an open-ended process. Don't plan to do it for just a few weeks and then stop. Foundation officers may or may not be up to date on all the current trends. It can only help you to stay current yourself, so you can educate them about your field, or simply appear more qualified and knowledgeable. Most important, when you finally get that funding and launch your project, you'll want to know everything you can that might help make it a success.

HOW TO SELL YOUR IDEA—AND YOURSELF

How can you sell your idea effectively? It's not as difficult as you might think. First, you want to convey your sense of passion and commitment. It's essential that you communicate this to funders in your proposal and in any other contact you may have with them. Of course, you also need to present your idea in an intelligent, cohesive, and logical fashion. Beyond this, you can use many kinds of supporting materials— testimonials, references, supporting documentation—to strengthen your proposal. This material can help communicate the timeliness of your idea, or the need for it, as well as conveying a sense of your talent and ability to carry it out. This is the most effective kind of "marketing" that you can do—and it's a good idea to start thinking about supporting material right from the beginning.

A word to the wise: don't feel that you have to use hard-core marketing or ingenious sales tricks to promote your project. In the nonprofit world, this kind of approach could backfire. You don't have to be a good personal salesman; this is not as important as the integrity of your idea, your commitment to it, and your ability to see it through. Don't worry if you're not used to selling yourself—it's your idea that's important. A great many original thinkers in all fields were basically shy or reserved people. It didn't stop them from pursuing their vision and putting it into action. The point is, you don't need sales skills so much as the commitment to doing the work necessary to get that grant.

SUPPORTING DOCUMENTATION

One kind of material you can start collecting right away is support documentation about yourself and the need for your project. If you are an artist or filmmaker, this would include any glowing reviews of your work and any good copy from festival programs, brochures, or announcements. If you're working in other areas, you may have copies of newspaper or magazine articles that relate to your work or mention it positively. Obviously, the more prominent the source, the more impressed the funder will be. But a glowing report from a local paper or newsletter *is* valuable. If you don't have such clippings, you might consider calling editors at a few publications and suggesting an article about you or your field. If you're a student, try your school paper. Or you might interest your hometown newspaper in a human-interest profile.

Aside from material about yourself, try to locate one or two very concise articles about the area you're working in, which discuss the problem your project will solve and stress the need for a solution. For example, if you are trying to start a day-care center in your home, find one or two articles that attest to the need for one in your community. If you are at work on an invention, find an article that discusses the problem it will solve. If you want to travel, find one that describes the need for a better understanding of the place you want to visit. You don't have to depend on chance to find these: go to the periodical index in your library and look up your subject area. Don't include an article just for filler—make sure it relates properly to your project and illustrates the need for it.

If you're a good writer, you might contact a newspaper or magazine and offer to do a column or a feature. This can turn you into an "instant expert" in your field as far as the public is concerned and provide useful support documentation at the same time.

ENDORSEMENTS AND RECOMMENDATIONS

Other people in your field can help your fund-raising greatly by supporting you with letters of endorsement or recommendation. They can support you in two ways: they can testify to your talent, skills, and abilities; and they can approve your idea and affirm the need for it. Try to get some of both kinds of support.

An endorsement is a statement from an individual or an organization that supports your idea. These don't have to be long or exhaustive—a brief statement from a well-known source can be very supportive. Do stick to sources in your field, and don't be shy about contacting prominent or well-known people. They may really get interested in your idea and give you the most effective endorsements. However, if you sense that someone is not that interested, and won't give you a glowing endorsement, don't bother. A lukewarm endorsement is not that helpful, no matter how famous the source.

This is not to say that you need a world-class authority to endorse your idea. It can be just as valuable to enlist the support of someone who is known and respected in your community, or who has solid professional credentials. If you have a theater project, contact a local theater critic. If you have an invention, try to find someone with professional credentials who can testify to the need or the feasibility— that the product could really be manufactured and widely used. Write some letters, make some calls. When you do get an endorsement, be sure to write a thank-you note.

It usually does help to get support that relates not only to what you are doing but also to the community you are working in. Contact organizations that work in your field, community groups, state or local government officials, schools, colleges, or universities. Institutional endorsements show that you are really reaching out.

You can also try to enlist commitments of real involvement or practical support. If you have an invention, contact someone in manufacturing or marketing. Try to get a letter from a manufacturer saying that when your project gets rolling, they will be happy to consider producing it. If you're working on a community project, get an organization to say they will help you do outreach by publicizing it among their members. If you're making a film, get a distributor to say they think there's a potential market, and would consider distributing it. If you're going to travel, get an organization to express interest in having you give a lecture on your return. You don't need a contract; a letter of interest or intent is sufficient. You may want to discuss the wording of the letter with the person who is writing it, so that you can get the strongest possible expression of interest. Get them to stress not just that they'll look at your project when it's done, but also that it sounds like an interesting idea, with real market potential. The more they write, the better.

Personal recommendations and testimonials are also important. If possible, get these from working professionals in your field. Letters from prominent people can be effective, but usually only if they really know you or get interested in your project. Someone who knows you well, has professional credibility of their own, and will write in some detail about your talent, skills, and integrity can give you very effective support. Ask a former teacher, employer, or business partner to testify to your organizational skills and your ability to follow through on a project, even if the work you did with them was different from your present idea. Be sure they know about your current work, though, so they can focus their comments in the right direction.

Get Started Early

You can start right away to collect supporting documents, recommendations, and endorsements. Don't wait until you are done with your funding research and are sitting down to write your proposal. It takes time to contact people and get responses. If you're contacting an organization for endorsements, a board of directors may have to approve it, and this will have to be brought up at a scheduled meeting. Starting early on endorsements and recommendations can be part of the market research in your area and may even lead to new funding ideas. It's also a way of beginning the process of outreach to your community. Remember, "outreach" should be interpreted broadly. If you're working on a solitary art project or research project, you still want to think about how and where your work will be presented.

What If You Have Trouble Getting Written Endorsements?

Some people may tell you that they like your idea but are too busy or for some other reason don't wish to provide a written recommendation. If you think they really do appreciate your idea, ask if you can use their name as a reference. Try to determine whether they are sincerely supportive or just don't like saying that they're not interested. You may run into people who seem to be phobic about writing letters of recommendation. Some may even suggest that you write a letter and they sign it. This is a tough one. You may sense that this person doesn't really want to support you, and it's possible. However, some professional people do get frantically busy, and some just hate to write. So if someone is willing to lend their name to help you, take them up on it. Ask them if there's anything they would suggest putting in the letter, and ask if they'll look at a draft, in case they want to make any changes. But get the letter.

SHOULD YOU DO A TRIAL RUN OR A PROTOTYPE?

You might wonder whether you should do a trial run of your project, or a sample of your work, or a prototype of your invention, to get funding. You may need to show some samples of previous work, but in most cases it's better not to start a project prematurely, unless you can get under way with limited resources. Trial runs, samples, and prototypes all cost money and take effort that might be better applied to your research, outlines, proposal, and budget. Do your thorough market research, draw up your detailed blueprint, and get your funding *before* you start work. Of course, if you have an invention that you're tinkering with, or a script you're writing, or a series of photographs that you've already started working on, go ahead. If you want to set up a project in your community, you might try holding a one-time workshop through an existing organization. This is all part of your subject research, and you'll have that much more evidence that you can do the project. But there's no need to do a large-scale effort before you have the resources.

DOLLARS AND SENSE — THE MONEY SIDE OF YOUR PROJECT

If you have a commitment to an idea that has been carefully thought through and developed, the money will follow. You are not going through this process just for the money but also because of your passion and commitment. Still, you do need money to put your idea into effect, so you have to think through the financial side of things as carefully as everything else. Since you are requesting money from a funder, it's important that the funder understands and appreciates not only what you are proposing but also the fact that you are realistic— that you are not asking for too little or too much, and that you have a realistic sense of what it's going to take to pay for your project.

DON'T UNDERESTIMATE YOUR NEEDS

I find that most people actually underestimate how much they will need for a project. This leads to two problems. First, the funders may conclude that you haven't thought your idea through; and second, if you do get funding based on a low estimate, you will be in trouble when you try to put your idea into effect.

You need to be very careful to plan on raising enough money to finish the project. You don't want to ask for too little, use up all the money, and then find you're unable to finish. *Don't ever be afraid to ask for too much.* If you're planning a complex project that will take place over a period of years and involve many people, you'll have far more credibility with funders if you show that you're doing realistic financial planning.

The main reason people underestimate their needs is that they haven't really sat down to make a point-by-point estimate of costs. Remember, you're not only going to need money for the actual con-struction of an invention, or the actual production of a theater piece, but for myriad related costs. You might need to rent separate office space and have enough to cover postage and mailing costs, telephone bills, copyright expenses, lawyers' fees, and so on. It's very important to make up a list of every aspect of your project that might involve expenses when you start considering how much money you will need to ask for.

What sort of things might you need to include in an expense list? It can certainly include a salary for yourself. If you are going to make a full-time commitment to your project, you need to have a salary. If you're going to be working with other people, you'll need to include salaries for them. If you want to hire an outside fund-raising consultant, put that expense in the budget. Consider the cost of space—office space, studio space, or whatever you need to carry out the project. Consider any special equipment you might need, or any travel ex-penses. Consider telephone costs, postage costs, office supplies. Don't forget to include the costs of printing, advertising, and publicity, if you're going to have to publicize your project. In fact, the best way to put together an initial budget is to go back to your outline and consider the costs involved in every part of the project.

You don't need to work up a detailed, line-by-line budget before you do all your funding research. But it helps to have a ballpark estimate of what your costs will be when you look at the giving patterns of funders. If your project will last for several years, you must take this into account. You can also start to accumulate budget information by getting price lists and estimates and putting them in a file, so you'll have them at hand when you're ready to sit down and do a detailed budget. I like to do the budget only after I've written the proposal. I like to start with the creative idea, and then fill in the dollars and cents. However, some people like to do the budget first, and then write the proposal from the budget. If you're the sort of person who naturally thinks about costs as you do your planning, you may find it easier to work this way. Everyone has their own style in dealing with money.

Are you good at handling money? Are you the sort of person who likes to do their own income tax, or do you have trouble every month balancing your checkbook? If you're not that comfortable handling money and your project will be costly or financially complex, you may want to consider getting assistance with this aspect. I have a friend who is very successful with her projects, but she is really not very good with money. She allows her husband to do the budgets, write the checks, and so forth. This works for her, because she wants to be more involved in the creative process rather than the day-to-day business. You don't have to have a handy spouse; you can include a bookkeeper's or treasurer's salary in your budget. You can also get help in preparing the budget. If your project is not too large, you may be able to find help from a service or membership organization in your community. There are plenty of nonprofit service organizations around, depending on your area of interest, and you may be able to contact officers who will offer consulting help, often free of charge. Some membership organizations make this part of their service, as well. For example, the Independent Feature Project, a filmmaker service organization, offers its members a certain amount of free consulting time with industry professionals.

How can you find out about these organizations? Some of this information will come out of your market research. You can also consult the *Encyclopedia of Associations* and other references to organizations given in the Appendix (page 336). Depending on your area of interest, you may be able to find reference books that will help you prepare actual budgets and financial plans.

If you do decide to affiliate with an existing nonprofit organization, you can certainly seek out the advice of the development officer or executive director. In fact, if your project is especially complex, if it will take place over a long period of time, or if many people will be involved, you may want to seriously consider affiliation. A fiscal sponsor can not only assist with the budget but also actually handle the funds for you, and do the bookkeeping and financial reporting. (More on this in Chapter 4.) If you're planning a big project but don't want to affiliate, you can certainly hire a professional to help you here.

But don't be too insecure about your own abilities. Say you're a homemaker who has a wonderful idea for a home business. You are probably already balancing your household budget, and believe me, that's no mean feat in these times. So if you do feel comfortable handling money, you can certainly manage a grant.

We've been talking about complex budgets, and the risks of under-estimating costs. Should you worry if your budget actually seems to be rather small? Not at all. There are plenty of funders who give grants in the range of a few thousand dollars or less. Still, raising grant money does take time and effort. If you don't need to raise more than a few hundred dollars, it might not be worth trying to get a grant.

THINK ABOUT MULTIPLE SOURCES

What if you come up with a budget that is really quite large, and you're afraid you won't find any funder willing to contribute that much? Should you scale back your project? Not at all. As a general rule, you're not going to find a single funder to underwrite your project completely; you're going to have to get money from several different sources. Some funders may give grants only in specific amounts. Others may want to assist your project but can't or don't wish to fund it completely. Some funders are happy to grant general "operating funds," the money you need to cover ongoing expenses, while others prefer to fund a specific part of a project, such as salaries or equipment purchase, or to contribute supplies or facilities instead of cash.

These are some of the reasons why you'll probably be applying to multiple funding sources. Try to be creative about this. For example, think about asking for basic operating funds from a foundation, or a donation of office equipment or supplies from a business. Ask a corporation to lend you use of a space or facilities. (This kind of donation is termed an "in-kind," or "noncash," contribution.) Perhaps you can get a city agency or a public radio or or television station to give you ad space on a bus, or air time for a public service announcement, as part of your outreach. Maybe you can get an advertising agency to make up a poster.

Funders are used to the idea of multiple sources. In fact, they even encourage it with such things as challenge grants and matching grants. A *challenge grant* is an initial grant that must be matched by another funder. It's not unusual for a foundation, a corporation, or a government agency to offer a gift that is contingent on a matching gift from another funder or funders. They might expect a match on either a one-to-one or a two-to-one basis. For example, a funder might give you $5,000, contingent on your getting a matching grant of $5,000 from another source. Or they might ask for a two-to-one match, which means you would have to raise an additional $10,000. The funder's original $5,000 gift might thereby inspire or initiate total funding of $10,000 or $15,000.

Donors like to do this for several reasons. It helps them stretch their own funding, by allowing them to assist more projects. It also lets them support a project that they can't fund completely. They do want to know that if they give you money, you will eventually raise all the funds you need and make the project actually happen. So if you get a challenge grant, you won't have access to these funds until you have raised the matching money. The great thing about a challenge grant is that it gets you started and it works as a kind of testimonial. Once a funder has given you its "seal of approval," so to speak, you'll find it easier to get other funders to contribute to your project.

Another similar grant is *seed money*, or *start-up funds*. This is money given by a funder to get your project started, perhaps on a limited scale, with the idea that you'll continue to raise funds for the full project. The big advantage of seed money is that you can use the funds right away, and it gives you a boost in your fund raising because someone has already seen fit to make an investment in you.

In some cases, funders like to see a promise of income generated by the project itself. For example, if you're putting on a play and you're going to sell tickets, then you can include an estimate of box-office receipts as income in your budget. Of course, many types of projects will not generate income. This is not a problem; don't try to invent income if it's not naturally part of the picture.

You Don't Have to Go It Alone

If you're undertaking a fairly simple project, you can easily manage all the details yourself, from the fund raising all the way through to putting your idea into effect. If you're planning a complicated project, though, you may feel the need for some kind of help with the grant-getting process, even if it's just calling on a friend for encouragement or moral support along the way. You may realize that you are going to want to collaborate with others when your project gets funded. You don't have to go it alone—you can turn to others for help with both the fund raising and the actual project. You can develop your own personal support group, or perhaps work with a collaborator. Or you can consider affiliating with a nonprofit organization, for support in both the grant-seeking process and managing your project. Or you can turn to a professional fund raiser for help in getting the grant. Let's consider some of these options.

Your Personal Support Network

If you have a family member or a personal friend who is very positive about your project, and who has some useful skills or a sense of the field that you are working in, they may be able to offer you a great deal of support. They can certainly provide moral support and encouragement. They can look through the various drafts and stages along the way, and serve as a sounding board for your ideas. However, a family member or an old friend is not always the best person to turn to for this kind of help. First of all, you need to have 100 percent positive support. If someone you are close to turns out to be lukewarm about your project, or expresses doubts, they are not going to be able to help you very much. More probably, they may simply not be familiar enough with your field, or the grant-seeking process itself, to be of much use. You may want to avoid leaning too much on friends or family, if only because they are not professionals in the field.

You may find much more valuable support by getting in touch with other professionals or groups in your field, to trade information, experiences, tips, and so on. Probably best of all is to develop a friendship with someone who is working in your field or a related one, perhaps pursuing similar goals but with a different project, and who is familiar with the general landscape that you are working in. This is not always possible, of course. Still, you may be able to turn to different friends and acquaintances for support with different aspects of your project. One friend may be good with fiscal matters and budgets, while a second might help you with organizational ideas, and a third may have a way with words and be able to help you edit or revise your proposal. Whatever you do, try to turn to people who show positive support for your idea. If they don't, they could drag you back instead of boosting you forward.

- **TIP:** If you're interested in other ideas about developing a personal support system, take a look at Barbara Sher and Annie Gottlieb's books. In their first excellent book, *Wishcraft*, they offer lots of useful tips for getting support for your long-term goals. They talk about networking, group brainstorming, over-coming family resistance, and developing a "buddy system" where you and a friend support each other with weekly "business meetings." Their second book, *Teamworks!*, describes a system of support groups that you can create or join to advance your long-term goals.
- *Wishcraft: How to Get What You Really Want,* by Barbara Sher and Annie Gottlieb. New York: Ballantine Books, 1983.
- *Teamworks! Building Support Groups That Guarantee Success,* by Barbara Sher and Annie Gottlieb. New York: Warner Books, 1989.

WHAT ABOUT THE COMPETITION?

If you do start networking and trading information in your field, sooner or later you're going to have the feeling that maybe you shouldn't be sharing absolutely every piece of information you come across. It's worth considering whether you might be sharing information too comfortably and giving a competitor access to something that's really perfect for you. Be aware of what you are revealing, and don't feel guilty about it. Remember that funding sources are not hidden. They're there to be found by anyone who does the research. So if you have a personal contact with a likely funding source and they are interested in your project, don't feel that you have to pass this along to someone who is looking to fund the same type of project. On the other hand, you shouldn't become paranoid about this. If a source is being widely publicized anyway, there's no harm in passing on the information to someone who hasn't heard of it yet. Generally, the more open you are with people, the more they will reciprocate by passing along tips to you.

Do You Want to Collaborate?

You may be thinking about the possibility of collaborating on your project, or taking on a partner, especially if it's a long-term, complex project. There are many advantages to collaboration—you can bounce ideas back and forth, you can share the work and the pleasures of fund raising and fulfilling a dream. If you and a collaborator have complementary talents or experience, this can make a grant proposal look stronger and a project more likely to succeed.

In fact, even if you're not going to undertake an equal collaboration, one of the best things you can have going for you when you ask for funding is a commitment from a few key people who have good professional credibility. This makes your project look solid, like one that is really taking shape. Of course, these commitments will be tentative, because you can't really have anybody clear their schedule or start work until you have the funding. But funders understand this and will appreciate your efforts.

On the other hand, you may feel more comfortable taking total responsibility for pursuing your personal vision. You don't necessarily have to work with a partner, even if you're planning a large and complex project. Remember, you can include salaries and fees in your budget for the backup and support people you might need. You can get funding to pay for a manager, a money person, even for other creative personnel. As you work on your project outline, keep thinking about what kind of support you'll need, and factor that in.

If you are thinking about collaborating, you are likely to have some possible partners already in mind—perhaps someone you have already worked with or whose work you know. You should have a sense of how your talents and skills complement each other's. You want to know that you and your partner will both keep going when the going gets tough. And of course you must have complete faith in your partner's integrity. A partnership is like a marriage—it has to be based on trust and a shared commitment. It's essential that you and your partner share the same passion and vision. You both have to feel that the project itself is more important than your individual egos.

THE AFFILIATION OPTION — WORKING WITH AN ORGANIZATION

There's another way that you can get substantial assistance with a project, but still retain a great deal of autonomy and control. That way is to affiliate with an organization. We'll examine this option in detail in Chapter 4, but you may find it helpful to begin thinking about this even before you start researching funders.

Thousands of foundations and government agencies will fund individuals directly, but many more will fund only nonprofit organizations. Many funders prefer to give money to organizations—it makes them feel more secure. These organizations can then act as *fiscal sponsors* and funnel the money to individuals. So one reason to consider affiliation is simply to get access to more possible funding sources. There's a second important reason to consider affiliation: you can draw on the expertise and resources of an organization to support your grant seeking and your project. Remember, it is not always necessary to have institutional affiliation. However, it is something you might want to think about because of the possibilities it opens up.

HOW IS THE APPLICATION PROCESS DIFFERENT?

Many funds that give individual grants use printed application forms. This is why it's easier for an individual to apply for a grant directly. The forms are much like college scholarship application forms, and you can sit down by yourself and fill them out. They are usually fairly straightforward.

If you work with an affiliate organization, you will have to spend a good deal of time with its officers or staff. First, you'll have to sell them on your project and convince them to work with you. You'll have to spend some time working with different staff members, learning the organizational guidelines, and sharing information about your project. When you get down to writing a proposal, though, this may be a little easier. Instead of filling out many different forms, you can make up a generic proposal that can be modified slightly for each funder (though if you're applying for government grants, you'll still have to fill out an elaborate application form). Still, there's no doubt that the overall application process will probably be more involved and take longer if you affiliate.

WHEN SHOULD YOU AFFILIATE?

Institutional affiliation does not even apply to many funding areas—for example, to undergraduate scholarships. If you are a painter and want to create new work, or if you are writing a book, or want to get a small-business-association loan, you will generally apply directly to the funders, and institutional affiliation will not be an issue. You'll be making a very simple, matter-of-fact application, and if you are applying only to foundations that fund individuals, then you can do the fund raising by yourself. Just follow the guidelines in this book.

However, even if you do want a grant to paint, or a postgraduate grant to do research, or if you want to develop an invention, you can pursue both individual funding and funding through institutional affiliation.

The more complicated your project and the more money you have to raise, the more you ought to think about affiliation. For example, if you have a scientific invention and will need laboratory space or specialized equipment or facilities, you may want to think about affiliation with a university, or perhaps a hospital. In certain areas, you will almost certainly have to have institutional affiliation. There are types of projects where funders really prefer to deal with an organization. If your project will involve a number of people working as more or less independent contributors—for example, when you are running a dance company or a large school—funders will usually want to see an organization involved.

This brings us to the second reason for considering affiliation: the kind of support it can provide for your project. One of the great advantages of institutional affiliation is that you can tap into the resources and pick the brains of the staff and officers of a nonprofit organization. This is a very important consideration, particularly for a first-time grant seeker. Nonprofits can offer resources and advice at every step of the way. They have experience with budgets, fund raising, managing grant money, and outreach. They may have a staff fund raiser or "development officer" who can assist you, or you may be able to work with the executive director, who runs the organization on a day-to-day basis.

When you do affiliate, there is generally some kind of trade-off or exchange between you and the organization. Usually they will take a portion of any grants received to cover their administrative costs for supporting your project (normal fees run from 3 to 7 percent of monies raised). Often they will want to involve your project in their outreach and their programming, but this is all to the good for you. They may also ask you to do a special workshop or performance for their membership.

How Can You Find a Sponsoring Organization?

How you find a sponsoring organization depends on what kind of project you are pursuing, and what kind of connections you may already have. If you are in the educational field—as a student, graduate student, or instructor—you may be able to work through your academic institution. If you're working independently, you can check out the service organizations in your field—some make it part of their mission to act as fiscal sponsors. If your project does not compete directly with the work of an existing nonprofit, you might ask if they will take you on as part of their overall program. If you have a community-oriented project, you could ask around in your community—talk to local United Way agencies and other local nonprofits. You can talk to people at your church or at a local school.

Affiliation is a big subject, and there are many types of affiliation agreements. If you think you might want to pursue this further, you'll find more details in Chapter 4, including tips on how to locate an appropriate sponsor.

Professional Fund Raisers

There's another way you can get help with your grant seeking: you can hire a professional fund raiser or a fund-raising consultant. In general, you should be thinking about this only if you're planning a very complex project and need to raise a large amount of money. As an individual artist, writer, inventor, or for a small start-up, you should be able to take care of things yourself. Remember, you may be able to get some of the assistance you might need at no cost through a service organization or an institutional affiliation. However, even for a smaller project, you might want to consider working with a freelance consultant on a limited basis. As a rule of thumb, the more money you want to raise, the more you should think about working with a consultant.

People often ask, "Can a fund raiser guarantee that I'll get a grant?"

The short answer is no. No good fund raiser would ever promise specific results, any more than a lawyer would guarantee that you'll win a case. However, what a professional fund raiser can do is offer his or her experience and expertise in doing good foundation research, analyzing your project, helping you to structure a well-written grant proposal, doing budgets, and so forth.

WHO ARE THE FUND RAISERS?

Most professional fund raisers work for nonprofit organizations, either on staff or on a consultant basis. They do what I call the bread-and-butter development work of raising money from private, corporate, and government sources. If they are on the staff of a nonprofit, they are called "development officers." If they are independent, the professional term is "fund-raising counsel." Professional consultants, as a general rule, prefer to work for organizations, though some will occasionally work for individuals on a for-hire basis. They will then bill on an hourly basis and usually charge fairly healthy fees. Many professionals avoid working with individuals, only because they simply cannot expect to make as much income as they can working for an organization. But there are professionals around that you can work with.

Professional fund raisers usually maintain a staff of researchers and assistants and are accustomed to conducting an entire funding campaign, from start to finish. Most work with all kinds of projects and all kinds of funders, though there are a few who will specialize, for example, in government grants.

Another kind of professional is the freelance consultant. These are people who have extensive background in one field and may offer their expertise, on a limited basis, to individuals. Usually, a freelance consultant will evaluate your project based on his or her experience with funders in your field and will help with preparing proposals and budgets.

WHAT A PROFESSIONAL FUND RAISER CAN DO FOR YOU

The professional fund raiser has good access to research materials and experience with funding sources. You would certainly save research time by hiring a professional. However, unless you want to invest a substantial amount of money in order to raise an even more substantial amount, I would suggest you think of using the professional fund raiser as a consultant only. It's going to get very, very expensive to use a professional for every stage of the process, and I would recommend against it.

Professionals may bill anywhere from $35 to $150 an hour for their time. If they are doing extensive research and putting together twenty or thirty individual proposals, you're looking at a lot of dollars. If money is no object, then of course you can hire a professional. I have worked with a number of individuals over the years, but I've often discouraged individuals from hiring me, only because it's so costly in billable hours, and that's how most fund raisers will work. No good professional will want to work "on spec" and wait for payment when funding comes through.

So, again, you can probably best use a professional fund raiser on a limited basis as a consultant. Get them to analyze how your campaign or your proposal should be structured, to critique what you have already done, and to guide you toward your next steps. You should be the one researching at the library, consulting with organizations, networking, writing up those proposals, and typing them out. *You* should be the one doing the legwork. If you work with a professional this way, you'll be investing a certain amount of money in your fund raising, and you'll be getting in return a good professional evaluation of your work. The more preparation you do before consulting a professional, the less of their time you'll pay for, and the more useful the results will be.

What a Freelance Consultant Can Do for You

An alternative to hiring a fund-raising professional is to work with a freelance consultant. This might be a professional in your field who has had some experience with fund raising and proposal writing, or it might be a development officer with a small nonprofit service organization in your field. The going rate for this kind of consulting is much lower, probably in the range of $35 to $75 an hour. If you use the person for a couple of hours—to look closely at your proposal, evaluate how funders may react to it, and make suggestions—this could well be worth the investment. If you know that writing is not your great strength, you might hire a freelance consultant to put together the whole proposal for you, in a form that could be easily changed or adjusted. (Of course, you will have to provide them with detailed notes and a project outline; no one will be able to conjure up a proposal out of vague ideas.)

How Can You Locate a Fund Raiser or Consultant?

The best way to locate a fund raiser is to talk to people in nonprofit organizations or people working in your field. Personal references are really ideal.

Evaluating Fund Raisers and Consultants

How do you know if a fund raiser is legitimate and good at what they do? First, talk with them, meet with them, and consider your own impressions. If you're going to be working with someone, you want to feel that you can communicate easily with them, that they understand your project, that you can understand their approach. So it's important to meet with the person and interview them as much as they're interviewing you. Even though they're the professional, you're the client, and the old adage says, "The client is always right."

If you do like someone and the chemistry seems good, ask for references and follow up on them. A slick brochure and a stellar list of clients is no guarantee of success. Find out what these former clients liked or didn't like about the fund raiser. Ask what the fund raiser offered that was especially valuable. Ask how much it ended up costing. And of course you'll be interested in what kind of results they got, what kind of funding the former clients did or didn't receive.

Other Support Systems — The Service Organizations

You may be able to find service organizations in your field that will offer fund-raising seminars, for varying fees; community colleges and other community organizations sometimes offer these as well. There are also a few organizations, like the Foundation Center, that have been set up to aid nonprofit organizations. Sometimes these can be of use to individuals as well. (See the next chapter for more on researching the fund-raising process itself and on service organizations.)

Approaching Funders

Market research, getting endorsements and recommendations, collecting support material, writing an effective proposal—these all contribute to a good funding campaign. But none of them will help if you do not communicate well with funders. You want to approach funders in a way that is efficient both for you and for them. There is an etiquette to dealing with funders, and you want to observe it. In fact, you may need to take different approaches when dealing with different types of funders, and we'll talk about these in the chapters that follow. Above all, you want to avoid sending any signals that you are not a serious prospect, that you haven't done your homework, or that you're going to waste a funder's time with inappropriate requests. This isn't difficult, but you must always keep it in mind as you go about your funding research.

THE FIRST CONTACT

First impressions are important, and so is your initial contact with a funder that you've targeted—usually to request guidelines or an application. I strongly discourage initial phone calls to most foundations, since they are often terribly understaffed. Unnecessary phone calls can be very annoying to staff members and program officers. So, after you've done your research, I recommend simply writing to request application guidelines and an annual report.

The "Big Daddy" foundations—a Rockefeller or a Ford Foundation—will have adequate staffing, so it's okay to call them and request their guidelines and materials. Government and public agencies are also usually set up to handle phone calls.

You don't need to say too much about your project. If you send a letter, just request the guidelines and annual report—you don't need to add anything at all about your project. If you do speak to a staff member by telephone, don't go into detail. If someone asks you, be very general; say, "It is a project for visual arts support," or, "It is a project for scientific support." Or use a phrase from their mission statement, which you've looked up. It's best not to say what it is that you want money for until you submit your formal proposal.

There are several reasons why you should avoid giving out information at this stage, whether in a letter or a phone call. First, you don't want a staff member making a snap judgment about whether your project fits within their guidelines. Second, there is the risk that if you start to describe your project, no matter how briefly, this may be misread by a foundation as a mini-proposal without your having been able to plan and submit a formal proposal. Finally, you want to present your idea in the best possible way, and first impressions are usually lasting. Submitting a preliminary idea either verbally or on paper before you've been able to refine it and work out all the details may create a weak impression that will haunt you when you make your formal proposal.

IF YOU HAVE QUESTIONS

After you receive the guidelines and application form, you'll be able to make a more informed judgment about whether you should continue to target this funder and actually submit a proposal. You may find something in the guidelines that contradicts what you found in your research, or indicates a change in funding patterns that might rule out this funder as a prospect. If this happens, go on to the next one on your list. However, after reading the guidelines, you may have some questions about the application procedures, or even about whether this is an appropriate funder for you. If your question is about procedures, and the funder is a Big Daddy foundation or a government or public agency, go ahead and call the staff. Government funders can be real sticklers about procedures, and you will want to follow their instructions to the letter. Smaller foundations, and especially family foundations, are usually not so picky about procedures, so it's better not to bother them on the phone about this. Just make your best guess of what they expect from you, and send in a good, strong proposal and budget. (Use the guidelines given in Chapter 9 to help you prepare a standard proposal and budget.)

If the funding interests or restrictions for any foundation seem ambiguous, you have to tread carefully. You don't want to make a judgment yourself that your project might not be appropriate, or have a staff member make the same snap decision. In this case, it's probably better *not* to ask for clarification of the funding interests or restrictions. If there seems to be a real possibility that your project might fit the funder's interests, go ahead and send in a proposal. You should add a paragraph that will slant it in the direction of their mission statement. I'm not suggesting you change or misrepresent the essence of your idea; just be sure to show clearly the connection to the funder's interests. For example, there's a small foundation that gives grants to "emerging filmmakers." Well, you could interpret "emerging" in many different ways, and wonder how much or what kind of past experience might rule a candidate out. The best approach would be to explain in what sense you are emerging. Perhaps you are switching from documentary to fiction, or you've done some shorts that have been shown, but never a feature. Give the funder the chance to make the decision. Let them make the final interpretation of their guidelines. Give them the opportunity to see a project that they might really be interested in, as long as it's not clearly ruled out by their stated restrictions.

So as a first-time grant seeker, stay away from initial telephone contact. Put in writing your request for guidelines, any application forms, and an annual report. Send in your written proposal. You will probably get a form letter sent out to all applicants that says something like, "We have received your proposal, it is under consideration, and we will be in touch with you about this at a later date." So just sit tight. If a funder contacts you after this and expresses interest, then you may start to have some phone contact with the foundation staff or program officer.

WHEN SHOULD YOU MAKE PERSONAL CONTACT?

As a rule, there's no need for any personal contact with funders unless they initiate it. And it's not appropriate for you to try to initiate it. Funders follow the old rule, "Don't call us, we'll call you"—it really does work that way. You usually won't hear from a foundation unless someone there is interested in your idea. They will get in touch if they want to speak to you. There is only one exception to this rule, and that is if you made the application on the basis of a personal contact—if someone introduced you to a funder, who told you to feel free to keep in touch about your proposal. Otherwise, unless someone says, "We would like you to call," or, "We've set up an appointment for you to call," don't do it. When they are interested in your work, some funders will be very accessible; that is all the more reason not to take advantage of the situation, and not to contact a foundation officer unless it is appropriate.

Once you've sent in a proposal, it's best not to bother the funder. Let them do their work. I once came across a funding source, in doing research, that I had never heard of before. We requested the guidelines and sent in a proposal. We had no phone contact, no meetings—and they gave $140,000 to the organization I was representing! So I do want to emphasize that personal contact is fine if you have it, but it's certainly not essential.

IF THE FUNDER CONTACTS YOU

If the funder is interested in your project, or wants to learn more about it, they may get in touch with you. (Though the fact that they don't does *not* mean they're not interested.) You may get a letter that says they are going to give your proposal serious consideration, or that the proposal is being forwarded to their Board of Directors or Trustees. (You do want to distinguish this from the form letter sent out to all applicants, saying the proposal is under consideration.) Once the funder has expressed this kind of interest, it is appropriate to make a phone call and talk to the person who signed the letter or the program officer in charge of the project. Foundations usually prefer personal contact by phone. They are inundated with requests for grants, and probably won't feel the need for a face-to-face meeting; further, they may be located in a distant city. There are exceptions, though. If your work is on display at a specific location, or if you're doing a public performance or theater piece, or if you have a scientific invention or research project with a special laboratory set-up, then the funder may decide that they want to see your work on location. But if there's no compelling reason for a visit and you want a grant to fund work in progress or the beginnings of a project, a phone call is usually sufficient.

Again, try to read between the lines. If it seems that personal contact is not being offered or is discouraged, pay attention. You have to strike a balance between being persistent and being pushy. Don't call constantly, or think you have to maintain contact. As a rule of thumb, one call is sufficient. Let the funder take the lead in terms of how much contact you should have.

It's a good idea to keep a log of all your calls to and from funders. Just jot down the date, the name of the foundation or corporation, the name of the person you spoke to, and whatever information you learned from the call.

How to Present Yourself

If it does turn out that you will meet directly with a funder, don't be too anxious about how to present yourself. I remember one client who came to me with a marvelous project that is now doing very, very well. A funder wanted to meet her, and she called me and asked, "What should I wear? I mean, how should I dress?" And I always smile when I think of this. Foundation people are basically interested in the project. Meeting with a funder is not like a job interview. No one is trying to see if you look a certain way. You are simply talking with a person who is very interested in what you have to say. If you feel you are not a good salesperson, if you are not very extroverted or aggressive, don't worry. Just talk about your project—what excites you about it, how you're going to follow through and put it into effect. Be yourself.

FOLLOW-UP

If you do have personal contact with a funder, follow-up is very important. I've seen too many people sit down for a meeting with a foundation, but not follow through and provide additional material that the funder requested. If the funder asks for additional documentation, or asks you to make a call or deliver something after the meeting, be sure to do it within a reasonable amount of time, usually a week to ten days. This is a real test of your commitment to the project and whether you will follow through if they grant you the funds. If they don't request anything further from you, be sure to write a note to thank them for their interest and their time. This not only makes people feel good, but shows that you do really care.

FUNDERS ARE PEOPLE

In my nonprofit work, I've found that funders can be very accessible, open people. They are interested in ideas, in social issues, in the arts and sciences. They like what they do, and if you think about it, it's wonderful to be able to give money to people with exciting projects who are trying to solve problems and make a difference in the world. Funders really deserve our admiration and appreciation. Above all, they are people who are interested in other people. So when you do have contact with funders, relax and be yourself. Whether or not you get a particular grant will ultimately depend on a funder's mission, policies, and interests, and not solely on your presentation. Relax and enjoy the process.

By now you should have a pretty good overview of the whole process of getting a grant. If you're not daunted by the process, if you're still committed to your idea and excited by the thought of forging ahead, then you're in the perfect frame of mind to get that grant. Let's go on to the next step: finding the right funder.

FINDING THE RIGHT FUNDER

A s you realize by now, there are thousands of foundations, cor-porations, and government funding sources out there that can provide you with free money. Your task is to find the funders who are most likely to support you. The real key to getting a grant is to research these sources thoroughly and discover those that best match your interests. When you find funding sources that support individuals like yourself, then you can begin ap-plying for support.

WHAT YOU NEED TO KNOW ABOUT FUNDERS

To apply successfully for nonprofit money, you need to match a specific type of purpose and project to the right type of funder. To do this, you need to know many details about possible funders—where they have given money in the past, what their areas of interest are, if they give grants to individuals or just to organizations, and what types of grants they give. You have to figure out if you do qualify for the kinds of grants that a funder does offer. Just because, for example, a funder gives to the arts will not necessarily mean that they give to theater or that they give to the visual arts. So it's important to learn more about each potential funder.

You also want to find out as much as you can ahead of time because you really can't write a proposal before you know whom you are addressing it to. You won't have to tailor every proposal from scratch for each individual funder; you will probably create a general proposal that you adapt to suit various funders. But the first step is to find out exactly what the funder is looking for.

In this chapter, you'll learn what you need to know in order to research funders: how to use the basic references to build a prospect list; how to organize your research; where to look for additional information; and how to start honing your prospect list. But first some general advice.

DOING IT YOURSELF

I always encourage individuals to do their own research, even when they hire my firm to assist with their fund raising. I believe that if you know what you want to do and how you want to do it, you will pick up on things that even a professional researcher might miss. You know your own field better than any professional, you will hear about things and get references from people you talk to.

How long will it take to do the research? Probably longer than you think. You have to be very patient and careful to be successful in your search for funders. This is the most arduous and time-consuming part of your quest for free money. You will probably need to spend between ten and forty hours of your time going to the library, poring over the grant books, taking careful notes, and keeping them organized. You will, however, save a good deal of time by using the references in this book (including the Appendix); a lot of information is right here at your fingertips. All that's left is for you to do the legwork of digging up the specific facts you need.

Yes, you can consider what a professional fund raiser might offer in terms of experience or contacts. As we saw, the more money you want to raise, and the more complicated your project, the more seriously you will want to think about this. As a result of having worked with many funders over the years, the professionals know the ins and outs, and the special interests, of various foundations and corporations. They have a rapport with these funders and an inside track on how they operate. But it just isn't necessary to hire a professional for research purposes. You really can and should do it yourself. Tracking down funders can be a fascinating process—you may even find yourself getting hooked by the thrill of the chase.

BUILDING YOUR PROSPECT LIST—A FOUR-STEP PROCESS

The first grant-seeking tool you will need to create is a prospect list of potential funding sources. This might include foundations, businesses and corporations, government agencies, even individuals. You will develop your prospect list by finding funders who have interests that match your project.

Building a prospect list is a four-step process:

1. You will need to locate lists of possible funders. There are many kinds of reference sources that list funders by various categories. Of course, you can also get names from the media, by word of mouth, and from other sources.
2. You will have to read and evaluate listings in reference sources to draw up a preliminary list of funders to write to for additional information. Since this follow-up takes additional time, you must consider carefully which prospects are really worth pursuing.
3. You will have to write to these potential funders for their funding and application guidelines and their annual reports. You may also want to do additional research on these sources by looking up the reports they must submit to the Internal Revenue Service.
4. Finally, you'll have to evaluate all this information and decide which funders to add to your prospect list and which to forget about.

HOW TO USE FUNDING CATEGORIES

The most useful way to research funders is to think always in terms of "funding categories." Foundations and other donors nearly always limit their grant giving to specific areas of interest. These may be defined by subject area, by geographic location, or by "population"— that is, by the type of individual or group that the funder wishes to support, such as students, the homeless, minorities, women, and so on. Throughout your research process, you'll be scanning lists and indexes to see which funders give grants in your subject area, in your community or region, and to your population group. Clearly, if you find a funder that matches you and your project in all three categories, this is a very strong prospect.

Subject area may be defined broadly or narrowly. A funder may simply give "to the arts," or, more specifically, "to support musical education, performances, and new compositions," or even more specifically, "to young composers who show promise and are recent graduates of a doctoral degree program in musical composition." Because of the many ways of defining subject area, you will need to read listings and guidelines very closely to rule out funders that give in your general subject area but not to your specific kind of project. Subject categories can be one of the most useful ways of narrowing your search. Many directories specifically list only the funders who give in a certain subject area, such as the arts, or filmmaking, or education.

Searching by region or geographic area can also be highly productive. A high proportion of private foundations and corporate funders prefer to give primarily or exclusively in their geographic region. Like subject area, geographic region can be defined broadly or narrowly. One funder might give in a multistate region, while another might give only to projects in eastern Massachusetts, for example, or primarily in Boston. Community foundations generally give only within a municipality, and a fund might give only to residents of a single county. So it's important to be on the lookout for very local funders. Some regional directories of funders are listed in the Appendix; you'll find geographic indexes in other directories, and geographic limitations noted in guidelines and listings.

Though this won't work for everyone, you should also try to narrow your funding search to any population group you belong to. There are grant programs directed specifically toward various minorities, women, the economically disadvantaged, people suffering from certain diseases, and so on. There are college scholarships that go to students of a given ethnic or national background, or even to those with a certain last name. Some directories list funders who support specific population groups, and you should keep an eye out for those indications in general listings and guidelines.

Finally, make sure you cover all the bases by researching each of the major funder types—private foundations, corporate funders, and government agencies. Some directories list grants available from all types of funders; others specialize in one or two. If you notice that you are only adding private foundations to your prospect list, make a special search for government or corporate funders that might also support your project.

What Types of Grants to Look For

To do effective research, you also need to know what types of grants are available. This is a good time for some basic definitions.

A *project grant* supports a particular project or program, of an individual or organization. It could fund a specific film, pay for you to travel to India for three months to take photographs, or support a six-week educational program of the Jacques D'Amboise Dance Company in an inner-city school in Detroit.

An *operating grant* is a grant made to an organization or individual to cover operating expenses for an ongoing program or project. This type of broad-based, unrestricted grant can cover anything from rent to the electricity bill to staff salaries or artist's fees—anything needed to keep the project going.

A *restricted grant* covers one specified part of a project, such as the fee for a musical score for your theater production.

A *general purpose grant* is a broad-based grant, not restricted to any particular purpose, to assist with the ongoing work of an organization. These are generally given only to organizations. An example: $10,000 to the Houston Opera to support their work.

Start-up funds or *seed money* are kinds of grants made to help an organization or individual start a new program or project. Seed money can cover salaries, operating expenses, and other expenses necessary to start a new venture, such as a new business or a theater company.

A *challenge grant* is an award that will be paid by a contributing organization if the grant seeker is able to raise a specified amount of funds to match the grant in question. For example, a foundation will give $10,000 to Joe Smith if he also raises $10,000 (or $5,000, or $20,000) on his own or through another grant.

A *matching grant* is similar to a challenge grant. A funder gives money to match funds granted by another organization. For example, the Ford Foundation may decide to match a $10,000 grant by the Rockefeller Foundation to help fund a particular research program.

A *regrant program* is an arrangement whereby a private foundation or a government agency gives funds to a nonprofit organization, which in turn administers a grant program with these funds, soliciting proposals and giving grants, usually on a local level.

An *in-kind donation or service* is a contribution to an organization or individual that might consist of materials or equipment, property, or free services of some kind. These could include computers, fax machines, other office equipment, office space, exhibition space, mailings, or any other kind of donation aside from direct cash gifts. This is sometimes called a *noncash grant*.

Technical assistance is aid in the form of free consulting services that are offered to nonprofit organizations (and sometimes to individuals). It may include fund raising or budgeting assistance, financial or legal advice, computer training, etc.

Grant periods are the time periods during which funds will be available, or during which they must be used. Grant periods vary according to the individual funding programs. A general-purpose grant might cover six months or one year of operation, at the end of which the organization or individual will generally have to report on the progress of the project.

Funding restrictions mean that grant monies may not be used for specific purposes, such as salaries, equipment, or real estate purchase. Limitations vary from program to program. A government grant might permit funds to be used for a wide range of expenses, excluding only equipment purchase. Another might give funds only for equipment purchase.

Fellowships are grants for educational studies or research, usually at the graduate or postgraduate level. They are always granted to individuals, though the funds may be channeled through a sponsor. The term "scholarships" strictly applies to undergraduates, although it's sometimes used loosely for both undergraduate and graduate grants. Although "fellowship" usually implies some sort of academic connection, several fellowships are available that support unstructured, unrestricted work. There are fellowships for writers, for example, that provide for living expenses while the person completes a novel or collection of poems. Research fellowships may permit original work either within or outside an academic environment.

Awards and prizes are grants given on a competitive basis, for specific accomplishments or achievements. They are usually initiated by the awarding organization, and individuals can't apply for them directly. However, there is often a nominating process, and an individual might be able to ask an appropriate person to nominate them.

How to Use the Basic References

The library is going to be your principal source of information, but you can adopt the right frame of mind even before you get there.

Start Thinking "Funders"

Before you open a book, you can start pumping up your awareness of who the funders are. When you read a newspaper article about a new school, or a theater, or a scientific venture, take note of who funded it. When you see an interesting public television program, notice the credit to sponsors. You may have seen a local announcement of an event or charity that included the words: "This was made possible by the generous support of XYZ Foundation." When you go to the library, look up a listing for the XYZ Foundation and see what else it funds and what its giving priorities are. If they give grants in your subject area, put the XYZ Foundation on your preliminary list of potential funders.

If you know other people working in your field, ask them what funding sources have given them grants, or which ones they have applied to. Or you might want to call some organizations in your area to get ideas. Don't be afraid to ask for advice before you even sit down at the library. The more you know about the world of foundations, the easier your research will be.

Libraries—The Place to Begin

You'll find at least some of the reference materials you need in a library. So make your first stop your local public library, a nearby university library, or other research facility. Many kinds of specialized libraries do keep funding references.

Once at the library, you can start sifting through reference guides and periodicals. Don't be discouraged by the vast number of sources that are out there, or the time you will need to spend to locate them. You can do much of your research with a few basic directories. *Remember, these references are your essential tools for getting that grant.*

You can get help building your initial list of prospects by talking to library staff members. They will point you to the appropriate reference section and to the specific books and directories you need to use. Ask about any special resources for funding research that may be available at your library, and about other libraries in your area that may have additional resources.

THE "BIBLES" FOR FUNDING RESEARCH

There are a few basic directories that you should start with. These can give you most of the information you need. Three of the most useful ones are published by the Foundation Center, the national service organization that disseminates information about private foundations (see later in this chapter, page 114, for more on the Foundation Center and what it does).

- *Foundation Grants to Individuals.* 7th edition, New York: The Foundation Center, 1991 (or latest edition). This is an extremely valuable directory that lists foundations making grants of at least $2,000 a year to individuals. It includes some smaller foundations that don't appear in other directories. It can save you lots of time by helping you focus your search on just those funders who give directly to individuals. The directory lists funders under several basic categories of awards— including educational, general welfare, arts and culture, grants to foreigners, awards and prizes by nomination, and company employee grants.

    This directory is probably the best starting point for you as an individual, and it contains useful bibliographies of other references, including all the publications and services of the Foundation Center itself. Entries give most of the details you need, including application guidelines (with limitations), addresses, contact names, and phone numbers. Unfortunately, you won't find this reference book in every local library, so you may need to go to one of the Cooperating Collections that keep Foundation Center materials (see page 115). You can also order *Foundation Grants to Individuals* directly from the Foundation Center, for the hefty price of $40.

- *The Foundation Directory.* New York: The Foundation Center, 1992 (or latest edition). This is a basic reference that fund raisers have used for thirty years. It gives detailed information on about 7,600 of the largest foundations in America, including both private and corporate foundations that hold assets of $1 million or more or make total grants of $100,000 or more each year. These foundations give out nearly $7 billion per year to institutions and individuals in areas that include education, research, travel, culture, health, and general welfare.

During 1985–86, grants by these foundations amounted to 92 percent of all foundation money given out.

The Foundation Directory gives detailed information on application procedures, types and amounts of grants awarded, names of foundation staff, addresses, and phone numbers. It has several indexes that list foundations by name, geographic area, areas of interest, and types of support provided, and even by names of foundation officers and donors. You'll find it at some larger libraries, and at the Foundation Center Cooperating Collections.

- **The Foundation Directory, Part 2: A Guide to Grant Programs $25,000–$100,000.** New York: The Foundation Center (latest edition). This directory is similar to *The Foundation Directory* and provides information on 4,200 mid-sized foundations which make grants ranging from $25,000 to $100,000. Listings are broken down by foundation geographical indexes, type of support, and subject area indexes.

- *National Directory of Corporate Giving.* New York: The Foundation Center, 1991 (latest edition). This directory has information about more than 1,500 corporate foundations and direct-giving programs. Listings are broken down by geographical location; type of charity (e.g., school, religious organization); type of recipient (e.g., youth); type of grant (endowment, seed money, cash awards, in-kind gifts); and amount of grants given. Of course it has all the necessary addresses and phone numbers, as well as a guide to corporate fund-raising techniques.

If your library doesn't have the *National Directory of Corporate Giving*, there are two other sources you can check out that also list grant-giving corporations:

- *Corporate 500: The Directory of Corporate Philanthropy.* San Francisco: Public Management Institute, 1991 (latest edition). This is a detailed directory that profiles 590 corporate giving programs. It is indexed by geographic region, subject, and funding areas. It offers information on application procedures, sample grants made, contact persons, corporate decision makers, giving priorities, and restrictions.

- *Corporate Giving Directory.* Rockville, MD: The Taft Group, 1992 (latest edition). This is a good sourcebook, detailing 571 of the largest corporate charitable giving programs, which provide at least $500,000 in grants. It features alphabetical listings of corporate foundations and giving programs, and information on whom to contact, size of grants given, type of grants, giving priorities, and sample grant recipients.

For grants by federal agencies, there is one master directory:

- *Catalog of Federal Domestic Assistance.* Washington, DC: Government Printing Office, 1992 (published annually). This is definitely not a user-friendly guide, but it does offer invaluable listings of all federal programs, projects, and services that offer aid to organizations and individuals. It lists many programs that individuals can apply to in a great number of areas. But the sheer size and bureaucratic jargon make it difficult to work with. If you want to try, see Chapter 7 for help with using this source.

To research government funding sources, you might find it easier to start with my own short guide:

- *Free Dollars from the Federal Government,* by Laurie Blum. New York: ARCO Publishing, 1991.

Other directories are listed later in this chapter and in the Appendix, but these are a good place to start.

How to Organize Your Research: The Basics

Once you've located a few of these references, you're ready to get started. There's a standard procedure you can follow to come up with potential funders for your prospect list. And of course you need to organize and keep notes on the information as you collect it. Let's start with these references, and begin our research by using the indexes and the funding categories.

Working with Categories

When you use a directory, always work with the major funding categories—funding by subject, funding by geographic location, and funding by population group. Look for indexes that categorize the funders, and try to do some cross-referencing—if you find a funder that gives in your subject area and geographic region, and supports a population group you belong to, you've found a very good prospect.

Since many foundations limit their giving to specific subject areas, start by looking at the subject index or at the subject divisions. For instance, if you are applying for a grant in the arts, look for the subject heading Arts and Humanities, or perhaps even more specifically, for Music, Dance, or Theater. In the index, under each subject heading, you will find a listing of those foundations that specifically fund these areas, and where in the directory to find the expanded listing for each foundation.

In some of the larger directories, you'll also find private and corporate foundations indexed by their locations, or by geographical areas where they offer funding. So if you are only looking for foundations based in Illinois, or that fund in Illinois, you may find them listed alphabetically in the geographical index.

The most important part of your research is your ability to identify sources that match your needs. Be creative in your search and take your time as you look under the various headings. Check to see what kind of indexes a directory might have in addition to subject and geographic indexes. Be sure to look at "population" categories and at other funding types. Look for indexes or sections that list funders under additional categories, such as Education, Youth, Research, Awards and Prizes, Company-Related Scholarships, Medical Expenses, and Welfare Assistance. Check to see if any of the special categories apply to you, and look at the listings of funding sources for those that do.

By looking through various categories and subcategories, you may find alternate funding sources you might not have considered before. If you want a scholarship, you would start looking under Educational Support or Scholarships. However, you might also look under Funding for Women or Funding for Minorities to locate specific scholarships that are directly focused toward your circumstances or interests.

CONSIDER THE DIFFERENT FUNDER TYPES

Even though you're starting your research by focusing on categories like subject area, make sure you consider all the possible funder types, or at least the major ones: private foundations, corporate funders, and government funders. Don't rule out any of the types because you think they may not be appropriate—you'd be surprised at the variety of projects and needs funded by corporations and the federal government. The only category you may not want to consider at all is that of individual donors, since they usually require the most effort to find and result in the least amount of funding. Still, there are exceptions, so don't rule out any possibility if you get a bright idea.

Some of the directories you will be using are compiled by funder type. As you proceed with your research, when you find you want to know more about a specific funder type, turn to Chapters 5 through 8 in this book. You'll find more details on how most effectively to research and approach each type in these chapters. But for now, get started by looking at the listings in the main directories.

Start Collecting Facts

Once you've picked out some likely funders in a directory, what should you look for? Here are some details you should check on to determine whether a funder might be right for you:

- Do your needs match the objectives or mission of the funder?
- Do they give grants in your *specific* subject area?
- Do they give grants in your geographical area?
- How much money do they have to give away, and what is the average size of their award? (A foundation that gives very small grants may not be worth the pursuit, if you have to raise a large sum.)
- What types of grants have they made over the last few years? Have they given any to projects like yours? (This will give you a better idea of whether they will fund your project.)
- Do they give to individuals or only to organizations? (Remember, you can possibly affiliate with an organization to receive some types of grants.)
- Are there any limitations on their grants that might rule out your project or you as a recipient?
- What are their application deadlines? If you missed the deadline for application, when is the next deadline and/or when does their Board of Trustees or Directors next meet?

If they do look like possible candidates for your prospect list, note down the program names, addresses, phone numbers, and contact persons. If you think that you meet all the requirements, then you'll want to go on to the next step and contact this source.

Before you move on to contact a funder, however, be sure that you clearly understand their limitations and giving priorities. If you are going to the trouble to sift through pages of information, don't waste your time by contacting or applying to a funding source that is an unlikely prospect for you. The best way to build a good prospect list is to weed out unlikely funders carefully. *Be sure to look for any special limitations.* Foundations will often tell you that they do not fund certain kinds of projects or expenses. If you are looking for a grant in the performing arts, for example, a funder's guidelines must clearly state that they support cultural projects or the arts. Applying to a foundation that isn't a good match for you wastes your time and theirs.

NOTE AFFILIATION REQUIREMENTS

You will find, as you look through the various directories, that some funding sources state that they don't make grants to individuals. If a listing says this, you know that you can't apply directly; however, you might still be able to apply under the auspices of a nonprofit organization. Even though some foundations will not give grants to individuals, they may support a person who is doing work at a non-profit institution like a university. You might therefore apply under the sponsorship of the university, and if a grant is awarded, the check will be delivered to the university, which in turn will disburse funds to you.

Accordingly, you may be able to meet your funding needs by associating yourself with a nonprofit institution that will accept funds from the foundation on your behalf. When you are doing your research, look to see if a funding source you're interested in provides grants to such institutions. You can then consider whether you want to find a formal sponsor to receive and manage your grant money for you. If you are a writer, artist, or researcher, you may even be able to use space or facilities provided by your sponsor. By affiliating with a non-profit institution, you can also increase the number of grants you can apply for. (More details on affiliation in the next chapter.)

ORGANIZE YOUR FINDINGS

It goes without saying that as you start to sift through all this infor-mation, you'll need to organize your findings so that you can make good use of them later and follow up on potential names for your prospect list. Here are some rules for keeping track of all these details:

- *Keep a record on each potential funder.* If you're working at a library with a photocopier, you can simply copy each page that has an interesting listing, and drop the copy into your active research file. Or you can note down the important information about each funder on a large index card, and put these in a card file. Or you can use letter-sized paper and keep at least one page for each potential prospect in a folder or looseleaf binder.

- *Note down the essential facts for each potential funder.* Make sure you collect the same important details for each prospect. These should include:
  Name of the funder
  Address and telephone number
  Areas of interest and giving priorities
  Financial data, including assets, number of grants given, and average amount
  Whether they give to individuals or just to organizations
  Any special limitations
  Name of contact person and board members
  Application procedures and deadlines

- *Use a data sheet.* If you think it will help, you can use a typewriter or word processor to make up your own data sheet with blanks. Photocopy your data sheet, take the copies with you to the library, and just fill in the blanks with the information listed above. (See sample data sheet opposite.)

If you keep track of the information you find in an organized way, with at least one page per prospect, it will be easy to follow up when you decide to dig for more information or to contact a funder. Your note page or data sheet then becomes the start of the prospect file that you keep for each funder you actually send a proposal to. If along the way you decide to rule out a prospect for any reason, just pull the data sheet or card from your active file and put it into a reject file. (Don't throw it out; you might be able to turn to this funder in the future or pass the information along to another grant seeker.)

FUND RAISER'S DATA SHEET

Funder's name: _____

Address: _____

_____

Contact person: _____

Financial data:

Total assets: _____

Total grants: _____

Grant ranges: _____

Subject focus: (in order of importance) _____

Geographic limits: _____

Population group(s) served: _____

Type(s) of support: _____

To individuals/org's? _____

Special limits: _____

People (officers, board members, staff): _____

_____

Application requirements:

Printed guidelines, report? _____

Method of initial approach: _____

Deadlines: _____

Board meetings: _____

Information source: _____

Date: _____

MAKE SURE YOUR INFORMATION IS UP TO DATE

It's very important to know that you are working with accurate and up-to-date information. As a general rule, foundations are pretty stable, but they do change their priorities and their personnel. It's not always easy to know whether the information you have is current or accurate. The references you are working with are usually one or two years old. Try to use the most current reference volumes—check with the publisher if necessary to make sure you are looking at the latest edition. *Never rely on files or directories that are more than a year old.* You will find that many libraries, even foundation libraries, stock volumes dating from the mid-1970s and early 1980s. These are practically useless. Remember that these books took one or two years to compile, so the information was already two or three years old on date of publication, as it is for even the most current editions you are consulting.

The only way to get current information on a funder—and you should definitely do this—is to locate its current annual report in a foundation collection, or write to the funder for the current report. You may well find that the current annual report indicates a change in guidelines or focus or that a contact person has changed. But again, until you do your homework in the library and go to a reference volume, do not contact the foundation. First, see if it is likely that you fit the funding profile; only then should you go on to the second step and request an annual report and application.

You can also try to keep up by reading special philanthropy journals, doing computer database searches, or seeking out the newsletters that are published by some of the larger foundations. However, you will probably have to go to one of the main foundation centers, or possibly a Cooperating Collection, to do this (more on these resources later in this chapter). So try to be thorough in your original research, and know that you can always confirm the information by writing to the funder directly.

The truth is, it can be quite difficult to find out certain types of information about funders, such as the average amount or number of grants they give to individuals. This is because many foundations do not publish information about more than just their best known and largest grants, and these usually go to nonprofit organizations. They simply do not list the grants that they give to individuals. The Guggenheim Foundation is one of the relatively few major exceptions. To make matters worse, when a foundation gives money to an individual through a sponsor or an institution, its listings will generally not reflect this type of grant either, making it even harder to discover their true giving patterns. The rule of thumb is, if an organization doesn't specifically rule out grants to individuals, don't cross it off your list—try to find out more. If it does rule them out, try to find out if it channels funds through sponsors.

HOW TO DIG DEEPER

You cannot always determine on the basis of a listing whether you will ultimately want to apply to a specific funder, or even whether you should bother to contact them. The listings will give you an idea, but you may need to do a little extra digging. Suppose, for example, you are trying to fund a play, and you find a listing for a funder that gives to the arts, but the listing doesn't specifically say that they give to theater. You should try to dig up additional information about this funder. See if you can find out about some of their past grants. If you see that they have primarily supported painters and sculptors, and have not given to theaters in the past, pass on the listing. This will again save you the time and trouble of contacting funders that are not really right for you. However, you may find it quite difficult to learn what specific grants a particular funding source has made in any given year.

Where can you look for more information? There are two primary sources: the foundation's own publications (including annual reports) and the reports it must file with the Internal Revenue Service.

THE 990-PF REPORTS

You may be surprised to learn that the U.S. Government has made things easier for you. All foundations are required by law to file an annual "private foundation information return," called a 990-PF, with the Internal Revenue Service. The PF stands for "Private Foundation." This form must state what the foundation's assets are and how many grants were given each year. The government requires this information because foundations' funds are tax-exempt. The 990-PF is a terrific research tool, because it will list at least some examples of grants given during the year, as well as actual recipients and amounts. Even more important, it is a way to find out about those small private foundations that might not appear in any directories or listings. If you do get the name of such a foundation, you can look up its 990-PF form to find out what its giving patterns are.

If you have access to one of the Foundation Center's main libraries, you can look at copies of these 990-PF forms for private and corporate foundations. Some Cooperating Collections keep 990-PF forms for local foundations and will help you order copies of forms from the main Center (see page 115 for details on the Foundation Center collections). You can also obtain these through some state attorneys' general offices, and you may purchase them directly from the IRS. Contact the Public Affairs Officer at your local IRS office.

- **TIP:** You can order foundation returns by contacting the Public Affairs Office at your local IRS headquarters. You will need to know the full name of the foundation, the city and state where it is located, and the year of the return you are ordering.

ANNUAL REPORTS AND NEWSLETTERS

For a very good resource, you can always turn to a foundation's or corporation's own publications. Individual foundations publish their own annual reports and giving guidelines. The annual reports will usually provide detailed information about a foundation's giving policies. They may summarize the foundation's history and why it was established, then outline the major kinds of programs and projects the company has funded. They will usually list the names of grant recipients, brief histories of their affiliations, and the amounts they received. Annual reports and guidelines provide the detailed information that can help you decide if you should apply to a particular foundation.

A small number of the bigger foundations also publish bulletins and sometimes quite elaborate newsletters. You may be able to find some of these publications in the Foundation Center's main or cooperating collections. If a larger foundation gets your request for an annual report and guidelines, they will most likely put you on a mailing list for bulletins or a newsletter. Some small foundations do not publish or distribute annual reports; to research these you'll have to stick to the listings and the 990-PF forms.

THE NEXT STEP—CONTACTING THE FUNDER

When you've done all the research you can from directories and other sources, and you really think you have found some likely prospects, go ahead and write to them. Just send a short letter requesting a copy of their annual report and a set of grant guidelines. If you know from your research that they use an application form, ask for that too. That's all you need to do at this point. Particularly if it's a smaller foundation, don't ask for anything else—you'll just bother the program officer.

When the material comes in, you can immediately check the information against your own information or data sheet to make sure your facts are up to date and accurate. You will then begin looking through the materials more closely to decide whether you want to keep this funder on your prospect list and eventually submit a proposal.

In the final section of this chapter (pages 130–33) you'll find more details on how to evaluate and act on the information you've collected. But first you may wish to do an even more thorough search for potential funders, going beyond the few major directories. In fact, there are a number of specialized resources you can use to zero in on the best funders for you, those most likely to give you a grant. The next section offers details on how you can find these resources and use them.

THE LARGER PICTURE: ADDITIONAL RESOURCES

Now that you know how to use a basic directory and manage your funder facts, you should consider some of the additional reference books and resources that are available. You can use these resources to dig deeper for additional information about specific funders or to track down obscure ones. You can also turn to specialized books and directories that focus on your own particular areas of interest.

GENERAL REFERENCES AND RESOURCES

Aside from the basic directories listed earlier, there are three other general references that you may wish to consult:

- *Annual Register of Grant Support: A Directory of Funding Sources,* edited by Linda Peterson. Wilmette, IL: National Register Publishing Co., 1990 (published annually). This is a valuable reference that offers more than just listings. It gives information on special programs sponsored by funding sources of all types, including professional associations and special interest organizations.

- *Awards, Honors and Prizes,* edited by Gita Siegman. Vol. 1: *United States and Canada.* Detroit: Gale Research Co., 1991 (latest edition). A comprehensive directory of over 22,000 awards, indexed by organizations, awards, and subject areas.

• *Encyclopedia of Associations,* edited by Deborah Burek. Vol. 1: *National Organizations of the United States.* Detroit: Gale Research Co., 1992 (published annually). Lists national organizations you may be able to affiliate with, including trade, business, environmental, government, health, athletic, etc. Includes addresses, publications of these organizations, and whether they hold conferences.

RESEARCH BY SUBJECT AREA OR CATEGORY

There is another direction you can take with your research that may prove especially efficient and productive. Start looking for specific references for your subject area, need, or "population." Many reference books deal with specific grants in various fields, such as education, the arts, company-employee grants from corporations, and grants by state.

The Free Money Books. I have a written a series of *Free Money* books which provide lists of funding sources that support individuals in many different fields—from college scholarships to grants in the arts to support for health care. Whether you use my books or others, I do suggest you pursue this idea of specific sourcebooks; it can save you a good deal of research time.

There are other specific guides on the market and in your local libraries. Ask your librarian to show you what he or she has in the reference sections. Scan the indexes of all these books to find the funding categories (subject areas, geographic areas, etc.) that might apply to your project. Be sure to read the introductions of all these reference guides for help as well. Introductions provide summaries of the various indexes and funding categories in each book.

The following is a selected sampling of some of the most useful specialized funding guides, listed by subject area in alphabetical order. You can find a more complete list in the Appendix, page 326.

THE ARTS

Free Money for People in the Arts, by Laurie Blum. New York: The Macmillan Co., 1991.

Guide to Corporate Giving in the Arts, edited by Robert A. Porter. New York: The American Council for the Arts, 1987.

Guide to Funding for Emerging Artists and Scholars, by Jennifer Sarbacher. Washington, DC: President's Committee on the Arts and the Humanities, 1991.

The National Directory of Grants and Aid to Individuals in the Arts, by Nancy A. Fandel. Arts Patronage Series, no. 15. Des Moines, IA: Arts Letters, 1989.

National Guide to Funding in Arts and Culture. 2nd edition. New York: The Foundation Center, 1992.

1992 Guide to Funding for Arts and Culture, edited by James Marshall. Alexandria, VA: Educational Funding Research Council, 1992.

(See the Appendix for additional subject guides for performing artists, filmmakers, musicians, visual artists, writers, and other.)

BUSINESS

Computer Grants Directory. 4th edition. San Francisco: The Public Management Institute, 1991.

Free Money for Small Business and Entrepreneurs, by Laurie Blum. 3rd edition. New York: John Wiley & Sons, 1992.

How to Invest in Real Estate Using Free Money, by Laurie Blum. New York: John Wiley & Sons, 1991.

EDUCATION

If you are looking for a scholarship and are already enrolled in or admitted to a college or university, your first stop should be the financial aid office of your school. Individual colleges and universities have many scholarships of their own for which you may qualify—for minorities, for women, for individuals with handicaps, etc. Your school's financial aid officer will be able to help you with these, as well as with information about other special scholarships, and will know about the many government grants in education. (And see complete listings in the Appendix.)

ARCO's College Financial Aid Annual, edited by John Schwartz. New York: ARCO Publishing, 1990.

College Blue Book. 23rd edition. New York: The Macmillan Co., 1991.

Financing a College Education: The Essential Guide for the 90s, by Judith B. Margolin. New York: Plenum Press, 1989.

Free Money for College, by Laurie Blum. New York: Facts-on-File, 1992.

Free Money for Private Schools, by Laurie Blum. New York: Simon & Schuster, 1992.

National Guide to Funding for Elementary and Secondary Education. New York: The Foundation Center, 1991.

Peterson's Guide to Four-Year Colleges 1991. Princeton, NJ: Peterson's Guide, 1990.

Scholarships, Fellowships and Loans 1992–93, by Debra McKinley. Detroit: Gale Research Co., 1991.

Foreign Study: See TRAVEL, below.

Graduate, Postgraduate, and Research

The Directory of Research Grants. Phoenix, AZ: Oryx Press, published annually.

Free Money for Graduate School, by Laurie Blum. New York: Henry Holt and Company, 1993.

The Graduate Scholarship Book: The Complete Guide to Scholarships, Fellowships, Grants and Loans for Graduate and Professional Study. Englewood Cliffs, NJ: Prentice-Hall, 1990.

The Grants Register. New York: St. Martin's Press, published twice a year.

U.S. Government Support

Directory of Federal Aid for Education: A Guide to Federal Assistance Programs for Education. Santa Monica, CA: Ready Reference Press, 1982.

The Federal Educational and Scholarship Funding Guide. West Warwick, RI: Grayco, 1989.

Free Dollars from the Federal Government, by Laurie Blum. New York: ARCO Publishing, 1991.

Student Guide: Five Federal Financial Aid Programs. Washington, DC: U.S. Department of Education, Government Printing Office.

State-by-State Support: Refer to the state funding directories—a complete listing appears in the Appendix.

ENVIRONMENT

Environmental Grantmaking Foundations 1992 Directory. Rochester, NY: Environmental Data Research Institute, 1992.

Environmental Grants: A Guide to Grants for the Environment from Government, Companies and Charitable Trusts, by Susan Forrester. London: Directory of Social Change, 1989.

National Guide to Funding for the Environment and Animal Welfare. 1st edition. New York: The Foundation Center, 1992.

HEALTH

AIDS Funding: A Guide to Giving by Foundations and Charitable Organizations. 2nd edition. New York: The Foundation Center, 1991.

Directory of Biomedical and Health Grants. 6th edition. Phoenix, AZ: Oryx Press, 1991.

Free Money for Diseases of Aging, by Laurie Blum. New York: Simon & Schuster, 1992.

Free Money for Heart Disease and Cancer Care, by Laurie Blum. New York: Simon & Schuster, 1992.

Handicapped Funding Directory, by Richard M. Eckstein. 7th edition. Margate, FL: Research Grant Guides, 1990.

National Guide to Funding in Aging. 2nd edition. New York: The Foundation Center, 1990.

National Guide to Funding in Health. 2nd edition. New York: The Foundation Center, 1990.

HUMAN SERVICES

Free Money for Day Care, by Laurie Blum. New York: Simon & Schuster, 1992.

Fundraisers Guide to Human Service Funding, by Susan Elnicki. 3rd edition. Rockville, MD: Taft Information, 1992.

HUMANITIES

Directory of Grants in the Humanities. Phoenix, AZ: Oryx Press, 1990.

MINORITIES

Directory of Financial Aids for Minorities, 1991–93, by Gail Ann Schlachter. San Carlos, CA: Reference Service Press, 1991.

Guide to Multicultural Resources, edited by Charles Taylor. Madison, WI: Praxis Publications, 1989.

RELIGION

Foundation Guide for Religious Grantseekers, edited by Kerry A. Robinson. Atlanta, GA: Scholars Press, 1992.

RESEARCH AND FELLOWSHIPS

Directory of Research Grants. Phoenix, AZ: Oryx Press, 1992.

Guide to Funding for Emerging Artists and Scholars, by Jennifer Sarbacher. Washington, DC: President's Committee on the Arts and the Humanities, 1991.

Guide to Research Support, edited by Kenneth Lee Honig. 3rd edition. Washington, DC: American Psychological Association, 1987.

SCIENCE

Directory of Biomedical and Health Care Grants. 6th edition. Phoenix, AZ: Oryx Press, 1991.

Directory of Grants in the Physical Sciences. Phoenix, AZ: Oryx Press, 1986.

Fellowships and Grants for Training and Research: To Be Offered in 1991– 1992. New York: Social Science Research Council, 1991.

Grants for Research and Education in Science and Engineering: An Application Guide. NSF, no. 90–77. Washington, DC: National Science Foundation, 1990.

SENIOR CITIZENS

The Caregiver's Guide, by Carolyn Rob. Boston, MA: Houghton Mifflin, 1992.

TRAVEL

Financial Aid for Research, Study, Travel and Other Activities Abroad 1990–1991, by Gail Ann Schlachter and R. David Weber. San Carlos, CA: Reference Service Press, 1990.

Financial Resources for International Study: A Definitive Guide to Organizations Offering Awards for Overseas Study. Institute of International Education. Princeton, NJ: Peterson's Guides, 1989.

Free Money for Foreign Study, by Laurie Blum. New York: Facts on File, 1991.

Fulbright and Other Grants for Graduate Study Abroad 1992–1993. New York: Institute of International Education, 1991.

Funding for Research, Study and Travel: Latin America and the Caribbean, edited by Karen Cantrell and Denise Wallen. Phoenix, AZ: Oryx Press, 1987.

The International Scholarship Book: The Complete Guide to Financial Aid for Study Abroad. 2nd edition. Englewood Cliffs, NJ: Prentice-Hall, 1990.

WOMEN

Directory of Financial Aids for Women 1991–1992, by Gail Ann Schlachter. San Carlos, CA: Reference Service Press, 1991.

Directory of Women's Funds. New York: Women and Foundations/Corporate Philanthropy, 1988.

Grants for Women and Girls. Grant Guide, no. 30. New York: Foundation Center, 1991.

This is just a sampling. More directories are listed in the Appendix, and you may come across others as you start to dig into your research.

RESEARCHING THE JOURNALS AND ANNUALS FOR YOUR AREA

Current journals and periodicals are a good source for up-to-date information about funding sources. Some magazines and newsletters have special sections on funding, including names, addresses, and deadlines. Many will run features on funding. Many organizations, and some journals, publish annual directories about their fields, with names of companies, services, organizations, etc. These can also be a useful source of information. Look into the specific publications that serve your area. (See the Appendix, page 337, for a listing of some of the major ones.)

PERIODICALS AND NEWSPAPERS

If you want to find out more about a funding source, check out the periodical index at your library for newspaper or magazine articles about the funder or the individual donor. You might run across an article on a particular foundation or organization that was assisted through a grant, or one on a business or corporation that you're interested in. You could also look for articles about your project area, to see if funders are mentioned. Also, take a look at indexes for periodicals that deal specifically with your project area.

There are a number of journals that deal specifically with philanthropy. These contain articles on such topics as who is giving, trends in philanthropy, latest grants awarded by particular foundations or corporations, and latest congressional rulings. If you can't find these in your local library, contact them directly to ask for a sample copy, or to find out which library might collect them (see the Appendix, page 337, for addresses and phone numbers). Some of the primary journals are:

- *The Chronicle of Philanthropy*
- *Corporate Philanthropy Report*
- *Foundation News*
- *Fund Raising Management*

- *Giving USA (annual and update)*
- *Nonprofit Times*

THE FOUNDATION CENTER — FOR IN-DEPTH RESEARCH

We've already mentioned the Foundation Center as the source of some of the most useful funding directories. If you are having trouble finding the directories you need, or if you want to do some in-depth research, the Foundation Center could help. This is a clearinghouse for information about the nonprofit world—for nonprofit management as well as for foundations themselves. It was set up as a national service organization in 1956, supported by a group of foundations, and its mission is to assist other nonprofit organizations with their fund raising. It keeps a valuable collection of information on philanthropy and foundation, corporate, and government giving. The Foundation Center publishes a multitude of reference books, directories, and reports that can answer virtually any question about philanthropy, and provide detailed information about the kinds of grants that corporations and foundations offer.

The Foundation Center maintains four principal reference collections—located in New York, San Francisco, Washington, DC, and Cleveland—but their directories are available in libraries throughout the United States. The collections are free and open to the public, and free orientation sessions are also given for nonprofit organizations (call for an appointment). Individuals can attend the orientation sessions. There are Cooperating Collections in nearly every state, and these too are open to the public, by appointment.

A word of caution, though: individuals are not turned away, but they are not really favored at the Foundation Center. It was not set up to service individuals; it exists primarily for the use of nonprofit organizations. You will not find the staff ready to hold your hand or offer you all the assistance you might get at your local library. If you do turn to the Foundation Center resources, be sure to study the orientation guides and information pamphlets about how to use the Center. Ask about the free orientation sessions, and try to take a course; this way you won't be bothering the staff with unnecessary questions.

There are two National Collections:

The Foundation Center	The Foundation Center
79 Fifth Avenue (8th Floor)	1001 Connecticut Avenue, N.W.
New York, NY 10003	Washington, DC 20036
212-620-4230	202-331-1400

And two field offices:

The Foundation Center	The Foundation Center
Room 312	Kent H. Smith Library
312 Sutter Street	1422 Euclid, Suite 1356
San Francisco, CA 94108	Cleveland, OH 44115
415-397-0902	216-861-1933

You can purchase Foundation Center publications at the National Collections, and place orders at the field offices. There are also more than 180 affiliated Cooperating Collections—one or more in nearly every state—and several abroad.

THE COOPERATING COLLECTIONS

The Cooperating Collections offer free public access to the basic collection of Foundation Center publications, and some offer access to computerized fields. These collections also provide free orientation sessions; in addition, they sometimes offer funding research guidance, and special workshops and orientations, though these are usually aimed at organizations. Some have sets of 990-PF forms for their state or region. Check with the Cooperating Collection near you to find out what they offer. (For the location of the collection nearest you, call the Foundation Center's toll-free information number, 800-424-9836.)

Because collection hours and services vary, it's best to call them in advance and make an appointment if you want to visit. You can also check with the Foundation Center at the same number toll-free to find out about new locations or get updated information.

What services exactly does the Foundation Center provide?

THE FOUNDATION CENTER LIBRARIES

First, the Center provides access to all of its own publications and references. In addition, you can find valuable publications provided by the foundations themselves, as well as other materials, such as the

IRS 990-PF forms provided by the U.S. Government. You'll find a core collection of references at each of the four main collections and at each of the Cooperating Collections. You can also order Foundation Center publications directly by writing to the New York office, or by calling the toll-free number and charging them to your credit card. Be forewarned: many of them are quite expensive. The major directories cost upward of $100 each. For information about any of the Center's services, call their toll-free information number: 800-424-9836.

- **TIP:** Call the Foundation Center's toll-free number, and ask them to send you their free catalogue, *Fundraising and Nonprofit Development Publications and Services.* This is a good orientation to their publication list and to the nonprofit world.

Here is a detailed listing of the core collection that you will find at each Foundation Center library:

- *The Foundation Directory.*
- *The Foundation Directory, Part 2: A Guide to Grant Programs $25,000–$100,000 (latest edition).*
- *Source Book Profiles: An Information Service on the 1,000 Largest U.S. Foundations.* New York: The Foundation Center, 1991. This directory offers in-depth information on the largest 1,000 foundations and their areas of interest and giving patterns.
- *National Data Book of Foundations: A Comprehensive Guide to Grantmaking Foundations.* New York: The Foundation Center, 1992 (latest edition). A comprehensive sourcebook on 34,000 large and small U.S. foundations.
- *National Directory of Corporate Giving.*
- *Foundation Grants to Individuals.* 7th edition. New York: The Foundation Center, 1991. Probably the best starting point for you as an individual.
- *Selected Grant Guides by Subject.* New York: The Foundation Center, published annually. These comprehensive guides break down foundation giving into many subject areas. The guides list actual foundation grants in thirty different subject areas; each guide shows listings of foundation names and addresses, the amount that was awarded and when, and who received the grant.
- *The Literature of the Nonprofit Sector.* This is a bibliography of books *about* fund raising, including those published by the

Center and elsewhere. Titles range from simple booklets to fairly technical studies on managing nonprofit organizations. The Center's main libraries have a broad selection of these books on hand, and you can find many of them at the Cooperating Collections as well.

- *Foundation Fundamentals: A Guide for Grantseekers*, edited by Judith Margolin. New York: The Foundation Center (latest edition). A concise guidebook that provides the beginning fund raiser with various information about foundations and philanthropy.
- *Foundation Giving: Yearbook on Facts and Figures on Private, Corporate and Community Foundations*. New York: The Foundation Center (latest edition). A good general data book, providing information about 33,000 U.S. foundations.
- *The Foundation Center's User-Friendly Guide: Grantseeker's Guide to Resources*, by Judith Margolin. New York: The Foundation Center, 1992. A revised edition that provides even more details about the grantmaking process to the novice fund raiser.
- *Directory of New and Emerging Foundations*. 2nd edition. New York: The Foundation Center, 1991. This sourcebook lists 1,000 new community, corporate, and private foundations in the United States, and also features information on 2,500 foundations, which make grants up to $2,500 each year.

Beyond the core collection, the National Collections, and some of the Cooperating Collections, contain other useful materials, such as:

- *Foundation files*. Annual reports, press releases, grants lists, application guidelines, and other materials provided on a voluntary basis by many major foundations.
- *IRS 990-PF returns*. The Center keeps on file the 990-PF returns of all 30,000 foundations required to file them (usually stored on microfiche). You can find a complete set of the 990-PF returns at the New York and Washington, DC, offices of the Center. The Cleveland and the San Francisco offices hold returns for the Midwestern and Western states, respectively. Some of the Cooperating Collections also contain the private foundation returns for their state or region. If one of these collections doesn't have a 990-PF return you are looking for, they can order it for you from the New York center.

Besides the library collections, the Foundation Center offers a few additional services, although these are mostly for the benefit of non-profit organizations:

The Associates Program. The Center has an Associates Program, which it calls "the direct line to fund-raising information." This is quite expensive—it costs $495 a year to be a member—but some organizations find that it saves many hours of research time. The program offers a toll-free telephone reference service, access to selected pages and files from the Center's references, and custom searches of the Center's computerized database. The Associates Program will help an organization (or an individual) to identify potential funding sources, target information, and write effective proposals.

This is certainly a good deal for many organizations—it's like having your own research staff—but I really don't recommend it for individuals. It's oriented toward fund raising for organizations, it's too expensive, and you can do this work quite effectively on your own. I've known a few small nonprofits that liked this service very much, but I've never known an individual who had any real use for it. (If you do want more information about this program, call the Center's toll-free number, 800-424-9836.)

On-Line Computer Databases. The Foundation Center supplies information through two on-line computer databases, available through DIALOG Information Services. These offer specialized information on funders and grants. This is one way to access the Foundation Center's resources and gain specific information on funding sources— their finances, giving interests, grants given, names and addresses, and application guidelines. The great advantage of searching a database is that you can specify very narrowly the type of information you are looking for.

Here are some examples of the kinds of questions that a database search might answer (taken from *Foundation Grants to Individuals*):

- Which New York foundations support urban projects? Who are their officers and trustees?
- What are the program interests of the ten largest corporate foundations? Which ones publish annual reports?
- Which foundations have given grants in excess of $100,000 in the past two years for continuing education for women?
- Which foundation would be likely to fund a cancer research project at a California hospital?

- Which are the ten largest foundations in Philadelphia by annual grants amount?
- What are the names and addresses of smaller foundations in the 441 zip-code range?

One of the databases, called "The Foundation Directory," includes information from the following publications: *The Foundation Directory; The Foundation Directory, Part 2*; the *National Directory of Corporate Giving*; the *National Data Book of Foundations*; *New York State Foundations*; and the *Directory of New and Emerging Foundations*. The second database, called "The Foundation Grants Index," contains records of grants to organizations of $5,000 or more. However, it does not list any grants to individuals. For more information on how to access these databases directly through DIALOG, call 415-858-2700, or 800-334-2564. To find out about what other on-line services provide access to DIALOG, or for free help in searching the files, call the On-line Support Staff at the Foundation Center at 212-620-4230.

There's one major drawback to using these database systems: the price. It costs $45 simply to access the database, plus $1.50 *per minute* to search records and 60 cents per minute to display them. So it would be easy to spend $100 on a simple search. My suggestion? Use the directories in the library.

If you do want to pursue this resource, and you are not set up with a computer to search the on-line DIALOG files yourself, you might try going through a third party. Some large libraries and information centers can also access these databases, and so can certain corporate libraries and some of the larger nonprofit organizations. Talk to the reference librarian at your local public or academic library to find out if a database search is available and at what cost.

You may find that your local library does not have access to the Foundation Center's data because the system is so costly. In that case, ask your librarian whether your library can access a system called "Easy Net" or the "GE Network of Information Exchange (GEnie)." Bear in mind that libraries will charge a fee for the service if they do provide it.

The Foundation Center's Associates Program also offers custom DIALOG searches as part of their services. But this too is a costly program, and you are not likely to want to sign up for it as an individual.

To find a library or other third party that could help you gain access to these databases, consult one of the following directories:

- *American Library Directory.* 43rd edition. New York: R. R. Bowker, 1990.
- *Directory of Special Libraries and Information Centers.* Vol. 1: A *Guide to Special Libraries, Research Libraries, Information Centers, Archives, and Data Centers,* edited by Janice A. DeMaggio. 14th edition. Detroit: Gale Research Co., 1990.
- *Online Database Search Services Directory,* edited by Martin Connors. 2nd edition. Detroit: Gale Research Co., 1987.

GOING BEYOND THE LISTINGS — CREATIVE RESEARCH

The listings, indexes, and directories are your primary sources of funding prospects, but you don't have to limit yourself to these. Keep your antennae up, keep your funder awareness activated, and try to go beyond the listings.

THINK CREATIVELY

How can you think creatively about funding? Think about the details of your project, brainstorm, make connections. Who is the audience for your project, whom will it affect, who will want to see it succeed?

With a PBS project I worked on, the producer was planning a program that was basically about books but with a real entertainment twist. And so his natural funders were booksellers, publishers, and literacy foundations—people who had a real interest in reaching and developing a reading public. Another wonderful project that reached out to booksellers is Garrison Keillor's American Public Radio show, "American Radio Company." Though the show is not strictly about books, Keillor has done specials on authors like Mark Twain and Willa Cather, and he always includes monologues and radio drama in the show. I am sure that he managed to convince the American Booksellers Association, a regular funder, that people who like to listen to radio stories (just words, not pictures) are also people who like to read books.

Here's another example of thinking creatively about sources that may not appear in any of the listings. Recently, a client of mine got a very large grant from Herb Alpert, whom he happened to know through a social connection. My client runs a private school, and he operates many arts programs in partnership with some of the public schools. As it turned out, Herb Alpert cares about the teaching of music to kids, and had never been approached for a contribution before. Thinking of him was a wonderful leap of the imagination and it resulted in a six-figure grant.

So creativity as well as common sense are certainly important when it comes to identifying possible funding sources. However, a word of caution. Do your traditional library research before making those leaps of imagination. It's your library research that will get the bread buttered; the creative flashes don't come every day.

KEEP UP WITH THE MEDIA

Read newspapers and magazines on a steady basis, especially magazines in your subject area. Keep a clipping file on projects that relate to yours. Even if they don't talk about specific funders directly, they may give you ideas about how to present your own project, creative ways that other people have raised money or reached out for funding. And you will come across some specific names to follow up on.

CONSIDER DIFFERENT TYPES OF AID

Don't limit yourself to going after cash grants. Cash is certainly preferable, but you should also think about in-kind donations of space, equipment, or services. In-kind donations can sometimes mean the difference between being able to do a project or not. Some years ago I raised the entire budget for a PBS documentary on women and the Constitution. The producer—a journalist—had been tearing her hair out trying to raise the money. In the end, a third to half of the budget came from Georgia Public Television, which gave us postproduction editing time, gave us tape, and gave us a lot of equipment and services that we would have had to pay top dollar for. Even though we did raise a fair amount of hard cash, the in-kind donations made it possible for us to get the project under way much sooner than expected, which was essential, since we had to meet a deadline for shooting an event that was crucial to the project. The in-kind services really made the difference and enabled us to do the project.

Don't be discouraged if you find that a corporation you've targeted does not want to give you money. Perhaps it's because their budget is spent, perhaps you are making too small a grant request, or perhaps they just don't choose to fund you at this time. Whatever the reason, they may well consider making an in-kind donation, so it's worth asking about this.

BE A DETECTIVE

Whether by reading newspaper articles or through word of mouth, you may come across the names of individual donors or small private foundations that you think might help you. And you may find it quite a challenge to track them down. They won't be listed in the major directories—and individual donors won't be listed anywhere as such. This part of funding research is like detective work. And like actual detective work (not the TV kind), it will take some real time and persistence digging for leads, trying different angles, sifting through information. You may have to go through newspaper articles, search periodical files on microfiche, talk to a local Chamber of Commerce, or hunt down those 990-PF IRS returns. It's hard work, but it's an adventure at the same time—and in the end you may find the perfect small foundation or donor that the people who stick to the directories will never come across.

What about a funder that you know of but can't find anywhere? I've had that happen, and believe me, it can drive you crazy. There's no rule of thumb about this—you really have to look under every stone. I had a client once who ran an animal shelter organization called Paws. She took in abandoned dogs and then flew them anywhere in the country she could find good homes for them. She had heard of a small foundation in Boston that supported this kind of work, but we couldn't find anything on it. My whole professional research staff couldn't turn anything up. But my client didn't give up; somehow she found out their address, and we finally got a seed grant from them for her project. The moral is: do make the extra effort to track down those difficult leads; it may be well worth your while.

STAY ORGANIZED—RESEARCH YOUR LEADS

Personal contact and word of mouth are wonderful, but don't neglect your homework. Just because someone gives you an inside reference to a foundation board member, don't think you can call them up and ask for money. You still need to collect your hard data—through the directories, a Foundation Center collection, newspaper articles, or a 990-PF. You must get the facts before you determine whether or not this is someone you should send a request for information. Follow the same steps that you would if you first found the source in a listing. Funders are swamped with requests from people who have heard of them, haven't done their homework, and have a project that really isn't appropriate for them. Even if you get a personal reference, make sure the funder is appropriate for you.

By the same token, if you see a tag line in a theater program that says "This production was made possible in part by a grant from the XYZ Foundation," that does not mean *your* theater project will qualify for a grant. Follow your step-by-step research plan. Go to a directory or specialized listing, find out what the foundation does, and decide whether your project fits their interests. If you think it might, write away for guidelines and an annual report. Only by looking at these will you know whether it's worth applying to them.

TALK TO PEOPLE

Never be afraid to ask for further assistance. If your local library does not provide as much information as you would like, and you've looked at the specialized guides but still have questions, go ahead and contact other people. Talk to the experts in your area. If you are an artist, talk to other artists in your community or to your state arts council. Go back and look over the sections in this book on market research, prepare your list of questions, then *get in touch*.

Talk to people in your community: community organizations, church groups, youth groups, anyone you have an affiliation with who might be able to help you. They might even be potential sponsors or funders themselves. But remember, you have to let them know how assisting or sponsoring you will benefit them. Perhaps your project will be good publicity for them, perhaps it will draw in new members and help them extend their outreach. Bear in mind that you are selling a product—even though it happens to be a nonprofit project.

Talk to people who are in fund raising. If you are a scholar or researcher, talk to people in a university development office. Talk to development officers of nonprofit organizations in your community. They may be able to give you some useful ideas about funding and the world of philanthropy. The more you know about this world, the more likely you will find a funder that is right for you.

KEEP EXPLORING

As your fund-raising awareness increases, you'll probably hear about courses, seminars, and workshops that are intended to assist the grant seeker. Some of these might help you, others might not. Unfortunately, aside from the basic orientation to research that the Foundation Center offers, there is not too much available in terms of low-cost general assistance for grant seekers. In fact, reading this book and following the guidelines in it carefully will probably give you as much as most basic courses can.

You may find that some organizations active in your field offer reasonably priced workshops from time to time. You might have to pay from $35 to $50 for an evening workshop, though you usually get a discount if you join the organization. These classes can be helpful. Although they will probably repeat some of the information given here, they will orient you to the standard practices and expectations of funders for your particular field and may direct you toward some specific possible funders. Some of these organizations may offer mini-courses that take place over several days; some may even offer workshops run by the program officers of foundations, who will talk about their programs and tell you how to apply. The best way to find out about such workshops is to seek out organizations in your specific field (see the next section, page 127).

There are also a few established organizations, such as the Grantsmanship Center in Los Angeles, that offer help with fund raising. However, their courses and materials can be quite expensive—and not always helpful, since they are directed toward organizations rather than individuals. Of course, if you have an organization and you want to raise a very substantial amount of money, you might find some of these services useful. You can also contact organizations that promote or support philanthropy and ask if they know of any workshops or assistance programs in your area. Some of these organizations are listed below.

The Grantsmanship Center.   The Grantsmanship Center in Los Angeles holds training programs and workshops in Los Angeles and around the country in grantsmanship, program management, fund raising, proposal writing, and so on. Their courses are quite expensive, $400 and up, and are targeted to nonprofit organizations. This is not an organization that's going to be of much help to individuals.

- The *Grantsmanship Center Whole Nonprofit Catalog* is published seasonally, and contains feature articles about fund raising and nonprofits, as well as information about the Center's programs and other publications. (It also lists various directories and publications that you can order.) The Center will mail this publication at no charge to staff members of nonprofit and government agencies, so if you can't find it at a Foundation

Center collection, ask someone you know at an organization if they would like to get it.

- For further information, contact:
The Grantsmanship Center
1125 W. Sixth Street (5th Floor)
P.O. Box 17220
Los Angeles, CA 90017
- 213-482-9860; Fax 213-482-9863

The Support Centers of America.   The Support Center of New York, which is the organization's main office, conducts management workshops for nonprofits in fund raising, human resources, finance, marketing, grant proposal writing, and so on. Again, these are really aimed at organizations and are not very useful for most individuals. However, for smaller organizations their fees are quite reasonable, ranging from $25 to $50. They offer special discounts to Latino organizations. The Support Centers of America is a network of sixteen offices throughout the country that offer similar training programs. See Appendix, page 352, for a complete list of Support Center offices.

- For further information, contact:
The Support Center of New York
305 Seventh Avenue
New York, NY 10001
212-924-6744

The American Association of Fund-Raising Counsel (AAFRC). This is a membership organization of fund-raising professionals that was founded in 1935 to promote philanthropy in the United States. Their mission is "to advance professional and ethical standards in philanthropic fund-raising consulting and promote philanthropy in general." The AAFRC also operates the AAFRC Trust Fund for Philanthropy, which works to advance research and education.

The trust publishes *Giving USA,* an annual report on philanthropy and charitable giving in the United States. It breaks down the sources of contributions in the United States according to individuals, foundations, corporations, and bequests. A second report, the *Giving USA Update,* promotes philanthropy at the undergraduate level with the assistance of the Association of American Colleges (which facilitates seminars and courses).

- For more information, contact:
American Association of Fund-Raising Counsel, and AFFRC
Trust for Philanthropy
25 West 43rd Street
New York, NY 10036
212-354-5799

Other Organizations in the Field of Philanthropy.   There are other organizations in the field that support the work of fund raisers, nonprofit organizations, and foundation executives, or do research or educate the public about philanthropy. If you are an individual seeking a grant, you are probably not going to find these directly relevant to your grant-seeking activities. Still, it's interesting to know they exist, and if you are involved with a nonprofit organization, some of them may be worth contacting. Here is a short list:

- American Prospect Research Association, 1600 Wilson Blvd., Suite 905, Arlington, VA 22200; 703-525-1191. Provides information about securing grants and charitable donations to nonprofit organizations.
- Council on Foundations, 1828 L. Street, N.W., Washington, DC 20036; 202-466-6512. Sponsors meetings for grantmakers, trustees, officers, and executives to keep abreast of current trends in the various fields of philanthropy.
- Independent Sector, 1828 L. Street, N.W., Washington, DC 20036; 202-667-9844. Conducts research and educates the public about the role of the independent nonprofit sector and its usefulness to society.
- National Charities Information Bureau, 19 Union Square West, New York, NY 10003; 212-929-6300. Works to maintain sound standards in the field of philanthropy and to aid sensible giving through advisory reports to contributors.
- National Society of Fund Raising Executives, 1101 King Street, Suite 3000, Alexandria, VA 22314; 703-684-0410. Holds periodic workshops and seminars dealing with all phases of fund raising.
- The National Volunteer Center, 1111 North 19th Street, Arlington, VA 22209; 703-276-0542. Assists communities and organizations to reinforce, expand, and improve the effectiveness of volunteer activities.

CONTACT ORGANIZATIONS IN YOUR FIELD

Organizations in your subject area are probably the best source of free or low-cost assistance with your fund raising. These are usually non-profit organizations set up to provide services to individuals in a specific field. Many publish journals or newsletters that announce grant opportunities, and some sponsor workshops and seminars on fund raising. Some organizations will channel grants to individuals, and some may themselves offer grants to individuals.

There are a number of service organizations around—more or less, depending on your area of interest—and their staff or officers will often be happy to offer consulting help, in many cases free of charge. Some will require membership for you to use their services, others will not. Some offer special consulting programs to members that enable you to consult with professionals in the field.

Every so often, an organization will conduct a *funding symposium* in a specific field, with multiple seminars and presentations, open both to individual grant seekers and to representatives from nonprofit organizations. I've gotten some really excellent funding sources through conferences and seminars. Still, you shouldn't feel obligated to attend a symposium just because you hope there'll be a potential funder there; go only if you think you'll get something out of the discussions and presentations.

HOW TO FIND ORGANIZATIONS

The quickest way to find organizations is to ask people in your field. And if you join one organization, or read one newsletter, you'll probably start finding out about others. Organizations are like people—they have their own unique characters, and you'll want to be in touch with those that seem sympathetic. If you join several organizations in a field, you may derive more benefits than from joining just one.

If you're having trouble locating an organization in your subject area or community, consult one of the following references, which are available in many libraries:

- *Encyclopedia of Associations*, edited by Deborah Burek, Vols. 1–3. Detroit: Gale Research Co., 1992. These reference books list 22,000 national and international organizations you may be able to affiliate with, covering nearly every conceivable interest area.

- *National Directory of Nonprofit Organizations.* Rockville, MD: The Taft Group, 1990. This directory lists 257,000 nonprofit organizations in the United States with annual revenues of $25,000–$99,000.

MAJOR NATIONAL ORGANIZATIONS AND PUBLICATIONS

You can also contact one of the major national organizations in your field. Many are open to individual members throughout the country, and they can refer you to regional or local organizations they are affiliated with. Here is a partial list:

THE ARTS

American Council for the Arts, 1285 Avenue of the Americas, New York, NY 10018; 212-245-4510.

Art Information Center, 280 Broadway, Suite 412, New York, NY 10007; 212-227-0282.

Business Committee for the Arts, 1770 Broadway, New York, NY 10019; 212-664-0600.

BUSINESS

American Business Association, 292 Madison Avenue, New York, NY 10017; 212-949-5900.

National Association for the Self-Employed, 2328 Gravel Road, Fort Worth, TX 76118; 800-232-6273.

National Business Association, 14875 Landmark Blvd., Suite 100, Dallas, TX 75240; 214-991-5381.

EDUCATION

American Council on Education, One Dupont Circle, N.W., Suite 800, Washington, DC 20036; 202-939-9300.

Council for Advancement and Support of Education, 11 Dupont Circle, N.W., Washington, DC 20036; 202-328-5900.

Council for Aid to Education, 51 Madison Avenue, New York, NY 10010; 212-689-2400.

National Association of Independent Schools, 18 Tremont Street, Boston, MA 02109; 617-723-6900.

ENVIRONMENT

Americans for the Environment, 1400 16th Street, N.W., Washington, DC 20036; 202-797-6665.

HEALTH

Association for Healthcare Philanthropy (formerly National Association for Hospital Development), 313 Park Avenue, Suite 400, Falls Church, VA 22046; 703-532-6243.

National Health Council, 1700 K Street, N.W., Washington, DC 20006; 202-785-3913.

HUMANITIES

American Council of Learned Societies, 228 East 45th Street (16th Floor), New York, NY 10017; 212-697-1505.

Council for International Exchange of Scholars, 3400 International Drive, N.W., Suite M500, Washington, DC 20008; 202-686-4000.

National Humanities Center, 7 Alexander Drive, P.O. Box 12256, Research Triangle Park, NC 27709; 919-549-0661.

MINORITIES

Minority Business Information Institute, 130 Fifth Avenue (10th Floor), New York, NY 10011; 212-242-8000.

National Association of Minority Women in Business, 906 Grand Avenue, Suite 200, Kansas City, MO 64106; 816-421-3335.

RELIGION

Global Congress of the World's Religions, 10 Dock Road, Barrytown, NY 12507; 914-758-6881.

The Interchurch Center, 475 Riverside Drive, Room 253, New York, NY 10115; 212-870-2932.

SCIENCE

National Research Council, 2101 Constitution Avenue, N.W., Washington, DC 20418; 202-334-2000.

SENIOR CITIZENS

American Association of Retired Persons, 1909 K Street, N.W., Washington, DC 20049; 202-872-4700.

TRAVEL

Academic Travel Abroad, 3210 Grand Street, N.W. (1st Floor), Washington, DC 20007; 202-333-3355.

Council on International Educational Exchange, 205 East 42nd Street, New York, NY 10017; 212-661-1414.

WOMEN

Ms. Foundation for Women, 141 Fifth Avenue, Suite 6-S, New York, NY 10010; 212-353-8580.

Women's Action Alliance, c/o Gail B. Chasin, 370 Lexington Avenue, New York, NY 10017; 212-532-8330.

HONING THE PROSPECT LIST—GETTING READY TO ACT

You've done your research, you've dug through those directories and files, you've written away to a list of potential funders. Now you are beginning to receive responses—your mailbox is jammed with envelopes from foundations—and you're starting to look through the guidelines and annual reports. This is an exciting moment: holding those guidelines in your hands starts to make this venture seem more real. You're at the point of making up your actual prospect list.

HOW TO EVALUATE MATERIAL FOR YOUR PROSPECT LIST

Once you receive the guidelines and reports you've requested, you can start to make final judgments about whether you should continue to target each funder and take the next step—actually send in a proposal. As you look through the material, you may find limitations or other factors that didn't appear in the directories or come up in your initial research. Sometimes, the new information may seem to rule out your project or suggest that a funder is not really for you. Don't get carried away by a glossy brochure, or by a letter addressed to you. If, after looking at the material, you're not convinced this is a potential funder, put it aside. This is the last stage of your research, and you need to be as careful here as you were in the beginning. Don't waste your time and theirs by applying to an inappropriate funder.

But if the potential funder still does seem appropriate, keep it on your prospect list; these are the funders that you are actually going to send proposals to.

What if you've read all of a funder's material and you still have a question about how to interpret the guidelines and whether your project fits? Should you contact the program officer for clarification? First, see if you can't possibly answer the question for yourself. If it's a matter of definition of terms, or interpretation, look up the item in this book or in one of the library references. Ask someone at an organization you've been in touch with, or someone you know who has applied for grants before. You do want to avoid bothering overworked program officers if you can, and you certainly don't want to convey the impression that you haven't done your homework or read the material carefully. If you still can't figure it out, and it's a larger foundation or a government agency, go ahead and contact the funder. Talk to the receptionist or the program officer, explain that you've read their guidelines but are still left with questions. If it's a smaller foundation, don't call. Write a brief note that clearly states your question, and ask for a short reply. Give your phone number and address, and let them respond to you.

FEED THE NEW INFORMATION INTO YOUR GRANT-SEEKING PLAN

There are two other ways you can use the information you've gathered by now, in addition to building your prospect list. First, look at the grant amounts that are available. If you need to raise quite a bit of money, and you see that only one or two or maybe none of your prospects can fund your whole project, you will realize right away that you can't rely on getting just one grant. Know from the start that you'll have to raise money from several sources and build this into your grant-seeking plan and project outline. There is no reason to conceal this fact from any potential funder; they like to see their money matched by other funders.

Second, take a close look at the funding deadlines and the notification times for grant awards. Some funders will notify you fairly quickly—within three to ten weeks—if you've gotten a grant. Others—including some government agencies—may take up to six months from submission of the application to notification of recipients. If your project requires you to act by certain key deadlines, you will have to take these long processing times into account.

WHAT ARE YOUR CHANCES FOR GETTING FUNDED?

It's going to be next to impossible to determine just what your chances of getting funded are. There are too many variables—the funder's current budget, shifting interests, proposals still under consideration from a previous grant cycle, other proposals that have come in. The best way to think about this is simply to prepare the best possible proposal package for those funders that seem likely, and take your best shot.

Do You Need to Know Someone?

You don't really need to know who makes the funding decision—whether it's a board, a single program officer, or a panel. And it doesn't matter as much as you think if you know someone on the Board of Directors or Trustees. I've had quite close friendships with some board members and decision makers and still haven't gotten all my proposals put through. These are responsible people, people with integrity, and if they're doing their jobs as they should, they will make their own well-considered judgments about what projects they are going to fund. They will choose the ones they feel best serve the mission of their foundation.

What About the Competition?

Usually you will have no way of knowing how much competition there is for funds. Sometimes you can get a rough idea—if you're applying to a program that tells you how many applications it received for the last grant cycle, and how many of these it funded. Still, competition is never a reason to eliminate a funder from your prospect list. You should only do this if the guidelines or limitations clearly rule your project out. So if you do fit a funder's guidelines and interests, give it your best shot. There is only one surefire way to increase the odds in your favor: apply to every good potential funder on your list, and don't rule any out because you're afraid of the competition.

If You Have a Hot Prospect

You may, in the course of your research, come across a potential funder that really seems likely for you. Maybe someone has referred you, or you've spoken to a program officer who seems very excited by your project. Maybe someone has even indicated that they would like to fund you. Should you stop pursuing other prospects? Not a good idea. Keep putting your prospect list together and considering other potential funders. Never put all your eggs in one basket, and never stop your grant seeking unless you have a definitive yes and a written commitment. You can lose not only time but credibility as well. Funders like to see that you aren't waiting for them, that you are pursuing other prospects. It shows that you aren't taking them for granted, that you're serious, that you're determined to get this project done no matter what.

Should You Do a Mass Mailing?

Absolutely never. Funding officers get really annoyed when they receive mass mailings. It suggests that you haven't done your research properly. They get all too many proposals that have nothing to do with their programs, or their missions. No matter what works in the world of direct-mail marketing, this is not an effective way to raise grant money. Do not send out a mailing based on the idea that you need only one or two funders to respond.

Second, don't even do a general mailing to your prospect list. You will end up creating the same impression—that you haven't done your homework—and will alienate the very funders that are best for you. Instead, you will need to tailor your proposal and application carefully to each funder.

Prepare Targeted Proposals

What you *can* do now is start planning your proposals. Build your proposal timeline, put up a wall chart with information on your likeliest prospects. Do any further market research that needs doing on the project, now that you know very specifically who your targeted prospects are. Gather your supporting materials and endorsements. If you're planning on working through a sponsor, be sure to read Chapter 4 of this book carefully. If you're specifically targeting private foundations, government agencies, corporate funders, or individual donors, be sure to read Chapters 5 through 8 on these funder types. And when you are ready to start working on your proposal, turn to Chapter 9.

You Don't Have to Go It Alone: Working with a Sponsor

I f the truth be told, the majority of grantmaking foundations
do not give grants directly to
individual applicants. Instead, they award grant monies to nonprofit
organizations, which, in turn, provide individuals with grants. This
is what I call "flow-through" funding—it is indirect in that the money
originates with a grant-making foundation, passes through a nonprofit
organization, and ends up in the hands of individuals. It may be that
the individual targeted the foundation with the help of the nonprofit
organization. Or the original funder may have set up a "regrant program" and given funds to a local or regional organization, which then
conducted its own grant-making operation to give money to individuals. Call it the trickle-down theory of grant making.

So how do you position yourself at the receiving end of this cash
flow? You have two options: create your own nonprofit organization
and seek incorporation and federal tax-exempt status; or establish a

sponsor relationship with an organization that already has these things going for it. Let's examine the sponsor arrangement first.

THE IDEA BEHIND SPONSORSHIP

There are several different terms for the sponsorship arrangement—"institutional affiliation," "organizational sponsorship," "fiscal sponsorship," "fiscal adoption." They all mean essentially the same thing. Although there are various forms of sponsorship (each of which will be discussed later in this chapter), the basic idea is that an individual and an organization get together in order to raise funds for the individual's project. This mutually beneficial (and primarily financial) relationship usually lasts for the duration of the project's life, whether that is one month or ten years.

WHY AFFILIATE?

Why should you bother to affiliate with a sponsor organization? The most obvious reason is to give yourself access to funding sources that do not award monies directly to individuals. If you can raise all the funds you need for your project with grants made directly to you, then you probably don't need a sponsor.

But there are other, less obvious reasons for institutional affiliation. Your project may require special equipment, laboratory facilities, or trained support personnel. In such a case, a sponsor organization (ideally a university or research institute) may be willing to provide you with access to its own facilities and staff. This is usually a much more efficient arrangement than trying to purchase expensive equipment and hire qualified staff members yourself.

One more reason for lining up a sponsor is that in the eyes of potential funders, the involvement and approval of an established organization lend credibility to your case. The fact that you have gotten a sponsor to agree to work with you means that others in your field think your idea is a good one.

This is especially valuable if your project is highly technical or on the cutting edge of your field. If you have an innovative, breakthrough idea, some funders may mistrust or fail to understand it, and will be unwilling to award grant money for it. But the same doubtful, uncomprehending funders will often respond favorably to the recommendations of established experts in relevant fields. And that is what a well-chosen sponsor organization can do: shift funders' dollars in your direction by giving your project an official stamp of approval.

THE SPONSOR'S SIDE

However, affiliation is not a one-way street. You're not going to reap all the benefits while the sponsor does all the work. This is a business relationship. The sponsor organization has its own reasons for allowing you to affiliate. To begin with, your project must serve the sponsor's overall purpose or mission. The sponsor is a nonprofit organization with specific goals; in an ideal individual/sponsor match, your project will help the sponsor meet those goals.

Along the same lines, the success of your project will bring the sponsor increased prestige. The sponsor thus achieves its own share of success through the association. A proud sponsor may boast of its support of your project in board meetings, annual reports, and media publications.

Further, your own quest for funding may bring your sponsor to the attention of previously untapped funding sources. This can be a strong motivating factor for the sponsor organization. The nature of your project, and the sponsor's support of it, may make the sponsor itself more attractive to foundations. In other words, you and your project may serve as a kind of magnet to attract new funders to your nonprofit sponsor.

As part of this business relationship, most nonprofit organizations that serve as sponsors will expect a small percentage of your grant money. This is a reasonable expectation; helping you prepare grant applications and providing support services during the course of your work can cause the sponsor to incur some additional administrative costs. Giving the sponsor a small share of your award helps defray their expenses.

WHY FUNDERS LIKE ORGANIZATIONS

So there are many ways in which institutional affiliation is good for you and good for the sponsor organization. What benefit does it offer the funder? Why are some foundations unwilling to award grants to individuals, yet eager to fund nonprofit organizations for the very same projects?

It stems in part from a congressional amendment in 1969 to the U.S. Tax Code, Section 4945, which set up the ground rules that private foundations must follow. The basic intent of the law was to ensure against arbitrary, whimsical, or personally motivated grants and to guard against people setting up self-serving foundations to give money to their relatives. The IRS code required that foundations must obtain reports at least annually from those they give grants to, and they quickly found that it was much easier to do the necessary monitoring and paperwork when they were giving to organizations than when dealing with individuals. So it became the general practice for foundations to deal only with organizations, simply in order to avoid headaches with recordkeeping and reporting.

Besides the recordkeeping issue, working with organizations is more efficient for many foundations. For a large foundation giving away millions of dollars, it would be an administrative nightmare to try to evaluate a flood of individual applications. And a small foundation may find that it simply costs too much to dole out the money in many small increments. Remember, this is business. It requires less administrative staff time to give a few large awards to nonprofit organizations, which can then turn around and share the wealth with individual grant seekers. By structuring their giving in this way, the foundations pass the administrative costs and some of the responsibility (along with the money) down to the nonprofit grant recipients.

I mention responsibility because there is a bit of risk involved. The individual grant recipient may abscond with the money and never actually begin his or her proposed project (it's been known to happen). An individual artist may use grant funds to create a sculpture that someone considers obscene. By funding the nonprofit sponsor rather than the individual, the grantmaking foundation protects itself from direct association with such problems.

But the foundation's reasons for preferring the sponsor arrangement are not all so selfish. More than anything, the foundation wants the projects it funds to be successful. In some cases, the involvement of a sponsor organization can improve a project's chances for success. For example, if your project requires specialized equipment, trained support personnel, or built-in technical evaluation processes, that project has a better chance for success if you have access to a sponsor's existing facilities. So especially when considering highly technical or scientific projects, foundations are predisposed toward funding nonprofit sponsors, which can provide adequate resources for the completion of the project.

TYPES OF AFFILIATION

There are several forms of fiscal sponsorship. I discuss them here in terms of levels of involvement. The greater the level of a sponsor's involvement, the more control it has over your access to the grant money and even the course of the project itself. I recommend that you seek a sponsorship arrangement that gives you the minimum level of affiliation necessary for you to obtain adequate funding. Retain as much control over your work as possible.

The Basic Fiscal Sponsor. At the low end of the affiliation spectrum is the individual working alone. If you are an artist, a researcher, an inventor, or a traveling scholar, you might use a nonprofit organization simply as a "conduit" to funnel grant money to you. You are essentially doing the project by yourself, and the organization you are affiliated with simply handles the money for you. For example, you are doing graduate work and a funder gives money to your university, which applies it to tuition fees and perhaps gives you a check for living expenses.

Umbrella Organizations. The next level of affiliation is umbrella sponsorship, which is well suited to short-term, seasonal, or one-time projects. This level of active, but not meddlesome, participation on the sponsor's part is often appropriate for educational projects, festivals, art shows, or theatrical performances. You conduct your project fairly independently, but the umbrella organization may handle things like bookkeeping and assist with publicity.

Institutional Sponsorship. This is a long-term arrangement requiring give and take on both sides. The sponsor gives you use of the resources you need, and in return you give the sponsor some degree of management power and a greater role in the project itself. This level of affiliation is appropriate for a scientist needing a laboratory, a researcher needing access to materials, or a television producer needing studio facilities and broadcast distribution.

Employment. The highest level of involvement is direct employment by the sponsor organization. This requires a surrender of autonomy, but the rewards are regular deposits into your bank account.

How the Different Types of Sponsorship Work

Sponsorship arrangements can be set up in many different ways. You might work with an umbrella organization that exerts a high degree of control over your project, or through an institutional affiliation that is rather loose.

Basic Fiscal Sponsorship—The Individual Working Alone

If your project truly is an individual pursuit, you should investigate sources of individual grant funding first. If you find you need additional support, however, then institutional affiliation may help you. Affiliating yourself—even loosely—with an educational institution or fellowship program can open up new funding opportunities as well as give you access to research facilities, libraries, rare-book holdings, special collections, and so on that can prove useful once you get started.

How It Works.   Look into forming a loose affiliation with a university, fellowship program, research institution, or other nonprofit organization appropriate to your needs. What you want is an organization willing to serve as a simple conduit for funding. You apply for funding through the organization and include a nominal administrative fee in your budget. Many universities and fellowship programs allow you nearly complete autonomy; they hand the grant check over to you and require only occasional reports on progress. Often, they even provide you with letters of introduction, giving you access to facilities that are off-limits to the general public. Another possibility is an existing "re-grant program" through a local service organization. Many arts and cultural organizations offer support to individuals by channeling money from a government agency or large foundation. If you find such a program, you apply for funds from the local organization.

Even with this loosest form of affiliation, you might benefit from some form of written agreement with your sponsor, addressing how the grant money will be handled and putting a time limit on the sponsor's involvement. In cases of established fellowship programs, you should clarify with the fellowship committee or representative just what is expected of you in the way of follow-up and financial recordkeeping.

The Fund-Raising Approach.   Once you have established a relationship with a sponsor organization, meet with that organization's fund-raising staff to discuss the financial requirements of your project and work out a grant-seeking strategy. Depending on the organization, you may be responsible for creating your proposal package, or the organization's staff may draw up the proposal for you. You may be responsible for researching potential funding sources, though the organization's staff may also give you some guidance here. In any case, you will be applying for project-specific funding through the sponsor's general fund-raising apparatus. This is because funding sources (those that do not fund individuals) require some hefty paperwork from the nonprofit organization that is submitting the application for you. At the very least they will want the IRS certification of tax-exempt status and audited financial statements—probably more.

When grant money is awarded for your project, the funder makes out a check to the sponsor organization. The sponsor at this point becomes your "fiscal agent" and will distribute the money to you, either as a lump sum or in installments. This fiscal agent may also keep track of your expenses, for eventual reports to the foundation granting the money. However, this is the extent of the sponsor's involvement. With this loose type of affiliation, the organization serves as a sponsor "in name only," exerting no control over your project itself. Bear in mind that it is still important for you to keep good records of your expenditures. This is not your money; it is public or private money that is given to you for a project, and you may be asked to account for it.

Sponsorship by an Umbrella Organization

An umbrella sponsor is a nonprofit organization that acts as your sponsor only for the duration of your project. This type of sponsorship is strictly short-term; it is most appropriate for seasonal or one-time projects, such as film productions, summer art fairs, theater festivals, or educational workshops. Projects that do involve some kind of community outreach require or benefit from an umbrella sponsor. If you want to do something in the community, such as setting up video workshops for young people, the very fact that a community group offers you space and assistance will strengthen your proposal and lend credibility to your project.

Any nonprofit organization can serve as an umbrella sponsor for fund-raising purposes, but it is best to choose a sponsor with federal tax-exempt status. Local groups such as church and school groups, arts councils, self-help groups, nonprofit clubs, and community organizations are ideal, especially if your own project is local in scope or promises to have some local impact.

How It Works.   The umbrella organization is more actively involved in your project than a basic fiscal sponsor and may assist you in outreach to the community and presentation of your work. They will want to work closely with you and may have some requirements of their own concerning management or direction. The relationship with the umbrella organization can take many forms, depending on their interests and the nature of your project.

In establishing that relationship, be sure to discuss all aspects of the arrangement up front. You and the sponsor should both state your expectations. Will you work on the sponsor's premises or your own? Will you have use of the sponsor's administrative staff and equipment? Will you have to make regular progress reports? Who is responsible for purchasing your supplies? Who will keep track of your project-related expenses? How is the money to be handled—is it to be given over to you in a lump sum or doled out as your work requires? What is the time limit on your financial relationship with the sponsor? What is the percentage of grant received or the amount due to the organization for administrative costs? Who is to have final artistic and administrative control? Who will own the finished work, if there is one? Will you or the sponsor have the option to renew or continue the project after the initial period?

All these details should be spelled out on paper, and it's a good idea to have an attorney draw up or review a contractual agreement. Both you and the sponsor should sign it and keep copies. This sounds like a lot of trouble, but stating your expectations up front can save you many headaches later on, and it is well worth the money to have an attorney look over your agreement. Remember, the umbrella organization is going to be receiving and handling the money for your project. You want to be as careful about this arrangement on your end as they are on theirs.

A few organizations that do re-granting may already have sponsorship guidelines, but most don't, or will be new to this, so you will still need to draw up an agreement in letter form. If the nonprofit organization has done this before (or even if they haven't), you can ask them to draw the letter up, but I do believe it is a good idea to have someone else look at it. You don't necessarily have to have an attorney draft the entire agreement, but you should have one review it and make comments. The more complex the project and the greater the sponsor's involvement, the more input you need from an attorney. If you are going to be using an organization's facilities and staff, if an original product will be produced, if ownership or use of a project name is involved—these circumstances all call for careful thinking. You'll want to establish how much freedom you are to have in directing your project, and just how much control or oversight the organization will have. Try to find an attorney who has some experience with nonprofit organizations, or in your own field.

- **TIP:** Call some of the law firms in your area, and ask if any of the partners do volunteer or pro bono work for nonprofit organizations. If you are working in the arts or a cultural area, contact the following organization, which offers free, arts-related legal assistance to those who can't afford private counsel and keeps lists of attorneys and volunteer groups around the country that do the same:
Volunteer Lawyers for the Arts
1 East 53rd Street (6th Floor)
New York, NY 10022
212-319-2787

Remember, you should have a comfortable, cooperative relationship with your sponsor. Don't let the process of putting the details down on paper throw you off. If certain things, such as the project start-up and ending dates, cannot be pinpointed, just make an estimate. Use the process to improve your communications with the sponsor; you both may find that creative ideas come out of it. Ultimately, your positive relationship with other individuals on the staff of the organization is what is going to make the sponsorship work and render your project successful.

The Fund-Raising Approach. To do successful fund raising, you'll need to make a cooperative effort with the organization's staff. You should meet to determine who will be responsible for creating the proposal package, and for researching potential funding sources. As with basic sponsorship, the proposal or application packages will be sent out from the sponsor's offices, since they have to enclose quite a bit of supportive paperwork.

Once you've received a grant, the sponsor takes on the role of fiscal agent. It's worth noting that an umbrella organization may take a more active role in administering funds, asserting more discretion and control over your use of the grant monies. You may have to justify and keep receipts for each project-related expenditure; you may also have to prove that all grant funds were spent only on the budget items for which they were intended.

So, it is very important, as always, to keep good financial records. When a nonprofit organization allocates funds to your project, they are taking on a fiscal responsibility and liability to both the original funder and the IRS. You want to be able to back them up, just as you would for your own tax return, and to provide receipts in order to prove how money was spent. And as your success reflects directly on the reputation of the umbrella sponsor, you may be under some pressure to keep the sponsor involved in and informed about your work.

INSTITUTIONAL SPONSORSHIP

When you have a long-term project, or one that requires a great deal of support in terms of staff or facilities, you might consider an institutional sponsor. As we have seen, working with an institutional sponsor means prolonged involvement and, often, some type of institutional management or control over your project. In return, you may benefit from the use of the sponsor's laboratory or studio facilities, special equipment, technical expertise, administrative services, and trained support staff.

If your idea is controversial or just brand new, your chances of funding will increase greatly if you apply through an institutional sponsor. Funders tend to look more favorably upon projects backed by established institutions; the sponsor's track record makes your project seem feasible. Funders are not usually in a position to evaluate controversial ideas within a field; they'll rely on the judgment of an institution.

Also, if your project is going to require high-tech, expensive equipment, special facilities, powerful computers, or the like, institutional sponsorship strengthens your position with funders. Funders want to know that you have access to the resources you will need to carry out your project.

And if you anticipate that your project will have significant community impact (for example, you might want to create a shelter for battered women), your funding position will be strengthened by an affiliation with a local community agency (in this case, a women's health organization or a family violence agency).

When you are looking for an institutional sponsor, you can go to some of the same nonprofit organizations that might serve as umbrella sponsors. You can also look to institutions that don't normally channel funds to individuals, and to larger national organizations, since your project may not be only locally based. Institutional sponsors include schools and universities, research institutions, professional societies, historical societies, art associations, museums, hospitals, health agencies, performing arts groups, sports clubs, community foundations, unions, veterans groups, civic leagues, Chambers of Commerce, and churches and religious groups.

How It Works. When you do your project with an institutional sponsor, you will be in constant communication about your activities, accomplishments, and financial status. Your project begins to resemble a program of the institution itself. In fact, this is a good way to think about this kind of sponsorship: you are essentially proposing to the institution a new program, which you will manage, as part of their overall activities. Expect to be making regular progress reports.

A clear written agreement is even more important with an institutional sponsor than with an umbrella organization. You need to create and sign an agreement detailing all aspects of the arrangement. This is not so much a sign of suspicion on anyone's part as an exercise in discovering and acknowledging your mutual expectations. It allows you and the sponsor to establish the ground rules for your long-term relationship.

You may not want to specify a time period for this relationship, as you are hoping to fund a long-term project. In fact, your arrangement may be permanent. But there are other issues that should be addressed and agreed upon now. Will you work on the sponsor's premises or your own? Will you have unlimited access to the sponsor's facilities and equipment? Will you have use of the sponsor's support staff and resources? Will the sponsor have any control over the progress of your work? Will the sponsor claim joint ownership of any invention/discovery you make during the course of your affiliation? Will the sponsor take responsibility for financial recordkeeping, or is that up to you? (Many foundations and government agencies require detailed records of how their grant money is spent, especially those that disallow funding for administrative salaries.) The most basic issue to settle is whether the sponsor organization will act as your fiscal agent, giving you relative autonomy while ensuring your appropriate use of grant funds, or whether it will adopt you, taking legal control over your finances and your work. Either arrangement is possible on a temporary or permanent basis.

The question of ownership may be one that you want to look at closely. Many institutions assert ownership over products and inventions that are developed under their auspices. Some will even claim copyrights of articles and material that are written with their support. If you start a project and at some point want to stop working with an institution, they may wish to carry on with your project under its original name. At the same time, if you have your own patent, copyright, or trademark as you go into a project, it's unlikely that an institution will try to take it over. Nonprofit institutions are not in business to rip off ideas, although they do like to find new sources of income to support their activities. Many kinds of relationships are possible with different institutions; you simply need to work things out based on what the institution is offering you and what you are bringing to them. Make sure you spell everything out clearly in a written agreement and have a lawyer who is familiar with the issues look it over and advise you.

If you are entering into a long-term association with an institution, keep in mind that officers or staff may change. If a new person comes in, the tone and interests of the institution can change. New officers may have a different level of enthusiasm about your project, or wish to move the institution in new directions. Even though it's an institution and you have a concrete project, everything is based on the relationships and interests of individuals. This is another thing that you will need to consider when structuring a letter of agreement, and another reason to make sure everything is crystal clear.

The Fund-Raising Approach. In an institutional sponsorship arrangement, the sponsor organization will probably want to be actively involved in the grant-seeking process. In fact, your project may be included in a larger, more comprehensive funding proposal for the institution as a whole. In this case, you would be responsible for supplying project-specific support material (a brief project description, biographies of the personnel involved, budget figures, etc.) for the larger proposal. If the grant-seeking process includes interviews with foundation representatives (as is often the case when large sums of money are being requested), you might be asked to participate in a discussion of your project. Be as cooperative as possible. Remember, you are in this for the long haul.

Once the money is awarded, you will either have relative freedom to pursue your project (if the sponsor simply acts as your fiscal agent), or your work will be closely watched and perhaps influenced (if you are adopted by your sponsor). If your project is being funded as part of a larger institutional grant, you may have to rely on appropriations from the institutional operating budget.

DIRECT EMPLOYMENT BY THE SPONSOR ORGANIZATION

When you go to work for a sponsoring organization, you are trading off some degree of autonomy for the institutional support and a steady paycheck. If this idea appeals to you, look for a creative environment for the work you want to do. Ideally, you can get a job at an institution already receiving grant funding, so that you are the indirect (and immediate) recipient of grant monies.

If you become an employee, there's still quite a wide range of possible involvement. At best, you might be paid to work on your project in an organization's office, or theater, or laboratory. You might also have to become a part-time fund raiser for the organization, helping to raise money for their other projects in order to get your own project off the ground. You don't have to consider the job a permanent one—there is quite a bit of turnover in some of these organizations, and sometimes people work at a nonprofit for a while, build up experience and connections, then move on to other projects. You might also consider working for a nonprofit on a consultant basis rather than as a full-time employee. You could try to get yourself hired to do a specific project—running poetry workshops in the schools, setting up a research lab for a university, and so on.

There are some potential drawbacks to the employee relationship. There's the issue of autonomy—how much control the organization will want to exercise over your work. It is likely that you will have responsibilities in addition to working on your own project. There's always the possibility of getting so caught up in other activities or projects that you are deflected from the work you want to do. You should weigh your eagerness to get your project done right away—maybe you can afford to proceed at a more leisurely pace as a nonprofit employee. You do want to make sure that you are going to work for an organization that is closely enough involved with the kind of work you want to do that you won't be permanently deflected. If you want to produce theater, for instance, you should work for an organization that does productions, or would like to, not an organization that only does research or provides information services.

The potential advantages, besides the steady paycheck, are several. For one thing, you will have easy access to and comfortable use of the facilities, because you are a part of the organization. You will also—and I think this is very important—enjoy the camaraderie and interaction with other professionals in your field. There is a great deal to be gained from this kind of day-to-day experience. And of course, it is a good way to establish credibility in your field. Funders will now consider you a professional.

Getting Hired, Getting Paid. If you have limited nonprofit experience, you will probably find that you have a better chance with a local, grass-roots organization. They will probably be more interested in hiring you if you can offer them services that they may not have other means of fulfilling. Perhaps they don't have a fund raiser, and you can offer to help with their other projects. Perhaps you have a particular idea for an outreach program that fits with their mission. If they like the idea and see that you have the expertise and passion to do it, they might be willing to hire you.

Now the catch is money. Often if you propose to work for a nonprofit organization on a project that they are really interested in, they will ask you to find the funding in order to pay your salary. They may have all kinds of institutional support they're happy to offer you, but no money in their budget for your salary. If you are going to have to raise the funds to pay your own salary, do think through the reasons you want to affiliate with the organization, and whether this still seems to have advantages over working independently.

If you are interested in pursuing the possibility of working directly for a nonprofit, see the references below for some books that may offer you guidance.

- *Careers for Dreamers and Doers: A Guide to Management Careers in the Nonprofit Sector,* by Lilly Cohen and Dennis R. Young. New York: The Foundation Center, 1989.
- *1990 Internships: On-the-Job Training Opportunities for All Types of Careers,* by Kathy Jobst. Cincinnati: Writer's Digest Books, 1990.
- *What Color Is Your Parachute?,* by Richard Nelson Bolles.

How It Works. Here again, you may need a contractual agreement. Many nonprofit organizations do offer contracts to their regular staff members. If you are going to work on a temporary, project-related basis, it's still important to spell things out in writing. If, for example, you will be working as an artist-in-residence for a nonprofit theater, you should lay down some ground rules as to what is expected of you during your tenure. This might take the form of an employment contract. Perhaps you will be required to direct one show during the course of the season. For the rest of your tenure (the remainder of the six-show season, let's say), you have an office, a computer, free access to the theater's support staff and resources, and unstructured time for the pursuit of your own project—writing a new play. In exchange for its generosity, the theater might want right of first refusal on the premiere production of your play.

If you and the theater can agree on the terms, then by all means draw up a formal agreement and sign it. Have a lawyer create the agreement or at least read over any standard agreement that the theater offers.

Do consider what could happen to programs you've been involved with if you should leave the organization. It's possible that the organization may want to keep using your idea or the names of your programs. After all, they have made an investment in these programs. Anything is possible; it all depends on the written agreement.

The Fund-Raising Approach. If you have the best of all possible arrangements, the organization is hiring you to do a project under their auspices, and already has funds, or will handle the fund raising. If you are coming to them with a new project, they may expect greater involvement. If the organization already has a development officer or a fund-raising staff, your involvement may be similar to independent affiliation with an institution or umbrella organization. You may be expected to do some funding research, write the basic draft of your proposal, and provide a budget and some supporting materials, while the staff prepares the additional paperwork.

If you are really coming in on the ground level, there is no development staff, and the organization is looking to you for some basic fund-raising assistance, you have your work cut out for you. In fact, you are almost in the position of someone operating their own nonprofit organization, except that the basic organization already exists. You are going to have to get familiar with a lot of bureaucratic details, and work closely with the secretary and treasurer or bookkeeper to come up with the various documents, budgets, and financial reports required by the IRS and by funders. If no one on the staff is familiar with all the procedures, you could ask the organization to send you to one of the seminars conducted by the Grantsmanship Center or the Support Centers of America (see pages 124 and 125). There are also some useful references available on management and fund raising for non-profits (see page 160).

HOW TO FIND A SPONSOR

When you have figured out which level of affiliation best suits you and your project, it's time to pinpoint those organizations you want to approach. Where do you look for names of potential sponsors? How do you even get started?

The best starting point is your own clubs, societies, and other affiliations. Think about all the organizations in which you are involved. Are any of these groups appropriate for sponsoring your project?

What about your friends' clubs and organizations? Ask around about their personal connections. There's nothing like a close friend's recommendation to get you in the door for sponsorship affiliation.

Research local nonprofit groups. If you've been doing market research in your field, you probably know of some of these already. Ask the organizations you know about for references to others in the field. To search further, see if your public library has a directory of local nonprofit groups in its reference collection. Larger, broad-based non-profits, such as the United Way, may be able to direct you to organizations whose goals and interests are in line with your own.

Also check into citywide, consortium-type associations, such as arts councils, if they are appropriate for your project. Your local Chamber of Commerce may be able to give you some leads in this area.

On a wider geographical scale, investigate national or regional organizations in your field. Look at the listings in Chapter 3 and in the Appendix, page 338, for some of the major ones; local professionals in your field may be able to refer you to others. A comprehensive list of national associations (arranged by subject) can be found in the *Encyclopedia of Associations*, a multivolume reference work available at most public libraries.

You can contact some of the major national organizations in your field to ask for references to similar local or regional groups. You will find a partial listing of these in Chapter 3, and a more complete listing in the Appendix, page 338.

At each step of your search, be sure to ask for referrals to other organizations that might serve as sponsors. Word of mouth is a powerful tool in nonprofit circles.

CHOOSING THE RIGHT SPONSOR

Begin by making an exhaustive list of potential organizations. As we saw in the section above, the best ways to create this list are through brainstorming and research. Think creatively. During this initial step, you will want to give yourself room to explore every possibility. Don't rule anything out yet; write it all down. You will thin out your list soon enough.

The second step is to evaluate the organizations on your list in order to determine just how helpful an affiliation with a specific organization would be in your search for funding. To make such an evaluation, you'll probably have to do a little research into each organization on your list, and we'll discuss ways to do this. First, however, let's consider the specific things you need to know about each sponsor:

1. Is the potential sponsor organization a nonprofit that is incorporated and designated as federally tax-exempt by the IRS? If the IRS considers it a bona fide tax-exempt organization, it will designate it as a charitable organization under Section 501(c)3 of the Internal Revenue Code. This arcane grouping of figures and letters may seem absurdly technical, but it's all-important for nonprofits. You'll hear nonprofit people freely talking about whether this or that organization has "501(c)3 status." If so, the organization is eligible to receive restricted foundation funding, and an affiliation would give you access to a new tier of funders; 501(c)3 status also means that individual donors can claim a tax deduction by contributing to your project through the organization. If the organization does not conform to this description, cross it off your list. You are best served by a sponsor that can lead you to new funding sources.

   You really do have to be a stickler about this. Not all nonprofit associations will have the tax-exempt status; although a community orchestra or a sports club probably will, a bird watchers' club probably won't. You *must* go through an organization that has a 501(c)3 tax-exempt status. Not a (c)4, not a (c)9, but a (c)3—this is essential. Even if an organization has applied for the tax-exempt status and the application is pending, they don't have a history of funding, so they're really in the same boat as you and probably could not offer you much more than you could get on your own. Most important, they will not be able to receive funds until their tax status is established. So don't waste your time. *Only go to an organization that has a 501(c)3 status.*

2. Do the activities and purposes of the organization reflect your own? If so, the organization is likely to be a good match for your project. Funding sources will perceive that your sponsor has a logical, fundamental interest in the success of your project. If your project doesn't seem to fit the purposes of the sponsor, you will confuse potential funders and weaken your proposal. Be sensitive to conflicts of interest in choosing a sponsor organization. If you do approach an organization that hasn't traditionally worked with projects like yours, there is probably a reason why not, but you might be able to convince them to work with you if your project relates closely to their overall purpose. If they are sincere and enthusiastic about moving in a new direction, they will have to do some extra explaining in their section of the proposal for your project.

3. Is the organization equipped and willing to support you in fulfilling your goals? This willingness may not be something you can determine before meeting with representatives. If you're looking for more than a simple fiscal agent, however, you should consider your support needs for the project. Will you need fund-raising assistance, facilities, office space, staff support, or equipment? You should have some sense of whether the organization will have the ability to meet those needs. It is as important for you as for the organization to determine whether this might be an appropriate marriage. The ideal sponsor will be able (and willing) to provide whatever you need to complete your project successfully.

4. Does the organization have a good reputation in the fund-raising world and a positive record of accomplishments in its field? This may be difficult to determine up front, but the organization's history and track record can make or break a grant request, especially where money management is involved. An organization that has mismanaged funds, failed to make regular progress reports, or otherwise disappointed fun-

ders will not help you make a favorable impression on grant committees. Worse, an organization that does not manage funds effectively may cause you problems with your own project if you do get funds and they become your fiscal agent.

Investigating Potential Sponsors.   How can you find out more about a potential sponsor? See if they have a good local reputation, if people like working with them, if they have community support. Talk to members or constituents and ask how they like dealing with the organization.

How can you find out if the organization has done successful projects? That's easy—they'll be telling everybody about them. They might not be publicizing the failures—but you can usually find out about this by talking to others in your community or at other organizations. Even national organizations may have regional offices or some kind of local presence.

Whom should you talk to in the community? The Chamber of Commerce is always a good place to start. Talk to the staff of other nonprofits who work in the same area, but realize, of course, that they may not say the most favorable things, since they are in competition. For the most part, though, nonprofit people really do cooperate with one another and form a community. Depending on the organization, you might also talk to the United Way. They can give you a good handle on what is going on with a nonprofit organization in your local community.

You can also talk to someone at your local Better Business Bureau if you have doubts, and ask them to look at an annual report or an audited financial statement. This doesn't have to be a federal investigation—you just don't want to walk blindly into a complicated situation.

APPROACHING A POTENTIAL SPONSOR

By doing a little investigation, you should be able to narrow your original list of organizations down to just a few. You may also be able to rank them in order of preference. Now, starting with your top-rated organization, set up meetings with representatives from each of the best, most appropriate organizations still on your list. Here is the best way to arrange such a meeting:

1. Send a letter outlining your project and requesting a meeting to discuss a sponsor affiliation.

2. Make a follow-up phone call (after you are sure the letter has been received) to schedule the meeting. If you plan to bring core project group members with you, mention this during the phone call. Their presence can help make you look serious and organized, but their unexpected arrival could be overwhelming. If possible, tell the representative how many people you will be bringing; he or she can then choose an appropriate meeting room.
3. When the time comes for the meeting, be prompt and professional. Bring support materials to help explain your project and demonstrate your serious commitment.

You can use this initial meeting as an opportunity to find out more about the organization, but don't start by asking what they are all about. You want to show first that you have done your homework and read their brochures and newsletters. Then discuss all aspects of the sponsor relationship. What would be the daily work arrangements? What administrative fees would the organization require? How would the money be handled (a lump-sum payment to you or cash as required)? What time limit would you set on the sponsor relationship? Has the organization participated in similar sponsor relationships in the past? How were they handled?

Be as specific as possible, especially about the items that most concern you. But don't commit yourself to anything yet. Both you and the organization are in a process of exploration and consideration. In fact, an organization will often have to present a new project to its Board of Directors or Trustees and get approval for supporting it. When you've discussed everything, you should have some sense of what their interest is and what they have to offer. Thank them for the meeting and say that you appreciate their time and consideration of your project and that you are exploring several possibilities; if they seem interested, suggest a time when you will be in touch again.

One of the most important things you can gain from a meeting like this is to get the feel of an organization—whether it's formal or informal, whether you have a rapport with the director or staff, whether communication is easy or difficult, and whether they seem genuinely interested in your project. This is important even if you don't end up affiliating with a particular organization; if they appreciate and respect your project, they may be able to help with an endorsement or a referral to other possible funders. Most of all, though, you want to have a sense of whether or not you could have a comfortable and effective working relationship with them.

After you have met with all the organizations on your short list, you should have compiled enough information to make a well-informed decision. Your best choice would be the organization that not only serves your needs but also shows real enthusiasm for your project. Call up the person you met with at that organization and tell them you would like to work with them. They may give you their decision immediately, or they may suggest another meeting or give you a time when they will let you know their decision. They may need to present your project to their Board of Directors for approval. Don't be disappointed if things don't work out with your first choice; they may still be able to offer you assistance or referrals.

When you *do* get an organization to agree to sponsor you, it's time to formalize the details of your relationship. If it's going to be a simple arrangement, draw up a letter of agreement. If it's going to be complex, work out the details in written agreement or contract. When your lawyer is satisfied that the document protects your interests, both you and the sponsor should sign it. Your sponsor affiliation is now official.

THE ALTERNATIVE TO SPONSORSHIP: FORMING YOUR OWN NONPROFIT ORGANIZATION

I'm mentioning this option last because it involves the greatest level of personal commitment (and the most work) and is appropriate only for very long-term projects. Incorporating yourself as a nonprofit can allow you as much autonomy as you have working as an individual, and many more funding prospects. But it requires a great deal of thought, initiative, and planning—and some initial expense.

Forming your own organization can get complicated; it can be not only time-consuming but expensive as well. Further, the statistics show that a great number of new nonprofit organizations collapse within the first few years. This may be partly because of competition for funds, but it's more likely because the founders simply didn't know what they were getting into. This is a step that must be taken with an eye toward the long-term future of your project. On the positive side, nonprofit incorporation will allow you to retain autonomy and control and give you more funding options.

What do you need to do to set up a nonprofit? First, be prepared to shell out some money for legal, accounting, and registration fees. This could amount to an outlay of several thousand dollars, which is one important consideration. To do this right, you will need to file for formal incorporation. And you'll need to apply to the IRS for official tax-exempt status. You are going to need to get other people involved, put together a board of directors, keep financial records, and have monthly meetings, keeping minutes. The process of getting started can take from six months to a year. This is not something that you do haphazardly. If you do not plan to continue this project for an extended period of time—several years, at the minimum—don't bother. I really recommend that people work with an existing nonprofit organization, or umbrella organization, before setting up their own. Working with an existing organization for a one-time, short-term project can save you a great deal of administrative work, time, and expense.

If you cannot find an existing organization that is really a good fit with your project, you may need to create a new entity. Remember, you do still have options other than the nonprofit mode. You should think about which would be better for you: a nonprofit, tax-exempt organization, or a for-profit business. If you have a marketable idea, product, or project, you may be able to turn it into a profitable business. You can pursue investors and loans and you can build up income and equity. It's important to think about this at the outset, because once you've started a nonprofit organization, it will not be able legally to transfer any assets, title, patents, or ownership to you as an individual or to a for-profit business.

Of course, a nonprofit corporation can earn income. It just has to plow any earnings back into its programs, to help serve its mission. It cannot distribute earnings to its directors or staff as bonuses or stocks. It can hire directors and staff, pay reasonable salaries, purchase health insurance for its employees, reimburse expenses, pay for advertising, and build up its facilities. The Children's Television Workshop, which produces *Sesame Street*, is a good example of a nonprofit organization that earns a good deal of money in the profit sector—in their case, by marketing toys and games. All these earnings then go back into the furthering of the Workshop's mission—to produce educational programs for children.

The relationship between an individual owner and a nonprofit organization can be complex. Individuals can sell goods or services to a nonprofit organization. A nonprofit can commission a writer to write a play, pay the writer's salary, and put on a performance, all while permitting the writer to retain copyright of the work. An individual may lend a trademark or patent to a nonprofit organization for its limited use without giving up ownership. At the same time, the government does not want individuals using nonprofit corporations as devices to build their individual careers. There has to be some kind of public service involved.

So if you do have an artistic, scientific, cultural, or social project that you would like to extend into the indefinite future—and it is not really a profit-making idea, and does not match any other existing program—then consider setting up your own nonprofit. Although the laws governing nonprofit organizations vary from state to state, there are two principle types: the unincorporated association and the nonprofit corporation.

THE UNINCORPORATED ASSOCIATION

Few legal requirements apply to the unincorporated association. There's no need for detailed articles of association—just some simple rules about procedures. This kind of organization is useful for neighborhood or community groups, such as a block association or a local homeowners' group. It has no legal identity separate from the individuals who make it up; the individual members share all financial and legal responsibilities and liabilities. This kind of association is easy to set up, but it's not very useful for grant seekers. Funders may perceive it as unstable, since the laws governing it are often vague. There can be problems with organizational credibility, and it can be difficult to do banking and establish ownership of property. A lawsuit or government inquiry will target the individual members.

Worst of all for the grant seeker, it can be difficult for an unincorporated association to establish its credibility with the IRS and gain the coveted 501(c)3 tax-exempt status. Although you can get limited funding without it, the 501(c)3 certificate is essential. Most funders require it; they won't give to nonprofits who don't have the IRS certificate (they would endanger their own tax-exempt status by giving to unqualified organizations). And of course, without the tax-exempt status, individuals cannot deduct their donations to such groups from their own income taxes. For these reasons, I do not recommend working through this type of nonprofit structure.

THE NONPROFIT CORPORATION

Unlike the unincorporated association, the nonprofit corporation is an independent entity, legally separated from its founders or board members as individuals. This offers several real advantages:

- *Limited liability.* This means that board members or directors are not individually liable for any lawsuits or debts that the nonprofit corporation may incur. This is especially important if the organization is operating in the public sphere, or managing large sums of money.

- *A greater sense of stability.* Board members, staff, and the community itself will have a stronger sense of commitment to the enterprise. Funders, government agencies, banks, and others will perceive the nonprofit corporation as more predictable, reliable, and likely to be around for a long time. This leads to the third advantage.

- *A greater likelihood of winning grants.* It's easier for a nonprofit corporation to earn the essential tax-exempt status, which makes it a legal recipient of foundation money and a legal write-off for individual donations. Funders will also respond to the appearance of commitment and stability.

There are many different types of nonprofit corporations, depending on different state laws. They can include business groups; political, trade, and service organizations; and charitable, educational, religious, scientific, and cultural organizations. They may include corporations established with a business purpose, such as a thrift shop set up to generate funds for a hospital or charity. If you seriously intend to set up a nonprofit corporation, you should work with a lawyer who can identify the best type for your purpose, under the laws of your state.

How It Works. Setting up any nonprofit organization involves taking a number of basic steps. (The specifics vary from state to state, so check with local authorities, and with a lawyer, before beginning the process.)

1. Choose a name and create a statement of purpose.
2. Create Articles of Incorporation and Bylaws. These should explain how the corporation may dissolve itself.

3. Form a board of directors. In most cases, the actual legal responsibility and control over the organization is held by the Board of Directors, not by an individual founder or project director. (Though the board may choose to follow this person's lead.)

4. Incorporate with the state government.

5. Begin financial recordkeeping and regular reporting to the state government.

6. Apply to the Internal Revenue Service for federal tax exemption.

• **TIP:** Call or write Volunteer Lawyers for the Arts at 1 East 53rd Street (6th Floor), New York, NY 10022, 212-319-2787, and order their short booklet on not-for-profit incorporation, *To Be or Not to Be: An Artist's Guide to Not-for-Profit Incorporation* (1986). Although this is addressed to artists and refers to New York State law, it gives a good overview of how the process is likely to work for any field and may help you decide whether you want to go ahead. The same organization can direct you to individuals and other volunteer organizations around the country that offer free or low-cost assistance with the process.

You might also contact the Small Business Administration for free advice and guidance on how to form and incorporate a nonprofit, tax-exempt organization. The SBA is a federal organization. Its address is 409 Third Street, S.W., Washington, DC 20416.

To ensure conformance with your state's requirements, you should also contact your state's Secretary of State or state Attorney General for detailed information on formal requirements, forms, and fees for setting up charitable or nonprofit corporations. And as with any business endeavor, you will benefit from the advice of professionals, including lawyers, accountants, and bankers.

The Tax-Exempt Status. Once you are incorporated, the first thing you want to pursue is the all-important tax-exempt status. Without a copy of written notification of this, it will be hard to get contributions or grants. Apply to the IRS, and expect to wait several months for your application to be processed. You will probably want the assistance of an experienced attorney in filing your application.

You have to supply information about the goals and history of your group, your Board of Directors, and your staff, salaries, and organizational structure. You also have to give detailed financial information, including a history of finances since you incorporated, projected budgets, and fund-raising plans.

The IRS will review and evaluate the information you supply and make a determination. To meet federal requirements, your organization must conduct activities that are in the public interest and must fit into one of the categories in Federal Tax Code Section 501(c), such as educational or charitable organizations. Your group can offer no privilege or benefit to individuals derived from its earnings. If it looks like your group is simply serving one individual's private career, the IRS may deny or revoke tax-exempt status. It can take three months or more to get a response.

- **TIP:** For detailed information on how to qualify for and receive an IRS certificate of tax exemption, order IRS Publication 557: *How to Apply For and Retain Exempt Status for Your Organization*. This is published by the U.S. Government Printing Office in Washington, DC, and you can order it through your local IRS office.

When your organization receives notification of 501(c)3 status, this means that not only will it pay no tax, but it also now has the right to receive grants from government and other tax-exempt organizations, including foundations. In addition, individuals who make donations to your organization can deduct these from their own income tax. This makes it legally possible for funders and motivated individual donors to help you.

Remember, there are different categories of nonprofit corporations, and the IRS does not treat them all the same. Some will require more stringent recordkeeping and reporting, and some do not allow individuals to deduct contributions to the organization. You should have professional help in applying for the proper category. In any case, you will have certain obligations to the government, including holding regular meetings and keeping minutes, making annual reports to the IRS and other government agencies, observing IRS regulations, and keeping up the activities for public benefit.

No Shortcuts to the 501(c)3! Are there other legal forms your group might take? Do you have to go through the whole process of getting tax-exempt status in order to be eligible for certain grants and donations? The short answer is, yes, you do. There are no shortcuts. Even incorporation is not enough—you still have to apply to the IRS.

The Fund-Raising Approach. Once you have established your own nonprofit, tax-exempt organization, you can start to seek funding for it. Your organization is qualified to seek and receive funding from a wide range of foundations. Just be sure to follow each foundation's application instructions carefully. You will have to supply documentation attesting to the tax-exempt status of your organization. (This usually means a copy of your IRS 501[c]3 certificate and audited financial reports.) Filing an institutional application can require more paperwork than filing an individual one. The added responsibility— and increased opportunity for funding—are now all yours.

Seeking funding for a nonprofit corporation is quite a bit different from seeking funding as an individual. Organizations like the Foundation Center, the Support Centers of America, and the Grantsmanship Center are really set up to serve organizations like yours (see pages 114 and 124). You can get more assistance from them and can attend seminars and workshops that are directed to you. (Of course, you may have to pay for these.) Here are some specialized references that you may find of use:

- *A Nonprofit Organization Operating Manual: Planning for Survival and Growth,* by Arnold J. Olenick and Philip R. Olenick. New York: The Foundation Center, 1991.
- *Raise More Money for Your Nonprofit Organization: A Guide to Evaluating and Improving Your Fund-Raising,* by Anne L. New. New York: The Foundation Center, 1991.
- *Securing Your Organization's Future: A Complete Guide to Fund-Raising Strategies,* by Michael Seltzer. New York: The Foundation Center, 1987.

The Foundation Center
79 Fifth Avenue (8th Floor)
New York, NY 10003
212-620-4230

The Foundation Center
1001 Connecticut Avenue, N.W.
Washington, DC 20036
202-331-1400

The Foundation Center
Kent H. Smith Library
1422 Euclid, Suite 1356
Cleveland, OH 44115
216-861-1933

The Foundation Center   The Grantsmanship Center
312 Sutter Street, Room 312   1125 W. Sixth Street (5th Floor)
San Francisco, CA 94108   P.O. Box 17220
415-397-0902   Los Angeles, CA 90017
                                     213-482-9860; fax: 213-482-9863

See Appendix, page 352, for a complete list of Support Center offices.
For further information, contact:

> The Support Center of New York
> 305 Seventh Avenue
> New York, NY 10001
> 212-924-6744

THE
FOUNDATIONS

When you started thinking about getting a grant, the first word that probably came to mind was "foundations." As you begin looking through the directories of grant givers, you'll find listing after listing of foundations. These are a major source of free money, and probably the one you've heard most about.

Everyone has heard of the Ford Foundation, the Rockefeller Foundation, and a few other of the "Big Daddies." But did you know that there are over 32,000 private foundations in the United States that give money to worthy causes? Many of these give to individual projects or needs like yours, either directly or through sponsors. They range from the major foundations, with their national—even global—and long-range concerns, to tiny foundations that give a few grants a year in very specialized areas or to specific kinds of recipients.

But what is a foundation? A private foundation is a nongovernmental, nonprofit institution created for the purpose of contributing to the common good. Foundations support charitable, educational, religious, and other activities, and focus on important social needs—in health, the environment, the arts, and so on. Foundations do their work by providing financial support, in the form of grants, to individuals or groups. Each foundation has its own independent Board of Directors or Board of Trustees that decides what kinds of issues it will grapple with and what kinds of projects it will support.

In pursuit of the common good, foundations can make grant awards to individuals, to assist with individual needs for health care or for education or with professional or creative goals, or to assist those who are helping and reaching out to others. Foundations set up procedures and guidelines for selecting those they'll give money to, and may have staff, program officers, or selection committees to advise the founders or Board of Trustees on these selections.

A LITTLE HISTORY

The idea of a "charitable trust" is very old. Even Plato had a kind of "foundation" that supported his Academy after his death. The modern American foundation is based on the nineteenth-century English model of charitable trusts that were set up to do good works, aid the unfortunate, improve education and medical care, support religion, and generally better society. The first American foundations were set up over two hundred years ago—Ben Franklin started his American Philosophical Society, which operated like a foundation, as early as 1743.

Other charitable trusts were put in place in the nineteenth century, most of them in support of specific institutions, but the real boom in establishing foundations took place around the turn of the twentieth century. The great tycoons and "robber barons," whether for personal or charitable reasons, began to concern themselves with social issues. Andrew Carnegie in 1896 set up the Carnegie Institute in Philadelphia to support education, and then the Carnegie Corporation of New York in 1911 to support libraries and medical education. Others—like Commodore Vanderbilt, Henry Ford, and John D. Rockefeller, Sr.—followed suit. The foundations of this period went beyond the support of specific institutions and began to address a wider range of issues and to support research to solve social problems.

From the beginning, these foundations were surrounded by some controversy and suspicion; people accused the founders of trying to conceal or "launder" their wealth. Nevertheless, American society would be much the poorer without their efforts.

A second boom took place in the 1930s. Millionaires like Andrew Mellon and Henry Ford set up foundations to escape giving up their profits to the graduated income tax and to avoid massive estate taxes.

The biggest boom of all came about immediately following World War II. The desire to shield their money from taxes again motivated many wealthy people to put it into foundations. Congress had voted massive increases in taxes on capital gains and high profits, and the 1950s were a time of high profits. The result was a great increase in donations to foundations—more than 90 percent of existing foundations were set up at this time.

In 1969, Congress passed a Tax Reform Act, and one of its major provisions was a set of rules to regulate foundations and control abuses. The Tax Reform Act prohibited the use of grants for private purposes or personal gain, restricted the kinds of programs that foundations could support, barred them from political lobbying, and required public disclosure of grant programs through the IRS 990-PF forms. The act also established clear definitions of which kinds of nonprofit organizations were private foundations and which were not. It distinguished "private foundations," which give away funds, from "public charities," which are tax-exempt organizations that solicit contributions and receive donations. It also distinguished private foundations from trade associations, political lobbying groups, and phony "foundations" that had nothing to do with the public good.

The Tax Reform Act established two clear and distinct types of foundations: operating and nonoperating. *Operating foundations* are limited to the function of supporting a single institution or program, like a hospital or research institute. *Nonoperating foundations* give away money in the form of grants to programs, organizations, or individuals. There are three basic types of nonoperating foundations: independent, community, and corporate.

Under the Tax Reform Act of 1969, foundations were permitted to make grants to individuals for "travel, study, or similar purposes," as long as they got approval in advance for their criteria and selection procedures and agreed to make detailed reports on their grantmaking. Many foundations chose not to go through this process and instead began to restrict their grants to nonprofit organizations with tax-exempt status. The same act set up the IRS 501(c)3 tax-exempt classification for these nonprofit organizations, which were called "public charities."

The last major law to affect foundations was the Economic Recovery Act of 1981, which required foundations to give away a minimum of 5 percent of their assets each year in the form of grants. This was to ensure that they really would fulfill their stated function. But foundations can still receive new funds, and they have the option to reinvest any investment income in excess of that 5 percent.

FOUNDATIONS TODAY

By the 1990s, there were over 32,000 private, corporate, and community foundations active in the United States. These foundations held assets of over $137 billion, and by 1992, total annual foundation giving had reached the $8 billion mark. Those contributing include not only the larger foundations, such as the Ford Foundation, the Lilly Endowment, the Andrew Mellon Foundation, the W. K. Kellogg Foundation, and the Rockefeller Foundation, but also smaller foundations. About one-fourth of these foundations held at least $1 million in assets or gave at least $100,000 in grants annually.

Foundations are located in every state of the Union, but the greatest concentration is in the Northeast, where the oldest and largest were originally set up. Those based in New York State alone hold about 23 percent of all foundation assets. This concentration of assets is offset by the fact that some of the very large foundations based in the Northeast distribute their funding throughout the whole country. Foundations in the Pacific region and South Atlantic states have been rapidly increasing in total assets recently.

As you begin to research foundations that might support your project, you should be aware of the various types in existence, since they often consider different types of requests, and sometimes handle them quite differently. The major categories, as defined by Congress, are the private or independent foundations, the community foundations, the corporate foundations, and the operating foundations. Of these, only the first three are set up to give grants to individuals or organizations that apply to them from the outside. There are also categories that reflect how a particular foundation operates, such as the pass-through type. Let's take a look at these different types.

PRIVATE FOUNDATIONS

Private foundations constitute by far the largest group. There are more than 28,000 of them, with total assets of nearly $120 billion, and they account for nearly 76 percent of the grant dollars awarded by all foundations. These are often termed "independent," or "family," foundations, because they have usually been funded or endowed by a single individual or family. Family members may be actively involved in guiding the foundation's program interests. Private foundations may limit their support to the specific cause, charity, or interests of the founder.

Private foundations are customarily divided into two categories: the large foundations—for example, the Ford, the Rockefeller, the Guggenheim—and the smaller independent or family foundations, which are scattered throughout the country. The distinction between the two is made according to an arbitrary cut-off point—usually $1 million in total assets, or $100,000 in annual giving. There is even a directory of so-called mid-sized foundations. For the individual grant seeker, the most important differences between large and small foundations are in how they are staffed and how they deal with the public.

The large foundations are among the oldest; they were set up by the major industrialists and millionaires of the late nineteenth and early twentieth centuries. Many are based in the Northeast, and they have long experience with addressing social needs and problems. They have national, even global concerns, and are interested in projects that can serve as models for dealing with long-term problems and needs. They may have a number of program officers who deal with specialized giving areas. Because of their high profiles, these large foundations get many proposals and have to be very selective about which ones they fund. Most give to large-scale projects administered by nonprofit organizations, though a few, like the Guggenheim, do give directly to individuals.

Large foundations generally have paid staffs that can review proposals and even seek out and develop projects. They make an active effort to communicate with the public by issuing guidelines, annual reports, and sometimes newsletters. They can respond easily to requests for information. It's easy to find out about the large foundations, and the big directories tend to focus on them.

The smaller foundations may have been set up as trust funds or started during a benefactor's lifetime. They usually focus on specific geographic areas. Their giving may be very closely tied to a local community or to the special interests of the founder. Perhaps a successful business person wants to give something back to the community, or to benefit individuals of the community, or individuals who share the founder's interests. Although they hold only about a third of total foundation assets, the smaller foundations actually give a greater number of grants than the large ones. The size of grants is usually smaller—ranging from perhaps $3,000 to $15,000—but they tend to give more toward ongoing operating expenses.

Many of the smaller foundations are unstaffed, and administered by a single director or trustee, who must process requests and present them to a board. Because of this, they often cannot actively reach out to the public, and it may be hard to find out about them and contact them. They do not have the facilities to respond easily to requests for information. They won't always appear in directories, but you can sometimes find them in specialized publications. If you learn of a small foundation in your region, you can research it by getting hold of its latest 990-PF form (see Chapter 3, page 105).

COMMUNITY FOUNDATIONS

Community foundations are set up to benefit a particular city or region. Their boards of directors are often representatives of the community. Unlike private foundations, they have been established with gifts and bequests from many different sources; in 1992, there were only about 330 of these, but they held assets of nearly $6 billion. Community foundations generally limit their giving to projects benefiting the immediate community, and to local residents. For example, the Marin Community Trust awards grants only to residents of Marin County, California. Some community foundations are classified as private foundations, reporting on IRS Form 990-PF, and some as public charities, reporting on Form 990. Their total giving is relatively small, amounting to only about 5 percent of all foundation grants. Still, they may be an important resource for the individual with community residence, or a locally based project.

CORPORATE FOUNDATIONS

Corporate foundations have been set up by profit-making corporations to support a variety of interests. They may give small grants to employees for education or general welfare, support projects that benefit their local communities, or back those that will serve as good public relations or advertising vehicles for the corporation. In 1992, there were over 1,500 company-sponsored foundations, with assets of nearly $6 billion. Their total giving amounts to between 15 and 20 percent of all foundation grants. These figures, however, do not reflect corporate giving programs that are administered through advertising or public relations departments, or discretionary funds.

Corporate foundations and giving programs both operate differently from other foundations. They have different mandates and different interests. They may support only their employees or employee family members. They may operate in a very free and entrepreneurial way with outside projects, and look for special benefits for the corporation. They may prefer to support projects with in-kind or donated services. Because of the variety of corporate funders, we'll consider them separately in the next chapter.

OPERATING FOUNDATIONS

Operating foundations are a special case, not directly relevant to the grant seeker. They are set up to support a single organization or institution, like a hospital, a research institute, or a community center. At the beginning of the 1990s there were about three thousand operating foundations in existence. Of these, about half did give small grants directly related to the work of their institution, but their total grant giving amounted to less than 2 percent of all foundation grants.

PASS-THROUGH FOUNDATIONS

This is not really a separate category but a way that a private foundation may operate. Pass-through foundations do not maintain an endowed fund or hold any real assets from year to year. Instead, they receive an infusion of funds each year, often from the founder, which they immediately pass on to other nonprofit organizations (they very rarely give grants to individuals). In a way, they are like a nonprofit organization that raises a budget annually but gives the money to other nonprofits rather than supporting its own programs. An example is the Fund for Psycho-Neuroimmunology, a former client of mine. This funds scientific fellowships and research and keeps its overhead close to the bone. The director doesn't take a salary, there are no office expenses, and all the money goes to other organizations. When you find a foundation listing that shows substantial annual giving but no real assets, it may well turn out to be a pass-through foundation.

WHO'S IN CHARGE?—RULES THAT GOVERN FOUNDATIONS

The principal laws that govern foundations are the Tax Reform Act of 1969 and the Economic Recovery Act of 1981. These define the basic rules and procedures that all foundations must follow. They must file the annual 990-PF reports with the Internal Revenue Service. They are allowed to give grants to individuals for "travel, study, or similar purposes." If they give grants to individuals, the IRS must approve their selection criteria and procedures, to ensure that the selection process is objective. They must supply extensive follow-up reports to demonstrate that the money was used appropriately and accounted for. A major impact of these rules has been to discourage many foundations from giving directly to individuals.

Curiously, foundations that do give to individuals do not have to have open and publicized calls for applications and proposals. They can even give grants to individuals that they know of, without any formal application, as long as the selection process is considered objective. The most well-known example of this kind of giving is the MacArthur Foundation "genius grant," which cannot be applied for, and which is awarded without the recipient being in any way involved in the process. Many smaller foundations give grants in a similar fashion.

The 1981 law required foundations to give away a minimum percentage of their assets each year. In periods of declining interest rates, this puts some family foundations and smaller foundations under pressure—they can see their overall endowment decline. In my experience, this seems to cause them to support a smaller number of organizations or individuals that they feel more strongly committed to. They tend to make somewhat fewer grants, but larger ones.

WHO GETS THE GRANTS?—FOUNDATION GIVING PATTERNS

How does a foundation decide who it is going to fund? Each foundation has its own unique giving priorities. The governing body of the foundation—the Board of Directors or Trustees—decides each year how to allocate funds. They may have more or less freedom to choose the kinds of projects they will support. *General-purpose* foundations have broad interests and can move into new areas. They may change their priorities to respond to new social issues or problems. Any new priorities must still fit within the original philanthropic intent of doing social or common good. *Special-purpose* foundations generally stick to an original mandate.

Foundations can channel their grants into many special categories, sometimes called *giving categories*. Some may focus on certain subject areas, such as the arts or education. They may specialize even more, and support only filmmakers in Kentucky, or medical education. Some are concerned with special populations—women, minorities, Native Americans. Some may support only certain types of organizations, such as schools or research institutes. Some may give only for certain types of activities, such as research or educational projects. They may specifically rule out certain categories, such as administrative salaries, equipment purchase, or new construction.

As you know by now, some foundations support both individuals and nonprofit organizations, and some support only one or the other. Certain private foundations, like government agencies, often do consider requests for renewed funding and multiyear grants, unlike corporate funders, who usually don't. In doing your research, you will need to look carefully at a funder's giving categories to decide if they will be able to support your project. You can find some of these categories in directories, but the final word appears in guidelines and annual reports.

Foundations can range from the clearly socially responsible to the unusual. Some are particularly concerned with such cutting-edge issues as the environment, and health and welfare in developing countries. At the same time, some of the older, more established foundations are also willing to address new and urgent issues. The Rockefeller Foundation is a good example. In fact, since the larger, more established foundations have huge assets, they are able and sometimes eager to take real risks. There are quirky foundations as well, that support things like the Frisbee scholarship at the State University of New York at Purchase. No matter how unusual your project or your background, you may find a foundation to support you.

- **TIP:** For radical, activist, and New Age projects, consult the *Oryx Guide to Alternative Foundations*. Phoenix, AZ: Oryx Press, published annually.

You might also try the *Directory of New and Emerging Foundations*. 2nd edition, New York: The Foundation Center, 1991.

THINKING GLOBALLY, ACTING LOCALLY—THE GEOGRAPHICAL FACTOR

While some foundations have national or even global interests, the great majority focus their giving in one geographical region. In fact, it's quite common for foundations to restrict their giving to their own state, or even to one part of a state. Many focus on a city, county, or local community. There are a few, like the Rockefeller Foundation, that concern themselves with such global issues as world population levels, but these are the exceptions. Only about one-third of the larger foundations give on a national or even regional basis. What does this mean for you as a grant seeker? You should direct a significant part of your grant research into local and regional funds—this can be as important as subject and population group research. In fact, you can combine these approaches to zoom in on your best prospects.

GRANTS TO INDIVIDUALS

In spite of the general trend, and the extra paperwork, some foundations do make a commitment to funding individuals. Why do they? There is usually a personal passion or experience that motivates such foundations. The founder or someone on the board may have a special interest in an area, whether it be painting, filmmaking, inventing, or ecology. Or someone may have had a difficult time in their own life, or cared deeply about someone who did, and were thus motivated to support general welfare grants or medical support grants for people in similar circumstances.

The Foundation Center's *Foundation Grants to Individuals* lists approximately two thousand foundations that specifically make grants to individuals. This is only one directory, and not a complete one. You can find many other grants to individuals listed in specialized directories for subject, population, and geographical area. Further, many foundations will fund individuals through a nonprofit sponsor. No one has ever tried to compile the statistics that would show how many grants flow through sponsors to individuals, but there are many.

Foundations make grants to individuals under a variety of specialized programs, including: scholarships, student loans, fellowships, travel internships, residencies, arts and cultural projects, general welfare grants, and program-related investment grants (PRIs). There are also many broad-based and generic types of grants to individuals. These are often less specifically defined than are grants to nonprofit organizations, which is an advantage for individuals seeking a grant.

The highest proportion of grants to individuals go for educational purposes, and the two highest categories are scholarships for undergraduates and fellowships for independent projects, research, or doctoral dissertations. In fact, over half of the funders that give grants to individuals specialize in educational support. Other important categories are corporate foundation grants to company employees and community residents; grants for general welfare and medical assistance; awards, prizes, and grants through nomination; and internships and residencies.

Still other grants to individuals can address a multitude of activities and subjects. They can support, just to pick some examples, accounting, agricultural sciences, anthropology, architecture, art, art education, biological research, business, cancer research, choreography, conservation, educational studies, foreign study, graduate study, journalism, medical research, music, poetry, teaching, women's studies, and writing.

A foundation's Board of Directors can always dictate where it will allocate its funds. It might decide to grant ten scholarships and adopt ten special projects in one calendar year. Or it might decide to fund an individual who has a program that will have a positive effect on other disciplines or groups the foundation wants to support. For example, a foundation may fund a choreographer whose work will affect a specific community, such as schoolchildren, or a multicultural audience.

Many foundations making grants to individuals are small, and may have limited funds for a modest number of grants. (This is why you will probably need to apply to several foundations.) You will also want to go beyond foundation funding and explore government programs—and don't forget fiscal sponsorship as a way to expand the funding prospects for your project. When foundations give grants to nonprofit organizations, they often prefer to fund a specific project of the nonprofit, rather than general operating expenses. This really works to your advantage if you have a fiscal sponsor, because your project becomes a specific project of the nonprofit sponsor.

You should bear in mind that some hot issues of the day—education, the environment, and health concerns are current examples—may claim a foundation's primary attention. They will tend to allocate the greater proportion of their grant budget for projects dealing with these choice issues. Still, I don't think you should do what I've seen many grant seekers consider—that is, alter or change your focus to match a foundation's priorities. Stick by your convictions. There has to be a funder out there that will match your needs! At the same time, keep thinking creatively about how to relate your project to a funder's interests.

GRANTS TO ENTREPRENEURS

If you are an entrepreneur looking for financial assistance, there are several grant categories you may find useful. Grant money can support research and development, employee training or hiring, and sometimes equipment purchase or real estate purchase. Grants cannot be used for debt reduction and certainly not for investment purposes. This is not a way to make a quick buck. It *is* sometimes a way to support a business that is also doing something for the common good.

You will need to think about how best to present your ideas to make them appealing or appropriate for nonprofit funding. Start by looking closely at the foundation's mission statement. Try to incorporate some of its wording or concepts into your own statement of need. I can think of a perfect case study. I had a client several years ago who was an excellent physician, a general practitioner who came up with a fabulously clever computer system for processing insurance claims much more efficiently. He needed a quarter of a million dollars for research-and-development expenses. So we approached medical foundations with the idea of streamlining health care and health insurance for foundations themselves. He made a fortune on the project, and saved medical foundations some money, too.

In some cases—and especially if you are an inventor, are developing a new product, or are starting up a new business—you can turn to foundations for help in getting started.

One form of funding is the *program-related investment (PRI)*. This is a low-interest loan or equity investment that a foundation makes in a project that helps the foundation further its own charitable objectives. Although some foundations make PRIs available only to nonprofit organizations, others provide funding to individuals and for-profit businesses, as long as the project at hand addresses the foundation's goals.

Keep in mind when applying for PRI funding that the foundation wants to make a bona fide investment in a business or project that promises to be successful. Return on investment may not be the foundation's first concern, but they certainly don't want to throw good money away either. If you are requesting program-related investment funding, you must address the director's concerns in real business terms. You will need to establish the financial viability of the project just as you would in any business plan. You will need to demonstrate that the PRI will allow you to get started, and that the project can then become self-sustaining and possibly even profitable. A one-time event, like a festival, is not appropriate for PRI funding.

HOW TO RESEARCH FOUNDATIONS

We've already outlined the basics about researching foundations and other funding sources in Chapter 3. You learned about some of the major directories, and you know that you need to use indexes and specialized directories to focus your search according to geographical location, subject area, and any population group you may belong to. You know you can use specialized directories, like my *Free Money* books, to find grants to answer specific needs. You know that you can find some basic information in directories, but will always have to write for guidelines and annual reports in order to tell whether a funder is really right for you.

When you start to research foundations, be sure you can express your own need and mission clearly. Look carefully at the giving categories and priorities of each foundation and make sure that your need and your qualifications match these. By weeding out inappropriate funders, you can make your grant seeking immensely more efficient and successful. This process begins as soon as you open a directory.

The following is a fictional sample of a typical foundation listing. If you are using a foundation directory or scanning an information sheet that a foundation has sent you, you may see the following information:

The XYZ Foundation
Address
Phone number
Incorporated in year: 1952
Donor: Joe Nations, Sr.
Officers (Board of Trustees): Joe Nations, Jr., President, Shirley
   Nations, John Powell, Harry Snow, Jane Rowe
Financial data (year ended '92): Assets, $3,000,000; gifts re-
   ceived, $3,000,000; expenditures, $2,750,000, including
   133 grants (high: $250,000; low: $1,500; average: $5,000–
   25,000)
Purpose and activities: Giving largely for higher education, arts
   and culture, community service, health care, civic orga-
   nizations, and individuals, minority opportunity and
   women
Types of support: operating budgets, seed money, endowment
   funds, scholarship funds, individuals, fellowships, general
   purposes, renovation projects, special projects, etc.
Limitations: Giving primarily in the state of California, with
   emphasis on southern California
Publications: Annual report, application guidelines, program
   policy statement, financial statement
Application information: Initial-approach letter
Deadlines: March 1, September 1
Contact: Shirley Nations
Number of staff: 3 full-time professional, 2 part-time

Let's consider what this information means to you as a grant seeker.

Officers. It's the listing of officers and the donor that tells you this is a family foundation. Apparently the founder's son and another family member are still active in the foundation. There isn't much else of significance to this section for you, unless you are lucky enough to know one of the board members.

Financial Data. $3 million in assets puts XYZ into the large foundation category, by the Foundation Center's reckoning. But it's still small compared with some of the real biggies. The large amount of gifts received means that this is a very active foundation, supported by its founder and/or others.

We can see from the financial profile that in 1992 the XYZ Foundation gave 133 grants, which ranged in size from $1,500 to $250,000. This amount of giving also puts XYZ in the large foundation category, since it clearly gives more than $100,000 a year. However, the average grant range of $5,000–$25,000 is more typical of mid-sized foundations. If the total expenditures were $2,750,000, this means that XYZ probably gave out quite a few grants. (Although expenditures could also include the foundation's own operating expenses or investments.)

Purpose and Activities.   The XYZ Foundation has very broad areas of interest. Education, arts, and culture cover a lot of activities, and so does community service. This suggests that the board will be taking a very active role in deciding what the foundation will fund on a case-by-case and year-by-year basis. Projects that combine more than one of the foundation's interests might attract special consideration. These might include minority training or education or support for a women's art program. Of course, the fact that they specify higher education might rule out education for younger children, and they may support only institutions and not offer individual scholarships. A scientific research project wouldn't seem strongly supported here, though it might somehow connect with the higher education or health-care interests. You would have to go to the guidelines, annual report, or 990-PF to find out. This listing just doesn't give you all the details you need.

Types of Support.   Individuals may apply to this foundation, but you would have to read the guidelines carefully to see exactly what types of support they qualify for. The foundation supports "scholarship funds," but this doesn't necessarily mean that it grants individual scholarships. It might or might not fund individual health care. Still, the small size of some of the grants suggests that there probably are a number of grants for individuals. The mention of support for minorities and women suggests that individuals from these groups might get special attention. In addition, there are grants for operating budgets, special projects, unique cases, seed money, renovation projects, and endowment funds, which a nonprofit organization could put aside in order to earn interest. XYZ will consider many different kinds of projects, and you would have to consult their guidelines for further details.

Limitations.   The principal limitation is geographical. The founder, Joe Nations, Sr., may have lived a long and successful life in southern California. It seems he wanted to make a contribution to others in his community; therefore, grants are restricted "primarily" to the state of California, with "emphasis" on southern California. How strict are these limitations? Does someone in San Francisco still have a chance? Yes, but not a very big one. The chances of someone in Arizona or Pennsylvania? Practically nil. If they have given any grants at all outside of the region, then they would list that information here. However, the grants that are given outside their primary region will probably be initiated by the foundation itself. So if you aren't based in southern California, or your project won't benefit the population of southern California, don't waste your time by applying to this foundation.

Publications. This foundation does make the effort to communicate openly about its activities. If it looked like a potential funder for you, you would write for the guidelines and annual report.

Application Information and Contact. You are given the name of a contact person to whom you should write for guidelines and an annual report. Once you've looked over the guidelines, if you believe your project would really qualify for funding, you will write your initial approach letter. (This would be either a three- to five-page letter following the format for the "letter of request," or a short, full proposal, outlined in Chapter 9 of this book.) Since this listing specifically indicates a letter, it would be a big mistake to go over five pages, which would start to look like a full proposal. Three pages would be fine. "Initial-approach letter" means that they may ask you to send a more elaborate proposal later, if you have a large-scale project. Or, if you write a great letter of approach, they may decide to give you funding on that basis alone.

Deadlines. The two deadlines suggest that the Board of Trustees will meet twice a year to decide what grants it will give. If you miss that September deadline, you won't have a chance to get funding from XYZ for another six to eight months. And remember, it's always better to get your proposal in earlier than the deadline.

Number of Staff. Since this is a staffed foundation, there will be someone there to send you guidelines, to possibly answer a question about limitations or priorities (after you've read the guidelines), and to talk to you about your project if you have sent a proposal they are interested in.

OTHER KINDS OF LISTINGS

Community Foundations. The listing will basically look the same for community as for family foundations. The annual report and guidelines may include some discussion of the multiple sources that donate funds to the community foundation.

Inactive Foundations. Since it takes several years to put a directory together, information can be out of date, and some of the listed foundations may have become inactive. This is another reason why you must always write to a foundation for guidelines or an application before sending them any form of request.

Guidelines and Annual Reports. Foundation guidelines will tell you more specifically what they are looking for and spell out any special limitations on funding. They will give you the essential details about the application process, including any special formats or procedures.

The annual reports provide detailed information about a foundation's giving policies. They may describe the history of the foundation and the purpose for which it was founded. They will outline the principal kinds of programs and projects the foundation has funded in the past. Often they will list names of grant recipients, giving brief histories of their affiliations and the amounts of money they received. Annual reports and guidelines give you the facts you need to know before deciding whether to apply to a foundation, and they tell you exactly how to apply.

HOW TO APPROACH FOUNDATIONS

Once you have received a foundation's guidelines and you believe you may qualify for funding, be sure to note the deadlines and methods of application. The Board of Trustees may only meet once or twice a year to decide where to allocate its funds; or the board may meet quarterly, and review applications every few months. If it's not clear in the guidelines, and this is a staffed foundation, do call to verify the deadlines. *It is crucial to get your proposal or application in on time.*

The guidelines will indicate the form of approach—whether a letter of request or a full proposal. If there is an application to fill out, this makes your job easier. (Before you fill out an application or send in a letter of request, be sure to read Chapter 9 of this book, to make certain you are presenting your strongest case.)

Some foundations will tell you in their guidelines that they do not accept unsolicited proposals. This means that they only consider invited proposals. How do you get invited? This is something that is not always easy or even possible. Sometimes you can simply call up and ask what the protocol is. Usually, though, you have to know someone who will recommend you to the foundation, and then if they are interested, they will get in touch with you. If you are fortunate enough to be invited to submit a proposal, the foundation will usually want to meet with you and give you guidance and suggestions to help you prepare your proposal.

How Foundations Deal with Grant Seekers

Foundations, both large and small, are swamped with requests for money. Letters and proposals come pouring in, month after month. It's a major job just to log them in and file them. This may seem like impossible competition. But the figures are somewhat misleading. The reason is that a large percentage of those thousands of requests are totally inappropriate for the foundations they are sent to. Many of them represent mass mailings from people who have done little or no research. A great many of the foundation officers I talk to complain bitterly that they receive floods of proposals from people who have absolutely no business even requesting guidelines. They complain that many people don't even bother to look carefully at a foundation listing. Most of their applicants will take a quick glance, spot their subject area, and do no further analysis to see if they fit even the listed guidelines. They don't look to see if the foundation funds individuals, they don't look for geographic limitations, they don't look for giving categories, and they don't request guidelines, which you, dear reader, always do.

What this means is that you have an immense advantage over thousands of other applicants, simply because you are doing your research properly. You are approaching only a carefully screened list of potential funders, and you are contacting them in a professional way. You will have thought through your project thoroughly, and after reading Chapter 9, you will have prepared a strong, professional-looking proposal. So don't worry about those other applicants—just make your proposal shine!

What Happens After You Apply?

Whether it's a large or small foundation, someone will log in your proposal and take a quick look to see if it really does fit the foundation's guidelines. At a large foundation, a program officer will look at it, and may pass it directly to the Board of Directors or Trustees, or perhaps to a preliminary evaluation committee. The evaluation committee will then decide whether to submit it to the board. If they do, you may get a call or a letter at this point, telling you that your proposal is "under consideration" or that it is up for a grant. The program officer may ask you to submit additional information.

At a small, unstaffed foundation, the foundation director or fund administrator may be the first one to look at your proposal. They will probably scan it quickly and make an initial decision as to whether they want to keep it under consideration. Or they may put it immediately into a reject file. After considering a number of proposals, the foundation director may make some preliminary decisions, or submit specific proposals to the board. Small, unstaffed foundations are generally incapable of even responding to every request they get, so you won't know whether you are under consideration or not. If you are going to be funded, you'll be notified. Smaller foundations do not always notify grant seekers whom they decide not to fund, and you may have to contact them again after the decision period has passed.

How long does it take to be notified? It all depends on the foundation and how it is structured. Many foundations will notify you within four to eight weeks of receiving your proposal; others may take up to three or four months. The foundation's guidelines may or may not indicate a decision period. If there is an application deadline, this means that the foundation expects to consider proposals during a certain period after the deadline. If there is no deadline, the decision time may depend on how often the foundation board meets to consider proposals. As a general rule, smaller foundations will meet less frequently than more heavily staffed foundations and may take longer to make decisions.

WHO MAKES THE DECISIONS?

The final authority for making funding decisions always rests with the Board of Trustees or Board of Directors, but that authority may be delegated in different ways. At the larger foundations, there may be a program officer who does some initial screening of proposals and requests, and a committee that does a second level of screening, passing only a few proposals on to the board. No matter how active an interest board members take in the decision process, they rely very heavily on program officers and staff for advice and judgment. So at a large foundation your proposal is being reviewed and passed by a number of people, and a consensus begins to develop along the way.

An unstaffed, small foundation may have a very small board, perhaps including relatives and personal friends of the founder, who will generally support the founder's wishes and interests even after his or her death. At small foundations, the actual founder or the director will often exert a great deal of influence over grantmaking decisions, or will essentially be making the decisions and passing them by the board for approval. An attorney or accountant who manages a trust fund may be making most of the actual decisions, but the board is always there as a counterbalance.

At the larger foundations, the board will always carefully consider the directions it wants the foundation to go in and the problems and issues it wants to address. It will decide beforehand, "Let's fund this type of project this year," and will make decisions in terms of those predetermined priorities. At smaller foundations, the board or director may be a little more flexible about dealing with new kinds of projects but will generally support their existing interests.

Sometimes people imagine that grants only go to personal friends or relatives of foundation board members. Though this might have occurred before the congressional rulings went into effect, these days it is just a lingering misconception. Foundations really do distribute grants with a sense of objective purpose and fair procedure.

Can you bring any personal influence to bear on a board or program officer? Not usually. You may have more opportunity to interact with the staff of a large foundation, but you will largely be supplying information that they request. The committees and boards will form their own judgments about whether they want to support you. Smaller foundations may be more susceptible to personal influence, just because they are small and don't have the same layers of staff members and committees. The board members of a small family foundation, or the individual founder, probably do respond to some personal influence. But it's much harder to communicate with these foundations, and unless you know board members personally, you can't hope to exert any influence. Just trust that they will support good projects when they see them, whether they know you personally or not.

If you do have a genuine personal relationship with someone on a board, or with someone who knows a board member, whether it's a large or small foundation, there's certainly no harm in mentioning that you have a proposal up for consideration. It won't necessarily help you, since the board does have to maintain the integrity of its own procedures, but it can't hurt. If you don't have a personal contact, it is a breach of etiquette, and could be counterproductive, to try to contact and influence a board member. Using personal influence isn't the way to get a grant. The way to do it is to develop a solid project, to research and target the right funders, and to send them a superb proposal.

CORPORATE
FUNDERS

T his program was made possible
by a generous grant from the
Triad Corporation." You've of-
ten seen or heard this kind of acknowledgment, related to television
and radio shows, printed on programs for public performances and
community events, or announced from a podium. What you may not
have realized is that your neighbor's children were helped through
college by their mother's employer, or that a corporation in your
community has been funding a drug-treatment center at the local
hospital.

The fact is that many businesses and corporations play a vital role
in communities throughout the United States by sponsoring events
or addressing problems in numerous fields, such as health care, culture,
and education. Many corporations have a sense of social responsibility to their employees and their community, and they act on this

by setting up corporate foundations or by giving funds directly from their operating budgets for worthy causes. They call it "corporate citizenship."

There are several distinct kinds of corporate funding. *Corporate foundations* are much like private foundations, except that their funds come from a different source and they have different kinds of interests. *Corporate giving* means that a corporation gives grants directly from its operating budget—through a formal program, a discretionary fund, or an advertising or marketing budget. Corporate giving programs operate differently from foundations. Corporations are permitted to give a percentage of their pre-tax income to charities in the form of direct tax-deductible contributions. Only tax-exempt organizations can receive these contributions, however.

Corporations and corporate foundations have their own mandates and concerns. Some support only their employees and employee family members; others give freely to individuals and projects in their communities. They often like to support projects that will give them good advertising or public relations value. They may support projects with in-kind donations or noncash grants. As a group, corporations are probably the most entrepreneurial of all funders. They can react more quickly and individuals can approach them more easily, and for these reasons they are an important group to pursue.

Corporate foundations do operate under the same IRS and Economic Recovery Act rules as private foundations. There is no specific legislation governing corporate giving programs, though of course they must comply with the normal IRS reporting procedures, as any business has to do. Ultimately, corporations always have to answer to their stockholders, so they do need to be businesslike about their giving programs. If their stocks are widely held, they must be able to justify grant giving as somehow of benefit to the corporation.

WHY CORPORATIONS GIVE GRANTS

Although some corporations have always given charitable gifts and contributions, they didn't get into the foundation business in any significant way until the early 1950s. When they did, it was for some of the same reasons that the great boom in private foundations occurred at this time. The government was imposing high tax rates on high business profits, and both individuals and corporations found that putting some of those profits into a foundation gave them significant tax savings. This was a more cost-effective way to do charitable work than making direct contributions.

Corporations have other reasons for preferring to work through foundations. They can hire specialists to make grants and do long-range planning, instead of depending on the instincts of a marketing manager. They can contribute more money to the foundation in good years and less money in lean years. And having a foundation that bears the company's name promotes good public relations.

Of course, there are those who raise questions about corporate philanthropy. They claim that corporate giving is really a way of promoting special interests and mounting public relations campaigns. They say it supports only projects that seem useful to the company instead of addressing pressing social issues. They are skeptical of corporate support of events like the Olympics, when television commercials use the giving to advertise the company.

I know of too much corporate giving that is practically anonymous, and too many worthwhile projects supported by corporations—when government or private funders wouldn't help—to criticize them for getting good p.r. out of it. Furthermore, since company foundations are completely separate legal entities, they cannot, by law, make grants that are solely of benefit to the company that sponsors them. They do give to many projects that have no connection with the corporation's business.

CORPORATE FUNDING TODAY

In 1992, there were over one thousand five hundred company-sponsored foundations, with assets of nearly $6 billion. Their total giving has amounted to between 15 and 20 percent of all foundation grants—in 1989, it reached over $1 billion. These figures, however, do not reflect direct corporate giving programs that are administered through advertising or public relations departments, or discretionary funds. In fact, it is impossible to produce statistics on the full extent of corporate giving, for reasons we'll address later.

CORPORATE FOUNDATIONS AND DIRECT CORPORATE GIVING

Corporate foundations and direct corporate giving represent two different styles and strategies of corporate funding. Still, both are guided to some extent by the same corporate policies, and they may even share the same staff, though they keep their operations separate.

Corporate foundations are registered with the IRS and must follow the same rules and procedures as any private foundation. The foundation makes its own grant-making decisions, establishes its own giving categories and restrictions, publishes its own guidelines and annual report, and must file the 990-PF form with the IRS. Like a private foundation, it can give grants to both individuals and tax-exempt organizations. Some officers of the parent corporation will usually sit on the Board of Directors, and the parent company can thus influence which grants are made. Since the corporate foundations have their own endowed funds, they can give grants somewhat independently of the business's ups and downs.

Direct corporate giving means that a company gives funds directly out of its operating budgets and treats them as regular business expenses. A company may give funds directly through an official *direct contribution program*, or through many different departments. Companies often grant funds from their advertising, marketing, or public relations budgets. They may also give to their own employees through an official *corporate contributions program* or *community relations program*. The CEO or other executives may have their own discretionary funds. Direct corporate giving always takes place on a discretionary basis, according to the judgment, decision, or impulse of some company executive, whether the president or marketing director. Smaller companies that do not have company foundations often give funds directly, and some larger corporations have both foundations and direct giving programs.

In direct corporate giving, a company can treat gifts as a business expense—say as an advertising cost—or as a charitable contribution. This is usually an accounting decision that has to do with the company's tax profile. It doesn't directly affect you as a grant seeker, except that a company can only make charitable contributions to tax-exempt organizations. A company has to treat direct gifts to individuals as business expenses, and would have to see a real advantage for themselves in such expenditure. Ultimately, if a company president wants to give money, it can be handled in many different ways.

Corporations can be much more responsive and flexible with direct giving. They can use discretionary funds to quickly support almost any kind of project that they feel will benefit them in terms of community goodwill or public relations, or for any other reason. If the company is doing well, more funds are available. In recessions, companies generally scale back their direct giving and discretionary grants, simply because there is less to give.

FOREIGN CORPORATIONS

A number of foreign corporations have set up shop in the United States in recent years—and not only the Japanese. These corporations operate factories or distribution systems, run publishing houses, and manage entertainment and communication companies. Like American companies, and for the same reasons, many have set up their own corporate foundations and direct giving programs.

For the most part, these companies give because they want to back up their employees and the communities that support them. Of course, corporations also operate giving programs because they want to create a positive image for themselves in the communities where they operate facilities. For such reasons, foreign corporate foundations have been steadily increasing their philanthropic giving in the United States.

In 1991, Japanese corporations, for example, gave over $400 million in grants throughout the United States, seeking high visibility and a positive public image. They want to be known as generous good guys who care about their American communities. Some have set up their own company-sponsored foundations with published priorities and guidelines. These include the American Honda Foundation in California and the Toyota Foundation and Hitachi Foundation in Washington, DC. These foundations are providing important services to their communities, issuing grants to improve American educational and health-care systems, the environment, and the basic quality of life for American citizens.

Japanese and other foreign corporations do not operate any differently from American corporations in their funding, nor do they seem to have any unique interests. Although philanthropy works in different ways in different countries, the foreign companies in the United States gradually learn the American system, set up foundations according to IRS guidelines, and operate in typical U.S. fashion. There are no special tricks to researching or approaching them. Just be aware that they too are potential funders for your project.

WHO GETS THE GRANTS? — CORPORATE GIVING PATTERNS

Like independent foundations, corporate foundations establish their own giving priorities. Companies that give directly are responding on an immediate and continuous basis to what they see as community needs and opportunities. Although they are in business to make money, some corporations do feel a social responsibility to their employees and their communities. They want to be perceived as good corporate citizens. Often, they see advantages and paybacks to offering support.

For example, by supporting educational initiatives or scholarship programs, companies are really supporting their future employees and the future work force. In the past ten years, corporations have taken an increasing interest in educational issues. Companies also support areas in which they have special interests or that are closely related to their own industries. For example, an insurance company like Metropolitan Life Insurance might support grants in the health field. Banks care about their image in their communities and might support programs for general community welfare.

At the same time, companies may freely support groups and institutions that operate quite independently of the funding corporation. For example, McDonald's Corporation set up the Ronald McDonald House as an independent charity, clearly with good public relations in mind. Nevertheless, this has become the single largest research facility in the United States for cancer research for children, and is now being supported by other foundations and individual contributions. The directors of Ronald McDonald House are not employees of McDonald's, and are not supervised or directed in any way by the founding company.

What areas do corporations give to? In recent years, according to the *National Directory of Corporate Giving*, corporate funding breaks down as follows:

1. Education (primarily higher education)—about 38 percent
2. Health care—about 26 percent
3. Culture and the arts—about 11 percent (some corporations have filled in for declining government support)
4. Community issues and the environment—about 14 percent
5. Miscellaneous—11 percent

To sum up, corporations support various areas for many different reasons. Most commonly, they want to support their own community, or they see a public relations value. Perhaps top management has some personal involvement with an issue, or they may simply become involved or identified with an issue and want to establish continuity of support. For example, American Airlines has continually sponsored events to help fight cystic fibrosis. Many corporations encourage their employees to do volunteer work, and then they contribute to the organizations their employees volunteer for. Finally, companies can always make discretionary grants to meet new needs or opportunities as they arise.

GIVING TYPES

What kinds of grants do corporations give? Corporations make loans to individuals, grant fellowships, help build endowment funds, provide seed money and equipment to new businesses, and even give loans to nonprofit organizations. In general, they place fewer restrictions on how their funds are used than private foundations or the government do. They often support specific programs rather than general operating and administrative expenses. Companies want to know they are helping a particular worthy cause. Corporate foundations may get more involved in renewed or long-term support, while direct corporate giving is usually targeted to immediate, short-term projects.

Corporate funders also support projects by donating products and services. These are called *in-kind* donations, or *noncash* grants. Some estimate that perhaps as much as 20 percent of corporate giving is in the form of in-kind services or resources. These could include supplies and equipment; facilities; meeting, exhibition, or performance space; support for mailings; or computer services. Such corporations may offer the expertise of their employees in the form of free legal assistance, or help with long-term planning, public relations, or marketing. They may even help with fund raising. Noncash grants and services are generally channeled through the corporate contributions program, rather than corporate foundations.

In addition, corporations have begun to forge cooperative projects with nonprofit institutions and are getting more involved in overseeing the projects they are funding. For example, they may pick the school districts where they will support arts-in-education programs. If they are contributing to a hospital, they may get involved with choosing which drug-abuse program they would like to see affiliated with it. They may choose to offer specific tutorial programs to their employees.

Corporations may also encourage their employees to join specific volunteer groups, or offer to sponsor special events that will involve employees. They are tending to sponsor more special events, such as health fairs, sports events, and arts festivals. You increasingly see corporate banners supporting a Walkathon for AIDS, say, or a free music festival.

GIVING RESTRICTIONS

Many corporate foundations and giving programs are set up to give specifically to employees. Probably half or more give only to their current or former employees, or to their employees' immediate families. Still, many others do give beyond this immediate circle, especially to individuals with institutional affiliation. And many companies are open to unique projects from their community, to which they can apply discretionary funds.

Geography also comes into play when you are researching corporate funders. Take note of any geographical limitations, as most companies will prefer to support programs in areas where they have operating facilities or plants and where programs will benefit their employees. This can encompass a wide region. Many companies operate throughout the country, handling grant requests through their regional centers.

CORPORATE GRANTS TO INDIVIDUALS

Corporate funders tend to give more to individuals than to private foundations, simply because they award many individual grants to their own employees. They can help with educational expenses, or sometimes provide emergency funds for medical bills. If you do have a connection with a corporation as an employee or an employee's family member, you should definitely explore the possibilities. The corporation may already have a specific program set up to assist you. Sometimes even a business connection with a corporation will provide an opening.

If you are planning a larger project—such as a theater piece, a health fair, or research work—then affiliation always helps, just as it does with private foundations. If you're applying directly to a company rather than a company foundation, affiliation can give them more possible ways to grant you funds. They can easily give a charitable contribution to a tax-exempt organization you're affiliated with. To receive funds as an individual, you will have to demonstrate that helping you offers them some clear business benefit.

How to Focus Your Idea Toward Funders

Whether you apply as an individual or through an affiliate, it's always good to think about how your project can benefit the corporation. Maybe you can provide them with good public relations by associating their name with your community project. Maybe your project will enhance the quality of life in their community, improving the business climate there. Maybe your project will reach out to their employees or their customers, or help them attract new customers.

I can think of many good examples of creative approaches to corporate funding. When tax revenues were down in the early nineties, New York State severely slashed its financial support for the Puerto Rican Traveling Theater, based in New York City. The theater's director immediately turned to the business community, and was able to raise substantial support from corporations that wanted to do business with the growing Hispanic population. Another example: a large southern California automobile dealership advertised that it would write a $100 check to a muscular dystrophy campaign for every new car it sold in a certain period of time. This offer gave them a unique advertising and promotion campaign, and at the same time contributed funds to a worthy cause. Corporations are always interested in funding projects that will benefit them and others. So think creatively about ways to attract their interest in your project.

How to Research Corporations

Your first step in researching corporate giving is, of course, to go to the basic directories. As with private foundations, you will then need to contact potential funders and request published guidelines and annual reports which outline the company's giving priorities. But to explore all the possibilities, you may need to go beyond the directories and contact companies that aren't in the listings. Let's look at these steps.

RESEARCHING THE CORPORATE FUNDER DIRECTORIES

There are three principal directories that will provide you with lists of hundreds of corporate funding sources in the United States:

- *National Directory of Corporate Giving.* 2nd edition. New York: The Foundation Center, 1991.
- *Corporate 500: The Directory of Corporate Philanthropy.* 10th edition. San Francisco: Public Management Institute, 1991.
- *Corporate Giving Directory.* 13th edition. Rockville, MD: The Taft Group, 1992.

You should also look into regional or state directories for your area, and pinpoint corporations based in your community. (See the Appendix, page 331, for a listing of state and regional directories.)

As you look through the directories, you will find corporate funders indexed by geographic location, subject, funding priorities, type of grant, type of recipient, and so on. As with all listings, check to see if you meet all of a funder's qualifications. If your project doesn't meet the restrictions or fit into the giving categories, don't put the funder on your prospect list.

You will find many listings for corporate or company foundations, and other listings for corporate giving programs or "corporate direct contributions programs." As you look through the directories, be aware that a company can be listed under its name, such as the Exxon Corporation, or under its foundation, such as the Exxon Foundation.

INTERPRETING THE LISTINGS

Let's look at a typical, fictionalized corporate foundation listing and analyze what you can learn from it.

METROPOLITAN BANK CORPORATION
Metropolis, New York

Business Activities: Bank holding company; commercial banks.

Financial Profile for 1993: Number of employees, 20,200; assets, $34,116,000,000; Fortune 12 (commercial banking); Forbes 35 (assets).

Corporate Officers: Thomas L. Jackon, Chair; Edison Ford, President and C.E.O.; Rockwell Carnegie, Executive V.P. and Treasurer.

Subsidiaries: Bismarck Corporate Center, Bismarck, ND; Metrobanc Financial Co., Metropolis, NY; Metrobanc Mortgage Center, Weston, MD; Metrobank New Jersey, Watergap, NJ; Locality Bank, Key West, FL; Delaware Hospital Trust, Easton, DL.

Giving Statement: Giving through a company-sponsored foundation and a corporate contributions program.

METROPOLITAN BANK CORPORATE GIVING PROGRAM
c/o Public Affairs Department
P.O. Box 0000
Metropolis, NY 00000 914-123-4567

Financial Data (year ended 12/31/92): Total giving, $2,072,795, including $844,620 for grants, $403,318 for employee matching gifts, and $824,857 for in-kind gifts.

Purpose and Activities: "Since its founding in 1830, Metropolitan Bank has considered it an essential part of its role to recognize community needs and channel its resources to most productively meet them." Metropolitan Bank seeks to help meet the financial needs and enhance the health and welfare of the communities the Bank serves, to improve educational programs and opportunities for all members of these communities, to help those who require special assistance to assume a full role in society, and to participate in major public policy issues that affect the well-being of the community. Metropolitan Bank supports civic and community organizations, culture and the arts, education, including higher education, health and hospitals, social services, in-kind services, and United Way. The Bank also administers an employee matching gifts program, and in 1990 started an employee community service program. Two international business units also contribute employee time, resources, facilities, and cash; and affiliate banks in New Jersey and Florida also operate their own contributions programs.

Types of Support: In-kind gifts, operating budgets, program-related investments, capital campaigns, endowment funds.

Limitations: Giving primarily in the Greater Metropolitan region, and two other regions in NY: Upstate and Downstate; affiliate banks in New Jersey and Florida have contributions programs in their own communities. No support for religious programs. No grants to individuals, or for research projects, conferences, forums, benefits, and similar events.

Application Information:

Initial Approach: Proposal; write to nearest branch

Copies of proposal: 1

Deadline(s): 6 weeks prior to Committee meeting

Board Meeting date(s): the Corporate Contributions Committee considers requests in March, June, September, and December

Write: Eleanor Eisenhower, Manager, Corporate Contributions

METROPOLITAN BANK CORPORATION CHARITABLE FOUNDATION
c/o Metropolitan Bank
Government and Community Affairs Department
100 Bank Street
Metropolis, NY 00000   212-123-2123

Trust established in 1965.

Donor(s): Metropolitan Bank Corporation.

Financial Data (year ended 12/31/92): Assets, $12,483,323; gifts received, $4,823,986; expenditures, $4,212,914, including $4,645,289 for 352 grants. High: $100,000; low: $1,000; average: $2,500–$7,500.

Purpose and Activities: Giving limited to community organizations with programs in education, health and hospitals, social services, arts and culture, and the civic community.

Programs:

United Way: United Ways of New York; $1,066,200 for 1 award, 31 percent.

Social Services: Emphasis on human services for youth, families, and the aged. Interests, include employment and job training, food and shelter assistance, recreation programs, and multiservice organizations; $731,092, 18 percent. High: $40,000; low: $5,000; average: $2,000–$10,000.

Civic and Community Affairs: Emphasis on neighborhood revitalization efforts, low-income housing and commercial development, training for community leadership, capacity building for not-for-profit organizations, and programs to improve the environment; $600,234 for 77 awards, 16 percent. High $45,000; low: $1,000; average: $2,000–$15,000.

Higher/Other Education: Strongly committed in the Greater Metropolitan region, major contributions to ongoing programs working to improve the public schools and to school partnerships. Support for institutions of higher learning is primarily given to campaigns conducted for the institution as a whole, rather than to individual programs or departments. In addition, Metropolitan Bank assists organizations that provide services to adult learners and to those with special needs: $555,219 for 62 awards, 15 percent. High: $100,000; low: $1,000; average: $3,000–$15,000.

Culture and the Arts: Major cultural institutions, as well as smaller performing and visual arts organizations, are supported. Some emphasis is placed on arts service organizations, which increase the impact of individual groups, and community arts organizations, which help to bring arts to local communities; $499,321 for 83 awards, 14 percent. High: $35,000; low: $11,000; average: $2,000–$20,000.

Health/Hospitals: Hospital support is usually confined to capital and/or endowment campaigns. Emphasis is placed on community health centers and on organizations that help families with health care planning and treatment; $257,284, 6 percent. High: $30,000; low: $5,000; average: $2,500–$15,000.

Types of Support: Annual campaigns, building funds, general purposes, matching funds, operating budgets, special projects, continuing support, capital campaigns, endowment funds, equipment, scholarship funds, renovation projects.

Limitations: Giving primarily in New York. No support for religious or partisan causes, fund-raising events, conferences, or forums. No grants to individuals, or for research or fellowships; no loans.

Publications: Annual report, corporate giving report (including application guidelines), grants list, informational brochure.

Application Information:

Initial approach: Proposal or letter

Copies of proposal: 1

Deadline(s): At least 6 weeks before meetings

Board meeting date(s): 3rd week of March, June, September, and December

Final notification: 2 months

Write: Eleanor Eisenhower, Manager, Corporate Contributions

Trustees: Thomas L. Jackson, Edison Ford, William Withers

Number of Staff: 2 full-time professionals; 1 full-time support.

There's a lot of information to be gleaned from this type of corporate listing. First of all, it's clear that this is a "Big Daddy" type of corporate funder, with substantial assets and some far-flung operations, that really wants to be seen as a good corporate citizen, with a high profile in its community. The Metropolitan Bank operates both a corporate giving program and a corporate foundation, and clearly wants the good public relations value that it can get from philanthropic giving. This is not one of the small private or corporate foundations that want to give to special interests without great fanfare. Let's look at some specific insights we can gain from the listing.

Corporate Giving Program. This represents funds that the "Metropolitan Bank" gives directly out of its operating budget.

Financial data. Notice that the Corporate Giving Program balances its giving almost equally between cash grants and in-kind grants. Corporate funders are especially fond of in-kind grants, which are a way for them to derive secondary benefits from their buildings, salaried employees, or equipment.

Employee matching gifts are grants that a corporation gives to match a gift that an employee may make to a charitable or nonprofit cause. For example, a corporation may match an individual's private donation to a public radio station. An employee community service program means that the corporation encourages its employees to donate their time and efforts to community projects, and may grant them paid released time from their normal work duties.

Purpose and activities. Metropolitan Bank sees itself as having a long history of being a good corporate citizen, actively involved in the affairs of its community. It supports a broad range of community projects and activities. Note that you might also apply directly to subsidiaries for funding.

Types of Support. Metropolitan Bank gives to certain kinds of long-term needs, such as endowments and capital campaigns, that many funders do not. "Program-related investments" means that an educational organization that wants to set up a money-making operation, such as producing and distributing educational videotapes, could go to Metropolitan Bank for start-up funds.

Limitations. The geographical limitation is unambiguous (though there are those subsidiaries). The Metropolitan Bank clearly wants to steer away from controversial projects that would support specific religious or political agendas, or even potentially controversial research or conferences. Their focus is on projects with an obvious community benefit. They do not fund individuals directly, but if you are working with a community organization, on a community-oriented project, you could apply for funds through the organization.

Applications. Metropolitan Bank uses its branch offices as processing centers for applications, which helps its image in the local neighborhoods.

The Corporate Foundation. Metropolitan Bank may derive some tax benefits by giving through a corporate foundation, though it has to adhere to stricter government regulations for this portion of its giving. You'll notice that there are close ties between the foundation and the corporation and its giving program. The corporation is the sole donor to the foundation; the foundations's trustees include the corporation's Chairman of the Board and its C.E.O.; a single Manager of Corporate Giving administers both programs; and the Foundation Board and the Corporate Giving Committee seem to meet on the same dates and to consider grant applications simultaneously. In fact, there is no clear distinction between funding areas for the two programs. In this case, you would simply address your proposal to the Manager of Corporate Giving, and let the corporation decide whether it might wish to fund you out of corporate giving or through its foundation.

Financial Data. This listing gives you very specific information about the total funds granted, the number of grants, and the range of amounts. You can see where your request might fit into this range.

Programs. Here you get even more specific information, including the percentage of giving to each type of program and the kinds of gifts to each, as well as the dollar range. It should be easy to see whether your type of project might fit into the bank's giving patterns and to estimate the amount you might request. Though there's no clear indication of this, Metropolitan Bank may be giving its larger grants to the endowments or capital campaigns of larger, established nonprofit organizations, and the smaller grants to smaller organizations with specific or short-term projects. Or it may be the other way around. You would have to look at their corporate giving report or grants list to get a sense of this.

Types of Support.   Again, we see a remarkable range of types of giving.

Limitations.   Again, the same geographic limitations, avoidance of controversial or partisan or research support, and the restriction of giving to nonprofit organizations. The focus is on the community— an individual would have to be pursuing a project of clear community benefit, and apply through an organization.

Publications.   Metropolitan Bank is really making an effort to get the word out about its programs, with a number of different informational publications. Write and ask for them all.

Applications.   Procedures are very straightforward, identical for both corporate giving and the corporate foundation. One application will serve for both sources.

Number of Staff.   If you think of it, this is a small staff for the amount of money the bank is giving away. There are only two full-time professionals, plus the Manager of Corporate Giving, and they share a single assistant. These people are working hard, and won't have a great deal of time for back-and-forth exchanges with applicants. They managed to give out 352 grants during the past year, which means about 90 grants were approved for each quarter that the Board and Committee met. And you can be sure that many more applications were received. This is a lot of sheer paperwork to keep track of, to say nothing of the careful evaluation that the staff must do for each application.

GUIDELINES AND ANNUAL REPORTS

Like family foundations, corporate foundations generally publish application guidelines and annual reports. In fact, since they are usually well staffed and well supported by the parent company, they may publish additional material, such as a corporate giving report or newsletter, a grants list, or an informational brochure. Official corporate giving programs will have guidelines, but usually not an annual report, which they leave to the corporate foundation. As you know by now, you should always request copies of these publications to help you decide whether you qualify for the funding programs. Oftentimes, companies will not provide enough information in a directory listing, because they don't want to be inundated with requests.

The annual reports provide detailed information about the corporation's giving policies. They may describe the history of the corporate foundation or contribution program, and for what purpose it was founded. They will outline the major kinds of programs and projects the company has funded. They usually list names of grant recipients, with brief histories of their affiliations and the amounts of money they received. Annual reports and guidelines will also provide information on how to apply.

You may find it much harder to get information about direct corporate giving programs. Unlike private independent foundations, which must file reports with the IRS, corporate giving programs aren't ruled by such regulations, and do not have to file any special reports or disclose any information to the public. When they make gifts from their operating budgets, they will not necessarily include these in any of their statistics.

Some of the very large corporations, like major banks that seek good community relations, will be happy to inform you about their giving programs. Smaller companies, and those without company foundations, may not wish to publicize their corporate giving. They may fear attracting an avalanche of requests, or alienating customers who might find some grants controversial. They may have no formal giving program at all and give solely on a discretionary basis, to people and projects they already know about, or to the few who seek them out.

Many giving programs will not have guidelines or annual reports, though you might find some reference to them buried in the annual report of the corporation itself. You may also find some reference to a giving program in a corporate foundation's annual report, but not necessarily. Funds may be channeled through an advertising, marketing, or public relations department and never appear in the company's financial reports as charitable giving. So how can you find out about this kind of corporate giving? You have to go beyond the listings and beyond the reports.

GOING BEYOND THE LISTINGS

When you are looking for corporate funding, it often makes sense to target companies in your community or companies that you think might respond to your particular project, and just approach them, even if they don't appear in funder listings. Small companies may not want to be listed in national directories; they may have no history of corporate funding, or simply prefer to respond to proposals on a discretionary basis.

If you have a community-based project, you might find several local companies who would be willing to support you. You might come up with an idea that would both support your project and provide a company with good public relations. Or you might look for a connection between the company's products and services and your own project. If you have a project involving children, for example, you might target a company that offers products or services for children or parents. Even when they have no traditional history of corporate giving, companies can suddenly decide to get involved. They're flexible enough to respond to immediate community needs and can come through much more quickly than private foundations and government funders.

How can you start to locate unlisted funders? The best place is in your own community. Look in the Yellow Pages, inquire at the Chamber of Commerce, and look through the newspapers, including the financial pages, to see which local companies are advertising. Check out any local business magazines or journals. You might look at some general business directories to identify local companies. Two that you might find useful are:

- *Standard & Poor's Business Directory*, which lists major companies in the United States.
- *Who's Who in Finance*. Try writing directly to some of these company officers.

When you do contact a company, inquire whether they have a foundation or a corporate contributions program, and who the appropriate contact person is. Sometimes a company will have both a foundation and a contributions department. If they are not listed in any directory and don't seem to have any official corporate contributions programs, ask for their public relations or community relations department. You can also try approaching their director of marketing or director of advertising. If it's a very small company, try to get through to the president. At any company you approach, remember to ask about noncash grants and in-kind donations as well. Be creative in thinking of corporations that might help you with goods and services.

One word of warning: it's essential to be as careful about judging an unlisted company's potential interest in your project as you are when you look at directory guidelines, funding limitations, and qualifications. Perhaps even more so. Try to decide if there really is some logical reason why a company would be interested in funding you. Rule out companies for whom this seems unlikely. You not only want to concentrate your efforts where they'll do the most good, you want to avoid harassing companies with inappropriate requests.

Carefully research the companies you're interested in approaching. Ask for any public relations literature about them, find out who their officers are, and what their major corporate divisions are. Do some research in your public library, or at the local Chamber of Commerce. Never, never send out mass mailings headed "To Whom It May Concern." Nothing could be more destructive to your fund-raising campaign. When you approach a local corporation, you want to show that you are a thoughtful, careful person, worthy of serious consideration for funding.

How to Approach Corporate Funders

After you have thoroughly researched corporate sources, you should have an idea of their giving priorities and restrictions. How you approach the corporation depends not only on your own project, but also on the way they set up their corporate giving. If they have a foundation, and you meet its qualifications, then you will apply to it just as you would to any other private foundation (see Chapter 5). If they have an official corporate contributions program, and you've researched guidelines and applications procedures for the program, then you simply follow the published procedures. If you are requesting in-kind services, such as the donation of computer equipment, office space, etc., then you will generally apply through a direct giving program.

If a company has a foundation but you don't qualify for its funding or you are interested in noncash donations, you may want to see if there is a corporate contributions program that you might qualify for.

You can write the foundation, or call if you know it's well staffed, to ask if there is such a program administered directly by the company.

It may be that you will need to approach a corporation that you haven't discovered in any listing and that doesn't publicize guidelines or information about its programs. In this case, it is okay to make an initial telephone call, since you need to identify the individual you should approach. If it's a large company, start with a community relations, public affairs, or public relations office, and ask whether the company has a corporate foundation or a corporate contributions program. If they do, ask for any published guidelines or information about the program that's available. If there are no published guidelines, ask for the name of an officer to whom you could write a letter about a project they might be interested in. Try to find out who handles the corporate contributions program. If there is no official program, find out the name of the director of advertising or public relations. If it's a small company, you may be told to write directly to the president.

You will need to approach a corporate giving program differently from the way you'd approach a corporate foundation. A corporate foundation is like a private foundation, and you will be submitting a proposal or application. When you approach a corporate giving program, especially if there are no guidelines, the best way to make contact is to write a simple letter of request to the officer whose name you've been given. (See Chapter 9 of this book for help with writing this letter.)

When you're dealing with corporate giving programs, as opposed to corporate foundations, you may want to go ahead and make brief telephone contact with the contributions officer. Ask if you can send a letter of request, or whether they might consider your type of project. You don't have to be as strict about sticking to written correspondence as you do with foundations. By making a call, you save yourself the trouble of writing a letter of request if they are out of funds at the moment, or if they do not fund in your area. If they don't have funds available, you might find out if there is another way they could support you, such as through in-kind services.

However, you want to be careful not to bother these very busy people. Corporate funders are constantly bombarded with requests, many of them inappropriate, just as the private funders are. If you do call, be sure you've done some research and careful thinking, so that you can quickly explain why you think your project might be of interest to this particular corporation. Let the program officer take the lead.

If you're lucky, you may develop a rapport with a program officer that can lead to valuable support. But never, never just launch into a long speech about yourself and your project without letting the officer get a word in edgewise. Summarize your project in two or three sentences, and ask if you could send them a letter describing it in detail. If they want to know more, they'll ask. Otherwise just thank them and get off the phone.

If you are contacting a large national corporation, try to make telephone contact with a corporate program officer at the regional office nearest you. Some corporations have locations and subsidiaries throughout the country, and there are usually program officers at these regional locations. Your local office will probably review your application, so it will help you to have a clear sense of the particular interests of the regional office.

You should never send a letter or proposal to several people at the same corporation. Never write separately to the advertising director *and* the director of public affairs. Pick one person for your initial contact, and go through them. If they don't think your proposal is likely, ask if there's someone else at the company you might contact. If they feel they should pass you along to someone else, let them make this decision. *Never approach two people at the same time.* It will look as if you are playing games and trying to manipulate people. This will only create a bad reputation for you at the company.

THE APPLICATION PROCESS

If you've received application guidelines for a corporate foundation or corporate contribution program, just follow the instructions. There's no one typical type of application. They may have an application form, or they may request anything from a simple letter to a full-blown proposal. If there are no published guidelines and you do talk to a corporate contributions officer, ask if there's any particular format they would like you to follow. Otherwise just use the "simple letter of request" described in Chapter 9.

If they are interested in you, they may contact you to arrange for a meeting. Generally, you will have a meeting with the corporate foundation or contributions staff only if they are seriously considering you for funding. They may also want to visit your facility or project, if you have one in operation.

Always be sure to verify deadlines, which are strictly adhered to because of budget allocations. If the contributions committee is meeting in December, that is when they will be allocating a specific amount of funds. This is similar to a meeting of the Board of Trustees at a private foundation.

HOW CORPORATIONS RESPOND

Corporate funders get swamped with requests, many of them inappropriate, just as the family foundations do. They too have to wade through hundreds of completely inappropriate requests from people who haven't bothered to read their guidelines. Even if you have carefully targeted a corporate funder and believe you fit within their guidelines, you will have to give them time to weed out the proposals that don't.

Corporate foundations generally have staffs, and the larger the corporation the larger the staff. This means that you will generally find it easier to get information from them than from other foundations. They will usually be able to track your proposal and give you a response. Established corporate contributions programs are also staffed. But if you are seeking discretionary funds from a company that doesn't have an established contributions program, you will have to be patient and especially considerate. People who have other full-time duties at the company may be looking at proposals on a volunteer basis. To deal with your proposal, they may have to shift their time and attention away from important corporate activities and enlist support from other corporate officers. Take this into account when you are contacting them or waiting for a response.

When you send a proposal to a corporate foundation, follow the same rules that you would with any foundation: read the guidelines about response time and wait for them to respond. If you are applying to a corporate contributions program or to another corporate department, it's okay to follow up your letter or proposal with a short phone call to the contributions office to make sure it has arrived. You can ask for an estimated response time if you can't find one in any published guidelines.

Corporate foundations generally operate the same way as private foundations in terms of response time and notifying applicants. Some corporate giving programs may have a somewhat quicker turnaround time and may want to have more personal contact with you, but it all depends on the particular company.

WHAT HAPPENS AFTER YOU APPLY?

Corporate funders process proposals in much the same way that private funders do. At corporate foundations, the process is the same: review by a program officer, review by a contributions committee, and final decision by the Board of Trustees. With corporate giving programs, a program officer will initially review your proposal, then recommend it to a contributions committee, which will vote on whether to fund it or not. It may or may not go to any higher level. If you submit a request where there is no formal contributions committee, a marketing director—or even the president, if it's a small company—may make the decision.

At a corporate giving program, it's often an individual who decides on your proposal, though it may go to a contributions committee or need to be approved by top management. Many times, corporate foundations and giving programs have different people making the decisions. And they do deal differently with decision making: the foundations will stick more closely to their mandate and mission, while the giving programs may respond to a wider range of projects.

With some of the larger national corporations, you will very often apply to a local or regional office, and that office may decide on your proposal. AT&T, for example, likes to work through its regional offices. The company feels that the regional office is simply better qualified than the national office to assess and react to the needs in a particular community.

You may have to research corporate funders a little differently than others. You will also have to think about how your project will benefit a corporation, directly or indirectly, and you may have the opportunity for a little more personal contact than with private foundations. In the end, though, any funds you raise from corporate sponsors will be one more important portion of your total funding.

7
GOVERNMENT FUNDERS

Budgets go up and budgets go down, but everyone knows that governments have deep pockets. Every year your local, state, and federal government together contribute billions of dollars to fund thousands of programs for individuals and organizations. Governments don't just repair roads and build bombers—they contribute money for scholarships, loans, community service programs, artists grants, research, and start-up costs for new business ventures. In fact, there is scarcely a region, a population group, or an aspect of contemporary life in which some governmental agency is not trying to make a positive difference.

Many different kinds of government agencies give grants. Indeed, so many do that it can be a little confusing to sort out the various levels of bureaucracy and the special programs. Let's just look at the federal programs, for instance. On one level, you have the major government departments like the Department of Energy and the Department of Health and Human Services. Within each of those departments, there are a number of separate agencies or "administrations," and sometimes offices within agencies. These lower-level agencies administer *federal programs*, which are authorized by acts of Congress. It's the federal programs that actually distribute grant money, and goods and technical assistance. They have names like "Promotion of the Humanities," "Travel to Collections," and "Minority Business Development."

In addition, there are free-standing, independent government operations that are not part of federal departments and agencies but that do give grants. These include institutions like the Library of Congress, the National Gallery of Art, and the National Institutes of Health; commissions like the Appalachian Regional Commission and the Commission on Civil Rights; and other entities like the Corporation for Public Broadcasting. All federal programs, no matter what agency or office administers them, have an individual federal program number, and all have been authorized either directly by Congress or indirectly by department policy. Some, like the Corporation for Public Broadcasting, disburse funds that are considered actual payments for product supplied rather than grants. These are not federal programs and do not appear in lists of grants with program numbers.

Though it may be the biggest in terms of sheer dollars, the federal government is only one part of the government funding picture. Myriad grant programs operate at the state, county, and municipality levels throughout the country. Many are official programs, like state arts councils. Others operate on an almost discretionary basis, especially through city and county governments. Cities and counties fund all kinds of special projects and events through offices like the parks and cultural affairs departments.

On the federal level, grant programs are authorized by Congress and must adhere to strict rules, procedures, and limitations. On the very local level, a mayor's office may have a good deal of discretion in supporting small projects.

A LITTLE HISTORY

Since President Roosevelt's New Deal in the 1930s, government funding has helped individuals buy homes, lease equipment, finance their education, hone their skills, and start businesses. Government funding has supported development of inventions, including the fax machine and other consumer products.

Broad-based government funding really flowered during the 1960s and 1970s, fueled by the social consciousness and economic surplus of the Kennedy and Johnson years. In those decades, lawmakers proposed that the federal government should take responsibility for basic societal needs—feeding the hungry, building low-income housing, underwriting the arts—and a great many programs were set up to fund both individuals and nonprofit organizations.

Under President Reagan, the 1981 Budget Reconciliation Act dramatically reversed this trend. In one fell swoop, this piece of legislation severely cut the overall amount of federal monies available and effectively killed the broad spectrum of federal funding programs established by the previous administrations.

However, the consensus of support for this funding shift soon crumbled, and the public called for the reinstatement of a broad base of socially responsive federal funding programs. During recent years, lawmakers have responded to the perceived needs of their constituencies, and have continued government support of the general welfare and specific initiatives through grant programs. Each year, of course, and at every level of government, the shifting political climate influences the level of support available for specific programs. Support levels are affected by which political party is in power, the popularity of certain causes with the public or the media, demographic shifts, and the strengths of competing social needs. All of these factors influence the amount of money available for things like environmental clean-up, AIDS research, support for the homeless, and support for the arts. While funding for some programs has dried up, other programs have sprung up to replace them. Budgets rise and fall, programs come and go, but government funding remains an important potential source for the grant seeker.

GOVERNMENT FUNDING TODAY

According to the *Catalog of Federal Domestic Assistance* (see page 208), in 1990 the federal government made available more than $735 million in grants, through nearly 1,200 federal assistance programs, administered by 52 federal agencies. Approximately 71 percent of these programs offer grants to individuals and nonprofit organizations through direct payments, direct loans, project grants, and other means. (Some of the government programs only fund state and local government projects.) State and local governments add their own contributions to this picture.

The Government Funding Maze

Private foundations all function pretty much alike, and are easy to identify. This is not true for government funders. Government funding is administered by a huge variety of departments, agencies, offices, commissions, and institutes; there can be agencies nested within other agencies, and multiple programs within departments, each with its own separate administrative structure. Similar programs can be administered by different agencies, which may or may not know about their counterparts. States have their own departments and agencies, which sometimes parallel the federal ones, but many have different names or missions. Counties and municipalities may have some similar offices, like parks departments, but can vary widely in their individual programs. Often the federal government will allocate monies to state or local governments, which will then administer programs locally.

This incredible variety of programs has its good and bad sides. On the positive side, there are a vast number of programs out there that can offer support to grant seekers and to projects of almost every imaginable description. On the other hand, it can be frustrating and difficult to thread your way through the maze of offices and agencies to find the specific programs that can help you. Just researching government programs can be difficult—the standard directory for federal programs has over 1500 pages, while state and local governments do not even publish such references.

Once you find a program that might help you, you may run into further difficulties. Though many procedures are standard from program to program, each agency or office will have its own peculiarities. Some are very good at dealing with the public, while at others you may find it difficult to get anyone on the phone or to get a response to a letter. Some program guidelines will be very clear, while others may use bureaucratic jargon and refer you to obscure government regulations and pamphlets. It can be difficult to get help in deciphering these guidelines. You will apply to some programs through a national office, but for others you will have to locate a regional office to process your application. Government application forms can be extremely detailed. You may have to break down your project and budget information differently for different programs. And government staff will go over them in detail, sometimes rejecting applications that don't follow instructions to the letter.

This is not to scare you off, because the government is a very important funding source for both individuals and organizations. There is a lot of money available, and government grants, unlike many private ones, can be large enough to single-handedly fund entire projects. Government grants can be renewed and can be extended to cover multiyear projects. But you will need to take extra time, and call on all your patience and perseverance, to pursue government funding. If you know what to expect going in, it is easier to adjust to the process of seeking government grants.

WHAT KINDS OF GRANTS DO THEY GIVE?

Government agencies help citizens meet their goals through a huge variety of different kinds of support. Besides outright project grants, these include loans, technical assistance, training grants, research or scholarship money, and planning grants for specific projects. The type of funding varies from agency to agency. Many programs offer technical assistance, which means they will help you manage or operate your project activities. They can help you raise funds, or budget and plan your project. They can give you legal or marketing advice and help with other aspects of project management. They don't only help with nonprofit activities—many programs assist small businesses.

As with private foundations, the largest number of individual federal grants are given for scholarships. Then comes money for fellowships, for independent projects or research, and for doctoral dissertations.

Government agencies, more so than private funders, do react well to requests for renewed funding and long-term support. Local governments sometimes help to fund special events, often in coordination with local businesses and private foundations.

GIVING LIMITATIONS

Geographical limitations clearly come into play for state and local governments. Federal grants are usually focused on subjects or issues and are available nationwide. Often, though, federal funds will be allocated on a regional basis to federal offices or local governments, and you will apply for funds through the regional office of an agency.

Even state governments may channel funding through regional or local offices.

Many government programs are available to the general public, but many others limit their giving to certain populations or industries, such as minorities, farmers, Native Americans, and the economically disadvantaged. If you meet the very specific requirements and criteria, you have a good chance of getting funding.

GRANTS FOR INDIVIDUALS

The federal government has a history of granting awards to individuals, and many departments and agencies do so. Grants go to individual artists, scholars, researchers, scientists, business people, and veterans. In comparison with private foundations, government agencies are remarkably willing to fund individuals. Of course, some programs will restrict their funding to organizations, but even here the range is very wide. Government grants go to both profit and nonprofit organizations and institutions, to public and private agencies, to businesses, partnerships, and joint ventures. So if a program you are interested in doesn't fund individuals directly, there are many institutions you can affiliate with to receive flow-through funding.

WHAT AREAS DO GOVERNMENT FUNDERS SUPPORT?

Government programs fund a great variety of activities, subjects, and social issues. These programs support the arts and literature, historical studies, business development, education, the environment, health care, medical research, and scientific research, among other things.

Government grants are a significant source of funding for nonprofit organizations in several key areas. In 1990, they provided about 40 percent of the budgets for social services agencies and about 35 percent of health organizations' budgets. They provided between 10 and 20 percent of the budgets for organizations working in the areas of education and research, and arts and culture.

As you begin your research, you will start to get a better feel for the multitude of government departments, administrations, agencies, and programs. But let's look at some examples.

Agriculture. The Department of Agriculture funds many different programs. Just a few examples: they offer housing and business loans to farmers who have suffered from a natural disaster; the Animal and Plant Health Protection Service protects U.S. agriculture from plant and animal diseases and offers project grants; the Distant Learning and Medical Link Grants (under the Rural Electrification Administration) provide funds to set up telecommunications and computer networks to provide medical and education benefits to people living in rural areas.

The Arts and Culture. The National Endowment for the Arts (NEA), which has persevered despite much controversy, fosters American art and new talent through the funding of choreographers, filmmakers, writers, performers, artists, opera singers, etc. The NEA operates many programs, and one must apply to the individual program—whether the Opera/Musical Theater Program, the Dance Program, or whatever. The NEA funds both organizations and individuals and supports arts education and special events as well as the creation of original work.

The National Endowment for the Humanities (NEH) operates a number of programs that fund projects in literature, history, languages, and the like. They support everything from original research to projects like Ken Burns's major television series, *The Civil War.*

Both the NEA and the NEH give funds to state arts agencies, historical societies, and nonprofit citizen councils, to support the arts and humanities on the state and local level.

Commerce. The Department of Commerce administers many different grant programs through its agencies. For example, the National Oceanic and Atmospheric Administration, which is part of the Department of Commerce, operates a program that helps compensate people in the fishing industry for damage or loss of their vessels caused by foreign fishing vessels.

Education. For students, the federal government offers five financial aid programs for higher education through the Department of Education. These are the Pell Grant Program, the Supplemental Education Opportunity Grants (SEOG), the Perkins Loan Program, the Guaranteed Student Loan, and the College Work-Study Program. All of these grants and loans are based on a student's financial need. The central Office of Student Financial Assistance in Washington, DC, works closely with colleges and universities to administer these programs.

Departments and agencies besides the Department of Education offer scholarships for specific areas. These include the Department of Health and Human Services, the Department of Energy, the Department of Housing and Urban Development, the Department of Justice, the Bureau of Indian Affairs, and the National Emergency Training Center. For example, the Department of Health and Human Services offers grants to repay educational loans of doctors and scientists who agree to do AIDS research.

Health. The Department of Health and Human Services administers many different grant programs that support health and medical projects. For example, it administers programs that research and address alcohol and drug abuse, such as the Demonstration Grants for the Prevention of Alcohol and Other Drug Abuse Among High Risk Youth. The National Institutes of Health also supports medical research and health projects.

Housing. The Department of Housing and Urban Development, better known as HUD, administers programs like the Home Equity Conversion Mortgages, which help elderly people convert their home equity into retirement funds, and the Home Ownership and Opportunity for People Everywhere program, which helps low-income people become homeowners.

Science. Departments and agencies that fund science projects include the National Science Foundation, the Department of Defense, the Department of the Navy, the Department of Energy, and others. For example, the Department of Commerce, through the National Oceanic and Atmospheric Administration, sponsors basic and applied research in clouds and precipitation, to help scientists who are trying to discover ways to induce rainfall. The same administration also supports research into both long- and short-term climate forecasting.

Another example: the Department of Health and Human Services provides research grants to small businesses to develop scientific information about potentially toxic or hazardous chemicals.

Veterans. The Department of Labor sponsors many programs to assist veterans, such as the Veterans Employment Program and regional programs to assist disabled veterans with jobs and job training. There is even an Assistant Secretary of the Department of Labor for Veterans Employment Training. The Small Business Administration (SBA) offers a program called Entrepreneurial Training for U.S. Veterans.

This is just a small sampling, but you get the picture: almost every government department or agency offers a range of grants to support individuals and groups, either directly or through research and projects that further the goals of the agency.

FUNDING FOR SMALL BUSINESSES AND ENTREPRENEURS

The federal government has a special interest in supporting American businesses, particularly small businesses. Many different agencies support small business ventures—through grants, loans, contracts, and technical services. Federal assistance helps small and new businesses provide new jobs in local communities and opportunities for people to better their lives. Federal grants help minorities and the disadvantaged by assisting them to start and run profit-making businesses that will contribute to the economic health of the community. The U.S. Government also gives selective research grants to businesses in order to further scientific and social aims.

State and local governments also understand the benefits of encouraging small businesses, and they assist with contracts, grants, and services. Some state programs even help entrepreneurs obtain venture capital—in other words, they lend a business money and become its partner. (Contact the Department of Commerce or Office of Business Development in your state to explore this type of funding.)

Many federal departments and agencies give grants and other direct support to small businesses in order to further their own particular goals. The National Institute of Mental Health, the Appalachian Regional Commission, the National Institutes of Health, the Department of Agriculture, the Department of Commerce, the Department of Transportation, the Department of Labor—all of these, and others, give grants to small businesses.

There is also a free-standing agency devoted entirely to the support of small businesses: the Small Business Administration (SBA), which has field offices throughout the country. The SBA administers special programs to support businesses owned by women, minorities, and the disadvantaged, as well as a wide range of general business development programs. It gives grants to assist research into business development and to provide services to business. It offers technical and management assistance through several programs.

The Small Business Administration also offers various kinds of nongrant support, including loans for special needs and circumstances. The Direct Loan Program, for example, offers low-interest business loans to creditworthy, low-income individuals and to privately held businesses located in areas of high unemployment, which have had trouble securing loans from commercial lenders. Direct SBA loans of up to $150,000 are available (the average loan is $68,000), and loan repayment can be structured over a long time period. (There are some restrictions on the types of businesses that can apply.) The SBA wants to help small business owners get started, but it also wants to make sure it gets its money back.

- **TIP:** For literature on federal business loans, write or call
  The Director, Loan Policy and Procedures Branch
  Small Business Administration
  409 3rd Street, S.W.
  Washington, DC 20416
  202-205-6570

Other government agencies offer grants and quasi-grants to support specific kinds of business projects. For example, the Corporation for Public Broadcasting, the Public Broadcasting Service, and the Independent Television Service all offer money to fund television programs and series. They may call for producers to address a specific subject or to come up with an original idea. These aren't strictly free grants, since they involve a contractual agreement to provide specified programming for broadcast on specified dates. There may be other restrictions on how the producer can show or distribute the work, and producers may have to come up with some of the money from other sources. But they generally do extend some rights of ownership to the producer, once the original broadcast schedule has been met.

HOW TO STEER YOUR IDEA TOWARD GOVERNMENT FUNDERS

Seeking government grants doesn't require creative thinking so much as very careful research to find the programs that are right for you. The process can be frustrating, but if you are patient and persevere, the rewards can be great. Many government funders programs are so narrowly focused that if you meet the application requirements, you may almost automatically receive a grant. Other programs are very competitive, with committees that make judgment calls on the proposals they receive, just as they do at private foundations. But you can win some grants just by going through those listings with a fine-tooth comb.

When you are seeking funding on a local, county, or municipal level, things may be a little bit looser. If you are seeking funding for a community-oriented project, it may be important to make some personal contact with local officials, have a meeting, or get them to visit a facility you are operating. You will need to show that your project is going to make a real contribution to the life of a neighborhood, community, or population group. It may be helpful to indicate that there is already strong community support or interest in your project. Local officials will often respond for purely political reasons when they see active community interest.

HOW TO RESEARCH GOVERNMENT GRANTS

It's almost mind-boggling to consider how many different departments, administrations, agencies, and programs in existence can provide you with funds. This adds to the amount of paperwork you'll have to wade through, and the number of people you'll need to contact for information. However, the best place to start, as always, is with directories and listings.

You can turn to various kinds of sources: (1) independent guides and directories to government funding; (2) directories for specific subjects, geographic areas, and population groups, which list federal and local government programs along with private funders; and (3) the master guide for federal programs, the *Catalog of Federal Domestic Assistance*.

For some useful general guides to government funding, you can refer to the following:

- *Financing a College Education: The Essential Guide for the 90s*, by Judith B. Margolin. New York: Plenum Press, 1989.
- *The Federal Educational and Scholarship Funding Guide*. West Warwick, RI: Grayco, 1989.
- *The United States Government Manual* (Washington, DC: Office of the Federal Register). This describes the broad responsibilities of all the major federal government departments and agencies. It doesn't list grant programs specifically, but it does list various publications that are offered by each agency. If you know that an agency gives grants—and many do—you can find useful information about them in some of these publications. You can contact the relevant agencies to have your name put on their mailing lists for program information.
- The U.S. Department of Education's *The Student Guide: Five Federal Financial Aid Programs* (Washington, DC: Government Printing Office). This describes federal assistance through Pell

Grants, college work-study programs, student loans, and other grants.

- *Free Dollars from the Federal Government,* by Laurie Blum. New York: ARCO Publishing, 1991.

- **TIP:** To get a free copy of *The Student Guide,* the official "bible" of the federal government's financial assistance programs, write to:

Federal Student Aid Program, Dept. J-8
Pueblo, CO 81009.

Or telephone the Federal Student Aid Information Center, Rockville, MD, at 301-984-4070.

For state and local funding, you'll need to dig a little deeper. Many state and local governments publish some kind of guide to their departments and agencies, similar to the *U.S. Government Manual.* These will have descriptions of program responsibilities and office addresses. You can also ask your local librarian to direct you to any reference materials about regional funding. You may even be able to get research help from the office of a state senator or representative.

Most guides that are not published by the federal government are fairly easy to use, and they will resemble the foundation directories you may already be familiar with. The biggest and most complete guide, however, is published by the federal government itself, and it's *not* so easy to use.

CATALOG OF FEDERAL DOMESTIC ASSISTANCE

The *Catalog of Federal Domestic Assistance* is the bible for federal funding. It lists every single federal grant program, and identifies the many departments and agencies that administer federal grants. (It's worth noting, though, that the *Catalog* does not list some sources of federal funds, such as the Corporation for Public Broadcasting and the National Institutes of Health. These do fund projects, but through their own procedures, not through official federal programs established by Congress.)

The *Catalog* is a massive resource. You can't even call it a book, since it is so big—about 1500 pages—that the government doesn't bind it. Instead, they offer it in looseleaf form, for purchasers to put into their own binders. It's revised every six months, so more pages keep coming. You can find it at well-stocked libraries, and it is also available from U.S. Government bookstores. Considering its size, the price is surprisingly reasonable: $46. Given the heft of this monster, though, you'll probably be grateful to your library for housing it. (If you do decide to purchase one, see the Appendix, page 324, for the phone number for the U.S. Government bookstores.)

The *Catalog* can be both a rewarding and an infuriating resource. The physical form is daunting, and not only because of its sheer size. It's printed on very thin paper, with two text columns per page, in very small type. There are no tabs, color coding, or anything to help you find your way through the sections. It's written in bureaucratic language, which is sometimes difficult to decipher. It does have some useful indexes, and others that may seem impenetrable or irrelevant. There is so much information, compared with other kinds of directories and listings, that it's difficult to wade through, and it can take time to digest what you find.

Still, you can find programs and resources here that you may find nowhere else. If you approach the *Catalog* with the right attitude, you will find it useful. The first step is to prepare yourself mentally and otherwise. You are going to have to spend a lot more time with this than with other directories, including some time just getting familiar with it. Use reading glasses, or a good reader's magnifying glass, to help with the fine print. If you have decided to buy your own copy of the *Catalog,* try to make it physically easier to use: get several large ring binders to hold the different sections, and use looseleaf dividers with tabs to mark off sections. Don't expect to find everything you are looking for in the first section or two. But rest assured—it gets easier as you get more familiar with it.

To help get you started, let's look at some specific sections of the *Catalog* that you will find useful.

The Indexes. These are at the beginning of the *Catalog,* instead of the end. Some are useful, others not. The first index lists government departments, subdivided by agency, followed by all the free-standing entities, like the Library of Congress. If you browse through this, you'll get a feel for the great variety of administrations and agencies, and may run across an agency that you want to look into. It's only useful as an index if you already know that an agency gives a grant that would apply to you but you don't know the program name. If you know the name of a specific program that an agency administers, you can find it in the second index, which lists programs by name. The third index, called the Applicant Index, lists departments and agencies again, with columns and checks to indicate types of grant recipients. You can scan these pages quickly to see which agencies give grants to individuals, for example. There is also a deadline index, which is not very useful, and an index that gives the functions of all departments and agencies, which you can refer to if you're interested in a particular one. Probably the most useful index is the last one, which lists specific program numbers by subject area.

As you browse through the first index—the Agency Index—you'll see that under each department heading, there are subcategories for agencies and programs. For example, under the Department of Agriculture, there are programs and grants in soil conservation, forestry, etc. There are also other agencies, such as the Forest Service and the Farmers Home Administration, which might fund similar projects. Carefully consider more than one agency for funding, since the giving interests of some agencies can overlap.

The Listings.   These make up the bulk of the *Catalog*. They're in two columns per page, in very fine print. Though they're hard to read, and you have to decipher the government-speak, they do offer a wealth of information about each program. These listings are much more thorough than typical foundation listings or third-party listings— they give you nearly all the information that you would find in a set of guidelines and an annual report from a private foundation. But you really have to concentrate to absorb all this information and decide if your project fits the guidelines. It's all there for you, but it takes time to pore over the details.

At the back of the *Catalog* you'll find several appendices, some of which are useful.

Appendix 4, Agency Regional and Local Office Addresses.   The program listing may not give a contact address, but instead refer you to your local or regional agency office. This is where you find it.

Appendix 5, Additional Sources of Information.   This section describes the Federal Information Center Program, with offices in seventy-two metropolitan areas, and a midwestern regional area, which you can call for general information about government programs.

Appendix 6, How to Develop and Write Grant Proposals.   This is a useful section, in larger type than the listings, that discusses the specific requirements of proposals for federal grants.

Connected with the *Catalog* is a computer database, called the Federal Assistance Programs Retrieval System (FAPRS), which allows grant seekers to search for the same program information by computer.

There are designated access points in each state where you can ask for a computer search of the database. You can also access the database through some commercial computer network companies. For more information, contact:

- Federal Domestic Assistance Catalog Staff
  General Services Administration, Ground Floor, Reporters Building
  300 7th Street, S.W.
  Washington, DC 20407
  800-669-8331; 202-708-5126

Let's look at an actual listing from the *Catalog*. This program does not have the complications that some listings do, but it does use terminology that you'll see in other listings. Since it is an actual listing, I must beg you, please, to note very carefully the specific restrictions that apply to this program. This is the kind of program that is focused so specifically that any applicant who meets the requirements is likely to get funded. It is also so specific that perhaps not more than one or two of the thousands of readers of this book would come close to qualifying. Please do not hinder this agency from going about its valuable work, and *do not* contact the agency unless you really are the one in a thousand readers who has all the specific credentials to apply.

15.114 INDIAN EDUCATION—HIGHER EDUCATION GRANT PROGRAM
(Higher Education)

Federal Agency: BUREAU OF INDIAN AFFAIRS, DEPARTMENT OF THE INTERIOR.

Authorization: Snyder Act of 1921, Public Law 67-85, 42 Stat. 208, 25 U.S.C. 13.

Objectives: To provide financial aid to eligible Indian students to enable them to attend accredited institutions of higher education.

Types of Assistance: Project Grants.

Uses and Use Restrictions: Grant funds are to supplement the total financial aid package prepared by the college financial aid officer. Funds are intended to assist students in pursuing regular accredited college courses necessary for achievement of a college degree.

Eligibility Requirements:

Applicant Eligibility: Must be a member of an Indian tribe or Alaska Native Village being served by the Bureau, be enrolled or accepted for enrollment in an accredited college, have financial need as determined by the institution's financial aid office.

Credentials/Documentation: Certificate of Indian blood; college financial aid package; statement of acceptance by college, Bureau of Indian Affairs grant application; high school transcripts and grades for each term.

Application and Award Process:

Preapplication Coordination: Acceptance at a college or university and application for financial aid from the college using their approved needs analysis system.

Application Procedure: Students must be accepted by a college or university. Application forms are completed by applicant in accordance with instructions available upon request from the area office, agency or tribal contractor administering the program for the applicant's tribal group. Completed forms are submitted to the student's higher education program office at the agency, area, or tribal contract office of higher education.

Award Procedure: When an award is granted, student is notified and funds are sent to the applicant in care of college or university financial aid office.

Deadlines: March 15 for next regular academic term. Students should also meet college financial aid office deadlines. This is usually March 15.

Range of Approval/Disapproval Time: 6 to 10 weeks when all required documents are submitted.

Appeals: From the administering office to agency/Area Education Program Administrator, to Director, Office of Indian Education Programs, to Assistant Secretary—Indian Affairs to Secretary of the Interior or through tribal appeal process for tribal contract programs.

Renewals: Grants may be continued through undergraduate or graduate levels if student maintains acceptable progress and academic standing. Renewal applications must be submitted yearly by March 15 with updated grades or transcript.

Assistance Considerations:

Formula and Matching Requirements: Students are expected

to take advantage of the campus-based financial aid programs offered to all students, and any other scholarships which may be available to them.

Length and Time Phasing of Assistance: Grants are generally made for the academic year on a quarter or semester basis. There is an 8 semester limit for undergraduate degree programs unless an exception is requested for a program that takes 10 semesters to complete.

Post Assistance Requirements: of academic progress, change of courses, dropout intentions, and graduation (degree received and date of graduation).

Reports: Grade reports of students applying for continuation of grants are to be submitted at the end of each semester or quarter.

Audits: None.

Records: None.

Financial Information:

Account Identification: 14-2100-0-1-501.

Obligations: (Total program funds including grants) FY 91 $27,635,000; FY 92 est $26,960,000; and FY 93 est $0 [figure not yet available].

Range and Average of Financial Assistance: Average for fiscal year 1990 $1,800; 1991 $1,402; Range $200 to $7,000.

Program Accomplishments: In fiscal years 1991 and 1992 it is estimated that 14,800 students will be assisted.

Regulations, Guidelines, and Literature: 25 CFR 40; Bureau of Indian Affairs Manual, 62, IAM 5.

Information Contacts:

Regional or Local Office: See area offices or agencies in Catalog Address Appendix IV.

Headquarters Office: Office of Indian Education Programs, Code 522, Room MS 3516, 1849 C Street, NW, Washington, DC 20245.

Related Programs: 15.108, Indian Employment Assistance.

Examples of Funded Projects: Undergraduate applicant (typical): Student, single, freshman; 41/64 Oglala Sioux; Black Hills State College, South Dakota; major/minor, Undecided; degree objective: BS; total budget $5740. Student Contribution $700, Pell $2200; BIA $2800. Married or advanced degree applicant (typical): Student, married with three family members, 1/2 Sioux Tribe; University of North Dakota; major-medicine/minor-Biology; degree objective: MD; total budget $12,245; Pell $1625, CWS $1200, NDSL $1200, SEOG $400, Student Contribution $700, BIA $5,900.

Criteria for Selecting Proposals: A member of an Indian, Eskimo or Aleut tribe served by BIA. Enrolled in an accredited institution in pursuit of a regular or advanced degree. Must have a demonstrated financial need as determined by the institution's financial aid office.

INTERPRETING A LISTING

As you can see, the catalogue listing offers a great deal of information. The listing format is the same for each program, and once you get familiar with it, you'll find it easier to interpret new listings. As in the listing above, program information is sometimes spelled out in several ways in different sections, so you should have no trouble determining if the program is right for you. Let's look more closely at some of the sections and subsections.

Program Title, Federal Agency, Authorization, Objectives. The program Title begins with the federal program number, which is used for referencing and cross referencing in the catalogue. You are told which federal agency and department administers the program, and which acts of Congress authorized it. There is a clear statement of the objectives of the program.

Types of Assistance. These include direct project grants, as above, grants through state or local agencies, direct payments of expenses, direct loans, technical assistance, or other types of assistance or services.

Eligibility Requirements. These are usually spelled out in great detail, as in the example above. Note that the applicant may be different from the beneficiary of the grant, although in this example they are the same. (A state government might apply for assistance to disabled toddlers, for example.) This section, including the Credentials/Documentation requirements, should make it clear whether the program is right for you. In this example, you must not only be a member of an Indian tribe served by the Bureau of Indian Affairs but must provide a certificate of Indian blood.

Application and Award Process. The whole process will be spelled out in detail, including deadlines, approval time, the appeals process, and the renewal option, if it exists.

Assistance Considerations. This spells out more details about the program and additional requirements.

Post-assistance Requirements. This details the sort of information and reports that you must supply to the granting agency if you do receive a grant. Note that for certain programs, you may have to supply financial records and submit to an audit.

Financial Information, Program Accomplishments. The financial information includes the total budget for the program, both actual and estimated for future fiscal years (FY's). (In the example, the budget was estimated only one year in advance.) The Program Accomplishments may tell you (in actual or estimated figures) just how many projects, programs, or individuals are served, what services are provided, or what percentage of eligible applicants are funded.

Regulations, Guidelines, Literature; Information Contacts. These sections tell you how to find out more about the program. You don't have to locate or decipher all the printed government regulations about a program; just contact the appropriate office and ask for any printed information or guidelines they may have. The example above refers you to local offices and agencies that are listed in one of the catalogue appendixes; you may also be able to contact a national office directly.

Related Programs. This will refer you to other federal programs that may offer support for similar needs or projects.

Examples of Funded Projects. As you can see from the example, this may spell out in some detail the kinds of projects that have been funded and the dollar amounts of funding. (This program's grants are identified by "BIA," Bureau of Indian Affairs. Unfortunately, not all agencies will offer such helpful details, or any examples at all.

Criteria for Selecting Proposals. As in the example, this may repeat information offered elsewhere, may list specific criteria, or may simply indicate that all eligible applicants will be funded. Or the agency may offer no further information about criteria.

CONTACT THE AGENCY

Once you have pinpointed one or more programs that are suitable for you, you will need to contact the agencies that operate them for more information. You can also try to glean information about other programs offered by the agencies you contact, and there may be other agencies that offer matching funds or similar programs. This is where you begin to negotiate the maze of government bureaucracy. Be patient, and remember that the money is there. You just need to locate the programs that will disburse it to you.

When you contact each agency and confirm that you are eligible for the program, ask them to send you their most recent guidelines and application forms. Also ask if there are any special publications with program announcements. Remember that deadlines, programs, or policies may have changed since the listing you read was published.

If you have trouble with some of the jargon in a listing or guideline, try to get someone at the agency to explain it to you.

GETTING MORE INFORMATION BY TELEPHONE

With federal programs you will often need to confirm that you are contacting the correct agency or department, so your procedure will differ a bit from the way you approach other funding sources. Some agencies, like the NEA and the NEH, have good, clear procedures for dealing with the public, and you may be able to pursue a grant entirely through written correspondence. With many government sources, however, you will need to use the telephone for some of your follow-up investigation. You'll need to get on the phone with Washington, or a regional agency office, or with your state or local government, to get guidelines and details about your eligibility for specific grant programs.

If you are working from a listing, start with the contact person mentioned in the reference directory. If it's a small or local program, this may be the program director. If it's a larger agency, you may talk to a program officer for a particular region or subject area. For example, if you're a writer, you'd talk to someone in the Literature Program at the NEA. Some federal programs may refer you to a regional office. Be patient but persistent in trying to get through to speak with someone.

When you do reach someone, you can be more open about your project than I've advised for private foundations. Ask for any information you still need, such as whether you meet their funding criteria. It's okay to offer a brief summary of your project or need. If the program officer does not think you should apply for funds from the agency, ask if they can refer you to another agency (though they won't always be able to).

Do not become flustered if you are put on hold, transferred to someone else, or asked to call back. Just keep asking, "Who can help me?" until you get through to someone with answers. You may run into dead ends, you may get shifted from department to department, or you may be told that everyone is on vacation this week. Be patient, and always be polite. Don't get annoyed and make speeches about your rights as a taxpayer. If you run into a dead end, call back the switchboard and ask if there is a different person you can talk to. As in most organizations, you'll reach some people who don't want to be bothered, and others who will take the time to talk to you and be helpful; if you are polite and persistent, you'll eventually get through to the helpful ones.

OTHER RESEARCH TIPS

- *Ask about previous grant recipients.* You may want to ask the agency you have contacted if they can send you a list of people or projects they have given grants to in the past year or so. This will give you a better idea of their funding priorities and the kinds of projects they like. As a general rule, most agencies are forthright about disclosing who they've funded in the past. Some, however, like the Small Business Administration, are just too large to do this easily. While it's true that agencies must legally disclose such information, it may be more trouble for you trying to get it than it's really worth. Just ask politely if they have such a list or have funded any projects like yours, and leave it at that. This is not something to make a big deal out of.

- *Agencies and programs can change.* Do keep in mind that government agencies and policies often change, and government programs can be canceled at any time. They are much more volatile than corporate or private foundations, which are solid entities with established giving priorities. You may find that when you call a government agency, the program you are interested in has been eliminated or its funding has been curtailed. Or the agency may have shifted its focus to another giving area.

  Do not stop when you hear this. Ask whether a different program has replaced this one or if there are funds from another agency that now support this area of interest. Very often, money for a given area can come from more than one department and be channeled through various agencies. This part of the bureaucracy can actually work for you. You may find several programs that will contribute to your project.

- **Explore other resources.** One last resource from which you can seek information is the Federal Information Center located in your state. Check your telephone directory, or ask your local librarian if there is an office providing information on federal programs in your state; most states have such information centers. You can also look up these centers in Appendix 5 of the *Catalog of Federal Domestic Assistance*. Or contact the main Federal Information Center office, listed below, to find the center nearest you:

  Federal Information Center
  P.O. Box 600
  Cumberland, MD 21501-600
  301-722-9098

- **Don't be discouraged.** Do not get discouraged by all of this detective work. Do not let regulations, policies, and application forms prevent you from applying for a government grant. The government does not always make it easy, and you may have to wade through paperwork, cope with policy procedures, and cut through red tape. But if you persist, you may well find the free money there waiting for you.

How to Approach Government Funders

Just as there are many different sources of government funds, there are many different ways to approach them. With some, you simply have to show that you meet their criteria. With others, you will have to prove that you are a good investment, since they have to be able to demonstrate that they are spending taxpayers' money responsibly and wisely. And with still others, you will face stiff competition, and your qualifications and project will have to compare well with those of other applicants.

With some agencies, you'll simply fill out the appropriate applications and wait for their response. With others, particularly at the county and municipal level, it may be important to make personal contact with someone at an agency.

Before you apply to any agency or program, ask yourself two key questions:

- Do you really meet all the requirements and fit within the limitations and restrictions of the program?
- Have you checked to see if there are other agencies or programs that offer similar support?

If you are eligible for several programs, do make multiple applications. This can only increase your chances.

Once you have researched your sources and contacted the appropriate agencies, and you know you meet their requirements, you are ready to submit an application or formal proposal. Government applications and proposals can be complicated, and may look different from those you send to private foundations. You'll find a special section on them in Chapter 9.

You'll need patience to fill out the detailed application forms and to prepare the requested credentials and supporting materials. In fact, it will help to be a little obsessive about this. You *must* follow directions to the letter. You may have to file applications in triplicate, put pages in a certain order, provide very specific credentials, and so on. Program staff will expect every "i" to be dotted and will put your application or proposal through a very thorough evaluation and review. So make sure your application follows all the rules.

When you are applying for a government grant, you may be competing for funding with many other individuals, businesses, or organizations. Your application must not only be perfect, but must also stand out from the rest. Don't give any staff member an excuse to put it in an "incomplete application" file. If you provide the agency with all necessary forms and materials, they will review your application and you will have a chance for approval.

HOW AGENCIES RESPOND

While some little-known programs get relatively few applications, many are flooded. The well-known agencies, like the National Endowment for the Arts and the Small Business Administration, process thousands of applications each year. And just like private funders, they get many applications that don't fit their guidelines and don't follow their instructions. This is why they are so quick to reject incomplete or inappropriate applications.

In general, government agencies have a longer, more thorough review process than private funders. It can take up to six months for an agency to notify you. Program guidelines usually clearly state waiting or notification times. Part of the reason for the extended waiting period is that many people will be looking at your proposal. Since these are public funds, agencies want to make sure that taxpayer money is allocated in a very even-handed and careful way. Your application or proposal will first be reviewed by a staff, to make sure it is complete and meets all the requirements. The staff may then split off sections of your proposal, and have specialists look at the different sections— a budget specialist may look at the budget, for example. This careful scrutiny means you should be very detailed and thorough in preparing your proposal.

After the initial staff review, your application or proposal goes to a committee or panel that will make the initial funding decision. The agency may use an internal committee, made up of government employees, or may call in an outside advisory panel of your peers or of experts in the field. The initial decision must still be confirmed by the chairperson or director of the agency, who may disapprove certain grants for political or policy reasons.

Established government programs must follow their basic requirements and mandates. Within their mandates, however, they can apply a great deal of discretion. They can judge individual applications according to many different criteria; they will look at your qualifications, the strength of your application, and the care and preparation that went into it. A committee or panel can have its own biases and interests and may be influenced by the general political climate. It's even possible for a panel to have interests and concerns that conflict with those of the agency or its director. In such cases, the director will always have the last say. A panel that chooses its own successors may perpetuate a particular viewpoint from year to year. A panel can also change quite radically if joined by one or two outspoken new members.

You cannot do anything about these factors—just remember that there is always turnover in government and that advisory panels change every year. You are, in a sense, stuck with the luck of the draw and the state of the agency at the moment you submit an application. Still, political factors change, and do not directly affect every program and agency. The majority of government programs will simply respond to your qualifications, the quality of your proposal, and the nature of your project—all factors that are under your control.

INDIVIDUAL DONORS

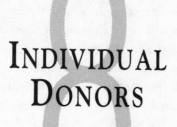

Surprisingly, individual donors, rather than foundations, give away by far the largest amount of money in the private sector. In 1989, for example, gifts from individual donors amounted to 84 percent of all private giving in the United States. At the same time, individual donors are probably the least likely prospect for you as an individual grant seeker, even if you are affiliated with a nonprofit organization. Let's examine this seeming paradox.

You may be an individual donor yourself—if you've ever put a dollar in a collection plate, made a contribution to United Way, responded to a telethon, paid a voluntary admissions fee to a museum, or written a check to a public radio or television station during a membership drive. More than half of all individual donations go to churches and religious organizations and are tax-deductible. Most of the rest go to other kinds of nonprofit organizations, from the American Cancer Society to the National Wildlife Federation—and these contributions are also tax-deductible. In fact, tax deductibility is a key factor in attracting donations, especially substantial ones. As an individual, you can't offer this benefit to potential donors.

There's another reason why individual donors are not a useful source of funds for most individual grant seekers, or even for many nonprofit organizations. It's just too difficult to identify and track down likely prospects and then get them to donate any meaningful amount of money. The wealthy individuals who do give substantial funds to worthy causes and projects are not easy to find. You can look up the names of thousands of foundations in directories, but there are few directories of wealthy donors. Even if you identify some prospects, it's not easy to make contact or arouse interest. Development officers at established institutions like colleges and museums sometimes devote years to cultivating a wealthy donor in order to get a substantial gift.

Even when an organization seeks smaller individual donations, the process is cumbersome and the rewards may be slim. It takes time to compile mailing lists, it's expensive to print up brochures and do mailings, and the return is often quite limited. Organizations may decide to do this anyway, as part of their general outreach effort, but it rarely makes sense for individuals.

Still, there are cases where individual donors may help your cause. In this chapter we'll look at some different ways to find and approach individual donors and to enlist their support, as well as some of the pitfalls to avoid. You will then be able to make the decision yourself as to whether this is an option worth pursuing, though I'll say again that in most cases it isn't.

There are three general types of individual donors, and three ways of approaching them. First, you can try to raise funds from multiple individual donors, asking each for a limited contribution or for whatever they wish to give. Many nonprofit organizations pursue this option. Second, you can try to identify and solicit a wealthy individual to act as a patron or principal contributor. Organizations often try to do this, and on rare occasions, a few individuals do succeed in finding a patron. Finally, you can try to identify bequests that are directed to give funds to individuals with your specific type of interest. Someone might decide to leave all or part of their estate in trust to support individuals from their own town who want to study medicine, for example, or the arts.

Since these three different types—multiple individual donors, patrons, and bequests—require different approaches, let's look at each of them separately.

MULTIPLE DONORS

Nonprofit organizations often seek to raise funds by approaching multiple individual donors. They may send out mass mailings or stage benefits to solicit contributions from many individuals. For example, a theater company I know of in New York City was facing a budget crunch. Its director sent out an appeal to 35,000 current and past ticket buyers whose names they had collected over the years. They got their largest check from the mayor, for $1,000; the rest of the response came in as a trickle of donations, ranging from $10 to $150 each. In the end, they received $8,000 in response to 35,000 letters of request. Although they raised only a small portion of their budget, they felt it was well worth the effort.

Approaching multiple donors does not make much sense for individuals. It takes time and work to develop mailing lists (and money, if you buy them), and it's easy to spend hundreds of dollars on postage. The usual rate of response to mass mailings is only about 1 to 3 percent. You will find it much more rewarding to put your time into grant research and proposal writing. Still, every once in a while you hear of an individual who decides to do a mailing like this and gets results. I recall the case of a young woman who wanted to raise money to pay for her university tuition and living expenses. She wrote a personal letter to absolutely everybody under the sun that she could think of, including perfect strangers as well as people she and her family knew. Believe it or not, she was very successful.

How to Research Potential Donors

A good starting point is the reference section in your library. You can refer to Who's Who, social registers, and other biographical and professional directories to get names of potential donors.

Start to build your own mailing list. Build on your address book, and add all the people you've already contacted about your project. Ask your friends for names and get mailing lists from groups whose members might be interested. If you ask a group for their list, you will either have to get their approval for your use of it or pay for it, or both. If you have access to a personal computer, use a database program to enter the names, so you can sort them and "merge" them with a letter of request. When nonprofits do direct-mail campaigns, they either use names from their own constituency base or they buy very targeted lists.

HOW TO APPROACH POTENTIAL DONORS

The standard method is a mass mailing, but this is a better tool for nonprofits. It doesn't usually make sense for individuals—the costs are too high, the returns too low. And an individual cannot offer the charitable tax deduction to contributors. However, if you are doing a community-focused project, a mailing might increase community awareness of your work. If you are affiliated with an organization, or can get this kind of support from one, see if they will assist you in doing a mailing or let you use their facilities. You might get the organization to accept contributions in its name, making them tax-deductible, and extend you support or services in exchange. Perhaps you can get a corporation to underwrite the cost of a mass mailing, which can run into hundreds or thousands of dollars, depending on the size of your mailing list.

There is another way to get individuals to give money to your cause—through benefits and special events. Again, nonprofit organizations do this all the time, staging benefit performances, demonstrations, and dinners. I am a big fan of benefits—as long as I don't have to do them. They take an enormous amount of work, but they can raise substantial funds and inspire a lot of goodwill. If this seems like a good way to raise money, you must ask yourself the all-important question: Will the benefit pay for itself? Halls cost money to rent, drinks and refreshment expenses add up. When organizations do benefits, they usually only raise money if somebody is making a contribution to the benefit itself—providing free space and refreshments, printing the invitations, etc.

For individuals, benefits or dinners are generally too much sheer work, and the fact that contributions aren't tax-deductible limits the amount that people will want to give. Still, you might consider throwing some kind of small-scale benefit or reception, or getting a friend to sponsor one in your honor. Or you might hold a private performance or presentation of your work: read from your poetry or novel-in-progress, show slides of your photographs, perform your music. Ask for voluntary donations, or charge something for admission. If you are not working through a nonprofit organization, make sure the guests

234 THE COMPLETE GUIDE TO GETTING A GRANT

know that their donations are not tax-deductible. Most people don't mind paying a modest amount for a reading or a performance even if they know they can't write it off.

In fact, you might think about ways of making your work partly self-sustaining. You could regularly sell tickets to your readings/performances or sell examples of your work, such as paintings, sketches, jewelry, quilts, and crafts. In many cases, this is your ultimate goal, anyway. A benefit or some other form of introductory event might help get you started.

If you do get contributions from individual donors, always recognize their generosity by sending them thank-you notes. Notes can be time-consuming, but it is very important to show your appreciation, and they can lead to an ongoing commitment.

INDIVIDUAL PATRONS AND MAJOR CONTRIBUTORS

Patrons are wealthy individuals who use their money and influence to support other individuals, usually (historically) artists, dancers, theater people, and the like. In most cases, a patron provides financial support to the artist by commissioning or purchasing his or her work. (In rare cases the patron supports the artist without claim to the work, but even that relationship is not without expectations.) Wealthy individuals can also take an interest in community projects and nonprofit organizations and offer major, sustaining support.

Patronage is a concept that has long been familiar to artists and creative people. Mozart had patrons; Beethoven had patrons; Fabergé had patrons. Even this century's great fashion designers—Chanel, Dior, Halston, Saint Laurent, and Givenchy—had patrons. In the twenties, Peggy Guggenheim supported some of the most talented Surrealist painters; in the seventies, Ralph and Ethel Skull supported Andy Warhol and other Pop Art painters. Raphael and Michelangelo had perhaps the wealthiest and most powerful patron of all—the Pope. In each case, whether the patron's clout was political, royal, social, or religious, you can be sure it was backed up with money. Individual patrons are best known in the arts, but they do support other areas, such as science and inventions.

HOW THEY CAN HELP

There are still patrons who support individual artists or make major contributions to nonprofit organizations. Some support individuals by commissioning work—from outdoor sculpture to personal and family portraits to architecture. A wealthy individual who purchases someone's work on a regular basis, or buys several pieces at once, is acting as a patron (just as a customer who "patronizes" your store regularly spends money there). Some patrons will even make outright gifts of money to support an individual.

Patrons can support an individual or organization in nonmonetary ways as well. These are not to be discounted, as they may have real practical value. Patrons can champion your cause by introducing you to other individuals who may make financial contributions. They can use media contacts to generate positive publicity for you and your work. They can offer you the use of an office, studio, or laboratory.

It is true that one wealthy individual could easily provide you with the funding you need to complete a project or to survive during a period of high creativity and low income. A patron could purchase your completed work, commission new work, provide you with a place to work, introduce you to other wealthy individuals, draw you into the media spotlight, or offer you outright financial support.

Why, then, are we discussing this funding approach so late in the book?

Because patrons are hard to come by. If you look at a list of the wealthiest men and women in America, it may seem that any one of them could cover your needs without missing what amounts to their spare change. But there are thousands of other people drawing the same conclusion, which is why the wealthy are often well insulated from unsolicited requests. You probably haven't run into too many people who are eager to support your ideas with money. What's more, why should they bother? Why should they take responsibility for your needs?

THE TAX QUESTION

Here is the crux of the problem: wealthy individuals have very little motivation to give money to other individuals, since gifts to individuals do not qualify for tax deductions. And tax deductions are the biggest incentive for charitable giving in the United States, no matter what socially conscious and idealistic reasons donors claim. If Madonna is going to give money away, don't you think she wants some tax credit for it? Her accountant certainly does.

This means that nonprofit organizations will always get more funds from wealthy donors than individuals will, though it's not easy even for them. There usually needs to be some kind of personal connection or interest; after all, there are thousands of nonprofit organizations out there looking for funding, just as there are thousands of individuals.

There are ways around the deductibility issue. If you do have a potential patron or major contributor in sight, you could always try to affiliate with a sponsor, or even set up your own nonprofit organization. I know of one performance artist who has been supported for years by a patron—the funds are channeled through the artist's own nonprofit organization. Of course, it certainly wouldn't be worth going through the trouble of setting up a nonprofit organization without already having interest from a likely prospect.

Wealthy individuals can themselves initiate something like a patronage relationship while retaining the tax deduction. They can set up their own private foundations, which are so closely controlled that they pick and choose the artists or recipients they want to support. This is done much more frequently than is generally known and really amounts to patronage. A wealthy business person could operate a corporate foundation in the same way. This is why many small foundations shy away from publicity; they want to be free to fund individuals or projects that the founder or founder's family has an interest in. There's nothing wrong with this—in our free society, everyone has the right to spend their money as they see fit. But it does explain why it's much easier to pursue foundations that publicly list their giving patterns and interests than to seek out individual donors.

WHAT MOTIVATES INDIVIDUAL FUNDERS?

Without the lure of tax incentives, what factors do motivate the wealthy to fund the work of others? They may be personally interested in your work, or they may want to link their name to your work in order to improve their public image. They may be looking for positive publicity. They may identify with your goals and, while lacking the talent, motivation, or ability to pursue such work, may want to somehow be involved with it. If they are contributing to your organization or community project, some of the same motivations may apply, or they may want to do some real social good. What might patrons expect of you, in return for their financial generosity? They may want your genuine and public gratitude, or they may insist on anonymity. They may want your allegiance in matters beyond the scope of your work. They may want to use their support of you to demonstrate that they belong to the cultural elite. They may want to claim you as a "discovery" or protégé.

These things seem harmless enough. But some patrons may want to induce an overwhelming sense of indebtedness (which makes them feel powerful). Or they may want to influence your work to such a degree that your integrity is compromised. Beware of such "generous" patrons.

In any situation with a patron or major contributor, you must try to anticipate your patron's expectations and decide whether or not they are acceptable to you—before you take the money. This can be difficult because patronage is usually an informal arrangement. There is nothing spelled out on paper. You've got to go on instinct. So try to get a sense of the patron's motivations.

In an ideal arrangement, a patron or major contributor can relieve you of financial concerns and allow you to devote all of your energies and attention to your project—or even to a series of projects, if the patron takes a long-term interest in your work.

HOW TO FIND PATRONS AND MAJOR CONTRIBUTORS

How do you find a patron? The wealthy are out there, but it can be difficult to contact them and even more difficult to get them interested in your work. The truth is, it often boils down to good timing and personal connections.

Begin by exploring your own network of friends and acquaintances. Do you already know anyone—or do they know anyone—who has the financial resources to support your work? If you know any lawyers or agents, they can be a good source of possible contacts. You may come up with one name or a list of names of potential patrons or contributors.

You can also use the reference books in your local library for information on potential donors. Look at the biographical compilations, professional directories, and social registers. Concentrate on your geographical area, but also seek out individuals you know to be interested in your field. Read the society pages and community pages of your local newspapers, noting who attends the benefits, who is supporting what kind of community efforts. Look in the periodical indexes for articles on prominent individuals. And study the following references to get ideas about the kinds of individuals you are looking for:

- *Biographical Dictionaries Master Index.* This gives information on different publications of biographical references to living individuals.
- *Current Biography.* New York: Wilson Company, monthly and annual.
- *Martindale-Hubbel Law Directory.*
- *Medical Specialists Directory.*
- *The Social Register 1992.* New York: Social Register Association, 1991 (and annually). Lists prominent families, with names and addresses; also clubs, organizations, and affiliations.
- *Standard & Poor's Register* for corporate executives.
- *Trustees of Wealth.* Washington, DC: Taft Corporation.
- *Who's Who.* Various volumes, by profession, population, and region. Consider which volumes might best lead you to potential donors.

It can be interesting to look through these lists, and you may find names that seem like likely prospects. But remember: ultimately, you will have to develop a personal contact. It's very easy to go off on flights of fancy and imagine that this person or that could support your project or need. But this is not the same as looking at lists of foundations, which have been set up for the express purpose of giving away money. You can spend a lot of time and effort writing to individuals or trying to make personal contact and never come up with anyone who really wants to contribute directly to an individual. So your first line of approach should always be to research the foundations and government programs. It's only worth trying to approach individual donors in those rare cases when you have some special kind of access, your work is known, or your project would be of particular interest to someone. Be realistic—don't waste your time dreaming about patrons if you can get real money through conventional grant programs.

HOW TO APPROACH POTENTIAL DONORS

If you are referred to a potential patron or contributor, plan to approach them with tact and restraint. It's certainly best to go through a personal contact or recommendation, and you should try to do it this way, even if it means going through a friend of a friend. Still, you can sometimes get through to someone by writing them cold. Be aware that many wealthy individuals are shielded by their personal or business staffs, private secretaries, or agents. Though you may think you'll have better luck if you can find a clever way to bypass these intermediaries, this can backfire. These people are performing a valuable service for their employers, protecting their privacy and shielding them from all kinds of demands. Even if you can get a personal recommendation or introduction on a social basis, you still may need to deal with secretaries or staff, so do so graciously. You may get a trusted employee on your side, which can only strengthen your case.

Find out what you can about prospective donors before you write to them or meet with them: What are their fields of business? What are their personal interests and hobbies? Are they familiar with you or your work? Based on the answers to these questions, is your project likely to be of interest to them? Do they have a history of supporting individual efforts?

If you can't arrange a personal introduction, you can always try writing a letter. This should touch on many of the points in the basic letter of request outlined in Chapter 9, though the format could be slightly less formal (but no less businesslike). You do want to explain your mission and supply some background about yourself and your project.

If you are lucky enough to get a personal introduction or recommendation, your chances are better. You might then be asked to send a letter or some background information, or a meeting might be set up. The first meeting could take place either socially or in a more formal context. You'll have to tailor your discussion to the nature of the meeting.

If you meet in an informal setting, don't make a heavy sales pitch unless you think it's expected, or you are asked. If you are an artist, you might arrange to meet someone at your studio or at a gallery where your work is being displayed. If you are a scientist, inventor, or community activist, think about creative ways to expose potential patrons to your work. Give a tour of your laboratory or facility, or invite them to a reading or performance. You'll do well with this informal approach to fund raising if you can carry on a conversation easily, think on your feet, and feel comfortable interacting with different kinds of people. At the same time, be yourself. Don't feel like you have to put on an act. You and the potential patron are sizing each other up. You want to make a good impression, but you also want to get a sense of what the patron's expectations are.

Talk about your work and your needs informally in the course of conversation. Potential donors will make their decisions based on the way you describe your work and your plans, their knowledge of your professional reputation, and their reaction to your work. If you can do so casually, remind them about any positive publicity you've received and your accomplishments or awards.

Remember, patronage can be an informal arrangement. Patrons or major contributors may simply hand you a check and wave you away, or they may buy several pieces of your work and give you no idea whether they have any interest in future support. On the other hand, they can behave as if they're buying a company and feel entitled to criticize or even make suggestions about the future direction of your work. Once you've got their money in your bank account, you may never see them again, or they may call you every day. If you're working on a theater production or a community project, they may want to get closely involved. Depending on the person and the kind of involvement, this could be extremely helpful or totally disruptive. Size up any potential patron or contributor according to your own good judgment. If your gut instinct tells you not to get involved with someone, steer clear. If you find someone who seems willing to help you with a minimum of interference, take advantage of your good fortune.

BEQUESTS

Individual donors can continue to extend their generosity even after they've gone. Aside from establishing large endowments for continuing fellowships and prize programs, wealthy individuals sometimes bequeath money for specific purposes or populations. These funds may not be well known, and are usually tied to very specific kinds of qualification, often supporting members of a local community. A wealthy individual with a passion for landscape design, for example, may bequeath money to encourage other people from his hometown to study horticulture after his death.

How can you seek out and connect with bequests? You really do have to poke around, and get lucky. Keep up with the local newspapers, chat with any bankers or lawyers you know. If you do identify a bequest, you may find that it is administered by an accountant, a bank trust department, or a lawyer. Usually a single trustee makes all the funding decisions, without going to a committee or board of directors. They handle requests in a similar way to small family foundations. You can ask about any special application procedures, but normally you will submit a letter of request, using the three-page format described in Chapter 9.

If there's a positive response, the trustee or administrator may want to interview you, but in general follow the same procedures and etiquette as you would with a foundation.

THE PROPOSAL

9

Your proposal is just one part of the fund-raising process, but it comes at the exciting moment when you are ready to "sell" your project to funders. Whether it's a simple letter, an application form, or a many-page proposal, all funders will want something in writing that tells them about you, your project, your mission, and what need you hope to satisfy or what you hope to achieve. You will use your proposal to convince a funder that you deserve a grant and that you merit funding over other viable candidates. A well-written proposal will communicate your goal and your plan for achieving it. If you can do this clearly, and show that you've thought things through, your proposal will attract attention and you will have a good chance to get funding.

Writing a proposal takes some thought and care, but there are no secret formulas or code words to use. However, there are some general rules and guidelines that fund raisers follow, that funders expect, and that will help sell your project. In this chapter, I'll show you how to construct an effective proposal from the ground up, and how to make it the best possible representation of your project. Bear in mind, preparing a proposal does require thought, effort, and time. But if you're serious about your project, this is where you begin to make your vision real.

Since proposal writing is not done by formula, what works for one person, or for one funder, will not work for all. Every project is unique, and funders recognize this. However, the guidelines in this chapter will help you effectively apply for most government, foundation, or corporate grants. It is worth noting that writing a proposal for a government grant is very different from writing one for a private or corporate foundation grant. Government programs often require you to fill out elaborate forms and package your information in specialized ways. That's why I've included a section in this chapter to help you specifically with proposals for government grants.

Doing a proposal is really not that daunting a task. It should flow naturally out of the planning you've been doing and the project outline that you've already prepared (back in Chapter 1). But it does take time. It's a little like doing a jigsaw puzzle—there are a number of components you have to piece together. As long as you have a clear vision and have thought through your project, you won't have a problem. As you start putting together a proposal, though, you may find that there are some things you haven't really thought through, some additional research you need to do. That's fine, and all part of the process; but it's also one reason why you need to leave plenty of time to work up your proposal. Don't push the deadlines.

HOW TO KNOW WHEN YOU'RE READY TO START

Before you sit down to write your proposal, make sure you've done all the necessary preparation. Here are some points that will help you decide when you are ready. Some have to do with your project development, some with your funding research.

PROJECT DEVELOPMENT

1. *You have a clear mission statement and outline for your project.*
   Remember, a good proposal starts with a good idea. You

need to have a clear understanding of how your idea will solve a problem or satisfy a need.

2. *You've developed your idea in outline form.*

If you haven't looked at your project outline (see Chapter 1) in a while, or if you have new details to add, go back and bring it up to date. Be sure you have thought through the exact locations where your project will take place, each step you'll have to complete, and a timeline or schedule you'll follow.

3. *You've done your basic budget research.*

You need to have looked up the basic costs of the materials, services, or salaries that you need the grant money to pay for. You may have collected some price lists and have them on hand, or you've called vendors for price quotes.

4. *You've thought about and contacted any essential personnel besides yourself who will be involved in the project.*

If other people will be involved, you have contacted them and received a commitment or at least an expression of interest. If you do have commitments from some key people, you've asked for copies of their résumés. If you're going to have to hire staff or pay for contracted services, you've researched what the salaries or fees will be.

In fact, one of the best things you can have going for you as you ask for funding is a commitment from a few key people who have good professional credibility. This makes it look like you have a solid project that is really taking shape. So do try to get some commitments lined up. Of course, these will be tentative, because you can't really have anybody clear their schedule or start work until you have the funding. But funders understand this, and will appreciate any efforts in this direction.

5. *You've collected the endorsements or supporting materials that you want to attach to your proposal.*

You don't want a massive amount of material, but if you have collected one or two key endorsements or articles, this is all on file.

FUNDING RESEARCH

1. *You've researched and refined your prospect list.*

   Before you even start to write a proposal, you need to know that your project does truly match the giving interests of your potential funders. Be sure that you've thoroughly researched each prospective funder still on your list and that you know their objectives, areas of support, and any limitations on giving. If prospective funders see that your project and proposal are closely attuned to their interests and practices, they will know that you have taken the trouble to find out about them, and they will consider your proposal and idea much more seriously.

2. *You've requested guidelines and an annual report.*

   Never consider sending out blind proposals to multiple funding sources without contacting them first. This is a sure-fire way to give your project a bad name in the nonprofit world. Only after looking at guidelines and an annual report will you be able to make a final decision about whether your project is right for a specific funder.

   Remember, when you write for guidelines and an annual report, do just that. If you start to say anything about your project, your letter may be treated as an informal proposal and rejected out of hand.

   What if you write to one of the very small private foundations and ask for guidelines and an annual report, and they simply don't respond? This is not so unusual. You may write to thirty-two foundations and get only twelve responses. Some of these small foundations are swamped with inappropriate requests, so if you haven't heard anything after six or eight weeks, you may want to drop them a polite two-line request for guidelines and a grant application. If you still don't get a response, cross them off your list and go on to the next prospect. It never pays to send in a proposal without some preliminary contact.

   Not every funder will have an annual report to send out. They will usually send you some sort of guidelines, even if it's a few lines in a form letter. If they have no guidelines, just send them the generic proposal (described later in this chapter).

3. *You have the name of the contact person for each funder you want to send a proposal to.*

I go nuts when people write me letters addressed to "Dear Sir" or "To Whom It May Concern," and so do program officers. Always, and I mean always, find out the name of the appropriate program officer to send your proposal to. Some funders will indicate one person that all proposals should go to. If you're targeting a large foundation, you'll need to find the officer who deals with your subject area or your type of funding. There may be one program officer for the social sciences, one for the medical sciences, and another for the arts.

You'll often find an appropriate contact person named in directories, but you should use the name listed in any guidelines you receive, since it will be more up to date. Always call to double-check on the name. Nonprofit people move around a lot, and the contact person may well have changed in the time since a particular directory was compiled. If you can't find a contact person's name, call and ask who is the appropriate person to send a proposal to. Don't talk about your project, just say that you want to send a proposal and ask who you should address it to. If you still can't find this out, don't send in a proposal. You just don't have enough information to approach this funder effectively.

4. *You've researched the average size of the grants that a funder gives, either through listings, annual reports, or the IRS 990-PF forms.*

You can't write a proposal without knowing how much you will request from each potential funder. If you ask for too much, you can turn off a funder—they won't take you seriously. If you ask for too little, you simply haven't maximized the return from all your efforts. You can't just make a guess as to how much a funder might offer. For most projects, you will have to put together funding from several different sources and usually cannot ask one funder to cover the total cost of your project. And you can't just divide the cost of your project by ten and apply to ten different funders. If you have a $50,000 project, you will probably end up piecing together the funding from different sources: $5,000 from this foundation, $7,500 from that one, $15,000 from another. How will you know what to request from each one?

You should base your request on the giving patterns of the funder. The key to knowing how much you can request is research. You have to tailor your request to what you have learned about the funder. Go back to your notes from the listings, go back to your notes from the 990-PF IRS forms. Look again at the range of grants given, and the average grant. If you don't have this information, you need to go back and dig it up.

How do you use the information? If you have a project with a relatively small cost, ask for an amount at the low end of the range. If you have an expensive project, ask for something at the medium point or just slightly above. Don't get greedy and request an amount equal to the highest grant given. Those grants are going to organizations, and very often to ones that have developed a relationship with the funder and have a track record. It is much better for you to get a modest grant in hand and go on seeking other funding than to get turned down because your request seemed arrogant or out of line. Remember, having one or two modest grants in hand makes your requests to other funders that much stronger; it's evidence that someone has confidence in you and your idea.

What if you just can't dig up the information about a funder's giving patterns? Go ahead and apply, but request a modest amount. For an individual project, ask for somewhere between $2,500 and $7,500. For a big-budget project, sponsored by an organization, ask for $5,000 to $15,000. Again, a smaller request will cause a lot less soul searching on the part of the board. You don't necessarily want board members balancing your larger request against all the other interests and commitments they may have. Let someone say instead, "It's an interesting project, and they're not asking for much money. Let's give it to them." Make it easy for a funder to give you the grant.

WHAT MAKES A GOOD PROPOSAL?

There are three things that a good proposal must do. First, it should convey all the vital facts about your project clearly and concisely. Second, it should make clear the importance of, or the need for, your project. And finally, it must sell you, succinctly and convincingly communicating your strengths to the reader.

It is essential to provide all the necessary information. If funders are going to consider your proposal seriously, they have to understand exactly what you are proposing. They will want to know why the project is needed, how you will meet that need, exactly how your project will be carried out, where it will take place, and how long it will take to see it through. They need to know who is applying for the grant, who will receive the funds and manage the project, and who will benefit from the grant ultimately. They need to know how much your project will cost, and how much you are asking them to contribute.

But facts alone are not enough. You also need to show them what makes your project exciting and unique and, ideally, to cause them to feel something of your own enthusiasm for it. Why is the need for your project pressing, what makes your solution especially creative or effective?

Finally, you must convince the reader that *you* are especially deserving of the funder's money. Foundations and corporations are bombarded with thousands of requests for funds. You need to show that *you* are in some way uniquely worthy of their financial support.

You'll find that if you have written a good mission statement, as described in Chapter 1, and you've outlined your project, a good proposal will follow naturally. Without the research and planning, there will be no proposal. You start with an idea, make a skeleton outline, and gradually flesh it out. If you approach the task seriously and meticulously, following the guidelines in this chapter, you will come up with a proposal that funders will consider seriously.

Is it essential to have an effective proposal? Yes. I've seen too many really good projects turned down because the proposals weren't clear, concise, or sufficiently developed. I have known the rare case, with a proposal submitted by a nonprofit organization, when a program officer so admired the project itself that he or she helped to redo the proposal. But this is something that they will seldom do for individuals. Your proposal is the first (and sometimes the only) sample of your work and evidence of your abilities that a funder will see. If you submit a good proposal, the funder will be predisposed to believe that you can follow through with a good project.

THE BASIC PROPOSAL—AND VARIATIONS

No matter what kind of funder you apply to—whether a private or corporate foundation, a government agency, even an individual donor—some aspects of the proposal will remain the same. You will always include something like a mission statement, you'll always need to provide basic information about the project, and you'll always have to explain your qualifications to do the project. Nevertheless, you may need to work up a few different variations on these basic themes.

Some proposals can take a relatively free form, and some will have to follow rigid guidelines. Government agencies have the most strict and demanding requirements, while private foundations may offer more room for creativity. Corporate foundations and giving programs are probably the most flexible in what they'll accept as a proposal. You may need to fill out preprinted application forms for some grants or supply some combination of application form and supplementary pages. If you are applying under the sponsorship of an organization, it will have to provide additional information.

Whatever form your proposal takes, you must follow the printed guidelines of each funder. Guidelines may ask you to use special formats, address specific questions, or provide particular supplementary documents. Whatever the guidelines ask for, you must provide it, even if it means cutting, pasting, and restructuring the proposal you've been sending to other funders. Follow the guidelines to the letter; they are not negotiable.

If a funder's guidelines differ from the suggestions you find in this chapter, follow the guidelines. Funders have reasons for asking what they do, and it's best to provide them with exactly what they want.

Let's look at some of the different kinds of proposals that you may need to prepare.

THE FULL-BLOWN PROPOSAL

Many foundations will not specify the form of the proposal, except perhaps to mention certain topics that they would like you to address. In these cases, you may submit a formal three- to ten-page proposal.

You will normally use this kind of full-length proposal only if you are applying through a sponsor, but in some cases you might use it for an individual grant application. I recommend you read the section on the full proposal later in this chapter (pages 271–98), even if you will be applying as an individual and filling out application forms. Many of the topics addressed in the full proposal can appear in some form on application forms, so it will help you to think these through beforehand. And if you are going to meet with a funder, it will certainly help to have thought about these issues and to have made some notes.

For a full proposal, you should submit a *proposal package* that includes your written proposal, along with a cover letter, your résumé, and any supporting documentation or sample work. It should reach the funder by the indicated deadline for their next funding cycle. (There might be one or several funding cycles each year.) Let's look at the basic elements.

1. **Cover letter.** You should write a cover letter after you have finished your entire proposal. This can be very brief, introducing your proposal, providing your mission statement, and indicating how much money you are requesting. We will discuss the cover letter in greater detail later in this chapter.

2. **Title page.** This gives the title of your project, and basic information about who is submitting the proposal, whether an individual or an organization. See later in this chapter for the correct format.

3. **Table of contents.** If you have more than about five pages, the table of contents will list the various sections of the proposal.

4. **Project summary, or introduction.** On one page, you'll give all the important information about your project: your mission statement, the problem or need, who you are, what you want to do, your total budget, and how much you are asking for. Here you fill in more details than are in the cover letter. Foundation staff, board members, and grant officers will read the project summary to get a quick sense of your proposal.

5. **Statement of need.** In this section you'll discuss the need for your project and, if applicable, the kind of problem that your project will solve. Describe the community that will be served and the long-range goals that will be achieved.

6. **Objectives.** What are the specific, immediate objectives that you wish to accomplish with your project (as distinct from long-range goals)?

7. **Plan.** Here you'll outline the plan or method you'll use to accomplish those objectives. Give the details of your project—where it will take place, the steps you'll go through, and the schedule or timeline for those steps. You will base this on your project outline.

8. **Evaluation.** Foundations want to know whether the projects they invest in are successful; your proposal should indicate how you will report on your project and what evidence of its success you will provide.

9. **Personnel.** This is where you attach your résumé. If it's a larger project, you might include the résumés of two or three other key people as well.

10. **Budget.** A one- or two-page budget, broken down into major categories.

11. **Other funding received.** If you've already received any funding when you send out a proposal, list it here to strengthen your request.

12. **Future funding and support.** If you are planning a project that will extend beyond the initial grant period, you should give some indication here of how you might keep the project going in the future.

13. **Official certification and signatures.** If you are applying through a sponsoring organization, you may be asked to provide a copy of the sponsor's 501(c)3 Internal Revenue Service certification, and some indication of the sponsor's support.

14. **Supporting documentation.** This is where you can include a relevant article about the need for your project, one or two letters of endorsement, and any reviews or articles on your work.

Not every proposal needs each of these components. If you're writing a short proposal for individual funding, you won't need the table of contents, future funding, and official certification. But you should include all the other items, even if your statement of need, objectives, and evaluation sections are only a few sentences in length. For personnel in this case, you'd simply insert your résumé. Your cover letter and project summary might be combined, and you would go into a little more detail for your plan. A budget is always essential, even if it's half a page in length. And if you have one or two pieces of supporting documentation, that's all to the good.

Later in this chapter, we'll take a closer look at each of these sections; but for now, let's consider some other forms of proposal.

THE SIMPLE LETTER OF REQUEST

Some foundations will ask in their guidelines for a simple letter of request rather than a more elaborate proposal. This might be defined as a *letter of request,* or a *letter of intent.* It calls for a brief two- or three-page letter containing all the basic information about you and your project. Very small foundations often prefer this type of informal proposal because they simply do not have the staff to handle large stacks of paper.

If they read the letter and are interested in your project, they may fund you directly or ask for more details.

How to Write a Letter of Request.   Follow these steps:

1. In the first paragraph, use your mission statement to introduce your project and indicate how much money you are requesting.
2. In a paragraph or two, describe the problem your project will solve (if applicable), the need for the project, your specific objectives, and the population you will serve or reach out to.
3. Next, explain your plan, including the location of the project and the time frame in which you hope to accomplish it.
4. Explain why you are qualified to apply for funding to this foundation and how you meet their guidelines. Also describe your qualifications for doing the project.
5. Attach a budget of no longer than one page (unless you are specifically requested not to) and your résumé.
   See also the sample Letter of Request on page 253.

To write an effective letter of request, you must be clear and succinct. In a way, you are condensing all the elements of a full-blown proposal into a few pages. The letter of request is really a combination of the cover letter and project summary. If you haven't explored all the points listed above in your project outline, or haven't already done a full-blown proposal, read the section in this chapter on how to do a complete proposal (pages 271–98) and use this as a guide. Write a paragraph to address each topic of the full-blown proposal, and condense as necessary to fit the important information within two or three pages.

SAMPLE LETTER OF REQUEST

Ms. June Wentworth
XYZ Foundation
St. Louis, MO

Dear Ms. Wentworth:

I am writing to obtain funding for a photo-documentary project, called, simply, *Farmer*. This will be a portrait of Midwestern farm life as it once existed. The project will be presented both as a gallery exhibition and in book form.

A way of life is dying out in America. From the earliest European settlements throughout the nineteenth century, farm life was at the core of the American identity. To many, it now seems a romantic, idealized way of life, a simpler, more honest way, the extended family living on the homestead, children and adults living and working together, in touch with the land, the seasons, producing whatever they needed from the land itself. In many ways, this was a true portrait. Yet it could also be a dangerous, fragile existence, at the mercy of storms and drought, an existence earned by grinding daily labor. By the 1920s more of the population was living in urban than rural areas, and the 1930s gave us indelible images of the harsh lot of backward and drought-stricken rural communities. Yet the heaviest pressure would come from economic forces, as vast agribusinesses, using high-tech machinery to manage thousands of acres of land with just a few hired hands, began to drive family farms out of business. International competition, energy prices, land taxes, interest rates—all conspired to bring an end to the family farm, and to a way of life.

Farmer is a project intended to preserve and document the shape and history of this vanishing culture. Focusing on the Midwest, where the farming way of life has lingered longest, the project will combine oral history, photographic impressions of living farms, farm people, and farming communities, and a collection of historical photographs, borrowed from family collections, which will be reproduced for gallery and book presentation. The project will feature a selected number of farm families and communities that are emblematic of the vanishing way of life. Though the emphasis will be on the past, the project will lead us through the recent transformation of farming into agribusiness, and feature one of the vast, capital-intensive operations that have replaced many smaller farms.

The project will take one year to complete, including collecting the oral histories, taking photographs, making archival masters of family photographs, and preparing for exhibition. Subjects will be sought in Indiana, Illinois, Missouri, Iowa, Kansas, Nebraska, and neighboring states.

Upon completion of the project, selected photographs, and excerpts from the oral histories, will be presented at the Capitol Gallery in the I——state capitol building. (The I——State Arts Council has already expressed interest in supporting this exhibition—see letter enclosed.) During the year, we will also be exploring possibilities for touring the exhibition to other venues in the Midwest and throughout the country. We will also prepare an edited text of the oral histories, along with selected photographs, for publication in book form. The University of I——Press, which published my previous book, *Tobacco Land,* has expressed strong interest in *Farmer.* (See enclosed letter.)

As author of a successful photo-essay book, *Tobacco Land,* and as a native Midwesterner, I feel I have a special understanding of farm culture and the people. In fact, the concept for this project arose from the many comments that people offered during research for my earlier book.

Since the XYZ Foundation has supported projects in the visual arts and oral history in the past, I am pleased to submit this proposal, and to request a contribution of $15,000 toward realization of this project.

I have enclosed a budget, and additional materials about my earlier work, including a résumé, along with letters from the I——State Arts Council and the I——University Press in support of this project. If you have any questions or need additional materials, please do not hesitate to call me at 987-654-3210.

Sincerely,
Ruth Miller

Farmer—Project Budget: $33,800
Salaries

Project director—half-time, one year:	$18,000
Part-time assistant:	$ 8,000
Supplies, equipment:	$ 2,800
Telephone, office expenses:	$ 800
Bookkeeper:	$ 200
Travel:	$ 2,000
Promotion and development (including fund raising):	$ 2,000
Total expenditures:	$33,800

THE PRELIMINARY LETTER OF INQUIRY

After you've written for guidelines and an annual report, you'll find that some foundations may request a preliminary letter of inquiry that briefly outlines your project. They will ask you to identify yourself in the letter and describe your intent to apply. If the foundation is interested in your project, they will then invite you to submit a full-blown proposal. On rare occasions they may give you suggestions that will influence the writing of your proposal. (They will generally only do this for organizations, however, not individuals. And the larger foundations are usually too swamped with proposals to offer this kind of personalized attention even to groups.)

How to Write a Preliminary Letter of Inquiry. This is easy—the letter of inquiry will look exactly like the simple letter of request described above. You can use the same two- or three-page format. Make sure you observe any restrictions on the length of the letter, and include any specific information that the guidelines request. Send it in, then stand by to see if the funder invites you to submit a complete proposal.

APPLICATION FORMS

Some funders will want you to fill in an application form rather than write a proposal. College scholarships and fellowships often require application forms. These are fairly clear; you just fill in the blanks. You won't have to do the outlining and structuring yourself. Still, you will sometimes run into forms that have large boxes or lined pages for you to fill in with text. They may ask you to attach supplementary pages, so that you are really doing a combined application form and proposal.

The first thing you should do when you get any application form is to make a copy of it to use as a rough draft. This is really essential. Fill in the blanks in pencil. When you come to a tough question, or a large box, work on your answer on a separate piece of paper, until you are satisfied with the wording. Type it out and make sure it will fit in the space given. If supplementary pages are required, type out finished drafts with clear headings at the top, using the same wording as in the guidelines or the application form. Attach these pages to the application form in the appropriate order.

Some forms may ask questions that directly relate to some of the major topics of a proposal. Review the later sections of this chapter to get a sense of what kinds of answers they are looking for.

Following are two sample application forms, the first for a private foundation, the second for a government agency.

THE INGRAM MERRILL FOUNDATION

POST OFFICE BOX 202, VILLAGE STATION, NEW YORK CITY 10014

APPLICATION FOR AWARD OR GRANT

Must be typewritten

Name   Anne   Elizabeth   Josephs
_____
        First   Middle name or initial   Last name

Address   132 West 28th Street, New York, NY 10010

Telephone no.   (212) 555-1379

I. PERSONAL HISTORY

Present occupation   Design Consultant

Place of birth   Yonkers, New York   Date of birth   4/27/49

Are you an American citizen? Yes   If you are a naturalized citizen
give date and place of naturalization.

_____

If you are not an American citizen, give country of which you are a citizen,
subject, or national.

_____

Are you now, or will you be at any time falling within the period of your project, a
representative, agent, or employee of any foreign nation or political subdivision,
or political party thereof? If so, give details.

  No

Number of dependents, other than yourself.   None

What is your estimated income from other sources in the year or years in which you
will be working on your project? A detailed answer is necessary.

Consultant in decorative arts and textiles - $20,000

Teaching - $2,000

II. ACADEMIC AND OCCUPATIONAL BACKGROUND

Summarize your academic background, listing colleges, universities, or other institutions of learning attended, with degrees, diplomas, and certificates held.

Syracuse University, School of Visual and Performing Arts

 — B.F.A. Degree 1970

Summarize your occupational background, indicating employer, position held, and dates of tenure.

Lawson Houston, Ltd.　　　　　Design Consultant and Writer
Aug. 1986-present

Cohama Riverdale　　　　　Director of Design
Oct. 1980-July 1986

Parsons School of Design　　　　　Part-time Instructor
Sept. 1983-present

Waverly Fabrics div./Schumacher　　　Design Director
Dec. 1974-Oct. 1980

List all fellowships, grants, and scholarships you have received, giving full details of each, including name of grantor, amount of stipend, and studies or work carried on thereunder.

　　　　None

List your publications, giving title, publisher, and date of publication of each. Submit copies of all of this work with your application, unless it is totally irrelevant to the present project. One copy of each is sufficient. Painters and sculptors should supply representative slides of their work. All applicants must enclose a stamped, self-addressed envelope for the return of materials submitted.

III. DESCRIPTION OF PROJECT

Concise statement of project ___We are writing a book on historical___

interiors and residences (18th—early 20th century) that com-

bines both Eastern and Western styles of design, becoming

hybrids of both worlds. It would be of significant interest to

design students, professionals, and decorative arts historians.

A more detailed statement of your project and of your plans for work may be attached.

When do you wish to begin your project? ___January 1991___

Give your best estimate of time required for its completion. ___1 year___

Give an estimate of the sum which you feel you will require from this Foundation in order to carry out your project.

___$7,500___

When do you desire payment? Keep in mind that funds are available once a year only; approximately the first of the year. Your application must be received by the 15th of August for consideration in that year.

January 1991

Have you applied elsewhere for a fellowship, grant, or scholarship for the same project or for another project for the same period of time? If so, give details.

John Simon Guggenheim Memorial Foundation, Rockefeller

Foundation Humanities Fellowships, Marguerite Ever Wilbur

Foundation, Graham Foundation for Advanced Study in the

Fine Arts

IV. REFERENCES

Give names of three or more persons who can supply further information with regard to your qualifications, and (if your project is of a scholarly nature) who can give expert opinion concerning the value of this project as a contribution to knowledge; ask them to write on your behalf as soon as you submit your application.

Mr. David Smith	Curator, Cooper-Hewitt Museum
Mr. Samuel Foley	Retired (1986) Dean of Continuing Education Parsons School of Design, Consult. to New York School of Interior Design
Ms. Katherine Johns	Editor, Simon & Schuster
Ms. Sarah Pickens	Professor, University of California at Davis
Mr. David Levy	Vice-President, Waverly/Schumacher

(If in any of the foregoing items sufficient space is not allowed for a full and complete answer, it is requested that the information called for be stated in a separate paper securely attached to this application form. Each such separate paper should be signed and dated by the applicant. The application, which must be typed, should be mailed to The Ingram Merrill Foundation, Post Office Box 202, Village Station, New York, NY 10014.)

Anne Josepke
_____
Signature

September 12, 1990
_____
Date

NOTE: Any false, misleading, or incomplete answer or statement in any of the items above shall be ground for the immediate termination of any scholarship or fellowship that may be awarded on this application.

Please note that the foundation does not grant personal interviews; applications are to be submitted by mail only.

Individual Grant Application National Endowment for the Arts	Visual Arts Program
Applications must be submitted in trip- licate and mailed with other required materials to the address indicated under "Application procedures" for your category.	Category under which support is requested: COLLABORATIVE PROJECTS

Name (last, first, middle initial) Brown, Joseph	U.S. Citizenship Yes X No Visa Number
Present mailing address/phone 123 Main Street New York, NY 12345 (212) 555-1111	Professional field or discipline Artist, Preparator (see background) Birth Date Place of Birth 1-1-53 Raleigh, N.C.

Permanent mailing address/phone
123 Main Street
New York, NY 12345
 	
(212) 555-1111
	Period of support requested
	Starting October 1, 1991
	            month day year
	Ending October 1, 1992
	            month day year

Career summary or background

Matthew Smith and Joseph Brown met while undergraduates at New
York University in 1972. Their past collaborations include
"REAPER-CUSSION," a musical performance for the Todd Ensemble
at the Picasso Art Gallery in Rochester, New York, in June 1990,
and, most recently, "Hyper-Space," a performance and installation at the Rosen-Fox Gallery in Buffalo, New York, in
September 1990.

Matthew Smith is currently teaching drawing and painting at the
State University of New York at Buffalo and is preparing for
the "Albright-Knox Invitational" this March. Please see
attached résumé.

Joseph Brown is working as a full-time artist and is a preparator
at the West Museum in New York City. Please see attached résumé.

Amount requested from National Endowment for the Arts $5,000.00

Education

Name of institution	Major area of study	Inclusive dates	Degree
New York University	drawing/printmaking	1972-1976	BFA
Yale University	drawing/sculpture	1976-1978	MFA

Fellowships or grants previously awarded

Name of award	Area of study	Inclusive dates	Amount

Present employment

Employer	Position / Occupation	Total income last calendar year
West Museum	Preparator, installationist	$7,200.00

Prizes / Honors received	Membership professional societies
Permanent collection—Missouri Art Center, 1977 Mural—Trade Center Observation Deck, 1979	

Description of proposed activity

(Do not complete this section if you are applying for an Artists', Craftmen's, or Photographers' Fellowship)

The goal of our collaboration is to produce a lively and harmonious relationship between the organic and inorganic aspects of our natural world.

Matthew Smith has created a series of drawings and musical pieces that express the atomic stucture of four elements taken from the Periodic Table of Elements (which is a mathematical inventory of the natural elements). The series is enhanced by the clean technical feel of the drawings and the "architectural" feel of the music, achieved by using Moog synthesizer and an electric piano in the building and reduction of tones.

Conversely, Joseph Brown's work projects the earthy textural resonance of animals as they interact among themselves.

The collaboration will involve the building of a scale environment (details are attached to the slide sheet). Through music, abstract depictions of animals will "interact" in the environment. The music will blend electronically synthesized sound with live recordings of animals, previously recorded on site in the Peruvian jungles. The drawings will be developed using the same methods as Matthew Smith's earlier works (using the Periodic Tables), by systematically scoring the pieces using the animals' spatial placement. The result will be a euphonious conversation between the living and nonliving world.

The interdisciplinary focus of the proposed installation will be amplified through the use of drawings, sculpture, and sound. The result will be a completely enveloping and engrossing environment.

Certification: I certify that the foregoing statements are true and complete to the best of my knowledge.

Signature of applicant _Joseph Brown_ Date _9/12/90_

PROPOSALS BY SPONSORING ORGANIZATIONS

If you are working with a sponsor, they will be submitting the proposal, and the format will be somewhat different from that of a proposal you would submit as an individual. There will be no application form, as a general rule, and you'll be applying as a project of an institution. The nonprofit organization will have to supply information about its history, its past funders, its current operating budget, and more. If it's a small nonprofit, and they haven't done much of this before, you may need to get very involved and educate yourself on how to prepare this kind of proposal. You can refer to the books mentioned in Chapter 4 (page 160), and in the Appendix, for help.

Usually, though, there will be a development officer or other member of the organization who has done proposals before and is quite familiar with the process. This person will tell you what you need to supply, and you should work quite closely with them. In general, if you can supply all the sections that you would normally put in your own proposal, that will give them enough material to work with. Go ahead and write these up, from project summary through budget, and show them to the development officer. Ask if you should type or prepare things in any special way. Usually, the more you give an organization to work with, the easier it is for them to generate a strong proposal. After all, you are the one who knows and cares the most about your project. Don't leave a development officer guessing how to present it.

HOW TO PLAN AND PREPARE YOUR PROPOSAL

There are some general considerations that apply to any proposal, from a simple letter of request to a ten-page monster. It *is* important that you plan the proposal-writing process. You will need to think through issues of style and tone, and to adjust your basic proposal for different funders. You'll need to prepare for proofreading and typing or word processing and to organize the physical preparation of your proposal package. You'll need to plan ahead to do all your preparation in time to meet important deadlines.

STYLE AND LENGTH—KEEP IT SIMPLE!

Follow the "Three-C" rule: be Clear, Concise, and Convincing. You don't need to write like a professional, you just need to explain your project in clear, simple language. Use short sentences, and a basic vocabulary. You are not trying to impress anyone with your style, just getting the information across. Don't be too vivid, don't use purple prose, don't try to tug at the emotions. If your project does have a moving, emotional side, just tell the story and let the facts back you up. If you are dealing with a technical subject, don't use professional jargon; this may confuse readers rather than impress them. Translate any technical terms into ordinary language, and remember, what is clear to you as a specialist may be obscure to a program officer who is a generalist.

Quality of writing is important, but you should be able to do an effective draft of a proposal even if you are not an experienced writer. Imagine that you are writing a letter to a friend, explaining your project to someone who is eager to listen. Try to be brief, clear, and to the point. Follow the proposal outline given in this chapter, step by step. If you get stuck, use wording from the sample letters and proposals in this book, substituting your own specifics.

If you are concerned about your writing, get help. Show or read your draft proposal to a friend and ask them if there's anything that they don't understand, or if it sounds like you are repeating yourself. Rephrase until they understand the material clearly, and cut out the repetitions. If you know you have real problems with writing, hire a freelance editor or consultant to help you. Or go through a local college or university and hire an English major or graduate student to do a second draft of your proposal.

Be sure to proofread your work for proper grammar and spelling. Your final proposal should look as perfect as a magazine article or professional brochure. This is a crucial test of your professionalism, and program officers will be turned off by substandard grammar or spelling. Even though writing may have nothing to do with your project, it is still the medium through which you must reach out for funds. Top executives in business don't have to be good writers, but they know they have to put out good writing to represent their company well. You don't have to do the proofreading yourself. You may be able to write effectively but have trouble with rules of grammar or spelling.

If this is the case, it's essential that you get a freelancer, secretarial service, or college student to do the proofreading for you.

- **TIP:** If you are a little unsure about your writing skills, you may find the following book helpful. It's one of the best and shortest books on writing style, and one that's been a standard for years: *The Elements of Style,* by William Strunk, Jr., and E. B. White. 3rd edition, New York: Macmillan, 1979.

Your proposal does not have to be a massive document. An effective proposal, again, can be anywhere from three to ten pages in length. It's impossible to be more specific, since the length will depend on your project and on what a funder asks you for. As a rule, anything over ten pages is too long. Foundations actually prefer shorter proposals, because they must sift through thousands every year.

In fact, I've seen more often than not that foundation officers will turn down proposals that are too long and wordy. Again, to make the strongest case for your project, be clear, brief, and to the point. Of course, if you are working on a full-blown proposal, this does not mean that you can just write up a few paragraphs and expect to get funding. You do have to cover all the points on the outline and answer any specific questions that the funder may pose in the guidelines. But strive for the simplest, clearest way to make each essential point.

When you are through writing your proposal, show it to a friend or adviser and get their response. Ask for positive criticism or feedback. Ask if all the points are clear, if there's any repetition, if there is a logical development from one section to the next. Go back and rewrite as many times as you have to until you think that you have the best possible presentation.

STRIKING THE RIGHT TONE

Funders who read your proposal will naturally begin to form a judgment about you as a person. It's important to strike the right tone in your proposal, so that you come across as a qualified, committed person who cares deeply about your project. It's okay to give a sense of your personal connection to the work, but your main goal should be an objective description of your project, the need for it, and your qualifications. It's good to write vividly, but avoid purple prose. Avoid overdramatizing needs, or appealing too baldly to emotions. Your passion and enthusiasm are important, but don't get carried away in describing your objectives and what you hope to accomplish. You need to have specific, achievable goals. Don't make grandiose promises that you might not be able to keep.

You may have a strong political perspective that motivates you to do your project, but try to keep this out of the description. Describe your mission, needs, and objectives in terms that don't have an obvious political slant—many proposals are rejected for doing this. Don't start blaming a corrupt or unjust political system in your community, or the country, for the problems you are trying to solve. Just describe the problem and say how you are going to solve it. If you are targeting a funder that clearly indicates a sympathetic political interest in their mission statement or interest areas, this is all the better for your project. But you should still avoid making politically based appeals.

Emphasize the positive. In your mission statement, project summary, and objectives, try to turn negative statements into positive ones. If you are proposing a television series, don't go on about the banal, predictable, condescending programming that already exists. Say that you want to create fresh, original, challenging programming that is unlike anything currently on the broadcast spectrum. If you want to start a day-care center, don't say that no one in the community is willing to contribute to this. Say that your project represents a great opportunity for the funder to do something in a financially strapped community. Don't say, "I can't go on without funding," but rather, "Look at all that I could do with funding!"

It helps to think positively about the foundation that you are addressing your proposal to, even if you've had no personal contact with them. Envision an individual who is going to take interest in your ideas and consider them seriously. Since you may not have much personal contact with a funder at the initial stages, it's easy to fall into the feeling that you are dealing with a large bureaucracy, where no one really cares. Since the funder has the power to approve or deny your request, you can also begin to imagine that you are in an adversarial relationship. Remember, people have gotten involved in the nonprofit sector because they want to make good things happen. They are trying to select worthy projects that fit their mission and overall funding strategy. And they are dealing with a great number of submissions. As an individual making a first-time application, you probably won't receive the kind of attention that an organization with a track record might get. But be assured that even at the largest foundations some individual, and maybe several, will be taking a close look at your proposal.

Physical Presentation—Make It Look Good!

Because foundations are swamped with proposals, you want yours to stand out from the pack. Readers will probably give your proposal a quick overall scan when they receive it, and their first impressions begin there. So make your proposal visually appealing. If you have it typed by a word-processing service, you can use large or boldface type for headings, use bullet points for lists, and emphasize key concepts with underlining or italics. If you are hand-typing your proposal, aim for a clean, uncluttered look. Double-space and use headings. Number the pages, and use page headings that identify your proposal by name. Don't go overboard with this, however; you don't need fancy covers with pictures, cute typefaces, colored paper or color graphics. The most important part of a proposal is the content, not the packaging. Your writing should speak for itself. The most important thing is still to express yourself clearly.

Read carefully any guidelines on packaging your proposal and note how many copies are requested. Don't use any bindings that can't be easily unfastened—a program officer may want to take out some pages to pass around or want to make extra copies of your proposal. For the same reason, never use staples—it really is annoying to have to remove them. Instead, fasten your pages with paperclips or binder clips.

It is essential to present your proposal in a neatly typed form with no handwritten corrections. Nothing, I repeat, nothing can be hand-written. This includes application forms. If you can't type, hire a typist. The physical form of your proposal must be near-perfect. Whatever its other merits, bad typing and rampant errors can single-handedly ruin a proposal's chances. You may not catch every last typo, but it's crucial to go through your final draft several times and check for errors.

If you have support documentation, make good, clear photocopies and attach these at the end of your proposal. Don't submit original letters or newspaper clippings. If an article doesn't fit easily on a page, do some cutting and pasting and set it up on letter-sized paper for photocopying. If you're asked to send in other kinds of documentation—slides, photographs, videotapes—make sure that everything is clearly labeled with your name and the project title. If you're submitting slides or photos, use plastic mounting pages that you can attach directly to your proposal. You should never submit originals; things do get lost, and foundations may not always return your materials.

FUNDER FOCUS—ADJUST YOUR PROPOSAL FOR DIFFERENT FUNDERS

Every funder will assume that you are applying to several sources. But even though they understand this necessity, you'll need to adjust your proposal slightly to focus on each funder's particular mission and interests. This doesn't mean that you are going to change your own mission or project in any way. You only want to show how they fit and could further the mission of each funder. This is why you should give each version of your proposal a special focus.

For example, say you've invented a process that will remove certain hazardous chemicals from water. There are several ways you could slant your description of this. For foundations that support scientific research in your region, you can stress that most of the R&D will be locally based. If you approach a foundation that supports environmental projects, highlight your project's ability to help clean up ponds or streams. For a funder interested in scientific education, explain that you will employ chemistry majors at the local university to help monitor trials of your process. Your basic plan remains the same, but you should adjust your statement of need and objectives to reflect the aspect of your project that each funder will be most interested in.

It's much better to integrate the funder focus into the body of your proposal in this way. Some grant seekers try to do this just in the cover letter, but I think this is the easy way out, and not as effective. You don't want to try to second-guess the foundation by making your project sound like something it isn't—there should be nothing manipulative or insincere about this process. What you want to do is put yourself in the funder's shoes and think about your project from the point of view of their mission and criteria. Write your proposal with an eye to making it clear why they in particular should give you a grant.

For example, I was recently working on a proposal for a public television series about books. Now, there are many directions one could go in with this kind of project, but I was targeting a foundation that is primarily interested in literacy programs, including media literacy programs. When writing the proposal for them, I directly addressed the concerns in the foundation's own mission statement. I talked about how this was a creative use of the television medium to get people motivated to read and make books seem more accessible. And it worked—we got the grant! (By the way, you should never tailor a proposal to make your project resemble other projects that have been funded by an organization. You should focus your writing only toward their mission statement.)

DEADLINES AND TIMING

Meeting deadlines is essential. Funders are extremely strict about this, and if you miss the deadline, you miss the chance for the grant. It really is that simple. You have to get your proposal into the funder's hands—a postmark by the deadline is usually not good enough. You can ask for an extension only if you have a history with the foundation, and even then they don't like to do this. Unless you have applied many times and have gotten grants from a foundation, forget about an extension.

In fact, it's best to send your proposal in advance; the early bird does get the worm. If you get your proposal in early, the staff will have time to make copies and distribute them to board members. Program officers and board members will have time to look over your proposal and think about it. It will already be in the back of their minds when they are looking at new proposals and thinking about priorities. And if the staff or a program officer wants to get in touch with you to clear up any questions, or to look at additional material, there's plenty of time.

So you shouldn't be trying to hammer proposals together at the last minute. You can't write an effective proposal the night before a deadline, though people have tried. Allow time for research, writing, and just carefully thinking through how you want to present yourself. Not to mention the time it takes to type up clean copies, or get work to a typist and back. If you are a first-time grant seeker, working on your first proposal, expect to spend ten or fifteen hours on it, perhaps over the course of a week. This takes into account writing time as well as thinking time. You need to let your ideas simmer.

Planning ahead to meet deadlines is a sign of professionalism in fund raising. I once knew of a small nonprofit organization that did very interesting work in the cultural field. Their principal funder was a state arts council. They had a unique program, but it seemed that every year they were sending someone to the post office at the very last minute to get their proposal in to their principal funder. This was emblematic of their approach to fund raising, and this is one organization that is not around any more. You should not be coming in at the eleventh hour.

I find the best way to effectively meet deadlines is to do a wall chart, as we discussed in Chapter 2. If you are applying to eight foundations, list all of them on the chart, list their deadlines, and designate a column for each section of the application. Mark your own deadlines for getting supplementary documentation and collecting résumés. Mark your personal deadlines for completing the basic proposal and having the budget done. Keep your deadlines well ahead of the funder's final deadline, so you have time for contingencies and can still get the proposal in early.

Now that you know some of the general considerations that apply to any proposal, let's take a closer look at the components of the full proposal package.

HOW TO PREPARE THE FULL PROPOSAL PACKAGE

If you are going to write up a full proposal, you can follow this outline in most cases. It is a standard approach that most funders are familiar with. Remember, though, that you *must* follow the funder's printed guidelines to the letter. If these differ in any way from this outline, don't worry; just follow the funder's guidelines.

The average proposal for an individual project will probably run from three to five pages in length, not counting the cover letter, the table of contents, or your résumé and supporting documentation. Keep it simple. The summary should never be longer than one page; the other sections each might run from a paragraph up to a page or two at most. Shorter is fine. If it starts to get too long, program officers will feel oppressed by all the verbiage, and this is not good for you. Of course, if you are proposing a complex, long-term project, the proposal will have to run a little longer. Explicate your ideas and plans, and don't lose sleep over the length.

1. COVER LETTER

This is where funders get their first impression of you and your project. It goes without saying that the cover letter is important. Be sure that you address it to the appropriate person—whether the head of the foundation, a program officer, or another contact person. You have double-checked that you have the right name (and spelling!), and that this person is still with the funder.

Say you're pleased to submit a proposal, and give the name of your project or organization. Your mission statement and the amount you are requesting should appear right in the first paragraph. Explain that you are writing "to obtain funding for . . ." and follow up with your mission statement. Next, state how much money you are requesting and what it would do. Your mission statement should really tell the whole story in a nutshell. Make sure it's clear and not too wordy. If you want, go back to Chapter 1 and review some of the samples of mission statements.

You can add a sentence here explaining where the project will take place and in what time frame. Say that you'll be happy to answer any questions or provide any further information. Thank the reader for their time and consideration, say you look forward to hearing from them, and leave it at that.

2. TITLE PAGE

The title page states your project title, your name, and the name of the funding source you are applying to. Center the project title and funding source near the top of the page. Think carefully about the title you give your project—and make it sound interesting.

Instead of simply:

PROPOSAL FOR FUNDING OF A DAY-CARE CENTER
Presented to the XYZ Foundation

you might call it:

THE FREEDOM TO WORK
A Request to the XYZ Foundation

In the lower right-hand corner of the page, include your full name, your address, your telephone number, and the date. If you have a sponsor or institutional affiliation, add the sponsor's name, address, and phone number under your own.

A catchy title might attract the reader's eye and pique some interest in your project, but it is not essential. What really matters in a proposal is the content of the project summary and the rest of the proposal. On a full-length proposal, I often include the mission statement and the amount requested on the title page.

3. TABLE OF CONTENTS

If your proposal runs five pages or longer, you should include a table of contents immediately following the title page. This would list the major sections, including Project Summary, Statement of Need, Objectives, Plan, Evaluation, Personnel, Budget, Future Support, and Supplementary Documentation. List the separate items that you are including under the Supplementary Documentation heading. If you are including more than one résumé, list the individual names in this section as well.

Even if you have a shorter proposal, you might include a simple List of Enclosures, itemizing such components as Project Summary, Proposal, Résumés, Budget, and Supplementary Materials.

4. PROJECT SUMMARY

Immediately following the cover letter or table of contents, you should provide a project summary. On a single page, outline your mission statement, the need for your project, your objectives, and your plan, and briefly describe yourself and your qualifications for receiving the grant. The project summary will give the funder's staff a quick sense of your project and tell them whether they want to read on.

Because it serves this important function, the project summary needs to arouse the reader's interest and provoke them to read further. It must also quickly convey all the essential facts about your project. Get as much information as you can into the first sentence. Again, begin with your request for funds and your mission statement: "This is a request to the XYZ Foundation from Jane Smith for a grant of $50,000 to enlist its support for the financing of her college education," or: "This is a request for a three-year grant totaling $110,000 to create a unique theater in Rapids City, South Dakota." Quickly describe the need for and the essential features of the project. You should be able to get most of the essential information into one paragraph. The project summary should never be longer than 250 words or one page.

In a new paragraph, explain why supporting your project is a good opportunity for the funder you are applying to. Make them feel that yours is a good cause. Explain how your project will have a positive impact, solve a problem, or satisfy a need. You can briefly provide some background on the community or context in which the project will take place, describe the outreach you will do, and tell why this will be important. If you are proposing to answer a need that no one else is addressing, you should stress this.

Finally, you can provide some background information on yourself and your qualifications. You might briefly describe your personal history if it is relevant to the project. If you are applying through a sponsor or institution, introduce them here. Mention anything about the past or present work or activities of the organization that relates directly to your project.

Try to come up with one or two key details that give evidence of your competence, or your unique qualifications to receive the grant. You should definitely mention any significant awards you have won, past funding, or any other outstanding accomplishments. Keep it short—this is not a résumé, and the whole project summary has to fit on one page. If you are a professional with much experience in the field, just say that, and let the reader flip to your résumé for more. If you're worried that you don't have much directly relevant experience, mention one or two positive facts that will indirectly support your case. If you're starting that day-care center, mention that you've done community volunteer work for your church, or been an officer in a Parent-Teacher Association.

Program officers will have a pretty good idea whether your project is feasible for them within a few minutes of reading your project summary. So keep it short, strong, and thought-provoking. If it's clear and to the point, your introduction will pique interest and induce the reader to read on. In the sections that follow you will be able to explain the needs, your objectives, and your plans in more detail.

5. STATEMENT OF NEED—PROBLEM STATEMENT

The body of your proposal begins with your statement of need. Keep this section, too, as concise as possible. The funder wants to know why you need the money, and whom the grant will help—whether an organization, a community, or you as an individual. It could be all three. The funder who sponsors you will want to know that they are having an impact upon a unique and urgent need. It could be your need as an individual or an opportunity for your community. Make the funder feel that you are a good "investment," that they will solve a problem or do good for society by giving you a grant.

Do emphasize the urgency of your need, and why your case may be unique. The need statement should be factual but it can help to dramatize a bit. Aim to have an emotional impact upon your reader, but don't overdo it. You need to find that delicate line between tugging on the heartstrings and presenting facts that speak for themselves.

Inject a sense of urgency. Show the funder that the problem you are addressing needs special attention and can be solved with *their* help. If current resources for dealing with the problem are inadequate, you should explain this. For an individual project, let them know if you don't have any alternative sources to turn to. For a community project, let them know if there are no other organizations or services addressing the need.

As you write your need statement, bear the following points in mind:

- Keep your need statement clearly connected to your mission statement. You are describing the need that the mission is designed to fulfill.
- Keep your need statement specific—localize it in time and space. You don't want to end up describing a huge social problem that your one project is helpless to solve by itself.
- The need statement is a good place to connect your project to the mission of each particular funder. Describe the need in a way that associates it as closely as possible with the kind of need the funder wants to address. Your project might in reality answer several needs, but emphasize the one that falls closest to the funder's interests.
- Emphasize the social need more than the strictly financial need. If an idea has integrity, the money will follow. So don't get as carried away with money as you do with your passion for the project.
- Don't focus on your personal life or personal need unless it relates directly to the larger problem. Try to cast personal need more in terms of positive opportunities than negative lacks. If you are applying for a scholarship, don't say that you are poor and don't have the money. Say that you have an incredible chance to enter this degree program, and that it's special because no one from your family, or your community, has ever had such an opportunity.
- You can mention some evidence to support your need statement, but you shouldn't go overboard on this. Just explain in an overview. Outline the causes or origins of the problem, and the current conditions or repercussions. You can briefly cite some statistics that support your need, if any are available.
- If applicable, mention the funding and support climate for your project. Is this a kind of project that has been neglected because resources have gone elsewhere? Is the need now becoming even more urgent because of the neglect?

- Don't overwrite. As long as it includes the necessary information, the shortest, clearest statement of need will be the strongest.

A strong statement of need will interest the funder in the next section of the proposal, which describes how you are going to fulfill the need.

6. OBJECTIVES

This section explains how your project meets the need you've just described. Here you want to list the goals you expect to achieve—the development of an invention to the point where it can be marketed, the completion of your college education, etc.

Your objectives will be unique to your project. Your objective may be personal and individual or it may reach out to the community. If you are going to do a research project, your objectives might include showing whether there's a clear correlation between two variables, publishing the results of your research, and establishing what the next course of research should be. If you are a performing artist, your objectives might be achieving a new level of skill in your craft, developing a new piece to perform at a certain theater, or developing new audiences for your work. A project may have one narrowly defined objective, or several related ones.

It's fine to itemize several objectives, as long as they develop in a logical, step-by-step way. Don't use this section to try to be all things to all funders. Stay focused, and be sure your objectives follow naturally and logically from your mission statement and statement of need.

Always go back to your mission statement. Your objectives are really a more detailed version of your mission. The mission statement gives a long-range, global vision of what you want to do. The objectives section goes into the specifics. I worked with one client whose mission was to bring free theater to children who normally don't have the opportunity to see it. When the client applied for funding, one of his specific objectives was to purchase a property for offices and performance space; another was to put on a particular show.

Above all, present your objectives in a positive way, as something that a funder should want to help you achieve. Don't just say you want to complete a series of twelve paintings for a public show; say you want to make twelve paintings that will grapple with a specific artistic problem, or will present the history of an oppressed community. Foundations want to know that something will change for the better because of their funding.

As you work on your objectives, keep the following in mind:

- Always include some kind of outreach among your objectives. You will bring people to the project, bring the project to people, or publish or disseminate results. If it's a community project, note how many people you hope to reach. If you are a filmmaker, explain that you will try to have your work screened at five festivals.
- If the need you describe is not being addressed by anyone else in the community, or the profession, be sure to mention this. This means that your project will have a special impact, and the funder will make a real contribution by giving you a grant.
- Regardless of your field or need, try to be as detailed and specific as you can. Show the foundation that you've thoroughly researched and thought through your project.
- Strike a positive note as you list your objectives. Convey the feeling that they can really be achieved. Include any information or evidence that will support this. If you have a community project, mention that you've done outreach in the community before and know what response to expect. If you're an artist, mention that you've completed commissions successfully.
- Your objectives should answer the needs you've described in specific, well-defined ways. In the need statement, you can talk about broad, long-standing needs. In the objectives section, discuss the short-term, readily achievable goals that you want to accomplish. In the need statement you can address the need for jobs and sophisticated work training for youth in your community. In your objectives, say that you'll provide fifty paying internships in high-tech local companies within the first year of your project.
- Don't confuse objectives with steps of your plan itself. Conducting a series of dance workshops with junior-high students in different inner-city schools is a method—part of a plan. Putting on a public performance of a new dance work with some of those students is an objective. Renting a space and

hiring teachers to care for children are two steps in a plan. Providing day care for twenty children during a specific calendar year is an objective.

- As with the statement of need, be clear, concise, and to the point. You shouldn't have a huge number of objectives, and you don't have to write at length about each one to get your point across. A sentence or two of explanation for each will do the trick.

Outlining your objectives will lead directly to the next sections of the proposal—plan and evaluation. Once you have described your specific objectives, you'll be able to lay out the methods by which you'll achieve them. And if your objectives are clear, it will be easy to evaluate your success at the end of the project.

7. PLAN—PLACE, METHODS, SCHEDULE

In this section, you should really dig into the details of your project. This will probably be the longest section of the proposal. It will be based on the project outline that you've been developing from the start. There are three major areas you will clarify in the plan. You'll explain where the project will take place; you'll describe the steps in the process, from start to finish; and you'll provide a schedule for accomplishing those steps.

You don't have to be creative about the writing, appeal to emotions, or explain how you chose your methods. Just write down exactly what you plan to do, clearly and in detail. The length of this section will depend on how complicated your project is. You don't have to belabor the obvious, but do explain any aspects of your plan that a funder might be curious about. In fact, this is a good way to proceed: Imagine that someone who knows nothing about you or your project is asking you specific questions, and answer them. If you've discussed the project with others, and some good questions have come up, be sure to answer them in this section.

As always, be organized, proceed step by step, and avoid lengthy discussions. The form of this section will be determined by the steps of your project, from start to finish. As you write this section, be sure to cover the following five aspects:

- **Place:** Where will you be doing the project? If you want a fellowship, explain where. If you want to travel, detail your itinerary. If you are working in a community, identify it by location, ethnicity, shared interest—whatever applies. If you are going to be doing scientific research at an institution, describe the facilities. If you are doing an artistic project, identify the studio where you'll be working, or the theater where you'll be rehearsing.

- **Method:** Go through the different stages of your project in step-by-step fashion.

    If your project is large, explain how you will administer, operate, and keep records on it. Discuss any special aspects of financial administration and bookkeeping.

- **Personnel:** If your project will involve other key people, identify them (if you know who they are) and the jobs they will be doing. This won't be a separate section—just explain what the others will be doing at each stage of the project. If you will be hiring an assistant or a staff, working with professional consultants, or hiring a specialist, explain all this here. You don't have to say who they will be, or, if you know, go on at length about them. Just attach their résumés.

- **Outreach:** Be sure to lay out the details of how you will bring people to the project, bring the project to people, or publish or disseminate the results.

- **Time:** Indicate the starting and completion dates for the project as a whole. If it's a complex or long-term project, indicate expected starting and completion dates for each stage. It may help to provide a chart or diagram showing when each stage of a longer project will take place. Include outreach and evaluation in your schedule.

8. EVALUATION

This may be the section you've thought least about, but it's important to funders. They want to have some means of getting feedback from you and of knowing that their dollars were well spent, that the project succeeded as planned, that their grant made a difference. For a simple project, the evaluation process might be as straightforward as writing up a short report for the funder. For a large or complex project, an evaluation might involve supplying progress reports, compiling figures or statistics, or receiving visits by independent observers. Funders may request specific evaluation procedures in their guidelines, or work these out with you once they've given you a grant. If the guidelines give any clues, write this section accordingly.

Be creative in thinking of ways to help the funder evaluate your project. At the very least, you should offer to write a report for the funder upon completion of the project. If you are doing any outreach, try to measure the impact of your project on the community. You can keep track of the number of people you've reached—through attendance records at your theater performance or enrollment records at your day-care center. You can record the number of young people who get full-time jobs after your internship program. If you will need ongoing feedback about your project, you might be planning to make up questionnaires or have an open discussion period. If your work is going to be publicized, you may be able to offer reviews or articles.

Some points to keep in mind as you write this section:

- For many projects, the evaluation will naturally be more subjective. If you've gotten a scholarship or a fellowship, you will simply have to describe your own understanding of the impact of your education on your life. If there will be any public presentation or publication of your work, do mention this, but it may be sufficient for you to write up a report.
- You can always base the evaluation on your original objectives—at the end of the project you should be able to tell whether or not you accomplished them. (Even if your methods of achieving them changed!)
- For some projects, having third parties evaluate your work will be a normal part of the process. If you are presenting a play, you'll naturally want reviewers to see it. If you are doing scientific research, you will certainly want to present your findings to a professional journal, which will review your work for publication.
- Think of a way to determine whether beneficial changes came about as a result of your project, and to identify any changes that might have had other causes. Remember, though, outside factors from the weather to the economic or political climate affect how well your project succeeds.
- If appropriate, discuss the kinds of conclusions you will be able to draw at the end of your project. If you are doing research, what should you be able to find out? If you are doing an experimental program working with young people, what

might the success of this program imply for other projects? You may be able to show that a new direction in research or social work will be especially fruitful for others.

9. PERSONNEL

If you are doing a small, individual project, this section is easy: just attach your résumé. Some funders will ask that you give them a biographical sketch instead of a résumé. (See page 282 for more on these.) If your project is larger, you should include the résumés of the other key people who will be involved. You've already introduced these people and explained what they will be doing in your plan, so here you just attach their résumés. You only need résumés for the most important people; three or four is probably the maximum.

If you've talked to some people about your project and already have a tentative commitment, ask them for copies of their résumés. If they aren't sure about this, ask if they mind your mentioning their names as possibilities. As long as this is okay with them, write up brief biographical sketches of the people you've contacted. Make it clear that these are only tentative commitments, and *never*, ever use anyone's name whom you haven't spoken to or who has said no. A funder may check up on this, word will get out, and your credibility will be zero.

On Résumés and Bios.   There are plenty of references available to help you work up a good résumé. If you already have a résumé, or if you're starting one from scratch, it is a good idea to give it a slant so that it better supports the project you are proposing. (Many people make up two or three versions for different purposes.) Emphasize and expand on the education or experience that relates most directly to your project.

Don't worry if you can't show a lot of professional experience that is directly related to your project. You don't necessarily need special qualifications if you can build your résumé to emphasize experience that indirectly supports your case. Even if you've worked in a completely different field, you can describe your duties and activities so as to feature general skills and experience that would also be useful in the project area. Maybe you've managed construction projects with complicated schedules and many independent contractors. This is the kind of management experience that can carry over to almost any other kind of work. Remember, you don't have to list only job experience on your résumé. You may have done volunteer work for a church, or an organization that involved community outreach. Maybe you've been very active in a school PTA, and have special understanding of some relevant educational issues.

On the other side, if you have substantial professional experience, don't go in for overkill. In the academic world it may be effective to have a fifteen-page résumé that lists every article you've ever published, but funders get weary of this. They don't want to wade through a résumé that's longer than your whole proposal. Summarize your accomplishments and list only the essentials and highlights. Funders will get the picture.

If you are including résumés of other people, take a close look at them to see if they will support your project. As project director, you must make this evaluation. Sometimes you'll get a résumé that is simply not well done or is slanted in the wrong direction. In such cases, you should consider rewriting the résumé to give it the spin that will help make your case.

- **TIP:** For help with preparing a résumé, take a look at:
  The Only Job Hunting Guide You'll Ever Need, by Kathryn and Ross Petras. New York: Poseidon Press, 1989.
  Writing a Job-Winning Resume, by John E. McLaughlin and Stephen K. Merman. Englewood Cliffs, NJ: Prentice-Hall, 1986.

Biographical sketches, or "bios," are a peculiar format, and not everyone is used to writing them. They generally convey the same information as a résumé, but in condensed, third-person prose. You normally structure them chronologically, to give a sense of the story of your life. Start with your name, and continue writing about yourself in the third person. Begin with your birthplace, summarize your education, then move on to your professional career, honors, and accomplishments. You might mention significant experiences that relate directly or even indirectly to your career or project. Bios can have more of a personal feel than résumés, but you don't want to take this too far. Avoid cuteness and melodrama, and focus on your professional career. Guidelines may tell you how long the bio should be, but they are usually shorter than résumés. One page is a maximum, and you may be asked for something even shorter. Writing a bio is a useful exercise, because it forces you to pick out the highlights of your career, your most significant experiences and accomplishments.

10. THE BUDGET—YOUR REALITY CHECK

Your budget is probably the most important part of your proposal, after the mission statement. It is going to tell funders whether you are being realistic or fanciful about your needs. The only time you shouldn't submit a budget with your proposal is when a funder specifically asks you not to. This will rarely happen. If there's no mention of a budget in a funder's guidelines, submit one.

Program officers will often turn to your budget immediately after reading your mission statement, to see how savvy and realistic you are. It's not hard to do a good budget—common sense is the rule of thumb. But you do need to prepare carefully.

You will normally prepare your budget after writing the rest of the proposal. Everything in the budget must be consistent with the objectives and plan you've laid out. Essentially, you will be breaking down your expenses into major categories. (We'll talk about these categories below.) However, the actual figures must be based on real research into costs and prices. You can't just estimate them. You need to collect price lists, make phone calls, get quotes, sit down with a calculator and start adding things up. You will not be able to put down exact figures for every item. Don't worry about this—just make an informed estimate. Funders know that you will probably need to modify your budget slightly as you get into the project. But do get as many exact figures as you can and make your estimates as accurate as possible.

The budget must be clear and concise. One or two pages at the most will be sufficient. Much of the research and thinking you do to construct a budget will not appear in the final form. You'll simply list the total figures for the various categories.

Nonetheless, it is important to do the detailed research. First, because you want to present an accurate budget that will seem realistic to funders. Second, because you want to be able to justify your figures if a funder should ask you for more details. And finally, because by putting together an accurate budget, you will be bringing your project that much closer to reality, and you will know that if you get the money you will really be able to make it work.

Some foundations will study your budget closely and compare it with your project summary, your objectives, and the steps listed in your plan. Be sure any major budget items are mentioned in your plan. If your plan is not specific enough and does not mention, for example, that you will need to rent or purchase office equipment, the funder may find no clear reason why you need this equipment. Finally, be sure that your expenses are clearly related to specific objectives. If you list a budget item that doesn't seem to support your objectives, funders will question this. You may not get a chance to justify your need for an expense if it's not clearly supported in your proposal.

Budget Format. To keep things clear, use a simple format for your budget. Put a title on your budget page, such as "Budget for the 'Make a Difference' Project," and use a two-column format. List the expense categories and items in the left-hand column and dollar amounts in the right-hand column. Round off to the nearest $10, $50, or $100. Make sure to line up all the figures in neat columns and subtotal each category that contains more than one amount. If you have just a few expense items in your budget, you can list each item by category. If you have a large budget that includes many individual items, just list the categories. As always, if the funder requests a specific budget format in the guidelines, follow their instructions. Below is a sample set of budget categories you can use to get started if the funder doesn't request a particular format.

- *Personnel* including salaries and wages. If you are putting someone on salary, you normally have to include fringe benefits, like unemployment insurance and health insurance. If you have an individual project, you can get around this by simply paying a professional fee to yourself or others involved in the project, as below. (For help with fringe benefits, see the references on pages 286–87.)

- *Consultants and professional services* fees for professionals and contracted services. You can pay most of the people who work for a project on a fee basis. They will simply report this as self-employment income on their IRS returns.

   If a development consultant or program consultant is getting a percentage of monies raised, this must be listed with a dollar amount.

- *Living expenses or per diem expenses* for a student on a scholarship, or a researcher who is traveling.

- *Expendable supplies* supplies that will be used in the course of your project. These could involve anything from office supplies to a scientist's glassware to a sculptor's clay.

- **Special contracted services** word processing, bookkeeping, film or photo laboratories, photocopying. If you think you'll be managing a lot of expenditures (or even income) once your project gets started, you might want to include a budget item for bookkeeping services. This doesn't have to be a big amount. You probably can get away with $100 or $150 monthly or quarterly, depending on how much needs to be done.

- **Space or facilities** rental of office space, studio space, etc.

- **Equipment** purchase and rental. Be aware, though, that some funders specifically bar the use of their funds for purchase of equipment.

- **Travel** foreign, domestic, local.

- **Communications** telephone installation or service, toll calls, faxes, messengers, postage, shipping.

- **Publicity and publications** advertising, printing of flyers, reports, programs, catalogues.

- **Promotion** special public relations events, receptions, dinners, entertainment.

- **Other costs** lump together here any miscellaneous expense items that don't seem to rate a category of their own.

These are only sample categories. Feel free to use others if they apply to your project and to drop any that don't apply. Also see the sample budgets on pages 255 and 296.

How long should a budget be? One page is usually sufficient—or two for a large project. I like to flesh out the budget and give a funder a little more detail, so that they can see what some of the important line items are. (*Line items* is budget jargon for one item on one line of a budget.) Have a few line items under each category. If you're paying three major professional or consultant's fees, list these under Personnel. List the major types or items of equipment. List the major categories of expendable supplies. You don't have to list every single supply or subcategory, but a budget with some detail shows funders that you have done your homework. They'll be able to judge whether you are being realistic financially.

If someone has offered you in-kind services, or will donate time to your project, and the commitment is really solid, you should show this in your budget. Just list the item under the appropriate category, and on the dollar side write "Donated" or "In-Kind." If you are going to donate your own equipment or facilities, enter this in the same way. Some funders might ask that you do this differently. They might want you to list the dollar value of the donated services, mark the items that are donated, and then subtract the total value of donated services from your budget total. Just follow their guidelines.

When you come up with your total, go back and adjust figures slightly to make your total a nice, round figure. Shave an amount here, supplement one there. A round figure will stick in funders' minds better—and will seem more realistic, since your budget does include some estimates. Make your budget total $7,500, not $7,350, $30,000 instead of $28,000.

DIRECT AND INDIRECT COSTS

If you are applying through a sponsor, many funders like you to break down your budget into two major categories: direct costs and indirect costs. Direct costs are those clearly connected with the actual project, such as salaries, fees, equipment, travel expenses, and publications. Indirect costs generally apply only to organizations and institutions and are a percentage of their overhead or general operating expenses. Indirect costs include items like rent and upkeep on facilities, administrative costs, a percentage of the salaries of the organization's officers, heat and electricity, and telephones and office supplies. Government applications and others for institutions usually ask for a breakdown of indirect and direct costs. They also may want you to break down some expenses into great detail—who exactly is being hired, what are their titles, job descriptions, etc.

If you are applying as an individual, you will have only direct costs. If you need to rent space, or include a budget line for telephone expenses, list these as direct costs. If you are applying through a sponsor, budgeting can get much more complicated, but there is usually someone on staff at the organization who can help you through the process. If there is no one experienced with this, you will need to do some research. See the books listed below for help with institutional budgets.

- *A Nonprofit Organization Operating Manual: Planning for Survival and Growth,* by Arnold J. Olenick and Philip R. Olenick. New York: The Foundation Center, 1991.

- *Raise More Money for Your Nonprofit Organization: A Guide to Evaluating and Improving Your Fund-Raising*, by Anne L. New. New York: The Foundation Center, 1991.
- *Securing Your Organization's Future: A Complete Guide to Fund-Raising Strategies*, by Michael Seltzer. New York: The Foundation Center, 1987.
- *Grants: How to Find Out About Them and What to Do Next*, by Virginia P. White. New York: Plenum Press, 1975.
- *Grants for the Arts*, by Virginia P. White. New York: Plenum Press, 1980.

Unless you are applying both as an individual and through an affiliate, you should be able to submit the same budget to most funders. Some, especially government agencies, may require special breakdowns. They may want you to itemize travel expenses in a certain way, or group together some categories and split others apart. In these cases, just read the guidelines and follow the instructions. For the most part, though, you'll be able to present the budget in the generic format that I've detailed in this section.

HOW TO MAKE BUDGETING EASIER

If you are not used to working with budgets, the process can seem a little daunting. A good way to proceed is to go to your stationery store, get a journal or ledger, and assign separate pages to different categories. Then you can enter in each expense as you research it. Many expenses will be linked to the projected time of your project. You'll have to estimate daily, weekly or monthly costs for certain items, and multiply to get totals.

If you have a personal computer, there are several simple money management programs available that will help you prepare quite elaborate budgets and do all the calculations automatically. If you're still at a loss, see if there is a service organization in your field that has a book or pamphlet on budgeting. Better yet, you might get someone from the organization to sit down with you for a consultation. As a last resort, you can hire a freelance consultant to prepare the budget. Look again at Chapter 2 for suggestions on how to do this. For the most part, though, preparing a budget simply requires common sense. Anyone who has done a household budget or prepared an income tax return should be able to do it.

How Fat or How Lean?

One question that grant seekers often fret over is just how big the budget should be. Can you fill it out with all kinds of perks and extras that would make life easier, or do you need to pare it down to the bare essentials? There's no easy answer to this. It depends on the funding climate in your subject area, on how innovative your project is, and on your personal qualifications. It helps to have some sense of what other projects in your area cost, though you can't simply reproduce someone else's budget request.

One of the problems in preparing a budget is the sometimes long lead time between the fund raising and start-up of a project. You have to be prepared for unexpected contingencies and cost increases. One way to factor this in is to pad each budget line a little. Don't base your budget lines on the most rock-bottom discount price you could find. Program officers expect a little bit of padding in a budget. Many organizations pad their budgets by 10 to 30 percent. This is not cheating—it's just being realistic. Everyone knows that prices can change by the time you have received all your funding and are ready to start up your project. You may need to take into account higher postage costs, higher rentals, higher personnel costs. On the other hand, program officers can spot excessive padding in two seconds. They are not stupid, and they'll throw out your budget, and your proposal.

Some guidelines will ask you to put down an amount for contingencies, and they may suggest a figure of up to 5 percent of your total budget. Do as they suggest, but you still shouldn't put down the rock-bottom price for each line item. Even if you like to work on a shoestring budget, make your costs look realistic.

If your fund raising stretches out over a long time, you may want to double-check your budget figures periodically. If some basic costs have gone up, factor this in, and adjust the total accordingly.

Program officers will be skeptical if your budget seems too low. They may suspect that you are not being realistic and conclude that you will never accomplish your project for this amount of money. They will worry that if they do give you money, it will be thrown away. So while it's good to be economical, don't underestimate your needs. Be honest with yourself, list all necessary expenses, and don't tell yourself that you'll solve that problem when you come to it, or that you can count on somebody to donate services. Even if you are used to working on shoestring budgets, use figures that reflect the going rate for goods and services. If you think you can do your project for less, you'll just have that much more flexibility.

Many grant seekers wonder about the issue of salary and compensation. You may be so excited about your project that you almost feel you'd like to do it without any compensation; but realistically, you probably need to support yourself. If it's a project with a limited time frame or scope, you can budget a professional fee for yourself, based on your estimate of the number of hours you'll be working on the project. If you will be managing a big project for a year and it will be your full-time job, put down a salary for the year. If this is the case, you'll probably be working through a sponsor, and you can get their help in figuring out fringe benefits.

When you are figuring salaries or professional fees, use the going professional rate, not the minimum wage that you might find somebody to work for. Remember, though, that the going rate in most parts of the nonprofit world, except at the very top, is somewhat lower than in the business world. It's not unusual for a project director of a cultural community project to earn between $25,000 and $35,000 annually. However, if you do have access to someone who is impassioned about the project and will work for union scale instead of their usual fee, or if you have someone who will volunteer time, by all means document this. The more money you can save, the stronger your chances of success.

If you are applying for travel grants, or there is a travel section in your budget, you will usually use a per diem figure that indicates basic daily expenses for lodging, meals, local transportation, etc. (This is exclusive of plane tickets and other intercity travel.) The per diem really depends on where you're going and what you consider a reasonable amount of money. A usual per diem is about $100 a day. The U.S. State Department lists the per diem it pays its employees in different cities in the world, so you might use this as a basis for budgeting international travel.

If you have one or two very expensive items in your budget, you don't have to explain or annotate them, as long as they are justified in your plan. If something is very unusual, you should explain in your plan why you are doing things this way. You should have good reasons for all your budget lines. If you get a meeting with a funder, they may well ask. You will not be turned down for a questionable item, but you may be questioned. If you do have a meeting, bring notes on how you arrived at your figures, so that you can answer such questions.

If you can get hold of some sample budgets for projects in your field, this may help you think through your own, and remind you of items that you might have overlooked. Of course, you can't copy someone else's budget format exactly, or base the size of your budget on someone else's. You have to build up your own budget from scratch, based on the needs of your particular project.

Similarly, you can't use a funder's grant guidelines or giving patterns to determine how big your budget should be. You will probably have to go to several funders to raise all the money for your project, and giving patterns can only help you decide how much of this sum to ask for from each funder.

11. OTHER FUNDING RECEIVED

If you have already received some funding at the time you send in a proposal, list it after the budget. Indicate the name of the funder and the amount of the grant. List any in-kind services or materials you've been offered here, too. This will help build your credibility—it shows that someone has already placed their confidence in you and that you are one big step toward getting your project done. Sometimes a funder will ask you to list other foundations or programs you are currently applying to, and you can list these after the budget as well, with an explanatory heading. Do this only if you are asked to—there is no need to volunteer this information.

12. FUTURE FUNDING AND SUPPORT

This is another optional section that usually only applies to institutional proposals. If you have an individual project with a definite completion point, you can skip it. If you are planning an ongoing, open-ended project, this is where you lay out any ideas you have about generating income to support the project, whether selling tickets, charging fees, or whatever. If this is a pilot project, you might discuss the stage at which you will start to do additional fund raising to continue the project, and how the results of the pilot will affect future fund raising. If you have an individual project that will continue after the initial grant period, you might plan to become part of an existing nonprofit organization, or to encourage your community to adopt the project.

You cannot usually go back to the same funder year after year. You have to go after a number of different sources and alternate them year to year. Some government agencies and large foundations will fund projects on an ongoing basis, but generally only for nonprofit organizations and institutions.

13. CERTIFICATIONS

If you're applying under an umbrella organization, you will usually be asked to supply a copy of its 501(c)3 IRS certificate of exemption. Some funders may also want an official statement of affiliation signed by officers of the organization or institution you are working with.

14. SUPPORTING DOCUMENTATION

Your supporting documentation might include one or two letters of endorsement (as discussed in Chapter 2), statistical evidence, a press release, a newspaper article about the problem or need, an article about you, or a review of your work. If you've been funded before, and this doesn't appear on your résumé, list it here.

Keep these documents to a minimum, and choose material that very directly supports your proposal. Don't pad this section. Many foundations are understaffed, program officers are overworked, and they can't wade through pages and pages to find the one or two telling documents. This is an area that many grant seekers abuse. As with the rest of the proposal, short and to the point makes the strongest impression.

If the guidelines address documentation, follow them very carefully. Funders may make very specific requests, or limit documentation. Do include anything they ask for. Most corporate and private foundations leave to you the judgment of what will best support your proposal. Government agencies may place very strict limits on what you can send them; don't send them anything but what they ask for, and send it in the form they request.

If you're applying under an umbrella organization, you normally add documentation about the organization itself. This will typically include a list of their supporters, major contributors, and past funders. The organization will supply these. Insert any reports, brochures, or other literature about your sponsor that is relevant to your project. Again, don't bloat your proposal with every piece of publicity material that your funder has produced.

If you get an expression of interest from a funder, or a meeting, they may request certain documentation. For a recent project, a funder asked to see very specific support documentation on how television influences individuals in their book-buying habits. I had to do some research to come up with material on this. But even when asked for something, don't go overboard.

Especially if you are doing creative work, funders may want to see samples of your work. If you want your work returned, they'll usually ask you to include a mailer with postage. But be warned: Over the years, I've raised a lot of money for visual artists, authors, and film-makers, and I'd say you should expect that your samples may not be returned. Even funders with good systems and fine intentions slip up. Never send original material, your only set of slides, or your only copy of something. Again, include only what's asked for. Less is more. Funders will ask for additional material if they need it.

SAMPLE PROPOSAL

This sample proposal comes from a nonprofit organization, but it will be equally instructive for individuals who are submitting full-blown proposals. It has several components: a cover letter; an introduction that includes the project summary, statement of need, and objectives; a plan of events that lays out the details of the project; a section on how the project's success will be evaluated; a summary; a list of the supporting documentation that would be attached to the proposal, including a list of personnel and information on other funding received; and the all-important budget. The title page and the table of contents are self-explanatory and thus are omitted here, but you should certainly include them in your proposal package—they'll make it both more professional-looking and more accessible.

Ms. Patricia Harrington
ZDF Corporate Foundation
Metropolis, NY

Dear Ms. Harrington:

We are honored to submit this proposal to the ZDF Corporate Foundation on behalf of VISIONQUEST, a nonprofit educational organization.

We are writing to obtain funding for the OPEN DOORS Career Conference and Workshop, a special one-week program designed to introduce minority and disadvantaged young people to career options in financial, service, manufacturing and media industries in the greater Metropolitan region. We are requesting a contribution of $10,000 to support this project.

If you should have any questions, need anything further, or would like to schedule a visit to any of our current programs, please don't hesitate to contact me.

Thank you again for your consideration.

Very truly yours,

Dr. Mara Lewis
Program Director
VISIONQUEST

I. INTRODUCTION [INCLUDES PROJECT SUMMARY, STATEMENT OF NEED, OBJECTIVES]

There are a number of thriving industries in the greater Metropolitan region, yet studies show that young people from minority and disadvantaged homes do not easily make their way into these industries, even at entry-level positions. Part of the reason has to do with expectations on the part of young people themselves, part with difficulties that many young people have in adjusting to the behavioral norms of the world of work. VISIONQUEST has addressed these issues in several of its programs, yet one hidden obstacle often remains: simple lack of information about the business world. While young people from middle-class or educated environments may know quite a bit about the career options open to them, as part of their general knowledge, the same cannot be assumed for many disadvantaged and minority young people.

These young people are in many ways cut off from information about the kinds of careers available, and they perceive limited options based on what they see in their neighborhoods, what they know of through friends and family members, and what they see on television. They may only know of jobs that seem either insecure and exploitive, or simply out of reach, and are thus unable to develop concrete goals and aspirations that would help motivate school study and personal development. With no information about challenging, rewarding work, many young people become increasingly alienated from the world of work, turning to dangerous, illegal activities, or simply giving up hope.

This is the need that the OPEN DOORS Career Conference and Workshop is intended to address. OPEN DOORS has three principal goals:

1. To introduce young people to the variety of occupations and careers that are available in the major industries of the region—financial, service, manufacturing, and media.
2. To provide each participant with a thorough understanding of how a selected one of these industries functions by the end of the one-week workshop experience.
3. To offer each participant individual counseling and information about further education, training, mentoring, and financial aid that might support their career goals or explorations. This would include information about the ongoing OPEN DOORS workshops in workplace habits and behavior.

VISIONQUEST is a ten-year-old educational organization, with experience in bringing together educators and businesspeople to enrich the educational process in the Metropolitan area. It began by forging links between specific high schools and colleges and the business community, bringing professionals into the schools to offer presentations on career options, and offering work-study mentoring and counseling on an individual basis. For five years it has successfully operated the OPEN DOOR Training Program, which is a rigorous training program for minority young people and adults in the culture, expectations, language, dress and behavior patterns of the workplace. Graduates of the Program are supported in active job searches, most of them successful. The OPEN DOORS Career Conference and Workshop is a natural expansion of VISIONQUEST's mission and activities.

II. PLAN OF EVENTS

The OPEN DOORS workshop will be hosted by Metropolitan University, at its central campus, and will begin with a "Career Fair," including exhibits, introductory presentations by academics and industry professionals, and counseling. This will be followed by three days of intensive exploration of an industry that each participant will select, including counseling focused on that industry. Participants will be able to meet and learn directly from prominent and successful professionals in various fields. They will visit active business locations: banks, law offices, factories, television stations, graphic design studios.

Young people of high school or college age will be able to register through their educational institutions or community groups, or directly through VISIONQUEST. Scholarship stipends will cover such costs as lunch and dinner each day in the Metropolitan University dining hall; chartered bus transportation, counselor supervision and guidance; college and career counseling provided by experienced Metropolitan University faculty; all program activities and seminar materials.

III. EVALUATION AND CONTINUATION OF PROJECT

It is anticipated that after initial funding, the OPEN DOORS Career Conference will be an annual event and will be continued for years to come.

Measurable results of the program will include an outreach campaign and an overall recruitment effort geared toward attracting disadvantaged and minority young people with potential. VISIONQUEST will disseminate news of the conference in various ways, including brochures and program materials; liaison with area schools, colleges, and community groups; and publicity/recruitment stories carried by the media, as well as through VISIONQUEST public relations efforts.

VISIONQUEST will maintain annual records documenting the numbers of young people participating in the program. A specific evaluation form will be designed for participants, and will induce individual appraisals of the program in the following areas: (1) if they feel the program enhanced their basic understanding of how the various industries work; (2) whether they are likely to pursue careers in those areas; (3) specifically what was of most interest to them; (4) what educational and career value they received from the program; and (5) their recommendations for improving the program to enhance the experience for future participants.

VISIONQUEST will also conduct follow-up surveys one, two, and three years after the program to identify any specific correlations between conference participation and educational or career choices.

IV. SUMMARY

Over the years, VISIONQUEST has received strong support from the Metropolitan educational and business communities. This support has been continued for the OPEN DOORS Career Conference, with Metropolitan University offering facilities and personnel and with members of the local business community offering their time and expertise, as well as financial support. We see this as an opportunity to make a real difference in the often-difficult lives of our young people, a way to offer them challenges and goals and to help bring them into the mainstream world of work.

LIST OF ATTACHMENTS (SUPPORTING DOCUMENTATION)

a. Budget for OPEN DOORS Career Conference and Workshop
b. Organizational budget for current and upcoming fiscal years
c. Copy of most recent financial statements
d. Proof of tax-exempt status
e. List of current supporting organizations (other funding received)
f. OPEN DOORS Training Program brochure
g. *Metropolitan Daily News* article on OPEN DOORS
h. Youth underemployment studies
i. OPEN DOORS Career Conference schedule of events
j. VISIONQUEST's Board of Directors (personnel)

OPEN DOORS CAREER CONFERENCE BUDGET

Salaries:

Conference director	$ 6,000
Administrative assistant	$ 4,000
Conference Week counselors	$ 6,000
Consultants	$ 3,000

Fringe benefits	$ 1,500
Administrative Overhead:	
Office expenses, telephone	$ 800
Bookkeeping	$ 300
Outreach, Advertising and Promotion:	
Fund raising, printing, postage, publicity	$ 3,000
Liability Insurance Rider:	$ 600
Fees:	
Metropolitan College facilities	$ 4,000
Food service and catering	$ 4,000
Transportation (buses)	$ 800
Program Materials and Surveys:	$ 1,000
TOTAL EXPENSES	$35,000

THE BIG PICTURE

When you've finished a draft of your proposal, look over the whole package to see how the various parts work together. Make sure there is a genuine progression. See that the needs or problems that you've described in your statement of need are clearly connected to your mission statement. Make sure the statement of need connects to the mission and interests of the funder as well. See if the objectives clearly answer the needs, and that your plan includes specific steps to achieve each objective. Make sure your plan justifies whatever will appear in your budget. Ask yourself if the evaluation will give the funder a sense of whether you will have achieved your objectives. Make sure résumés or bios seem relevant to your project, and put supporting documentation to the same test. Also take the following six final steps:

1. Look over your cover letter, and your statement of need, to be sure that you haven't been too emotional or melodramatic in stating the need for your project. Make sure that you've avoided leaning on political arguments or taking a political position. A simple statement of facts will be the strongest support for your project.
2. Look again at your objectives, and check that they are clear and attainable, not vague, long-term goals that simply restate your mission. Make sure, too, that you are not merely listing steps in your plan.

3. Make sure your plan includes the three basic elements: location of the project or activity, steps for accomplishing the objectives, and a timeline or schedule.

4. Make sure that your résumé clearly conveys your qualifications to do the project. Check your supporting documentation. Don't pad this section—use relevant documents only.

5. Look again at your budget, and be sure you have followed any guidelines from the funder about budget items or format. Make sure the need or use for line items has been clearly stated or implied in your plan. Make sure you've added all your figures correctly!

6. Look over the whole proposal once more and make sure that you are giving the funder all the information that they need to make a decision. Make sure that you've included outreach ideas wherever they fit. You can discuss outreach in the statement of need, objectives, plan, or evaluation. Depending on your project, outreach might even be part of your mission statement.

Don't do this right before sending out a proposal, but as you're working on the draft, you might want to show it to one or two *experienced* people for constructive criticism or response. "Experienced" means someone familiar with proposal writing and the nonprofit field. You might also want to have a freelance consultant look over your work. (See Chapter 2 for more on this.) Don't wait till the last minute—you don't want someone to devastate you with criticism the day before you have to send out your proposal.

A SPECIAL CASE: GOVERNMENT APPLICATIONS

Government applications are quite a bit different from private and corporate-style proposals. Instead of supplying the agency with your basic proposal, you'll have to fill in the blanks on complicated application forms. These often ask you to separate out and break down information in very specific and seemingly peculiar ways. You may have to do a lot of cutting and pasting and rework the material from your basic proposal to fit the government requirements. You may also have to do some additional research.

The forms can be quite long, require detailed information, and include specific requests and limitations. You may have to make multiple photocopies and add several attachments. Some of these intricacies can be intimidating even to the seasoned professional. But don't worry. Just follow the instructions in a step-by-step way and you won't have any problems.

It's a good idea to make your own photocopies of the blank forms, so that you can do rough drafts before typing up the final versions. Just go along, following the instructions and filling in the blanks. You *must* fill all of them in. If a question is not applicable, type N/A in the blank.

Government forms are usually broken down into sections. They may follow the format of the generic proposal, with boxes or blank lines for a project summary, objectives, timeline, budget, future funding, or other funders applied to. Or they may use different headings. Break up your proposal into the parts they ask for. This is almost like filling out a tax form, although the results may be more pleasant. The application may give you less space than you'd like to respond to a question. You really have to boil down your information into the clearest, briefest, strongest statements. Tinker with the wording of your responses until you get the best version you can.

There may be boxes that you can fill in with a paragraph or two, or just a few lines. You can type up a response on a blank page or a word processor, and cut it out to see if it will fit in the space provided. Cut and reword until you make it fit. The application guidelines will often warn you in dire terms not to go outside the allotted space, so do be careful. Sometimes you'll have the opportunity to attach a page in support of a particular entry on the form. If you do this, make sure you head the page with exactly the same entry name and number that appear on the application form. Type "See attached" on the form. Put your name and the agency to which you are applying on each separate attached page, in case it gets lost or separated from the rest of the application.

Government budget forms can be extremely detailed and may require you to enter information in ways that seem awkward and nonintuitive. You may have to rework your budget quite a bit to get it into the required form. Government budget forms demand extreme precision, requiring you to calculate all costs down to the last penny (though some will ask you to round off figures). You'll have to break down any travel expenses on a per diem basis.

You'll find that government application guidelines are usually very specific about what kind of support documentation is required or permitted. You may be asked to submit testimonials, endorsements, press clippings, photos, videos, artwork, etc. Send in only what's requested or specifically allowed, and in the specified format.

When you are ready to do the final draft of the application, type carefully, neatly correct any errors, and proofread for typos. You'll usually be asked to submit the application in duplicate or triplicate. You should also make copies of everything you are submitting for your own files. Carefully follow any guidelines on the physical format of the application. Use a removable binder if permitted, or just use paperclips or binder clips for each set of copies. Send the entire application in one folder or with a big binder clip to keep it together. Address it as the guidelines indicate.

The forms and guidelines aren't always clear, and you may be stumped by something as you are filling out an application or getting ready to submit one. You can try calling up the agency to see if there is someone on the staff who can help you. Some of the larger agencies can seem very impersonal and you may find it difficult to get anyone to listen to your questions. Be persistent if you truly have a question that you cannot answer yourself. You can also get in touch with someone at a nonprofit or service organization that is familiar with this program and ask them for advice.

WRAPPING IT ALL UP AND SENDING IT IN

So you've finally put all the pieces together and you have your complete proposal ready to send out. Before you send it, do some last-minute checking, as every good development officer does. Look at the checklist below, and make sure you have included every element that you need.

1. *Cover Letter.* Double-check that you have addressed this to the right person. If it's been three or four weeks since you got their name, call right before submitting your proposal. The contact person might have changed in the meantime.
2. *Title page*
3. *Table of contents*
4. *Project summary*—maximum one page!

5. *Statement of need*
6. *Objectives*
7. *Plan*—location, steps, timeline
8. *Evaluation*
9. *Personnel*—your résumé or bio and any others
10. *Budget*
11. *Other funding received*—if applicable
12. *Future funding and support*—if applicable
13. *Official certification and signatures*—if applicable
14. *Supporting documentation.* Don't pad—include relevant items only.

If all the components are there, proofread the proposal one last time for spelling and typos. Check for general neatness and retype pages if you have to. If the funder has asked for additional copies, make them, and *always* make one for your files. Be sure you have a copy of each piece of supporting documentation as well. Put your copy in the file you are keeping for this funder, and note on the file folder the date you send the proposal out. If you are using a wall chart or calendar, mark the date on that as well.

I had a personal experience that demonstrates exactly why you must make a copy of each proposal you send out. Some years ago, a client of mine was up for a major grant. The foundation was interested in the project but couldn't find their copy of the proposal we had sent them. We were close to the deadline, we had to get them a copy of the proposal, and it turned out that somebody in my office had sent it to them without making a copy. I went nuts. Luckily, the foundation found it, or we would have lost the grant. So foundations can misplace things; you *must* make copies of proposals.

Your proposal is ready. Now you look at your wall chart or calendar and see that you still have time before the deadline. You can send it by regular first-class mail, or perhaps U.S. Priority Mail. I don't like to send proposals certified—return receipt requested or not—because I think it annoys the funder. The nonprofit world is still a little bit in the nineteenth century, and you need to follow different rules than in normal business. If you're down to the wire, you could send your proposal by U.S. Express Mail, or by Federal Express, but you shouldn't be pushing the deadline like this. Don't send the proposal by messenger, or hand-deliver it, unless you are at the eleventh hour. It's best just to send it through the regular first-class mail, well in advance of the deadline. The low-key, low-pressure approach works best with funders, and sending your proposal in early shows that you've got your act together.

THE WAITING GAME

You've put a lot of time, care, and consideration into writing your proposal. Once you have submitted it, though, there's nothing to do but wait. Some foundations will send you a reply card or form letter to let you know that your proposal has been received and that you will be notified of its status shortly. If a foundation has not contacted you after twelve weeks, you should call them, just to make sure they have received the proposal. Making one follow-up call shows that you are on top of things; if you start making too many calls, you'll be seen as pushy and overly eager. Do not make more than one, unless a funder has given you the go-ahead to call them.

Sometimes funders will contact you if they have questions about your project, or if they want to meet with you about it. If you have the opportunity to meet with a grant officer, this is a chance to create a good personal impression and to explain your project in detail. You should prepare for such a meeting carefully and bring any supporting materials that might be useful, including more detailed budget notes.

On the other hand, many funders will advise you not to call them but to wait until their Board of Trustees meets and makes its decision. The larger foundations in particular are so inundated with proposals that they do not want to be bothered with any questions. Their guidelines will usually specifically instruct individuals not to contact them until a few months after the submission of the proposal. If a funder's guidelines state, "No personal calls whatsoever," you should respect this. If it seems that the decision period has passed and you've heard nothing, you could send them a brief note, saying that you sent them a proposal on such-and-such a date and you just want to confirm that they received it. If you never do hear from a funder, just assume that they weren't for you and go on to the next one. This is why you send proposals to a number of different funding sources.

Don't feel discouraged if funders seem remote and unavailable. This is the way they must operate in order to be able to process the vast number of proposals they get. Also, don't feel discouraged if they don't contact you about your application. Most people who get grants simply send in their proposals, wait until the funder makes a decision, and receive notice of their grant at that time.

The waiting game requires patience. If you have been thorough in working up your mission statement and your plan, if you've been careful about selecting the right funders to apply to, if you've written the best proposal you can, then you have a good chance of getting a grant. When you're notified whether you got the grant or not, take a look at the next chapter to consider how to proceed.

FOLLOW-UP

YOU ARE AWARDED A GRANT!

Congratulations! You may receive the news through the mail or, more informally, over the telephone. If it's by telephone, wait for your formal notification letter before beginning your project. And hang on to that letter. Put it in the funder's file, which has just advanced from potential to actual status.

Your notification letter should indicate the amount you've been granted and the schedule of payment. The grant check may be enclosed with the notification letter, or it may follow close behind (usually through the mail). If you are working with a sponsor organization, the check will probably be made out and mailed to them. In any case, don't spend your own money on the project before receiving the promised grant funds. Wait until all the details are settled before moving ahead.

Once you have received formal notification of funding, you should write a brief thank-you letter to the funder. Expressing your gratitude will help you build a positive relationship with the funder. You want to stay on good terms not only for the funding period but afterward, in case you later seek additional funding from the same source, or referrals to other funding sources. If you receive the check some time after the notification, write again just to let them know it has arrived.

LITTLE GRANTS AND BIG: THEY ALL ADD UP

You may have been fortunate enough to be awarded a grant but still feel discouraged because it wasn't as much as you requested, or isn't enough to fund your whole project. Do understand, most funders do not expect to underwrite an entire project. The only time a funder will pay for your whole project, and do so exclusively, is when they want to take full credit for it. A perfect example is Mobil Oil's single-handed support of "Masterpiece Theater."

Usually, though, grant amounts are based on what funders feel they can give, or want to give, to your project. So if you requested $10,000 and they only give you $5,000, don't be disappointed. It is simply that they want to make awards to a certain number of different applicants. Getting any grant is an honor, and you should be pleased to be one of the recipients.

If you can't complete your project with what you have been given, I advise you to accept the partial funding and pursue additional funding elsewhere. Yes, it is tough to keep on trying to raise money, but it's not impossible. Receiving one grant makes your case stronger for other funders. If you have raised a good percentage of the funding, chances are good that you will raise the rest of the money—as long as you keep trying.

I once worked with a television producer who had a very timely project, which we had to find support for quickly. She had a budget of $120,000; after quite a bit of hard work I managed to raise $70,000 for her, but it was time to start production. She was so discouraged by not having raised the whole sum that she seriously suggested returning all the money, thinking she just couldn't do it for that amount. I couldn't believe it. Fortunately, I was able to line up additional in-kind services that made it possible for her to finish the project. The point is: if you get a substantial part of the funding you need, there is usually a way to go ahead with your project, even if it's on a smaller scale.

ARE THERE STRINGS ATTACHED?

Before you start spending the grant money, establish where there are special restrictions or requirements regarding expenditures. Usually these will be very carefully spelled out in your award letter, or have already been announced in the guidelines. If you're not sure about a restriction, ask the funder for clarification. Many of the points below will apply only to complex, sponsored projects, but some may come into play for the individual.

Be sure you understand *any restrictions on the types of expenditures* you are allowed to make with the grant money. For example, some foundations will not let their funds be used for administrative salaries, or to purchase equipment. Others may forbid use of their funds for advertising or press releases.

There may be *time* restrictions on the grant. You may be expected to use all the funds within a certain period. If you've been awarded a challenge grant, or another kind of restricted grant, you may not be able to use the money immediately. (See Chapter 2 for more on challenge grants and matching grants.)

Content restriction is a special problem that has been much in the news, and the debate continues. In the past few years, a few artists and arts organizations awarded government grants were asked to sign a statement that they would not produce or present work that might be considered obscene. Some signed and some did not; eventually the requirement was removed. Recently, subject restrictions have started to appear in the humanities and scientific fields as well.

Some funders have *operating* restrictions that apply to the way scientists can do research or the kinds of materials they can use. Usually, though, these come into play when the funding decision is made, and recipients are not always required to sign agreements.

People have different views about some of these restrictions. Some feel that if you are going to accept money from a patron, whether public or private, it's realistic to expect to accept any restrictions they might impose. Others feel that the principle of freedom of speech should apply to government funding. They draw an analogy to academic freedom in colleges and universities. This is very much a matter of personal opinion.

You should be aware, though, that if you refuse to accept content or operating restrictions, you may have to give up the grant. This may also affect your future funding possibilities, though in unpredictable ways. It could jeopardize your future funding with the particular agency, or with other agencies. On the other hand, some people who have turned down grants on this basis have suddenly found themselves offered awards from private sources.

If you do have problems with this issue and want to talk to others who are concerned with it, you can contact:

- People for the American Way
  2000 M Street, N.W., Suite 400
  Washington, DC 20036
  202-467-4999

Even when project content is not an issue, you will on rare occasions be asked to sign an *agreement* with the funder. Usually this simply means agreeing to whatever restrictions or requirements are listed in the guidelines. If you don't understand all the terms, talk to someone at the program or foundation. This is a very civilized business, and dialogue is welcome at this point of the process. If you're still unsure, do have a lawyer, or someone knowledgeable in the field, look at it.

Check on the *method of payment*. Will the funder send you one lump-sum check or pay out the grant in installments? Are installments keyed to the calendar or to stages of your project? If a sponsor is acting as your fiscal agent, they may receive the grant as a lump sum and dole out limited amounts to you. You should clarify this with your sponsor.

Financial recordkeeping is another important matter to clarify. What kinds of records will the funder require? If you have a sponsor, they may be responsible for keeping these records—but don't assume so. Discuss this point with your sponsor, as well as with your funder.

If you have a sponsor, you should set up a meeting to discuss *accounting procedures*. There may be some grant-related details to take into account, details not anticipated when you drew up and signed your formal letter of agreement. The person you should meet with at this point is the sponsor organization's fiscal officer (i.e., business manager), rather than the individual(s) with whom you arranged the sponsorship.

Find out whether or not the funder requires you to make regular *progress reports,* and if so, how often. How formal must these reports be? Is there a recommended or required format, or specific topics you must address? Get all the details you can—if you know beforehand about special requirements, you can keep appropriate notes as you go along and use these to create the progress reports.

Check on how your project will be *evaluated.* Does the funder require or prefer any specific type of evaluation process? Do they want to be involved, or will you be solely responsible for evaluating your success? When will you be expected to provide or participate in an evaluation?

USE YOUR FIRST GRANT TO GET MORE

One of the great benefits of getting the first grant is that it can help you raise more funds. If it's all right with the funder, you should certainly make public announcements about your grant in your field's local or professional papers. This may attract other funders, as well as increase your profile and credibility. And be sure to include this information in any new proposals you send out.

Can you ask for referrals to other funders after you've received a grant? Usually only if you are having a lot of dialogue with the funder and they broach the subject first. If a program officer is musing out loud, "This is the sort of thing that ABC likes to support," then you can definitely say, "Oh really, who should I approach over there?" But if you are having minimal contact with the funder, and they don't offer help first, don't bring it up yourself.

You also want to update any foundations or government agencies that are considering funding you. Send a brief letter of announcement to these funders, and add the information to your résumé as well.

There are occasions when a funder will not want you to announce your grant. This is rare, but you should always check with the funder before you publicize it or tell other funders. If your project receives any media attention, or if you plan to send out press releases (either announcing your grant award or just mentioning it in connection with a publicized opening or show), be sure to clear all public mention with the funder (and in some cases with the sponsor) beforehand. Many corporate foundations prefer that all their press coverage be coordinated through their own PR offices. Some funding sources avoid all media attention. Respect the wishes of the funder.

Likewise, if you are planning to use the funder's name in any brochures or programs, you should definitely get their approval first. Years ago, a client of mine got money from a major oil company for a series of symphony concerts. We printed up thousands of brochures, and then it turned out they did not want their name mentioned as underwriting the project. We were dumfounded (they had never minded before), but had to reprint the whole lot without their name. You don't have to clear all press releases and public information about your project with the funder, just those that mention them.

FORGING AHEAD—WORKING WITH THE FUNDER

After getting funded, it's important to maintain a good professional relationship with your funders. Keep them abreast of any new information about your project—send a brief note from time to time, telling of your progress. If you hold any kind of performance or public event, you should certainly invite them. If you are doing community outreach, send them a copy of any brochures or press releases. At the same time, remember that the funder's function is really to provide the support and then sit back and enjoy the results. Even if they've been helpful and cooperative, you shouldn't expect them to be interacting with you on a daily or weekly basis. If you encounter problems in doing your project, go to your sponsor, or try to get help through a service organization in your field. Don't ask a funder for more help than they've already given you.

With funding in hand, you are finally ready to forge ahead. As you devote your attention to the project itself, reserve some time for the paperwork and recordkeeping that funders, and perhaps the IRS, require. It's a good idea to set aside a specific time each week to do this.

FINANCIAL MANAGEMENT

It's extremely important to administer your grant in a professional, responsible manner. You have been privileged to receive grant money, and some responsibility comes along with it. You want to manage the finances professionally so that not only will your project succeed but you'll also be in a position to apply for further funding in the future.

Good financial management requires good recordkeeping. If the funder will ask for financial accounting, you need to keep records of all of your grant-related expenditures. Save receipts, make entries in a ledger book, do whatever it takes to create a complete and organized record of your grant spending. Behave as if you expect an audit. Your funder will appreciate accurate records of how their money was used. For smaller projects, though, the funder may expect only minimal accounting or none at all. Check your award announcement and guidelines carefully.

One way to keep good records is to get a ledger book with columns and use one column for each of your budget categories. Write checks, use credit cards, or keep receipts for your expenditures, and every week or two go through your receipts and checkbook, entering each expense in the appropriate column. Depending on your project, you may need to have a credit column (or columns) where you record funding received, or other income generated by your project.

- **TIP:** If you use a personal computer, a simple money management or checkbook program will help you keep track of your expenditures. You can set up an account or "check register" for your project and enter all expenses, dates, check numbers, and expense categories, and the program will automatically prepare reports with exact figures and category breakdowns.

If you received a very large grant and your project is complex, do set up a good, simple bookkeeping system such as any small business would use. For certain government grants, or a very large or long-term project, you will definitely be expected to provide detailed financial accounts. You might explore the possibilities of hiring a professional bookkeeper, which could cost from $100 to $150 a month, and which should be built into the budget. If you are working with a sponsor, they will already be taking care of most of this.

Do you have to worry about mingling grant monies with your other personal funds? Not necessarily. If you have received a small grant such as a scholarship, or several thousand dollars for a personal project, it isn't necessary to set up a separate bank account. You can deposit and write checks from your regular bank account as long as you keep separate records of your expenses.

If you're looking at more than a few thousand dollars in funding, you should consider setting up a separate bank account for the project. This can cost a little extra money, but you will have very clear records of all income and expenditures, and your balanced checkbook will itself be a good financial record.

TAXES

The bad news is that most grants, prizes, and awards to individuals are taxable, whether they come from private foundations, the government, or nonprofit organizations. This is another reason why you will want to keep careful records of all grant income and project-related expenses. The good news is that some of your grant expenditures may be deductible or even exempt.

The portion of the grant that covers your professional fee or salary is always taxable. If you are working on a career-related project, however, many of your expenditures may be deductible as business expenses. If you're a writer, a painter, or a researcher, and you sometimes earn money from your work—or plan to—you can deduct such expenses as the cost of materials, research expenses, tools and equipment, and project-related travel. The usual way to deduct these expenses is to file an IRS Schedule C form, on which you declare business income and expenses. However, detailed tax advice is really beyond the scope of this book. You should consult a qualified accountant or tax preparer, or do some research on your own. If you do decide to work with a professional, get someone who is familiar both with your field and with grants. There are also a number of printed references you can turn to for help with proper tax procedures. A few are listed below.

- *The Artist's Tax Guide and Financial Planner,* by Carla Messman. New York: Lyons and Burford.
- *J. K. Lasser's Your Income Tax.* New York: Simon & Schuster (published annually).
- *J. K. Lasser's Tax Guide for Small Business.* New York: Simon & Schuster (published annually).
- *Tax Guide for College Teachers.* College Park, MD: Academic Information Service (published annually).

If you are funded through a sponsor, you are shielded from some tax liabilities because the sponsor is the actual recipient of the grant and is a nonprofit organization. This can simplify your recordkeeping a great deal—you may not have to get involved with business deductions. Still, any fees or salaries paid you by the sponsor are taxable.

There are other complications for individuals receiving grants. There is a special place to list grants, prizes, and awards on the IRS 1040 form. Fellowships and awards are taxable as income but are not subject to Social Security tax. They cannot be used as part of earned income for IRAs. Fulbright fellowships are taxable, but foreign income tax credit can be used to offset some tax liability. You get the picture— it's a complex situation, and you need to either have help or do the research.

The tax rules for students and graduate degree candidates can get even more complicated. Grants for tuition and related instructional expenses such as fees, books, supplies, and equipment are generally tax-exempt. Tuition remission is tax-exempt. However, grants for room, board, and living expenses are considered taxable income. The rules are different for degree and nondegree candidates, and there are special rules regarding Social Security tax exemption. The definition of whether you are receiving a scholarship or a fellowship becomes important—fellowships and assistantships are considered taxable income. Gifts are tax-free, while grants, prizes, and awards are subject to tax rules. There are special places to report tax-free grants on a tax return, and ways to report scholarships and grants to minimize the chance of an audit. Again, there is much more to this than we can cover here. You should find a good tax reference guide, or consult a specialist, or perhaps someone in your school's financial aid office can help with these issues.

PROGRESS AND PROJECT REPORTS

If your project is not too big, you may be asked to write an informal report at the end or deliver some kind of material as evidence and record of what you did. If it's a larger, more complex project, you may be asked to file formal progress reports, which you would send to your funder at regular intervals during the course of your project. The grant guidelines will spell out the reporting requirements, or a program officer will explain them when you are awarded the grant. Reporting requirements vary from funder to funder. If you're asked to file reports, put a little time and effort into making them readable and informative. Turn them in promptly. Make your funders feel that you are pleased by their interest and eager to share news of your project. Remember, you and the funder are now in a working relationship. You need to hold up your end of the bargain—especially if you might have to request additional funding in the future, for this project or others.

Even if formal reports aren't required, you should still keep your funders up to date about your project. One or two informal phone calls a year is sufficient. You don't want to overwhelm funders with your enthusiasm or intrude on their time. Even if it's not a requirement, do invite funders to any performances, shows, or demonstrations related to your project. This lets them see firsthand what their money has enabled you to accomplish.

IF YOU RUN INTO PROBLEMS

The most usual problems you might run into are delay in getting your project started, perhaps because you are still raising funds, or delay in finishing your project. If reports or evaluations are due at a certain time and you're just not ready to submit them, do write to the funder, explain the reason for the delay, and ask for an extension. Give an interim summary of progress, explain what stage you're at, and give an estimated schedule for completion. If grant payments are tied to calendar dates, or to stages of your project, ask for an extension of the scheduled payments beyond your original schedule and explain in detail the reasons for the delay. (We're not talking about additional payments, just about making scheduled payments beyond an initial cut-off date.) If funders see that you are committed to the project, working at it, and delayed by circumstances beyond your control, they will usually continue to support you. They want to see the project completed successfully.

What happens if you get grant monies, you start a project, disaster strikes, and you can't continue? Should you offer to give back part of the money? Not unless it is required, but it depends on the circumstances. You have probably spent some of the money developing the project. If you don't raise the entire budget, do you have to return the money? No, with the caveat that you must use it toward the project; you can't use it to buy groceries or pay your mortgage. If the project doesn't fly, the project doesn't fly. If there is a balance remaining that you haven't spent, I would encourage you to return it. It's a sign of professional responsibility, and it will stand you in better stead if you ever want to raise funds again.

Remember, funders have placed a high degree of trust in you and made a real commitment. You must deal with your funding responsibly. I once knew of a highly respected but rather unpredictable artist who got a prestigious government grant, used the money somehow, but never seemed to have really pursued the project he got the grant for and never made any kind of final report to the granting agency. They gave him the money and never heard from him again. This was a serious, committed artist, who was certainly not getting rich off grants, but he was blacklisted in the funding world for years. So you do want to follow up on your reporting, even if you run into problems.

This raises another question: What if in the middle of the project you suddenly get hit with a massive, unanticipated expense, or something affects your budget? Should you tell the funder? Yes and no. Chances are the funder will not increase your funding. Continue anyway, even if you can't do the complete project. You're going to have to shave expenses. I've seen this happen to project after project. You can also try to raise more funds. People are always dealing with the unexpected when working on big projects. When one budget category balloons, you just have to cut back on another.

IF YOUR REQUEST IS TURNED DOWN

A rejection notice is always disappointing.

Worse, some foundations don't even notify unsuccessful applicants. They only contact those to whom they are making awards. This limits administrative costs, especially when they are swamped with applicants. In most cases, you can find notification policies listed in the funder's application guidelines. If you have heard nothing, but the decision should have been made by now, call the funder to check on the status of your request. Be prepared for bad news. Remain polite and thank the individual on the phone for helping you.

WHAT DOES THIS MEAN?

How should you respond to being rejected by a funder? It's important to be realistic and not be thrown off course. You must realize that this is not a personal slight on your project. Perhaps the funder was over-committed. Perhaps it just wasn't meant to be for this cycle. Instead of dwelling on negativity, look at your proposal and project and see if they can be made to work better, or if you just need to keep trying with other funders.

Often, you'll find that a corporation, or even a foundation, that can't give you cash will think about making an in-kind donation.

Still, there are some legitimate, logical reasons why a funder might turn you down:

1. *Funding area.* The most common reason given in a rejection notice is that your project doesn't fit the guidelines or granting areas of the funder. This is something you shouldn't be getting too much of, since you did your research and should have ruled out any inappropriate funders. Still, you may have interpreted guidelines or announcements to mean something different from the funder's intentions. There isn't much you can do about this one; there's no point in trying to argue with a funder about their guidelines. Pack your bags and move on. But you might want to look again at your proposal. Did your statement of need clearly fit with the funder's mission? Consider this carefully for your next proposal.

2. *Lack of affiliation.* Another common reason for rejection is that the funder does not accept proposals from unaffiliated individuals. Again, this is a problem that you should have avoided through research and screening. Still, you may have applied to a funder that didn't clearly state their restrictions. There's nothing you can do about this except to go back again through a sponsor.

3. *Proposal problems.* It may be that your proposal simply wasn't strong enough to sell the funder on your idea. If you think this might be the case, go back to Chapter 9 again and measure your proposal against its recommendations. Look again at "The Big Picture" on page 297 and evaluate your proposal in terms of these guidelines and potential problems. If you think you have a proposal problem, consider having a freelance consultant look it over. Remember, a proposal problem could reflect a problem with your mission statement or the plan itself. Make sure these are carefully thought through.

4. *Budget problems.* The funder may have had a problem with your budget or with the cost of your project. They may have felt your budget was unrealistically small, or not reflective of actual costs in the field. Or they may have felt your budget was excessively padded, too luxurious, too big for a person of your experience to handle, or just so big that it would be too difficult to raise all the funds you would need. They won't always tell you this, but if you suspect it might be the problem,

you can sometimes try to get the information out of the funder. (See the next section, Finding Out Why.) Some of these determinations simply represent a judgment call on the funder's part, and another funder might not have the same problem. If you think your budget might be the trouble, though, take a careful look at it.

5. *Your idea or approach.* A more unpredictable reason for rejection is that the funder may have some negative history with your type of project. They may know that other people have tried the idea or approach you are proposing and it hasn't worked. Or they may disagree philosophically with it. They may even have a similar project under consideration, from someone with more experience or better credentials.

There isn't much you can do about this, and it's hard to find out if it's the problem. All you can do is to research your field and make sure you know about the kinds of projects that other people have done. If you suspect that others may be proposing similar projects, be sure to present your unique insights and skills in your proposal. If you know that your idea has been tried before but was never successfully implemented, do try to clarify in your proposal and plan what will give it the edge to succeed. Never, however, directly compare your project to failed projects. You might end up scaring a funder that hadn't even heard of the failures.

6. *Your qualifications.* Another problem, and perhaps the most frustrating, is that the funder may like your idea and your approach but feel that you don't have the experience or qualifications to do it. You won't find it easy to learn if this is the problem, and it's not an easy one to solve. If lack of experience is indeed the case, you still may find another funder willing to take a chance on you. You can try to bring in a collaborator with more experience to back you up. If you are applying as an individual, you can consider going through a sponsor, which will add its credibility to yours.

7. *Your sponsor.* The funder may like your idea but feel that your sponsor is somehow not the right one. If the problem is the sponsor, this gets sticky, and it's hard to even find this out. A funder may think your sponsor is too inexperienced in your project area, or that your sponsor's mission doesn't really fit with your project. If you have done your research and selected

your sponsor carefully, you shouldn't run into such trouble. Don't be too quick to change a sponsor. You have spent some time building up this relationship, and there are many other reasons why a proposal can be rejected. Still, if you get some very clear feedback that there is a problem with your sponsor, and you feel that this could influence other potential funders, you should consider a change.

FINDING OUT WHY

It is not easy to get frank details on why you were turned down; in fact, usually it is just impossible. Sometimes, however, you can get hints or clues from a funder. You are in a stronger position to get information if a funder informed you that you were under consideration, and the board then didn't approve your project. In such a case, program officers may be willing to speak with you in some detail. Usually, though, finding out the reasons behind a rejection is very hit-or-miss. It may be more worthwhile for you to put your energies into pursuing other prospects.

Still, you may be able to glean something that will help you. If you are informed by telephone that your proposal has been rejected, gently try to find out why. Make it clear that you aren't trying to change anyone's mind, but you would like some constructive criticism to improve your chances next time.

If you get a form letter turning you down, the letter itself may give you a clue. If it tells you that the funder doesn't give to individuals, or that your project isn't in the funder's area of interest, just fold up your tent and move on. And be more careful in evaluating future potential funders. If the letter says that they "had many fine proposals and just couldn't fund all of them," it may be impossible to find out more.

Again, the only time I really recommend that you talk to a program officer is if you were told that you were being considered for funding and you then got turned down by committee. In this case it's appropriate to call the funder and try to find out more information. If you got a simple rejection letter at the outset, do not call the foundation. If you were under consideration, call up and ask for the program officer who signed your rejection letter. Very briefly ask if there was something you could have done, or should do in your next application, to improve your chances. Don't be defensive, don't argue points, just take it all in. Write down notes as you're talking, so you don't miss anything because of an emotional response to what you are hearing. Be sure to tell the program officer that you appreciate their taking the time to talk to you.

If you are dealing with a government agency, especially if it's a huge bureaucracy, it can be difficult to get any response. However, if your project reached a certain level of consideration, and you were in touch with officials about it, you may be able to get some feedback. If you were dealing with a state or local agency, such as an arts council, it may be easier. Try calling up and speaking to a staff person. Ask if they can give you the gist of a panel's assessment of your project. Explain that you are just trying to glean any information that might help you proceed with the project.

REFERRALS AND RESUBMISSIONS

There are cases when you should consider reapplying to a funder. This depends on the funder's reason for rejecting your application. If your project was outside their mission or area of interest, just move on to other funders. If your project was recommended to the Board of Trustees or Directors for consideration but not approved, then it's worth resubmitting.

Don't just send the proposal back immediately; wait until the next grant cycle. If you do plan to reapply, ask the funder if a resubmission of the same idea is allowed in the next funding cycle. (Some foundations prohibit this.) Make any revisions that you think might improve the proposal and add any new information about funding received. Many people do get funding on the second or third application. The funder sees that you are serious about the project, and if they've been considering other projects before yours, yours has now moved to the head of the line.

Depending on the reasons for rejection, you might be able to ask for referrals to other (perhaps more appropriate) funding sources. The nonprofit world has its own intricate interconnections. One funding organization may be able to direct you to several other organizations— organizations not known to much of the general public. Again, you should only ask about this if your proposal was under serious consideration, made it through the initial screening, and was up for a decision by the board. If you are a first-time grant seeker and just got a standard form letter, don't bother the foundation about this.

On rare occasions, you may be rejected for being outside the funding criteria, but it seems that you really do fit in, according to all that you read in the guidelines. If this is an initial turndown, it did not go to committee, and you were not considered by the board, you might consider reapplying. It may be that a staff member took a quick look at your proposal and misread or misunderstood it. Do look again at the guidelines, make sure you understand them clearly, and make sure your proposal and cover letter clearly state how you fit within the funder's mission and criteria. Don't bother calling program officers about this, but rework your proposal as needed and try again for the next funding cycle.

Some government agencies and private foundations convene special panels, sometimes called *peer panels*, to make their funding decisions. Very often some of the panelists change from funding cycle to funding cycle. You can usually find out about this by reading guidelines or reports. If you're rejected by a panel for one cycle, it may be worth reapplying for the next. New panelists may have a different and more positive view of your project. Sometimes, though, depending on how panelists are chosen, a panel can develop a character or perspective that persists even though the individuals rotate. Still, you might get lucky and have an individual panelist really support your case. So it can be worthwhile to reapply two or three times to some funders.

WHAT TO DO NEXT

Failing to get a grant does not make your idea worthless. As we've discussed in this chapter, there are many factors that can cause a funder to turn down a proposal. Sometimes ideas are timely and sometimes they are not. Luck definitely plays a part in getting a grant. I often light candles.

If you do get turned down, you may feel anger and self-doubt, but you cannot let this get to you. You have to focus again on the worth of your project and your passion for it, and this will keep you going.

What should you do next? Look again at the possible reasons for a turndown listed in this chapter. See if you think any of these apply to you and whether you can adjust your proposal and fund-raising campaign. If you can get any reasons at all, try to apply them. If it seems appropriate, ask for referrals or revise and resubmit your proposal.

You may also want to revise or adapt your idea to the current funding climate—that is, to the kinds of issues that funders are currently concerned with. It may be that you can refocus your statement of need, or find a new application for your idea. I remember my client with the low-cost shelters, who shifted from the need for international disaster relief, which had little funding interest, to the need for shelter for the homeless, which was a timely problem. Or the client who got funding for hiring personnel by focusing on hiring recovering alcoholics. Or the client with the water-purifying filter who tied his project to environmental concerns. See if you can connect your idea to a need that funders want to support.

One of the toughest problems to solve is the funders' perception that your qualifications or experience are not adequate to the project. If you are passionate enough, and do enough good planning and preparation, you may be able to overcome this. It may help to work as an intern in your field, building up contacts and experience. You can also consider teaming up with more experienced collaborators.

If you are just getting started in a field, you may simply need to develop your work and ideas further and build stronger evidence of your abilities. You may want to try doing something on a low-budget, speculative, or volunteer basis to get more experience, or to create work that shows your abilities. If you are an artist, painter, or choreographer, you may have to develop a greater body of work, a record of shows and performances, or stronger samples. It can sometimes be very refreshing to step back from the grant-application grind and really focus on what you want to do, on a smaller scale and a more independent basis.

If you are rejected by all the funders you apply to, should you give up? It depends on how passionate you are about the project. Independent filmmakers confront this issue all the time. Some will never work on a project if they don't have the money up front; others will work on smaller projects, or plunge in and try to get a film started even without all the funding in place. Many have spent years raising money for their projects, and have kept on working at them without any idea where the rest of the money would come from. Sometimes the films have been completed and sometimes they haven't. It all depends on the extent of your commitment and your passion, on your willingness to take certain risks. I think of Julie Dash, an African American independent filmmaker who took seven years to complete her first feature, *Daughters of the Dust*. Along the way, she enlisted support from all kinds of people who believed in the project, and she finally got the completion funding from American Playhouse, which permitted her to go ahead and finish the film. If you believe in your project, and you do have a good one, you should eventually get funding. It just may take a while.

APPENDIX: BOOKS AND RESOURCES

GUIDES TO FUNDERS—GENERAL GUIDES

Annual Register of Grant Support: A Directory of Funding Sources, edited by Linda Peterson. Wilmette, IL: National Register Publishing Co., 1990, 24th edition (published annually).

GUIDES TO FUNDERS—BY FUNDER TYPE

FOUNDATIONS

Directory of New and Emerging Foundations. New York: The Foundation Center, 1991, 2nd edition.

Foundation Giving: Yearbook on Facts and Figures on Private, Corporate and Community Foundations. New York: The Foundation Center, 1991 edition.

The Foundation Directory. New York: The Foundation Center, 1992 edition (or latest edition).

The Foundation Directory, Part 2: A Guide to Grant Programs $25,000–$100,000. New York: The Foundation Center, 1990, 1991/1992 edition (or latest edition).

Foundation Grants to Individuals. New York: The Foundation Center, 1991, 7th edition (or latest edition).

National Data Book of Foundations: A Comprehensive Guide to Grantmaking Foundations. New York: The Foundation Center, 1992, 16th edition.

Public Media Center's Index of Progressive Funders. San Francisco: Public Media Center, 1985.

Selected Grant Guides by Subject. New York: The Foundation Center, published annually. A series of thirty guides to foundation giving. Each guide covers one subject or population. Contact the Foundation Center for specific titles.

Source Book Profiles: An Information Service on the 1,000 Largest U.S. Foundations. New York: The Foundation Center, 1991.

CORPORATIONS

Corporate 500: The Directory of Corporate Philanthropy. San Francisco: Public Management Institute, 1991, 10th edition (or latest edition).

Corporate Giving Directory. Rockville, MD: The Taft Group, 1992, 13th edition (or latest edition).

National Directory of Corporate Giving. New York: The Foundation Center, 1991, 2nd edition (or latest edition).

GOVERNMENT

Catalog of Federal Domestic Assistance. Washington: Government Printing Office, 1991, published annually.

Free Dollars from the Federal Government, by Laurie Blum. New York: ARCO Publishing, Inc., 1991.

The United States Government Manual. The Office of the Federal Register. This describes the broad responsibilities of all the major federal government departments and agencies. It doesn't list grant programs specifically but does list various publications that are offered by each agency. If you know that an agency does give grants—and many do—you can find useful information about them in some of these publications. You can contact the relevant agencies to have your name put on their mailing lists for program information.

Government Assistance Almanac 1992–93, by J. Robert Dumouchel. Detroit: Omnigraphics, Inc., and Washington, DC: Foggy Bottom Publications, 1992, 6th edition.

Guide to Federal Grants & Financial Aid: For Individuals and Nonprofit Organizations, edited by Calvin Fenton and Charles Edwards. Dubuque, IA: Kendall/Hunt Publishing Co., 1985, 2nd edition.

1992 Guide to Federal Funding for Governments and Nonprofits, edited by Charles Edwards. Vols. 1 and 2. Arlington, VA: Government Information Services, 1992.

To find your local U.S. Government Bookstore, call 202-512-0132.

To order U.S. Government publications by mail write:

U.S. Government Printing Office
Superintendent of Documents
Washington, DC 20402

For general information about U.S. government programs, contact, the Federal Information Center nearest you. The main office is:

Federal Information Center
P.O. Box 600
Cumberland, Maryland 21501-600
Tel.: 301-722-9098

Federal Assistance Programs Retrieval System (FAPRS). There are designated
access points in each state where you can ask for a computer search of
the database. You can also access the database through some commercial
computer-network companies.

For more information, contact:

Federal Domestic Assistance Catalog Staff
General Services Administration, Ground Floor, Reporters Building
300 7th Street, S.W.
Washington, DC 20407
Tel.: 800-669-8331, 202-708-5126

For literature on federal business loans, write or call:
The Director
Loan Policy and Procedures Branch
Small Business Administration
409 Third Street, S.W.
Washington, DC 20416
Tel.: 202-205-6570

SMALL ORGANIZATIONS, PRIZES, AWARDS

Awards, Honors and Prizes, edited by Gita Siegman. Vol. 1: *United States and
Canada.* Vol. 2: *International & Foreign.* Detroit: Gale Research, 1991,
9th edition.

INDIVIDUAL DONORS

Biographical Dictionaries Master Index. This gives information on 53 different
biographical references to living individuals.
Current Biography. New York: Wilson Company, monthly and annual.
Martindale-Hubbel Law Directory.
Medical Specialists Directory.
"The Richest People in America, The Forbes Four Hundred," *Forbes.*
The Social Register 1992. New York: Social Register Association, 1991 (and
annually). This lists prominent families, with names and addresses, clubs,
organizations, and affiliations.
Standard & Poor's Register for corporate executives.
Trustees of Wealth. Washington, D.C.: Taft Corporation.

Who's Who. Various volumes, by profession, population, and region. Consider which volumes might best lead you to potential donors.

GUIDES TO FUNDERS—BY SUBJECT AND POPULATION GROUP

THE ARTS

General

ARIS Funding Messenger: Creative Arts and Humanities Report. San Francisco: Academic Research Information System. Special rates for individuals, 8 issues per year.

Artist's Market: Where and How to Sell Your Artwork, edited by Lauri Miller. Cincinnati: Writer's Digest Books, 1991.

The Business of Art, edited by Lee Evan Caplin. Englewood Cliffs, NJ: Prentice-Hall, 1989, 2nd edition.

Free Money for People in the Arts, by Laurie Blum. New York: Macmillan Press, 1991.

Grants for the Arts, by Virginia P. White. New York: Plenum Press, 1980.

Guide to Funding for Emerging Artists and Scholars, by Jennifer Sarbacher. Washington: President's Committee on the Arts and the Humanities, 1991.

The National Directory of Grants and Aid to Individuals in the Arts, by Nancy A. Fandel. Arts Patronage Series, no. 15. Des Moines, IA: Arts Letters, 1989.

National Guide to Funding in Arts and Culture. New York: The Foundation Center, 1992, 2nd edition.

1992 Guide to Funding for Arts & Culture, edited by James Marshall. Virginia: Educational Funding Research Council, 1992.

Performing Arts

Dramatists Sourcebooks: Complete Opportunities to Playwrights, Translators, Composers, Lyricists and Librettists, edited by Angela E. Mitchell and Gillian Richards. New York: Theatre Communications Group, 1989.

Money for Performing Artists, edited by Suzanne Niemeyer. New York: American Council for the Arts, 1991.

Money for Performing Artists: A Guide to Grants, Awards, Fellowships, Artists Residencies, and More, edited by Suzanne Niemeyer. New York: American Council for the Arts, 1991.

Film and Video

The Independent Film and Videomaker's Guide, by Michael Wiese. Studio City, CA: Michael Wiese Productions, 1990, revised edition.

Money for Film and Video Artists, edited by Suzanne Niemeyer. New York: American Council for the Arts, 1991.

Museums and Collections
Funding for Museums, Archives and Special Collections, by Denise Wallen and Karen Cantrel. Phoenix: Oryx Press, 1988.
Official Museum Directory, by American Association of Museums. Wilmette, IL: National Register Publishing Co., 1988.

Music
Musical America: International Directory of the Performing Arts. New York: ABC Consumer Magazines, 1989.

Visual Arts
Money for Visual Artists, edited by Suzanne Niemeyer. New York: American Council for the Arts, 1991.

Writers
Grants and Awards Available to American Writers, edited by John Morrone. New York: PEN American Center, 1990.
Publication Grants for Writers & Publishers: How to Find Them, Win Them, and Manage Them, by Karin Park and Beth Luey. Phoenix: Oryx Press, 1991.

BUSINESS

Computer Grants Directory. San Francisco, CA: The Public Management Institute, 1991, 4th edition.
Free Money for Small Business & Entrepreneurs, by Laurie Blum. New York: John Wiley & Sons, 1992, 3rd edition.
How to Invest in Real Estate Using Free Money, by Laurie Blum. New York: John Wiley & Sons, 1991.
Pratt's Guide to Venture Capital Sources, edited by Jane Morris. Wellesley Hills, MA: Venture Economics, 1989, 13th edition.
Venture Capital, Where to Find It. Membership Directory. Washington: National Association of Small Business Investment Companies, 1985.

EDUCATION

General and Undergraduate
ARCO's College Financial Aid Annual, edited by John Schwartz. New York: ARCO Publishing, Inc., 1990.
Chronicle Student Aid Annual: For 1990–91 Schoolyear. Moravia, NY: Chronicle Guidance Publications.
College Blue Book. New York: Macmillan, 1991, 23rd edition.
Financing a College Education: The Essential Guide for the 90s, by Judith B. Margolin. New York: Plenum Press, 1989.
Free Money for College, by Laurie Blum. New York: Facts on File, 1992.

Free Money for Foreign Study, by Laurie Blum. New York: Facts on File, 1991.

Free Money for Private Schools, by Laurie Blum. New York: Simon & Schuster, 1992.

National Guide to Funding for Elementary and Secondary Education. New York: The Foundation Center, 1991.

1992 Guide to Funding for Education, edited by James Marshall. Virginia: Educational Funding Research Council, 1992.

Peterson's Guide to Four-Year Colleges 1991. Princeton, NJ: Peterson's Guides, 1990.

Scholarships, Fellowships and Loans 1992–93, by Debra McKinley. Detroit: Gale Research, 1991.

Graduate, Postgraduate, and Research

The Directory of Research Grants. Phoenix: Oryx Press, annual.

The Graduate Scholarship Book: The Complete Guide to Scholarships, Fellowships, Grants and Loans for Graduate and Professional Study. Englewood Cliffs, NJ: Prentice-Hall, 1990.

The Grants Register. New York: St. Martin's Press, published twice a year.

U.S. Government Support

Free Dollars from the Federal Government, by Laurie Blum. New York: ARCO Publishing, Inc., 1991.

ENVIRONMENT

National Guide to Funding for the Environment and Animal Welfare. New York: The Foundation Center, 1992, 1st edition.

Environmental Grantmaking Foundations 1992 Directory. Rochester, NY: Environmental Data Research Institute, 1992.

Environmental Grants: A Guide to Grants for the Environment from Government, Companies and Charitable Trusts, by Susan Forrester. London: Directory of Social Change, 1989.

HEALTH

AIDS Funding: A Guide to Giving by Foundations and Charitable Organizations. New York: The Foundation Center, 1991, 2nd edition.

Directory of Biomedical and Health Grants. Phoenix: Oryx Press, 1991, 6th edition.

Free Money for Diseases of Aging, by Laurie Blum. New York: Simon & Schuster, 1992.

Free Money for Heart Disease and Cancer Care, by Laurie Blum. New York: Simon & Schuster, 1992.

Handicapped Funding Directory, by Richard M. Eckstein. Margate, FL: Research Grant Guides, 1990, 7th edition.

National Guide to Funding in Aging. New York: The Foundation Center, 1990, 2nd edition.

National Guide to Funding in Health. New York: The Foundation Center, 1990, 2nd edition.

Scholarships and Loans for Nursing Education. New York: National League for Nursing, 1990.

HUMANITIES

Directory of Grants in the Humanities. Phoenix: Oryx Press, 1990.

National Endowment for the Humanities Annual Report. Washington: National Endowment for the Humanities, 1991.

HUMAN SERVICES

Free Money for Day Care, by Laurie Blum. New York: Simon & Schuster, 1992.

Fundraisers Guide to Human Service Funding, by Susan Elnicki. Rockville, MD: Taft Information, 1992, 3rd edition.

Towards a Solution to Homelessness: An Annotated Funding Directory. San Francisco: HomeBase, 1990.

MINORITIES

Black Americans Information Directory, 3d edition, edited by Julia C. Furtaw. Detroit: Gale Research, 1993.

Directory of Financial Aids for Minorities, 1991–93, by Gail Ann Schlachter. San Carlos, CA: Reference Service Press, 1991.

Guide to Multicultural Resources, edited by Charles Taylor. Madison, WI: Praxis Publications, 1989.

RELIGION

Religious Philanthropy 1992, edited by Bernard Jankowski. Rockville, MD: The Taft Group, 1992, 5th edition.

Foundation Guide for Religious Grantseekers, edited by Kerry A. Robinson. Atlanta: Scholars Press, 1992.

RESEARCH AND SCHOLARSHIPS

Annual Register of Grant Support, edited by Linda Peterson. Illinois: National Register Publishing Co., 1990.

Directory of Research Grants. Phoenix: Oryx Press, 1992.

Fiscal Year 1989 Awards by State and National Science Foundation Directorate. Washington: National Science Foundation, 1990.

The Graduate Scholarship Book: The Complete Guide to Scholarships, Fellowships, Grants and Loans for Graduate and Professional Study, by Daniel J. Cassidy. Englewood Cliffs, NJ: Prentice-Hall, 1990.

Research Centers Directory, edited by Karen Hill. 2 vols. Detroit: Gale Research, 1991, 16th edition.

SCIENCE

Directory of Biomedical and Health Care Grants. Phoenix: Oryx Press, 1991, 6th edition.

Fellowships and Grants for Training and Research: To Be Offered in 1991–1992. New York: Social Science Research Council, 1991.

Grants for Research and Education in Science and Engineering: An Application Guide. NSF, no. 90-77. Washington: National Science Foundation, 1990.

Grants for Science and Technology Programs. Grant Guides, no. 27. New York: Foundation Center, 1991.

TRAVEL

Financial Aid for Research, Study, Travel and Other Activities Abroad 1990–1991, by Gail Ann Schlachter and R. David Weber. San Carlos, CA: Reference Service Press, 1990.

Financial Resources for International Study: A Definitive Guide to Organizations Offering Awards for Overseas Study, by the Institute of International Education. Princeton, NJ: Peterson's Guides, 1989.

Free Money for Foreign Study, by Laurie Blum. New York: Facts on File, 1991.

Fulbright and Other Grants for Graduate Study Abroad 1992–1993. New York: Institute of International Education, 1991.

The International Scholarship Book: The Complete Guide to Financial Aid for Study Abroad. Englewood Cliffs, NJ: Prentice-Hall, 1990, 2nd edition.

WOMEN

Directory of Financial Aids for Women 1991–1992, by Gail Ann Schlachter. San Carlos, CA: Reference Service Press, 1991.

A Directory of Selected Research and Policy Centers Working on Women's Issues, compiled by Mary Anne Jorgensen. Washington: Women's Research and Education Institute, 1989.

Grants for Women and Girls. Grant Guide, no. 30. New York: Foundation Center, 1991.

FUNDER GUIDES—BY GEOGRAPHY

ALABAMA

Alabama Foundation Directory. Birmingham: Birmingham Public Library, 1990.

ARIZONA

Arizona Foundation Directory. Phoenix: Junior League of Phoenix, 1991.

ARKANSAS

The Guide to Arkansas Funding Sources, edited by Earl Anthes and Jerry Cronin. West Memphis, AK: Independent Community Consultants, 1990.

CALIFORNIA

Guide to California Foundations, by Carol Fanning. San Francisco: Northern California Grantmakers, 1988, 7th edition.
San Diego County Foundation Directory. San Diego: San Diego Community Foundation, 1989.

COLORADO

Colorado Foundation Directory. Denver: Junior League of Denver, 1990.

CONNECTICUT

The Connecticut Foundation Directory, edited by Michael Burns. Hartford: Development and Technical Assistance Center, 1990, 6th edition.

DELAWARE

Directory of Delaware Grantmakers: 1990. Wilmington: Delaware Community Foundation, 1990.

FLORIDA

The Complete Guide to Florida Foundations, edited by Lonna J. Myers Hord. Miami: John L. Adams, 1991, 4th edition.
Foundation Guide: N.E. Florida. Jacksonville: Volunteer Jacksonville, 1990.

GEORGIA

Foundation Profiles of the Southeast: Georgia, by James H. Taylor. Williamsburg, KY: James H. Taylor Associates, 1983.

HAWAII

Directory of Charitable Trusts and Foundations for Hawaii's Non-Profit Organizations, compiled by Marcie Hanson. Honolulu: Volunteer, Information and Referral Service, 1990, 2nd edition.

IDAHO

Directory of Idaho Foundations. Caldwell, ID: Caldwell Public Library, 1990, 5th edition.

ILLINOIS

The Directory of Illinois Foundations, edited by Marty Bowes. Chicago: Donors Forum of Chicago, 1990, 2nd edition.

Chicago's Corporate Foundations: A Directory of Chicago Area and Illinois Corporate Foundations, by Ellen Dick. Oak Park, IL: Ellen Dick, 1990, 2nd edition.

INDIANA

Directory of Indiana Donors. Indianapolis: Indiana Donors Alliance, 1989.

IOWA

Iowa Directory of Foundations, by Daniel Holm. Dubuque: Trumpet Associates, 1984.

KANSAS

The Directory of Kansas Foundations, edited by James Rhodes. Topeka: Topeka Public Library, 1991, 3rd edition.

KENTUCKY

A Guide to Kentucky Grantmakers, edited by Nancy Dougherty. Louisville: Louisville Foundation, 1982.

LOUISIANA

Citizen's Handbook of Private Foundations in New Orleans, compiled by Joseph Lazaro. New Orleans: Greater New Orleans Foundation, 1987.

MAINE

Directory of Maine Foundations. Portland: University of Southern Maine, 1990, 8th edition.

MARYLAND

Index of Private Foundations, 1989. Baltimore: Attorney General's Office, 1990.

MASSACHUSETTS

Massachusetts Grantmakers. Boston: Associated Grantmakers of Massachusetts, 1990.

Worcester County Funding Directory, edited by Jane Peck and Charlene Sokal. Worcester, MA: Worcester Public Library, 1991.

MICHIGAN

The Michigan Foundation Directory. Grand Haven, MI: Council of Michigan Foundations, 1991, 7th edition.

MINNESOTA

Guide to Minnesota Foundations and Corporate Giving Programs: 1991–92. Minneapolis: Minnesota Council on Foundations, 1991, 6th edition.

MISSOURI

The Directory of Missouri Foundations, compiled and edited by Wilda Swift. St. Louis: Swift Associates, 1991, 3rd edition.

The Directory of Greater Kansas City Foundations, edited by Linda Talbott. Kansas City: Clearinghouse for Midcontinent Foundations, 1990.

MONTANA

Montana and Wyoming Foundations Directory, compiled by Travis Grossman and edited by JoAnn Meide. Billings, MT: Eastern Montana College Library, Grants Information Center, 1991.

NEBRASKA

Nebraska Foundation Directory. Omaha: Junior League of Omaha, 1989.

NEVADA

Nevada Foundation Directory, compiled by Vlasta Honsa and Mark Stackpole. Las Vegas: Las Vegas—Clark County Library District, 1989.

NEW HAMPSHIRE

Corporate Philanthropy in New England: New Hampshire, edited by Michael Burns. vol. 2. Hartford: D.A.T.A., 1987.

NEW JERSEY

The Mitchell Guide to Foundations, Corporations, and Their Managers, edited by Wendy Littman. Belle Mead, NJ: Littman Associates, 1990.

NEW MEXICO

The New Mexico Funding Directory, edited by Denise Wallen. Albuquerque: University of New Mexico, 1990, 2nd edition.

NEW YORK

New York State Foundations: A Comprehensive Directory. New York: The Foundation Center, 1992, 2nd edition.

NORTH CAROLINA

North Carolina Giving: The Directory of the State's Foundations, by Anita Gunn Shirley. Raleigh: Capital Consortium, 1990.

OHIO

Charitable Foundations Directory of Ohio, by Lee Fisher. Columbus: Attorney General's Office, 1991, 9th edition.
The Cincinnati Foundation Directory, by Frances Martindale and Cynthia Roy. Cincinnati: MR & Co., 1989.

OKLAHOMA

The Directory of Oklahoma Foundations, compiled by Mary Deane Streich. Oklahoma City, OK: Foundation Research Project, 1990, 3rd edition.

OREGON

Guide to Oregon Foundations, by Marc Smiley and Nancy Bridgeford. Portland, OR: United Way of Columbia–Wilmette, 1991.

PENNSYLVANIA

Directory of Pennsylvania Foundations, compiled by Damon Kletzien. Springfield, PA: Triadvocates Press, 1990, 4th edition.

RHODE ISLAND

Directory of Grant-Making Foundations in Rhode Island. Providence: Council for Community Services, 1983.

SOUTH CAROLINA

South Carolina Foundation Directory, edited by Guynell Williams. Columbia, SC: South Carolina State Library, 1990, 4th edition.

SOUTH DAKOTA

The South Dakota Grant Directory. Pierre, SD: South Dakota State Library, 1992.

TENNESSEE

The Tennessee Directory of Foundations and Corporate Philanthropy. Memphis: City of Memphis Bureau of Intergovernmental Management, 1985, 3rd edition.

TEXAS

Directory of Texas Foundations, edited by Mary Elizabeth Webb. San Antonio: Funding Information Center of Texas, 1990, 11th edition.

VERMONT

Vermont Directory of Foundations, edited by Christine Graham. Shaftsbury, VT: CPG Enterprises, 1991, 4th edition.

VIRGINIA

Directory of Virginia Private Foundations. Hampton, VA: Hampton Public Library, 1991.

WASHINGTON

Washington Foundation Directory: How to Get Your Slice of the Pie, by Mardell Moore and Charna Klein. Seattle: Consultant Services Northwest, 1991.

WASHINGTON, D.C.

Directory of Foundations of the Greater Washington Area. Washington: Community Foundation of Greater Washington, 1991.

WISCONSIN

Foundations in Wisconsin: A Directory, edited by Susan Hopwood. Milwaukee: Marquette University Memorial Library, 1990, 10th edition.

WEST VIRGINIA

West Virginia Foundation Directory. Charleston, WV: Kanhawha County Public Library, 1987, 2nd edition.

WYOMING

Montana and Wyoming Foundations Directory, compiled by Travis Grossman and edited by JoAnn Meide. Billings, MT: Eastern Montana College Library, Grants Information Center, 1991.

SERVICE ORGANIZATIONS—DIRECTORIES AND PUBLICATIONS

GENERAL DIRECTORIES

American Library Directory. New York: R. R. Bowker, 1990, 43rd edition.

Directory of Special Libraries and Information Centers, Vol. 1: A Guide to Special Libraries, Research Libraries, Information Centers, Archives, & Data Centers, 2 vols., edited by Janice A. DeMaggio. Detroit: Gale Research, 1990, 14th edition.

Encyclopedia of Associations, edited by Deborah Burek. Vols. 1–3. Detroit: Gale Research, 1992.

National Directory of Nonprofit Organizations. Rockville, MD: The Taft Group, 1990.

Online Database Search Services Directory, edited by Martin Connors. Detroit: Gale Research, 1987, 2nd edition.

DIRECTORIES BY SUBJECT AREAS

Audiovisual Market Place, R. R. Bowker Company, 121 Chanlon Road, New Providence, NJ 07974. Tel.: 908-464-6800.

Dance Magazine—Summer Dance Calendar Issue, Dance Magazine, 33 W. 60th Street, New York, NY 10023. Tel.: 212-245-9050.

Religious Organizations Directory, American Business Directories, Inc., American Business Information, Inc., 5711 S. 86th Circle, Omaha, NE 68127. Tel.: 402-593-4600.

Fine Arts Marketplace, American Business Directories, Inc., American Business Information, Inc., 5711 S. 86th Circle, Omaha, NE 68127. Tel.: 402-593-4600.

Photomarket, PhotoSource International, Pine Lake Farm, Osceola, WI 54020. Tel.: 715-248-3800.

Scientific Directory & Annual Bibliography, National Institutes of Health, Department of Health and Human Services, Building 31, Room 2B03, Bethesda, MD 20892. Tel.: 301-496-4143.

Stern's Performing Arts Directory, Dance Magazine, 33 W. 60th Street, New York, NY 10023. Tel.: 212-245-8937.

Who's Who in Finance and Industry, 1989–90, 26th rev. ed. Wilmette, IL: Marquis, 1989.

Writer's Digest Books, 1507 Dana Avenue, Cincinnati, OH 45207. Tel.: 513-531-2222.

Journals and Periodicals

BCA News
(quarterly)
Business Committee for the Arts
1775 Broadway, Suite 510
New York, NY 10019-1942
Tel.: 212-664-0600

The Chronicle of Higher
    Education
(weekly)
1255 Twenty-third Street, N.W.
Washington, DC 20037
Tel.: 202-466-1212

Crain's New York Business
(weekly)
Crain Communications Inc.
220 E. 42nd Street
New York, NY 10017
Tel.: 800-678-9595

Currents
(monthly)
Council for Advancement and
    Support of Education
11 Dupont Circle, Suite 400
Washington, DC 20036
Tel.: 202-328-5900

Forbes
(biweekly)
Forbes Inc.
60 Fifth Avenue
New York, NY 10011
Tel.: 800-888-9896

Fortune
(weekly)
Time Inc.
Time & Life Building
Rockefeller Center
New York, NY 10020-1393
Tel.: 800-621-8000

F[or]. Y[our]. I[nformation].
(quarterly)
New York Foundation for the
    Arts
155 Avenue of the Americas
New York, NY 10011
Tel.: 212-366-6900

Health Funds Development Let-
    ter
(monthly)
Sharing Information on Federal
    and Foundation Fund Services
Health Resources Publishing
Brinley Prof. Plaza
3100 Highway 138
Wall Township, NJ 07719-1442
Tel.: 908-681-1133

The Independent Film & Video
    Monthly
(monthly)
Foundation for Independent Video
    and Film
625 Broadway
New York, NY 10012
Tel.: 212-473-3400

National Science Bulletin
(monthly)
National Science Foundation
1800 Sixth Street, N.W.
Washington, DC 20550
Tel.: 202-357-7861

Poets & Writers Magazine
(six times a year)
72 Spring Street
New York, NY 10012
Tel.: 212-226-3586

Dance Magazine
33 W. 60th Street
New York, NY 10023
Tel.: 212-245-9050

SERVICE ORGANIZATIONS—BY SUBJECT AREA

THE ARTS

American Council for the Arts
1285 Avenue of the Americas
New York, NY 10018
Tel.: 212-245-4510

Art Information Center
280 Broadway, Suite 412
New York, NY 10007
Tel.: 212-227-0282

Business Committee for the Arts
1770 Broadway
New York, NY 10019
Tel.: 212-664-0600

People for the American Way
2000 M. Street N.W., Suite 400
Washington, DC 20036
Tel.: 202-467-4999

Volunteer Lawyers for the Arts
1 E. 53rd Street, 6th Floor
New York, NY 10022
Tel.: 212-319-2787

See also:
*Volunteer Lawyers for the Arts
National Directory.* New York:
VLA.

BUSINESS

American Business Association
292 Madison Avenue
New York, NY 10017
Tel.: 212-949-5900

National Association for the Self-
Employed
2328 Gravel Road
Fort Worth, TX 76118
Tel.: 800-232-6273

National Business Association
14875 Landmark Boulevard, Suite
100
Dallas, TX 75240
Tel.: 214-991-5381

Patent Research Associates,
8826 Washington Boulevard
Jessup, MD 20794
Tel.: 800-548-3721

EDUCATION

American Council on Education
One Dupont Circle, N.W., Suite
800
Washington, DC 20036
Tel.: 202-939-9300

Council for Advancement and
Support of Education
11 Dupont Circle, N.W.
Washington, DC 20036
Tel.: 202-328-5900

Council for Aid to Education
51 Madison Avenue
New York, NY 10010
Tel.: 212-689-2400

National Association of
Independent Schools
18 Tremont Street
Boston, MA 02109
Tel.: 617-723-6900

ENVIRONMENT

Americans for the Environment
1400 Sixteenth Street, N.W.
Washington, DC 20036
Tel.: 202-797-6665

FEDERAL GOVERNMENT

Federal Information Center
P.O. Box 600
Cumberland, MD 21501-600
Tel.: 301-722-9098

HEALTH

Association for Healthcare
Philanthropy (formerly
National Association for
Hospital Development)
313 Park Avenue, Suite 400
Falls Church, VA 22046
Tel.: 703-532-6243

National Health Council
1700 K Street, N.W.
Washington, DC 20006
Tel.: 202-785-3913

HUMANITIES

American Council of Learned
Societies
228 E. 45th Street, 16th Floor
New York, NY 10017
Tel.: 212-697-1505

Council for International
Exchange of Scholars
3400 International Drive, N.W.,
Suite M500
Washington, DC 20008
Tel.: 202-686-4000

National Humanities Center
7 Alexander Drive
P.O. Box 12256
Research Triangle Park, NC
27709
Tel.: 919-549-0661

INVENTORS

Patent Research Associates
8826 Washington Boulevard
Jessup, MD
Tel.: 800-548-3721

MINORITIES

Minority Business Information
Institute
130 Fifth Avenue, 10th Floor
New York, NY 10011
Tel.: 212-242-8000

National Association of Minority
Women in Business
906 Grand Avenue, Suite 200
Kansas City, MO 64106
Tel.: 816-421-3335

RELIGION

Global Congress of the World's
Religions
10 Dock Road
Barrytown, NY 12507
Tel.: 914-758-6881

The Interchurch Center
475 Riverside Drive, Room 253
New York, NY 10115
Tel.: 212-870-2932

SCIENCES

National Research Council
2101 Constitution Avenue, N.W.
Washington, DC 20418
Tel.: 202-334-2000

SENIOR CITIZENS

American Association of Retired
Persons
1909 K Street, N.W.
Washington, DC 20049
Tel.: 202-872-4700

TRAVEL

Academic Travel Abroad
3210 Grand Street, N.W., 1st
Floor
Washington, DC 20007
Tel.: 202-333-3355

Council on International
Educational Exchange

205 East 42nd Street
New York, NY 10017
Tel.: 212-661-1414

WOMEN

Ms. Foundation for Women
141 Fifth Avenue, Suite 6-S
New York, NY 10010
Tel.: 212-353-8580

Women's Action Alliance
c/o Gail B. Chasin
370 Lexington Avenue
New York, NY 10017
Tel.: 212-532-8330

FUNDRAISING RESOURCES

FOUNDATION CENTER OFFICES

The Foundation Center
79 Fifth Avenue, 8th Floor
New York, NY 10003
Tel.: 212-620-4230

The Foundation Center
1001 Connecticut Avenue,
N.W.
Washington, DC 20036
Tel.: 202-331-1400

The Foundation Center
312 Sutter Street, Room 312
San Francisco, CA 94108
Tel.: 415-387-0902

The Foundation Center
Kent H. Smith Library
1422 Euclid, Suite 1356
Cleveland, OH 44115
Tel.: 216-861-1933

FOUNDATION CENTER AFFILIATES

A list of the phone numbers of
regional affiliates appears on
pages 352–53.

ALABAMA

Birmingham Public Library
Government Document
2100 Park Place
Birmingham, AL 35203
Tel.: 205-226-3600

Huntsville Public Library
915 Monroe Street
Huntsville, AL 35801
Tel.: 205-532-5940

University of South Alabama
Library Reference Department
Mobile, AL 36688
Tel.: 205-460-7025

Auburn University at
Montgomery Library
7300 University Drive
Montgomery, AL 36117-3596
Tel.: 205-244-3653

ALASKA

University of Alaska Anchorage
Library
3211 Providence Drive
Anchorage, AK 99508
Tel.: 907-786-1848

Juneau Public Library
292 Marine Way
Juneau, AK 99801
Tel.: 907-586-5249

ARIZONA

Phoenix Public Library
Business and Sciences Department
12 E. McDowell Road
Phoenix, AZ 85004
Tel.: 602-262-4636

Tucson Public Library
101 N. Stone Avenue
Tucson, AZ 85726-7470
Tel.: 602-791-4393

ARKANSAS

Westark Community College
Library
5210 Grand Avenue
Fort Smith, AR 72913
Tel.: 501-785-7000

Central Arkansas Library
System References Services
700 Louisiana Street
Little Rock, AR 72201
Tel.: 501-370-5950

Pine Bluff-Jefferson County
Library System
200 E. Eighth

Pine Bluff, AR 71601
Tel.: 501-543-2159

CALIFORNIA

Ventura County Community
Foundation
Community Resource Center
1355 Del Norte Road
Camarillo, CA 93010
Tel.: 805-988-0196

California Community Foundation
Funding Information Center
606 S. Olive Street, Suite 2400
Los Angeles, CA 90014-1526
Tel.: 213-413-4042

Community Foundation for
Monterey County
177 Van Buren
Monterey, CA 93942
Tel.: 408-375-9712

Riverside Public Library
3581 Seventh Street
Riverside, CA 92501
Tel.: 714-782-5201

California State Library
Reference Services, Room 301
914 Capitol Mall
Sacramento, CA 94237-0001
Tel.: 916-654-0261

Non Profit Resource Center
Sacramento Central Library
516 K Street Mall
Sacramento, CA 95812-2036
Tel.: 916-264-7131

San Diego Community
Foundation
101 W. Broadway, Suite 1120
San Diego, CA 92101
Tel.: 619-239-8815

Non Profit Development Center
1762 Technology Drive, Suite 225
San Jose, CA 95110
Tel.: 408-452-8181

Peninsula Community Foundation
1700 S. El Camino Real
San Mateo, CA 94402-3049
Tel.: 415-358-9392

Volunteer Center Resource Library
1000 E. Santa Ana Boulevard
Santa Ana, CA 92701
Tel.: 714-953-1655

Santa Barbara Public Library
40 E. Anapamu
Santa Barbara, CA 93101-1603
Tel.: 805-962-7653

Santa Monica Public Library
1343 Sixth Street
Santa Monica, CA 90401-1603
Tel.: 213-458-8600

COLORADO

Pikes Peak Library District
20 North Cascade Avenue
Colorado Springs, CO 80901
Tel.: 719-473-2080

Denver Public Library
Sociology Division
1357 Broadway
Denver, CO 80203
Tel.: 303-640-8870

CONNECTICUT

Danbury Public Library
170 Main Street
Danbury, CT 06810
Tel.: 203-797-4527

Hartford Public Library
Reference Department
500 Main Street
Hartford, CT 06103
Tel.: 203-293-6000

D.A.T.A.
70 Audubon Street

New Haven, CT 06510
Tel.: 203-772-1345

DELAWARE

University of Delaware
Hugh Morris Library
Newark, DE 19717-5267
Tel.: 302-451-2432

FLORIDA

Volusia County Library Center
City Island
Daytona Beach, FL 32014-4484
Tel.: 904-255-3765

Nova University
Einstein Library—Foundation
    Resource Collection
3301 College Avenue
Fort Lauderdale, FL 33314
Tel.: 305-475-7497

Indian River Community
College Learning Resources
    Center
3209 Virginia Avenue
Fort Pierce, FL 34981-5599
Tel.: 407-468-4757

Jacksonville Public Library
Business, Science and Documents
122 North Ocean Street
Jacksonville, FL 32206
Tel.: 904-630-2665

Miami–Dade Public Library
Humanities Department
101 W. Flagler Street
Miami, FL 33130
Tel.: 305-375-2655

Orlando Public Library
Orange County Library System
101 E. Central Boulevard
Orlando, FL 32801
Tel.: 407-425-4694

Selby Public Library
1001 Boulevard of the Arts
Sarasota, FL 34236
Tel.: 813-951-5501

Tampa Hillsborough County
Public Library System
900 N. Ashley Drive
Tampa, FL 33602
Tel.: 813-223-8865

Community Foundation of Palm
Beach and Martin Counties
324 Datura Street
West Palm Beach, FL 33401
Tel.: 407-659-6800

GEORGIA

Atlanta-Fulton Public Library
Foundation Collection—Ivan
Allen Department
1 Margaret Mitchell Square
Atlanta, GA 30303-1089
Tel.: 404-730-1900

HAWAII

Hawaii Community Foundation
Hawaii Resource Room
222 Merchant Street
Honolulu, HI 96813
Tel.: 808-537-6333

University of Hawaii
Thomas Hale Hamilton Library
2550 The Mall
Honolulu, HI 96822
Tel.: 808-956-7214

IDAHO

Boise Public Library
715 S. Capitol Boulevard
Boise, ID 83702
Tel.: 208-384-4024

Caldwell Public Library
1010 Dearborn Street
Caldwell, ID 83605
Tel.: 208-459-3242

ILLINOIS

Donors Forum of Chicago
53 W. Jackson Boulevard,
Room 430
Chicago, IL 60604
Tel.: 312-431-0265

Evanston Public Library
1703 Orrington Avenue
Evanston, IL 60201
Tel.: 708-866-0305

Sangamon State University
Library
Shepard Road
Springfield, IL 62794-9243
Tel.: 217-786-6633

INDIANA

Allen County Public Library
900 Webster Street
Fort Wayne, IN 46802
Tel.: 219-424-7241

Indiana University Northwest
Library
3400 Broadway
Gary, IN 46408
Tel.: 219-980-6582

Indianapolis-Marion County
Public Library
40 E. St. Clair Street
Indianapolis, IN 46206
Tel.: 317-269-1733

IOWA

Cedar Rapids Public Library
Funding Information Center
500 First Street, S.E.
Cedar Rapids, IA 52401
Tel.: 319-398-5123

Southwestern Community College
Learning Resource Center
1501 W. Townline Road
Creston, IA 50801
Tel.: 515-782-7081, Ext. 262

Public Library of Des Moines
100 Locust Street
Des Moines, IA 50308
Tel.: 515-283-4152

KANSAS

Topeka Public Library
1515 W. Tenth Street
Topeka, KS 66604
Tel.: 913-233-2040

Wichita Public Library
223 S. Main
Wichita, KS 67202
Tel.: 316-262-0611

KENTUCKY

Western Kentucky University
Helm-Cravens Library
Bowling Green, KY 4201-3576
Tel.: 502-745-6125

Louisville Free Public Library
301 York Street
Louisville, KY 40203
Tel.: 502-561-8617

LOUISIANA

East Baton Rouge Parish Library
Centroplex Branch
120 St. Louis Street
Baton Rouge, LA 70802
Tel.: 504-389-4960

Beauregard Parish Library
205 S. Washington Avenue
De Ridder, LA 70634
Tel.: 318-463-6217

New Orleans Public Library
Business and Science Division
219 Loyola Avenue
New Orleans, LA 70140
Tel.: 504-596-2580

Shreve Memorial Library
424 Texas Street
Shreveport, LA 71120-1523
Tel.: 318-226-5894

MAINE

University of Southern Maine
Office of Sponsored Research
246 Deering Avenue, Room 628
Portland, ME 04103
Tel.: 207-780-4871

MARYLAND

Enoch Pratt Free Library
Social Science and History
  Department
400 Cathedral Street
Baltimore, MD 21201
Tel.: 301-396-5320

MASSACHUSETTS

Associated Grantmakers of
  Massachusetts
294 Washington Street, Suite 840
Boston, MA 02108
Tel.: 617-426-2606

Boston Public Library
666 Boylston Street
Boston, MA 02117
Tel.: 617-536-5400

Western Massachusetts Funding
  Resource Center
Campaign for Human
  Development
65 Elliot Street
Springfield, MA 01101
Tel.: 413-732-3175

Worcester Public Library
Grants Resource Center
Salem Square
Worcester, MA 01608
Tel.: 508-799-1655

MICHIGAN

Alpena County Library
211 N. First Avenue
Alpena, MI 49707
Tel.: 517-356-6188

University of Michigan—Ann
   Arbor
209 Hatcher Graduate Library
Ann Arbor, MI 48109-1205
Tel.: 313-764-1148

Battle Creek Community
   Foundation
One Riverwalk Centre
34 W. Jackson Street
Battle Creek, MI 49017
Tel.: 616-962-2181

Henry Ford Centennial Library
16301 Michigan Avenue
Dearborn, MI 48126
Tel.: 313-943-2330

Wayne State University
Purdy-Kresge Library
5265 Cass Avenue
Detroit, MI 48202
Tel.: 313-577-6424

Michigan State University
   Libraries
Reference Library
East Lansing, MI 48824-1048
Tel.: 517-353-8818

Farmington Community Library
32737 West 12 Mile Road
Farmington Hills, MI 48018
Tel.: 313-553-0300

University of Michigan—Flint
   Library
Reference Department
Flint, MI 48502-2186
Tel.: 313-762-3408

Grand Rapids Public Library
Business Department
60 Library Plaza, N.E.
Grand Rapids, MI 49503-3093
Tel.: 616-456-3600

Michigan Technological
   University Library
1400 Townsend Drive
Houghton, MI 49931
Tel.: 906-487-2507

Sault Ste. Marie Area Public
   Schools
Office of Compensatory Education
460 W. Spruce Street
Sault Ste. Marie, MI 49783-1874
Tel.: 906-635-6619

Northwestern Michigan College
Mark & Helen Osterin Library
1701 E. Front Street
Traverse City, MI 49684
Tel.: 616-922-0650

MINNESOTA

Duluth Public Library
520 W. Superior Street
Duluth, MN 55802
Tel.: 218-723-3802

Southwest State University
   Library
Marshall, MI 56258
Tel.: 507-537-7278

Minneapolis Public Library
Sociology Department
300 Nicollet Mall
Minneapolis, MN 55401
Tel.: 612-372-6555

Rochester Public Library
11 First Street, S.E.
Rochester, MN 55902-3743
Tel.: 507-285-8000

St. Paul Public Library
90 W. Fourth Street
Saint Paul, MN 55102
Tel.: 612-292-6307

MISSISSIPPI

Jackson-Hinds Library System
300 N. State Street
Jackson, MS 39201
Tel.: 601-968-5803

MISSOURI

Clearinghouse for Midcontinent
    Foundations
University of Missouri
Block School of Business
5110 Cherry Street, Suite 310
Kansas City, MO 64112
Tel.: 816-235-1176

Kansas City Public Library
311 E. 12th Street
Kansas City, MO 64106
Tel.: 816-221-9650

Metropolitan Association of
    Philanthropy, Inc.
5615 Pershing Avenue, Suite 20
St. Louis, MO 63112
Tel.: 314-361-3900

Springfield-Greene County
    Library
397 E. Central Street
Springfield, MO 65801
Tel.: 417-866-9400

MONTANA

Eastern Montana College Library
1500 N. 30th Street
Billings, MT 59101-0298
Tel.: 406-657-1662

Bozeman Public Library
220 E. Lamme
Bozeman, MT 59715-3579
Tel.: 406-586-4787

Montana State Library
Reference Department
1515 E. 6th Avenue
Helena, MT 59620
Tel.: 406-444-3004

NEBRASKA

University of Nebraska
106 Love Library
14th and R Streets
Lincoln, NE 68588-0410
Tel.: 402-472-2848

West Dale Clark University
Social Sciences Department
215 S. 15th Street
Omaha, NE 68102
Tel.: 402-444-4826

NEVADA

Las Vegas-Clark County Library
    District
1401 East Flamingo Road
Las Vegas, NV 89119-6160
Tel.: 702-733-7810

Washoe County Library
301 S. Center Street
Reno, NV 89501
Tel.: 702-785-4012

NEW HAMPSHIRE

New Hampshire Charitable Fund
1 South Street
Concord, NH 03302-1335
Tel.: 603-255-6641

Plymouth State College
Herbert H. Lamson Library
Plymouth, NH 03264
Tel.: 603-535-2258

NEW JERSEY

Cumberland County Library
800 E. Commerce Street

Bridgeton, NJ 08302-2295
Tel.: 609-453-2210

Free Public Library of Elizabeth
11 S. Broad Street
Elizabeth, NJ 07202
Tel.: 908-354-6060

The Support Center
17 Academy Street, Suite 1101
Newark, NJ 07102
Tel.: 201-643-5774

County College of Morris Masten
    Learning Resource Center
Route 10 and Center Grove Road
Randolph, NJ 07869
Tel.: 201-328-5296

New Jersey State Library
Governmental Reference
185 W. State Street
Trenton, NJ 08625-0520
Tel.: 609-292-6220

NEW MEXICO

Albuquerque Community
    Foundation
3301 Menual, N.E., Suite 22
Albuquerque, NM 87107
Tel.: 505-883-6240

New Mexico State Library
325 Don Gaspar Street
Santa Fe, NM 87503
Tel.: 505-827-3824

NEW YORK

New York State Library
Cultural Education Center
Humanities Section
Empire State Plaza
Albany, NY 12230
Tel.: 518-474-5355

Suffolk Cooperative Library
    System
627 North Sunrise Service Road

Bellport, NY 11713
Tel.: 516-286-1600

New York Public Library
Bronx Reference Center
2556 Bainbridge Avenue
Bronx, NY 10458
Tel.: 212-220-6575

Brooklyn in Touch
One Hanson Place, Room 2504
Brooklyn, NY 11243
Tel.: 718-230-3200

Buffalo and Erie County Public
    Library
Lafayette Square
Buffalo, NY 14202
Tel.: 716-858-7103

Huntington Public Library
338 Main Street
Huntington, NY 11743
Tel.: 516-427-5165

Queens Borough Public Library
89-11 Merrick Boulevard
Jamaica, NY 11432
Tel.: 718-990-0700

Levittown Public Library
One Bluegrass Lane
Levittown, NY 11756
Tel.: 516-731-5728

SUNY/College at Old Westbury
    Library
223 Store Hill Road
Old Westbury, NY 11568
Tel.: 516-876-3156

Adriance Memorial Library
93 Market Street
Poughkeepsie, NY 12601
Tel.: 914-485-3445

Rochester Public Library
Business Division
115 South Avenue
Rochester, NY 14604
Tel.: 716-428-7328

Onondaga County Public Library
at the Galleries
447 S. Salina Street
Syracuse, NY 13202-2494
Tel.: 315-448-4636

Utica Public Library
303 Genessee Street
Utica, NY 13501
Tel.: 315-735-2279

White Plains Public Library
100 Martine Avenue
White Plains, NY 10601
Tel.: 914-422-1480

NORTH CAROLINA

Asheville-Buncomb Technical
Community College
Learning Resources Center
340 Victoria Road
Asheville, NC 28802
Tel.: 704-254-1921, Ext. 300

The Duke Endowment
200 S. Tryon Street, Suite 1100
Charlotte, NC 28202
Tel.: 704-376-0291

Durham County Library
300 N. Roxboro Street
Durham, NC 27702
Tel.: 919-560-0100

North Carolina State Library
109 E. Jones Street
Raleigh, NC 27611
Tel.: 919-733-3270

The Winston-Salem Foundation
310 W. 4th Street, Suite 229
Winston-Salem, NC 27101-2889
Tel.: 919-725-2382

NORTH DAKOTA

North Dakota State University
The Library
Fargo, ND 58105
Tel.: 701-237-8886

OHIO

Stark County District Library
715 Market Avenue N.
Canton, OH 44702-1080
Tel.: 216-452-0665

Public Library of Cincinnati and
Hamilton County
Education Department
800 Vine Street
Cincinnati, OH 45202-2071
Tel.: 513-369-6940

Columbus Metropolitan Library
96 S. Grant Avenue
Columbus, OH 43215
Tel.: 614-645-2590

Dayton and Montgomery County
Public Library
Grants Information Center
215 E. Third Street
Dayton, OH 45402-2103
Tel.: 513-227-9500, Ext. 211

Toledo-Lucas County Public
Library
Social Science Department
325 Michigan Street
Toledo, OH 43623-1614
Tel.: 419-259-5245

Ohio University—Zanesville
Community Education and
Development
1425 Newark Road
Zanesville, OH 43701
Tel.: 614-453-0762

OKLAHOMA

Oklahoma City University Library
2501 North Blackwelder
Oklahoma City, OK 73106
Tel.: 405-521-5072

Tulsa City—County Library
System
400 Civic Center
Tulsa, OK 74103
Tel.: 918-596-7944

OREGON

Oregon Institute of Technology
Library
3201 Campus Drive
Klamath Falls, OR 97601-8801
Tel.: 503-885-1772

Pacific Non-Profit Network
Grantsmanship Resource Library
33 N. Central, Suite 211
Medford, OR 97501
Tel.: 503-779-6044

Multnomah County Library
Government Documents Room
801 S.W. Tenth Avenue
Portland, OR 97205-2597
Tel.: 503-248-5123

Oregon State Library
State Library Building
Salem, OR 97310
Tel.: 503-378-4277

PENNSYLVANIA

Northampton Community College
Learning Resources Center
3835 Green Pond Road
Bethlehem, PA 18017
Tel.: 215-861-5360

Erie County Public Library
3 South Perry Square
Erie, PA 16501
Tel.: 814-451-6927

Dauphin County Library System
101 Walnut Street
Harrisburg, PA 17101
Tel.: 717-234-4961

Lancaster County Public Library
125 N. Duke Street
Lancaster, PA 17602
Tel.: 717-394-2651

The Free Library of Philadelphia
Logan Square
Philadelphia, PA 19103
Tel.: 215-686-5423

University of Pittsburgh
Hillman Library
Pittsburgh, PA 15260
Tel.: 412-648-7722

Pocono Northeast Development
Fund
1151 Oak Street
Pittston, PA 18640-3795
Tel.: 717-655-5581

RHODE ISLAND

Providence Public Library
Reference Department
150 Empire Street
Providence, RI 02903
Tel.: 401-521-7722

SOUTH CAROLINA

Charleston County Library
404 King Street
Charleston, SC 29403
Tel.: 803-723-1645

South Carolina State Library
Reference Department
1500 Senate Street
Columbia, SC 29211
Tel.: 803-734-8666

SOUTH DAKOTA

Non Profit Grants Assistance
Center
Business and Education Institute,
East Hall
Dakota State University
Madison, SD 57042
Tel.: 605-256-5555

South Dakota State Library
800 Governors Drive
Pierre, SD 57501-2294
Tel.: 605-773-5070
Tel.: 800-592-1841 (SD
Residents)

Sioux Falls Area Foundation
141 N. Main Avenue, Suite 500
Sioux Falls, SD 57102-1134
Tel.: 605-336-7055

TENNESSEE

Knox County Public Library
500 W. Church Avenue
Knoxville, TN 37902
Tel.: 615-544-5750

Memphis & Shelby County Public
Library
1850 Peabody Avenue
Memphis, TN 38104
Tel.: 901-725-8877

Public Library of Nashville and
Davidson County
8th Avenue N. and Union Street
Nashville, TN 37203
Tel.: 615-862-5843

TEXAS

Community Foundation of
Abilene
Funding Information Library
500 N. Chestnut, Suite 1509
Abilene, TX 79604
Tel.: 915-676-3883

Amarillo Area Foundation
700 1st National Place One
800 S. Fillmore
Amarillo, TX 79101
Tel.: 806-376-4521

Hogg Foundation for Mental
Health
University of Texas
Austin, TX 78713-7998
Tel.: 512-471-5041

Corpus Christi State
University Library
6300 Ocean Drive
Corpus Christi, TX 78412
Tel.: 512-994-2608

Dallas Public Library
Grants Information Service
1515 Young Street
Dallas, TX 75201
Tel.: 214-670-1487

El Paso Community Foundation
1616 Texas Commerce Building
El Paso, TX 79901
Tel.: 915-533-4020

Texas Christian University Library
Funding Information Center
Fort Worth, TX 76129
Tel.: 817-921-7664

Houston Public Library
Bibliographic Information Center
500 McKinney Avenue
Houston, TX 77002
Tel.: 713-236-1313

Lubbock Area Foundation
502 Texas Commerce Bank
Building
Lubbock, TX 79401
Tel.: 806-762-8061

Funding Information Center
507 Brooklyn
San Antonio, TX 78215
Tel.: 512-227-4333

North Texas Center for Nonprofit
Management
624 Indiana, Suite 307
Wichita Falls, TX 76301
Tel.: 817-322-4961

UTAH

Salt Lake City Public Library
Business and Science Department
209 E. Fifth South
Salt Lake City, UT 84111
Tel.: 801-363-5733

VERMONT

Vermont Department of Libraries
Reference Services
109 State Street
Montpelier, VT 05609
Tel.: 802-828-3268

VIRGINIA

Hampton Public Library
Grants Resources Collection
4207 Victoria Boulevard
Hampton, VA 23669
Tel.: 804-727-1154

Richmond Public Library
Business, Science & Technology
101 E. Franklin Street
Richmond, VA 23219
Tel.: 804-780-8223

Roanoke City Public Library
    System
Central Library
706 S. Jefferson Street
Roanoke, VA 24016
Tel.: 703-981-2477

WASHINGTON

Mid-Columbia Library
405 S. Dayton
Kennewick, WA 99336
Tel.: 509-586-3156

Seattle Public Library
1000 Fourth Avenue
Seattle, WA 98104
Tel.: 206-386-4620

Spokane Public Library
Funding Information Center
West 811 Main Avenue
Spokane, WA 99201
Tel.: 509-838-3364

Greater Wenatchee Community
Foundation at the Wenatchee
Public Library
310 Douglas Street
Wenatchee, WA 98807
Tel.: 509-662-5021

WEST VIRGINIA

Kanawha County Public Library
123 Capital Street
Charleston, WV 25304
Tel.: 304-343-4646

WISCONSIN

University of Wisconsin—
    Madison
Memorial Library
728 State Street
Madison, WI 53706
Tel.: 608-262-3242

Marquette University Memorial
    Library
1415 W. Wisconsin Avenue
Milwaukee, WI 53233
Tel.: 414-288-1515

WYOMING

Natrona County Public Library
505 E. Second Street
Casper, WY 82601-2598
Tel.: 307-237-4935

Laramie County Community
    College Library
1400 E. College Drive
Cheyenne, WY 82007-3299
Tel.: 307-778-1205

Teton County Library
Community Resource Library
320 S. King Street
Jackson, WY 83001
Tel.: 307-733-2164

AUSTRALIA

ANZ Executors & Trustees Co.
Ltd.
91 William Street, 7th Floor
Melbourne, VIC 3000
Australia
Tel.: 03-648-5764

CANADA

Canadian Centre for Philanthropy
1329 Bay Street, Suite 200
Toronto, Ontario M5R 2C4
Canada
Tel.: 416-515-0764

ENGLAND

Charities Aid Foundation
114/118 Southampton Row
London WC18 5AA
England
Tel.: 71-831-7798

JAPAN

Foundation Library Center of
Japan
Elements Shinjuku Bldg. 3F
2-1-14 Shinjuku, Shinjuku-ku
Tokyo 160
Japan
Tel.: 03-350-1857

MEXICO

Biblioteca Benjamin Franklin
American Embassy, USICA
Londres 16
Mexico City 6, D.F. 06600
Mexico
Tel.: 905-211-0042

PUERTO RICO

University of Puerto Rico
Ponce Technological College
Library
Box 7186
Ponce, PR 00732
Tel.: 809-844-8181

Universidad del Sagrado Corazón
M.M.T. Gueverra Library
Correao Call Loiza
Santurce, PR 00914
Tel.: 809-728-1515, Ext. 357

THE SUPPORT CENTERS OF AMERICA

The Support Center of New York
305 Second Avenue
New York, NY 10001
Tel.: 212-924-6744

REGIONAL PHONE NUMBERS OF FOUNDATION CENTER AFFILIATES

CALIFORNIA

Palo Alto, CA
Tel.: 415-323-0873

San Diego, CA
Tel.: 619-292-5702

San Francisco, CA
Tel.: 415-552-7584

COLORADO

Denver, CO
Applied Research and
Development Institute
Tel.: 303-691-6076

GEORGIA

Atlanta, GA
Tel.: 404-688-4845

ILLINOIS

Chicago, IL
Tel.: 312-606-1530

MASSACHUSETTS

Boston, MA
Tel.: 617-338-1331

NEW JERSEY

Newark, NJ
Tel.: 201-643-5774

NEW MEXICO

Santa Fe, NM
National AIDS Support Center
Tel.: 505-986-8337

NEW YORK

New York, NY
Tel.: 212-924-6744

OKLAHOMA

Oklahoma City, OK
Tel.: 405-236-8133

Tulsa, OK
Tel.: 405-236-8133

RHODE ISLAND

Warwick, RI
Tel.: 401-781-3338

TEXAS

Houston, TX
Tel.: 713-739-1211

WASHINGTON, DC

Washington, DC
Tel.: 202-833-0300

National/International
Tel.: 202-296-3900

OTHER ORGANIZATIONS

AAFRC Trust for Philanthropy
25 W. 43rd Street
New York, NY 10036
Tel.: 212-354-5799

American Prospect Research
    Association
1600 Wilson Boulevard, Suite 905
Arlington, VA 22200
Tel.: 703-525-1191
    Provides information about
securing grants and charitable
donations to nonprofit
organizations.

Council on Foundations
1828 L Street, N.W.
Washington, DC 20036
Tel.: 202-466-6512
    Sponsors meetings for
grantmakers, trustees, officers, and
executives to keep abreast of
current trends in the various fields
of philanthropy.

The Grantsmanship Center
1125 W. 6th Street, 5th Floor
P.O. Box 17220
Los Angeles, CA 90017
Tel.: 213-482-9860
Fax: 213-482-9863

Independent Sector
1828 L Street, N.W.
Washington, DC 20036
Tel.: 202-667-9844
    Conducts research and
educates the public about the role
of the independent nonprofit
sector and its usefulness to society.

National Charities Information
    Bureau
19 Union Square West
New York, NY 10003
Tel.: 212-929-6300

Seeks to maintain sound standards in field of philanthropy and to aid wise giving through advisory reports to contributors.

National Society of Fund Raising Executives
1101 King Street, Suite 3000
Alexandria, VA 22314
Tel.: 703-684-0410
Holds periodic workshops and seminars dealing with all phases of fund raising.

The National Volunteer Center
1111 N. 19th Street
Arlington, VA 22209
Tel.: 703-276-0542
Assists communities and organizations in reinforcing, expanding, and improving the effectiveness of volunteer activities.

FUNDRAISING—PUBLICATIONS AND REFERENCES

GENERAL REFERENCE BOOKS

The Foundation Center's User-Friendly Guide: Grantseeker's Guide to Resources, by Judith Margolin. New York: The Foundation Center, 1992.

Foundation Fundamentals: A Guide for Grantseekers, edited by Judith Margolin. New York: The Foundation Center, 1991, 4th edition.

Grants for the Arts, by Virginia P. White. New York: Plenum Press, 1980.

Grants: How to Find Out About Them and What to Do Next, by Virginia P. White. New York: Plenum Press, 1975.

The Individual's Guide to Grants, by Judith B. Margolin. New York: Plenum Press, 1983.

REFERENCE BOOKS—FOR NONPROFIT ORGANIZATIONS

Careers for Dreamers and Doers: A Guide to Management Careers in the Nonprofit Sector, by Lilly Cohen and Dennis R. Young. New York: The Foundation Center, 1989.

"How to Apply For and Retain Exempt Status for Your Organization." IRS Publication 557. This is published by the U.S. Government Printing Office in Washington, DC, and you can order it through your local IRS office.

A Nonprofit Organization Operating Manual: Planning for Survival and Growth, by Arnold J. Olenick and Philip R. Olenick. New York: The Foundation Center, 1991.

Raise More Money for Your Nonprofit Organization: A Guide to Evaluating and Improving Your Fund-Raising, by Anne L. New. New York: The Foundation Center, 1991.

Securing Your Organization's Future: A Complete Guide to Fund-Raising Strategies, by Michael Seltzer. New York: The Foundation Center, 1987.
To Be or Not to Be: An Artists Guide to Not-for-Profit Incorporation. New York: Volunteer Lawyers for the Arts, 1986.

JOURNALS IN THE NONPROFIT FIELD

The Chronicle of Philanthropy
1255 Twenty-third Street, N.W.
Washington, DC 20037
Tel.: 202-466-1212

Corporate Philanthropy Report
3218 Fuhrman Avenue E.
Seattle, WA 98102-9938
Tel.: 202-329-0422

Foundation News
1828 L Street, N.W.
Washington, DC 20036
Tel.: 202-466-6512

Fund Raising Management
224 Seventh Street
Garden City, NY 11530
Tel.: 516-746-6700

Giving USA (Annual and Update)
American Association of Fund-Raising Counsel
25 W. 43rd Street
New York, NY 10036
Tel.: 212-354-5799

Nonprofit Times
190 Tamarack Circle
Skillman, NJ 08558
Tel.: 609-921-1251

PERSONAL DEVELOPMENT AND ORGANIZATION

The Seven Habits of Highly Effective People, by Stephen R. Covey. New York: Simon & Schuster, 1989.
Flow: The Psychology of Optimal Experience, by Mihaly Csikszentmihalyi. New York: Harper & Row, 1990.
Learned Optimism: How to Change Your Mind and Your Life, by Martin Seligman. New York: Alfred A. Knopf, 1991.
Wishcraft: How to Get What You Really Want, by Barbara Sher and Annie Gottlieb. New York: Ballantine Books, 1983.

Copyright, Patent, Licensing and Legal Issues
A Writer's Guide to Copyright. New York: Poets and Writers, 1990.
How to Be a Successful Inventor, by Gordon D. Griffin. New York: John Wiley, 1991.
Licensing Art & Design, by Caryn R. Leland. New York: Allworth Press, 1990.
Protecting Your Songs and Yourself, by Kent. J. Klevens. Cincinnati: Writer's Digest Books, 1989.
Trademark and the Arts, by William M. Borchard. New York: Center for Law and the Arts, Columbia University School of Law, 1988.
VLA Guide to Copyright for Musicians and Composers, 1987.
VLA Guide to Copyright for the Performing Arts, 1987.
VLA Guide to Copyright for Visual Artists.
Volunteer Lawyers for the Arts National Directory.

To order VLA publications, contact:

Lynn E. Richardson
Volunteer Lawyers for the Arts
1 E. 53rd Street, 6th Floor
New York, NY 10022
Tel.: 212-319-ARTS, Ext. 25

Jobs and Résumés

1990 Internships: On-the-Job Training Opportunities for All Types of Careers, by Kathy Jobst. Cincinnati: Writer's Digest Books, 1990.

What Color Is Your Parachute?, by Richard Nelson Bolles.

The Only Job Hunting Guide You'll Ever Need, by Kathryn and Ross Petras. New York: Poseidon Press, 1989.

Writing a Job-Winning Résumé, by John E. McLaughlin and Stephen K. Merman. Englewood Cliffs, NJ: Prentice-Hall, 1986.

Personal Computers

Introduction to Personal Computers, by Peter Stephenson. New York: John Wiley & Sons, 1991.

Personal Computers for the Computer Illiterate, by Barry Owen. New York: HarperCollins, 1991.

Your First Computer, by Alan Simpson. Alameda, CA: Sybex, 1992.

Tax Assistance

The Artist's Tax Guide and Financial Planner, by Carla Messman. New York: Lyons and Burford.

J. K. Lasser's Your Income Tax. New York: Simon & Schuster, annual.

J. K. Lasser's Tax Guide for Small Business. New York: Simon & Schuster, annual.

Tax Guide for College Teachers. College Park, MD: Academic Information Service, annual.

INDEX